International Financial Centres
of Europe, North America and Asia

International Financial Centres of Europe, North America and Asia

Edited by

Richard Roberts

Lecturer at the School of Social Sciences
University of Sussex

INTERNATIONAL FINANCIAL CENTRES

An Elgar Reference Collection

Published by
Edward Elgar Publishing Limited
Gower House
Croft Road
Aldershot
Hants GU11 3HR
England

Edward Elgar Publishing Company
Old Post Road
Brookfield
Vermont 05036
USA

British Library Cataloguing in Publication Data
International Financial Centres
I. Roberts, Richard
332.15

Library of Congress Cataloguing in Publication Data
International financial centres / edited by Richard Roberts.
p. cm. — (An Elgar reference collection)
Includes bibliographical references and index.
Contents: v. 1. International financial centres: concepts, development, and dynamics — v. 2. Global financial centres — v. 3. International financial centres of Europe, North America, and Asia — v. 4. Offshore financial centres.
1. International finance. 2. Central places. I. Roberts, Richard, 1952– . II. Series.
HG3881.I60727 1994
332′.042—dc20 94–21487
CIP

ISBN 1 85898 154 9
1 85278 758 9 (4 volume set)

Printed in Great Britain at the University Press, Cambridge

Contents

Acknowledgements

The editor and publishers wish to thank the following who have kindly given permission for the use of copyright material.

American Banker for figures included in excerpt: Richard McGahey, Mary Malloy, Katherine Kazanas and Michael P. Jacobs (1990), 'Front Office Competition Among US Financial Centers', *Financial Services, Financial Centers: Public Policy and the Competition for Markets, Firms, and Jobs*, Chapter 5, 187, 188.

Austrian National Bank for excerpt: Georg Winckler (1991), 'Vienna as an International Financial Centre', *Challenges for European Bank Managers in the 1990s*, Adolf Wala (ed.), Internationale Schriftenreiche der Oesterreichische Nationalbank, Volume 3, 165–78.

Basil Blackwell, Inc. for article: James O. Wheeler (1986), 'Corporate Spatial Links With Financial Institutions: The Role of the Metropolitan Hierarchy', *Annals of the Association of American Geographers*, **76** (2), June, 262–74.

Canadian Association of Geographers for article: Donald Kerr (1965), 'Some Aspects of the Geography of Finance in Canada', *The Canadian Geographer*, **IX** (4), 175–92.

Carfax Publishing Company for article: Michael A. Goldberg, Robert W. Helsley and Maurice D. Levi (1989), 'The Location of International Financial Activity: An Interregional Analysis', *Regional Studies*, **23** (1), 1–7.

Centre for Economic Policy Research for article: Vittorio Grilli (1989), 'Europe 1992: Issues and Prospects for the Financial Markets', *Economic Policy*, **9**, October, 388–421.

Paul Chapman Publishing Ltd for excerpt: Andrew Leyshon and Nigel Thrift (1989), 'South Goes North? The Rise of the British Provincial Financial Centre', *The North–South Divide*, J. Lewis and A. Townsend (eds), 114–56 and references.

Department of Finance, Canada for excerpt: L. Rasminsky and R.W. Lawson (1986), *Canada as an International Banking Centre*, 1–19, 21–4.

Dow Jones & Company, Inc. for figure included in excerpt: Richard McGahey, Mary Malloy, Katherine Kazanas and Michael P. Jacobs (1990), 'Front Office Competition Among US Financial Centers', *Financial Services, Financial Centers: Public Policy and the Competition for Markets, Firms, and Jobs*, Chapter 5, 189.

Euromoney for figure included in excerpt: Richard McGahey, Mary Malloy, Katherine Kazanas and Michael P. Jacobs (1990), 'Front Office Competition Among US Financial Centers', *Financial Services, Financial Centers: Public Policy and the Competition for Markets, Firms, and Jobs*, Chapter 5, 191.

Federal Reserve Bank of Chicago for article: Paul L. Kasriel and Randall C. Merris (1983), 'Chicago: City of the Big Straddles', *Economic Perspectives*, January/February, 3–7.

Federal Reserve Bank of San Francisco for article: Hang-Sheng Cheng (1976), 'US West Coast as an International Financial Center', *Economic Review of the Federal Reserve Bank of San Francisco*, Spring, 9–19.

Fortune for figure included in excerpt: Richard McGahey, Mary Malloy, Katherine Kazanas and Michael P. Jacobs (1990), 'Front Office Competition Among US Financial Centers', *Financial Services, Financial Centers: Public Policy and the Competition for Markets, Firms, and Jobs*, Chapter 5, 192.

Frank Cass & Co. Ltd for article: Youssef Cassis (1991), 'Financial Elites in Three European Centres: London, Paris, Berlin, 1880s–1930s', *Business History*, **XXXIII** (3), July, 53–71.

Institut für Kapitalmarktforschung for excerpt: Ralf-Joachim Götz and Johannes Müller (1990), *Frankfurt – A Banking and Financial Services Centre*, 3, 5–48, 50.

International Monetary Fund for excerpt: Benedicte Vibe Christensen (1986), *Switzerland's Role as an International Financial Center*, iii–v, 1–40.

Y.C. Jao for his own article: (1980), 'Hong Kong as a Regional Financial Centre: Evolution and Prospects', *Hong Kong Dilemmas of Growth*, Leung Chi-keung, J.W. Cushman and Wang Gungwu (eds), 161–94.

Journal of Business Administration for article: Kam-Hon Lee and Ilan Vertinsky (1987/88), 'Strategic Adjustment of International Financial Centres (IFCs) in Small Economics: A Comparative Study of Hong Kong and Singapore', *Journal of Business Administration*, **17** (1 and 2), Special Issue, 151–72.

Kluwer Academic Publishers B.V. for article: Philip G. Cerny (1989), 'The "Little Big Bang" in Paris: Financial Market Deregulation in a *Dirigiste* System', *European Journal of Political Research*, **17**, 169–92.

Lo Fung Learned Society for excerpt: Y.C. Jao (1993), 'Hong Kong as an International Financial Centre: Evolution and Prospects', *The Asian NIEs: Success and Challenge*, 39–82.

New York Times Company for figure included in excerpt: Richard McGahey, Mary Malloy, Katherine Kazanas and Michael P. Jacobs (1990), 'Front Office Competition Among US Financial Centers', *Financial Services, Financial Centers: Public Policy and the Competition for Markets, Firms, and Jobs*, Chapter 5, 222.

Oxford University Press (Hong Kong) Ltd for excerpt: Richard Yan-Ki Ho (1991), 'Hong Kong as an International Financial Centre', *The Hong Kong Financial System*, Richard Yan-Ki Ho, Robert Haney Scott and Kie Ann Wong (eds), 381–405.

Prentice Hall of Australia Pty. Ltd for excerpt: Yoon S. Park (1982), 'A Comparison of Hong Kong and Singapore as Asian Financial Centres', *East Asia Dimensions of International Business*, Phillip D. Grub, Tan Chwee Huat, Kwan Kuen-Chor and George H. Rott (eds), 21–8.

Royal Bank of Scotland plc for article: Richard Dale (1990), '1992–2002: The Future Evolution of Financial Markets in Europe', *The Royal Bank of Scotland Review*, no. 165, March, 3–15.

Royal Dutch Geographical Society for article: H.W. Ter Hart and J. Piersma (1990), 'Direct Representation in International Financial Markets: The Case of Foreign Banks in Amsterdam', *Tijdschrift voor Economische en Sociale Geografie*, **LXXXI** (2), 82–92.

Runzheimer for figure included in excerpt: Richard McGahey, Mary Malloy, Katherine Kazanas and Michael P. Jacobs (1990), 'Front Office Competition Among US Financial Centers', *Financial Services, Financial Centers: Public Policy and the Competition for Markets, Firms, and Jobs*, Chapter 5, 204.

Van Nostrand Reinhold for excerpt: Max Iklé (1972), 'The Origin of the Swiss Financial Center', *Switzerland: An International Banking and Finance Center*, Chapter 1, 3–30.

Weltwirtschaftliches Archiv for article: Charles P. Kindleberger (1963), 'European Economic Integration and the Development of a Single Financial Center for Long-Term Capital', *Weltwirtschaftliches Archiv*, **90** (2), 189–208.

Westview Press, Inc. for excerpt: Richard McGahey, Mary Malloy, Katherine Kazanas and Michael P. Jacobs (1990), 'Front Office Competition Among US Financial Centers', *Financial Services, Financial Centers: Public Policy and the Competition for Markets, Firms, and Jobs*, Chapter 5, 183–228.

Every effort has been made to trace all the copyright holders but if any have been inadvertently overlooked the publishers will be pleased to make the necessary arrangement at the first opportunity.

In addition the publishers wish to thank the Library of the London School of Economics and Political Science, and the Marshall Library of Economics, Cambridge University for their assistance in obtaining these articles.

Introduction

The global financial centres London, New York and Tokyo constitute a top tier among international financial centres. The essays in this volume focus on the set of financial centres that occupy a second tier of the hierarchy, centres that will be called *regional international financial centres*. The relatively smaller size and range of international financial activities distinguishes them from the global centres. A regional sphere of operations, for example, Europe for Paris, the US West Coast and the Pacific Basin for Los Angeles, and Asia for Hong Kong, is characteristic of these second-tier centres. The international dimension of their activities distinguishes them from a further tier of financial centres, the domestic centres that predominantly serve a local hinterland. The regional international financial centres have strong ties with the global financial centres, particularly the global centre in their region or time zone. Many have also established their own inter-continental links, though these are much less developed than those of the global centres.

This collection contains essays about Amsterdam, Berlin, Canada, Chicago, Frankfurt, Hong Kong, Los Angeles, Paris, San Francisco, Singapore, Switzerland and Vienna. Unfortunately, suitable studies on other regional international financial centres, for instance Brussels, Luxembourg, Houston or Boston, are unavailable. But references to the full range of regional international financial centres is to be found in the comparative and thematic essays which comprise the rest of the collection.

Europe

An historical perspective on the development of Paris, Berlin and London, the leading European financial centres at the turn of the century, is provided by the article by Geneva University business historian Youssef Cassis (1991). Although a comparative study of the banking communities in these three cities, it includes a survey of the principal activities of each centre from the 1880s to the 1930s. This demonstrates the considerable gulf between the scale and scope of international financial business in London, the global centre, and the two continental centres. Together they constituted the bulk of the international capital market, but London had the lion's share of new issues and of secondary market dealings. Trade finance was a significant function of each centre, but whereas London served a world-wide clientele, including many French and German merchant firms, Paris and Berlin financed only their own nationals. In international banking London was again at the forefront, having 30 foreign bank branches in 1914 while Paris hosted only 20. In the same year, British banks had 2 000 overseas branches, whereas French and German banks had only 500 each.

The First World War curtailed international financial business in all three centres. London re-emerged as a global international financial centre after the war, but now experienced vigorous competition from New York which had developed a global reach during the hostilities. The position of Paris as a financial centre was not only restored but enhanced in the inter-war years, when it was indisputably the leading regional international financial centre of continental Europe. Its pre-eminence was facilitated by the demise of competition from Berlin, which due to Germany's post-war economic and financial problems did not resume a role as a significant international financial centre, though becoming more important as a domestic financial centre.

Paris in its late 19th century and early 20th century hey-day as an international capital market, its foremost activity as an international financial centre, is the subject of the chapter by economist Margaret Myers, which is taken from her book *Paris as a Financial Centre* published in 1936. In the decades prior to the First World War, demand for foreign bonds was buoyant, continental investors being attracted by the high yields relative to domestic government securities, despite their higher risks. In the 1920s and 1930s Paris resumed its role as an important international capital market, although in these years the volume of domestic issues significantly exceeded that of foreign issues. The leading foreign borrowers in the Paris market were the governments of French Allies in central and eastern Europe, Turkey and China. In the inter-war years the Paris Bourse was much the most important secondary market of continental Europe for the trading of securities, and Myers provides a full account of its operations.

The Second World War put paid to Paris's role in international financial activities and disrupted the Bourse. The post-war decades saw little revival of either activity, since governments of both the Left and the Right ignored the financial markets and pursued *dirigiste* policies characterized by technocracy, indicative planning and state-sponsored industrial development. The banking system, three-quarters of which had been nationalized since 1945, not the capital market, was the French state's chosen agency for the provision of finance to industry. Moreover, the Bourse of the 1950s and 1960s was parochial and, first and foremost, concerned with the protection of its members' privileges. The mid-1970s saw a fundamental re-evaluation of the role of market forces in France, leading over the following decade or so to the revival of the capital market as a source of industrial finance, reform of the Bourse and the partial denationalization of the banking system. Philip G. Cerny (1989), a York University political scientist, investigates the causes and consequences of the deregulation of the French financial system in the 1970s and 1980s. The reforms promoted the internationalization of the French financial markets, drawing foreign banks to Paris and enhancing its role as a regional international financial centre. The late 1980s saw ambitious plans to establish a Paris-based computerized pan-European securities trading system – modelled on NASDAQ – to rival London, though at the time of writing the reality was that probably 50 per cent of the turnover of leading French stocks was taking place in London.

Germany's foremost international financial centre in recent years has been Frankfurt. The city has a long history as an important financial centre. As early as 1200 a mint of the Holy Roman Empire was established there, and the first bank was founded in 1402 to service the money exchange requirements of the merchants who attended the major trade fairs held in the city. The Frankfurt Exchange, the forerunner of the Frankfurt Stock Exchange, was established in 1585, trading at the time focusing on fixing the exchange value of nine different types of coin. The 18th century saw an increase in the number of Frankfurt banks and in the range of their activities, developing expertise in trading bills and issuing bonds and promissory notes. The mid-19th century saw a further strengthening of Frankfurt's position, with the establishment of a number of new institutions, such as savings banks and credit associations. But its position was undermined by the rise of Berlin as Germany's leading financial centre, following its establishment as the political capital in 1871, and as the home of the Reichsbank, the newly formed German central bank, in 1876. The inter-war years saw more centralization of German financial activities in Berlin, further diminishing Frankfurt's importance.

Since the Second World War, however, Frankfurt has enjoyed a remarkable revival. This has had its origins in two decisions of the immediate post-war years: the choice of the city as the location for the offices of the economic administration of the occupying Allied forces, and the establishment there of the Bank Deutsche Länder, the forerunner of the Bundesbank, in 1948. The presence of the central bank led many of Germany's leading banks and other firms to locate their headquarters there. Ralf-Joachim Götz and Johannes Müller (1990) of the Frankfurt-based *Institut für Kapitalmarktforschung*, present a comprehensive survey of the German financial sector at the end of the 1980s, paying particular attention to the role of Frankfurt. They also detail Frankfurt's labour market, commercial property market and infrastructure, drawing attention to the scale of the financial services industry in Frankfurt (it employs 53 000 people – 10 per cent of the city's workforce) and its superior communications (the airport being continental Europe's busiest, handling 27 million passengers per annum).

Amsterdam was Europe's, and the world's, foremost financial centre in the 17th and 18th centuries. Invasion by France in 1795 put paid to its international prominence, but since the mid-19th century it has functioned as a regional international financial centre. Today it houses the head offices of most Dutch banks, a respectable number of foreign banks, the Dutch Stock Exchange, the European Options Exchange and a range of supporting professional services. The 1970s and 1980s saw the establishment of offices by a growing number of foreign banks, despite its relatively close proximity to London where they could have enjoyed the advantages of operating in a global financial centre. This development, seemingly contrary to what might be expected given the formidable external economies that are characteristic of the financial services industry, led Amsterdam University geographers H.W. Ter Hart and J. Piersma (1990) to investigate the strengths and weaknesses of this 'second-tier financial centre' through a survey of Amsterdam bankers. They identify a number of financial services in which physical proximity to clients remains an important advantage despite improvements in communications technology, drawing conclusions about the impact of modern communications technology that are optimistic for regional international financial centres such as Amsterdam. They argue that, as financial information becomes available to anyone, anywhere, to get an edge over competitors it is more and more important to stay close to clients and investors. This requires a tangible presence and personal representation in regional and even local markets.

Vienna's prospects of becoming a regional international financial centre in the 1990s is the subject of the essay by Georg Winckler (1991), Professor of Economics at the University of Vienna. He identifies in the opening up of Eastern Europe a rare opportunity for Vienna to develop as a centre providing international financial services; the Austrian capital's banks enjoy a geographical and historic comparative advantage in knowledge of the region, especially in relation to individual firms. He stresses that the economies of scale inherent in the international financial services industry necessitate prompt action so that Vienna is a leader in the development process and attains a level of activity that allows it to enjoy the benefits of increasing returns ahead of rival centres. He identifies a number of policy measures that must be taken to allow Vienna to seize its moment of opportunity to make the transition from a domestic financial centre to a regional international financial centre.

Britain's provincial domestic financial centres are the subject of the essay by Nigel Thrift and Andrew Leyshon (1989) of the Geography Department of Bristol University. The years from the mid-1970s to the mid-1980s saw rapid growth in financial services employment in some British provincial cities, especially Edinburgh, Bristol, Leeds, Norwich, Brighton, Reading, Southampton, Cardiff and Northampton. There were three reasons: the expansion of local financial and producer services firms; the establishment of offices by large non-local financial and producer services firms; and the decentralization of the back-office activities of London-based banks and other financial services sector firms. The authors pay close attention to the expansion of the large multi-locational accountancy, commercial property and investment banking firms in the provincial centres. Another trend, though still in its infancy, is the establishment of a presence by overseas banks, particularly in Manchester. It is suggested that this is leading to the development of an international dimension to the activities of some British domestic financial centres.

Switzerland

Switzerland has a unique history and its significance as an international financial centre is likewise *sui generis*. An historical introduction to the development of Switzerland as an international banking and finance centre from the Middle Ages to the 1960s is provided in the chapter by Max Iklé (1972), a long-serving Swiss central banker, while the essay by Benedicte Vibe Christensen (1986), an economist with the International Monetary Fund, analyses its modern functions. Ideally, this volume would also include an essay on the role of Luxembourg as an international financial centre, which in many respects in recent decades has paralleled that of Switzerland. Since nothing suitable for this collection is available, readers are referred to the annual reports of the *Institut Monetaire Luxembourgeois*.

Swiss bankers were prominent in international finance for many centuries, being particularly engaged in channelling Swiss savings into financing the French monarchy in the 17th and 18th centuries. Thus the French Revolution of 1789 was a disaster and in Geneva disgruntled investors even passed the death sentence on a prominent banker who was held responsible for their losses. Capital exports resumed after the Napoleonic Wars, since Swiss savings usually exceeded the country's investment requirements, even despite the demands of industrialization and railway building. The Franco-German war of 1870–71 saw large financial inflows from the belligerents on Switzerland's borders, the funds being re-lent to France through Swiss investment institutions to meet the post-war reparations bill. The episode constituted the commencement of Switzerland's role as a haven for flight capital and as an *entrepot* financial centre mediating international flows. Swiss banks participated profitably in the international bond-issue boom of the early 20th century, but the First World War brought hardship, and the government even resorted to raising funds abroad in New York.

Switzerland's safe haven role for foreign funds came to the fore in the turbulent inter-war years, its political and financial stability contrasting markedly with other countries. The maintenance of the gold standard until 1936 appealed greatly to international investors, as did the new bank secrecy law of 1934. Foreign financing resumed in 1947, Belgium being the earliest beneficiary. The 1960s and 1970s saw an enormous expansion of international financial transactions, notably the recycling of petro-dollars, in which Switzerland played a leading part as an intermediary. Its prosperity, low inflation, external surpluses, sound government finances, political neutrality, bank secrecy, central geographic position and the language skills of its population gave it an unrivalled set of advantages for many investors and borrowers.

Christensen's paper presents a detailed analysis of the modern Swiss banking industry and the investment management, foreign exchange and bullion dealing activities of Swiss financial institutions. He pays particular attention to the increased importance of foreign banks since the mid-1970s, a development encouraged by the Swiss banking authorities to promote the competitiveness of the financial services sector. Addressing the issue of the competitiveness of Switzerland as an international financial centre, he notes that the promotion of offshore banking operations and the reduction in taxes on financial transactions in other countries has somewhat diminished its comparative advantage, the 1980s witnessing a marginal reduction in market share. At the time of writing, the structure and level of taxes levied on financial transactions was a live policy issue in relation to Switzerland's future as a leading international financial centre.

European Economic Integration and European Financial Centres

This short section opens with an article by the distinguished MIT economist Charles Kindleberger (1963) that was a forerunner to his pioneering study, *The Formation of Financial Centers* (1974), which is included in the companion volume, *International Financial Centres – Concepts, Development and Dynamics*. Written in 1962, only eight years after the signature of the Treaty of Rome that began the process of European economic union, Kindleberger's article is of interest for the light it sheds on contemporary views of the process and its prospects. He comes to the conclusion that none of the European centres will emerge as the pre-eminent centre of a European capital market and foresees that the function will be fulfilled by New York. This prediction was soon proved to be spectacularly mistaken, since even as he wrote London was beginning to develop the Eurobond market and New York's role as an international capital market was about to be curbed by US government controls.

Writing almost three decades later, economist Richard Dale (1990) of the University of Southampton examines the implications for Europe's financial services industry of the advent of the Single Internal Market in the European Community in 1992. As regards retail banking services, he anticipates that markets will remain national in character for the foreseeable future, though characterized by greater concentration and intensified competition. At the wholesale level, he expects further integration of capital markets, this development in Europe being part of a wider global integration. He ponders whether the process of regulatory convergence in the international financial markets will lead to a decline in Euromarket activity, since in large part the offshore markets are products of regulatory disparities. With a common regulatory framework across European markets, the Eurodeutschmark and Euroguilder markets, for instance, might be repatriated, bolstering Frankfurt and Amsterdam as financial centres. Declines in the level of international financial business conducted in London, Luxembourg and Switzerland, the leading European Euromarket centres, would be the consequence. But potentially much more threatening to them is regulatory reform in the US, that might in future undermine the Eurodollar deposit and bond markets.

Vittorio Grilli (1989) of Yale University also examines the issues arising from the advent of the European Single Internal Market in 1992 and arrives at conclusions highly congenial to London. His analysis, which gives pride of place to the importance of 'thick-market externalities' (external economies of scale), suggests that the liberalization process will strengthen the global centres London and New York. The dismantling of regulatory barriers will allow residents of countries with relatively small financial markets to have access to the more sophisticated centres, making the latter's markets even larger, more liquid and more appealing. He is sceptical about the ability of smaller centres to defend themselves against this process, even by the adoption by their governments of aggressive policies to do so. Grilli, like Dale, draws a distinction between the impact of market integration upon wholesale and retail financial markets. His empirical study of international bank deposits suggests that the wholesale market is highly susceptible to economies of scale and will migrate to the larger centres. The retail banking market, however, may well be unaffected, a conclusion consistent with Ter Hart and Piersma's article about Amsterdam discussed above.

North America

New York is the foremost North American international financial centre, but not the only one. Its principal rivals in recent times have been Los Angeles and Chicago, though Houston, San Francisco, Miami, Atlanta, Washington DC, Dallas and Seattle are also hosts to significant numbers of foreign banks. The development of Los Angeles as a financial centre is discussed in the article by Hang-Sheng Cheng of the Federal Reserve Bank of San Francisco (1976) and the chapter by Richard McGahey, Mary Malloy, Katherine Kazanas and Michael P. Jacobs (1990), the staff of the Governor of New York State's Advisory Panel on Financial Services. The challenge from Chicago is analysed in the article by Paul L. Kasriel and Randall C. Merris (1983), economists with the Federal Reserve Bank of Chicago, and in the above-mentioned chapter by McGahey, Malloy, Kazanas and Jacobs (1990).

Underlying the rise of Los Angeles and San Francisco as regional international financial centres has been the dynamism of the Californian economy and the countries of the Pacific Basin, the Los Angeles region having the 11th largest gross national product of the world's economies at the beginning of the 1990s. Los Angeles and San Francisco were the headquarters of four of America's top ten bank holding companies, measured by asset size. Moreover, Los Angeles was the headquarters of several of America's largest savings-and-loans, four of its top 50 life insurers and three of the top 50 diversified financial companies. During the 1980s many New York-based securities houses and investment banks established a presence in Los Angeles, complementing the indigenous firms. Trading on the Pacific Stock Exchange was boosted by technical innovation and the establishment of a presence by a number of New York brokerage houses.

The integration of the West Coast into the international banking market proceeded rapidly from the late 1960s, the foreign assets of the West Coast banks rising from $7 billion in 1969 to $32 billion in 1974; moreover the number of foreign bank branches and representative offices in Los Angeles and San Francisco grew from 16 in 1969, to 50 in 1975, 165 in 1981,

180 in 1985 and 190 in 1988. Much of the foreign bank activity in the Los Angeles region was Japanese, and by the end of the 1980s Japanese banks had built up a 22 per cent share of the California loan market. The 1990s are likely to see further enhancement of the importance of Los Angeles as an international financial centre servicing the rapidly growing economies of the Pacific Basin.

Chicago's importance as an international financial centre is due to its leadership and dominance of the financial futures and options markets. Its pioneering role in relation to these markets has lengthy historical roots. As early as 1848 the Chicago Board of Trade was organized for the purpose of trading forward contracts in grain, becoming a fully-fledged futures exchange in 1865 when a clearing-house was established. Futures trading in perishable agricultural products was initiated by the Chicago Mercantile Exchange in 1919. In more recent times, a major milestone was the beginning of trading of foreign currency futures in 1972 on the newly established Chicago-based International Monetary Market. This pioneered the concept of trading futures in something other than a physical commodity. The following year saw yet another important innovation – exchange-traded options in equities at the newly created Chicago Board Options Exchange. The 1980s saw further developments; the Chicago exchanges consistently leading the field in the development of new futures and options products. The rapid growth of derivatives business in the 1980s was much to the advantage of the Chicago exchanges and at the start of the 1990s they accounted for almost 80 per cent of the US and 60 per cent of the global futures market. Naturally, such success has spawned rivals, notably in New York, London and Tokyo, and it may prove impossible for Chicago to sustain its pre-eminence.

Another measure of a US city's significance as a financial centre is the proportion of total employment in the FIRE (Finance, Insurance and Real Estate) sector. Naturally, New York City is the leader with 15.1 per cent in 1988, the nearest rival being San Francisco with 11.8 per cent and then, in descending order, Dallas, Wilmington, Boston, Chicago, Atlanta, Los Angeles, Charlotte, Pittsburgh and Jersey City. Despite the great Wall Street boom of the years 1982–87, the cities with the fastest growth in employment in the FIRE sector in these years were in fact Wilmington and Jersey City, which were the favoured relocation sites for back-office and data-processing activities by New York banks, a phenomenon similar to that discussed in the article by Thrift and Leyshon in relation to London. Readers interested in pursuing this development should consult Chapter Six of *Financial Services, Financial Centers* (1990) by Richard McGahey, Mary Malloy, Katherine Kazanas and Michael P. Jacobs.

The articles by James O. Wheeler (1986), of the Department of Geography, University of Georgia, and Michael A. Goldberg, Robert W. Helsley and Maurice D. Levi (1989), of the Faculty of Commerce and Business Administration, University of British Columbia, both explore aspects of the spatial distribution of US financial centres. Wheeler's study focuses on ties between major US corporations and US financial institutions. He quantifies the commonsensical proposition that larger corporations demand more sophisticated financial services, preferring those provided by New York-based firms over local alternatives. His research shows that the relationship is strongest for investment banking, somewhat less strong for foreign banking and weakest for commercial banking services. Goldberg, Helsley and Levi ran a series of regressions in which the dependent variables were measures of the level of financial activity in individual US states. They establish that the level of international financial activity is statistically positively and significantly related to per capita income, the level of imports and the number of corporate headquarters. Their results indicate that international trade is intensive in its use of financial services and that financial activity tends to be exported along with goods.

Canadian financial centres are the subject of the studies by Donald Kerr (1965), a geographer at the University of Toronto, and the economists L. Rasminsky and R.W. Lawson (1986). Kerr's essay, which is a notable early contribution to the literature on financial centres, uses a number of yardsticks to measure the level of financial activity in a variety of Canadian cities: employment in finance; bank assets; cheques cashed at clearing-houses. These commercial banking criteria identify Toronto and then Montreal as the top financial centres by a wide margin, the other significant domestic centres being, in descending order, Winnipeg, Vancouver, Calgary, London and Kitchener-Waterloo. Data on securities underwriting and securities dealing reinforce Toronto's leading position and Montreal's secondary role, though Kerr notes that in many ways the interconnections between Toronto and Montreal are so strong that they should be regarded as constituting a single financial centre.

The study by Rasminsky and Lawson is a report conducted in the mid-1980s at the request of the Canadian Department of Finance into the pros and cons of initiatives to promote Canada as an international banking centre. This was inspired, like similar enquiries elsewhere that are discussed in the companion volume *Offshore Financial Centres*, by the introduction in 1981 of International Banking Facilities in the United States. These are special arrangements whereby banks can conduct Eurocurrency banking business without being subject to the full regulatory rigours that govern their domestic operations and with fiscal concessions. They were intended to win back Eurocurrency banking business for US financial centres from offshore financial centres. Canadian banks being major participants in the Eurocurrency markets, accounting for 4–5 per cent of total transactions, Rasminsky and Lawson divine opportunities for repatriating offshore bookings through modest adjustments of the tax structure. But they are doubtful that it would give a big boost to employment in the banking sector, since the conduct of even large Eurocurrency transactions is not labour-intensive. They argue against a bold strategy of aggressive tax and regulatory concessions to compete directly with the offshore banking centres, a move which would introduce undesirable laxity into the Canadian regulatory regime and would be countered by intense competition from existing and aspiring offshore centres.

Hong Kong and Singapore

Hong Kong has been an important regional international banking and financial centre throughout the 20th century, save for the years of the Second World War. From the turn of the century to the 1930s it was Asia's leading centre and ranked fourth in global significance behind London, New York and Paris. In the 1930s it was overtaken by Yokohama and Shanghai, though the challenge from these centres proved short lived due to Japan's defeat in the war and the Chinese revolution. The post-war era saw the re-emergence of Hong Kong as the leading Asian regional international banking centre, though Tokyo and Singapore soon became significant rivals.

Y.C. Jao of the University of Hong Kong is the leading authority on the development of Hong Kong as a financial centre. He is the author of numerous publications on the subject, two of which are reproduced in this collection. His essay entitled, 'Hong Kong as a Regional Financial Centre', published in 1980, details the city's dynamic development in the 1970s. Jao identifies 1969–70 as an important turning point, these years seeing a concurrence of favourable factors: a shift of attention on the part of the multinational banks to the Asia Pacific region; the extension of the Eurocurrency market to Asia; the stock market boom in the major markets of the area, which provided lucrative underwriting opportunities; and the reduction of political uncertainty because of China's new-found desire for a *rapprochement* with the West. Hong Kong's first merchant bank was established in 1970 and such firms rapidly proliferated, as did the presence of American and European commercial banks as well as international money brokers, securities houses and exchange dealers. Insurance was another boom industry due to the influx of foreign companies, and Hong Kong became the leading insurance centre of the Asia Pacific region. These developments had favourable consequences: employment in the financial services sector more than doubled from 18 000 in 1969 to 39 000 in 1978; the financial sector's share of GDP increased from 9.3 per cent of GDP to 12 per cent; and funding was readily available for a number of large capital-intensive projects, such as the city's mass-transit railway system.

Jao's essay entitled 'Hong Kong as an International Financial Centre: Evolution and Prospects', published in 1993, analyses developments in the 1980s and early 1990s. Liberalization was an important theme of these years, beginning in 1978 with the relaxation of the restrictions on the establishment of branches by foreign banks in response to pressure from international banks and competition from Singapore. As a result, foreign bank branches increased from 40 in 1978 to 135 in 1990. This was one of the reasons for the rapid growth and transformation of the Hong Kong banking system over these years, the banking sector's aggregate balance sheet increasing by 263 times. Other financial services also expanded rapidly: by the early 1990s the foreign exchange market was the world's sixth largest and the gold market the fourth largest; the securities market was sixth largest in the Asia Pacific region; and the Hong Kong futures market, established in 1977, was one of the earliest in the region. The outcome was that total employment in the financial services sector tripled over the years 1975–90, at the latter date accounting for 4.5 per cent of the total labour force.

'What kind of financial centre is Hong Kong?', asks Jao following a discussion of the typology of financial centres. He strongly takes issue with the 'widespread practice' of describing Hong Kong as an 'offshore centre', emphasizing that it has none of the latter's typical characteristics: it is not a tax haven; it is not a mere 'paper centre' or 'booking centre'; nor is the onshore financial sector artificially insulated from the offshore sector. Since its firms and markets have dealings with every major financial centre and every continent, it is plainly not a 'domestic' or 'national' centre whose activities are largely confined within its territorial limits. But the core of its business is the Asia Pacific region, serving especially the requirements of South China, Taiwan and Macau. Jao writes that the appropriate term for Hong Kong is *regional financial centre*.

Richard Yan-Ki Ho's (1991) essay places Hong Kong in the context of the development of international financial markets in the 1970s and 1980s. He identifies and discusses Hong Kong's three main financial centre functions: financial intermediation, inter-bank activities and maturity transformation. His points are illustrated by a wealth of useful statistical information. Both he and Jao conclude their essays with examinations of Hong Kong's problems and prospects, paying particular attention to its competitive position *vis-à-vis* other

Asian financial centres and to the impact of the end of British rule in 1997. Jao argues that the political uncertainty created by the '1997 syndrome' may well prove harmful to Hong Kong's standing as an international financial centre.

The common historical heritage of British colonial rule, the geographical similarities as city-states, and the parallels between their roles as providers of financial services, prompts comparison between Hong Kong and Singapore as financial centres in the Asia Pacific region. Detailed studies of Singapore form part of the companion volume *Offshore Financial Centres*, but two comparative essays, by Yoon S. Park (1982), a George Washington University Professor of International Finance and Banking, and Kam-Hon Lee and Ilan Vertinsky (1987/88) of, respectively, the Chinese University of Hong Kong and the University of British Columbia, are included in this collection. Park explores the individual identity of each centre but also the complementarity of their financial services to the Asia Pacific region. Lee and Vertinsky's article is based on a survey among leading bankers in the two centres of their assessments of supply and demand factors in the environment in which they operate. The survey reveals a marked consensus between the two communities of bankers about the attributes of a financial centre that are important for its success. They conclude optimistically that the globalization of markets offers opportunities for smaller regional international financial centres so long as competitiveness is maintained through advantages such as lower transaction costs, lower service costs and lower taxes. They argue that such centres may achieve profitable niches in the supply of international financial services by accommodating the needs of regional or special markets.

Richard Roberts

Part I
Europe

[1]

Financial Elites in Three European Centres: London, Paris, Berlin, 1880s–1930s

YOUSSEF CASSIS

University of Geneva and
Business History Unit,
London School of Economics

Bankers, and more generally financial elites, are rarely included in the discussions on entrepreneurs and the main questions they raise, whether in terms of ownership and management or in terms of social mobility. The object of this article is to consider the financial elites of the three major European economies from the 1880s to the 1930s. The differences between the English, French and German banking systems are relatively well known and the relationships between financial structure and economic development have been for several decades a central issue in economic and business history. Bankers and financiers have remained absent from these debates and analysis. An important question is whether a different type of banker and financier, defined both in terms of professional activity and social status, existed in London, Paris and Berlin; and if there were significant differences, to what extent they were the product of the banking system prevailing in each country, and in turn whether the socio-professional characteristics of a financial centre had any incidence on the interaction between finance and the 'real' economy.

These questions will be considered in a comparative perspective. It will be argued that the earlier emergence of a professional banking elite in Germany appears unlikely to have had long-term economic implications. In a first section, the main attributes of London, Paris and Berlin as financial centres will be briefly discussed. In a second section, the professional and business positions of bankers and financiers in the three centres will be examined, and in a third section their social status. Some conclusions will be drawn in a fourth seciton. The notion of financial elite will be primarily applied throughout this article to senior bankers and financiers, and to a certain extent to merchants and other professional groups which are found on the boards of the joint stock banks. Other groups, such as stockbrokers, money dealers, insurance brokers, commodity brokers and so on, although they will occasionally be referred to, cannot be included in the financial elite. In the first place, only a handful of them belonged to the highest ranks of the financial world; secondly, they were to be found in much greater number in the City of London than in the two other centres, particularly in Berlin, where these activities were usually undertaken by bank officials.

I

As financial centres, London, Paris and Berlin present both many contrasts and many similarities. Although all three were the financial – as well as the political – capitals of countries of comparable size, the scope of their financial activities varied considerably. This was due to the form of financial organisation prevailing in each country, their degree of development and sophistication, as well as to the role of each city as an international financial centre. In hierarchical order London came first followed by Paris and then Berlin. This order did not change throughout the period under review and indeed has not changed up to this day.

Before 1914 the position of London as the financial centre of the world meant that world trade was financed through the medium of bills of exchange drawn on London, whereas bills on Paris or Berlin were only used in order to finance the commerce of these countries.[1] The capital exported from Britain – between £3.5 billion and £4 million in 1913 – considerably exceeded the capital exported from France – about £1.8 billion – and from Germany – about £1.1 billion.[2] As a consequence, London was the leading centre for the issue of foreign loans and equity. The London Stock Exchange was larger than the Paris and Berlin stock exchanges put together; however, Paris emerged in the second half of the nineteenth century, alongside London, as an international market covering in particular Europe and the Mediterranean era, whereas Berlin had to compete with both Frankfurt and Hamburg and never managed to dominate, although it was considered to have the edge.[3] The insurance market was also much bigger in London, with the emergence, to a greater extent than in the two other centres, of large composite companies with offices in several cities in North and South America, Australia and other parts of the empire.[4] Only two German insurance companies, and not a single French one, had premium incomes in excess of £2 million in 1910 as against ten in Britain. With over £12 million premium income that year, the Prudential the largest insurance company in Britain, was twice as large as its German counterpart, the Victoria zu Berlin.[5] London's dominance of the world of insurance was also due to the unique role played by Lloyd's, first and foremost in the field of marine insurance, but also and increasingly from the early twentieth century through its capacity to insure new risks.[6] Many commodities were traded primarily if not exclusively in London, and markets such as the Baltic Exchange or the London Metal Exchange had no equivalent in the two continental centres.

These business opportunities attracted many foreigners to London, whether individuals or institutions. It has been observed that in the foreign governments bonds market of the London Stock Exhange, French and German could be heard as often as English[7] and that the foreign exchange business in the City of London was almost entirely in foreign hands. From the 1870s on, all the leading European and American banks opened a branch in London; the number of branches of foreign banks in the City amounted to about 30 in 1913.[8] The London bankers were fully aware of the attractions the City offered to foreign banks. Alexander Goschen, a partner in the merchant bank Frühling & Goschen and a director of the London Joint Stock Bank, considered that there was a bigger market for everything in London and that many operations undertaken by foreign banks in the City could not be done by British banks in a European centre. According to Goschen, this explained why the English clearing banks were so reluctant to open branches abroad.[9] The overseas banks, however, ensured that many more multinational banks were based in London than in Paris or Berlin. The number of foreign branches of British banks has been estimated at 2,000 in 1913 as against 500 for French and German Banks.[10] The attractions of Paris to foreign banks should not, however, be underestimated, as about 20 of them had opened a branch there in 1914.[11]

Despite these differences at the international level, London, Paris and Berlin showed greater similarities on the domestic banking scene. In the three centres there remained until 1914 a financial aristocracy based on old family partnerships. The largest joint stock banks were also of the same size: in 1913, Lloyds Bank and the Midland Bank in London, the Crédit Lyonnais in Paris, and the Deutsche Bank in Berlin all had total assets amounting to about £100 million. The continental banks, however, worked with a larger capital than their English counterparts which, in turn, had higher deposits.[12] One reason for this difference in the structure of their liabilities lies in the banking organisation of each country. As is well known, the English banking system was much more specialised than those existing on the Continent. The English joint stock banks confined themselves to deposit banking, other operations being undertaken by the discount houses, the merchant banks, the overseas banks and the investment trusts, whereas in Germany the so-called 'universal' banks undertook all sorts of financial operations including long-term investment and the issue of securities on behalf of industrial companies. In France, the commercial banks modelled themselves on the English joint stock banks and, even though the system was less specialised than in England, there was a clear difference between the *banques de dépôts* (deposit banks) and the *banques d'affaires* (investment banks). It is nevertheless interesting to note that, although the City of London was the world's leading financial centre, and despite the beginning of Britain's relative industrial decline, the largest companies in Britain, measured in terms of paid-up capital, were not banks but manufacturing industries, whereas the reverse was true in France and Germany.[13]

The First World War put an end to London's unrivalled financial supremacy, as a result of the sale of part of British overseas investments, its abandonment of the Gold Standard and the difficulties of returning to it between 1925 and 1931, and more generally Britain's weakened economic position. However, the challenge to London's world leadership came from New York, not from Paris and even less Berlin, and this challenge was only gradual, for if the capital was henceforth in New York, experience and expertise remained in London.[14] Berlin's position was considerably weakened by defeat, inflation and reparations. The situation of Paris was somewhat different: although it never developed the range of financial services which would have enabled it to challenge London seriously, the gold reserves and the sterling assets held by the Banque de France, as a result of the overvaluation of the pound and the undervaluation of the franc, put Paris in a strong position *via-à-vis* London and enhanced its international status, particularly in the immediate aftermath of Britain's departure from gold in 1931.[15] Otherwise, despite the loss of its financial supremacy in favour of New York, London actually widened the gap which separated it from the two continental centres, and from Berlin in particular. In 1938, the capital exported from Britain amounted to $22.9 billion, as against $3.9 billion for France and $700 million for Germany.[16] The London Stock Exchange remained far larger than its continental counterparts, as did the insurance market and the insurance companies. As far as the clearing banks were concerned, after the amalgamation movement of 1918 which gave birth to the 'Big Five', they now outdistanced in size their French and German competitors, both in terms of capital and deposits.[17]

II

The professional position of financial elites in London, Paris and Berlin can be compared at three levels: firstly, the respective role played by individual and corporate initiatives; secondly, the place of the '*haute banque*'; And thirdly, the management of the joint stock banks.

Because of the specialisation of the English banking system and the confinement of the clearing banks to traditional banking operations such as short-term loans, discounts or overdrafts, the City of London offered many more business opportunities for individuals or private firms, particularly in new areas of financial activity. The contrast is particularly striking between London and Berlin. Company promotion is a revealing example. In the City of London before 1914, no type of bank or financial institution such as the investment trusts were undertaking this type of operation. So the field was left open for the company promoter who mainly acted as an independent financier. Some had a reputation for honesty, like Osborne O'Hagan, others were notorious adventurers, like Ernest Terah Hooley or Whitaker Wright.[18] In Berlin, by contrast, the place of the company promoter was taken by one of the big banks' senior executives. At the Deutsche Bank, for example, Carl Klönne, one of the six members of the executive board, was responsible for industrial finance; he joined the Deutsche Bank in 1899 after having spent 20 years with a bank in Cologne, thereby acquiring a solid experience of the Ruhr industry.[19]

The differences between London and Berlin were as pronounced in the field of international finance. In England, new initiatives were taken by private firms of merchants, bankers or financiers, whereas in Germany these initiatives were usually taken by the big banks. In the oil industry, for example: in England, the Shell Transport and Trading Co. was founded and managed by Marcus Samuel, later Lord Bearsted, and his partners, whereas in Germany Deutsche Petroleum was founded in 1904 under the auspices of the Deutsche Bank; Deutsche Erdöl, however, was created by an individual entrepreneur, Rudolf Nöllenburg.[20] The financing of the Baghdad railway was taken in charge by the Deutsche Bank, whereas its counterpart in England, until the prospect of a collaboration collapsed in 1903, were Baring Brothers & Co., J.S. Morgan & Co. and Ernest Cassel.[21] In mining finance, A. Goerz & Co., a company registered in London, was backed by the Deutsche Bank, the Berliner Handelsgesellschaft and Jacob S.H. Stern, while a firm like Wernher, Beit & Co. was owned by its two partners Julius Wernher and Alfred Beit, who were originally German businessmen who had settled first in South Africa and then in London.[22] The British overseas banks were founded in the mid-nineteenth century by merchants and bankers independently from the joint stock banks, whereas their German counterparts, established a few decades later, were all subsidiaries of the big banks.[23] Whether an independent financier in the City of London fared better than a director of a large bank in Berlin will be discussed later. The question of the economic effects of each system has been for some time an open debate in English historiography, and cannot be dealt with here.[24]

The situation changed somewhat after the First World War without, however, being radically transformed. In England, individual initiatives clearly diminished with the decline of the company promoter, both in domestic affairs or in international finance. His role, however, was taken over by the merchant banks, directly or through the medium of finance houses specially set up for that purpose,[25] and not by the clearing banks despite the latter's greater involvement in industrial finance following the 1918–20 boom, or their control over overseas banks, with the creation, for example, of Barclays Bank D.C.O. in 1925 or the controlling interest of Lloyds Bank in the Bank of London and South America.[26] Where the old established private banks capable of holding their own in the same way in Paris and Berlin?

At the beginning of the period under review, the banking aristocracy, or '*haute banque*' was in the foremost position in the three centres, whether in terms of social and professional prestige or in terms of wealth and business activities. In Paris, where the word originated, the '*haute banque*' was made up of a certain number of old Protestant family banks, such as Mallet, Vernes, Hottinguer, de Neuflize or Mirabaud, with a network of European connections, in particular in Switzerland. In parallel to the *haute banque protestante*, there was a Jewish *haute banque*, whose most prominent member was of course Rothschild, as well as a Catholic *haute banque*. In Berlin, the term refers to a few private banks, mainly Jewish, such as Bleichröder, Medelssohn or Warschauer, the last one being taken over by the Darmstädter Bank in 1904. The German *haute banque*, however, was not confined to Berlin; some of its members were to be found in centres such as Frankfurt, with the Speyer and the Rothschild until the disappearance of the German branch of the family in 1901, Hamburg with the Warburgs or Cologne with the Oppenheims. The business of these banks, both in France and Germany, corresponded more or less to that of the English merchant banks, that is issuing foreign loans and financing international trade, although the German private banks were also engaged in commercial banking.[27]

In the City of London, until the last decade of the nineteenth century, two types of private banks co-existed: the private deposit banks and the merchant banks, and both can be considered as members of the *haute banque* on the basis of the wealth and social status of their partners. By the early twentieth century, nearly all the London private banks, with the exception of a few exclusive West End banks, had been taken over by the joint stock banks.[28] The London *haute banque* thus became much more similar, as far as its functions were concerned, to its continental counterpart. But the London *haute banque* was to prove the most resilient: it remained in the inter-war years, and indeed up to this day, a decisive component of the English banking sense, whereas it had lost almost all significance in Berlin and had entered a period of decline in Paris.

The financial aristocracy was stronger in London because its existence rested on a banking speciality which was not undertaken by the joint stock banks. As is well known, the two specialities of the merchant banks were the accepting and issuing businesses, and, even though competition was growing in the early twentieth century, the merchant banks were not really threatened until the First World War. After the war, they compensated for their loss of international business by turning to the domestic market, where they met with little competition from the joint stock banks.[29]

The situation was different in Berlin where the big banks were engaged in all the activities which constituted the private banks' speciality. Incidentally, it is not without interest to note that in the City of London itself the German big banks were amongst the strongest competitors of the English merchant banks in the accepting business, in particular the Dresdner Bank and the Disconto-Gesellschaft.[30] The result was that only a few very strong and very wealthy private banks could survive, at least at the top of the league. There remained about 460 private bankers in Berlin in 1902, but they were small firms, many of them being in fact brokers and commission agents on the Berlin Stock Exchange,[31] and cannot be considered as part of the financial aristocracy. In the inter-war years, after Bleichröder had become 'a shadow of itself',[32] Mendelssohn remained the only major Berlin private bank, while Warburg of Hamburg, thanks in particular to its New York connections, rose to international prominence. During the Nazi period, M.M. Warburg & Co. was 'Aryanised' in 1938 and its name changed to that of Brinckman, Wirtz & Co. in 1941, while the Mendelssohns preferred to join the Deutsche Bank in 1938.[33]

The Parisian *haute banque* remained very rich and very powerful until 1914 and beyond, and this was in no small way due to the international character of Paris as a financial centre. However, the activities of the *banques d'affaires*, the most important of which was the Banque de Paris et des Pays-Bas, were certainly encroaching on the traditional banking specialities of the *haute banque*, particularly the issue of foreign loans. It is significant, for example, that in the various Argentine loans that they issued between 1907 and 1914, Baring Brothers dealt, for the portion of the loans to be issued in Paris, with the Banque de Paris et des Pays-Bas and its two associates, the Société Générale and the Comptoir d'Escompte; in Germany, Baring's partners were the Disconto-Gesellschaft, associated with the Deutsche Bank.[34] The same is true about the financing of foreign railways, mining companies and others. In the Far East, the Banque de l'Indochine became the privileged instrument of French foreign policy, and the Banque de Paris et des Pays-Bas played the same political role in Morocco.[35] However, as David Landes showed some 35 years ago, the 'new bank' was very much a product of the old one.[36] There were members of the *haute banque* on the board of the Banque de Paris et des Pays-Bas and another important *banque d'affaires*, the Banque de l'Union Parisienne, was created and owned by the *haute banque*. Members of the *haute banque* also filled the boards of the major insurance companies, in particular the biggest one, the Compagnie d'Assurances Générales where, as late as 1926, the chairman was the Baron de Neuflize and the vice-chairman Ernest Mallet. The *haute banque* was also strongly represented on the boards of the railway companies and, most importantly, among the directors of the Banque de France. The semi-nationalisation of the Banque de France in 1936, that of the railway companies the following year and the nationalisation of the commercial banks – but not of the *banques d'affaires* – and insurance companies in 1944–46 undoubtedly diminished the control exerted by the *haute banque* over the financial sector of the French economy.[37]

Such a control was even more impressive in the City of London, where the most prominent merchant banks and merchant houses were represented, through their partners, on the boards of the major joint stock banks, overseas banks, insurance companies and investment trusts as well as on the Court of Directors of the Bank of England. This situation put the private firms in a position of collective control over the funds of huge financial institutions and gave them an economic power which went far beyond the size of their private firm.[38]

Contrary to their English and French counterparts, the German private bankers did not succeed in keeping control over the large financial institutions they had themselves created. The founders of the Deutsche Bank in 1870 were private bankers and the evolution of its relationships with one of them, Delbrück, Leo & Co., is revealing in that respect. At first, all the issue business was jointly undertaken, but as the Deutsche Bank grew stronger the relationships increasingly cooled, with the director general, Georg Siemens, having the edge over the chairman of the supervisory board, Adelbert Delbrück.[39] The identity of functions between private and joint stock banks as an explanatory factor has already been discussed. Another explanation lies in the higher status enjoyed by professional bankers in Germany, which is reflected in the differences between the management structure of the English and French banks on the one hand and of the German banks on the other hand.

In England and France, a clear demarcation separated the directors from the managers. The directors were concerned with defining the general policy of their bank and supervising its management. This supervision could be very close, through committees of the board which met regularly to control one aspect of the bank's activity. The responsibility of running the day to day business of banking was left to the managers whose ultimate status was therefore that of subordinate to the directors.

Socially, there is no doubt that the managers, including the general manager, enjoyed a lower status than the directors. The former often came from a lower middle-class social background and made their entire career in the same bank of which they were full-time salaried employees; the latter were partners in a merchant or banking firm, company directors, retired businessmen, men of independent means, sometimes former civil servants or political notabilities, and devoted only a part of their time to the bank. There were differences between the English and French banks – for example the board of directors was more involved in the management of the bank in England, whereas the social status of the managers could be higher in France. However, they were minor in comparison to the German model.[40]

Such a social and professional division did not exist in Germany. As is well known, after 1870 German companies were required to have, in addition to their executive board (*Vorstand*), a supervisory board (*Aufsichtsrat*).[41] It would be a mistake to compare the members of the executive boards to the managers of an English company and the members of the supervisory board to the directors. The members of the executive board were not only responsible for the daily routine of banking activities; they were the real heads of their bank, deciding its long-term strategy as well as its short-term tactics. They were rather in the position of the managing directors of an English bank while the members of the supervisory board could be compared to non-executive directors in England. The example of the Deutsche Bank is the most striking. In 1907, it was managed by an executive board of six members. Among them, Arthur Gwinner, usually considered as the unofficial head of the bank, was in charge of external affairs: foreign loans, foreign investments, in particular the Ottoman railway. Carl Klönne, already mentioned, was in charge of industrial finance. Rudolf Koch was responsible for the current and deposit accounts as well as the relationships with provincial banks, while Paul Mankiewitz was responsible for Stock Exchange operations. Significantly, the chairman of the supervisory board was Wilhelm Herz, at the time over 80 years old, one of the most prominent merchants in Berlin.[42]

It is important to bear in mind that the members of the executive boards were not subordinate to the supervisory board – as managers of an English or French bank with similar share of responsibility would be to the directors – and that they enjoyed the same social status. This is shown, for example, by the fact that two of them were ennobled, Arthur Gwinner and Rudolf Koch; no manager of an English bank was ever raised to the peerage during that period. Rudolf Koch was on the central committee of the Reichsbank, alongside private bankers such as Albert von Oppenheim, Julius Bleichröder or Paul Schwabach, as well as representatives of the other big banks. Apart from the fact that a clearing banker could not become a Director of the Bank of England, bank managers in England hardly ever represented their bank on the board of other companies, unlike the members of the executive boards of the German banks who could chair several supervisory boards, in particular of industrial companies. The higher social status of the members of the executive boards of the German banks in Germany is also reflected in their personal wealth. The richest of them, men such as Carl Fürstenberg, of the Berliner Handelsgesellschaft, Eugen Gutmann, of the Dresdner Bank, or Arthur Gwinner, of the Deutsche Bank, had fortunes estimated at around 16 million marks in 1911, that is £800,000. This is the sort of fortune left by a rich merchant banker in the City of London: such considerable City figures as Henry Huck Gibbs, later Lord Aldenham, or Alexander Kleinwort did not leave as much as that. Among the less wealthy, Ernest Russel, of the Disconto-Gesellschaft, had an estimated fortune of two to three million marks in 1911, that is between £100,000 and £150,000, which is well above the average fortune of the general manager of an English bank: 66 per cent of those active betwen 1890 and 1914 left an estate valued at less than £50,000.[43] This is not to suggest, however, that banking fortunes were higher in Berlin than in London. On the contrary. We will come back to that point in the next section.

The status of the professional bankers in England and France improved from the beginning of the twentieth century and in particular after 1914. An increasing number of general managers became chairman of their bank. One of the earliest and most spectacular examples is that of Edward Holden, who became chairman and managing director of the Midland Bank in 1908. Another is Frederick Goodenough who became chairman of Barclays Bank in 1917, the most private of the British clearing banks, after having been secretary and then general manager. In France, in the same year, Adrien Mazerat, general manager of the Crédit Lyonnais between 1882 and 1905, succeeded Henri Germain, the founder of the bank, as chairman. At the Société Générale, Louis Dorizon, who had started as an office boy in 1874, rose step by step to become manager in 1896, general manager in 1909 and finally chairman in 1914. Senior managers also increasingly tended to hold the position of managing-directors rather than general managers. At the Midland Bank, after Holden's death in 1919, three joint managing directors were appointed. At the Crédit Lyonnais, after Germain's death in 1905, his two sons-in-law, Edmond Fabre-Luce, originally a diplomat, and Baron Brincard, became joint managing directors, the latter becoming chairman in 1919. In France, an important factor in the rise of the professional bankers was the higher proportion of university-educated managers. In particular, the banks increasingly recruited finance inspectors to fill senior managerial positions. In the course of time, especially after World War II, this *grand corps* was to become the main supplier of French senior bankers.[44]

The integration of full-time professional bankers to the financial elite took place earlier in Germany than in England and France. All the descriptions of Berlin *Hochfinanz* before 1914 put side by side private bankers and top salaried managers of the big banks.[45] This took another generation to happen in France, and even longer in the City of London. But was this closely-knit German banking community as integrated to the upper-classes as the English and French financial aristocracies?

III

Wealth is a first indicator of social status, although not necessary a sufficient one as it usually takes a second generation to gain full social acceptance. In the three countries, bankers and financiers were the wealthiest business group in the early twentieth century. In England, according to Rubinstein's figures, 51 per cent of the non-landed millionaires and half-millionaires deceased between 1900 and 1919 were engaged in banking, commerce and other services; the proportion is 47 per cent for those deceased between 1920 and 1939. The figures are very similar for Germany: according to Dolores Augustine, the tertiary sector accounted for 47 per cent of businessmen with estates of six million marks – that is £300,000 – or more in 1911. Bankers, with 27 per cent, were the largest single group and, interestingly, formed a larger proportion than their English counterparts who accounted for 22 per cent of the businessmen worth £500,000 or more deceased between 1900 and 1919 and 19 per cent of those deceased between 1920 and 1939.[46] This reflects the wider spectrum of business opportunities existing then in the British economy rather than a greater strength of the financial sector in Germany.

Wealthy bankers and financiers – with say £300,000 or more – were in fact more numerous in Britain. The level of their fortune was also higher, although not of a different order of magnitude. The richest bankers in Berlin in 1911 were Hans von Bleichröder, with £1.5 million, Robert von Mendelssohn, with £1.3 million and Paul von Schwabach, with £1 million. Many more City of London bankers were millionaires and the largest fortunes were in the region of £2.5 million, as in the case of Lord Rothschild, the second Lord Revelstoke, or Everard Hambro. The fortune of the most successful financiers could reach greater heights, for example Sir Ernest Cassel, who left £7.3 million in 1921. Compared to London, Berlin was handicapped because of its more recent accession to the position of Germany's financial capital. The largest German banking fortunes were not in Berlin, but still in Frankfurt, with Maximilian von Goldschmidt-Rothschild, worth £8 million in 1911 – he had married the daughter of Willy von Rothschild, the last male member of the Frankfurt branch – and Eduard Beit von Speyer, worth £4.4 million. The aggregate fortune of the Rothschilds and Goldschmidt-Rothschilds in Frankfurt in 1911 reached £19.2 million:[47] the family fortune long outlived the banking house, which closed in 1911. There are unfortunately no equivalent figures for France, as the studies undertaken so far refer to businessmen as a single category without further differentiation. However, considering the concentration of millionaires in Paris and the huge fortunes of some of the directors of the Banque de France studied by Alain Plessis for an earlier period, there is some indication that banking and finance accounted for a fair share of the French millionaires.[48] Comparative analysis of the levels of fortune after 1914 remains for the moment impossible.

Education cannot be readily used as an indicator of social status. For England, education at a public school is usually considered as a criterion of absorption into the upper classes, but this can hardly be said of education at a German *Gymnasium* or a French *lycée*, even though a very small percentage of the population obtained a *baccalauréat* or an *Abitur*. Education, on the other hand, has often been linked to business performance, and in that respect the most striking feature is the comparatively low level of education of German bankers. For 1907, a sample of 20 bankers, mostly members of the executive boards of the four 'D' banks shows that the training of half of them consisted in a banking apprenticeship, while 25 per cent went to university. In England, although only four per cent of managers studied at a university during the period 1890–1914, 42 per cent of directors did so, mostly at Oxford or Cambridge. For 1927, in Germany, the proportion of apprenticeships rises to 59 per cent, 23 per cent being universityeducated; details of education are unknown for only 18 per cent. In England, for the same year, the analysis of the education of the chairmen, vice-chairmen, general managers or managing directors of the 'Big Five' produces almost identical results: 60 per cent did not go beyond secondary education, while 20 per cent studied at a university, the details of education of the remaining 20 per cent being unknown; the percentage of university-educated cases, however, rises to 40 per cent if only the chairmen and vice-chairmen are considered. In France, from a sample of bankers established on the same basis, it appears that a third pursued their studies at a university, but with no available information for more than half of the cases, the percentage is most probably underestimated.[49] Whatever the influence of German bankers on industry, it was not due to any superior level of education.

In the three capitals, bankers and financiers led an aristocractic way of life. They lived in a fashionable area such as Mayfair or Belgravia in London, the *8ème* or the *16ème arrondissement* in Paris, or the western area near the *Tiergarten* in Berlin, coupled with a seat in the country. Membership of a prestigious club was also a mark of upper-class status, primarily in London, but also in Paris; as far as Berlin was concerned, there were no such clubs and on the whole the German capital had a less active social life than the British and French ones. In the three capitals, the banking elites were geographically and socially close to the political and administrative elites, and had their entrées into higher government circles.[50]

Despite these apparent similarities, bankers and financiers in London, Paris and Berlin did not enjoy the same social and professional status in their respective country. In Britain, City bankers clearly were the most prominent business group, being on the whole richer, more integrated into the aristocracy and closer to political power than industrialists.[51] The separation between what we could call a national bourgeoisie, based on the capital, and a provincial bourgeoisie, coincided to a large extent with the separation between the City and industry, although this distinction tended to diminish from the inter-war years as the largest industrial companies increasingly moved their head office to London and the most successful industrialists were gradually integrated into the upper classes.[52]

The differentiation between a national and a provincial bourgeoisie applies even better to France. However, contrary to England, the national bourgeoisie included from an earlier date various categories of businessmen. Paris was not only the home of the *haute banque* and the large financial institutions, but of any company of some significance in France. French top industrialists were more integrated to the upper classes than their English counterparts. Members of the old industrial dynasties fully belonged to the Parisian society, the best known examples being Eugène Schneider and François de Wendel, the steel magnates.[53] The cohesion of the French business elite was certainly facilitated by the fact that the largest companies, whether financial or industrial, were often headed by former senior civil servants. However, as far as bankers were concerned, whatever their wealth and status, they could not escape the persistent hostility that the French felt towards banks, although it was more characteristic of the lower middle and rural classes than of the upper classes.[54]

Berlin, despite being the political and financial capital of the Reich, was not the home of the most important business group in Germany. Despite their involvement in industrial finance and their massive presence on the supervisory boards of industrial companies, German bankers never enjoyed the same status as their English counterparts who kept away from industry. In Imperial, as well as in Weimar, Germany the Ruhr industrialists were undoubtedly the business group enjoying the highest prestige and capable of exerting the strongest political pressure.

Their base, however, was in Düsseldorf, Cologne or Essen, although they had powerful antennae in Berlin, in particular through their professional organisations. As Gerlad Feldman put it: 'the pre-war power and prestige of German banking ... lay in its enthusiastic participation in the adventure of German industrialization'.[55]

A difference between London, Paris and Berlin, which partly explains the position of bankers in English society, is that the City aristocracy was not primarily composed of members of religious minorities. That was certainly true of the London private bankers; although they included a not insignificant contingent of Quakers, a great proportion of the latter had joined the Church of England during the period under review. But it was also true of the merchant bankers, at least as far as the most prestigious firms were concerned, apart from the Rothschilds who were in every respect an exceptional case. It is true that many of these firms had been established by foreign immigrants during or after the Napoleonic Wars, but from the second generation most of them were totally integrated into the English upper classes; they were no more part of a network of relationships characteristic of the religious minorities, but rather of a network of relationships linking together the old banking families and a number of landed families. If one adds to the merchant banks the most important merchant houses which, at least until 1914, must be considered as part of the financial aristocracy on the basis of their membership of the Court of Directors of the Bank of England, the result is that the impact of the religious minorities was much more limited in London than in Paris and even more in Berlin. As already noted, the *haute banque* in Paris was composed of several religions, but with a strong Protestant and Jewish element, while it was virtually entirely Jewish in Berlin.[56]

Not only the banking, but more generally the business elite, was less integrated into the upper classes in Germany before 1914. There was no unified dominating elite in Germany, such as the 'establishment' in Britain or the '*grand monde*' in France, based on the merger of top businessmen with another elite group. there might have been a new elite in Imperial Germany, in the sense that the aristocracy was henceforth sharing its power with the *Grossbürgertum*, that they increasingly led the same way of life, met socially and that intermarriage was becoming more frequent; the two groups might also have been functionally integrated. However, contrary to England, a complete merger, leading to the formation of a single social group, did not take place. On the other hand, the links between German big businessmen and other bourgeois elite groups were not as close as in France, where in any case the bourgeoisie did not have to share its power with any other social group. The reasons for this difference between Germany on the one hand, and England and France on the other hand, are numerous and include Germany's later industrialisation and the federal structure of its state as well as the nature of the German *Junkertum*. The specific position of the financial elites within the upper classes provides another element of explanation. As it has been suggested earlier in this article, there was no real German equivalent to the English or French financial aristocracy. In England and France, bankers were the first business group to be integrated into the upper classes, whereas in Germany the banking community was largely Jewish and so could not be absorbed fully into the dominating elite.[57]

IV

To summarise: economic power and social status do not necessarily move together and in the same direction. Despite the strong influence of the banks in the German economy, German bankers never enjoyed the same social status as their English counterparts. On the other hand, the German business community appears to have been more homogeneous, in the sense that the separation between 'owners' and 'managers' was less marked than in Britain and France.[58] German professional bankers were therefore earlier integrated to the financial elite than their English and French counterparts. The reasons for this early integration are mainly to be found in the position of the middle classes (the *Bürgertum*) in Imperial Germany. However, this integration was certainly facilitated by the existence of a supervisory board alongside the executive board, as both owners and managers basically enjoyed the same social and professional status. In addition, the existence of a supervisory board might well have helped the passage from family to managerial capitalism in Germany,[59] as it was easier than in Britain for owners to retain a certain degree of control over their enterprise without hampering the rise of salaried managers. Although this would apply more to industry than banking, there is no doubt that the subordinate status of managers in England contributed to the lasting dominance of the financial world by a City aristocracy.[60]

One should not conclude, however, that German bankers were more 'professional' than their English and French counterparts. English bank managers ran their business in a thoroughly professional manner and generated higher profits than their Continental competitors.[61] The lack of expertise of the British clearing banks in industrial financing has often been noticed[62] but must be attributed to the absence of tradition and experience in that particular field rather than to a lack of professionalism. As far as the French banks were concerned, it should be remembered that the Crédit Lyonnais was one of the very first banks to create a financial analysis department, as early as 1871,[63] and, as has been noted earlier,

French bank managers had on the whole a higher level of education than their English and German counterparts. And whatever the forms of organisation of the German 'universal' banks and their representation on the supervisory boards of innumerable industrial companies, German bank directors were very conservative during the 1920s and apparently lacked entrepreneurial spirit.[64] In any case, the management structures of the joint stock banks have so far attracted little attention from historians, especially in comparison with manufacturing industry; this should prove a fruitful field of investigation, not only at the level of the financial elites, but also of the lower strata of the banking hierarchy.

NOTES

An earlier version of this article was presented at the Metropolitan History Seminar, Institute of Historical Research, University of London. I should like to thank the participants for their helpful comments.

1. On the City of London before 1914, see Y. Cassis, *La City de Londres, 1870–1914* (Paris, 1987).
2. United Nations, *International Capital Movements during the Interwar Period* (New York, 1949).
3. R.C. Michie, 'Different in Name Only? The London Stock Exchange and Foreign Bourses, c. 1850–1914', *Business History*, Vol. XXX (1988), pp. 55–7.
4. See B. Supple, 'Corporate Growth and Structural Change in a Service Industry: Insurance, 1870–1914', in B. Supple (ed.), *Essays in British Business History* (Oxford, 1977), pp. 70–1.
5. *Post Magazine Almanac*, 1911.
6. On Lloyd's of London, see D.E.W. Gibb, *Lloyd's of London: A Study in Individualism* (1957); C. Wright and C.E. Fayle, *A History of Lloyd's* (1928).
7. D. Kynaston, 'The London Stock Exchange, 1870–1914: An Institutional History' (unpublished Ph.D. thesis, University of London, 1983), p. 200.
8. Cassis, *City de Londres*, pp. 40–2.
9. Bodleian Library Oxford, Milner Papers, Vol. 481, ff. 10–14. On the clearing banks abroad, see G. Jones, 'Lombard Street on the Riviera: The Clearing Banks and Europe, 1900–1960', *Business History*, Vol. XXIV (1982).
10. Z. Aliber, 'International Banking', *Journal of Money, Credit and Banking*, Vol. 16 (1984), pp. 661–2. These figures are most probably overestimated. According to G. Jones, the number of foreign branches of British banks amounted to 1,286 in 1913. 'Competitive Advantages in British Multinational Banking since 1890', in G. Jones (ed.), *Banks as Multinationals* (1990), p. 31.
11. L. Dufourcq-Lagelouse, *Les banques étrangères en France* (Paris, 1922), p. 32.
12. In 1913, the total assets of the London City & Midland Bank amounted to £109 million, of Lloyds Bank to £107 million, of the Crédit Lyonnais to £99 million and of the Deutsche Bank to £92 million. However, the paid-up capital of the Deutsche Bank was £12.5 million and the Crédit Lyonnais £10 million as against £4.35 million for the Midland Bank and £4.2 million for Lloyds Bank.
13. In 1905, Imperial Tobacco, with a capital of £17.5 million, was the largest industrial company in Europe if measured in terms of nominal capital. In that year another 26 industrial companies had a larger capital than that of the largest bank, namely the Midland Bank whose capital was £3.14 million; for lists of the largest industrial companies in Britain, see P.L. Payne, 'The Emergence of the Large-Scale Company in Great Britain', *Economic History Review*, 2nd series, Vol. 20 (1967), and L. Hannah,

The Rise of the Corporate Economy (2nd ed. 1982). In Germany, the largest company in 1907 was the Deutsche Bank, with a capital of 200 million marks, closely followed by Krupp with 180 million marks (unpublished list of the largest German companies in 1907 kindly communicated to me by Jürgen Kocka). The gap between the largest banking and industrial companies was wider in France: in 1907, the largest industrial companies were Saint-Gobain and Thomson-Houston, with a capital of 60 million francs, as against 250 million for the Crédit Lyonnais and 200 million for the Société Générale.

14. See K. Burk, 'Money and Power: 'The Shift from Great Britain to the United States', in Y. Cassis (ed.), *Finance and Financiers in European History, 1880–1960* (Cambridge, 1991). A good example of the lasting importance of London's expertise is given in her recent study *Morgan Grenfell, 1838–1988: The Biography of a Merchant Bank* (Oxford, 1989), pp. 86–90.
15. See P. Coste, *Les grands marchés financiers: Paris, Londres, New York* (Paris, 1932), pp. 37–71.
16. W. Woodruff, *Impact of Western Man* (New York, 1966), pp. 156–7.
17. In 1928, the capital and total assets of the largest English, French and German banks were as follows:

	Capital	*Total assets*
	in £million	
Barclays Bank	16	345
Lloyds Bank	16	395
Midland Bank	13	434
Société Générale	4	85
Crédit Lyonnais	2	78
Deutsche Bank	7.5	116
Dresdner Bank	5	98

18. On the company promoter, see J. Armstrong, 'The Rise and Fall of the Company Promoter and British Industry', in J.J. van Helten and Y. Cassis (eds.), *Capitalism in a Mature Economy: Financial Institutions, Capital Exports and British Industry, 1870–1939* (Aldershot, 1990).
19. *Neue Deutsche Biographie*; E.W. Schmidt, *Männer der Deutschen Bank und Disconto-Gesellschaft* (Düsseldorf, 1957).
20. See R. Henriques, *Marcus Samuel, First Viscount Bearsted and Founder of the Shell Transport and Trading Company, 1853–1927*, (1960); J. Riesser, *Die deutsche Gross banken und ihre Konzentration* (Iena, 1912), p. 342; F. Pinner, *Deutsche Wirtschafts-führer* (Berlin, 1924), pp. 232–5.
21. See J.G. Williamson, *Karl Helferrich, 1873–1924: Economist, Financier, Politician* (Princeton, 1971), pp. 78–110.
22. P.H. Emden, *Money Powers of Europe in the Nineteenth and Twentieth Century* (1937); entries on Alfred Beit and Julius Wernher in D.J. Jeremy (ed.), *Dictionary of Business Biography*, 5 vols. (London, 1984–86).
23. See A.S.J. Baster, *The Imperial Banks*, (1929); idem, *The International Banks* (1935); D. Joslin, *A Century of Banking in Latin America* (1963); G. Diouritch, *L'expansion des banques allemandes à l'étranger* (Paris, 1909), P. Hertner, 'German Banks abroad until 1914', in Jones (ed.), *Banks as Multinationals*.
24. I have recently discussed this question in 'British Finance: Success and Controversy', in van Helten and Cassis (eds.), *Capitalism in a Mature Economy*.
25. See an interesting case study in S. Diaper, 'The Sperling Combine and the Shipbuilding Industry: Merchant Banking and Industrial Finance in the 1920s', in van Helten and Cassis (eds.), *Capitalism in a Mature Economy*. See also Burk, *Morgan Grenfell*, pp. 91–8.
26. See D. Ross, 'The Clearing Banks and Industry – New Perspectives on the Interwar Years', in van Helten and Cassis (eds.), *Capitalism in a Mature Economy;* S. Tolliday, *Business, Banking and Politics: The Case of British Steel, 1918–1939* (Cambridge, MA,

1987); J. Crossley and J. Blandford, *The D.C.O. Story (1925–1939)* (Cambridge, MA, 1975); Joslin, *Century of Banking*.

27. See A. Plessis, *Régents et Gouverneurs de la Banque de France sous le Second Empire* (Geneva, 1985); F. Stern, *Gold and Iron* (New York, 1977); W. Treue, 'Das Bankhaus Mendelssohn als Beispiel einer Privatbank im 19. und 20. Jahrhundert', in C. LowenthalHensel (Hg.), *Mendelssohn Studien*, Bd 1 (Berlin, 1972); E. Rosenbaum and A.S. Sherman, *M.A. Warburg & Co., 1798–1938: Merchant Bankers of Hamburg*, (1979).
28. See Y. Cassis, *Les banquiers de la City à l'époque edouardienne, 1890–1914* (Geneva, 1984), pp. 23–38.
29. See S.D. Chapman, *The Rise of Merchant Banking*, (1984).
30. Ibid., pp. 121–5.
31. W. Treue, 'Der Privatbankier an der Wende vom 19. zum 20. Jahrhundert', *Tradition*, Vol. 5 (1970), p. 230.
32. Stern, *Gold and Iron*, p. 547.
33. Treue, 'Bankhaus Mendelssohn'; Rosenbaum and Sherman, *Warburg*.
34. Baring Brothers Archives, 73, Argentine Internal Gold Loan of 1907.
35. See J. Thobie, *La France Impériale, 1880–1914* (Paris, 1982).
36. D. Landes, 'Vieille banque et banque nouvelle: la révolution financière du XIXème siècle, *Revue d'histoire moderne et contemporaine*, III (1956).
37. See A. Plessis, 'Bankers in French Society, 1860s–1960s', in Cassis (ed.), *Finance and Financiers*.
38. I have discussed this point in a previous article in this journal; 'Management and Strategy in the English Joint Stock Banks', *Business History*, Vol. XXVII (1985).
39. Carl Fürstenberg, *Die Lebensgeschichte eines deutschen Bankiers* (DüsseldorfWien, 1968; 1st ed. 1938), p. 209.
40. For England, see Cassis, *Les banquiers*; for France, see Plessis, 'Bankers in French Society'.
41. See N. Horn, 'Aktienrechtliche Unternehmensorganisation in der Hochindustrialisierung (1860–1920). Deutschland, England, Frankreich und die USA im Vergleich', in N. Horn & J. Kocka (eds.), *Recht und Entwicklung des Grossunternehmen im 19. und frühen 20. Jahrhundert* (Göttingen, 1979).
42. See Schmidt, *Männer*.
43. R. Martin, *Jahrbuch der Millionäre in Berlin* (Berlin, 1913); Cassis, *Les banquiers*, pp. 28–40.
44. Cassis, *Les banquiers*; Plessis, 'Bankers in French Society'; A.R. Holmes and E. Green, *Midland: 150 Years of Banking Business*, (1986); J. Rivoire, *Le Crédit Lyonnais: Histoire d'une banque* (Paris, 1989).
45. See for example E. Achterberg, *Berliner Hochfinanz: Kaiser, Fürsten, Millionäre um 1900* (Frankfurt am Main, 1965).
46. Percentage calculated from W.D. Rubinstein, *Men of Property: The Very Wealthy in Britain since the Industrial Revolution* (1981) pp. 62–5, and D. AugustinePerez, 'Very Wealthy Businessmen in Imperial Germany', *Journal of Social History*, Vol. 22 (1988), p. 304.
47. W. Mosse, *Jews in the German Economy: The GermanJewish Economic Elite, 1820–1935* (Oxford, 1987), pp. 172–217.
48. See A. Daumard, *Les fortunes françaises au XIXe siècle* (Paris, 1973); Plessis, *Régents et Gouverneurs*.
49. Samples of English, French and German bankers for the years 1907 and 1928 established by the author.
50. Cassis, *Les banquiers*; Plessis, 'Bankers in French Society', C. Charle, *Les élites de la République, 1880–1900* (Paris, 1987); Achterberg, *Berliner Hochfinanz*: Stern, *Gold and Iron*.
51. See Cassis, *Les banquiers* and 'Bankers in English Society in the late Nineteenth Century', *Economic History Review*, 2nd series, Vol. XXXVIII (1985).
52. See P. Stanworth and A. Giddens, 'An Economic Elite: a Demographic Profile of Company Chairmen', in P. Stanworth and A. Giddens, *Elites and Power in British*

Society (Cambridge, 1974).

53. See L. Bergeron, *Les capitalistes en France, 1780–1914* (Paris, 1978); Charle, *Elites de la République*; A. Roy, *Histoire de la maison Schneider et du Creusot* (Paris, 1962); J.N. Jeanneney, *François de Wendel en République: L'argent et le pouvoir 1914–1940* (Paris, 1975).
54. Plessis, 'Bankers in French Society'.
55. G. Feldman, 'Bankers and Banking in Germany after the First World War: Strategies of Defence', in Cassis (ed.), *Finance and Financiers*. On the weight of the heavy industry see his *Iron and Steel in German Inflation, 1916–1923* (Princeton, 1977) among many other works on the subject.
56. Cassis, *Les banquiers* and 'Bankers in English Society'.
57. For further developments on this point, see Y. Cassis, 'Wirtschaftselite und Bürgertum: England, Frankreich, Deutschland um 1900', in J. Kocka (ed.), *Bürgertum im 19. Jahrhundert. Deutschland im europäischen Vergleich*, 3 vols. (Munich, 1988), Vol. 2.
58. On the salaried managers in Germany, see J. Kocka, 'Les entrepreneurs salariés dans l'industrie allemande à la fin du XIXe et au début du XXe siècle' in M. LévyLeboyer (ed.), *Le patronat de la seconde industrialisation* (Paris, 1979).
59. On the general question of ownership and management in the United States and major European economies, see the essays in A.D. Chandler, Jr. and H. Daems (eds.), *Managerial Hierarchies* (Cambridge, MA, 1980) and A. Chandler's latest book, *Scale and Scope* (Cambridge, MA, 1990).
60. Y. Cassis, 'Profits and Profitability in English Banking, 1870–1914', *Revue international d'histoire de la banque*, Vol. 34–35 (1987).
62. See for example Tolliday, *Business, Banking and Politics*, p. 179.
63. J. Bouvier, *Naissance d'une banque: le Crédit Lyonnais* (Paris, 1968), pp. 126–9.
64. Pinner, *Deutsche Wirtschaftsführer*, pp. 184–5. See also H. James, *The German Slump: Politics and Economics, 1924–1936* (Oxford, 1986), pp. 139–46.

[2]

Excerpt from Margaret G. Myers, *Paris as a Financial Centre*, 135–56.

CHAPTER VI

PARIS AS AN INVESTMENT CENTRE

THE investment market plays a far more important *rôle* in Paris than the money market, from the foreign as well as from the domestic point of view. Personal savings and investments are a national habit in France, and the surplus of wealth in the country, accumulated in small individual amounts, has for a century furnished a steady stream of capital flowing into the securities market. One may say that the Frenchman is proud of what he saves, in contrast with the American, who is proud of what he spends.

The most striking aspect of French saving is the proportion which has always gone into foreign investment. To a certain extent this is inevitable in a country which is industrially far advanced, but in France, foreign investment seems to have occurred earlier and in larger amounts than in other countries in a comparable stage of development. A number of circumstances serve to explain this situation. The small scale upon which many French concerns were organised made it unnecessary for them to float securities in order to obtain their capital. The family of owners, or a group of partners provided the initial capital, and additions and improvements to the plant were paid for out of profits. Such enterprises were quite independent of the investment market.

On the investors' side, there was relatively small demand for the industrial shares, and instead a preference for government bonds with a fixed yield. Since many foreign governments paid a higher rate than the French, their issues were easily placed among investors who were primarily interested in revenue. French banks, through which most small investors purchase their securities, earned higher commissions in placing foreign issues, and therefore pushed them more zealously. Moreover, the French Government itself, for political reasons, took an interest in the flotation of certain foreign securities. In view of all the factors which favoured foreign investments as against domestic, it is not surprising that French producers often experienced difficulty in obtaining new capital.

The total volume of securities held by investors in France, and the volume of foreign investments, have been estimated for various dates before the war as follows :—*

TABLE XVI

Securities Owned in France

(In Millions of Francs)

	French.	Foreign.	Total.	Per cent. of Foreign to Total.
1850 . .	6,627	2,500	9,127	27
1869 . .	20,869	10,000	30,869	32
1880 . .	40,914	15,000	55,914	27
1890 . .	53,677	20,000	73,677	27
1899 . .	59,882	27,000	86,882	31
1908 . .	66,446	38,000	104,446	36
1914 . .	—	45,000	—	—

The lower proportion of foreign securities after 1869 is explained largely by the payment of the French war indemnity of five milliard francs, which was accomplished by selling French foreign investments. After 1890 the proportion of foreign to domestic issues increased again. Between 1890 and 1908 the volume of foreign issues nearly doubled, while the volume of domestic securities increased by little more than one-fourth. Expressed in another way, less than half of the net increase during this period was in the holdings of domestic securities.

This flood of foreign issues into France drew criticism not only because of the prejudice which it caused to French

* André Théry, "*Les grands établissements de crédit français, avant, pendant et après la guerre.*"

borrowers,* but also because of the poor quality of many of the securities. There was no adequate supervision over them, either by the banks which handled the issue, or by the Government. The banks were little interested in the intrinsic value of the bonds they handled. Few were kept in their own portfolios. The Government was more concerned with the taxes to be derived from them than with safeguarding the investor. Indeed, the legal regulations for these issues were of such a nature that they tended to lower rather than raise the quality, inasmuch as they increased the cost of issue. Every foreign security issued in France had the choice between two tax systems. Either it paid an initial tax of 2 per cent. of par value, which when added to the other costs of emission (3 or 4 per cent.) made a total cost of 5 or 6 per cent.; or it came under the *abonnement* system, which avoided the initial 2 per cent. tax, but had to guarantee, for the whole life of the security, the payment of all French taxes—stamp, transmission and revenue. These requirements added so much to the cost of issue that the best securities were always able to find better terms in another market, and it was often true that only those of second quality were willing to pay the price of admission to the French market. The small-investing public, which bought its securities for the most part over the counters and at the recommendation of the big banks, was not competent to judge the quality of the issues, and was more interested in the rate of interest than in any other feature.

It was not until the years immediately preceding the outbreak of the World War that the increase in foreign investments was halted. In those years the international political situation became so obviously explosive that even high interest rates could no longer attract French investors to foreign issues. The revolutions in Mexico and South American countries, the Moroccan crisis, the Balkan wars, and the increasing tension between the great Powers, were accompanied by an economic crisis in many countries which

* Lysis, "*Les capitalistes français contre la France,*" and Testis, "*Le rôle des établissements de crédit en France; la vérité sur les propos de Lysis.*"

still further discouraged the flotation of foreign bonds in France. The volume of new foreign issues, which had been more than twice as great as that of domestic issues in the years 1908–11, fell off sharply in 1912, and in 1913 was very little larger than the domestic.

TABLE XVII *

New Issues of Securities in France
(In Millions of Francs)

	Government and Municipal.		Industrial.		Total.		
	French.	Foreign.	French.	Foreign.	French.	Foreign.	All.
1908	97	1,040	634	1,709	731	2,749	3,480
1909	155	809	1,630	1,700	1,785	2,509	4,294
1910	106	1,628	779	3,098	885	4,726	5,611
1911	7	989	807	2,893	814	3,882	4,696
1912	312	430	1,648	2,651	1,960	3,081	5,041
1913	151	754	2,018	2,004	2,169	2,758	4,927

During the war the French market was practically closed to foreign issues in order to turn the investment resources of the country toward French Government loans, and to prevent an export of capital with consequent depreciation of the franc. The *Bourse* had been closed upon outbreak of the war, and did not re-open again until December 7th, 1914. Several months later, in order to prevent speculation against the French *Rentes* by foreigners, the brokers themselves decided (following the example of London brokers about the same time) not to accept selling orders unless given by persons of French nationality, residing in France, and actually in possession of the stocks which they wished to sell. Foreigners were thus practically prevented from reselling their former investments on the Paris *Bourse*.

New foreign issues were not legally excluded until the law of May 31st, 1916, which forbade their introduction or sale unless specifically authorised by the Minister of Finance. This law has never been repealed, and although the Minister

* E. Théry, "*Economiste Européen,*" December 27th, 1913, p. 810.

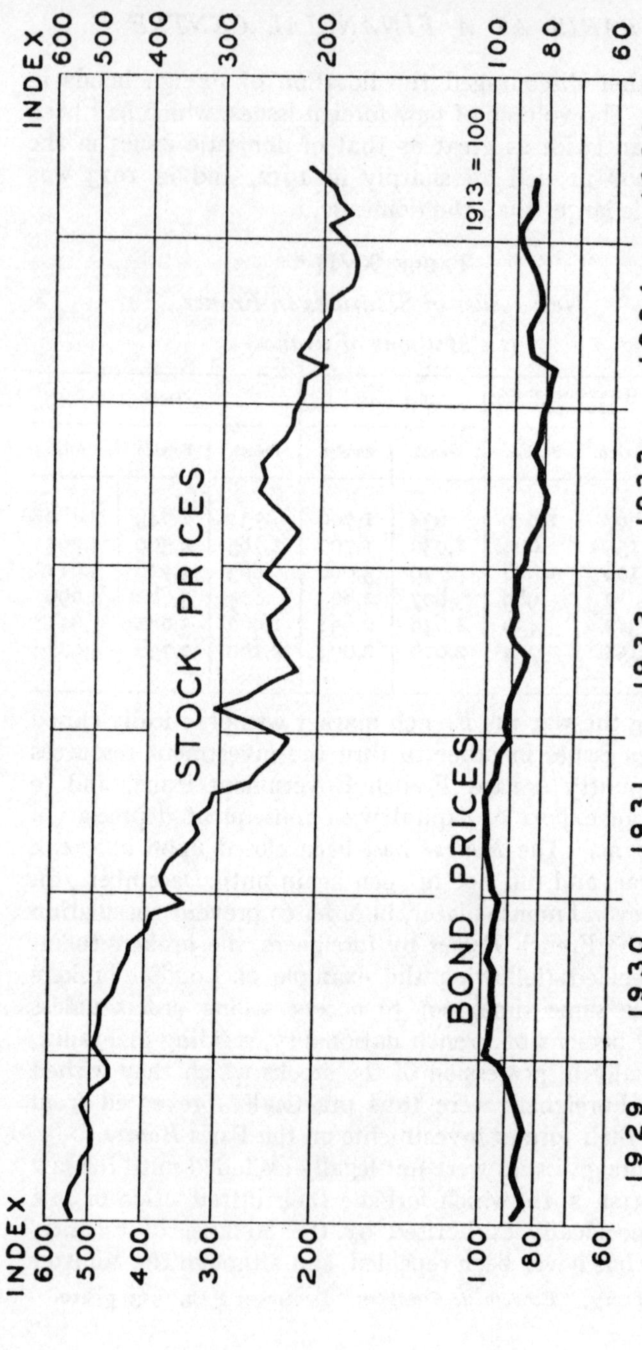

CHART III.—Index Numbers of French Security Prices. The index of bond prices includes 12 rails, 19 industrials, 2 Government issues and 2 mortgage bonds. The index of stock prices includes 300 issues.
Source: *"La France Economique."*

of Finance had always had the right to interfere with foreign issues, the necessity of his formal approval has been a decided deterrent since 1916. In addition to this requirement, foreign issues were further handicapped by the very high taxes placed upon them during the war and afterwards. In addition to transmission and stamp taxes, the revenue from foreign securities was subject to an annual tax up to 25 per cent., as compared with a tax of 18 per cent. on domestic issues.

Foreign Issues after the War

In the years after 1926, as France recovered from the war and the inflation, there was again a surplus of savings available for foreign investment. There had actually been a favourable balance of trade for France ever since 1921, but the flight of capital had more than counterbalanced it. After 1926 the normal surplus arising from trade was increased by several unusual circumstances. Not only did the capital which had taken flight away from the depreciating franc return to France after the stabilisation, but a large amount of foreign funds also came to France—at first between July, 1926, and January, 1927, to speculate in a rise of the franc, and later, when the position of the franc was assured, in flight from other currencies. A stream of gold set in toward France which threatened to flood the money market.

The efforts to cope with this tide of gold have been elsewhere described.* The plans to make of Paris a great money market for the financing of international trade was the central point of a scheme which, it was hoped, would give an outlet for the funds dammed up in Paris and redistribute them throughout the world. The investment market had its place also in the plans; foreign issues were to be moderately encouraged by the reduction of the tax on dividends from 25 to 18 per cent. (in comparison with a 16 per cent. tax on French issues). At the same time, certain technical improvements of the *Bourse* were to be carried

* See p. 24.

out,* which would facilitate trading in foreign as well as in domestic securities.

It is doubtful if such feeble efforts could have been successful in any case, but they were completely useless in the face of the unwillingness of the average investor to risk any more money abroad, especially in bonds, and in view of the fact that the law of 1916 was still in force. The French investor was quite right in his judgment, as the Americans learned later to their cost, but the result of the French failure to lend out their surplus produced an accumulation of gold in France which, perhaps fortunately, brought the world crisis more quickly to a head.

TABLE XVIII

Securities Issued in France, 1926–32†

(*In Millions of Francs*)

	French Government.	French Industrial.	Total French.	Foreign Government.	Foreign Industrial.	Total Foreign.	Total.
1926	—	—	—	—	—	—	9,182
1927	—	—	—	—	—	—	18,487
1928	—	—	—	—	—	—	25,070
1929	5,416	15,107	20,522	—	—	—	20,522
1930	8,335	21,877	29,412	3,111	c. 800	3,911	33,323
1931	8,147	16,386	24,533	3,400	c. 350	3,750	28,283
1932	23,393*	6,424	29,817	1,400	—	1,400	31,217
1933	20,657	3,600	24,257	1,008	—	1,008	25,265
1934	20,450	4,095	24,545	—	—	—	24,545

* Including 6091 millions of short-term Treasury issues.

The number of foreign loans, and their volume, has never gone back to anything like its pre-war dimensions, and after 1930 the amount fell off again even from the moderate peak of that year. Such loans as were made were largely government issues. Some of them aroused criticism because they were made to France's political friends, although this type of loan is neither new nor exclusively French. It will be

* See p. 153.

† "*La France Economique*" for each year.

seen from the following list that the largest loans were those made under the Dawes Plan and the Young Plan, and the loan to Great Britain. Some of the issues represented funding operations, and did not therefore represent a demand for new credit.

TABLE XIX

*Foreign Government Loans Floated in Paris, 1919–33**

1919. China—23,000,000 francs, 7 per cent., Lung-Tsing-Uha; Railway.
1922. Hungary—63,846,500 francs, 6 per cent., Consolidation Loan.
1923. China—$43,893,900, 5 per cent., Industrial Bank of China.
Austria—170,000,000 francs, 6½ per cent., Stabilisation Loan.
Belgium—400,000,000 francs, 6½ per cent.
Roumania—£6,943,160, 4 per cent., Consolidation Loan.
1924. Germany—£3,000,000, 7 per cent., Dawes Plan Loan.
1925. Austria—71,172,500 francs, 5 per cent., Funding Loan.
Bulgaria—44,360,000 francs, 6½ per cent.
1926. Austria—25,090,000 francs, 5 per cent., Funding Loan.
Austria—60,000,000 francs, 5 per cent., Funding Loan.
1927. Poland—$2,000,000, 7 per cent., Stabilisation Loan.
Hungary—96,000,000 francs, 6½ per cent., Funding Loan.
1928. Turkey—99,945,000 francs, Consolidation of notes of Ancient Empire.
Turkey—670,216,500 francs, payment of Cumulated Annuities of Public Debt.
Roumania—50,929,000 francs, 5 per cent.
Roumania—269,353,000 francs, 4 per cent.
1929. Roumania—561,638,000 francs, 7 per cent., *Caisse autonome des monopoles de Roumanie.*
Bulgaria—130,000,000 francs, 7½ per cent., Stabilisation Loan.
1930. Chile—35,000,000 Swiss francs, 6 per cent.,
Germany—2,515,000,000 francs, 5½ per cent., Young Plan Loan.
Hungary—59,650,000 francs, 6 per cent., Funding Loan.
1931. Roumania—575,000,000 francs, 7½ per cent., *Caisse autonome des monopoles de Roumanie.*
Yugoslavia—675,000,000 francs, 7 per cent.
Great Britain—2,500,000,000 francs, 4·25 per cent. Treasury Notes.

* Source: *Temps*, March 2nd, 1932, and "*La France Economique.*"

Yugoslavia—250,000,000 francs, Treasury Notes.
Hungary—354,000,000 francs, Treasury Notes.
1932. Belgium—800,000,000 francs, 5½ per cent., twenty-five years.
Czechoslavakia—600,000,000 francs, 5 per cent., five years.
1933. Belgium—600,000,000 francs, 5½ per cent., thirty-five years.
Austria—408,125,000 francs, 5½ per cent., twenty years.

TABLE XX

French Balance of Payments
(In Milliards of Francs)

	1928.	1929.	1930.	1931.	1932.	1933.	1934.
Payments made to foreign countries :							
Excess of imports (including colonies)	4·5	10·0	13·0	13·3	10·0	9·0	6·9
Immigrant remittances	2·2	2·5	2·5	1·8	1·2	0·8	1·0
Government payments (interest, etc.)	2·3	0·6	0·9	0·7	0·5	0·3	—
Purchase of securities or repurchase of previous French issues	2·2	2·2	5·4	2·1	0·5	—	—
Foreign issues in France	0·6	1·1	1·4	7·3	3·8	1·3	—
Bank of France credit to foreign central bank	—	—	—	3·8	—	—	—
Purchase of devisen by Bank of France and Treasury	10·9	1·5	—	—	—	—	—
Other invisible capital exports	—	—	—	—	—	1·5	0·2
Gold imports (net)	6·1	8·5	11·5	18·5	17·7	—	1·5
Total	28·8	31·4	34·7	47·5	33·7	12·9	9·6
Payments made to France :							
Freight, insurance, transport	3·7	3·6	3·1	2·7	2·3	2·1	1·6
Tourist expenditures in France	7·5	8·5	8·5	6·0	3·0	3·0	2·5
Reparations (including Young Plan Loan of 1930)	5·2	6·7	7·1	2·6	—	—	—
French securities issued abroad or repayment of previous French loans	0·2	0·2	—	—	6·9	0·2	0·5
Interest on capital invested abroad	3·5	5·8	5·1	4·0	1·7	2·0	2·5
Invisible capital imports	8·7	—	6·8	25·8	2·0	—	2·5
Sales of devisen by Bank of France and Treasury	—	6·6	4·1	6·4	17·8	3·6	—
Gold exports (net)	—	—	—	—	—	2·0	—
Total	28·8	31·4	34·7	47·5	33·7	12·9	9·6

Source : " *La France Economique* " for each year.

The amount of all these loans was quite insignificant in comparison with the surplus which accrued to France from the annual balance of payments with the rest of the world. This balance, which is estimated every year in *La France Economique* by Pierre Meynial, makes it possible to trace the changes in the import and export trade, in the export of capital, in reparations payments and in the other items which make up the national balance of payments. It will be observed that in spite of an increase in the unfavourable *trade* balance of France in the years 1928–31, the total balance of *payments* was favourable because of off-setting invisible items, notably the "invisible import of funds," which reached a peak of 25 milliard francs in 1931.

In many respects the balance of payments for the year 1929 was very similar to that for the year 1913. That is, the balance seemed to be swinging back to its pre-war normal level, with foreign governments and private concerns coming to France for long-term loans as they had done before the war. If it had not been for other forces largely beyond the control of France, which brought about banking and currency crises in many countries, the efforts of France to redistribute the funds clogging her market might have succeeded.

Domestic Issues

The total amount of domestic industrial issues in France can be seen in Table XVIII. In the rapidly declining total after 1930, bank and railway securities maintained their level better than the manufacturing and mining issues. The industries most severely affected by the crisis were, in France as elsewhere, the textiles, gas, rubber and chemicals.

Stock prices had begun to decline in France early in 1929, even before the Wall Street panic of that year. The drop was not as pronounced as in the United States, but it continued almost without interruption through 1931, and after several short periods of improvement, reached a new low in the summer of 1934. The total drop in the index of prices was from 540 to 190, while the index of transactions fell from 1,121 to 160 in the same time.*

Bond prices, which had been rising since 1926, continued upwards until the middle of 1931, and after that declined almost steadily as interest rates rose. In 1934 the upward movement was again resumed.

The decline in the price and volume of sales was greater in the case of stocks than in that of bonds, for after May, 1929, public demand shifted back to bonds, that is, to issues with a fixed revenue, and away from stocks of which the revenue varies. This may be considered the normal state of affairs in France, where the small investor predominates. During the period of inflation, stocks had served to protect the investor to a certain extent from the effects of the depreciated currency, since their varying dividends permits the price of stocks to rise as the currency depreciates. Once the franc was stabilised, this advantage was lost and the end of the speculative period brought an end to the preference for stocks.

The Technique of Marketing Securities in France

One of the principal features in the issue of new securities and the exchange of old ones in France is the prominent part played by banks. The position and functions of the investment banks have been discussed in a previous chapter †; they serve not only as houses of issue when a new group of securities is to be introduced, but they, and the commercial banks as well, sell a very large amount of securities over their counters, in small lots, to customers who accept the advice of the banker in investment matters.

Even for those securities which are traded in by the banks, however, the quotations depend upon those which are set by the transactions of the *Bourse*. In the *Bourse*, the heart of the investment market, can be observed most clearly the special characteristics of the French investment system, and the differences between the Paris market and the London and New York Stock Exchanges.

* Index of "*Statistique Générale.*"
† See p. 107.

The organisation of the Paris *Bourse* has a semi-official character which is quite different from the private-club status of the New York Stock Exchange. The Society of Exchange Agents (*Compagnie des Agents de Change*), which is ordinarily known as the *Parquet* from its meeting place in the central hall of the *Bourse*, has been the official market since 1141, when Louis VII. granted a charter to the Guild of Money-changers, giving them the right to operate on the Great Bridge of Paris. Through a historical evolution of functions, the *Parquet* now enjoys a legal monopoly of stock selling, and the other markets operate only under its suffrance.

Since 1898 the number of its members has stood at seventy, in spite of many proposals to increase it. Thanks to the monopoly which the members enjoy, they are looked upon to a certain extent as public officers, with definite responsibilities towards their profession and the Government. A member may not carry on transactions for his own account, but is limited to carrying out the orders of customers. The members are legally responsible for the validity of the quotations which appear on the official list published daily at the close of trading, the listed securities being divided up among "specialists" for this purpose. The form of accounting to be used by brokers is prescribed by law, but the actual records are protected by the law regarding professional secrecy.

The qualifications for membership in the *Parquet* are carefully established by law. The applicant must be a French citizen at least twenty-five years of age, with four years of practical experience in banking, business, or law. In his own name he must possess enough capital to pay at least one-fourth the price of the seat he is purchasing. Until recently this price was fixed at 1,500,000 francs, but now it is set by the association according to the particular circumstances of each sale. In addition, the new member must contribute 250,000 francs to the guarantee fund of the association. This fund, which includes the proceeds of the sale of seats and certain other payments, is used for the protection of the customer in case any member is unable to meet his contractual obligations. If the guarantee fund is inadequate to the charges upon it all the members are liable to further assessments up to the amount of their total personal fortune. The obligation towards this fund is perhaps the most onerous of all those attached to membership in the *Parquet*. This type of guarantee does not exist outside of the official market, and it gives to that market a reputation for conservatism and solidity. It is a strong incentive to the small investor to choose his holdings from the issues listed on the *Parquet*, and it encourages the *Parquet* to prudence in the admission of new securities to its list, since the failure of any broker due to dealings in worthless stock would bring heavy penalties upon the whole membership.

When the prospective member has met all preliminary requirements he is permitted to come up for examination by a committee of members ; if he passes this test his name is submitted for approval to the association and to the Minister of Finance before he is finally admitted. Members are not permitted to have an interest in any commercial enterprise.

The official character of the *Parquet* is evidenced not only by the participation of the Minister of Finance in the admission of new members, but also by the necessity for his approval of new security listings. He is kept in touch with the market through the committee of eight members known as the *Chambre Syndicale*, which has executive and disciplinary functions. Every company which wishes its stock to appear on the official list of the *Parquet* must submit to this committee a number of documents and reports. French corporation reports are generally inadequate. The documents submitted to the *Parquet* committee are quite distinct from the announcement which must be made for every issue of new stock in the *Journal Officiel*, and which has nothing whatever to do with the listing of the stock on the exchange.

If the stock to be listed is a foreign one it must have the approval of the Minister of Foreign Affairs as well as of the Minister of Finance. The offerings of foreign shares have, however, been so rare in recent years that he is seldom called upon. The political scandal resulting from the approval

L 2

of the S. N. I. A. Viscosa, an Italian company for the manufacture of artificial silk, has made Cabinet Ministers ever since wary in their attitude towards industrial shares from abroad.* This has undoubtedly been another factor accounting for the absence of foreign shares in the French market.

The stocks listed on the *Parquet* are traded in either for immediate cash settlement (*marché au comptant*), or on time (*marché à terme*). In the cash market, securities are paid for upon delivery, which takes place on the day following purchase or any day thereafter, depending upon arrangements between the individuals concerned. This is the market in which the largest part of the transactions is made. Since purchases are paid for at once, there is no trading on credit, and consequently little speculation. There is no limit to the number of securities which can be traded at a time, and " odd-lot " trading therefore falls in this market. All the securities listed on the *Parquet* are eligible for trading on the cash market ; at the beginning of the year 1930 these were about 2,500 in number. In spite of the relatively large volume of business transacted in the cash market it contributes less to the picturesque confusion of the sessions of the *Bourse* than the time market, largely because cash orders are not called out, as in New York, but are simply entered by the brokers in their note-books.

The term market is that in which purchases are made for settlement twice a month. Here securities are handled only in lots of twenty-five or its multiples, and brokers' commissions are lower than in the cash market. This is the market for large-scale and speculative trading, since credit is very largely employed. In placing the order a margin of 20 per cent. in cash is customary, or 30 per cent. in approved securities (valued at 10 to 20 per cent. below the market price). The broker has the right to increase the margin requirements, as was done during 1926 and 1931, for example, up to 40 per cent., or to demand securities or funds to cover the transaction before he executes the order.

* The hearings on this case were published in the Paris *Temps* during December, 1930.

The purchases and sales made in the time market are settled twice a month, during three days at the middle and end of the month, much as in London. Credit which is extended to purchasers to enable them to hold securities from one settling day to another goes under the name of *reports* or carrying loans. These are the nearest French equivalent for the American call loans, but there are very important differences between them.*

The term market was at one time the most important section of the *Parquet*, but it has been declining in relative importance ever since 1900, and rapidly since the war. At the outbreak of the war, French Government *Rentes* were withdrawn from the *marché à terme*, in order to prevent as far as possible speculation against them. It was not until 1927 that the continued rise of the *Rentes*, in view of the stabilisation of the franc, seemed to make it safe to reopen the term market to them. At first only the 3 per cent. and 5 per cent. Amortisables were added to the list; later other *Rentes* were included, but the market has never regained its pre-war scope. Of the total list of 2,500 issues on the *Parquet*, only 100 at the beginning of 1930 were eligible for term trading.† The lack of new foreign issues has also been an important factor in the decline of the term market, since foreign industrials were frequently among the popular speculative securities. The actual number of shares traded in at term is, however, not a fair indication of the volume of trading in this market, for the more speculative issues which figure in it have a very much more rapid turn-over than the issues which are traded in exclusively for cash. In periods of active speculation such as that which preceded the Oustric crash, the term market may still account for a very large part of the total trading on the Paris *Bourse*.

The question is often raised as to the value of a term market in the *Parquet*, a question which resolves itself into the more general one of the value of speculation in any securities market. It is recognised that the operations on

* See p. 158.

† Report of the *Comité parlementaire du commerce* (1929–30), p. 53.

term are far more dangerous for the public than those on account, but it is also pointed out that the term operators are to a large extent professional traders who are presumably able to take care of themselves, and it is felt that a certain amount of speculation forms a useful cushion for the market by absorbing the floating supply of securities.

Speculation as such has never been the problem in Paris that it is in New York. This is due in large part to the fact that there is not a close connection between the Paris banks and the *Bourse* which would bring the banks into jeopardy with every drop in security prices on the *Bourse*. Another factor is that a larger proportion of the trading is done for investment in France, where saving and investing are widespread. The problem in France has been the protection of the small investor from worthless speculative stocks, rather than from losses due to speculation in relatively good stocks. It would be impossible to improve the situation in New York by merely copying certain features of the French set-up, since the whole legal and economic background of the two countries is different. Reform in New York will have to be accomplished rather by changes suited to the particular situation there. It is noteworthy that the feature of the Paris *Bourse* which is sometimes advocated as a solution for the speculative problem in New York—the term settlement—is precisely that feature which permits speculation in Paris. There is no reason to think that if transplanted to New York it would serve to reduce speculation.

The second great division of the Paris *Bourse* is the *marché en banque*, or *Coulisse*, which takes its name from the fact that it meets in the corridor outside the *Bourse* proper. It is comparable to the Curb market of New York in many respects. The *Coulisse* has had a somewhat checkered career, and has always been obliged to content itself with what was left over from the *Parquet*, in the way of business. For many years the *Parquet* fought to exterminate the *Coulisse* altogether, but in 1901 the two groups finally signed an agreement and since then have inhabited the same building in peace. The *Parquet* agreed to share its monopoly of trading with the *Coulisse* in return for a sharing of commissions. The *Coulisse* recognises the legal right of the members of the *Parquet* to all transactions in securities on the official list. When a member of the *Coulisse* has an order for one of these issues, he transmits it to the specialist of the *Parquet*, who executes it for him at a rate much lower than an ordinary customer would be charged. As much as 40 per cent. is deducted from the usual commission in the case of some term transactions, and 20 per cent. on *reports*. On these terms the two groups cooperate with mutual profit.

The number of members on the *Coulisse* is not limited, as is that of the *Parquet*, and the requirements for membership are less exacting. The proposed member must be of French nationality, and must be possessed of a capital of 2,500,000 francs, either personal or corporate. With these relatively simple qualifications he may be admitted upon two-thirds vote of the association. On the *Coulisse* a member may trade for his own account, in contrast with the *Parquet* where such action is strictly forbidden. The *Coulisse* has also a guarantee fund, but it is intended only to protect the members from any loss incurred in dealing with a colleague; the customer, legally and in theory, is protected only by the capital of his own broker, but in fact it happens that the *Coulisse* indemnifies the customer also, in order to protect its own reputation.

The *Coulisse*, like the Curb market, is pre-eminently the place for new issues and for old ones which have not been found suitable for the official list of the *Parquet*, or which have been left to the *Coulisse* by courtesy of the *Parquet*. Although the requirements for entry on the list of thes *Coulisse* list are not onerous, the number of listings has greatly declined during the past few years. The list is being constantly shortened by losses at both ends. The best issues of the list are taken over by the *Parquet*, ninety-seven securities having been transferred from the *Coulisse* to the official list between 1919 and 1930. At the other end the *Coulisse* is obliged to strike off the poorest issues as companies fail or lose their standing; more than 100 were dropped in the house-cleaning of 1930–31.* These losses have recently not been compensated, as they should be in normal times, by the constant addition of new issues. The *rôle* of the *Coulisse* before the war consisted largely of introducing foreign issues, acclimating them, and passing them on to the *Parquet*. But in recent years the influx of foreign shares has been almost totally cut off, and the new domestic issues have not appeared in sufficient volume to fill the gap. A large part of the new issues in 1930–32 were made by the Treasury itself or the Government-guaranteed railways, and appeared therefore on the official list.

One of the results of the decline in activity on the *Coulisse* was the reorganisation of that market. The members were formerly grouped into two *Syndicats*, one for term operations and the other for cash trading. Since most of the members who belonged to the term market were also connected with the cash market, the division had little value, and on January 25th, 1932, the two were combined into one *Syndicat général des Banquiers en Valeurs près de la Bourse de Paris*, with a *Chambre syndicale* or executive committee of twelve members.† The reorganisation changed very little in the actual functioning of the market, but represented an economy in administration. Term settlements continue to be made monthly as before, instead of fortnightly as on the *Parquet*. The long period which elapses between settlement dates on the *Coulisse* is an element of grave danger not only to customers but to brokers as well.

Besides the *Parquet* and the *Coulisse*, there is also a *marché hors cote*, a sort of curb market for the curb market, which handles trading in securities not listed by either of the organised exchanges. For many years this market was quite unregulated, but repeated scandals finally brought about a modicum of organisation, under rules which went into effect on February 4th, 1929. The section of the *Bourse* corridor where these brokers had been accustomed to meet was recognised as their especial domain ; a " list " of traded securities was established, and quotations published daily.

* *Journal des Finances*, January 22nd, 1932.
† *Journal de la Bourse*, January 30th, 1932.

The information regarding this market is, however, always meager, and in periods in which speculation is little active, its transactions are relatively unimportant.

The whole organisation of the securities markets in Paris was brought under scrutiny in 1929–30 when the movement of funds into Paris was beginning to attract attention, as a part of the effort to develop Paris into an international financial centre and thus find employment for its surplus funds. During October, 1929, conferences were called between the Minister of Finance (then Monsieur Chéron) and the members of the *Parquet* and the *Coulisse*, in an effort to plan changes which would facilitate trading. The suggestions made for the *Parquet* ranged from such relatively superficial reforms as the elimination of confusion from the trading floor, to more important matters like the extension of telephone connections to provincial exchanges, the regularisation of quotations, and the better organisation of credit so that on settling days the rate of interest on *reports* would show less violent fluctuations. The recommendations made for the *Coulisse* included the reduction of brokerage charges, the reorganisation of credit, and the organisation of a stock exchange clearing house.

At about the same time, a Parliamentary committee was occupying itself with the same problems. This committee also recommended improvements in the physical organisation of the *Bourse*, but was especially concerned with the more fundamental problems. The creation of a national organisation to provide publicity for corporate activities was stressed, since corporation reports in France are extremely unsatisfactory from the point of view of the investor and the general public. Further legal regulation of plural-voting stocks was another recommendation. The most radical of all the innovations suggested was the unification of the *Parquet* and the *Coulisse*, but it seems to have received no serious attention from either of the bodies most concerned.*

The suggestion which bore the most immediate fruit was

* *L'Economiste Européen*, October 11th, 1929; *London Economist*, November 2nd, 1929; Report of *Comité parlementaire français du commerce* (1929–30); Marseilhan, *La Coulisse et sa Réorganisation*.

that for the reduction of brokerage charges, which went into effect early in the year 1930. At the same time the unit of trading for certain securities in the term market was reduced to lots of five and ten, instead of lots of twenty-five as had previously been required. The hoped-for increase in *Bourse* activity could not be stimulated by merely reducing the cost of trading, and after two years' trial of the new rates, the old ones were restored. These, as published in 1932, were as follows * :—

Cash Transactions

0·15 per cent. of the amount of the transaction, for French *Rentes* with a minimum of 0·75 francs.
0·15 francs per share, for shares quoted at less than 50 francs with a minimum of 2·50 francs.
0·30 francs per share, for shares quoted at 50–100 francs with a minimum of 2·50 francs.
0·30 per cent. of the amount of the transaction, for securities quoted at more than 100 francs.

Term Transactions

0·30 francs per security, for securities quoted at less than 200 francs.
0·60 francs per security, for securities quoted at 200–400 francs.
0·25 per cent. of the amount of the transaction, for securities quoted at more than 400 francs.

The *Bourse*, instead of developing, as had been hoped for, into an international securities market, saw its volume of business declining steadily, and the quoted value of its listed securities falling off.

Relations between Investment Market and Short-term Money Market

The funds with which operations on the Paris *Bourse* are financed are quite different from those in New York, and it has already been pointed out that there is in Paris nothing corresponding to the call loan market in New York. There

* *Journal Officiel*, March 31st, 1932.

is, in the first place, no such volume of funds available for day-to-day loans in Paris, since the branch banking system of France makes it unnecessary for provincial banks to keep reserve funds on deposit in the banks of Paris. And in the second place, because the speculation in Paris is for the most part carried on in the term market, with settlements at the end of each fortnight, there is little demand for day-to-day credit from stock exchange operators.

The loans made in order to carry stocks from one settling day to another, called *reports*, may be made in either securities or money. On the *Parquet* their duration is for two weeks, on the *Coulisse* for one month, because of the difference in settling periods in the two exchanges. The funds may come from a number of sources. Many brokers make a practice of lending a part of their own capital in this way, and many receive also deposits from customers for this purpose. Banks usually keep a part of their short-term funds loaned on *reports*, since the period of the loan is short and repayment is almost certain. In addition there are several small institutions, such as the *Société Française de Reports et de Dépôts*, which specialise in accepting funds for placement in such loans.*

The amount of *reports* is not published, but is undoubtedly small in comparison with the total volume of trading, and varies with the proportion of speculative activity to the whole. The rate is fixed by the executive committees of the exchanges, and is published regularly. It varies widely from one settlement day to the next, but is always lower at the *Parquet* than the *Coulisse* because of the shorter settlement period. Part of the variations may be ascribed to the varying lengths of the period between settlements, due to the occurrence of Sundays, holidays, and longer months. During 1928 the rate went as high as 7 per cent. on the *Parquet*, and 8½ per cent. on the *Coulisse*. In the following year, as a result of the flooding of the Paris market with short-term funds, it fell off to as low as one-sixteenth of 1 per cent. The commission charged by brokers for placing such loans is relatively high, standing at 1·80 per cent. for securi-

* Chapoutot, "*Les Dépôts de Fonds en Banque.*"

ties, and at $\frac{1}{20}$ per cent. for cash. Besides the commission, there is also a tax on such operations. Speculation with borrowed money is, therefore, expensive in Paris, and this is a minor factor in the smaller volume of speculation at Paris as compared with New York or London.

[3]

European Journal of Political Research 17: 169–192, 1989

The 'Little Big Bang' in Paris: financial market deregulation in a *dirigiste* system

PHILIP G. CERNY
University of York, United Kingdom

Abstract. French *dirigisme* since World War II has been identified at four levels: economic planning; the dominance of a *neo-colbertiste* civil service elite; Gaullism and the Fifth Republic; and a state-led, credit-based system for financing industry. The last of these was seen by Zysman (1977, 1983) as the strategic core of *dirigisme,* as in Japan, through state control of industrial purse strings. Paradoxically, it was the Socialist Governments of 1981–86, in response to deregulation elsewhere, which initiated extensive capital market reforms intended to replace the state-led, credit-based system with an 'arms-length' financial market system. These continued under the right-wing Chirac Government. However, the reform process itself has been state-led rather than market-led; and both rigidities in the markets and shortcomings in the reforms have been highlighted by the October 1987 crash. Much *dirigisme* of a tactical kind remains, but the state's potential for strategic intervention has been reduced.

In studying state economic intervention in France, analysts have long been concerned with analysing a venerable *dirigiste* tradition dating from the 17th century. This has been seen as having undergone a renaissance after the Second World War, at several levels: first, the planning system; second, the development of a new technocratic ethos in the higher reaches of the civil service; third, the *étatiste* policy orientation of the Gaullists and the Fifth Republic more generally; and fourth, the financial system and the way in which money has been provided to the economy, especially for industrial modernisation.

The most thorough presentation of this thesis is to be found in the work of John Zysman (1977; 1983), who emphasises the fourth level of the financial system. In effect, Zysman's model of a state-led, credit-based system of nurturing and managing industrial development took its cue not only from European state theory and the French model, but also from a not entirely unfavourable comparison with the interventionist 'developmental state' which he and other authors have described in Japan (cf. Johnson, 1982).

Most critiques of this model focus on the first three levels. Financial deregulation is potentially a difference of kind, however. Deregulation, in theory, means more than just removing regulations: it implies both the removal of restraints on market forces inside the national economy; and opening up the economy to transnational market forces. Deregulation undermines *dirigisme*. This is all the more pertinent if we accept Zysman's argument that the cornerstone of the strategic state is the financial system.

However, to undermine *dirigisme* effectively, financial deregulation would have to change behaviour at other levels, enforcing competitive, market-oriented norms on bureaucratic, economic and political vested interests. And if such interests are secured by a *dirigiste* regime, then state actors may have to force deregulation on them. As Moran (1987) points out, state officials may decide to enforce deregulation on other officials and on state-sponsored corporatist bodies like stock exchanges, and may even impose deregulation on market actors like banks or industrial and commercial firms previously shielded from the full blast of the market – especially the international market.

Indeed, the 'strategic state' may pursue financial market deregulation as part of an internationalist strategy in the era of May Day and the Big Bang – to shake up ossified market structures and unadventurous market actors. But, in so doing, does the state thereby undermine its own *modus operandi* and even its *raison d'être?* Does the very concept of the 'strategic state' lose its plausibility in the era of the international 'financial revolution'? And if so, then what does this mean for theories of state intervention in general – and for the politics of both Left and Right – in the late 1980s?

French *dirigisme* and the financial markets

In the late 19th century, the Paris Bourse was the equal of the London Stock Exchange (Sassier and de Witt, 1985). Its 20th century decline reflected the destruction of the First World War, the stagnation of the interwar period, and the growing role which the state came to play in providing finance to industry in the post-Second World War period. The new *dirigisme* of the 1960s and 1970s was mirrored by the stagnation of financial markets, seen as the outdated legacy of the Third Republic's *mur d'argent.* Derided by the Left, they were also shunned by 'modernising' fractions of the Right, who preferred technocracy, indicative planning and state-sponsored industrial development.

Of course, this was not the whole story of France's postwar development. Cheap labour, the 'Korean War boom', European integration, a 'virtuous' inflationary circle and general Western prosperity all increased demand and lowered factor costs. But the role of the state was being simultaneously transformed by the pragmatic use of specific instruments of control, wielded by a self-styled modernising elite, who differed over party politics and the constitution, but who were agreed on the need for structural transformation.

Four instruments were of particular importance. One was a battery of postwar price controls, credit controls, exchange controls, etc., many of which lasted much longer. A second was nationalisation of certain basic industries and large parts of the financial system. Given wide managerial autonomy, they were expected nevertheless to reflect priorities of government policy on investment and growth. A third was control of new funds for investment, especially from Marshall Plan aid and later through the national *caisses* which invested funds from the national savings system. Bringing all of these together was the Plan, which worked through a combination of bilateral corporatism, Walrasian 'auctioneering', the targeting of specific government sanctions and incentives, and quite effective technocratic exhortation.

With the advent of the European Economic Community and the Fifth Republic in 1958, came a new step for *dirigisme*. Postwar reconstruction was national; now the state wished to make French capital competititive internationally. The most important element was the use of regulation, subsidies and control of credit flows for restructuring and industrial development. The Government's power of 'regulation' under the constitution – free from direct control by the National Assembly – gave it wide power over resource allocation. This helped ensure that recipients confirmed to state policy priorities, while E.E.C. entry, Kennedy Round tariff cuts, decolonisation, etc., provided the impetus for a shift away from protection towards support for internationally competitive sectors.

Subsidies cushioned the growing rural exodus while structural measures hastened it. The 1963 miners' strike speeded substitution of imported oil for coal. Spending on defence and nuclear weapons channeled funds into aeronautics, electronics, civil nuclear energy and scientific research in general. Backing for industrial concentration came through subsidies, loans, guarantees, procurement, etc., directed towards specific firms (especially those under French control) or sectors such as, steel, oil and electronics (Zysman, 1977, and Berger, 1981). The Fifth Plan, while systematising the new 'industrial imperative', also widened the ambitions of planning in the social field to deal with the consequences of restructuring. But the government's intention to end exchange controls and to move towards a more flexible monetary policy were thwarted by the Events of May 1968 and the financial instability which followed.

The 1970s were more paradoxical. Planning was overtaken by short-term policy, as economic disruptions falsified forecasts and undermined credibility. But at the same time the state took a stronger role in controlling the provision of finance to industry. New financing bodies such as the Institute for Industrial Development (I.D.I.) were established, major state-funded projects extended and closely targeted micro- and meso-economic policies adopted, first under the presidency of Georges Pompidou, and then – despite a 'liberal' façade – under Giscard d'Estaing from 1974. Interministerial committees took on a more comprehensive coordinating role (Green, 1983).

But one of the most important innovations arose almost accidentally, in the context of the international monetary perturbations of 1971. This was the establishment of credit ceilings – the *encadrement du crédit* system – not only for quantitative control of the money supply, but also to control the *direction* of financial flows. A number of analysts – Zysman (1983) in particular – have argued that, given the underdevelopment of alternative sources of finance, especially the small size and stagnation of the financial markets, ceilings ensured that there was a shortage of credit for investment which could only be satisfied by selective exemptions. The criteria for granting exemptions were overseen by the Finance Ministry, which ensured overall coordination of policy.

Together with direct government financing, subsidised interest rates and other incentives, the potential of credit policy for achieving other aims was increased. Combined with a *colbertiste* culture of state promotion of industry, a technocratic civil service linked with modernising fractions of capital, and greater political control of the policy process through the institutional arrangements of the Fifth Republic, Zysman concluded, such a state-led, credit-based supply-side approach put France into the 'strategic state' category.

Other writers have not seen the *encadrement* system as quite so coherent. What they suggest is that the French state is divided by competing policy networks and lacks the coordinating capacity of a strategic state like Japan, although it is none the less still highly *dirigiste* in each sector (cf. Hayward, 1986, and Machin and Wright, 1985). Intrastate cleavages are especially significant where they reflect competition between different economic sectors. State 'patrons' may identify with the interests of their 'clientele', but state actors, with their *grands corps* old boy networks (predominant in the private sector too) and control of the purse strings, still exert the greater influence.

A more important intrastate cleavage exists between ministries, state agencies and *grands corps* whose outlook is said to reflect an 'industrial logic', and those with a 'financial logic'. The first represent the *colbertiste* tradition of state promotion of industry and infrastructure in their priority for modernisation, production, research and development, and technology. Their post-war institutional base was in the planning system, but this shifted to the Ministry of Industry (and perhaps the Ministries of Defence and Foreign Trade); and their *grands corps* base would be in the *Corps des Mines,* the *Corps des Ponts et Chaussées,* the prefects and the civil administrators.

The second represent what in Britain would be called the 'Treasury view', giving priority to the control of government expenditure and its effects on the *grands équilibres* – inflation, the balance of payments, the government budget deficit, the percentage of G.D.P. taken in tax and compulsory contributions, etc. Not surprisingly, this outlook would be found in the Ministry of Finance, and the *Trésor* in particular; and its coporate identity would be firmly rooted in that most prestigious of *grands corps*, the *Inspecteurs des Finances.*

Now these contrasting logics are still both *dirigiste:* state elites dominate in their narrower spheres of competence; the private sector is still enmeshed in special relationships of a quasi-corporatist nature (Cerny and Schain, 1980, 1985; Cerny, 1987), while the public sector still plays a leading role in restructuring and modernisation; and the system of financial allocation is still predominantly state-controlled and credit-based. But the implications of financial market reform are far-reaching in both cases.

This image of state intervention in France has not really been challenged in the 1980s. Investment had been falling since the mid-1970s, and, despite a temporary upturn in 1980, its medium-term downward trend continued. Socialist policy after May 1981 did not dismantle existing instruments, but reinforced and complemented them through increased state funding of investment, direct control of major sectors through nationalisation, an expansion of planning, and reflationary social measures, all intended to set off a virtuous circle of growth and restructuring (Cerny and Schain, 1985). The residual consequences of the second oil shock, plus the deep international recession of 1982, however, undermined the French state's capacity to pursue its full range of goals.

The consequent shake-out of 1982–83 led to a new austerity ('socialist rigour') and a new emphasis on managerial autonomy and profitability in both public and private sectors. Huge losses in 1981–82 by the very firms being nationalised required extra funding as well as compensation for shareholders (a burden increased by the Constitutional Council). Private investment continued to stagnate, and only state-funded investment prevented a more precipitous fall.

In an apparent paradox, Socialist goverments took measures to strengthen private capital markets: at first to supplement the state-based system; but later as part of a more comprehensive policy – not only deregulating markets but also modifying the *dirigiste* system itself. But these changes were also seen as imperative for maintaining competitiveness in a volatile and rapidly evolving international financial environment. The Fabius Government of 1984–86 took a quantum leap forward in financial market deregulation, although the consequences were not visible until 1986, just as the Socialists were voted out.

After March 1986 the Chirac Government, elected on a 'neo-liberal' platform implicitly critical of earlier Gaullist and Giscardian *dirigisme* as well as of the Socialist variety (Berger, 1986; Schmidt, 1986), continued the deregulatory process. However, events in 1987, especially the global stock market crash, have highligted the fragility of deregulation so far. This can be seen at two levels: the difficulty of undermining *dirigisme* sufficiently to lead to a genuinely 'arms-length' financial market sytem; and the elusive objective of turning Paris into a competitive financial centre in the integrated, 24-hour global financial marketplace of the late 1980s.

French financial markets in the postwar period must therefore be seen in the context of the development of the French financial system as a whole. Stagnant through the 1940s, the Bourse rose rapidly in the expansive 1950s, peaking with the end of the Algerian War in 1962 (for long-term trends, see the graphs in *La Vie française,* 16 February 1978 and 27 January–2 February 1986). However, from 1962 onwards, the C.A.C. index (100 in late 1961) rarely went above its base level, with troughs in 1967 and 1974. From 1961 until 1982, then, the Bourse was stagnant or worse. This stagnation paralleled the development of the state-led, credit-based financial system which the Fifth Republic evolved on top of the postwar controls and the planning system.

In 1972, one government loan mopped up three times the entire amount of new issues on the Bourse for the year (*Financial Times,* 26 January 1973). In 1976, the major institutional investors (primarily the state *caisses*) represented 80% of daily business (*Le Point,* 18 October 1976). In 1977, I.B.M. alone was capitalised at twice the amount of all shares quoted on the Bourse (L'Express, 16 May 1977); and in the same year, the state, through the *Caisse des dépôts et consignations,* the *Caisses d'épargne* and other public establishments held 55% of French shares (*L'Unité,* 3 June 1977). However, returns for investors were high, as many firms were seriously undercapitalised compared with profits (*L'Express,* 16 May 1977), reflecting the closed and protected structure of the Bourse itself and the *rentier* character of shareholding. Bond markets, though scarcely more active than share markets in the mid-1970s, were considerably better capitalised and had significant tax advantages.

From a structural point of view, then, the Bourse was fairly irrelevant to French economic development in this period. Indeed, broadly-based private sources of capital for industry were crowded out at a number of levels. Capital and investment funds, especially for expansion and restructuring, were more readily available from the state, and on favourable terms too, for both public and private sectors, despite the 'queueing' system created by credit controls. The investment banking system was limited in its resources, and the interbank market was closely controlled by the *encadrement* system.

French commercial banks, the biggest of which were nationalised, and which attracted the lion's share of deposits, concentrated on extending their branch networks to become the largest *per capita* in the world; given their dependence on large numbers of small transactions, overhead costs were high and they made inefficient sources of capital. The private bond market was a better bet than the share market, partly due to preferential treatment from the state, but this only reflected the weight of state issues and institutions. Exchange controls limited the interpenetration of the French financial system with foreign finance. And the structure of the Bourse itself was an obstacle.

The Bourse was run in an *étatiste* manner reflecting French traditions. The main actors were much more than mere stockbrokers. They were (and still are) *agents de change,* positions first established as venal offices of state under Louis XIV to raise the huge borrowings required to finance 17th century wars. Subjected to the vicissitudes of state fortunes under the *ancien régime* and temporarily abolished after 1789, they were given a monopoly over exchange transactions by Napoleon I, a monopoly which, while having lost its functions on the interbank market, remained intact in the securities field until the establishment of the 'new money market' in 1985 and subsequent reforms.

Thus they were more than just a 'corporatist' body in the current sense – a private body granted public status. They were, and are, a public body, but in effect with quasi-private status – the other side of the traditional corporatist token. The regulations of their corporate body, the *Chambre syndicale des agents de change* or C.A.C. (whence the index), have had the status of regulations issued by the Ministry of Finance, and require Ministry approval. And yet their activities have been significantly more restricted than those which have been available to investors in other major stock markets.

Charges have remained artisanal, often family, firms, passed down through generations, while outsiders have faced a corporate veto. More importantly, however, *agents de change* were not permitted to trade in the market on their own account. Thus the Bourse has had, in effect, only half of a system of dual capacity – brokers trading directly on others' accounts, but no jobbers or market makers. And as *charges* have not been highly capitalised in the past, the development of specialisation, research, etc., has been limited. This has also placed severe physical contraints on the volume and composition of trading, seriously restricting the liquidity of the markets, limiting economic efficiency.

Deregulation has therefore come as a major structural shock. The most visible change occurred in the equities sector, where the C.A.C. index, from a base of 100 in 1982, reached 460.4 on 26 March 1987 – the high point of the French bull market. Average share prices thus quadrupled over five years, while West German prices trebled and New York and London prices little more than doubled. Total transactions of shares rose from 26 billion francs in 1976 (62.8 billion in 1982) to 411.2 billion in 1986; bond transactions rose from 28.2 billion francs in 1976 (151.3 billion in 1982) to 1.673 *trillion* francs in 1986.

Stock market capitalisation rose from 9% of Gross Domestic Product in 1978 to 13% in 1985 and 25% in 1986, putting it in the same league as other major industrial economies (*Financial Times,* 11 March 1987; 'CSFB Annual Financing Report', *Euromoney* supplement, March 1987). Privatisation greatly inflated some of these numbers in 1987 prior to the October crash. Less visible changes, including the introduction of new financial instruments, the ending of the *agents of change* monopoly, banking reform, and the end of the *encadrement* system, will have an important long-term structural impact, even after the crash. But will all this undermine the *dirigiste* system at its heart?

The state and the financial markets, 1978–84

The objective of deregulation is to increase the efficiency of markets by reducing barriers to exchange and widening the range of both goods and market actors involved. Paradoxically, this may actually require expansion of the role of the state – for example if the state, by integrating markets, undermines traditional socio-economic structures and promotes commodification, or where the state acts to counter the uncertainty inherent in the interplay of myriad market signals (see North, 1981, for a 'neo-classical' argument in this vein). The state's role can be particularly significant for financial markets, which have frequently grown up not to meet private demand for capital but government demand for borrowing, as in 17th century France and 19th century Britain.

This role must also been seen in the context of potential weaknesses identified in *private* capital markets. For example, they have frequently been criticised for 'short-termism', harming the longer-term efficiency of other (e.g., product or labour) markets. This has been a key argument for *dirigisme* in Imperial Germany, Japan and Gaullist France. The analysis of deregulation policy, therefore, concerns not only whether it derives from 'state preferences' or private market demand, but also whether the impact of that policy actually works to promote wider market efficiency. With regard to recent French financial market reforms, the first question can be answered more readily than the second. These reforms clearly derive from state policy: domestic market forces provided little autonomous impetus for change; and international market forces have had a more direct impact on state policy than on domestic markets.

The second question is more problematic. Is the financial logic of state actors, influenced by external market forces, in fact leading to the replacement of the state-led, credit-based supply-side financial system with one based on private and open capital markets, and what will this mean for *dirigisme* itself? Is France moving towards an 'arms-length' relationship between the state and the financial system? If the state wished to turn back the clock, could it succeed, given international constraints and growing interpenetration of the international monetary system (see Strange, 1986)? There is a third possible outcome, however: financial market deregulation could provide an opportunity to rethink the 'fault line' of contemporary state/economy relations, blurring the distinction between public and private in the 'competition state' (Cerny, 1988).

Before 1976 the revival of the Bourse, as we have seen, was not a major issue, although attempts to reduce exchange controls and reform monetary policy in the late 1960s were thwarted by financial and economic instability in France and the collapse of the Bretton Woods system abroad. Valéry Giscard d'Estaing, Finance Minister for most of 1962–73 and President of the Republic after 1974, proposed financial market reforms as early as 1973 (*France-Soir*, 17 March 1973), but did not really challenge *dirigiste* methods. And coalition politics in the mid-1970s, with the Right in the National Assembly still dominated by the Gaullist party under Jacques Chirac (Prime Minister, 1974–76), meant that the policy legacies of the Gaullist years were not easily dismantled.

But the first oil shock of 1973–74 exposed the inflationary potential in the financial system. Planning was left to decline, undermined by the volatility of the period (Green, 1978); and the appointment of Raymond Barre as Prime Minister in 1976 pushed the freeing of market forces to the forefront of political debate, although *de facto* state microeconomic interventionism continued to grow (Green with Cerny, 1980). After the 1978 elections, Barre was able to take new policy initiatives such as the lifting of some price controls still in place from 1945 – or even since the Revolution, in the case of bread prices.

Also in 1978, Economics Minister René Monory introduced the measure which is now seen as the beginning of the process of financial market reform – an income tax deduction of 5,000 francs for *new* purchases of French shares. This measure proved immensely popular. Banks responded with new SICAVs (mutual funds or unit trusts) designed to conform with the act. Share transactions doubled in 1978, partly because the Right's electoral victory reversed a flight of capital, and partly because of the *loi Monory (Le Monde*, 2 January 1979).

Between 1978 and 1980, the *Commission des Opérations de la Bourse* (C.O.B.) estimated, the number of households owning shares through SICAVs doubled, to over half of the estimated total of 1.8 million shareholding households – itself up from around 1 million in the early 1970s. Shareholders were becoming younger since 1978, where previously they had been aging. Whereas in 1978 one French person in 31 was a shareholder, by 1980 this had increased to one in 23, the same proportion as in Britain (*La Croix*, 23 May 1981; *Le Monde*, 30 June 1981). A new trend towards 'popular capitalism' can thus be traced from 1978.

Minor reforms were enacted in late 1980, but although bond issues boomed and capitalisation increased, share issues stagnated through 1980 and early 1981 and the number of quoted companies dropped (*La Croix*, 23 May 1981). Anticipation of the presidential election of 1981 revived splits in the Right and

178

the challenge of the Socialist Party overshadowed financial market reform. The Socialist victories were not received well; shares lost about one-sixth of their value in 1981 despite an end-of-year recovery, both share and bond issues stagnated and market capitalisation fell (*Les Echos,* 31 December 1981).

Although share markets were relatively stagnant in 1982, with transactions falling slightly, bond transactions in contrast rose 83%. More important, however, were political shifts taking place within the government in 1982 and the beginning of deeper structural change in financial policy. Paradoxically, policies adopted during the 'honeymoon' period in 1981, along with changes in the market environment at home and abroad, cast a new spotlight on the Bourse (*Le Monde,* 9 February and 9 March 1982; *Le Matin,* 6 February and 25 May 1982).

The extensive nationalisation programme, approved in early 1982, was the main spur. In the light of large losses by 'nationalisable' firms, the Constitutional Council's decision to increase compensation terms seemed a bit of a windfall, and their shares rose dramatically. Even once the shares had been withdrawn from the markets, trading in the firms' indemnity bonds proceeded at a lively pace. Nationalisation thus had the unintended consequence of stimulating the Bourse: despite a reduction of 30% in share capitalisation, new capital was attracted; and, after compensation, existing capital was redistributed to other outlets on the exchange. New 'glamour stocks' emerged from the pack.

In addition, other investments became less attractive: gold prices were falling, and the government lifted the provision which allowed gold transactions to remain anonymous; property markets were in disorder and savings accounts showed little return. Securities also became more attractive. New shorter-term and floating rate bonds attracted a new clientele. The secondary bond market flourished too. The Monory reforms were still working. But the closed nature of the Bourse and the unfavourable general economic climate still dissuaded unquoted firms from applying for listing.

Rising inflation and pressure on the franc led to drastic measures in June 1982 – a prices and wages freeze, including dividends; devaluation; tighter exchange controls; and a new austerity in government expenditure – depressing the markets and wiping out most of the year's gains. Shares stagnated, but bond markets improved, mainly thanks to increased government borrowing and new short-term and floating rate issues (*Les Echos,* 3 January 1983). At the same time, however, a sea change was taking place in government policy.

Recession and austerity undermined industrial policy after nationalisation. Nationalised firms' losses drained funds for restructuring. The Industry Ministry's aim to get firms under its *tutelle* to draw up comprehensive plans for negotiating future allocations of state funds stagnated. Austerity meant that both sides focused on rationalisation, not expansion. The world crisis worsened competitiveness. Thus the heart of the Socialists' programme – social reforms, already cut back in mid-1982, and industrial modernisation, where they had hoped to out-Gaullist the Gaullists – was thwarted. But this situation partly obscured an emerging shift in power from supporters of an 'industrial logic' represented by the Industry Minister, Jean-Pierre Chevènement, and the Minister for Foreign Trade, Michel Jobert (a prominent ex-Gaullist), towards the Ministry of Finance, headed by Jacques Delors (another ex-Gaullist).

Delors incurred the wrath of some Socialist colleagues with his call for a 'pause' in reforms and his 1982 austerity package. But the clash lead in March 1983 to a major reshuffle, the resignation of Chevènement and Jobert, a currency realignment in the European Monetary System and more austerity. A new tone was reflected in Mitterrand's 1983 New Year message: it was necessary to restore profitability in industry; management, whether in the private sector or the public sector, had to be given the necessary autonomy; and only when financial balances had been restored – including the *grands équilibres* – could expansion safely proceed. The Mitterrand Presidency Mark I was over.

Delors's package of financial measures was passed in early 1983. This included both traditional credit-based mechanisms – tax-free savings accounts whose funds would go into subsidised loans to high-tech industries – and more market-oriented measures, from authorisation for public sector firms to issue new hybrid debenture stocks (*titres participatifs*) and non-priority non-voting shares (*certificats d'investissement*) which counted as capital, to setting up a new *Second Marché* or unlisted securities market. Both nationalised firms and reluctant smaller and medium-sized businesses were brought into the private capital markets. Continuing austerity, which was rapidly reducing inflation, the bottoming out of the recession and the new measures, together had the effect of setting off a new, long-term upward trend in the markets.

A further element was the government's changing relationship with the banks, 75% of which had been in the public sector since 1945. It had been assumed by the Socialists that nationalisation of the rest (including the major investment banks) would make it possible to increase the supply of funds to industry. However, the banks, heavily committed in a period of recession – and by far the biggest of which, the commercial banks, had expensive branch networks and high overheads – were reluctant to play along. Government pressure became increasingly ambivalent. The result was an agreement that the banks would provide one major injection of new capital to the public sector, but that thereafter there would be no further pressure. Thus bank nationalisation failed to expand the state-led, credit-based financial system. Chevènement wanted a separate national investment bank to coordinate expansion, but this was vetoed.

However, measures to stimulate the development of private capital markets were maintained, and reform proposals brought out of desk drawers. Rules were simplified for new flotations, new financial instruments authorised, the 'monthly settlement' market reformed, securities 'dematerialised' – no more bond and share certificates by the end of 1984, only computerised records – and financial market authorities' powers strengthened (*Journal des Finances*, numerous articles, February-July 1984; *Le Monde*, 16–17 October 1983). The bond markets were stimulated by public sector deficits – a new structural factor in France after 1981 and often a major force in stimulating financial markets elsewhere. By 1984, then, French financial markets were poised to make a structural breakthrough as domestic and international trends converged.

The 'financial revolution' and the emerging momentum of reform

In 1984, two elements predominated. Firstly, there was an even more important change of government. Laurent Fabius, the new Prime Minister and long a close adviser to Mitterrand, had been Budget Minister and Chevènement's successor as Industry Minister. He had increased managerial autonomy in the public sector and speeded the rationalisation of older industries. The new Minister of Finance was Pierre Bérégovoy, who as Social Affairs Minister had presided over the 'pause' in social reforms. The Communists, who supported social reforms and industrial expansion to combat unemployment, withdrew.

In the second place, however, Europe was becoming aware of changes in the world financial system. In 1981–82, Delors and other European finance ministers had attempted to deal with capital flight and high interest rates by calling for concerted action by the major industrial countries to reduce rates and for a more managed exchange rate system. But volatility was increasing with First World recession and the Third World debt crisis, and the Reagan Administration was even more opposed to such measures than the Carter Administration had been.

Following the move to floating exchange rates in 1973, the United States had begun deregulating its financial markets. Under Reagan, financial deregulation and the growth and diversification of American financial institutions were bound up with the more freewheeling environment created by broader deregulation and extensive tax cuts. Furthermore, tax cuts created budget and trade deficits which required financing. High interest rates were the key to financing the deficits out of capital flows from abroad. The rising dollar created an impression in the U.S. of America's financial 'muscle', and rising demand for imports was seen as a contribution to European recovery.

But European policymakers saw their lack of sufficient investment capital as the main obstacle to recovery. American demand for European imports tended to concern cheese and wine rather than capital goods or products with high technological content or value added, while Europe was seen to have a major financial supply-side problem. Capital market deregulation would be necessary to compete with the U.S. for international funds. In 1983 Britain started the process which would lead to the Big Bang three years later.

United States pressure on Japan in the same year to open its financial markets – for America's own competitive reasons – faced strong opposition at first, until Japan began to adopt its own strategy to take advantage of deregulation elsewhere to benefit Japanese institutions. Other countries too experimented with financial deregulation. International capital flows were increasing (and increasingly volatile), while new negotiable instruments were successfully competing on a large scale with credit finance. A state which wished to both retain a sufficient share of domestic capital for investment and attract foreign capital would have to enable its public and private sectors alike to compete for funds in rapidly integrating global securities markets.

The unregulated Eurobond market, for floating-rate notes in particular, was growing rapidly in the wake of the collapse of Eurodollar loan markets with the Third World debt crisis. New instruments for currency and interest rate hedging and speculation – U.S. Treasury bills, futures, options, commercial paper, swaps, etc. – began to be widely copied as bank intermediation came under pressure. High real interest rates – growing as inflation fell – made hedging through securitisation an ever more crucial tool of the company treasurer's trade. At the same time, nominal interest rates began to fall, prices of securities rose, and the secondary market became more atractive and competitive.

Indeed, the whole structure of profitability from financial transactions was changing. To reduce costs, the burden was shifting from interest income to commissions (to the detriment of bank loans). Pressure increased from large issuers and investors to shave commissions. Arbitrage between increasingly interpenetrated markets made it impossible for financial institutions to stay aloof. Disintermediation and securitisation gained an international momentum and created an appetite for more and more new instruments.

These external pressures converged with the aims of French policymakers, making financial market deregulation seem not only an attractive alternative to the credit-based system, but also the only alternative to a siege economy. But the situation was full of pitfalls. Capital markets had previously been closed and isolated, resistant to reform; they were crowded out by credit-based *dirigisme,* and they were organised by a tight corporate group of artisanal brokers, who were themselves often bypassed as a means of raising capital.

Indeed, the Bourse was so small in international terms that for some time new international trends passed it by and headed for larger and more dynamic financial centres, while at home it was juxtaposed with an undercapitalised and overextended banking system, itself uncompetitive and constrained by the *encadrement* system. Even minor reforms created tensions. However, once the French state became interested in the markets, it was characteristic that policymakers should attempt to marshal state authority in favour of reform. Thus the objectives of state actors came to define the parameters of reform.

It is clearly critical that 'financial logic' had already won the day in government and civil service circles through what were widely perceived as the 'lessons' of trying to pursue 'socialism in one country' in 1981–82 (Hall, 1985). But industrial logic also played an interesting role. The rationale presented by Bérégovoy for deregulation was that it would reduce interest rates charged to industry for investment and modernisation (see his preface to the *Livre blanc sur la réforme du financement de l'économie,* 1986; interview, December 1986). His claim to have reduced interest rates by 2% as a result is widely accepted.

This convergence of the two logics enabled the authoritative resources of the state to be effectively mobilised, through the Ministry of Finance, in favour of financial market reform – first under the Socialists, and eventually under the 'neo-liberal' right too. Rather than setting the markets a task and simply overseeing their attempts to fulfill it, as in the classic self-regulatory mode, the French state has imposed reform in a step-by-step manner. Although not all steps have been worked out in Cartesian fashion, a certain logic *has* emerged.

The reform process, 1984–1987

In November 1984, in order to focus public attention on the new policy direction, Bérégovoy became the first Minister of Finance to visit to the Bourse since 1962. Reforms introduced since 1983 fall into six major categories: authorisation of new financial instruments and decompartmentalisation of various capital markets; extension of the negotiability of commissions; tightening of regulatory supervision; privatisation; modifying the role of the *agents de change;* and attempts to start a process of internationalisation.

The introduction of new financial instruments was the first major step. At first these were mainly longer-term, intended to raise new capital for industry and trade on the Bourse in traditional fashion – *titres participatifs, certificats d'investissement,* warrants and variable rate and exchangeable instruments (see the *revue Banque,* April 1984). The next stage, in line with trends abroad, was a range of more flexible medium and short-term instruments which could be freely traded by banks and other institutions as well.

A key innovation was the introduction of negotiable bank certificates of deposit, encouraging banks to raise capital beyond their deposit base, reducing overheads and encouraging a closer alignment of interest rates between securities and credit. The French financial community was at first generally opposed to C.D.s., and Bérégovoy's announcement was made without consultation with the profession. Fears that competition from banks would soak up liquidity led to a noted but temporary fall on the bond markets (*Le Monde*, 7–8 December 1984 and 20–21 January 1985). This was the first really significant step in a state-led deregulation process (Noyer, 1985).

More new instruments were to follow in rapid succession (see Guimbert, 1987). Short-term instruments included bills issued by specialised financial institutions, Treasury bills 'negotiable on current account' and commercial paper. The market for these (including C.D.s) rose from 31 billion francs at the end of December 1985 to 155 billion by 30 September 1986, with the lion's share (75%) taken up by negotiable Treasury bills (Marchetti, 1986). New instruments for interest rate and currency hedging were copied from international markets: forward rate agreements; interest rate, currency and stock market futures and options; swaps; etc. A new caisse for mortgage refinancing was set up (Saglio, 1986). And a variety of new banking institutions emerged – *banques de trésorerie, banques de marchés* and *banques d'arbitrage* (see *International Financing Review*, 8 April 1986, and Bertier, 1986) – to operate in the 'new money market' which, although outside both the Bourse and the old interbank market, was open to actors from both (see Beaufils, *et al.*, 1986).

Probably the most important structural breakthrough was the 1986 opening of the Paris financial futures market – the *Marché à terme des instruments financiers*, or M.A.T.I.F. Despite limitations on the market – it started with only the equivalent of a long gilts contract – it structural impact was huge. It symbolised the coming of age of French markets on the international scene. The *Journal des Finances* headlined its opening as 'When Pierre Bérégovoy gets his inspiration from Chicago', with the apparent paradox that 'Under a Socialist government, and with elections just three weeks away, Paris sees the opening of a futures market: the last word in capitalism' (22–28 February 1986).

Furthermore, although real competition with Chicago's futures markets is not feasible, the M.A.T.I.F.'s main contract has become competitive with the London International Financial Futures Exchange (L.I.F.F.E.) (de la Martinière, 1986; *Financial Times*, 27 January 1987). The new exchange quickly had to move to new and more spacious quarters. Most importantly, with only half of the seats reserved to the *agents de change*, the M.A.T.I.F. represented the first major breach of the brokers' monopoly in an integral part of the Bourse itself – and the reverberations have been felt all around the financial system.

The second major set of reforms concerned the fixing of commissions for financial services. This has been a key structural issue in the reform of other securities markets (Moran, 1987). Fixed commissions have not been eliminated in France, but were reduced following a 1984 report by M. Bernard Tricot, a *grand commis de l'Etat* and former president of the C.O.B.; indeed, the Finance Ministry went well beyond his recommendations. Commissions on bond issues became freely negotiable first for the private sector in March 1985, and for the public sector in December of that year. Brokerage commissions are still fixed on transactions of less than 2 million francs for shares and less than 10 million francs for bonds; commissions on larger transactions are freely negotiable on the entire transaction. This attests to the tendency of deregulated markets to favour the largest (and highest-rated) borrowers and investors.

The third major set of reforms involves the extention of the powers of the main regulatory body, the C.O.B. (as well as the *Commission bancaire* and the *Conseil de la concurrence*). The C.O.B. is a statutory body and not a self-regulatory organisation (see Choinel and Rouyer, 1986). Formerly financed by the states, its budget now mainly derives from a charge on new issues and compulsory contributions from market institutions. it has a brief to oversee the Bourse, with a general power of regulation, certain specific prerogatives and an auxilliary judicial role. In recent years it has concentrated on trying to increase transparency by requiring secretive French firms and institutions to provide more information than in the past, including improved accounts.

Its role has been expanding in the area of insider trading, but its resources are limited, with 100 employees and a budget of 30 million francs. Insider trading has not yet had as much attention in France as elsewhere (Gherardi, 1987). However, its brief has widened with the new financial market reform act (*loi du 22 janvier 1988*). As for other regulatory bodies, the *Commission bancaire* was revamped in the 1984 banking reforms, and the powers and remit of the *Conseil de la concurrence* are being extended in the areas of price fixing, information and control of takeovers (*Le Monde,* 5 November 1986).

A fourth major change has been to privatise public sector firms. The first privatisations, of the Saint-Gobain conglomerate and the Banque Paribas, were very successful, with the former attracting 1.5 million shareholders and the latter 3.8 million. But with no requirement to apply for a minimum number of shares, many applications were for single shares, maximising 'popular capitalism' at the expense of institutions and foreign applicants (*Financial Times,* 3 March 1987) – other than the 'hard core' (see below). French small shareholders are more likely to hold on to their shares rather than sell them for short-term gain. But the October 1987 crash and the upcoming presidential election have halted the privatisation programme at the time of writing.

The main impact of the privatisations on the Bourse was that the markets could not cope with the volume of early trading, with brokers unable to make a price in the new shares. Indeed, it was estimated 'that as much as 15% of the daily turnover in French stocks now takes place in London, where six houses make a market in leading French shares without transactions passing through the Paris stock exchange' (*Financial Times,* 11 March 1987), and it is likely that over half of the turnover of the biggest French stocks takes place in London. This leads us to consider the fifth major set of reforms.[1]

The brokers' monopoly has been the main obstacle to opening market structures. A protected profession, well off but not particularly dynamic – there is only one *agent de change* in *L'Expansion*'s 1987 list of the one hundred richest people in France – is faced not only with adaptation and expansion but also a major shake-out of firms. There has always been a significant minority prepared to adapt in order to expand their own businesses, and many existing positions have been undermined because the *charges* are so undercapitalised. The banks have long been pushing to play a greater role in the markets, but while the main competition was merely the French commercial banks, with their own problems of competitiveness, the brokers were able to resist.

Again it was state pressure combined with international market forces which forced the pace. The flood of new financial instruments and decompartmentalisation of markets have led to a search for greater competitiveness, which means a need for larger firms and higher capitalisation. The reduction of commissions and the sheer number of markets to deal with all the time require higher turnover, and this means more personnel, more highly qualified personnel (with higher salaries) and investment in computerisation. Particularly significant for brokerage methods has been the development of continuous trading on the Bourse, which by the beginning of 1988 concerned over 100 shares (expected to reach 200 by 1989). And expanding market activities will eventually require participants to make markets themselves – a very underdeveloped activity in Paris – and to engage in arbitrage.

This leads to the final factor, the lack of international competitiveness of, and foreign participation in, the French markets. As *Euromoney* headlined on its cover in October, 1986: 'Welcome to Paris, if you're there already.' There are at the time of writing 105 official positions of *agent de change* (*Euromoney,* January 1988), and they until quite recently maintained individual practices. However, mergers among *charges* have been increasing in pace, the number of firms failing to 61 (45 in Paris markets and 16 on regional bourses). Only a small number of *charges,* perhaps 10, carry out the majority of business, although statistics are not available. But by 1986 it had become clear that *agents de change* were facing serious difficulties with new challengers even in their own bailiwick, the share market. Restructuring became imperative.

Indeed, an end to the *agents de change* monopoly seemed inevitable. The reform announced by Finance Minister Édouard Balladur in March 1987 – later to become the *loi du 22 janvier 1988* – was intended to do just this, but in a gradual way. Since 1 January 1988, 30% of the capital of a *charge* may be owned by outsiders; from 1st January 1989, up to 49%; and from 1 January 1990, 100%. Outsiders, French or foreign, will be vetted by the new Stock

Exchange Council (*Conseil des Bourses*) – which along with a new clearing house has replaced the C.A.C. – and the Treasury. *Charges* can expand in the money market, and can register under the Banking Act to provide a full range of investment banking services. A small percentage of the firms' capital can be floated publicly.

The monopoly will formally end on 1 January 1992, at the same time as the European Community's 'single market', which includes financial services, is due to come into effect. The *Conseil des Bourses,* with a larger membership, can authorise firms to engage in brokerage activities; its shares are distributed among existing *charges. Agents* who find it impossible to adapt will eventually be indemnified by the new authority. The reform, negotiated between M. Balladur and M. Xavier Dupont, President of the C.A.C., has been compared with the British Goodison-Parkinson agreement of 1983, although there are significant differences. But the real question is whether state-imposed reform has effectively been translated into a consensual solution which will be sufficient to create a self-sustaining, internationally competitive dynamism in French financial markets. The 1987 crash and its aftermath may have exposed significant problems here.

The final stage is to promote internationalisation of French financial markets in the future. All the above reforms have been justified indirectly by the need to compete internationally, but there is a long way to go (Fourcans *et al.*, 1987; Dupont, 1987; de Gournay, 1988). The most important direct step, however, was the agreement by E.E.C. finance ministers in 1986 on a package of liberalisation measures in the context of the 'single market' to remove exchange controls on long-term credit and on buying and selling unlisted securities, unit trusts, etc.; new financial instruments are to be included. Delors, now President of the Commission, also proposed that all transactions on E.E.C. money markets be freed from control – covering all flows, and not just those related to commercial transactions (*Financial Times,* 18 November 1986).

This is particularly important in the light of proposals, taken seriously by French brokers and bankers, for setting up a computerised continental European market, possibly centred on Paris, linking all existing major European exchanges – on the model of the American N.A.S.D.A.Q. system – in order to rival London on the global marketplace. Such a market would have an advantage in relaying trading from the Far East, as it would be able to open an hour ahead of London, but at the moment it is still a gleam in the eye of the French.

Concomitant changes have also been taking place since 1984 outside the financial markets. The structure of banking has been changing drastically. Banks have been moving into securities in a major way. A greater proportion of their own income has been coming from commissions rather than interest, and they have also faced problems of capitalisation, restructuring, computerisation, training, etc. In this process, however, the banks (with the exception of the newly-established capital market banks) have had to do unpopular things such as shed labour, reclassify existing workers, rationalise their branch networks, and campaign for bank charges on current accounts (still blocked by the government). And the international French banking network, the world's second largest until 1985 when it was overtaken by the Japanese, has had to be rationalised as well; it too was based on extensive branch networks and volume of business rather than on high capitalisation and profitability.

At the same time, the state-sponsored credit system has changed. The key has been a cutback in subsidised loans. In 1979, three-quarters of all loans to business came from state or para-state institutions, including nationalised banks ans subsidiaries; 43% were subsidised by the state. Most state support came through direct subsidies and privileged refinancing arrangements which institutions such as the Crédit Agricole or the Banque Française du commerce extérieur had with the Bank of France (*La Vie française*, 27 July 1981).

In 1982–83, the government began to 'banalise' these loans as market rates fell (*Les Echos*, 10 October 1982 and 22 September 1983). Total subsidised loans dropped by about a quarter from 1983–86, while budget costs fell from 45 billion francs in 1985 to only 16 in 1986. Only one of six original categories was left in 1986, a 9.25% rate for small and medium-sized firms; its budget allocation dropped from 38 billion francs in 1984 to 12 in 1986 (*Témoignage Chrétien*, 24–30 March 1986). Support for exports has shifted from subsidised loans to direct subsidies and pure guarantees (*revue Banque*, November 1986 and March 1987). Thus the extension of the financial markets has parelleled the decline of the credit system. Industrial policy, however, has in some ways remained resilient; cuts in direct subsidies have been difficult to make despite announcements to the contrary (Bertier, 1987).

Exchange controls have been all but lifted since 1985. The only major exchange control measure remaining is a limit on franc loans to non-residents, seen as a minimal safeguard against the vulnerability of the franc, caught between the falling dollar and a strong deutschmark. This, however, also limits expansion of the Eurofranc market, which none the less took a 2% share of the Eurobond market in 1986. (Paris has also been a centre for some time for the growing Euro-ECU market, which took a 4% share [*Euromoney* supplement, March 1987]). And perhaps the most crucial component of that *dirigiste* strategy in the 1970s, the *encadrement du crédit* system, was phased out between 1985 and 1987. The government has adopted an open market system of money supply and interest rate control which has had its teething trpubles, but which is developing (*revue Banque*, January 1987; *Le Figaro*, 22 January 1987).

The crash and the future of *dirigisme*

All of these changes have the potential to undermine the *dirigisme* of the French state. There are two major questions, however. The first is whether the reforms themselves will stick. Our conclusions on this point have to be nuanced in light of the events of 1987 – even before the October crash. The second is whether they will alter *dirigiste* state/economy relationships in any quasi-paradigmatic way. Here, too, conclusions must be nuanced: the role of the state as prime mover is still critical since market reform is so recent; and the weaknesses exposed in 1987 point to both a reaffirmation of state-led reform and a shift of *dirigisme* to the micro-level.

In the first place, it is clear that the financial market boom in France between 1982 and 1986 was more fragile than in the major internationalised marketplaces. Once the C.A.C. index had peaked in March 1987, it began to decline, more than six months before the crash. A bear market in bonds, noted in the United States as a sign that a stock market crash might be coming, started earlier and was more severe in France than elsewhere. By mid-September 1987, *Le Point* asked in a major survey: '*Faut-il quitter la Bourse?*'. By the end of November, capitalisation had slumped and the C.A.C. index was at 293.9; it was to fall further in January and early February 1988, before stabilising at around 300, an important psychological level. With a fall of over a third from its peak, and a over a quarter from its pre-crash level, the Bourse was hit far harder than New York or London, but about the same as other major continental markets such as Milan, Frankfurt or Zurich (*The Banker,* January 1988; *Euromoney,* January 1988; *Le Monde,* 29 December 1987 and 9 January 1988).

At the time of writing, trading has recently been thin (except for a flurry of takeover activity in mid-late February), and uncertainties surrounding the presidential election seem to be dampening the markets. Foreign interest in buying stakes in French brokage firms was already declining before the crash, and is unlikely to pick up rapidly. American firms do not like the conditions for setting up in Paris (preferring London) and the Japanese are standing on the sidelines; only British firms have been buying in. However, the process will probably accelerate as the European 'single market' approaches. And the Bourse has been hit by the worldwide post-crash syndrome of 'coming home', which in the French case means that foreign investors, so recently won by the reforms, have cut their holdings from an estimated 25% to around 14% of share capital.

The M.A.T.I.F. and the more recent traded options market have stabilised after some serious difficulties (*Financial Times,* 10 March 1988). The bond market has been the strongest, having benefitted, like bond markets elsewhere, from a 'flight to quality' since October and from the small downward trend in interest rates (due, as elsewhere, to government policy) since then. Perhaps the biggest victim was the privatisation programme, which has been completely stalled since the crash, and will remain so until the presidential election.

Strong suspicions remain that privatisation, rather than just bringing cash to the markets, also had the perverse effect of soaking up existing liquidity and crowding out other market activity – contributing to the severity of the crash when it came. Future sales will suffer from the fact that privatised firms have done badly out of the crash; at the end of November, only five of the eleven denationalised companies were trading above the issue price. On the other hand, the controversial government strategy of selling significant interests to friendly shareholders – the 'hard core', attacked by the Left as neo-Gaullist clientelism (see *L'événement du jeudi,* 17 September 1987) – has probably been a stabilising factor, along with small shareholder loyalty.

Finally, the reforms so far have been gradual, step-by-step ones. Trading is still limited to the exchanges during opening hours (the 'single price' policy), which further limits any embryonic market-making; this can be seen either as an attempt to prevent the premature drain of trading towards London (and other centres), or as a leftover of pre-reform corporatism. And the brokers' monopoly will not be lifted until 1992, despite provisions for opening ownership. Thus although the state has raffirmed its commitment to the reform process, the future is uncertain. Will some of the current weaknesses prove to be strengths in the longer run? If French financial markets are seen as 'infant industries', being nurtured in a transitional period towards future international competitiveness, then possibly so; if market habits can only be learned in the rough-and-tumble of open competition, then perhaps not.

But what will happen to the French economy – and to *dirigisme?* There will be advantages for firms which are in a position to raise funds on the capital markets. However, debate is fierce among economists as to whether expansion of financial markets actually helps or hinders the 'real economy', and the manufacturing base in particular.[2] It is often said that financial markets reinforce tendencies towards 'short-termism'. This can partly be overcome by arbitrage and rolling over debt, but that is not what firms which need investment to modernise find most useful. And it has been argued that open financial markets privilege the 'best risks' – big firms with high ratings.

Brokers and bankers require high turnover to make profits while large borrowers can negotiate low commissions on big transactions. This may lead to a 'dual market' mentality, where the markets engage in securities transactions with multinational firms and large banks, while other borrowers are required to find loans from hard-pressed banks (which would themselves prefer to move 'upmarket' – or queue for state subsidies). World markets would seem to be going in this direction. Finally, it is often said that the best risks – the big borrowers – are more interested in recycling old debt through hedging than raising new investment capital.

Dirigisme, in this context, loses its macroeconomic function. What would be left would be a mixture of indirect, open market instruments, middle-level clientelism and microeconomic policies for small and medium-sized firms. But financial markets provide opportunities for new forms of state/economy concertation too. Indeed, one of the main beneficiaries may be public sector firms. On bond markets, the most favoured borrowers are sovereigns and public sector firms with a state guarantee. Prior to privatisation in France, the Socialists seemed to see financial market reform as compatible with a dynamic public sector which would no longer be a burden on the state. The British Labour Party seems to have adopted a similar approach to public sector funding in its industrial strategy in the mid-1980s.

At this stage, then, France seems to be replacing 'strategic' *dirigisme* with 'tactical' *dirigisme* – or what might be called 'arms-length *dirigisme*' . . .[3] In fact, such tactical *dirigisme* has probably been more characteristic of state/economy relations through French history than the strategic pretensions of *neo-colbertisme* would admit. But in a world context where even Japan is experimenting with deregulation, this may reflect international constraints rather than domestic choice. Indeed, the French Government sees international policy cooperation, on the quasi-Gaullist model of the Louvre Accords, as the model for future intervention.

It may be for this reason, more than any other, that the period when the choice was between '*la Bourse ou l'emploi*' (*L'Humanité,* 14 February 1986) is over. Traditional conceptions of state intervention on both Left and Right are already changing (Cerny, 1988). The financial revolution is here to stay, and the state will inevitably adjust its line of fire, even if it has itself to evolve in order to do it.

Acknowledgments

An earlier version of this article was presented to the Workshop on Deregulation in Western Europe, Joint Meetings of Workshops, European Consortium for Political Research, Amsterdam, 10–15 April 1987. Fieldwork was aided by a small grant from the Nuffield Foundation as well as travel funding from the University Association for Contemporary European Studies and the Department of Politics, University of York. I should like to thank M. Serge Hurtig of the Fondation Nationale des Sciences Politiques, Dr. William Wainwright and his colleagues at the Banque Arabe et Internationale d'Investissement, Mr. George Graham of the Paris bureau of the *Financial Times* and

Ms. Valerie Thompson of Euromarket Trading Consultants for their help and support.

Notes

1. This section has benefited greatly from interviews with MM, Xavier Dupont, President of the Chambre syndicale des agents de change, Jean-Jacques Burgard, Délégué Général of the Association Française des Banques, and Jacques Moreau, President of the Crédit coopératif, December 1986.
2. Interview with M. Jean-Marcel Jeanneney, Director of the Observatoire français des conjunctures économiques, December 1986.
3. Term coined by Will Hutton of B.B.C. Newsnight, private conversation, February 1988.

References

Berger, S. (1981). 'Lame Ducks and National Champions: Industrial Policy in the Fifth Republic', in Andrews, W.G. and Hoffmann, S. (eds.), *The Fifth Republic at Twenty*. Brockport N.Y.: State University of New York Press).

Berger, S. (1986). 'French Politics at a Turning Point?', *French Politics and Society*, No. 15. pp. 3–8.

Beaufils, B., Py, G., Richard, B., Thiry, B. and Guimbert, J.-P. (1986). *La banque et les nouveaux instruments financiers: la pratique des marchés*. Paris: la *revue Banque*, Éditeur.

Bertier, E. (1986). 'Drôle de banques', *L'Expansion*. 7–20 November, 106–113.

Bertier, E. (1987). 'Couper les aides? Pas si facile . . .', *L'Expansion*, 20 March–2 April, 84–91.

Cerny, P.G. (1988). 'From the Welfare State to the Competition State: British and French Industrial Policy in Perspective', in C. Farrands, (ed.), *Industrial Intervention in France and Britain* (in press).

Cerny, P.G. (1987) 'Reconceptualising Corporatism: State Structures and Patterns of Interest Intermediation', paper presented to the annual conference of the Political Studies Association (U.K.), University of Aberdeen, April.

Cerny, P.G. and Schain, M.A. (eds.) (1980). *French Politics and Public Policy*. London: Pinter.

Cerny, P.G. and Schain, M.A. (eds.) (1985). *Socialism, the State and Public Policy in France*. London: Pinter.

Choinel, A. and Rouyer, G. (1986). *Le marché financier: structures et acteurs*. Paris: la *revue Banque*, Éditeur.

Dupont, X. (1987). 'La réforme de la Bourse', *Revue Banque*. November, 1042–1044.

Estrin, S. and Holmes, P. (1982). *French Planning in Theory and Practice*. London: Allen & Unwin.

Fourcans, A., Hubert, V. and Pène, D. (1987). 'Paris: la grande place financière de demain?', *revue Banque*. May, 438–443.

French, M. (1988). 'Un tout petit boum', *Euromoney*. January, 95–100.

Gherardi, S. (1987). 'Délit d'initié', *L'Expansion*. 23 January–5 February, 98–103.

Gournay, C. de (1988). 'Paris, place financière européenne pour vos placements monétaires et obligatoires', *revue Banque*. March, 290–294.

Green, D.M. (1978). 'The Seventh Plan – The Demise of French Planning?', *West European Politics*. 1: 60–70.
Green, D.M. (1983). 'Strategic Management and the State: France', in Dyson, K. and Wilks, S., *Industrial Crisis*. Oxford: Blackwell, 161–192.
Green, D.M. with Cerny, P.G. (1980). 'Economic Policy and the Government Coalition', in Cerny and Schain, 1980.
Guimbert, J.-P. (1987). 'Exploitants et nouvelles techniques de marchés', *revue Banque*. March, 224–233.
Hall, P.A. (1986). *Governing the Economy: The Politics of State Intervention in France and Britain*. Oxford: Polity Press.
Hayward, J.E.S. (1986). *The State and the Market Economy: Industrial Patriotism and Economic Intervention in France*. Brighton: Wheatsheaf.
Johnson, C. (1982). *M.I.T.I. and the Japanese Miracle: The Growth of Industrial Policy, 1925–1975*. Stanford: Stanford University Press.
Kuisel, R.F. (1981). *Capitalism and the State in Modern France: Renovation and Economic Management in the Twentieth Century*. Cambridge: Cambridge University Press.
La Martinière, G. de (1986). 'Le Matif après quatre mois', *revue Banque*. October, 839–846.
Machin, H. and Wright, V. (eds.) (1985). *Economic Policy and Policy-Making under the Mitterrand Presidency, 1981–84*. London: Pinter.
Marchetti, L. (1986). 'Les titres de créances négotiables à court terme', *revue Banque*. December, 1100–1104.
Ministère de l'Économie des Finances et du Budget. (1986). *Livre blanc sur la réforme du financement de l'économie* . Paris: Documentation Française.
Moran, M. (1987). 'Deregulating Britain, Deregulating America: The Case of the Securities Industry', paper presented to the Workshop on Deregulation in Western Europe, European Consortium for Political Research, Joint Meetings of Workshops, Amsterdam, April.
North, D. (1981). *Structure and Change in Economic History*. New York: Norton.
Noyer, C. (1985). 'Les certificats de dépôt', *revue Banque*. July, 693–698.
Saglio, D. (1986). 'La réforme du marché hypothécaire', *revue Banque*. January, 31–34.
Sassier, P. and de Witt, F. (1985). *Les Français à la corbeille*. Paris: Robert Laffont.
Schmidt, V. (1986). 'Neo-Liberal Laissez-faire vs. Socialist Dirigisme: An Evaluation of the Contemporary French Debates on the Role of the State in the Economy', paper presented to the annual meeting of the American Political Science Association, Washington, D.C., August.
Strange, S. (1986). *Casino Capitalism*. Oxford: Blackwell.
Zysman, J. (1983). *Governments, Markets and Growth: Financial Systems and the Politics of Industrial Change*. Ithaca: Cornell University Press.
Zysman, J. (1977). *Political Strategies for Industrial Order: State, Market and Industry in France*. Berkely and Los Angeles: University of California Press.

[4]

Excerpt from Ralf-Joachim Götz and Johannes Müller, *Frankfurt – A Banking and Financial Services Centre*, 3, 5–48, 50.

FRANKFURT - A BANKING AND FINANCIAL SERVICES CENTRE

Contents

The authors are particularly grateful to Prof. Dr. Karl Häuser, director of the institut für Kapitalmarktforschung, who generously shared his time and knowledge in encouraging the project and affording useful critical suggestions.

1 THE FINANCIAL SECTOR IN THE FEDERAL REPUBLIC OF GERMANY

1.1 FINANCIAL FRAMEWORK

Germany is well known as an economic power and so is Frankfurt, its centre for banking and financial services. The city hosts more than 400 banks from all over the world, including the headquarters of the leading German credit institutions. The most important German stock exchange, with a share of more than 60 percent of all equity turnover and more than 70 percent of all bond turnover, is located in Frankfurt as well. Furthermore, the first and only German Futures and Options Exchange (DTB) has recently started operation in Frankfurt. The city also serves as the domicile of the Deutsche Bundesbank, the German central bank, which is highly respected world-wide and plays a leading role in international foreign exchange activities.

The stability and growth of the German political, economic and financial system has enabled the Federal Republic of Germany, in more than 40 years of existence, to develop into one of the leading economic and financial powers in the world. In terms of gross national product, Germany ranks third in the world behind the United States and Japan. The German current account balance has been positive for years and reached a record surplus of almost DM 100 billion in 1989, whereas most other countries have been confronted with deficits in their current account. The inflation and unemployment rates in Germany have been among the lowest throughout the world during the 1980s. Low government debts and a remarkable degree of monetary stability are highly esteemed in today's Germany - a reaction to two hyper inflations and currency reforms in the first half of the twentieth century. Throughout its more than four decades of existence, the Federal Republic of Germany has only once experienced an inflation rate in excess of 6 percent.

This strength of the German economy is also emphasized in the monetary sector where the Deutsche Mark has developed into the second most important international currency for transactions, interventions, capital investments and reserves. The German currency represents some 17 percent of the world reserves in foreign exchange and some 30 percent in the ECU-basket of the European Monetary System. Monetary decisions made by the German central bank have a direct impact on the external value of currencies and interest rate levels of other European countries.

The German banking system is among the most efficient in the world. As the majority of German banks offer all sorts of banking and other financial services generally, including jobbing and investment banking, they are often referred to as universal banks. Banking services in Germany are supplemented by a wide range of special banks such as mortgage banks or building and loan associations. The 1989 business volume of all banks included in the banking statistics of the Deutsche Bundesbank exceeded DM 4.2 trillion, not counting the increasing amount of off-balance sheet transactions. There are more than 44,000 bank offices all over the Federal Republic of Germany; the density of banks is 1,400 inhabitants per bank office which is equivalent to the bank density in Switzerland, but nearly double as dense as, for instance, in Great Britain. Due to the growing importance of the German financial markets, more and more foreign banks open branches, subsidiaries or representative offices in Frankfurt, Germany's financial centre. By December 1989, there were more than 400 credit institutions present in Frankfurt, some 270 of which were foreign.

Germany can also rely on very efficient money and capital markets although some improvements still have to be made. The German equity market ranks fourth in the world in terms of market value. It does, however, only account for some 3 percent of the world's market capitalisation. If measured in turnover, the German bond market ranks second in the world behind Great Britain in spite of the almost complete absence of private issuers. Steps toward liberalisation and deregulation, still only partially implemented, will enable the German financial markets to compete even more with other European markets which - regarding market capitalisation, eligible financial instruments, futures and options trading, transaction costs etc. - still benefit from Frankfurt's need to catch up. The German financial community meanwhile has realised the necessity to jointly promote the further development of the German financial markets.

The following chapters describe the main actors affecting the financial markets as well as the markets themselves, the market mechanisms, financial instruments, and innovative steps, which all are responsible for the smooth functioning of the financial sector in the Federal Republic of Germany.

-7-

1.2 BANKING SYSTEM

As mentioned above, banks in Germany generally operate as so-called universal banks. In contrast to separation banking systems like in the United States or Great Britain, the majority of German banks usually offer all kinds of banking and other financial services, including the securities business and investment banking services. German universal banks, acting as principal bankers, put a great emphasis on an overall relationship with their private and corporate customers.

The German Banking Act (Gesetz über das Kreditwesen) defines the following banking activities as feasible: taking deposits, granting loans and acceptance credits, discounting bills of exchange, promissory notes and cheques, deposit banking, administrating securities on account of others, dealing in securities, investment banking, acquiring claims in respect to loans prior to their maturity, and executing cashless payment transactions. It should be understood that these provisions enable German banks to act as brokers and dealers on the stock market. Besides those activities, there are several universal banks issuing their own bonds, arranging bond or equity issues for their clients, dealing in foreign exchange and precious metal transactions as well as playing an active role in the mergers and acquisitions business. During the past few years, universal banks have even extended their activities to fields that in the past were strictly separated from banking, e.g. the insurance business and the building and loan sector.

This wide-spread activity of universal banks in all sectors of the economy is offered by a large variety of institutions of different legal form, organisation, business structure and focus on business activity. According to the statistics of the Deutsche Bundesbank*), which covers the vast majority of credit institutions operating in Germany, the total market share of universal banks expressed as a percentage of the total business volume reaches some 77 per cent; the remaining market share is comprised of those specialized institutions that are reporting to the Bundesbank, such as mortgage banks, banks with special functions or postal savings and giro banks.

*) All figures as to business volume, market share as well as number of banks and branches are taken from the statistics of the Deutsche Bundesbank as per December 1989, unless otherwise stated.

There are three major categories of universal banks in the Federal Republic of Germany: private commercial banks (Kreditbanken), savings banks (Sparkassen) and credit associations (Kreditgenossenschaften).

Private commercial banks currently hold a market share of around 24 percent. The group of private commercial banks is very heterogeneous and comprises more than 320 credit institutions. Four subcategories can be distinguished: firstly, the three big banks (Deutsche Bank, Dresdner Bank and Commerzbank) and their legally independent Berlin subsidiaries, secondly, around 170 regional banks which, however, do not necessarily merely operate regionally, thirdly, around 90 private bankers, and finally, some 60 branches of foreign banks.

The three big banks and their Berlin subsidiaries amount to a business volume of around DM 400 billion which represents a market share of approximately 9 percent. Each of them has the legal form of a stock corporation (Aktiengesellschaft, AG), offers its services nation-wide and maintains an international network of branches, subsidiaries and representative offices. Furthermore, they hold shares largely in other companies which supplement their range of services, such as mortgage banks or investment institutions, and have also established a seemingly close relationship with insurance companies, building and loan associations and international banks abroad. With regards to the business volume and the nation-wide operation of banking activities, there are at least four other German banks - Bank für Gemeinwirtschaft, Bayerische Vereinsbank, Bayerische Hypotheken- und Wechselbank and BHF-Bank - that might be comparable to the big banks. The Bundesbank statistics, however, rank them in the category regional banks which is described next.

The category regional banks (Regionalbanken) comprises all private commercial banks organized as stock corporations, partnerships limited by shares (Kommanditgesellschaft auf Aktien, KGaA) or limited liability companies (Gesellschaft mit beschränkter Haftung, GmbH) unless operating as a big bank. The 170 regional banks contribute roughly 12 percent of the total business volume of all German banks. Most of these institutions concentrate their business activity on a certain region of Germany, whereas only some of them operate nation-wide, as stated above. Due to their expertise and knowledge of regional problems, needs and peculiarities, regional banks are particularly esteemed as business partners among small and medium-sized enterprises.

Private bankers, the third subcategory of private commercial banks, are the most traditional credit institutions in the Federal Republic of Germany. In fact, German universal banks historically emerged from individually owned banks. Due to a well-known historical trend towards concentration in the twentieth century, there operate nowadays only 89 private bankers compared to 1,221 in 1913. Private bankers are organized as sole proprietorships (Einzelkaufmann), general partnerships (offene Handelsgesellschaft, OHG), or limited partnerships (Kommanditgesellschaft, KG). In spite of their relatively small market share of less than 2 percent their services are especially appreciated by wealthy clients and corporate customers looking for individual services in fields like investment banking, export financing, money and trust management as well as industry and trade financing. Private bankers generally show a high degree of specialisation and expertise, which helps them to maintain their position in an increasingly competitive environment.

Foreign banks increasingly engage in German financial markets and have particularly concentrated on Frankfurt as their German base. More than 400 banks are currently present in Frankfurt, Germany's financial centre, of which only some 140 are domestic banks. Foreign credit institutions have different possibilities to participate in the Frankfurt banking market: while almost 50 foreign banks have chosen the legal form of a branch of dependent legal status, 85 credit institutions situated in Frankfurt are either majority-owned or wholly-owned by foreign banks and other foreign enterprises, and can be considered as legally independent banks under German law. Around 130 foreign financial institutions carry out their business in Frankfurt through representative offices. The entire market share of all foreign banks recorded in the different banking categories of the Bundesbank statistics amounts to nearly DM 200 billion or 5 percent of the total business volume of all banks.

During the past few years, there has been a tendency towards establishing a subsidiary instead of a branch. This is mainly due to developments in European banking regulations and the German banking law. According to the German Banking Act, as amended in 1985, the Federal Banking Supervisory Agency (Bundesaufsichtsamt für das Kreditwesen) may refuse a banking licence

-10-

to the branch of a foreign bank unless reciprocity is guaranteed by its country of origin. This provision to refuse a banking licence does not apply in the case of a subsidiary. Besides, several banking activities in Germany are not allowed to be conducted by branches of foreign banks, such as the lead management of DM-denominated bond issues, the acting as principal paying agents for DM-bond issues or the membership in the Federal Bond Consortium (Bundesanleihekonsortium) which is solely responsible for arranging for the underwriting of German Federal bond issues. A representative office, as another form of presence of a foreign bank in Germany, does not need a banking licence, but on the other hand is not authorized to be engaged in any of the banking activities as specified in paragraph 1 of the German Banking Act.

Savings banks (Sparkassen) represent a second group of credit institutions in the Federal Republic of Germany acting as universal banks. Most of the savings banks operate under public law and are owned by local authorities. In general, savings banks are obliged to concentrate their activities in the area of their guarantors. As savings banks operating under public law are guaranteed by these authorities, they do not need equity capital and only rely on dotation capital. The Bundesbank statistics reveal that the savings banks, including their head institutions, have the largest share of the market at some 37 percent. The savings banks themselves, of which there are roughly 580, are responsible for around 22 percent of the total business volume, whereas the head institutions account for the remaining 15 percent. The 10 regional head institutions are owned by the respective savings banks and the states in which they operate. They usually act as central banks and clearing houses for the savings banks and also supplement the range of services the savings banks offer, e.g. by maintaining branch offices abroad or offering underwriting services. They are particularly actively involved in the German capital market as investors and issuers. This can also be said about the Deutsche Girozentrale-Deutsche Kommunalbank, the central giro institution of the savings bank sector on the national level.

The more than 17,000 branches of savings banks throughout Germany guarantee the savings banks a good access to personal savings and the real estate business, their traditional domains. Savings banks, however, have participated in the development of the present-day universal banking system in Germany, providing nearly the same banking services nowadays as other competitors, although some transactions, like the international and securities business, still play a minor role. Some apparently more risky activities, such as investing in equities, are not permitted either.

The largest network of bank offices - more than 3,300 legally independent banks and almost 16,000 branches - is maintained by credit associations (Kreditgenossenschaften), the third major group of banking in the Federal Republic of Germany. They can be either commercial credit associations (Volksbanken) or rural credit associations (Raiffeisenbanken) and represent three quarters of the number of German banks. As their market share amounts to roughly 12 percent of the total business volume of all banks, it is evident that credit associations generally are of small size and concentrate their business activity away from the main financial centres. Credit associations are organised in the legal form of co-operatives. Initially they supplied banking services to their members, but have in the meantime extended their activities to non-members too. They have also developed into universal banks, but due to their tradition, they still predominantly deal in accepting savings and lending in the short and medium-term.

The universal banking system is supplemented by a wide variety of specialised banks, some of which are not included in the Bundesbank statistics, such as building and loan associations (Bausparkassen), clearance banks for securities (Wertpapiersammelbanken/Kassenvereine; in late 1989 the regional securities clearance banks merged to one nation-wide operating institution) and investment companies (Kapitalanlagegesellschaften), which operate under special laws or regulations. This inhomogeneous group, aggregated, contributes around one quarter of the total business volume of all German banks. They cover a very heterogeneous field of business activity.

Some three dozen institutions of this category concentrate on the mortgage loan and municipal loan business. Mortgage banks (Realkredit-institute) raise their funds by selling mortgage or municipal bonds on the capital market. Mortgage banks operate either under private law (private Hypotheken-banken), mostly owned by universal banks, or under public law (öffentlich-recht-liche Grundkreditanstalten). Their aggregated market share is around 14 percent. They have to maintain high quality standards as required by the two German mortgage bank acts.

Most of the banks with special functions (Kreditinstitute mit Sonderaufgaben), another subcategory of specialized banks, were created in the immediate post-war period by special legislation in order to primarily promote the restructure of the German economy. As new problems arose, they took on new activities, such as export financings, aid to Third World countries, ecological projects or the implementation of government loan programs. Their services supplement the range of banking products offered by regular banks. They are also very active issuers of bonds. Examples of these credit institutions are Kreditanstalt für Wiederaufbau (Reconstruction Loan Corporation), Deutsche Ausgleichsbank (Equalisation of Burdens Bank), Industriekreditbank (Industrial Loan Bank) and Landwirtschaftliche Rentenbank (Agricultural Mortgage Bank). Together, all these institutions represent a market share of less than 7 percent.

Two postal savings banks and 13 postal giro banks offer services through the extensive network of post offices throughout Germany. Together, they total 1 to 2 percent of the total business volume of the banking sector. Acting mainly as deposit banks for sight and savings deposits, they are serious competitors for regular banks in the deposit business with their attractive debit and credit conditions and their low fees.

1.3 THE CENTRAL BANK AND BANK SUPERVISION

The central bank system was originally set up in 1948, the date of the currency reform and the introduction of the Deutsche Mark. The central bank at that time (Bank deutscher Länder) was subsequently transformed into the Deutsche Bundesbank by the Bundesbank Act (Gesetz über die Deutsche Bundesbank) of July 26, 1957. According to this law, the Bundesbank "shall be required to support the general economic policy of the Federal Government" (§ 12) when pursuing its duties, i.e. to "regulate the amount of money in circulation and of credit supplied to the economy, using the monetary powers conferred on it by this Act, with the aim to safeguarding the currency" (§ 3). This aim is commonly understood as the maintenance of monetary stability.

-13-

Frankfurt is the domicile of the Deutsche Bundesbank, also the home of its predecessor, the Bank deutscher Länder. In more than four decades of existence, the German central bank has regulated the money and credit supply in such a way that a high degree of monetary stability, i.e. low domestic inflation rates and a strong currency, has become the basis for the economic and financial strength of the Federal Republic of Germany.

Due to the Bundesbank's commitment to safeguarding the currency internally and externally it has also promoted Frankfurt's rise to the leading financial centre in Germany and continental Europe by attracting banks and other financial institutions from all over the world. Due to its stability, the Deutsche Mark has become the most important international currency for monetary transactions, interventions, investment and reserves after the US-Dollar with a share of around one fifth of the world foreign exchange reserves. The German currency also serves as an anchor in the European Monetary System with a weight of 30.1 percent in the ECU basket after the recent inclusion of Spain and Portugal. Monetary policy decisions made by the Bundesbank, therefore, influence the external value of the currencies as well as the interest rates of Germany's western European neighbours.

The German central bank is a Federal corporation under public law, owned by the Federal Government. According to the Bundesbank Act, the central bank has to draw up a balance sheet similar to a stock corporation showing its status, including profits or losses. Consequently, profits have to be transferred annually to the Federal budget. In spite of this formal ownership, the Bundesbank's independence while pursuing its monetary policy has to be respected by the Federal Government.

The three decision units of the Bundesbank are the Central Bank Council (Zentralbankrat), the Directorate (Direktorium) and the Managing Boards (Vorstände) of the State Central Banks (Landeszentralbanken). The Central Bank Council decides on the credit and monetary policy of the Bundesbank, sets the guidelines for the conduct of the bank's business and administration, and determines the responsibilities of the other decision units unless stipulated by law. The Council usually meets every other Thursday in Frankfurt and consists of the President and the Vice-President of the Deutsche Bundesbank, the other members of the Directorate, a maximum of eight people, and the Presidents of the 11 State Central Banks.

The Directorate of the Bundesbank with currently 7 members, including the President and the Vice-President of the Bundesbank, acts as the central executive body of the Bundesbank and is situated in Frankfurt as well. Like the Central Bank Council it has the status of a Federal authority. According to the Deutsche Bundesbank Act, the Directorate is primarily responsible for implementing the decisions of the Central Bank Council as well as managing and administrating the bank. In particular, the Directorate is in charge of transactions with the Federal Government and its Special Funds (Sondervermögen), transactions with banks that have central functions in the Federal Republic of Germany, foreign exchange and external transactions as well as open market operations. The members of the Directorate, including the President and the Vice-President of the Bundesbank, are appointed by the President of the Federal Republic of Germany, having been nominated by the Federal Government in consultation with the Central Bank Council. Their tenure of office ranges between two and eight years; reappointment is possible, but a removal from office because of political reasons is excluded.

The Managing Boards of the State Central Banks are the third governing body of the Bundesbank. Each of the 11 states in the Federal Republic of Germany, including West-Berlin, has its own regionally operated State Central Bank which, in general, concentrates on transactions with its state governments as well as with the banks in its area. Together, the State Central Banks maintain around 200 branches all over the Federal Republic of Germany; this extensive network of branches facilitates the implementation of the Bundesbank's monetary policy, the control of the money circulation, the supply of liquidity to the banking system and the handling of cashless payments. The Managing Boards are composed of a President, a Vice-President and, in the larger State Central Banks, an additional member. The President of each State Central Bank automatically becomes a member of the Central Bank Council. The government of each state proposes the President of its State Central Bank via the Bundesrat, Germany's second Chamber of Parliament; after consultation with the Central Bank Council, the President is then appointed by the President of the Federal Republic of Germany. In contrast, the Vice-President and the other members of the Managing Board are appointed by the President of the Bundesbank, having been initially nominated by the Central Bank Council. This pluralistic form of appointing the Bundesbank officials, which at first glance seems to be rather complicated, reflects the federal character of this institution on the one hand and its political independence on the other.

The Bundesbank has the monopoly to produce and to issue banknotes which are the only unrestricted legal tender in the Federal Republic of Germany. Although the coinage prerogative is reserved for the Federal Government, the Bundesbank is in charge of putting the coins in circulation. The Bundesbank thus buys the coins at their nominal value from the Government, crediting the seigniorage to the Federal budget. The Coinage Act (Münzgesetz) places a limit on the issue of coins, which can only be exceeded with the consent of the Bundesbank. This provision, as well as the monopoly to issue banknotes guarantees the Bundesbank's control of the cash supply of money and thus represents the cornerstone for its monetary policy. The cash supply also influences indirectly the level of deposits held in the commercial banking sector. At the end of 1989, the total amount of currency in circulation was DM 162 billion, DM 11.5 billion of which were coins. Money stock indicator M1, which includes not only currency in circulation but also domestic sight deposits of non-banks reached around DM 450 billion; currency in circulation therefore represents almost 40 percent of M1.

According to the Deutsche Bundesbank Act, the central bank is also lender of last resort and responsible for supplying sufficient funds to commercial banks in order to ensure the solvency and liquidity of the banking system as a whole, while maintaining monetary stability at the same time. The Bundesbank thus not only supplies central bank balances to the money market, but also indirectly controls monetary and credit expansion.

For more than one and a half decades the Bundesbank has pursued a policy of monetary targeting, setting an annual growth rate for the central bank money stock (Zentralbankgeldmenge) at the end of the preceding year. The central bank money stock consists of currency in the hands of non-banks and the banks' required minimum reserves on domestic sight deposits, time deposits of up to four years and savings deposits at statutory notice; the required minimum reserves are calculated at the constant reserve ratios of January 1974. Due to some statistical problems and other considerations the Bundesbank switched its policy indicator two years ago from central bank money stock (Zentralbankgeldmenge) to a slightly different money stock, M3, which consists of currency, sight deposits, time deposits and savings deposits at statutory notice, all of domestic non-banks. The monetary target is determined annually in December for the forthcoming year and is defined as a percentage growth of M3 or central bank money stock. The growth target of M3 for 1990 was set on December 14, 1989 and is intended to be between 4 and 6 percent.

The money stock indicator can be influenced directly by the central bank's policy decisions on the money market but is nevertheless closely linked to the ultimate economic variables; it thus represents a key element in the complex monetary transmission process. The annual setting of the monetary target for the following year is based on the Bundesbank's assumption that, in the long run, inflationary developments are only possible if there is an extensive growth in the money stock. This publicly announced emphasis of the Bundesbank's commitment to a stability-orientated monetary policy also helps the central bank to convince all decision-makers, including the government, the unions and the employers, of the monetary framework available for the nominal growth of their expenditures. The expected growth of the production potential, the intended increase in the utilisation of the production potential, the unavoidable inflation rate and the expected development of the velocity of money circulation are the variables that are taken into consideration by the Bundesbank when calculating the monetary target.

In order to follow a stability-orientated monetary policy and to achieve the monetary target, the Deutsche Bundesbank has a set of monetary instruments at its disposal. Besides, using this legal frame, the Bundesbank has developed specific fine-tuning instruments in order to influence both short-term interest rates and money market conditions in particular. Apart from minimum reserve requirements, all monetary instruments given to and used by the Bundesbank are market-orientated; credit ceilings, interest rate controls and similar administrative or regulatory measures used in many other countries, have not been used in the Federal Republic of Germany for decades.

The Bundesbank's monetary instruments used to influence both interest rates and bank liquidity include the setting of the discount and lombard rates as well as the quantitative and qualitative variation of the banks' access to rediscount and lombard credit (refinancing policy), minimum reserve policy, open market policy, the infusion of public funds into the money market (deposit policy), and liquidity policy as a result of Bundesbank interventions on the foreign exchange market. During the past few years, refinancing policies and especially open market policies in the form of repurchase agreements, have become the major instruments used by the Bundesbank, whereas minimum reserve requirements have been drastically reduced and were changed for the last time almost 4 years ago. A detailed description of the Bundesbank's monetary instruments and their impact on the money market will follow in the next chapter.

Furthermore, the Bundesbank assists the banking sector as a clearing house for the handling of cashless payments through its extensive network of branches, which is widely used for interbank transactions and even for interregional transactions within one bank. In general, the central bank offers attractive credit and debit conditions, and its clearing house services are generally free of charge.

The Bundesbank also participates in bank supervision. According to the Banking Act (Gesetz über das Kreditwesen), the Bundesbank is obliged to assist the Federal Banking Supervisory Agency (Bundesaufsichtsamt für das Kreditwesen) in the supervision of the banking sector. This cooperation includes mutual consultation and the exchange of information as well as the use of the Bundesbank's local branches and their employees, especially for the analysis of the current monthly statements and annual accounts that all German banks have to submit. The establishment of a bank, a branch or a subsidiary requires a banking licence which can only be obtained from the Federal Banking Supervisory Agency. This governmental agency safeguards the standards set by the Banking Act with regards to legal form, capital and liquidity requirements, management qualification, allowed business, ceilings for credits, and auditing provisions. The agency is also authorized to withdraw a banking licence, dismiss bank managers or control a bank's conduct of business should a bank violate the law or experience financial difficulty. Far-reaching amendments of banking regulations by the Supervisory Agency, however, need the consent of the Bundesbank.

The Bundesbank also serves as principal banker for the Federal Government and - to a lesser extent - the state governments. Furthermore, the bank acts as a fiscal agent by heading the Federal Bond Consortium (Bundesanleihekonsortium) and by supporting the Federal bonds market to avoid erratic price fluctuations. It should be understood that, by intervening in such a way, it is not intended that market trends be diverted and, that the interventions differ, in this way, from the Bundesbank's open market operations.

Serving as a principal banker, the Bundesbank also has to offer short-term advances to the Federal Government, the State Governments, and the Special Funds (e.g. the Federal Railways or the Federal Post Office). Paragraph 20 of the Deutsche Bundesbank Act, however, sets ceilings for those grants to avoid the involuntary creation of central bank money.

With regards to the external position of the Federal Republic of Germany, the Bundesbank administers and guards the official German foreign exchange reserves including gold, the International Monetary Fund special drawing rights and the claims on the European Monetary Cooperation Fund. The Bundesbank is also in charge of interventions within the European Monetary System and foreign exchange markets in general.

1.4 MONEY MARKET

The markets for money and capital play a major role in Frankfurt's economic activity. In general, the money market is the market-place for issuing and trading short-term debts, while the capital market encompasses markets for longer maturities. Both markets are interlinked in many ways, despite their apparent differences.

In fact, the Frankfurt money market is mainly an interbank market, where banks deal in central bank balances with different maturities. The banks aim to balance their surplus or deficits resulting from daily transactions, by distributing their central bank deposits amongst each other. Furthermore, the Bundesbank, pursuing its open market policy in order to influence interest rates and liquidity, affects the Frankfurt money market by offering repurchase agreements (Pensionsgeschäfte) in bills and bonds as well as selling and buying money market papers to and from banks. Such money market papers could be Treasury bills (Schatzwechsel), Treasury discount papers (Schatzanweisungen) and prime acceptances (Privatdiskonte). Since 1967, when the control of interest rates was abolished and non-banks were permitted to purchase money market papers, large industrial corporations have increasingly entered the money market as investors as well as borrowers. Their market share is, however, relatively small so that the money market can be regarded primarily as a means for horizontal liquidity adjustment within the banking system. Due to the different business structure of the various banking groups in the Federal Republic of Germany, this bridging of foreseen and unforeseen liquidity surpluses and deficits usually works efficiently and generally without any problems.

As the money market is not institutionalised and there is no "floor" or physical meeting-point, dealing is done via telephone, usually between 9 and 11 o'clock daily. During this time, supply and demand are matched by the interbank money market rates. Money market rates are not fixed or quoted officially, although the Bundesbank publishes average rates in its monthly report. One representative indicator for interest rates on the Frankfurt money market is FIBOR (Frankfurt Interbank Offered Rate).

There are several market segments for interbank deposit loans depending on maturity and withdrawal notice. The most important for money market transactions between banks, is day-to-day money (Tagesgeld). It is usually lent and borrowed on a day-to-day basis without any security, mainly to regulate the required minimum reserves within a calendar month. Some participants in the market offer two-way-prices while the majority of players are either borrowers or lenders. Money market rates tend to fluctuate during a business day as well as during a week or a month. If money is not lent on a day-to-day basis, but in the longer term, ranging from 7 days to some 12 months, it is called Termingeld (time deposit). Interest rates in these longer-term markets tend to be much less volatile than in the day-to-day market.

The market volatility mainly results from the liquidity needs of banks, which in turn depend on their specific financial activities as well as on their minimum reserve requirements. In this context, specific weekly dates are of importance when banks have to report their liquidity position to the Bundesbank. In addition, there are other dates which influence the money market rates, such as major tax payment deadlines or ultimo positions. Another impact may come from the foreign exchange market, partly resulting from the Bundesbank's interventions in foreign currencies. Last but not least, the official monetary policy of the Bundesbank influences the money market development fundamentally. In particular, the Bundesbank's interest rate policy, which is mainly the setting of the discount and the lombard rates, as well as its repurchase agreements in securities, can be held primarily responsible for the level of interest rates in the money market.

The Bundesbank grants discount credits exclusively to credit institutions by buying either trade bills that satisfy certain minimum quality requirements or Treasury bills. The Bundesbank also limits the total amount of discount loans available to credit institutions by stipulating rediscount quotas for the entire banking sector and calculating standard quotas for each bank. Quotas can be raised or reduced, for instance, in order to achieve the goals of the Bundesbank's monetary goals. In the event of a raise in the rediscount quotas, the banking sector is confronted with additional unutilised rediscount facilities which, depending on the tightness of the money market and possible compensatory monetary policy actions of the Bundesbank, might reduce the interest rate level.

As during the past few years rediscount quotas have in general been almost fully utilised, German money market rates have exceeded the central bank discount rate permanently. This also shows that the official discount rate is far from being a true market rate. Yet, the setting of the discount rate usually signals the Bundesbank's intentions for its monetary policy. In the past seven years the discount rate has ranged between 2.5 and 6 percent compared to 3.13 to 7.86 percent for day-to-day money (average monthly rate). As discount credits may be granted up to three months, discount rate policy not only affects very short-term interest rates but also influences medium-term conditions and even capital market interest rates.

In contrast to the discount rate, the lombard rate usually surpasses market rates. Lombard credit is offered against the collateral of certain bonds, bills, discount papers and Debt Register claims. The Bundesbank Act specifies the credit limits for each kind of collateral. Although there is usually no limit to lombard loan access, warning marks or lombard ceilings have been used in times of very tight market situations. The lombard rate is usually changed simultaneously with the discount rate and has in recent years stayed 1.5 to 2 percentage points above the discount rate. Changes have, nevertheless, a certain signalling effect, particularly if the normal spread is altered. The Bundesbank generally regards the lombard credit as an exceptional or occasional form of refinancing and has sometimes been obliged to stress this role to the banking sector by suspending the lombard credit or by replacing it through a special lombard loan on a daily basis. Since 1982, lombard loans have been unrestricted. Normally, the lombard rate may be considered an upper limit for the interest rate for day-to-day money. However, shortage of liquidity may push the latter rate above the lombard rate.

As mentioned above, the Bundesbank is also buying and selling securities as well as offering repurchase agreements in securities. In the 1980s, repurchase agreements became the most important monetary instrument influencing money market rates. Under such an agreement, the Bundesbank purchases securities from banks on a tender basis, either defined as interest tenders or volume tenders. Papers sold to the Bundesbank this way must be eligible for collateral loans. These securities are purchased from the Bundesbank for a short-term period along with a repurchase agreement signed by the banks. These agreements are an effective instrument for influencing liquidity and interest rates in the market and have served primarily as a fine-tuning instrument. They nowadays also ensure the role of the lombard credit as a form of exceptional or occasional refinancing instrument, whereas, in the past, lombard rate developments had a predominant impact on money market rates.

A further monetary instrument, though less frequently used, is open market policy by means of money market papers, such as Treasury bills (Schatzwechsel), Treasury discount papers (Unverzinsliche Schatzanweisungen), and prime acceptances (Privatdiskonte). Treasury bills and Treasury discount papers are issued by public authorities. Their maturity ranges from 30 to 90 days, and they are sold as one-off issues to the banking sector. The size of the issue depends on the needs of the treasury as well as the Bundesbank's open market policy. Treasury discount papers are discounted like treasury bills, but have a longer maturity of up to two years; they are discounted when issued and are repayable at par. Although no secondary market for trading exists, some types of Treasury discount papers included in the Bundesbank's money market regulation arrangements may be resold to the Bundesbank prior to maturity and at prevailing market rates of discount. During the past few years, only Treasury discount papers without this option (N-Papiere) have been sold to the public. Acting in the money market, the Bundesbank sets selling rates for Treasury bills and Treasury discount papers according to its intended monetary policy. Prime acceptances (Privatdiskonte), as another money market paper, represent a special kind of banker's acceptances, issued by companies of prime standing and used to finance import, export or merchanting transactions. Their maturity remaining may not exceed 90 days if they are to be bought by the Bundesbank. The central bank purchases prime acceptances either through its regular discount business with credit institutions or on the open market, to regulate the money market. In the latter case, only the Privatdiskont AG is accepted by the Bundesbank as a business partner.

Due not only to the German exchange turnover tax (Börsenumsatzsteuer), but also to existing regulatory restrictions, other money market papers, especially of private issuers, such as certificates of deposit or commercial papers that are quite popular in other countries, are still of minor importance in Germany. It is hoped that the abolition of this tax, scheduled for January 1991, will promote new money market papers and probably also increase the number of participants in this market. So far, market participants engaged in money market papers besides the Bundesbank are mainly credit institutions, and - to a much lesser extent - certain public bodies and a few non-banks.

1.5 CAPITAL MARKET

Capital markets can generally be divided into two main subsections - the bond market and the stock market. In Germany and particularly in Frankfurt, the bond market is far more important than it is in other countries which sometimes leads to the capital market being identified with the "Rentenmarkt", the German expression for bond market.

Due to its magnitude, the bond market regularly surpasses the stock market not only in market capitalisation, but also in turnover and number of listed securities. With some 15,000 listed securities the German bond market is world leader. If measured in turnover, it ranks second. The 1989 bond turnover reached nearly DM 2 trillion according to officially reported turnover data. These figures only cover transactions registered at German stock exchanges. But there is also an important over-the-counter bond market in Germany whose turnover is estimated to be some four times higher than those transactions registered at the German stock exchanges. By the end of 1989 the German bond market totalled more than DM 2 trillion bonds in circulation, of which domestic bearer bonds accounted for some DM 1.2 trillion, loans against borrowers' notes for more than DM 500 billion, registered bonds for some DM 200 billion, foreign issues for DM 200 billion, and new instruments for less than DM 50 billion. In terms of bonds in circulation, the German bond market ranks third in the world, behind the United States and Japan. In 1989, gross sales of domestic bonds on the primary market exceeded DM 250 billion, but due to a high volume of redemptions, net sales in this period reached only DM 80 billion.

The importance of the German bond market is even more remarkable if the almost complete absence of domestic bonds issued by private enterprises is taken into consideration. The bulk, or more than 60 percent, of domestic bearer bonds were bank bonds, the remainder were public bonds since very few industrial bonds exist. Consequently, apart from foreign bonds only two groups of debtors can be found, - credit institutions and public authorities. Yet, in Germany, public credit is less intensively used than in most other countries, and financing debts through direct borrowing from banks via loans against borrowers' notes (Schuldscheindarlehen) is generally preferred. Less than 40 percent of domestic bonds in circulation were issued by the public sector. With some DM 380 billion of fixed interest securities outstanding at the end of 1989 the Federal Government is the largest single issuer; its bonds are commonly understood as "Bund". Other public bonds are issued by the Federal states, the Federal Railways and the Federal Post Office. Coupons and maturities of their bonds are comparable to those of the Federal Government, though in smaller volumes. Of course, Federal bonds are the most popular ones and normally preferred to all others so they are considered to be the most marketable and of a high liquidity. As a consequence, private bonds often have some 0.2 to 0.6 percent higher interest rates than comparable "Bund" papers.

Although more publicly than privately issued domestic bonds have been sold during recent years, the opposite had been the case previously. In fact, private papers dominate in terms of total bonds issued, although domestic industrial bonds have not been issued for many years. Private bonds are issued by banks, mainly mortgage banks (Hypothekenbanken) and central head institutions of the savings banks (Landesbanken-Girozentralen; as described in chapter 1.2.), which offer mortgage bonds (Pfandbriefe) and municipal bonds (Kommunalobligationen). Sales of municipal bonds treble that of mortgage bonds with some DM 370 billion municipal bonds in circulation compared to about DM 140 billion mortgage bonds, as per December 1989. Both categories of bonds are issued on tap.

The almost complete lack of industrial bonds may be regarded as a particular feature of the German capital market. This deficiency, as mentioned previously, is mainly a consequence of taxation, the complicated procedure of government approval as well as of transaction costs.

Turning from issuers to investors, focus is directed on four main groups of lenders - banks, foreign institutions, domestic private households and institutional investors, such as investment funds and insurance companies.

Banks hold some 40 percent of all outstanding bearer bonds and are by far the most important group of institutional investors in bearer bonds. Their demand is mainly determined by the liquidity situation in the market, i.e. the monetary policy of the Bundesbank and the customer demand for loans. Banks prefer types of bonds with a deep market, a coupon slightly above market level and a maturity of between 1 and 5 years. Usually the minimum bargain size in over-the-counter transactions between banks is DM 5 million.

Domestic purchases of foreign bonds or foreign purchases of domestic bonds prevailed in rather erratic fluctations, due to exchange rate expectations, tax rate changes and interest differentials between domestic and foreign bonds, mainly Dollar denominated. Whereas in 1986 two thirds of the total amount of newly issued domestic bonds were sold to foreigners (DM 59 billion out of a total of DM 87 billion), in 1988 hardly any German bonds went abroad and far more foreign bonds than the total volume of all domestically issued papers were imported (DM 54 billion against DM 35 billion).

-25-

Private households represent another important group of investors on the bond market. As small investors they are usually involved in bargains of up to DM 10,000 and primarily engaged in medium or long-term maturity periods. Their investment behaviour often lags behind or is even contrary to the policies used by the banks, which means that private investors are less sensitive to interest rate changes than banks normally are. Due to taxation, private households often prefer bonds with a long maturity and a coupon below market level, as price differentials remain tax free.

Investment funds and insurance companies form the final group of investors. Insurance companies hold some 10 percent of outstanding bearer bonds, but prefer direct loans against borrowers' notes or registered bonds that are not subject to writeoff under German law, unless by default. Insurance companies do not usually buy above par value and prefer papers with longer maturities in bargains of DM 1 to 10 million, sometimes with up to 1 year forward values. Investment funds, still of minor importance in Germany, normally prefer foreign bonds to domestic ones. However, 2 percent of the German bond volume is in the funds' portfolios.

As to the bond market there are some rules to be taken into consideration:

In general, public bonds are sold by subscription through a banking consortium, whereas private bonds are normally sold directly to the public by the issuing institution without the service of a consortium or intermediary. While mortgage banks and other banks granting communal loans are constant issuers and usually offer on tap, most other private bonds of banks or companies are still subject to individual approval under German civil law, §§ 795 and 808a. In the latter case, the Federal Ministry of Finance has to approve creditworthiness. This complicated procedure of individual approval is one of the reasons why German companies prefer to issue bonds on the Euromarket rather than on the domestic market.

The issue of Federal Government bonds is managed by a permanent Federal Bond-Issuing Syndicate (Bundesanleihekonsortium), its membership consisting of the Bundesbank as lead manager and more than 70 banks. Whenever an issue is launched, the members of this syndicate receive a selling commission for their services. However, if those bonds are sold to the

Bundesbank within a year after issue at a rate equal to or lower than the issue price, the respective bank has to repay the received commission. This incentive system encourages members of the Federal Bond-Issuing Syndicate to try to place their tranche with long-term orientated investors.

All occasional issues of bonds, i.e. those not sold on tap, normally pass a special panel called the Central Capital Market Committee (Zentraler Kapitalmarktausschuß). It is a self-governing body which was inaugurated for some kind of steering recommendations to prevent any overstrain on the market. In this committee, which functions as a gentlemen's agreement, representatives of the major issuing banks assemble and, in cooperation with the Bundesbank, recommend timing and volume of new issues. These procedures do not apply to loans against borrowers' notes (Schuldscheindarlehen), which is one reason for that market's growth and its popularity among borrowers. The Central Capital Market Committee is not involved in private placements, which are not listed on the stock exchange, or DM-foreign bonds and DM-Euro bonds. Usually denominated in large amounts these papers bear low issuing costs. While Euro-DM bonds are primarily sold to institutional investors, the DM-foreign bond market has traditionally been a more retail-orientated market; therefore, private placements only play a limited role there. Since January 1990, domestic banks have been allowed to issue foreign currency bonds and to sell them directly to German investors in the primary market. With this step towards further deregulation, the Bundesbank intends to repatriate and activate the international bond market and also stimulate the market for bonds of industrial corporations.

The Frankfurt capital market offers a variety of debt instruments for borrowers and lenders. Some are described below:

Loans against borrowers' note (Schuldscheindarlehen) are long-term direct credits with fixed interest rates and, preferrably, with a maturity between one and ten years and with a minimum amount of DM 1 million. This instrument has been and still is used widely by public authorities for obtaining large amounts of credit. The Federal states (Länder), as well as the municipalities, make almost exclusively use of borrowers' notes when increasing debts, whereas the Federal Government has reduced this kind of borrowing in recent years, preferring loans. Although not quoted on the stock exchange, the transfer of title is possible by written assignment. Private firms also make use of negotiable debt in the form of loans against borrowers' note because the issuing cost is much lower than for bonds and other securities, the issuing procedure is simpler, handling is faster, and transfer is exempt from capital transfer tax. The level of loans raised by public authorities against borrowers' notes amounted to more than half of the total public debt outstanding of some DM 900 billion.

In addition to loans against borrowers' note, public authorities meet their financial demand by issuing several types of bonds, though this is almost exclusively done by the Federal Government and other Federal authorities.

Straight bonds (Anleihen) are the most popular type of bonds issued as bearer securities with maturities of usually ten years, sometimes up to 15 years and in times of capital shortage even as low as 4 years. They are mainly issued by the Federal Government, the state governments, the Post Office and the Railways. The bonds are issued from time to time in issue sizes between DM 4 and 5 billion (Bund) and DM 1 to 2 billion if issued by the Federal Railway or Post Office. The most liquid and actively traded papers are Federal bonds (Bundesanleihen) with a maturity of 10 years. Interest on bonds is paid annually, and redemption is either by random withdrawal or in full at maturity. Straight bonds are issued to the public on the primary market through a banking consortium dominated by the major domestic banks. The consortium underwrites the whole issue under firm conditions and then places the bonds among customers. Generally, the consortium offers the bonds through public subscription. Federal bonds are placed on the market by the Federal Bond-Issuing Syndicate (Bundesanleihekonsortium), as mentioned before. By the end of 1989 there were about DM 220 billion bonds issued by the public sector in circulation, DM 195 billion of which were so-called "Bunds" or Federal bonds (Bundesanleihen). It should be mentioned, however, that Federal bonds, as with all other Federal securities, are not certificated but exclusively exist as loan stock rights which are transferred by security clearing only.

The Federal Government also issues special bonds with a maturity of 5 years (Bundesobligationen) to finance public investments and to promote private savings. Consequently, the denomination is DM 100 only or any multiple thereof. These fixed-interest papers are constantly issued with a selling period of several months and at variable prices adjusted to market yield. Five-year-special

Federal bonds are listed on the stock exchange. While primary purchase is reserved exclusively to individuals and non-profit organisations, anyone can buy these bonds on the secondary market. By the end of December 1989, there were DM 94 billion 5-year Federal bonds in circulation. These bonds are quoted and traded on the secondary market of the stock exchange, but most of the dealing is done on the over-the-counter market offered by banks. Trading is very active in Frankfurt, but relatively inactive among non-banks due to the exchange turnover tax which, incidentally, will be abolished by the end of 1990. There are no purchase restrictions for non-residents.

Treasury notes (Kassenobligationen) are medium-term fixed-interest instruments with a maturity of 3 to 6 years and a minimum amount of 5,000 DM. Treasury notes are issued by tender without the intermediary of a syndicate. The Bundesbank acts as agent for the issuing public authorities and invites bids for new notes from investors, which are almost exclusively given by banks. The final selling price is fixed by the Bundesbank according to the bids received. There are no purchase restrictions whatsoever, and even foreigners may buy. Like straight bonds, Treasury notes are listed on the stock exchange, but trading is mainly done over-the-counter. Public sector indebtedness in this financial instrument was some DM 50 billion at the end of September 1989 .

Finally, the Federal Government issues savings bonds (Bundesschatz-briefe); their primary acquisition is also reserved to individuals and non-profit organisations. There are two types, A and B, with a maturity of 6 or 7 years respectively. Type A distributes interest annually, whereas type B accumulates it. Federal savings bonds are primarily intended to be sold to small investors. Though not traded in the secondary market, sales and redemptions are possible through credit institutions. Some DM 33 billion were in circulation at the end of 1989.

As shown above, bonds are the most dominant segment of the German capital market. Apart from the most popular type of bonds, i.e. straight bonds in all the modifications as described above, other bonds, different from straight bonds, exist too, such as convertible bonds and option bonds.

Convertible Bonds (Wandelschuldverschreibungen) provide the holder with the right to exchange the respective bonds for shares at predetermined prices within a given period of time. Interest is lower than for bearer bonds, but may be compensated by a prospective cheap exchange for shares. This instrument is used increasingly by stock corporations to provide equity capital particularly in times of a bearish stock market.

Option bonds or warrants (Optionsanleihen) are fixed-interest instruments with warrants attached, giving the right to purchase shares at predetermined conditions. The warrants may also be traded separately as securities.

In order to complete the view on the German bond market, some remarks have to be made on trends and prospective changes in this market. In recent years, the German capital market has seen several reforms and steps towards liberalisation to strengthen its international competitiveness. These changes, which affected the Frankfurt markets for DM-denominated debt instruments of all kinds especially, were influenced and motivated by a similar trend towards deregulation in other European countries.

The abolition of the 25 percent withholding tax on coupon payments for domestic bonds held by foreigners in August 1984 was the first among a number of significant reforms to support the DM bond market as a whole. From May 1985 onwards, floating rate notes, zero bond coupon issues and issues with multi-currency options or swaps were permitted for the first time. From the same date onwards, the Bundesbank also allowed the subsidiaries of foreign banks to lead-manage DM-denominated bonds. By announcing these steps towards liberalisation, the Bundesbank explicitly emphasized that it wanted the international DM market to be German-based, requiring foreign lead managers to operate through a German legal entity. Generally, liberalisation also requires reciprocity, which means that the same right to conduct a certain business is also to be given to German banks in the foreign bank's country of origin.

The obligation to notify the Deutsche Bundesbank of international DM-bond issues prior to the scheduled day of issue was repealed in July 1989. At the same time, the Bundesbank also reduced the minimum maturity of five years for public issues and three years for private placements to two years in both cases.

-30-

Turning now to the German equity market, focus is directed to different characteristics and developments. Seen from the outside, it may be surprising that the German equity market is much less important than the bond market. This can be proved in terms of turnover as well as volume or total market value of securities. German shares quoted on a stock exchange at current prices constitute no more than roughly a quarter of GNP, whereas in the UK it is nearly on a par and in Japan it outstrips GNP. This is also illustrated by the number of stock corporations quoted. Less than 600 domestic companies have a listing in Germany while more than 2,600 can be found on British quotation lists.

It is commonly believed that German shares are notoriously undervalued. It is also obvious, however, that the return on shares in terms of dividends is not very attractive as explained below. Nevertheless, undervaluation can be detected in terms of intrinsic value, notably for the most reputed shares. This comes from the considerable amounts of undisclosed reserves which are a characteristic feature of German stock corporations. Although this could give rise to takeovers, it has rarely occurred before, due to institutional impediments not treated here.

The German stock market has never reached the potential one might expect from such an economy. Several reasons can be listed as being responsible for the German situation, some of which are given below:

Firstly, the German tax system favours outside capital rather than equity capital much more than in most other countries. Apart from high marginal tax rates for both personal income and corporation income (withheld), there are two additional taxes mostly unknown in other countries: a property tax (Vermögenssteuer) and a trade tax (Gewerbesteuer) levied on capital as well as on return.

Secondly, the existence of certain legal provisions favours bonds against equities. This is particularly true for insurance companies whose investments in equities are much more restricted compared to those in bonds. But this also applies to quite a number of other cases, in particular when money has to be handled in a trustworthy manner.

Thirdly, the universal banking system itself prefers bonds to equities as instruments for finance and investments. Although this may differ from one sector to another, it applies in particular to savings banks and their central giro institutions (Landesbanken-Girozentralen).

Fourthly, in Germany the everyday private investor seems to be rather risk averse compared to American, Japanese or British private savers. Most people in Germany associate investments in shares with risk and speculation. Consequently the private saver prefers to invest in a monetary claim rather than in a direct investment. The everyday German saver generally leaves the final decision on an investment to the experts of a bank. He therefore lends his money to banks rather than to companies. Due to this investment behaviour, only 5 percent of the private financial assets in Germany are held in shares, and approximately less than 10 percent of private households have shares in their portfolio, although, on average, households in Germany hold close to DM 100,000 in financial assets (Geldvermögen).

Fifthly, dividends do not necessarily reflect profits of the respective companies. In fact, many companies prefer to distribute about half of their profits and traditionally pay relatively constant dividends as long as profits do not fluctuate too much. As a consequence, small investors in particular compare dividends with interest. As dividends rarely return more than interest, it does not seem worthwile purchasing shares unless an increase in share prices is expected.

Finally, in addition to private investors' preference for bank deposits, insurance policies, or fixed-interest securities, there also is a lack of demand for equities from the institutional side. Savings and investment schemes as well as pension funds, designed to make provisions for senior citizens, are almost unknown in Germany or play only a minor role in the capital market.

Yet, with a market value of more than DM 600 billion at the end of 1989, the German stock market ranked fourth in the world behind Japan, the United States and the United Kingdom, although it only accounts for some 3 percent of the world's market capitalisation. In 1989, the total market value of domestic equities sold on the primary market reached a peak of nearly DM 20 billion, which could be interpreted as the beginning of a more prosperous development.

The issuing side of the equity market is dominated by large industrial corporations along with banks and some insurance companies. While Germany hosts some 350,000 private companies of limited liability, there are only some 2,200 stock corporations, less than a quarter of which are quoted on the stock exchanges. While the 20 largest stock corporations in Germany account for some 50 percent of the market capitalisation, most companies fall into the middle market segment. The structure of the market, with the dominance of a few major shares, is another reason why the equitiy market as a source of corporate finance is relatively small.

Many German stock corporations are interlocked either partly or wholly with other equity holding companies. Thus, the main investors in equities are industrial corporations with a market share of some 40 percent, with private households having over 20 percent, foreigners with some 13 percent, banks with more than 10 percent and insurance companies with less than 10 percent.

In general, German shares are bearer shares, but some insurance companies issue registered shares. They are denominated and consequently listed in blocks of DM 50 of the nominal capital stock. Although this does not really matter for quotation, it sometimes causes some kind of money illusion with respect to the actual price of a share which seems to be "high" or "low".

Instruments traded in the equity market are common and preferred shares, profit-sharing certificates, convertible bonds, options and warrants. While the warrants market has grown considerably in recent years, the options market has remained small due to legal and other restrictions. With the opening of the German Futures Exchange (Deutsche Terminbörse, DTB) on January 26, 1990, a liquid market for traded options on 14 major German stocks was introduced.

There is some hope that the German equity market will be able to keep up with the other large world markets, provided that some still existing impediments, as described in this brochure, will be removed soon.

-33-

1.6 THE STOCK EXCHANGE

Federalism, as one of Germany's constitutional elements, not only prevails in governmental affairs but also in the organisation of the German stock exchanges. As a result, Germany has eight different stock exchanges with trading-floors, located in Frankfurt, Dusseldorf, Munich, Hamburg, Stuttgart, Hanover, Berlin and Bremen, ranked thus, according to their respective market volume. While Frankfurt is dominant without a doubt, Dusseldorf still ranks far ahead of the remaining exchanges. Nevertheless, the other exchanges, although of minor importance, operate as local or regional centres in their respective area.

Since January 26, 1990, the German Futures Exchange (Deutsche Terminbörse, DTB) in Frankfurt has operated as Germany's ninth exchange. It is fully computerised, and has no trading floor. The DTB currently is specialised in traded options on 14 major German stocks, but will introduce further options as well as a future contract, based on the German Stock Index (DAX), and a future on a synthetic Federal bond later this year. Further products are in the pipeline. The DTB is based in Frankfurt, but trading is conducted by a computer system which links market participants regardless of where they are located. The DTB computer centre collects the orders of the participants and then matches and settles them. Membership is open to all German banks and brokers as well as to subsidiaries or branches of foreign banks. In addition, there are three other computerized securities price information systems for the cash market (IBIS, MATIS and Midas) which were either implemented recently or are in the pipeline.

While the Frankfurt Stock Exchange is responsible for some two thirds of the country's turnover in shares and about three quarters of it in bonds, Dusseldorf has a market share of almost 20 percent; the six other exchanges remain well below 10 percent each. The eight German stock exchanges are represented by the Federation of the German Stock Exchanges (Arbeitsgemeinschaft der Deutschen Wertpapierbörsen). This federation of stock exchanges accounted for a turnover of some DM 3,300 billion in securities in 1989, of which almost DM 1,400 billion was in equities. This clearly indicates the predominance of the bond market. Up until the present day, the German stock market has been the largest one in continental Europe. On average every share has changed owner once in the past year. The most actively traded shares were those of Deutsche Bank, Siemens, Volkswagen, Bayer and Thyssen. These five leading shares as measured by turnover in 1989 constitute around one fifth of the total turnover of equities on the German stock exchanges. The average daily turnover on the German stock exchanges amounted to DM 13 billion in 1989.

Since Frankfurt can be considered Germany's representative stock exchange, it will be treated here. Turnover on the Frankfurt Stock Exchange reached nearly DM 2,200 billion in 1989, some DM 750 billion, or 34 percent, of which was done in equities. Around 8 percent of the turnover in equities and some 7 percent of the turnover in bonds on the Frankfurt Stock Exchange is in foreign securities. The market value of all domestic equities listed in Frankfurt reached more than DM 560 billion by the end of 1989. At the end of 1989, there were 850 equities, 390 of which were foreign, and 6,835 bonds, 993 of which were foreign, listed on the Frankfurt Stock Exchange. Going by the number of listed bonds, Frankfurt is the leading stock exchange in the world.

As mentioned above, the Frankfurt Stock Exchange is by far the largest stock exchange in Germany and is strongly supported by the large concentration of banks in the city. According to German law, banks are the main trading members. Currently, there are more than 130 members of the Frankfurt Stock Exchange. Its main building with the trading floor is located in the centre of Frankfurt and only a few minutes walking distance from the banking sector. The Frankfurt Stock Exchange is organised according to the auctioneer system and not like market maker systems found in the United States or Great Britain. As a consequence, there are no spreads. The auctioneer system on German Stock Exchanges particularly attracts investors in shares of smaller companies which usually have a wide spread in market maker systems. Margin trading and short sales are not possible on the Frankfurt Stock Exchange, although banks might grant their customers loans to purchase securities in exceptional circumstances. The introduction of a securities lending system, as in the Euromarket, is on the agenda for reform discussions. A huge increase in business activity since the beginning of the eighties as well as the internationalisation of markets and competition has made it necessary to enlarge the trading floor of the Frankfurt Stock Exchange and to install the most modern information and communication technology.

-35-

According to its Rules and Regulations, the Frankfurt Stock Exchange is managed by a Board of Governors (Börsenvorstand) which consists of at least 19 and at most 22 members who are elected for three years. The Board of Governors is responsible for the admission of persons and enterprises to the stock exchange, monitors compliance with laws and other rules, and lays down and controls trading conditions. Other bodies of the Frankfurt Stock Exchange are the Admission Board (Zulassungsstelle) for the admission of securities to official listing, the Arbitration Board (Schiedsstelle) for settling disputes arising from transactions between members of the Stock Exchange, and the Chamber of Official Brokers (Kursmaklerkammer), a public law entity representing the official brokers (Kursmakler).

According to the terms of the German Stock Exchange Act (Börsengesetz), the Frankfurt Stock Exchange is subject to supervision by the state government, i.e. the Government of Hesse. It approves the establishment, rules and regulations as well as the list of fees, appoints the official brokers and supervises the stock exchange via a state commissioner. The Stock Exchange itself (administration, equipment etc.) is financed by fees levied on the admission of persons and the admission or introduction of securities to trading.

Types of instruments traded on the Frankfurt Stock Exchange are common and preferred stocks, warrants, bonds, securities options, gold (spot only) and currencies (spot only). The Frankfurt exchange is the guiding market (Leitbörse) for currency quotations in Germany. Trading hours on the Frankfurt Stock Exchange are 10.30 a.m. to 13.30 p.m., Monday to Friday. Fixing of shares starts at noon daily, fixing for non-continiously traded bonds half an hour earlier.

The following three markets for securities exist in Germany:

The "Amtlicher Handel" is the official market for the listing and trading of the major and large blue-chip companies and government bonds. It has the most stringent listing requirements which are subject to the Stock Exchange Act (Börsengesetz) and the Stock Exchange Admission Regulation (Börsen-zulassungs-Verordnung). 540 equities with a nominal value of DM 180 billion and 6,236 bonds with a nominal value of DM 810 billion were listed in the official trading in December 1988. Principal requirements for admission of securities to the official trading are an expected market value of at least DM 2.5 million for equities and more than DM 0.5 million par value in the case of other securities. The issuer of shares should have existed as a company for more than three years and is obliged to publish an interim report. At least 25 percent of the shares admitted have to be offered to the public. Furthermore, a prospectus has to be published, which enables the public to assess the issuer and the securities appropriately.

The "Geregelter Markt" is the second or regulated market which was opened in May 1987 to encourage smaller companies to go public. It replaced the former "geregelter Freiverkehr" which was a regulated unofficial market. Most of the companies listed on the latter market had joined the "Geregelter Markt" by the end of 1987, the others trade on the third market segment (Freiverkehr) nowadays, which is described later. The regulated market is more attractive to smaller companies because its listing requirements are based on the same principles but are less stringent than those of the "Amtlicher Handel"; joining is therefore easier und less costly. In 1988, there were 51 equities with a nominal value of DM 1 billion and 541 bonds with a nominal value of DM 86 billion listed on the regulated market. A listing on the regulated market requires a minimum nominal capital of DM 0.5 million. Besides, a company report must be published prior to introduction. The application for a listing must be filed by the issuer in cooperation with a bank or another eligible institution.

"Freiverkehr" as the third stock market is an unregulated market. On this market, shares are traded on the floor as well as off the floor. Trading is active in unlisted shares; they are quoted using the same procedure practiced on the other two markets. At the end of 1988, there were 180 equities and 6 bonds listed on this market.

Trading on the Frankfurt Stock Exchange requires membership. In Frankfurt, banks are direct members of the stock exchange. This is mainly due to the fact that banks in Germany play an active and important role in securities trading, acting not only for their own trading account but also as brokers for private and institutional clients. Only they are allowed to bring buying and selling orders to the Frankfurt Stock Exchange. There are currently 131 banks with membership to the Frankfurt Stock Exchange, 61 of which are foreign. Apart from banks, there are 35 official brokers (Kursmakler) who also are members of the Frankfurt Stock Exchange. Kursmakler act as intermediaries for transactions in those securities that are admitted to official trading. They receive buying and selling orders from banks and then determine official prices. Official brokers set a standard price for every security officially listed, according to supply and demand and with a view to the price which will guarantee them the greatest turnover possible. This price-setting system works like an auctioneer system. Apart from standard price quotation there is a variable price quotation in certain equities and bonds which are very actively traded. As soon as the official broker has determined an official price, he inputs this price into the computer of the KISS price information system. KISS transmits real time prices of all officially listed securities via screens to the trading floor as well as to the offices of banks, news agencies and other institutions.

In addition to the official brokers, there are 43 free brokers (Freimakler) who also have membership to the Frankfurt Stock Exchange and are allowed to act as intermediaries in any dealings in securities. They are entitled to intervene as brokers, parallel to and in competition with official brokers.

Settlement of securities transactions in Frankfurt is very efficient. The predominance of bearer shares and the use of modern computers for processing and settlement allows a ready transferability of securities and a low scale of fees. Until now orders are transmitted to the stock exchange via telephone or telex and then passed on to the broker who issues a sales note. This sales note, which names the banks involved as partners in each transaction, is the basis for the settlement of a transaction. The securities traded on the Frankfurt Stock Exchange are stored in a collective deposit with the Frankfurter Kassenverein which acts as a securities clearing house and settlement bank. Usually, delivery of securities has to be made the second working day after the transaction, and is executed via book entries from one account to another. The processing is performed by the DWZ Deutsche Wertpapierdaten-Zentrale which serves the German stock exchanges with centralised software and hardware support.

The order routing system BOSS was recently introduced in some market segments and has already undergone a testing period there. It will be in operation for all securities transactions by April 1991. It offers electronic order routing during trading hours with an immediate settlement of the transaction.

The main advantages of the German stock market, besides its very efficient settlement and clearing system, are the low transaction costs for the private client with small transactions. Securities transactions on the Frankfurt Stock Exchange are subject to a commission charge payable to the bank. The bank commission is stipulated independently by the individual bank, but is negotiable. The smaller investor is usually charged a commission of 1 percent with a minimum charge of some 10 to 25 DM for equities and 0.5 percent for bond orders. In addition, there is a brokerage fee payable to the official broker (Kursmakler), which amounts to 0.08 percent of the value for equity transactions and between 0.075 and 0.0003 percent for bonds, depending on the size of the bargain. The brokerage fee is eliminated if securities change hands over the counter and no official broker is involved.

Currently, there still exists a turnover tax for equity transactions. It is 0.25 percent and halved if the buyer or seller resides abroad. Stock exchange turnover tax for bonds is, as a rule, 0.1 percent. Turnover tax on securities transactions will be abolished on January 1st, 1991.

In 1989 the Frankfurt Stock Exchange showed a performance increase of 35 percent according to the DAX (Deutscher Aktienindex), a continously (i.e. every minute) updated German stock index which was introduced in 1988 and comprises the 30 most actively traded German shares. By April 1990 a new bond index called REX (Deutscher Rentenindex) will be introduced at the Frankfurt Stock Exchange. Rex was created by the Federation of the German Stock Exchanges and the Frankfurt Stock Exchange in view of the needs of the recently opened German Futures Exchange (DTB). Rex represents a portfolio of national bonds with 5-year and 10-year Federal bonds as its basis. The portfolio is structured in ten different categories of maturities (from one year up to ten years) and three different types of coupons (6 percent, 7.5 percent and 9 percent). Rex should become a kind of "official" bond index for the German market. In addition, a new European stock index called EURAX is in the pipeline.

In order to supplement the existing floor of the Frankfurt Stock Exchange, new electronic markets for securities have either been established recently or are to be implemented in the near future:

-39-

IBIS, an interbank information system, was launched by German banks in December 1989. IBIS is a new electronic price information system which currently distributes prices of 14 blue-chip shares. Banks offer two-way indicative prices and deal with each other off floor via the telephone. IBIS will serve the German Futures Exchange (DTB) as an underlying spot market. It is planned that IBIS will become an electronic market with obligatory prices in 1990, under the roof of the Frankfurt Stock Exchange.

Apart from the banks, the official brokers also established a competing securities trading system called MATIS (Makler-Tele-Informations-System). MATIS is an electronic system, distributed via Reuters, which offers firm one-way prices for the leading German shares as well as for some most traded bonds. Prices offered via MATIS are subject to a brokerage fee.

A further electronic information and trading system will be established by the free brokers and is called MIDAS. It is planned by the free brokers to offer prices of some 600 securities to banks, insurance companies and other institutional investors via MIDAS. The distribution of prices will be offered through the Quotron electronic network, while clearing will be managed by Citibank.

Until recently there has been no financial futures market in Frankfurt although there is a forward market for currencies outside the Stock Exchange. Options trading in Frankfurt took place on the Frankfurt Stock Exchange in 69 stock options and 14 bond options, but due to legal restrictions, access to and liquidity of the market was rather poor. In August 1989, the German Stock Exchange Act was amended to permit the new German Futures Exchange (DTB), which was described above, to be established. By means of this overdue implementation, Frankfurt is getting a new and efficient trading centre for options and futures contracts without a physical trading floor.

To strengthen its international competitiveness the Frankfurt Stock Exchange is planning to change its legal form into a stock corporation. Despite the schedule for the integration of IBIS under its roof, the Frankfurt Stock Exchange will participate in a European price information and trading system which is currently in the pipeline.

To conclude, it can be said that the Frankfurt Stock Exchange is the leading German stock exchange with an international approach and a very fast growing market, both in terms of turnover as well as new listings. During the past six years, 126 new issues of shares have been introduced to the market. But still relatively few corporations in Germany are listed on the Frankfurt Stock Exchange. Furthermore, market capitalisation in relation to Gross National Product is still rather low (below 25 percent). One reason for this phenomenon is the top-heaviness of the Frankfurt financial market. Because of historical reasons, like currency reforms, which were an obstacle to the development of the issuing business, too many credits are still granted and too few securities issued. Besides, the Frankfurt stock market is influenced more than other markets in the world by international investors because the distribution of private sector savings, as well as the portfolios of domestic institutional investors, still show a preference for fixed income securuties, savings accounts or, more recently, mutual funds. German private investors are rather risk averse as to the ownership of equities. Roughly 40 percent of German equities are held in non-traded blocks by banks and other companies. Pension funds and insurance companies own around 12 percent of the shares listed on the Frankfurt Stock Exchange. One step to considerably improve the management of the save custody accounts of both institutional and private investors has been the permittance of stop-orders since the beginning of 1989. Further steps to attract investors are mentioned above, so conditions are favourable that Frankfurt can consolidate and even extend its position as the international German stock market and centre for securities transactions in continental Europe.

2 FRANKFURT

2.1 HISTORICAL BACKGROUND

During more than a thousand years of existence, Frankfurt has evolved into a centre for trade, commerce and finance. This development was promoted through its favourable geographic location at the crossroads of major trade routes.

Frankfurt gained considerable political importance when in 1356, it was appointed by law as the place for the election of German kings and in 1562, also became the place of their coronation. Long time before that, Frankfurt's role as a trade fair centre was founded. Around 1200, a mint of the Holy Roman Empire was established in Frankfurt. In 1402, Frankfurt's first bank, called "Wessel" started operating due to the necessity to offer money exchange services to travelling merchants during the trade fairs regularly held here. By the early 16th century, Frankfurt had already gained a reputation as a leading financial centre. At that time, it had the status of a Free City of the Holy Roman Empire.

In 1585, more than 400 years ago, the Frankfurt Exchange was founded, the predecessor of the Frankfurt Stock Exchange. Trading at that time concentrated on the fixing of the exchange value of nine different types of coins. In 1790, the Frankfurt Exchange became the Frankfurt Stock Exchange. Throughout its lifetime, the Frankfurt Exchange and Stock Exchange have always been accessible to foreign borrowers and investors. In the early 19th century, for example, Austria was a major borrower. Some decades later, the US Government as well as foreign railway companies were among the leading market participants wanting to borrow.

In the 18th century, more and more banks were established in Frankfurt. Whereas up to then, most banks had had their roots in the commodity trading business, other forms of financial needs, such as serving the haulage and commission business, trading in bills as well as negotiating and placing government bonds and promissory notes, promoted the development of new banks. Around the middle of the 19th century, even more banks in new legal forms were established, such as saving banks and credit associations.

-42-

After the foundation of the German Empire (Deutsches Reich) in 1871 and the subsequent establishment of the central bank (Reichsbank) in Berlin in 1876, Frankfurt lost some of its importance in several financial fields. The growth of the big banks in Berlin meant that the role of private bankers, predominantly residing in Frankfurt, also began to decline. Frankfurt was, however, able to maintain its role as a leading stock exchange in foreign securities.

Throughout this century Frankfurt has experienced both a deep depression and a surprising recovery. Inflation after World War I deprived financial markets of their role and consequently, affected Frankfurt extremely hard due to the devaluation of money and bonds. A further decline in Frankfurt's financial importance at that time was caused by the continuing centralisation towards Berlin and the exodus of Jewish bankers during the Nazi dictatorship shortly after. World War II brought an almost complete devastation of the German economic and financial system. The city of Frankfurt was also heavily destroyed. The recovery of Frankfurt after the war was fostered by its historical traditions but was also helped by the political decisions of the American and British military with the selection of Frankfurt as the headquarters of the Bizonal Economic Administration.

In the course of the currency reform of 1948, which implemented the Deutsche Mark as legal tender in West Germany, the central bank (Bank Deutscher Länder), the predecessor of the Bundesbank, was established in Frankfurt. This decision represented the cornerstone for the post-war rise of Frankfurt into Germany's leading financial and banking centre. Subsequently, many credit institutions moved their headquarters to Frankfurt, whereas before World War II, none of the ten largest banks had its main office here. Besides the big banks, the central head institutions of the credit associations as well as the savings banks chose Frankfurt as main base for their business. In addition, the Frankfurt Stock Exchange became the leading market place in Germany for securities.

2.2 ECONOMIC STRUCTURE AND INFRASTRUCTURE

Frankfurt's economic activity is often associated with its role as Germany's most important financial centre, as continental Europe's busiest airport and as a main centre for trade fairs. However, there are also other sectors of the economy that contribute to Frankfurt's economic performance. In 1988, Frankfurt's gross value added as an indicator of its economic performance amounted to more than DM 60 billion and thus represented more than one quarter of the gross value added of the State of Hesse. Only 25 percent of Frankfurt's gross value added accounted for in the production of physical goods, although reputable industrial companies have their headquarters in Frankfurt. Another 20 percent is contributed by trade and traffic, while more than half of Frankfurt's economic performance is related to public and private services. Frankfurt thus is often quoted as Germany's capital for services. These services include the activities of the banking community, which was responsible for some 20 percent of all domestic banking transactions as well as for nearly half of the German capital and money movements with other countries. The total business volume of the banks with headquarters in Frankfurt exceeded DM 900 billion in 1988. Credit institutions nowadays offer more than 53,000 jobs, some 10 percent of the Frankfurt working population.

The Frankfurt Stock Exchange is by far the most important German market place for securities, representing a turnover of more than half of all shares and nearly three quarters of all bonds traded in Germany. Insurance companies, investment companies, advertising agencies, high tech companies and an increasing number of other supporting and related industries supplement the tertiary sector in Frankfurt.

Due to its geographic location in the centre of Europe and of Germany, Frankfurt has become one of the busiest traffic centres. Its airport is the most frequented in continental Europe with nearly 27 million passengers and more than one million tons of freight every year. Its main railway station is the second largest in continental Europe. Two of Europe's most vital highways intersect in Frankfurt. Last but not least the Main river connects Frankfurt to the Rhine, Europe's busiest river for cargo ships; the Main-Danube canal, which is to be opened in the near future will increase the waterway transportation business in

Frankfurt. Every year, up to 10 million visitors, 30 percent of them foreigners, come to Frankfurt.

But it is not only economic or financial benefits that have increased Frankfurt's attractiveness. During the past few years, Frankfurt has also increasingly gained a cosmopolitan and open-minded atmosphere. Furthermore, it offers lots of opportunities in the leisure sector.

2.3 HUMAN RESOURCES

The banking and financial services business requires adequate know-how and human resources. Due to the high standard of education and training in Germany, Frankfurt can meet these standards of the financial services sector, although with many foreign banks operating in Germany, competition for professional staff has increased enormously and led to a temporary shortage in some special sectors. This competition creates substantial problems for recruiting and renumeration practices. However, there are still some rules that are, in general, accepted and respected in the Frankfurt banking community, such as not hiring staff from direct competitors. Yet, it is quite common to rely on the services of professional agencies.

By tradition, German employees are more closely linked to their employing company than in anglo-saxon countries, but globalisation of markets, as well as new competitors, who are prepared to pay higher salaries nowadays, stimulate the flexibility of German employees to change company when it seems attractive to do so. Although Deutsche Angestellten-Gewerkschaft (DAG) and Gewerkschaft Handel, Banken und Versicherungen (HBV) are strong unions, the level of organisation of the Frankfurt bank and financial services clerks is rather low compared to other sectors of the German economy. Nevertheless, there are many specific labour regulations concerning working time (currently 39 hours per week in the banking sector), co-determination, job environment as well as agreements with the unions, to be considered. The social security system in Germany is of a high standard and provides for pension, health, disability, unemployment and workmen's compensation. Half of the social security contributions are usually paid for by the employer and the other half by the employee, except in the case of workmen's compensation, which is paid in full by the employing company.

Salaries paid in Frankfurt are in some cases substantially higher than those in other European countries, and foreign banks, particularly, are forced to pay a premium for staff with extra qualifications such as language skills and international experience. Bank cashiers in London or Paris, for example, earn some 20 to 25 percent less than they would in Frankfurt. On average, the gross income of an employee in the Frankfurt banking sector reached DM 4,300 (DM 4,800 for men and DM 3,800 for women) per month in 1988 with an average nominal growth rate of more than 4 percent per year since 1983. Salaries spread widely, however, depending on the job. Some representative salary levels are DM 140,000 to more than DM 300,000 p.a. for branch managers, DM 120,000 to more than DM 200,000 for foreign exchange managers or chief dealers, DM 55,000 to DM 80,000 for loans administration clerks and DM 40,000 to DM 70,000 p.a. for secretaries.

Employees are usually paid monthly with one or sometimes two extra months' salaries payable before Christmas or vacation period. Six to seven weeks annual vacation are normally granted. Social security contributions usually cost the employer 25 to 30 percent of the salary. Management often receives a share of the company's annual profits which may easily reach 50 percent of the annual basic salary. Other tringe benefits offered to attract qualified personnel include some, or all, of the following: pension-schemes, overtime payments, luncheon vouchers, preferential loans, insurances, and a company car.

Employment contracts between employer and employee are subject to specific labour laws and regulations and, generally speaking, may be terminated by either party with at least six weeks' notice, but there is a tendency to agree upon longer-term arrangements for senior staff.

Although Frankfurt as a banking and financial centre has experienced a rapid change and a substantial growth in recent years, it has not built up huge overcapacities of banking facilities and employment like other financial markets. Frankfurt has a population of some 620,000 people, 135,000 or 22 percent of whom are of foreign nationality. As Frankfurt offers jobs for more than 460,000 people, it benefits from the human resources of the entire Rhine-Main area where some 2.5 million people reside. Due to the prosperity of the Frankfurt economy, unemployment is reasonably low (6.4 percent at the end of 1988). Some fifty percent of the population are between 15 and 60 years old.

A university (Johann Wolfgang Goethe-Universität) with more than 30,000 students, specialised colleges for business administration, the German apprenticeship system, and various trainee programs laid on by banks and insurance companies guarantee a high standard of qualification of the employees available for the financial services sector. Employment in Frankfurt's banks and insurance companies has grown by more than 1,000 people per year over the past 10 years and has now reached nearly 58,000 people, so that more than 10 percent of the Frankfurt working population are currently employed by banks and some 2 percent by insurances. The presence of financial institutions in Frankfurt has also attracted other services such as advertising agencies, management consultants, legal advisers, media and high tech companies. They also compete with credit institutions for skilled and qualified staff on the Frankfurt labour market. Due to the internationalisation and growth of the Frankfurt services sector, this market will also offer unique opportunities in the future for both employers and employees.

2.4 THE OFFICE-LETTING MARKET

The Frankfurt office-letting market has experienced rapid growth in recent years and emphasizes Frankfurt's attractiveness as an office location. The continuing expansion of the financial services sector is producing an increasing demand for office space, not only from foreign banks but also as a result of the expansion of domestic banks. Demand by far exceeds the existing capabilities of the development sector. In many ways the development market has been "caught out" by the extraordinary high level of current demand for prime office space in Frankfurt. Planning delays as well as the political situation have exacerbated the situation. Although take-up of office accommodation has increased steadily from some 200,000 m^2 annually in recent years, to more than

300,000 m^2 in 1989, it could not prevent an unprecedented growth of rents for first-class accommodation which have reached over DM 70 per m^2 per month in the centre of Frankfurt, an increase of some 40 percent in just one year. This has also had an impact on rents in peripheral markets in other parts of Frankfurt, as well as in the entire Rhine-Main area.

The level of rents for small units, which in 1989 was reached for new tenancy agreements of prime office space, is likely to also be valid for larger units of accomodation in the next year. Due to the fact that rents for office space in Frankfurt are still quite reasonable compared to other financial centres like London, Paris or New York, participants in the markets expect a further growth of up to DM 100 per square metre per month in the forthcoming years.

Although, as mentioned above, the take up of office space increased considerably in 1989, the new political leadership, supported by a coalition of social-democrats and green party in the local parliament of Frankfurt prevents expansion of office space becoming too extreme and uncontrolled. In spite of the Messe Turm, which with a height of 256 metres will be the tallest office building in Europe when completed in 1991, and further "skyscraper projects" in the pipeline, the expansion of office space will probably slow down due to the new political environment. In view of this limited growth potential for office space supply, and an expected increase in demand, a further rise in the level of rents can be predicted.

While rents for prime office space in the Westend or the banking quarter have broken the barrier of DM 70 per square metre per month, there is still office space available in some parts of the city at between DM 22 and DM 50, and outside the centre in areas like Niederrad or Eschborn at less than DM 30 per square metre per month. The sharp rise in rents in Frankfurt's banking and Westend areas has inspired many tenants, especially those companies who do not feel bound to the city and do not require a central Frankfurt address, to move to alternative locations. The movement of these companies might, in the future, function like a velve to decrease the pressure in an overheating office-letting market. Nevertheless, it is anticipated that with rising rents and demand still high, many German as well as foreign investors might still acquire real estate in Frankfurt and will be prepared to pay prices which require a considerable further growth in rents to guarantee an adequate yield. Although the Frankfurt real estate market is still healthy, the danger of "overheating" cannot be ignored.

Related to the envisaged development of Frankfurt into continental Europe's leading market for banking and financial services and the growing number of employees in this sector, the market for flats and private homes has also experienced a sharp rise of prices and rents during the past few years. While official figures for Germany only show a reasonable increase of rents and housing prices, Frankfurt as a booming centre of economic activity shows a dramatic increase in this sector, way above the average. The demand concentrates on one- or two-family houses in a quiet and attractive neighbourhood, preferably in exquisite quarters of Frankfurt or in smaller towns located in the Northwest of Frankfurt like Bad Homburg, Kronberg, Königstein, or Bad Soden. The price of a terraced house or a semi-detached house in exquisite areas was between DM 500,000 and DM 700,000 or more, at the end of 1989, while potential buyers of a villa in high-class suburban districts have to pay DM 750,000 and sometimes even up to DM 1.5 million. Beside the demand for houses there also is a strong demand for flats in exquisite areas. The price of a new flat in and around Frankfurt ranges between DM 3,500 and DM 7,000 per square metre, with a high concentration between DM 4,500 and DM 6,000. The rent for a flat, sized 60 to 80 square metres, is between DM 12 and 20 per square metre per month.

The authors of this brochure estimate that the demand for office accomodation and housing in and around Frankfurt will be further stimulated by Frankfurt's economic development, its preparations for "Europe 1992" and the globalisation of markets. Although recent developments in Eastern Europe could strengthen the position of Berlin as the national centre for politics and culture, the international approach of Frankfurt with its know-how, adequate human resources and infrastructure, as well as the city's development into continental Europe's centre for banking and financial services, are not endangered.

FIGURE: THE GERMAN BANKING SYSTEM

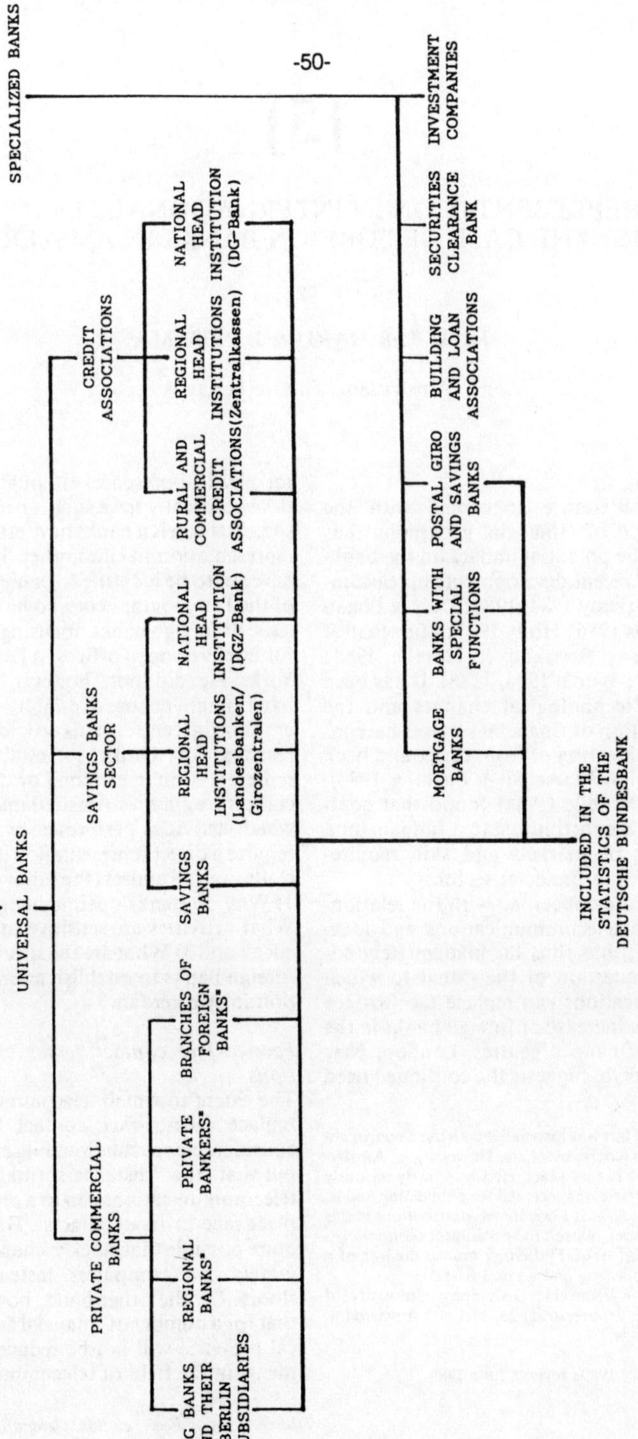

Note: Foreign banks operating in the Federal Republic of Germany are categorized in one of the banking groups marked by * depending on their legal status.

[5]

DIRECT REPRESENTATION IN INTERNATIONAL FINANCIAL MARKETS: THE CASE OF FOREIGN BANKS IN AMSTERDAM

by

H. W. TER HART† & J. PIERSMA*

Amsterdam, The Netherlands

Introduction
The recent literature concerned with the emerging field of 'financial geography' has focused on the potential impact on the banking sector of recent developments in telecommunications (Daly 1984, 1989; Daly & Logan 1986; Daniels 1986; Holly 1987; Marschall & Bachtler 1984; Bertrand & Noyelle 1984; Noyelle 1987; Würth 1986, 1988). It has been shown that technological changes and the computerization of financial services have influenced the location of front office and back office activities (Marschall & Bachtler 1984). Bertrand & Noyelle (1984) found that computerization is contributing to a fundamental restructuring of markets and skill requirements within the financial sector.

The literature concerned with the relationship between telecommunications and location, however, has thus far inadequately addressed the question of the extent to which telecommunications can replace face-to-face contacts. The increase of foreign banks in the three major financial centres, London, New York, and Tokyo, suggests the continued need for physical presence, although which activities specifically have such a need and the reasons that foreign banks have established direct representation in cities other than these three have yet to be identified. Daniels (1986) is one of the few geographers who has addressed the issue of foreign banks, focusing on the reasons for banks to open offices in London and New York. He did not, however, consider why banks might choose to establish offices in other financial centres. This article focuses on the reasons for banks to establish a direct representation in a second or third tier financial centre such as Amsterdam and identifies which activities performed by foreign banks require a direct representation abroad. Specifically, we will address the following questions: 1) Why do banks operate internationally? 2) What activities are sensitive to physical presence? and 3) What are the specific reasons for foreign banks to establish a direct representation in Amsterdam?

Face-to-face contact versus telecommunications
The extent to which telecommunications can replace face-to-face contact has generated considerable speculation. Finsen (1985) points out that 'the "distance-shrinking" nature of telecommunications can to a certain extent replace face-to-face contacts'. For example, it is quite possible that stock exchanges might ultimately use computers instead of trading floors. On the other hand, however, it seems that for a number of financial activities, physical presence will not be reduced by developments in the field of telecommunications. As

† Dr. Henk Ter Hart was associated with the Department of Economic Geography of the University of Amsterdam for nearly twenty years. He was already seriously ill when this article was accepted for publication and he passed away in August 1989. In his contributions to this journal he showed himself to be a diligent economic geographer. All of us at *Tijdschrift* mourn the loss of a stimulating colleague and a good friend.

* Department of Economic Geography, University of Amsterdam, Jodenbreestraat 23, 1011 NH Amsterdam, The Netherlands.

Received January 1989; revised June 1989.

Wango (1987) states, 'The more information networks we build, the less people rely upon them and the more important direct face-to-face communication becomes. Everyone seems to believe they can only get the really important information – the right perspective, or the private, missing piece of data that someone is carrying around in his head or briefcase – by staying in close, face-to-face contact with the sources'.

The physical presence hypothesis

On the basis of earlier research of banking and foreign banks in Amsterdam (Catz 1975; Van den Bosch 1976; Schneider 1984; Ter Hart & Lambooy 1984; Lambooy, Van Geuns & Ter Hart 1985; Ter Hart 1987), we hypothesized that for some activities, physical presence in any foreign financial market is a necessity because telecommunication is unsuitable for acquiring essential inside information. For obtaining that kind of information, regular face-to-face contacts with reliable colleagues are a conditio sine qua non.

To test this hypothesis, we opted for the technique of open interviews with key figures, a technique best suited for inquiries into the intricate problems of strategic corporate policy decision making. Such problems are often so complex and companies are so varied that large-scale questionnaire surveys are useless. Therefore, we selected a limited number of bankers (Dutch and foreign) who are regarded by their colleagues as experts on foreign banks in Amsterdam and the role of Amsterdam as an international financial centre; these bankers were interviewed between October 1987 and April 1988. From these interviews we learned that although the objectives and strategic choices may differ, certain activities in foreign markets indeed do require physical presence and face-to-face contacts, while other activities can very well be handled by the various means of telecommunication.

The internationalization of banking

The internationalization of banks is a rather recent phenomenon. Until the 1950s, the international transactions of most banks were limited to financing the international operations of domestic industrial corporations and trade firms, and for that purpose most banks had established 'correspondent relations' with foreign banks. Only banks from countries with a colonial background had branches or subsidiary offices abroad. During the 1960s, however, an increasing number of banks opened their own offices abroad, to serve the needs of large multinational corporations which were their clients in the home country. Since then a fundamental revision of the world's capital markets took place, a process which began with the shortcomings of the Bretton Woods system and the rise of the Eurocurrencies (Daly 1984; Daly & Logan 1986).

The internationalization of industrial corporations was theoretically explained by Dunning (1981), whose well-known concepts to explain the internationalization of banking institutions, were used by Cho (1983). This author cited three advantages of internationalization: (1) ownership-specific advantages; (2) locational advantages; and (3) internationalization advantages.

Re (1) – *ownership specific advantages:* Not every bank can profit from representation abroad. Factors influencing this are the amount of assets involved, the experience in international operations and foreign markets, and the number of foreign establishments. Foreign banks can also offer a number of specific advantages to corporations which have their headquarters in the host country, e.g. a thorough knowledge of their home market, cheaper loans in their own currency, and the ability to transfer issuances of securities to investors in their home market. In addition, some banks (e.g. Citicorp and Chase Manhattan) can offer more sophisticated cash management systems. Through satellite connections, multinational companies have 'real-time' information about their worldwide cash positions, currency exposures, and liabilities.

Re (2) – *locational advantages:* These may refer on the one hand to differences between the home and the host country with regard to the rates of interest, shares, and foreign exchange, and on the other hand to differences in legislation. As an example of the latter the foreign expansion of US banks can be mentioned. This process was stimulated by the tight rules existing in the US, which forbade American banks to operate outside their home states. Another locational advantage can be the presence of multinational corporations in the host country. Locational advantages may also be connected with market expectations, i.e. clients who want to be able to talk to their bank advisers face-to-face. Furthermore, they need to be confident that their advisers know the market they are operating in. This may not only require direct representation, it may also require inputs from the local labor market.

Re (3) - *internationalization advantages:* In this respect, Cho (1983) argued that by replacing correspondent relations with their own offices, banks could organize the transfer of money more efficiently and faster than through external channels, and, more importantly, information could reach the headquarters faster and 'unfiltered'. The disadvantages of international market imperfections (e.g. delayed and distorted information) could thus be overcome by internalizing functions which formerly were carried out by others.

Therefore, the multinational operation of banks can be seen as a way to circumvent (or to profit from) international market imperfections. These imperfections may be of three kinds: (1) differences in rules and regulations; (2) differences in rates of interest, shares, and foreign exchange; and (3) imperfections in the transfer of information.

During our interviews, we have learned that the importance of the first two of these imperfections is decreasing as a consequence of deregulation and improvements in communication technology. Therefore, the relative importance of the third factor, internationalization in order to secure the flow of 'unfiltered' information, is increasing.

Activities of foreign banks and physical presence

In studies concerning the (multinational) banking sector, banking activities are usually classified as lending, the taking of deposits, and the generation of commission. However, if we want to establish the degree of sensitivity to information and personal contacts, we need a different classification. Therefore, we introduce the following classification, based on the various kinds of transactions:

(1) interbank transactions;
(2) transactions between banks on the one hand and companies and institutions on the other; and
(3) transactions between banks, investors, and the stock exchange.

Each of these categories covers several financial activities, which will be elaborated on below (see Table 1).

As to *interbank transactions,* the banking world is characterized by a 'competitive/co-operative paradox': banks are competitors, but they need each other much more than do companies in other industries. Co-operation between banks is frequent for interbank payments, for dealing in stocks and foreign exchange, and for swap-transactions[1]. Most interbank transactions are executed by telephone or by telex, and increasingly also by computer networks. Here, physical proximity is hardly necessary, but we found that nevertheless dealers prefer to deal with people

Table 1. *International banking transactions.*

(1) Interbank transactions
- dealing in foreign exchange
- arranging, managing, and participating in syndicated loans principally to international borrowers
- swap activities

(2) Transactions between banks and companies and institutions
- dealing in foreign exchange
- arranging, managing, and participating in syndicated loans principally to international borrowers
- international payment services such as money transfers, collections, etc.
- international cash management
- financing international trade
- taking deposits in local and other currencies and providing current account facilities
- granting and taking loans in foreign currencies with related financial swap transactions
- consultancy vis-à-vis mergers, acquisitions, and management buy-outs
- stocks issues

(3) Transactions between banks, investors and the stock exchange
- trade in shares and bonds at the local stock exchange commissioned by investors and on own account
- managing, underwriting, and placing Eurobond and other issues, and dealing in the secondary market

Source: Peat Marwick (1984); Piersma (1988).

they know and with whom they have an established relationship. How do these people get to know each other? We found that bank managers who visit their correspondent relations are often accompanied by their dealers. This gives them an opportunity to get to know each other. Moreover, dealers frequently change jobs, after which they continue to deal with their former colleagues. Furthermore, they all attend the yearly FOREX (Foreign Exchange) meetings, where dealers in currencies from all over the world get together. Dealers in bonds have a similar organization: the Association of International Bond Traders (AIBT). Once the dealers know each other, however, dealing is no longer very sensitive to location, due to telecommunication and computer facilities.

A situation in which contact patterns are rather more complicated is the syndication of banks for large loans to companies, or for the issue of their bonds and equity. In a syndicate, banks are involved with three different kinds of partners: the other participating banks, the corporate client, and, when issuing shares into circulation, the investors who will buy the stock. This latter relation will be dealt with in the next section.

Banks can take different roles in a syndicate: the lead manager and a restricted number of co-managers vouch for the take-up of the amount of money or stock the company is in need of. The managers then distribute their share among a larger number of banks, the so-called 'participants'. The conditions of the arrangements are negotiated between the lead manager and the corporate client. Further details and the division of shares will then be arranged among the banks themselves.

According to some authors (e.g. Kindleberger 1974) and to some of our respondents, the physical proximity of banks on the one hand, and of banks and the client on the other, is not necessary. As one banker said: 'I think it does not make any difference whether a foreign bank participating in a syndicate for a Dutch company is located here (i.e. Amsterdam) or not. Distances are so short; by air you are in London or Paris within the hour'. Yet, it can be observed that banks co-operating in a syndicate often are located in the same financial centre. For New York and London this may seem obvious, because virtually all banks operating internationally are located there. For a city like Amsterdam, however, this is not obvious at all. Yet, analysis of a number of recent issuing syndicates showed that most participating banks were actually located in Amsterdam[2]. For the lead manager, it is absolutely necessary to have physical proximity to the client: the company has to have faith in the capabilities of the bank, and the arrangement of the syndicate is a complex and time-consuming matter. Often the company asks the lead manager to choose a number of co-managing and participating banks, with which the company already has a good relationship. When an issue is involved, the company will also indicate in which countries, in what way, and by which banks its securities will be offered to investors. For building up this relationship, physical proximity between the participant and the client may be instrumental. Those participating banks that are not present in the home country of the corporate client may have established a relation with the client through its overseas activities or they may have an established relation with the lead managing bank. Thus, most participating banks can be found in one financial centre, because physical proximity to the client is required by the managing bank, and because it may be instrumental for participants. For the latter, however, it is not a prerequisite. Once a syndicate has been formed, negotiations about conditions and the division of shares among banks do not require the physical proximity of the banks. If necessary, the large amount of money or stock involved in a syndicate will justify the cost of travel by air to a central meeting point.

The second category we distinguished relates to *transactions between banks on the one hand and companies and institutions on the other.* We found that physical proximity to the customer is important for three consecutive stages of establishing a position in a foreign market, viz. (1) obtaining knowledge of the local market, (2) establishing personal contact with clients; and (3) supporting existing relations.

Knowledge of the local market is a prerequisite for identifying market opportunities. To obtain local knowledge, a representative of a bank ought to be on the spot. Through local representatives, foreign bankers may learn seemingly trivial, but nevertheless important facts. For instance: the fact that C&A Brenninkmeyer does not publish an annual report (a fact which is common knowledge in the Netherlands) came as a surprise to a Japanese banker, who wanted to have basic financial information about this well-known Dutch multinational retail company. Similarly, despite the very short geographical distance between the Netherlands and Belgium, a Belgian banker did not know that the relative absence in the Netherlands of medium-sized companies is the cause for the small amount of commercial paper issued in this country. In order to get into contact with clients, formal and informal networks are of the utmost importance. In the third stage, in which contacts with existing relations have been established, physical proximity is required for consultations and negotiations. 'Bankers point out that the size and complexity of large financial agreements require direct personal interaction among the parties (borrowers, lenders, accountants, attorneys, project engineers, special consultants, and so on). They consider it extremely important to be able to look the other participants in the eye, to observe their behavior, to assess their character, and to evaluate their competence' (Reed 1981, p. 56).

However, transactions between banks and corporate customers do not all require physical presence in the same measure. We have already mentioned the different requirements for banks (lead) managing or participating in syndicates. Dealing in foreign currency with the client can be done by telephone or telex. This is a kind of activity which hardly needs face-to-face contacts. In international cash management, physical proximity is required even less: once relations have been established, completely automated communications are possible. At present, the development of electronic cash management in the Netherlands is not widely accepted yet, but it may become important in the near future. However, traditional banking activities, like financing international trade (by way of Letters of Credit, Bills of Exchange, etc.), require the presence of a bank for psychological reasons. Or, as one Japanese banker said: 'You can't very well finance Japanese-Dutch trade from Brussels. There you are, psychologically, too far away'. The same holds true for lending activities: a treasurer of a corporation prefers to do business with somebody (a bank) nearby. A banker explained this as follows: 'It is very inconvenient for a treasurer of a Swiss company located here, if he has to call Zurich every time he needs money. It's not the price of the call which bothers him; it simply is annoying. So he prefers to do business here'. The acquisition of deposits requires an even more personal and intensive approach because of confidence which has to be built up (Cho 1983, p. 23). For other bank/corporate customer transactions, like swap transactions, the issuing of stocks, and consultancy in relation to mergers, acquisitions, and management buy-outs, direct contacts between a bank and its corporate customers is more intensive than the relative standard procedures of trade- and credit-oriented activities. Therefore, it requires physical proximity even more.

In conclusion we can say that physical proximity, however important it may be at certain moments, is not as important to all forms of financial services rendered to companies. In the search for possibilities and in establishing the first contacts with a potential customer, physical proximity plays an important part in all activities, with the possible exception of participation in syndicates. Once relationships are established, physical proximity may be convenient for corporate customers. If contacts between banks and corporate customers are non-standardized, as is the case with lead management of syndicates, or consultancy, the physical proximity to and face-to-face contacts with the corporate customer will be imperative.

As far as *transactions between banks and investors* are concerned, it was said before that foreign banks may play an important part in the introduction of stocks and bonds of corporations of the host country in their home markets (a primary market activity). As a secondary market activity, they also trade in stock commissioned by investors and for their own account. Some banks specialize in optimizing their buying and selling of shares for investors, an activity known as 'portfolio management'. It will be evident that this activity requires as many and as intensive contacts between the investor and its banker as was the case with some forms of financial services to the corporate client. Traditionally, this stock could only be purchased at the stock exchange, exclusively through members of the stock exchange, like banks and specialized stock brokers. However, since the early 1970s, a number of technological developments have changed the scene profoundly. In the stock trade, the introduction of NASDAQ (the National Association of Security Dealers Automated Quotations) in the United States was an

Table 2. *Sales of the five largest stock exchanges in 1986.*

Exchange	Volume (in billions of US$)
New York	1,374.3
Tokyo	958.1
NASDAQ	378.2
German exchanges	150.8
London	134.3

Source: De Jonge 1987, p. 3.

important step towards electronic dealing. Banks and brokers, but also large (institutional) investors, are 'on-line', connected by computers and telephone lines. NASDAQ provided professional dealers with the possibility to feed their buying and selling prices into the computer, after which the actual deal could be concluded by telephone. NASDAQ - a non-floor exchange - became the third largest exchange in the world (Table 2). The system is constantly being improved upon. The deal itself can be done by computer now, and since April of 1988, London can deal directly with NASDAQ.

These technological developments imply that the stock exchange, as a meeting place for traders dealing on behalf of investors, is now under discussion. Various authors suggest that screens may well replace the traditional stock trading floors; others, however, expect that the trading floor, with its possibilities for face-to-face contacts, will be indispensable in the near future. 'It is not that the screen cannot provide the excitement of the floor: for a whole generation of traders the changing figures on a terminal are a much more natural form of dealing than the chaos and noise of a trading floor. But gossip and rumour, and the proximity of like-minded people, are essential to a market' (Hamilton 1986, p. 49). The now famous 'Big Bang' in London made the floor redundant. In contrast, the Midwest Stock Exchange in Chicago has computerized, but did not replace its trading floor. The administrative handling of the deals will be done by computer, but the dealing room as a meeting place for dealers has been retained and is now attracting more people than ever before. The Amsterdam Stock Exchange, after a recent reconstruction of its dealing room, has also maintained its auction system floor-based, rather than screen-based, by introducing a modified version of the Chicago system.

In conclusion, we do expect that in transactions between banks and investors, more often than not, face-to-face contacts will continue to be indispensable, whereas transactions between stock traders are likely to be computerized in various degrees.

Determinants of physical proximity

We have shown that the degree to which physical proximity is required for transactions in international financial markets depends on the type of transactions involved. On this basis, we have constructed a continuum ranging from transactions like interbank payments, which need no physical proximity at all, to transactions like lead management of syndicates, with a high sensitivity to physical proximity (Fig. 1). This sensitivity to physical proximity is determined by four factors, which may be summarized as follows:

(1) *The intensity of contacts* - This intensity is nil in international cash management, is weak in standard procedures like international money trade, and is strong in consultations related to, for instance, mergers and acquisitions.
(2) *The balance between rapidity and intensity* - In the trade of money and stocks, and in international cash management, rapidity is of utmost importance; in other cases, the possibility of consultations and a personal approach are more important.
(3) *The scale of the transaction* - The influence of this factor is not univocal. The larger the amounts involved in lending or issuing, the more important the personal contact between the parties concerned may be. But, on the other hand, the scale of transactions may also justify business trips.
(4) *The party one is dealing with* - Once contacts are established, most interbank relations can be maintained by telecommunication. Syndicates may be considered as interbank customer-related contacts, which do not always require physical proximity. With the exception of international cash management, bank/customer and bank/investor transactions require physical presence in the home country of these customers.

Foreign banks in Amsterdam

In June of 1988, a total of 49 foreign banks had offices in the Netherlands, whether as representations, branches or subsidiaries, or

Fig. 1. *Continuum of sensitivity to physical proximity in international banking transactions.*

LOW		MEDIUM	HIGH
– Interbank – payments – foreign exchange – credits – deposits – stock trade in small amounts and in stock not locally listed – International cash management for corporate customers – Participation in syndicates for corporate customers	– Participation in issuing	– Credits – Trade related finance	– Lead management of syndicates – Deposit taking – Mergers and acquisitions – Management buy-outs – Portfolio management for investors – Swap transactions – Stock trade in large amounts and in locally listed shares

as participations with a foreign interest of at least 50% (Table 3). Of those 49 banks, 43 have offices in Amsterdam, whereas eight have offices in Rotterdam and only one has an office in The Hague (three banks have offices in both Amsterdam and Rotterdam).

For centuries, Amsterdam has been an international centre of trade and finance. At the end of the 18th century, 'it was still Amsterdam, and not London, which was the world's main financial centre' (McRae & Cairncross 1984). As a result of the Napoleonic Wars, Amsterdam lost its leading position. Since then, the position of Amsterdam was influenced by changes in the economic tide, but the city still is the country's financial heart. It is the home of the head offices of most Dutch banks, including De Nederlandsche Bank (the Dutch central bank), most foreign banks, the

Table 3. *Number of foreign banks in the Netherlands and in Amsterdam.*

	1979	1984	1988
Representative offices	5	19	8 (8)
Branches	16	19	18 (16)
Subsidiaries	13	17	21 (17)
Participations	12	6	2 (2)
Total	46	61	49 (43)

Source: Peat Marwick (1984), NIBE (1988).
Note: The number for Amsterdam in 1988 is shown in parentheses.

Stock Exchange, the European Options Exchange, almost all Dutch stock brokers, and various interprofessional services (Ter Hart 1987). However, it is very difficult to establish the position of Amsterdam as an international financial centre. Each of the various criteria which could be used to rank centres like Zurich, Frankfurt, Paris, Brussels, Luxembourg, Milan, and Amsterdam, such as international reputation, number of banks, employment, value added, etc., fail to give an overall assessment. Therefore, on the European continent, what we might call a single, dominating financial centre is not to be found. However, Amsterdam has been recognized as the best possible location for foreign banks who want to operate in the Netherlands.

However, whether a country will be regarded as profitable is a matter of strategic banking policy. The profitability of the Dutch market is related to the presence of four categories of customers: foreign companies operating in the Netherlands, internationally active Dutch companies, foreign investors willing to buy Dutch, and Dutch investors willing to buy foreign shares and bonds. We will now briefly discuss each of these four categories.

The number of *foreign companies in the Netherlands* is considerable. In 1986, over 3,500 foreign companies were operating in the Netherlands, through participations, acquisitions, joint ventures, or new establishments they own These companies accounted for 15%

Table 4. *Number of companies listed on stock exchanges, 1986.*

	Total	Domestic	Foreign
(1) London	2,685	2,101	585
(2) New York	1,575	1,516	59
(3) Tokyo	1,551	1,499	52
(4) Australian exchanges	1,193	1,162	31
(5) Paris	677	482	192
(6) German exchanges	673	492	181
(7) Amsterdam	509	267	242
(8) Zurich	339	145	194
(9) Brussels	331	191	140
(10) Italian exchanges	184	184	–

Source: Fédération Internationale des Bourses de Valeurs, 1987.

of all employment in manufacturing, and 7% in the trade and service sector. Most foreign companies in the Netherlands are trade or service companies who realize the larger part of their sales on the Dutch market. Foreign manufacturing companies operating in the Netherlands are oriented more towards the European rather than the Dutch market. Since the Second World War, US direct investments have predominated. However, this share diminished from 51% during the period 1946-1959, to 37% of the number of establishments in the period 1975-1984. On the other hand, the number of Japanese firms increased from 7% in the period 1960-1975 to 13% in the period 1975-1984 (Loeve 1986). Correspondingly, American and Japanese banks now dominate the scene of foreign banks in the Netherlands. The year of establishment in the Netherlands of the seven US banks (five of which still exist) and that of the seven Japanese banks is highly correlated with the period in which manufacturing, trade, and service firms located here: American banks came in the 1950s and 1960s, whereas most of the Japanese banks arrived in the 1970s. At present, these banks have to compete with the Dutch banks, who increasingly operate on the international market.

Due to the small size of their home market, many *Dutch companies are export-oriented.* It should be stressed that the Netherlands is the homeland of a number of (very) large multinational companies, such as Royal Dutch (part of the Royal Dutch Shell oil major), the food group Unilever, the electronics giant Philips, and the chemical conglomerates Akzo and DSM. These and other internationally active companies frequently use the services of foreign banks and stock brokers for issuing on foreign markets. Moreover, the Netherlands has an important transit function.[3] All this together results in the fact that there are a lot of international firms in the Netherlands to render banking services to.

We now have to turn our attention to the *relations between banks and investors.* The position of Amsterdam as an international financial centre is often illustrated by the international character of its stock exchange. Next to London, Amsterdam has the highest number of foreign listings (Table 4) and the most active and modern system of trading foreign stocks within Europe. However, this importance should not be overrated. The large num-

Table 5. *Volume of shares and bonds, 1986 (in $1,000,000,000).*

	Total	Domestic	Foreign
(1) New York	1,347.5	*	*
(2) Tokyo	819.6	813.7	5.9
(3) Zurich	266.8	*	*
(4) German exchanges	130.3	117.2	13.1
(5) London	113.0	*	*
(6) Paris	46.7	44.2	3.3
(7) Italian exchanges	38.4	38.4	0.0
(8) Amsterdam	26.1	25.8	0.2
(9) Australian exchanges	22.6	*	*
(10) Brussels	5.6	3.7	1.9

* Data not available.
Source: Fédération Internationale des Bourses de Valeurs, 1987.

ber of foreign companies has historic causes. In the 19th century, a large number of developments in the US were financed with Dutch capital. As a consequence, up to this very day a lot of US companies have a listing on the Amsterdam Stock Exchange. But Table 5 shows that these foreign companies represent only a small fraction in terms of volume. Moreover, Amsterdam suffers from severe competition by the London Stock Exchange. For large institutional investors (such as Shell Pension Fund), London is a cheaper and therefore more attractive place to deal. As a consequence, the London Stock Exchange has attracted part of the trade in Dutch stocks. Measures are now being taken to try to get (part of) this trade back to the Amsterdam Stock Exchange.

From an investor's point of view, the liquidity of the Dutch money and capital market is rather limited. However, some recent deregulations, like the introduction of 'bullet bonds' and commercial paper, have made the Dutch market more attractive for foreign investors. From the perspective of a foreign bank, the limited liquidity and the limited size of the Dutch consumer market may at the same time be considered to be both disadvantages and advantages. Just like Dutch manufacturers, Dutch investors are looking for new possibilities beyond the national borders. They invest large amounts in other countries. In doing so, these 'institutionals', as they are called, attract foreign banks and broker firms. Dutch institutional investors are in fact the big carrot for foreign banks and brokers. As an indication, Dutch pension funds hold 40% of the total assets of all pension funds on the European continent. The Dutch capital market, although sophisticated, is not deep enough for Dutch institutional investors.

Recently, Dutch institutional investors have shown an increased interest in foreign stock, whereas at the same time foreign investors are showing a growing interest in Dutch shares and bonds, especially since 1980 (Fase & Huijser 1988). According to foreign banks and brokers, Dutch shares are undervalued and, therefore, cheap in relation to the profit made by the issuing firms. Also the fact that the largest Dutch (state) pension fund, Algemeen Burgerlijk Pensioenfonds (ABP), is now allowed to invest abroad is greatly welcomed by foreign banks and brokers. In relation to this growing cross-border traffic of securities, foreign banks and brokers have expanded their activities in the Netherlands. In 1986 Citicorp, which according to US law is not allowed to trade in shares and bonds, created a new, legally independent unit: Citicorp Investment Bank, which became the first foreign member of the Amsterdam Stock Exchange. In 1987, Nomura also increased its stock activities in Amsterdam, which is another indication of the importance of physical proximity to the corporate customer. 'Formerly, Nomura contacted Dutch institutional investors from its London office. That, however, hampered expansion of these activities in the Netherlands. The new department (in Amsterdam) is in a better position to direct orders to the Japanese market' (*Het Financieele Dagblad,* 3 March 1988). Another indication of increased interest for the Dutch stock market is the opening in 1988 of a research department of the British broker firm James Capel in Amsterdam, which put this firm in a better position for monitoring developments on the Amsterdam Stock Exchange. And, finally, in April 1988 Nikko Securities, the last of the four big Japanese brokers that was not yet present in the Netherlands, also opened a representative office in Amsterdam, to become a full banking subsidiary within a year.

Conclusion

In a world which has been reduced by telecommunications and satellites, by fibre optics and silicon chips, one would perhaps not expect banks to open offices in second-tier financial centres abroad. Yet, the number of offices of foreign banks in Amsterdam – a city situated close to London – has increased considerably over the last few decades. From our survey, it became clear that for some specific banking transactions, physical proximity is required, whereas for other kinds of banking transactions, physical proximity is of less or no importance.

A continuum of banking transactions has been constructed, indicating the degree of sensitivity of the various banking activities to physical proximity. This continuum shows that the necessity of physical proximity is not a straightforward concept, but rather one that needs differentiation. At the one end, we find transactions like interbank payments, which need no physical proximity at all; at the other end, we find transactions like lead management of syndicates, which require physical proximity for an adequate performance.

Against this background, the continuing internationalization of banking is not contradictory to the rapid developments in telecommunications and computer technology; on the contrary, internationalization may even be further stimulated by these developments. On a worldwide scale, almost anyone can obtain ever increasing amounts of financial and other information on his computer screen. But to get an edge over competitors, one needs to gather the really important information. Screens can provide detailed information on stock prices, interest rates, and past performances of companies; but information on future needs and plans of companies and investors can far better be monitored on the spot. Hence the correct observation of Wango (1987) we cited earlier: that nowadays 'Everyone seems to believe they can only get the really important information... by staying in close, face-to-face contact with the sources'. Often this will require a direct representation in the market one is interested in.

Acknowledgements:

The authors are greatly indebted to H. G. Advokaat (emeritus professor at the University of Amsterdam and former member of the Managing Board of AMRO Bank, Amsterdam), who provided comments on the thesis of J. Piersma on which part of this article is based, and to the following experts who generously gave up some of their time for interviews: W. L. Benard (De Nederlandsche Bank), S. Chubert (Banque Nationale de Paris), R. O. Fuchs (Amsterdam Stock Exchange), N. B. Gelissen (ABN Bank), G. A. Koenders (Dai-Ichi Kangyo Bank), C. D. Van Rappard (Citibank), R. Van Rappard (Citicorp Investment Bank), O. L. Roëll (ABN Bank), and R. Soeting (De Nederlandsche Bank).

Notes:

1 Swap: The exchange of debt obligations between two counterparties to take advantage of differing interest rates or currency opportunities that each can obtain (Hamilton 1986, p. 252).

2 Five foreign banks participated in a syndicate issuing bonds for Van Ommeren Company in 1987, three of which have offices in Amsterdam (Citicorp, Commerzbank, and Swiss Bank Corporation); the remaining two (Kredietbank and Mitsubishi Bank) are located in Belgium. In February 1988, a 'multi-currency syndicated revolving credit facility' was arranged for Ahold Company. With one exception (Deutsche Bank), the foreign banks involved (Citibank, Crédit Suisse (through Crédit Suisse First Boston), Dai-Ichi Kangyo Bank, and J. P. Morgan) are located in Amsterdam. In March of that same year, the same banks (with the exception of Mitsubishi Bank) were involved in a bonds emission. A syndicate placing bonds for Dutch Railways in the same month consisted of six foreign banks, all of which were located in the Netherlands.

3 In 1984, the share of the Netherlands in the sum total of the GNP of England, Germany, France, Switzerland, the Netherlands and Belgium amounted to 6.9%. For intracommunal road transport this figure was 31.9%, for incoming and outgoing transport in seaports it was 28.7%, and for incoming and outgoing transport at airports the share of the Netherlands amounted to 15.0% (source: McKinsey report 'Gateway Holland', 1986).

References:

Bertrand, O. & T. J. Noyelle (1984), *Changing Technology, Skills, and Skill Formation in French, German, Japanese, Swedish and US Financial Service Firms. Preliminary Findings.* (A report to the Center for Educational Research and Innovation of the OECD).

Catz, P. (1975), *Buitenlandse Banken in Nederland.* Deventer: Kluwer.

Cho, K. R. (1983), *Multinational Banks. Their Identity and Determinants.* Ann Arbor: UMI Res. Press.

Daly, M. T. (1984), The Revolution in International Capital Markets: Urban Growth and Australian Cities. *Environment & Planning A* 16, pp. 1003-1020.

Daly, M. T. (1989), Transactional Economic Bases: From the Mass Production Society to the World of Finance. (Unpublished paper.)

Daly, M. T. & M. I. Logan (1986), The International Financial System and National Economic Development Patterns. *In:* D. Drakakis-Smith, ed., *Urbanisation in the Developing World,* pp. 37-62. London: Croom Helm.

Daniels, P. W. (1986), Foreign Banks and Metropolitan Development: a Comparison of London and New York. *Tijdschrift voor Economische en Sociale Geografie* 77, pp. 269-287.

De Jonge, J. (1987), De Visie van een Institutionele Belegger. (Unpublished seminar paper.)

Dunning, J. H. (1981), *International Production and the Multinational Enterprise.* London: Allen & Unwin.

Fase, M. M. G. & A. P. Huijser (1988), Financiële Internationalisering en Wereldwijde Vervlechting van Effectenbeurzen. *Economisch-Statistische Berichten* 73, pp. 326-331.

Finsen, S. (1985), The Impact of Technology Change on the Location of Banks: the Case of the City of London. London: London School of Economics (M.Sc. thesis).

Hamilton, A. (1986), *The Financial Revolution.* Harmondsworth: Penguin.

Holly, B. P. (1987), Regulation, Competition, and Technology: The Restructuring of the US Commercial Banking System. *Environment & Planning A* 19, pp. 633-652.

Kindleberger, C. P. (1974), *The Formation of Financial Centers.* Princeton: Princeton University Press.

Lambooy, J. G., R. C. Van Geuns & H. W. Ter Hart

(1985), *Oplevend Amsterdam.* Amsterdam: AMRO Bank.

Loeve, A. (1986), Buitenlandse Ondernemingen in Nederland. *Economisch-Statistische Berichten* 71, pp. 220-225.

Marschall, J. N. & J. F. Bachtler (1984), Spatial Perspectives on Technological Changes in the Banking Sector of the United Kingdom. *Environment & Planning A* 16, pp. 437-450.

McRae, H. & F. Cairncross (1984), *Capital City; London as a Financial City.* London: Methuen.

nibe (1988), *Bankenboekje,* editie 1988. Amsterdam: Nederlands Instituut voor het Bank- en Effectenbedrijf (nibe).

Noyelle, T. J. (1987), New York City in an Era of Global Financial Markets. (Unpublished paper.)

Peat Marwick (1984), *Banking in the Netherlands.* Amsterdam: Peat Marwick Nederland.

Piersma, J. (1988), De Rol van Fysieke Nabijheid in Financiële Markten. Een Onderzoek onder Buitenlandse Banken in Amsterdam. Amsterdam: University of Amsterdam. (thesis.)

Reed, H . C. (1981), *The Pre-Eminence of International Finance Centres.* New York: Praeger.

Schneider, A. M. (1984), Het Vestigingsbeleid van Banken in Nederland. Amsterdam: University of Amsterdam. (thesis.)

Ter Hart, H. W. (1987), Amsterdam: Het Financiële Hart van Nederland. *In:* H. van der Wusten, ed., *Postmoderne Aardrijkskunde; de Sociografische Traditie Voortgezet*, pp. 117-134. Muiderberg: Coutinho.

Ter Hart, H. W. & J. G. Lambooy (1984), Amsterdam Amongst the Ranks of European Capitals. Amsterdam: Economisch-Geografisch Instituut/Universiteit van Amsterdam. (Unpublished paper.)

Van den Bosch, R. A. R. (1976), Buitenlandse Banken in Nederland. *Economisch-Statistische Berichten* 61, pp. 280-281.

Van Wensveen, D. M. N. (1989), *Het Europese Bankwezen op weg naar 1992.* Amsterdam: Nederlands Instituut voor het Bank- en Effectenbedrijf (nibe).

Wango, R. J. J. (1987), *PHP Intersect* (Tokyo), January.

Würth, M. (1986), Telematik im Schweizerischen Bankgewerbe – eine Raumbezogene Analyse. *Dokumente und Informationen zur Schweizerischen Orts-, Regional- und Landesplanung* 85, pp. 15-21.

Würth, M. (1988), Finanzplatz Schweiz: Eine Beurteilung unter Berücksichtigung regionaler Aspekte. *Dokumente und Informationen zur Schweizerischen Orts-, Regional- und Landesplanung* 93, pp. 5-12.

[6]

Excerpt from Adolf Wala (ed.), *Challenges for European Bank Managers in the 1990s*, 165–78.

Vienna as an International Financial Centre

Georg Winckler

Professor of Economics
University of Vienna

1. The emergence of international financial centres today

1.1. Factors determining the emergence of international financial centres

Historical studies about the formation of financial centres usually stress the role of three factors (see e.g. Kindleberger, 1974): an existing trading place, sustained surpluses or special regulations.

At the international level, important financial centres emerged *as a consequence of international trade.* The handling of trade between different continents or states, especially with planned economies, or international trade with raw materials or agricultural products, has generally required specific know-how and specific methods of financing. Hence banks and other financial institutions which provided these services, followed the trade activities of companies to the trade centres. International trade centres which have become important international financial centres are New York, Chicago, Hong Kong, London or Frankfort.

A second cause for the emergence of international financial centres is *the existence of sustained domestic surpluses (current account surpluses)*[1]: In countries with domestic surpluses such as Japan, Germany or Switzerland, lenders look for international investment opportunities. Foreign borrowers come to these countries to get cheap credits.

In history, examples of the opposite development may be found too. A country with high current account deficits needs credits to finance these deficits. Hence an international centre may be formed or may gain importance where such financial operations are transacted (Vienna in the 18th century, see Baltzarek, 1980; probably New York in the 1980s).

A third cause are *special tax exemptions and regulatory freedom:* In the past, many countries tried to attract international financial business by liberalizing it within their own boundaries. They reduced the amount of banking supervision (e.g. by reducing the obligations to publish records, by stipulating low ratios for equity capital or liquidity) or implemented banking secrecy laws. Another way to attract international financial business was to grant tax exemptions. Such measures can typically be found in off-shore financial centres. They are present in places like Luxembourg or Liechtenstein.

Generally, the production of financial services is characterized by *economies of scale.* Economies of scale can occur at the level of the firm (e.g. in the management of assets or liabilities) or there are increasing *social* returns to scale due to external effects[2]. Positive external effects may be the reason why institutions like the stock market emerge or why it is profitable to concentrate financial activities at specific centres.

1.2. Two modifications

This list of factors explaining the formation of international financial centres needs two modifications. The first one is in line with the recent studies on industrial organization dealing with the phenomenon of economies of scale in the context of international trade. The second one is a consequence of portfolio theory.

The first modification refers to the fact that the services offered in financial centres are differentiated products and subject to economies of scale due to high fix cost and low marginal cost. Hence, for each differentiated product it is profitable to concentrate all activites in one centre to best exploit the benefits of economies of scale. Whether this or that centre offers a specific differentiated product is largely arbitrary, a result of initial locational advantages and coincidence. Chicago has specialized in one range of differentiated goods (e.g. the trade of futures), because futures have been important in the trade with agricultural products for many years. London offers another range of differentiated goods, because the Eurodollar market started there by coincidence in the early 1960s.

Since entry (in the sense of the theory of industrial organization) is free and since there is competition among the centres, each centre only receives an amount of (monopoly) rents which is low enough not to induce others to set up an alternative financial centre offering the relevant range of differentiated products. Of course, each centre strives to develop new differentiated products in order to receive high monopoly rents, at least for a while.

What is important in this context is the kind of reputation a financial centre has acquired. This reputation is closely linked with the type of products a centre offers. New centres need — in order to give clear signals — to overemphasize what kind of centre they would like to be in the long run (tax haven or innovative centre). In the language of the theory of signalling, they need this emphasis in order to gain a profile which clearly "separates" them from other centres. They do not want to have their profiles "pooled" with those of other centres. They can only expect to attract business to the degree at which economies of scale become important, if their profiles are clearly set apart from those of other centres.

The second modification comes from the theory of portfolio management. This argument refers to the fact that the rate of return on credits, equities etc. varies systematically from region to region. This regional variation in the rates of return may be due to many factors: market segmentation, regional business cycles, different demographic processes, varying savings ratios or inflation rates, different economic policies, etc. Given this regional variation of the rate of return, it is individually rational to diversify portfolios. Hence it is generally advantageous to invest in the stock markets of Tokyo, New York and Vienna at the same time, since the rates of return of the stocks in these centres have different probability functions and therefore allow a diversification of risk.

The portfolio argument runs counter to the prediction based on what one would expect due to the effects of economies of scale. The latter presumes an ongoing concentration of financial activities on few places. The former, however, postulates a more diversified pattern of emerging international centres. Probably, both arguments put together can explain the existing structure of financial centres in the world fairly well.

1.3. The effect of Europe '92

As is well known, the European Community (EC) aims at establishing a single European financial market. Several Directives of the Council specify the subject and the extent of the liberalization of capital transactions (24th of June 1988, No. L178, 7/8/1988) as well as the provision of a single legal framework for the functioning of banks (15th of Dec. 1989; 18th of Dec. 1989; L386, 12/30/1989). In addition, the Bank for International Settlements, within the Cooke Committee, passed a document which also constitutes an important step towards harmonizing the rules of banking supervision[3].

From an economic point of view, the most important consequence of European integration in the financial sector will be that legally established market segmentations will cease to exist, at least in most of the countries in the EC. Probably that change is already sufficient to intensify competition among banks in Europe decisively (see the Price Waterhouse study within the Cecchini Report). The outcome may well be, given economies of scale, that financial activities will be more and more concentrated at a few centres only, such as London, Paris or Frankfort. Luxembourg may lose importance, since its profile is based on liberalized regulation, the third factor mentioned above (see 1.1.). Hence an important question will be which financial centre will emerge with what range of differentiated products in Europe in the near future[4)].

1.4. The effect of opening up Eastern Europe

The reforms in Eastern Europe will very likely cause its countries' creditworthiness and their willingness to repay their debts to deteriorate. Their creditworthiness will decline due to imminent economic difficulties. Willingness to repay debts will decrease because they will try to profit from the awareness of the West that the ongoing political and economic reforms in Eastern Europe justify the delay of debt repayments today.

Yet, despite these pressing problems of creditworthiness and willingness to repay, there are plenty opportunities for Western banks in Eastern Europe. Due to the decentralization of economic planning and the potential of joint ventures and privatization, it has become highly worthwhile to look at the *individual* firm in Eastern Europe.

Evaluating individual firms there, picking out the most promising ones and providing them with adequate financial means (equity and/or loans) will become a prime business for Western banks in Eastern Europe in the future. Since Eastern European countries have and will continue to have many regulations (not only in the field of financial markets) and since the convertibility of their currencies will remain quite limited in the near future, the task of financing Eastern European firms will require a lot of specific know-how. Hence the question arises in which financial centre the knowledge of picking the profitable firms and of dealing with the financial regulations in Eastern Europe will be concentrated.

2. The past discussion about Vienna as an international centre

2.1. Factors important for Vienna

About ten to fifteen years ago, there was discussion in Austria about how to make Vienna an international financial centre. From the very beginning of this discussion it was clear that Vienna was not to become an international centre by granting tax exemptions or by abolishing regulations. Consequently, the question was what role other factors (international trade, domestic surpluses or deficits, financial innovation) could play.

Austria's domestic surpluses or deficits could hardly be of importance. Austria's current account was in balance until 1975 and again from 1982 on. Between 1976 and 1981, the current account posted considerable deficits: 4.5% of GNP in 1977 and, on average for this period, 2% of GNP. However, in terms of international standards, in a world which tried at that period to adjust to oil-price shocks and which experienced huge current account imbalances, these Austrian sums were negligible. After the second oil shock, for example, the Austrian current account deficit amounted to only US$ 1.7 billion in 1980 compared to a deficit of nearly US$ 48 billion for the Group of Ten and US$ 59 billion for the developing countries (without OPEC countries). Hence Austria was not an important net lender or net borrower; it could always obtain the means to finance its current account deficits wherever it wanted, even at Zurich.

Nor was financial innovation a factor to rely on. Austrian financial institutions were not keen on introducing financial innovations, preferring protected domestic markets instead.

Yet the first factor, international trade, seemed to be highly promising. In handling East-West trade, Vienna had and still has comparative advantages due to traditional know-how. The following example may serve to indicate this comparative advantage: Most of the foreign banks in Austria (more than twenty) were founded in the 1960s and 1970s, when these banks followed their worldwide clientele to the "distant" region of Vienna as Vienna emerged as one of the centres of East-West trade.

It is interesting to note that most of the banks founded then had American or Eastern European institutions as owners. German, Swiss or Italian banks were hesitant to establish branches in Vienna at that time, because they disposed of their own know-how in East-West trade or relied on information provided by existing Austrian banks as their traditional correspondents.

The importance of Vienna as a centre of East-West trade can be evaluated by looking at so-called transit trade (export or imports via a third country, in this case via Austria). Austrian transit trade boomed in the mid-1970s and reached its peak about 1980 (when transit exports and imports reached US$ 4 billion). This means that exports by the West, especially by Germany, to Poland, Hungary, Romania, and Yugoslavia (only marginally to USSR) were mediated in Vienna. The emphasis of Austria's mediation was focused on exports from the West to East European states (except the USSR) rather than on Eastern exports to the West (Stankovsky, 1981).

Another indicator of Vienna's East-West role was the emergence of Austrian banks as financial intermediaries between East and West. Austrian banks then started to accumulate claims against Eastern European states (Soviet Union, East Germany, Poland, Hungary, Czechoslovakia and Bulgaria)[5)] and to hold liabilities to Western Europe, since the domestic financial sources in Austria were too weak to finance the banks' claims.

2.2. Advantages and disadvantages of making Vienna an international financial centre

An important expected advantage was the positive employment and qualification effect. This effect is calculated using a simple method. One assumes that the domestic banking business of Austria is comparable to the domestic banking business of — say — Switzerland or

Belgium. One further assumes that the banking system in Austria is affected by internationalization in a similar fashion as were these countries. One knows the total amount of foreign assets and foreign liabilities of banks in these countries. In addition, employment figures and the figures about value added in the banking industry are known. Hence one can estimate by how much an increase in foreign assets and liabilities raises employment and value added.

The following expectations for Austria were drawn up nine years ago (Tichy, 1981). If Austria, i.e. Vienna, had succeeded in becoming an international financial centre as attractive as the Swiss centres, about 15,000 new (especially highly qualified) jobs would have been created in the banking industry. The ratio of those employed in the banking industry to overall employment in Vienna would have risen from 3.3% to 5.2% (Tichy, 1981, p.45). Of course, more insurances, more lawyers, more computer services etc. would have emerged too. The estimate of the overall employment effect was 25,000–30,000 new jobs.

Other advantages were not so important. The current account effect, for one, was regarded as negligible: On the one hand, the interest balance would have been activated due to better portfolio management and to services of financial intermediation; on the other hand, the positive employment effect would have generated higher imports. Tax revenues were not expected to rise considerably: Due to the international competition among financial centres, most of the activities in international banking would have benefited from tax-exemption.

2.3. Main opposition

The most important opposition to the idea of making Vienna an international financial centre came from the Austrian National Bank. There were two arguments: (1) Austria's risk exposure would be increased; (2) Austria's so-called hard currency policy would be endangered.

The first argument refers to the fact that Austria's current account has never shown considerable surpluses. As a consequence, the financial institutions operating in Vienna would need *foreign* liabilities to match *foreign* claims. But who are the foreigners *to whom* you grant credits and *from whom* you get your deposits? As already mentioned, the problem with the international financial intermediation of Austrian banks was (and still is) that due to the boom in East-West-trade in the 1970s, its main debtors were and are Eastern European states like Poland or Hungary, both of which have considerable problems repaying their debts. On the other side, Austria's main creditors were Swiss and German institutions.

Of course, in limited cases, the Austrian National Bank could allow domestic banks to go bankrupt, if they ran into solvency problems due to international financial intermediation. Yet, in order to avoid consequences fo the domestic markets, the Austrian National Bank wanted banks operating in these markets to refrain from expanding too fast in international financial business. Hence it did not favour the formation of an international financial centre, since it feared that domestic banks would be induced to act too imprudently otherwise (paternalistic argument of the Austrian National Bank).

The second argument concerned the so-called hard currency policy. This policy mainly consists in fixing the DM/Austrian Schilling exchange rate. In order to pursue this policy of a fixed exchange rate to the DM, the Austrian National Bank has aimed — at least until 1989 — at keeping foreigners' assets and liabilities denominated in Schilling and domestic assets and liabilities denominated in foreign currency as low as possible. A means to reach this goal was to prevent the liberalization of capital movements from and to Austria, although the IMF and OECD have frequently requested this liberalization[6)].

The only variant not subjet to the opposition of the Austrian National Bank consisted in allowing foreign-owned banks which do *not operate in the domestic markets* to do international business in foreign currencies. But why would they come to Austria?

Opposition was also raised by Austrian banks. In the beginning they visualized the growth or profit potential of an expansion of international business. But then they realized that the coming of foreign banks to Austria meant that these banks wanted to participate in the domestic markets (credits *and* deposits) too. That would have increased the competition among banks in Austria considerably. Hence, in order to keep foreign banks out of the domestic markets, domestic banks were no longer interested in the internationalization of the Austrian financial markets.

Consequently there was a tacit compromise about ten years ago: foreign banks were effectively kept out of the Austrian markets by not allowing them to collect savings depostits and thus by forcing them to raise funds in the (expensive) interbank market[7]. On the other hand, domestic banks accepted the limits set by the Austrian National Bank to curb their international business ("Auslandslimes").

However, in order to attract cheap and long-term money from abroad (which is not subject to currency speculation), the banking secrecy law was strengthened by a broad national consensus; Austria now provides more anonymity to clients than even Switzerland has ever done[8].

3. Vienna as an international financial centre today

3.1. The importance of Vienna today

When looking at the statistics provided by the Bank for International Settlements (BIS), one can easily determine the negligible role of Vienna as an international financial centre: At the end of 1988 and 1989, total foreign claims of all banks in Austria[9] amounted to only 1.1% of all foreign claims by banks reporting to the BIS (compared with nearly 20% in the case of England/London, 16% Japan/Tokyo, 12% USA/New York, 6% France/Paris, 4% Luxembourg)[10]. If one looks not at the place of banking, but at the nationality of banks, the Austrian role is roughly the same[11] (Japanese banks lead by 38%, the share of U.S. banks is 15%, of German banks 8%)[12].

The role of foreign banks operating in a financial centre can be assessed by comparing the two statistics mentioned above: if 20% of the total international banking business is transacted in England/London, but British banks only dispose of a share of 5%, one can easily imagine the role of foreign (esp. Japanese) banks in London. In Austria, the second figure exceeds the first (foreign branches of domestic banks do more foreign business abroad than domestic branches of foreign banks do in Austria)[13]. Foreign banks operating in Austria are still doing a negligible international job (about AS 60 billion at the end of 1989). Hence Vienna cannot be regarded as an international financial centre today. In addition, the Austrian Schilling is not an international currency. Its role is so modest that it is not even reported in the international statistics.

With regard to differentiated products, Vienna as an international financial centre does not dispose of any specific profile except perhaps in the case of those products which typically arise as a consequence of strict banking secrecy laws (although the methods of modern portfolio management are not well known in Vienna). However, even this profile of offering safe and anonymous investments may come under attack when the international efforts to ban money laundering become more effective.

3.2. Will Vienna be an international financial centre tomorrow?

In the first part of the paper, the importance of economies of scale, the concept of differentiated products and the theorem concerning a seemingly random pattern of specialization among financial centres were mentioned. Why were these arguments stressed?

The point is that in a world with economies of scale and differentiated products, economic reasoning tells us that the existence of comparative advantages only plays a role at the very beginning, when a market evolves. After a while, when economies of scale have already started to take effect, comparative advantages lose momentum. Hence, if Vienna wants to exploit its geographical and historical comparative advantage in offering special know-how by picking profitable Eastern European firms and by finding the best method of financing them, *Vienna must move quickly* in order to attain a level of activity at which economies of scale start to get important. Otherwise other cities, like Berlin or Budapest, will move ahead and will be the first to profit from increasing returns.

What does this imply for economic policy? The implications seem to be clear: Try to internationalize the financial markets in Vienna as quickly as possible.

(I) If foreign banks want to move to Vienna, let them enter and even allow them all domestic business (as an extra incentive). Of course all banking has to meet the general standards of solvency and liquidity.
(II) It is important to make the Vienna Stock Exchange as attractive as possible (e.g. sophisticated order routing and clearing systems, a ban on inside trading, which could harm its reputation).
(III) Tax harmonization in all areas touching upon the financial markets (income tax, property tax, stock market turnover tax).
(IV) Liberalization of all kind of services which are relevant for the functioning of financial markets (management consulting, legal services, communications services). Such liberalization may help to increase the specialization and internationalization of the service sector in Austria.
(V) Attracting foreign workers who dispose of special know-how in international banking.

Today, the chances of overcoming internal opposition to an internationalization of Vienna's financial markets may be excellent: the hard currency policy has gained a very good reputation, so that the segmentation of markets is no longer needed to avoid speculation against the Schilling. In addition, banks now seem to be ready to meet the European challenge and hence to accept competition by foreign banks in Austria.

4. References

Baltzarek, F.: "Finanzplatz Wien — die innerstaatliche und internationale Stellung in historischer Perspektive", *Quartalshefte der Girozentrale 15* (no. 4/1980).

Bank for International Settlements (BIS), *Annual and Quarterly Reports.*

Helpman, E.; Krugmann, P. R.: *Market Structure and Foreign Trade. Increasing Returns, Imperfect Competitions, and the International Economy,* MIT Press, Cambridge/Mass, 1985.

Kindleberger, Ch.: "The Formation of Financial Centers: A Study in Comparative Economic History". *Princeton Studies in International Finance no. 36,* Princeton 1974.

Peubey-Kronsteiner, M.: "EG 92: Der Gemeinsame Bankenmarkt und seine Auswirkungen auf Österreich", *Bank Archiv 38* (no. 2/90).

Stankovsky, J.: "Finanzierung internationaler Warenströme in Österreich", *Quartalshefte der Girozentrale 16* (no. 4/9181).

Stanzel, A: "Bankenrecht und Bankenaufsicht im Hinblick auf die Europäische Integration", in W. Stadler, K. Völk (eds.), *EG-Binnenmarkt & Banken. Bankenwissenschaftliche Schriftenreihe* no. 70, Vienna 1989.

Tichy, G.: "Die volkswirtschaftliche Bedeutung eines Finanzplatzes Wien", *Quartalshefte der Girozentrale 16* (no. 4/1981).

Notes:

1) See the fundamental equation: Savings minus investments equals exports minus imports (= current account).

2) The presence of economies of scale at the level of the firm implies that markets cannot be perfectly competitive (the price behaviour of firms can then be explained by the theories of contestable markets, of monopolistic competition, or of oligopoly). The idea of introducing increasing social returns due to external economies in a model with constant or decreasing returns to scale at the level of the firm was developed by Marshall. For a good survey of the consequences of assuming economies of scale see Helpman/Krugman (1985), pp. 32.

3) Obviously there is a need to change Austrian laws (KWG, DevG), see Peubey-Kronsteiner, 1990, pp. 108, and Stanzel, 1989.

4) In a recent article in the "Economist" (April 28, 1990), it is reported that the rivalry among the eight financial centres (Börsenplätze) in Germany will end by giving a dominant role to Frankfort. Frankfort thus has good chances of becoming the leading financial centre in Europe after London and Paris.

5) Total claims of Austrian banks were about US$ 10 billion at the end of 1988.

[6] See OECD, Economic Survey "Austria", 1986, p. 50. Thus the Austrian National Bank hoped to avoid any currency speculation which could endanger its hard currency policy. In Austria, the liberalization of capital movements did not start before 1989.

[7] This restricted entry is possible due to the Banking Act (Kreditwesengesetz): The establishment of branches was liberalized; however, when establishing new banks one has to prove that there is a "need" for them. It was argued at the time that there is no need for banks that collect savings deposits.

[8] Note, however, that the emergence of Vienna as an international centre by strengthening banking secrecy law does not exploit the specific know-how of East-West-trade. It is based on the third factor mentioned above (see 1.1.).

[9] Thus excluding the foreign branches of Austrian banks, but including the domestic branches of foreign banks.

[10] BIS, Annual Reports, Section V, and the quarterly reports "International Banking and Financial Market Developments".

[11] At the end of 1989 the foreign claims of the domestic branches reached AS 60.8 billion, whereas the foreign claims of the foreign branches of domestic banks amounted to AS 162.7 billion.

[12] See footnote 11.

[13] See footnote 11.

[7]

Excerpt from J. Lewis and A. Townsend (eds), *The North–South Divide*, 114–56.

5

SOUTH GOES NORTH? THE RISE OF THE BRITISH PROVINCIAL FINANCIAL CENTRE

Andrew Leyshon and Nigel Thrift

Introduction

This chapter examines one aspect of the north-south divide, the rise of financial services to a position of some prominence in the British economy. According to some commentators (for example, Gillespie and Green, 1987; Howells and Green, 1988), the growth of financial and producer services has only strengthened the north-south divide in terms of employment, occupational mix and a host of other indicators. We take limited issue with this interpretation of the British space economy by considering the rise of the provincial financial centre in the 1970s and 1980s. It may seem a strange idea to talk of the provincial financial centre. The term conjures up an image of all but outmoded practices of commerce, such as the provincial stock-exchange, but the evidence is there. The provincial financial centre is on the rise and not just in the south.

The evidence is set out in the first section in which we identify the leading urban centres of financial and producer service activity in Great Britain and chart their growth from the mid-1970s to the mid-1980s. However, the explanation for the rise of the provincial financial centres is paradoxical. Although part of the explanation lies in the strength of certain regional economies and their emergent demand for financial services, another important determinant has been decentralization processes emanating from Central London. Office decentralization is one of these processes. Another is the expansion of London-based firms in opportunist searches for new business. These firms have also acted as a catalyst for local financial-service activity. In the second section we consider both indigenous expansion and these two 'south goes north' processes. The last section documents some of the local impacts of financial and producer service growth, paying particular attention to the consequences of the in-migration of offices of large London-based financial and producer service firms.

The growth of provincial financial centres in Great Britain, 1974–84

Defining financial centres

There are several ways in which the relative importance of a financial centre may be determined. These include the number of key financial functions located within a centre; the demand for office space in a centre as reflected in local office-rental values; the importance of finance-related occupations within the overall employment structure of a centre; and total employment within financial and producer service industries.

First, the relative importance of financial centres may be assessed by way of an examination of the spatial distribution of key financial functions (Table 5.1). Only six British cities - London, Birmingham, Manchester, Liverpool, Glasgow and Edinburgh - possess stock exchanges. It is not surprising that these centres of capital formation and exchange also contain relatively large proportions of stockbroking firms. The headquarters of the ten British clearing banks are based in only four cities - London, Edinburgh, Glasgow and Manchester. Merchant banks are overwhelmingly located in the City of London and only seven such banks were actually located outside the capital. Other banks and deposit-taking institutions are also predominantly located within London, although they displayed a greater level of spatial dispersal, with Manchester, Edinburgh and Nottingham containing important concentrations. The functional importance of a financial centre will also be influenced by the number of institutional investors that are located there, given that such organizations are the principal users of stock exchanges and are the most important clients of stockbrokers. The spatial distribution of the headquarters of insurance companies, investment trust companies, unit trust managers, pension fund management groups and self-investing pension funds is illustrated in Table 5.2. These too are primarily located in large cities with London and Edinburgh containing by far the largest concentrations of investment institutions. Smaller concentrations occur in Liverpool, Norwich, Birmingham, Bristol, Croydon and Manchester.

A more indirect measure of the relative importance of financial centres may be derived from the level of demand for office space as reflected by office-rental values. Of course, rental values give only a very broad indication of a centre's functional importance since many activities other than financial and producer services occupy office space within urban areas. Nevertheless, financial and producer service firms are major occupiers of office space in towns and cities and one would intuitively expect the prevailing rental value of office property to be related to the demand for floorspace generated by such firms. In 1986 the demand for office property in England and Wales was considerably greater within centres located within the south. Rental values in Central London were £35 per square foot per annum. In the rest of Greater London they averaged £11 per square foot per annum, while in suburban cities of the South East the mean annual rental value was £10.25 per square foot. The highest annual rental values outside the South East were recorded in Birmingham and Bristol where office property was valued

Table 5.1 Locations containing stock exchanges or at least two headquarters of British stockbroking firms, clearing banks, merchant banks and other banks and deposit-taking institutions

Centre	Stock exchanges	Stockbrokers	Clearing banks	Merchant banks[1]	Other banks, deposit-taking institutions	Total number of firms
London	1	108	6	64	194	372
City of London	1	106	6	61	128	301
Rest of Central London	0	2	0	3	66	71
Manchester	1	12	1	0	8	21
Birmingham	1	10	0	1	1	12
Edinburgh	1	3	2	3	4	12
Glasgow	1	7	1	1	3	12
Liverpool	1	6	0	0	2	8
Bristol	0	3	0	0	3	6
Nottingham	0	2	0	0	4	6
Leeds	0	4	0	0	1	5
Bournemouth	0	3	0	0	2	5
Bradford	0	2	0	0	2	4
Aberdeen	0	2	0	0	1	3
Cardiff	0	1	0	0	2	3
Croydon	0	0	0	0	3	3
Exeter	0	1	0	0	2	3
Harrow	0	0	0	0	3	3
Norwich	0	1	0	0	2	3
Sheffield	0	2	0	0	1	3
Hull	0	1	0	0	1	2
Leicester	0	1	0	0	1	2
Lincoln	0	1	0	0	1	2
Newcastle	0	2	0	0	0	2
Slough	0	0	0	0	2	2

Notes
1. Members of Issuing and Accepting Houses Committees.

(*Source: The City Directory*, 1984–5.)

Table 5.2 Locations containing at least four headquarters of institutional investment organizations

Centre	Insurance companies	Investment trust companies	Unit trust managers		Pension fund management		Pension funds (self-investing)		Total firms
			No.	Funds (£m)	No.	Funds (£m)	No.	Funds (£m)	
London	229	154	72	21,928	34	90,898	37	45,500	526
City of London	193	126	58	19,762	30	88,552	12	12,566	419
Rest of London	36	28	14	2,166	4	2,346	25	32,932	107
Edinburgh	9	33	14	2,857	13	13,344	1	428	70
Liverpool	7	1	1	98	0	0	2	349	11
Birmingham	5	5	0	0	0	0	0	0	10
Glasgow	4	0	3	119	3	2,538	0	0	10
Norwich	8	0	1	353	1	769	0	0	10
Bristol	2	0	1	228	2	281	4	2,213	9
Croydon	7	0	0	0	1	400	1	173	9
Manchester	5	0	3	119	0	0	0	0	8
Dorking	6	0	1	61	0	0	0	0	7
Tunbridge Wells	4	0	1	36	1	68	0	0	6
Bournemouth	4	0	1	61	0	0	0	0	5
Dundee	0	5	0	0	0	0	0	0	5
Exeter	2	0	1	43	1	350	1	83	5
Milton Keynes	4	0	0	0	0	0	1	250	5
Aberdeen	0	4	0	0	0	0	0	0	4
Halifax	3	0	0	0	0	0	1	260	4
Perth	3	0	0	0	0	0	1	352	4
Stratford-upon-Avon	2	0	1	9	1	350	0	0	4

(*Source: City Directory*, 1984–5; *Crawford's Directory of City Connections*, 1986; Pensions Management, 1987.)

at £8.50 per square foot. The only other provincial centre outside the South East where office property values exceeded £8.00 per square foot per annum was Swindon.

Third, some indication of the functional significance of a financial centre may be gauged by the relative importance of key 'financial occupations' within the employment structure of the travel-to-work area (TTWA) within which centres are based. The extent to which the occupational groups of 'chartered and certified accountants', 'underwriters, brokers, investment analysts', 'taxation experts' and 'economists, statisticians, actuaries' formed a greater proportion of the resident workforce than was the case in Great Britain as a whole can be judged with the Location Quotient (LQ).[1] Out of a total of 322 TTWAs in Great Britain, financial-service occupations were over-represented in only 40, according to the residence of respondents to the 1981 Population Census. Of these, 30 TTWAs were located in the south (defined here as the South East, South West, East Anglia), and 20 were based in the South East region. The seven highest concentrations of financial-service occupations were all in the South East, with Tunbridge Wells (LQ = 3.15), Crawley (2.62), Southend (2.38), London (2.10) and Chelmsford and Braintree (2.06) possessing the largest over-representations. Of the ten northern TTWAs containing over-representations of financial-service occupations, the highest-ranking northern centres were Harrogate (LQ = 1.68), Warwick (1.37) and Edinburgh (1.29). However, these were ranked only 8th, 15th and 17th respectively. Therefore, not only was there an over-representation of financial service occupations in more southern centres than northern centres, but also the relative concentration of such employees tended to be greater in the south than in the north.

Although such data may be indicative of the functional importance of a centre, it is important to bear in mind that the location quotients indicate only the relative importance of financial and producer service occupations and say nothing about the absolute numbers of employees. More importantly, the data used are residence-based and allowances need to be made for people working in one labour-market area and commuting to another. This problem is of particular significance within the South East region. For example, while the Tunbridge Wells TTWA contained the highest proportion of financial-service occupations within its overall employment structure, it is located firmly within the City of London commuter zone (see Thrift, Leyshon and Daniels, 1987). Indeed, the 'London effect' is probably a major determinant of the over-representation of financial and producer service occupations in many of the South East TTWAs.

The most direct measure of the functional importance of financial centres is the number of employees directly employed within financial and producer services. Financial-service industries are those that are fundamental to the functioning of a financial centre. Using the 1980 revision of the Standard Industrial Classification these industries include Banking and bill discounting (Activity Heading 8140), Other financial institutions (8150), Insurance (8200), Activities auxiliary to banking and finance (8310), Activities auxiliary to insurance (8320), and Accountants, auditors and tax experts (8360)[2]. Producer service industries in this context are taken to be secondary business services that assist in the successful functioning of a financial centre. These include House and estate agents (Activity Heading 8340), Legal services (8350), Advertising (8380), Computer services (8394) and Business services (8395). Following Reed (1981), the 25 leading centres have been classified as either pre-eminent, regional or sub-regional financial centres[3]. Although Reed's original analysis of international financial centres was multi-dimensional, time and data availability constraints forced our classification to be posited solely upon the numbers employed within either financial or producer services. Nevertheless, despite the one-dimensional character of the classification it served to confirm our earlier attempts to arrive at a functional definition of financial centre by possession of key financial operations.

Figure 5.1 reveals the extent to which London is Britain's pre-eminent financial and producer service centre in terms of numbers employed within such industries. In 1984 the city contained around 14 times as much financial and producer service employment as the next largest financial centre. Consequently, over 60 per cent of all financial and producer service employment within the 25 centres in 1984 was located within London. The supremacy of London resulted in large part from the importance of the international financial enclave that is the City of London. Some 37 per cent of the 560,000 people employed within financial and producer services in the capital worked in the City. However, other areas of the capital were also important centres of financial and producer service employment. For example, if component employment-office areas of London were considered as separate financial centres in their own right then - after the City of London - Westminster, Marylebone, King's Cross and Croydon would respectively rank as the second, fourth, ninth and tenth largest such centres in Britain. Over 148,000 employees worked in financial and producer service industries in these employment-office areas in 1984. London's pre-eminent status in terms of financial and producer service employment is a product of not only its sheer size - one in seven of Britain's entire population live in the capital (Champion *et al.*, 1987, p.10) - but also of its importance as a locational base of key international financial and producer service organizations (Leyshon, Daniels and Thrift, 1987; Leyshon, Thrift and Daniels, 1987).

Financial-service employment is clearly a major component of overall producer service employment in a centre. Figure 5.1 reveals that financial-service employees outnumbered other producer service employees in 23 of the 25 centres. Financial-service employment was particularly important in Bootle, Southend and Norwich where over three-quarters of financial and producer service employees were employed within financial-service organizations, while over two-thirds of financial and producer service employees were employed in financial-service industries in Brighton, Northampton, Bradford and Bournemouth.

Despite London's clear pre-eminence as a centre of financial and producer service employment, its relative dominance in Britain has in fact been in decline in recent years. This has resulted not from employment decline in the capital but from rapid employment growth in certain regional and sub-regional financial centres. The following section analyses the processes of financial and producer service employment change within the largest 25 centres in Britain between 1974 and 1984.

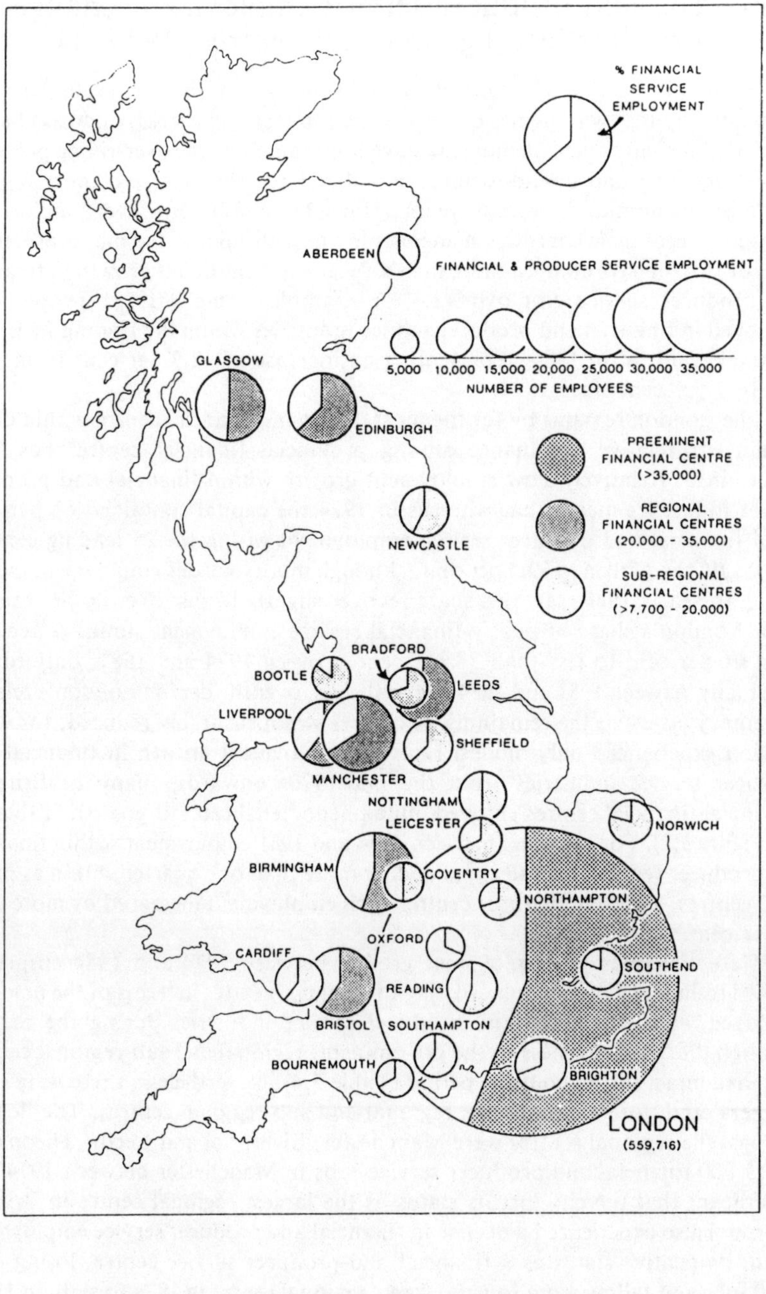

Figure 5.1 *Distribution of financial and producer service employment, 1984 (Source*: Census of Employment, *1984, as from the National Online Manpower Information System)*

Financial and producer service employment change in Britain's leading financial centres, 1974–84

The economic history of urban Britain during the 1970s and 1980s has been dominated by the twin themes of large-scale job loss and sharply-increased levels of unemployment. These phenomena have been caused by the over-riding processes of restructuring and de-industrialization that have characterized most western capitalist economies in recent years (Hausner, 1987). However, amidst the widespread economic contraction and employment shrinkage, the major provincial cities of Britain have enjoyed more than a decade of continuous growth in financial and producer service employment. For example, some 931,251 people were employed in financial and producer service industries within the leading 25 British 'financial centres' in 1984, representing an increase of 12.9 per cent from 1981 and 16.9 per cent since 1974.

While London remains by far the most dominant financial centre within Great Britain, its relative dominance among provincial financial centres has been undermined. Relatively-slow employment growth within financial and producer service industries meant that whereas in 1974 the capital contained 63 per cent of all financial and producer service employment within the 25 leading centres, by 1981 this had fallen to 59.5 per cent, although more vigorous employment growth during the early 1980s saw this share recover slightly to just over 60 per cent by 1984. London's share of purely-financial service employment similarly declined from 61 per cent to less than 58 per cent between 1974 and 1981, only to rise marginally between 1981 and 1984. Nevertheless, over the decade London's relative supremacy *vis-à-vis* the remaining 24 centres was measurably reduced, for while London experienced only modest rates of employment growth in financial and producer service industries from the mid-1970s onwards, many of Britain's provincial financial centres enjoyed quite phenomenal rates of growth (Table 5.3 and Figure 5.2). For example, between 1974 and 1981 employment within financial and producer services overall expanded by more than one quarter within as many as 12 centres, while within three centres such employment increased by more than 50 per cent.

Differential rates of employment growth between 1974 and 1984 ensured a marked reshuffling of the rank ordering of financial centres in terms of the numbers employed within financial and producer service industries during the period, although the distinctiveness of the pre-eminent, regional and sub-regional centres remained intact throughout the period (Table 5.4). Nevertheless, there were clear 'winners' and 'losers' among the regional and sub-regional centres. The 'losers' amongst the regional centres were Manchester, Liverpool and Leeds. The loss of over 5,000 financial and producer service jobs in Manchester between 1974 and 1984 meant that the city lost its status as the largest regional centre in Britain. Liverpool also experienced a decline in financial and producer service employment and in its relative status as a financial and producer service centre, losing over 1,000 jobs and falling from fourth-largest regional centre in 1974 to sixth in 1984. Leeds, meanwhile, became the smallest regional centre in 1984, even though its financial and producer service employment base actually expanded by more than

Table 5.3 Financial and producer service employment change, British provincial centres: (a) 1974–81

Financial and producer service employment change			Financial-service employment change		
Rank	Centre	(% change)	Rank	Centre	(% change)
1	Bootle	(88.8)	1	Bootle	(78.0)
2	Coventry	(55.1)	2	Sheffield	(56.3)
3	Aberdeen	(51.0)	3	Brighton	(50.2)
4	Brighton	(39.9)	4	Bournemouth	(44.2)
5	Southend	(38.9)	5	Aberdeen	(43.5)
6	Norwich	(38.2)	6	Southend	(41.8)
7	Bristol	(37.6)	7	Bristol	(40.1)
8	Sheffield	(35.0)	8	Reading	(36.7)
9	Northampton	(34.2)	9	Norwich	(38.2)
10	Leeds	(31.2)	10	Southampton	(29.2)
11	Bournemouth	(30.1)	11	Northampton	(26.5)
12	Southampton	(21.5)	12	Coventry	(22.2)
13	Oxford	(20.8)	13	Edinburgh	(21.3)
14	Reading	(20.1)	14	Newcastle	(20.5)
15	Leicester	(17.8)	15	Leeds	(16.9)
16	Birmingham	(16.9)	16	Oxford	(15.9)
17	Cardiff	(16.8)	17	Glasgow	(12.5)
18	Edinburgh	(16.7)	18	Birmingham	(10.7)
19	Glasgow	(9.8)	19	Leicester	(10.6)
20	Newcastle	(9.4)	20	Bradford	(6.7)
21	Bradford	(7.8)	21	London	(4.8)
22	London	(2.5)	22	Manchester	(4.1)
23	Liverpool	(−2.4)	23	Cardiff	(2.9)
24	Manchester	(−8.9)	24	Nottingham	(−9.8)
25	Nottingham	(−10.8)	25	Liverpool	(−11.1)

Continued overleaf

Table 5.3 (cont.): (b) 1981–4

Financial and producer service employment change			Financial-service employment change		
Rank	Centre	(% change)	Rank	Centre	(% change)
1	Aberdeen	(38.0)	1	Southend	(18.6)
2	Oxford	(32.6)	2	Brighton	(16.0)
3	Reading	(26.0)	3	Cardiff	(15.7)
4	Southend	(21.6)	4	Southampton	(14.3)
5	Northampton	(20.5)	5	Northampton	(13.8)
6	Birmingham	(19.9)	6	Reading	(13.4)
7	Edinburgh	(18.2)	7	Aberdeen	(11.2)
8	Brighton	(17.1)	8	Edinburgh	(10.8)
9	Newcastle	(15.8)	9	Coventry	(9.8)
10	Cardiff	(15.7)	10	Birmingham	(9.1)
11	Southampton	(15.0)	11	Leeds	(8.0)
12	Nottingham	(14.6)	12	Bradford	(7.8)
13	Coventry	(14.4)	13	Oxford	(7.0)
14	London	(14.1)	14	London	(6.6)
15	Bournemouth	(9.7)	15	Bournemouth	(5.6)
16	Leeds	(7.7)	16	Bootle	(4.8)
17	Bristol	(6.4)	17	Norwich	(4.3)
18	Bradford	(6.1)	18	Nottingham	(3.0)
19	Norwich	(6.1)	19	Newcastle	(2.4)
20	Liverpool	(4.8)	20	Leicester	(0.3)
21	Glasgow	(4.4)	21	Bristol	(−0.1)
22	Bootle	(3.3)	22	Liverpool	(−1.5)
23	Manchester	(1.3)	23	Glasgow	(−4.3)
24	Sheffield	(−3.5)	24	Sheffield	(−6.6)
25	Leicester	(−5.0)	25	Manchester	(−6.8)

(*Source: Census of Employment*, 1974, 1981, 1984, as from the National Online Manpower Information System.)

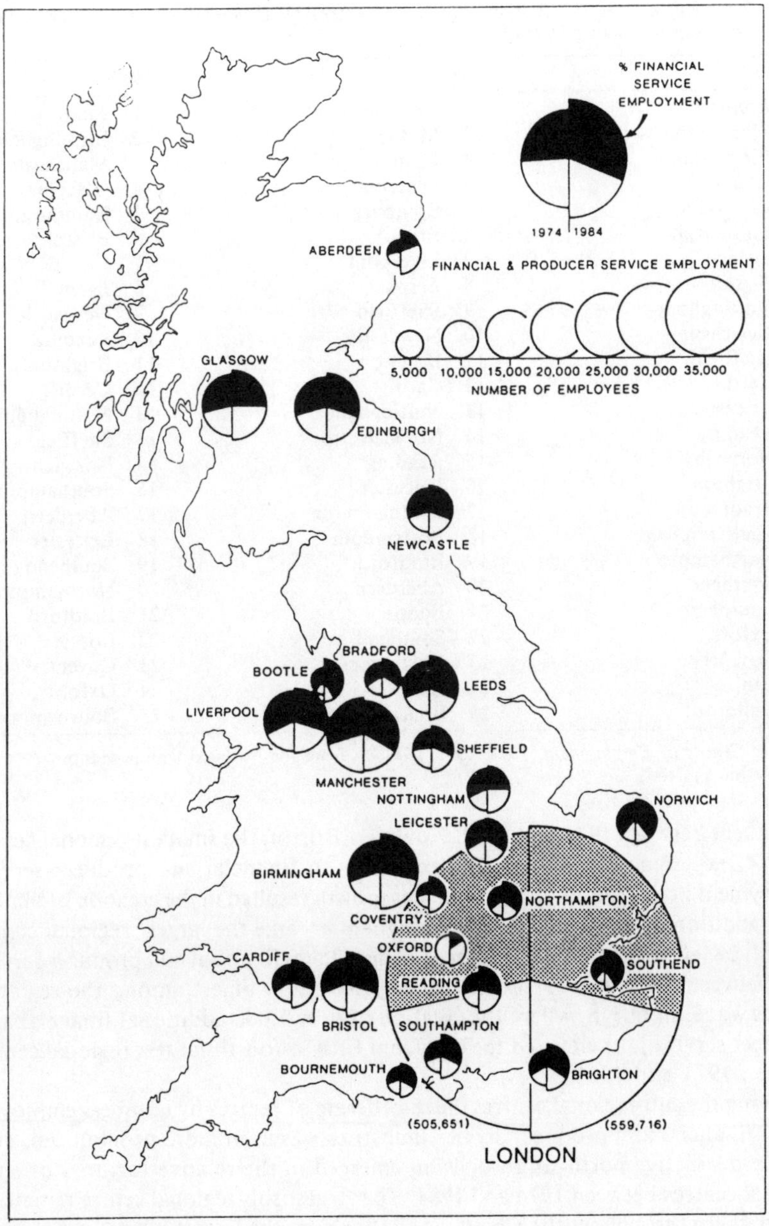

Figure 5.2 Change in the distribution of financial and producer service employment, 1974–84 (Source: Census of Employment, *1974, 1984, as from the National Online Manpower Information System)*

Table 5.4 Rank order of British provincial centres by financial and producer service employment, 1974–84

1974		1981		1984	
1	*London*	1	*London*	1	*London*
2	Manchester	2	Manchester	2	Birmingham
3	Birmingham	3	Birmingham	3	Manchester
4	Glasgow	4	Glasgow	4	Glasgow
5	Liverpool	5	Edinburgh	5	Edinburgh
6	Edinburgh	6	Bristol	6	Bristol
7	Leeds	7	Liverpool	7	Liverpool
8	*Bristol*	8	*Leeds*	8	*Leeds*
9	Nottingham	9	Sheffield	9	Newcastle
10	Newcastle	10	Newcastle	10	Reading
11	Sheffield	11	Brighton	11	Brighton
12	Cardiff	12	Cardiff	12	Cardiff
13	Leicester	13	Nottingham	13	Nottingham
14	Reading	14	Norwich	14	Sheffield
15	Norwich	15	Reading	15	Norwich
16	Brighton	16	Leicester	16	Southampton
17	Bradford	17	Southampton	17	Aberdeen
18	Southampton	18	Portsmouth	18	Leicester
19	Northampton	19	Bradford	19	Southend
20	Southend	20	Aberdeen	20	Northampton
21	Bournemouth	21	Bootle	21	Bradford
22	Oxford	22	Southend	22	Bootle
23	Coventry	23	Northampton	23	Coventry
24	Hull	24	Hull	24	Oxford
25	Guildford	25	Bournemouth	25	Bournemouth

(*Source: Census of Employment*, 1974, 1981, 1984, as from the National Online Manpower Information System.)

23 per cent between 1974 and 1984. However, Bristol, the smallest regional centre in 1974, experienced a 49 per cent expansion in financial and producer service employment in the period up to 1984. This growth resulted in the creation of almost 8,000 additional jobs in the city. Birmingham became the largest regional centre in 1984, benefiting from the creation of almost 7,500 financial and producer service jobs between 1974 and 1984. The other principal 'winner' among the regional centres was Edinburgh, where the creation of over 7,000 additional financial and producer service jobs elevated the city from fifth to fourth-largest regional centre between 1974 and 1984.

Among the sub-regional centres the re-ordering of centres by numbers employed within financial and producer service industries was even more pronounced, and a fairly-distinctive north-south division emerged in the relative fortunes of sub-regional centres between 1974 and 1984. The largest sub-regional centre remained non-southern throughout the period, as Nottingham, the largest sub-regional centre in 1974, was supplanted by Sheffield in 1981, which in turn was replaced by Newcastle in 1984. Employment in financial and producer services in Newcastle expanded by over 28 per cent over the period. However, the southern boom-towns of Reading and Brighton emerged as clear winners among the sub-regional centres.

Financial and producer service employment in these towns increased by 59 and 67 per cent respectively between 1974 and 1984, elevating them to second and third place among Britain's sub-regional centres. Other southern centres to expand their financial and producer service employment bases and to increase their relative standing among sub-regional centres included Southampton. However, those centres that experienced a decline in their relative standing among sub-regional centres were predominantly non-southern towns and cities. For example, while the financial and producer service employment bases of Nottingham, Sheffield, Leicester, Bradford and Northampton all increased over the period, all five centres were relatively less important in terms of such employment in 1984 than they were in 1974.

Therefore, a considerable re-ordering of regional and sub-regional financial centres took place between 1974 and 1984, in terms of financial and producer service employment. Although 'winners' and 'losers' could be identified, within only 2 of the 25 leading centres - Manchester and Liverpool - did employment within financial and producer service industries actually decline.

A closer analysis of employment change within the component industries of the financial and producer service industries indicated that those centres that grew fastest were dependent initially upon the rapid growth of usually just one financial sector. First, there were those towns and cities that grew fastest in terms of financial-service employment between 1974 and 1981 - centres such as Bootle, Sheffield and Southend were dependent largely upon the expansion of the banking and bill-discounting sector. The number of employees within this sector in the three centres increased by 84, 127 and 62 per cent respectively. Financial-service employment growth in Bootle has been caused almost exclusively by the *in situ* expansion of the operations of the national Girobank, while Southend is now the administrative centre of the Access credit-card organization (owned jointly by the major clearing banks). Second, centres such as Bournemouth, Bristol, Reading and Norwich, on the other hand, had their financial-service employment growth fuelled by the expansion of the insurance sector, within which employment increased by 122, 57, 98, 45 and 37 per cent respectively. The insurance labour-market in these centres is dominated by a relatively small number of large employers. For example, a handful of large nationally-orientated insurance companies - Phoenix, Sun Life, Clerical Medical and General, London Life and the insurance subsidiary of NatWest - accounted for over half of all insurance employment in Bristol in 1983 (Boddy, Lovering and Bassett, 1986). The insurance labour-market in Norwich is concentrated to an even greater extent. Although Sedgewick, the UK's largest insurance broking firm, operates within the city, local insurance employment is dominated by the Norwich Union insurance company. The firm has been based in the city since the 18th century and is now one of the world's *premier* insurance companies. The company employs around 4,000 people making it Norwich's largest private-sector employer (Reeves, 1987b). Some 60 per cent of all those employed within the insurance industry in Norwich work for Norwich Union, as do 42 per cent of all those who work within financial-service industries. Finally, much of the financial-service employment growth in Brighton was dependent upon the expansion of the 'other financial institutions sector', where employment increased by more than 132 per cent over the period. One component of this growth is the expansion of the Alliance and Leicester Building Society, which is headquartered in the town.

However, while between 1974 and 1981 financial-service growth in the fastest-growing centres could be attributed to the influence of employment expansion in just one financial-service industry, between 1981 and 1984 growth seems to have been more equitably distributed across the range of financial-service sectors. For example, Brighton, Southend and Reading also figured among the ten fastest-growing centres between 1981 and 1984. However, in each case the relative specialization of their financial-service employment base actually declined, and within each centre the level of dependence upon one, key, growth sector was reduced.

Determinants and mechanisms of growth

This section attempts to identify both the determinants and mechanisms of financial and producer service employment growth within British provincial centres since the mid-1970s. Accordingly, the section is in two parts. The first part considers the implications of an elementary regression model that measures the degree to which local levels of consumer and business demand are linked to the level of financial and producer service employment within provincial centres. The second part of this section identifies the processes of financial and producer service employment growth within the provincial centres of Britain.

Determinants of financial and producer service employment growth within provincial centres: an exploratory analysis

Using employment data for 1984, an attempt was made to determine the extent to which the level of financial and producer service employment in provincial centres was related to the local level of local consumer and business demand. A proxy for 'consumer demand' was calculated by multiplying the 1984 average, gross weekly income of full-time male and female employees (*New Earnings Survey*, 1985) by the respective number of male and female employees employed within the TTWA in which the centre was located (*Census of Employment*, 1984). A proxy for 'business demand' was derived from the relevant county Gross Domestic Product figures for 1984 as calculated by the Central Statistical Office (CSO, 1988). The use of these variables is, of course, fraught with problems and it must be stressed that this is merely an exploratory analysis. The interpretative value of the analysis is tempered by a quite considerable list of caveats[4]. In addition to these caveats the analysis omitted two centres: London, because its relative size would have distorted the analysis and because, in any case, the functional importance of London's financial and producer service industries beyond local demand levels can be taken as read, given the importance of the city as an international financial centre; and Bootle, because of the impossibility of deriving meaningful values of local consumer or business demand from the data available, in the light of its dependence on the national demand for the services of the Girobank.

The regression analysis revealed that the local level of consumer demand and business demand was an extremely good predictor of the level of financial and producer service employment within provincial centres (Figures 5.3 and 5.4). The level of consumer and business demand was found to explain 65.2 per cent of the variation in financial-service employment and 76.3 per cent of the variation in financial and producer service employment in British provincial centres. It was, therefore, not surprising to discover financial and producer service employment increased fastest in those centres that were for the most part located within TTWAs and counties where consumer and business demand experienced the greatest increases (Table 5.5).

Having established that the level of financial and producer service employment within British provincial centres appears to be closely related to prevailing levels of local demand, the next section outlines the three major processes by which financial and producer service employment has grown within these centres. First, employment has increased as a consequence of the growth of local financial and producer service firms. A second process of employment growth has been the in-migration to provincial centres of offices belonging to large London-based multi-locational financial and producer service firms. The third process of financial and producer service employment growth has been the decentralization of offices from central London.

Mechanisms of financial and producer service employment growth

Growth of local firms

The most immediate effect of rising regional demand for financial and producer services has been to stimulate the growth of financial and producer service firms 'indigenous' to provincial centres. It is clear that the local business-service communities of many provincial centres have undergone something of a renaissance in recent years, and an important component of this renaissance has been the willingness of local firms to extend the range of services they offer. Anyone who regularly reads the British financial and business press cannot have failed to notice the recent eagerness with which financial journalists have reported the growing confidence - and growing profitability - of provincial financiers and business professionals. In this respect there is no north-south divide since the growing prominence of local financial and producer service firms is as evident in the provincial cities of the north as it is in those of the south. Indeed, this has created something of a paradox in the writings of several financial journalists. On the one hand, they continue to transmit the prevailing governmental line that unfavourable socio-economic conditions in the north are due in large part to the absence of a suitable entrepreneurial culture among the people who live there (see Massey, 1988). Yet much of the credit for the resurgence of provincial financial centres is attributed

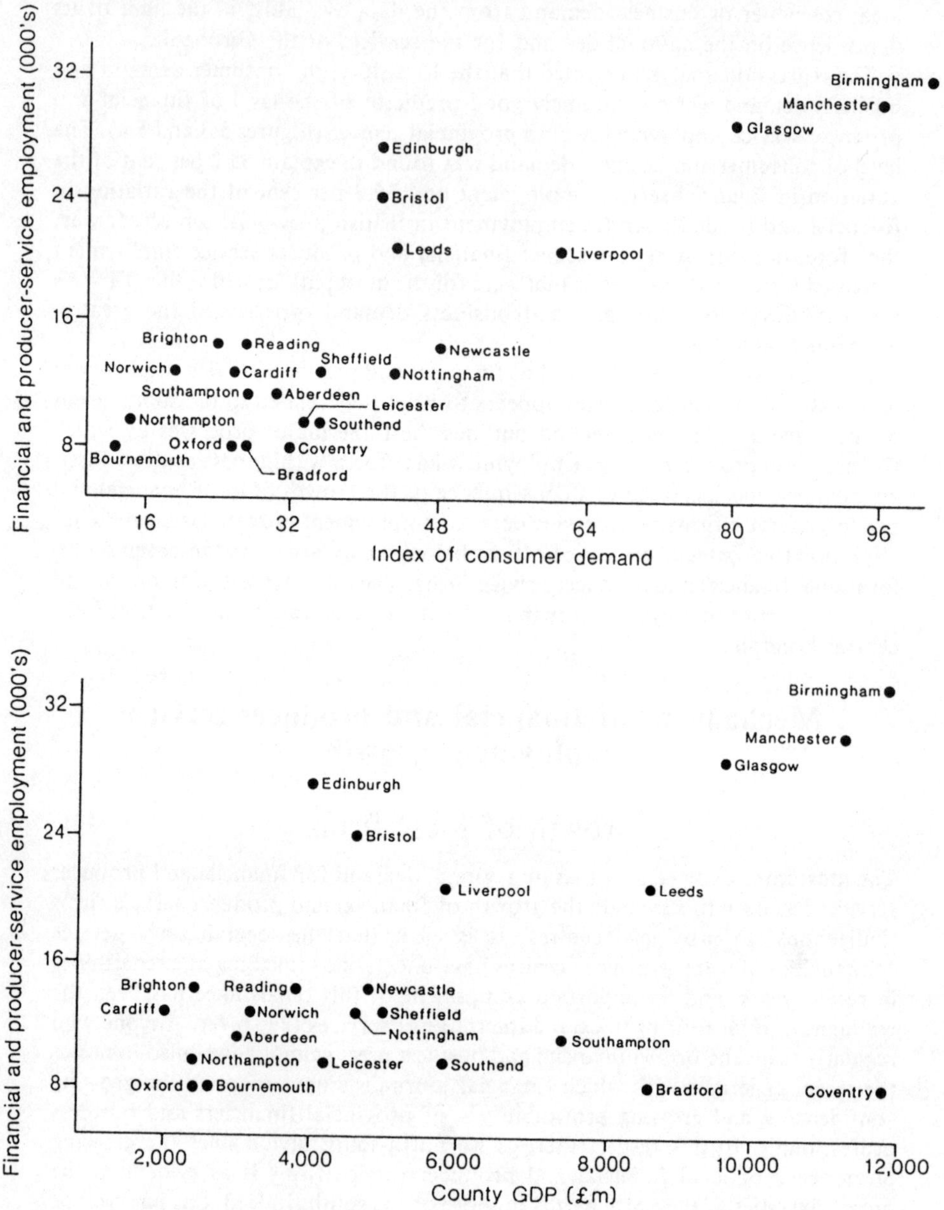

Figure 5.3 *Relationship of financial and producer service employment to measures of demand*

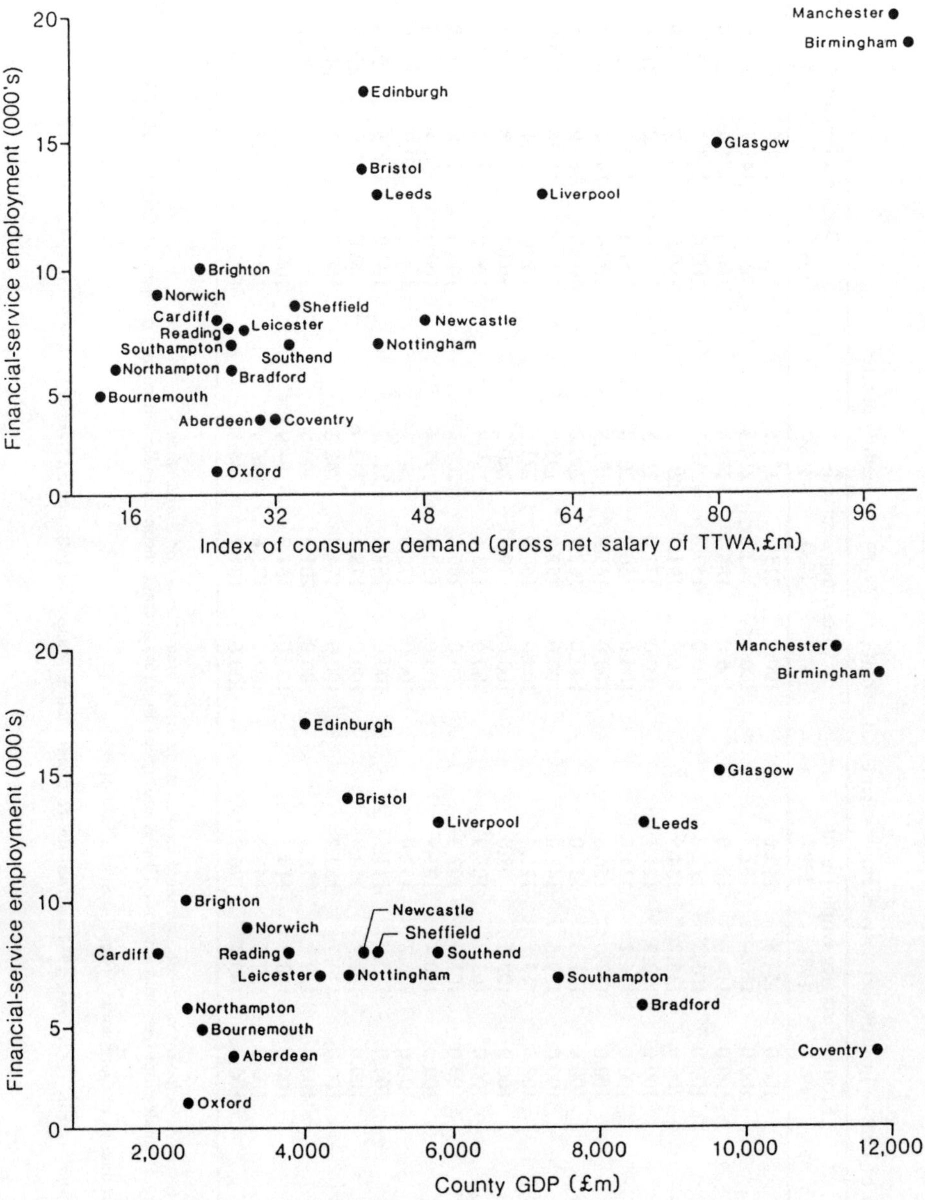

Figure 5.4 Relationship of financial employment to measures of demand

Table 5.5 Indices of change in producer service employment and demand, 1977–84, 23 leading centres

Centre	Producer service employment[1]			Consumer demand[2]			Business demand[3]		
	1977	1981	1984	1977	1981	1984	1977	1981	1984
Aberdeen	100.0	154.8	213.6	100.0	213.7	331.5	100.0	184.5	255.7
Birmingham	100.0	110.4	132.3	100.0	163.3	216.3	100.0	141.7	175.0
Bournemouth	100.0	114.9	126.0	100.0	185.5	248.4	100.0	171.4	223.4
Bradford	100.0	105.8	112.2	100.0	157.8	211.3	100.0	157.1	195.2
Brighton	100.0	115.2	134.9	100.0	191.3	286.3	100.0	185.7	221.9
Bristol	100.0	113.8	121.1	100.0	171.0	211.5	100.0	168.2	217.0
Cardiff	100.0	116.1	134.6	100.0	156.2	207.8	100.0	159.2	210.4
Coventry	100.0	137.0	156.8	100.0	145.8	192.5	100.0	141.7	175.0
Edinburgh	100.0	111.6	132.0	100.0	182.7	240.2	100.0	165.9	212.5
Glasgow	100.0	139.8	148.0	100.0	152.7	195.5	100.0	154.4	184.9
Leeds	100.0	113.1	121.8	100.0	168.0	223.1	100.0	157.1	195.2
Leicester	100.0	103.2	98.0	100.0	179.9	240.5	100.0	173.8	226.1
Liverpool	100.0	103.9	108.9	100.0	153.6	188.8	100.0	148.2	175.7
Manchester	100.0	101.0	102.3	100.0	165.0	209.8	100.0	155.8	187.8
Newcastle	100.0	110.4	127.8	100.0	150.0	195.4	100.0	154.4	182.5
Northampton	100.0	126.2	152.0	100.0	178.9	247.2	100.0	160.9	219.9
Nottingham	100.0	120.9	117.9	100.0	169.6	211.7	100.0	170.1	203.5
Norwich	100.0	122.9	130.3	100.0	178.3	242.9	100.0	166.9	219.8
Oxford	100.0	114.7	152.2	100.0	174.7	242.2	100.0	169.3	212.0
Reading	100.0	139.9	175.1	100.0	201.0	304.8	100.0	169.3	212.8
Sheffield	100.0	118.3	114.1	100.0	161.9	194.9	100.0	156.1	173.8
Southampton	100.0	127.8	146.9	100.0	173.6	246.4	100.0	177.9	212.0
Southend	100.0	140.4	170.7	100.0	181.7	246.5	100.0	175.9	210.7

Notes

1. Number of producer service employees by amalgamated employment office area (*Census of Employment*).
2. Number of male and female employees and relevant TTWA multiplied by gross average income in relevant county (*Census of Employment; New Earnings Survey*).
3. Gross domestic product in relevant county (Central Statistical Office).

(*Source: Census of Employment*, 1977, 1981, 1984 as from the National Online Manpower Information System.); *New Earnings Survey*, 1977, 1981, 1984; Central Statistical Office, 1988.

to the efforts of northern-based financiers and professionals, who have responded to the increasing level of demand for financial and producer services by enterprisingly extending the range of services on offer. For example, the following statements were both included within a recent report on Sheffield:

> The worry among professionals is that many of the manufacturing workforce ... are not going to be entrepreneurial enough. They have been too used to being employees in big corporations. ... What is ... apparent from doing the rounds of Sheffield's professional and financial community ... is that this community contains some impressive entrepreneurs in their own right. What other explanation is there for the survival of firms of solicitors such as Rogers and Howe which has been in continuous business in the same building since 1800?
>
> (Hamilton Fazey, 1987a, p.4)

That financial and producer service firms are able to survive and even thrive in regions more commonly associated with processes of economic decline should not really be surprising. For example, a still-important component of accountancy practice is insolvency work, where firms earn fee income from the management of company receiverships and liquidations. Insolvency also creates work for solicitors who are employed by creditors to act on their behalf in presentation of winding-up petitions to the court. Therefore, such firms are able to remain profitable in times of economic downturn as well as in times of growth. However, in recent years local financial and producer service firms, even in northern provincial centres, have been faced with sharply-growing levels of demand for a whole suite of business services. Firms have responded by extending the range of their existing services while at the same time new firms have emerged to fill market niches.

There would seem to be three important causes of the upsurge in demand for financial and producer services within provincial centres. First, there is the general trend within the economy towards externalization and the vertical disintegration of production (Marshall, 1988), where activities that were previously performed in-house are contracted out to specialist firms. For example, economic pressures have forced many companies to dispense with specialist management advisory positions, preferring instead to buy in such services as and when they are needed, a development that has benefited the management consultancy departments of accountancy firms in particular (see Leyshon, Daniels and Thrift, 1987).

Second, advances in communications technologies have had the effect of undermining the functional importance of location for certain financial-service activities. For example, the installation of the automated SEAQ (Stock Exchange Automated Quotations) system in London in October 1986 has allowed regionally-based stockbrokers to participate within the domestic securities market on a more or less equal footing with firms based in the City of London. Witness the comments of a Manchester-based financial professional quoted in a recent press report:

> 'The Big Bang has been very good for Manchester and has brought business back. Local stockbrokers are working all the hours there are and doing very good business.' With Manchester Britain's most important financial centre after London, the electronics revolution has given it direct, instantaneous contact like never before. Anyone wanting to deal might as well be in Manchester 1 as London EC4.
>
> (Hamilton Fazey, 1987b, p.3)

The third cause of growing demand for financial and producer services in provincial centres also results from changes taking place within the City of London. The restructuring of the City in 1986 confirmed its new role alongside New York and Tokyo as one of the three transactional centres of the New International Financial System (Thrift, Leyshon and Daniels, 1987; Thrift and Leyshon, 1988). In the hours between the closing of the Tokyo financial markets and the opening of the New York markets, London is the international financial centre of the world economy. As the volume of capital flowing through London has increased so some City-based organizations have increasingly tended to concentrate upon satisfying the demand for their services emanating from multinational corporations and international financial institutions, and many City firms have embarked upon substantial internal expansion programmes in an effort to keep up with demand. However, in the scramble for highly-valued internationally-orientated business, the needs of smaller domestic clients have become very much of secondary importance. Therefore, the functional take-off of the City has presented regionally-based financial and producer service firms with the opportunity to fill the growing lacunae in local financial and business-service markets. And local firms are indeed responding to the opportunities that have arisen from the increasing scale of operations in London. For example, take the case of Manchester:

> Increasingly when companies in the [North West] issue their company reports or prospectuses, the addresses of their professional and financial advisers are Manchester ones. When it comes to flotations and buy-outs in the North West, the list of advisers will be Manchester-based. Partly it is a question of scale. While Manchester ... is a big league player in financial circles, even £100m companies are small by London standards ... . A Northern industrialist visiting his (*sic*) London merchant bank will nowadays find it difficult to see much of a senior partner, if at all. But he can reach Manchester from almost anywhere in the North-West in less than an hour – and be guaranteed the attention he wants and deserves.
>
> (Hamilton Fazey, 1987b, p.3)

However, the best illustration of the benefits that have accrued to many local financial and producer services firms as a result of the transformation in the City has been the spectacular growth of regionally-based corporate legal practices. The largest corporate legal practices in Britain are all based in London, and the largest of these in the City of London. These firms have long provided corporate legal advice to companies throughout Britain, and are hired as much for the prestige their appointment brings as for the quality of their services. Interviews conducted with partners of City law firms by the authors in the summer of 1987 confirmed their increasing orientation towards the international capital markets. Although the City firms had all expanded rapidly in the face of growing demand, several of the partners interviewed admitted that they had been forced to turn work down since they were already overloaded. Regional lawyers have not been slow to seize the market opportunities this presents. They have quickly tapped into the regional demand for corporate legal services and are beginning to cut off the flow of business that traditionally has gone to London:

> 'The London firms are so bombed out with work for very large national companies or international clients that even a £10m capitalised Yorkshire company is pretty small beer

to them. Yorkshire directors quickly catch on - 200 miles is a long way to go to see a newly qualified solicitor different from the one they saw last time.'

(Bradford solicitor, quoted in Hamilton Fazey, 1987c, p.5)

Indeed, the orientation of City law firms towards very large-scale corporations has meant that provincial corporate legal practices are not only shoring up their own regional markets for legal services, but in some cases are also encroaching into the medium-sized firm corporate legal market within London and the South East where firms too are feeling neglected by their former advisers. For example, Bristol legal practice Osborne Clark possesses many London-based clients. A recent review of corporate legal practice in Scotland suggested that in the near future Scottish law firms would soon begin to expand into London to 'stop the more lucrative Scottish business haemorrhaging out to the English jurisdiction' (Fennell, 1987b, p.36). Two trends that are becoming increasingly important are those of centralization and spatial expansion both within and between provincial centres. With regional demand for corporate legal services increasing as City-based firms move off into the distance of the international markets, so local firms are eschewing organic growth in favour of more rapid accretional expansion so as to pool those resources necessary for the provision of services of the scope and sophistication required by their increasingly-numerous clients. There are many examples of centralization among corporate legal practices within provincial centres. For example, merely within the first half of 1988 two new enlarged firms were created in Leeds as A. V. Hammond merged with Last Suddards (to form Hammond Suddards) and Walker Morris & Coles merged with Scott Turnbull & Kendal (to form Walker Morris Scott Turnbull) (Fennell, 1987a). In many cases, merger activity is combined with spatial expansion providing the firms with more comprehensive geographic coverage. Thus, Liverpool-based practice Alsop Stevens expanded the spatial extent of its operations by opening an office in Manchester in 1984 (Hamilton Fazey, 1987b), while Bristol firm Burges Salmon is forging an office network running parallel with the M5 from Plymouth to Birmingham (Alexander, 1987). In Scotland, Glasgow firms are increasingly looking for Edinburgh practices with which to merge because the location in the capital of the Supreme Court allows firms located there direct access to counsel. This was an important motive in the recent creation of the Glasgow-Edinburgh practices of Bishop and Robertson Chalmers in 1986 and Bird Semple in 1987 (Fennell, 1987b).

However, it would be wrong to assume that the vigorous growth displayed by provincial corporate legal practices is paralleled by all provincial financial and producer service firms. Although there is an undoubted increase in demand for financial and professional business services in such centres, provincial lawyers have enjoyed the comparative luxury of being free from the very real competitive pressures exercised by the regional operations of multi-locational London-based financial and producer service firms. In other sectors, local financial and producer service firms have not been so fortunate to find themselves in competition only with one another. As demand for financial and producer services has grown in provincial centres, local firms have been forced to compete for market share with branch offices of large international practices. Therefore, while there has most assuredly been a renaissance of financial and producer service activity within provincial centres, it would be wrong to overstate the importance in this movement of locally-based firms.

The geographical expansion of large multi-locational financial and producer service firms

The extent to which large London-based financial and producer service firms have embarked upon the construction of branch-office networks varies quite markedly between sectors. At one extreme are the corporate lawyers who operate almost exclusively out of their London offices. In contrast, there are the large accountancy firms who have relentlessly pursued a policy of geographical expansion so that most now possess almost comprehensive national coverage. Below we examine the spatial impacts of the expansion of the office networks of large accountancy firms and of large firms within two other sectors - commercial property agencies and merchant and investment banking.

The accountancy profession in Britain is characterized by a three-tiered organizational structure. The bottom two levels are characterized by many thousands of small firms (usually consisting of no more than two or three partners) and a decreasing number of medium-sized firms. The upper strata of the accountancy profession is characterized by a handful of international practices that dominate the accountancy market worldwide (Bavishi and Wyman, 1983). Between 1978 and 1986 the British operations of these large accountancy firms experienced substantial growth in fee-income, professional employment and profitability. As these firms have grown internally they have also comprehensively extended their office networks throughout the UK. For example, in 1985 the 20 leading firms collectively operated some 492 offices in the UK, an increase of over 62 per cent from 1975 (Leyshon, Daniels and Thrift, 1987). Between 1975 and 1985 the leading firms entered 128 previously-unserved locations while consolidating their position in established markets, and in 1985 12 cities contained the offices of at least 11 of the leading 20 firms (Table 5.6).

There were four interrelated spatial determinants of large accountancy-firm office growth during the period. First, offices were opened by firms in an attempt to claim UK market share through the construction of nationwide office networks that include most of the major cities. In 1975 some of the leading firms still ran their UK operations solely out of their London office. Cities such as Glasgow and Edinburgh, for example, have particularly benefited from this process of office-network development. Second, offices have been opened in response to business opportunities that arise in areas of industrial expansion. Aberdeen, the Thames Valley and Cambridge all witnessed a significant increase in the number of offices operated by the leading firms as they moved in to secure new clients. Third, the stagnation of the audit market during the period encouraged many large accountancy firms to cast their client-net wider to encompass the small-firm sector. The desire to capture an increased share of the small-firm accountancy market

Table 5.6 UK office distribution of large accountancy firms, 1975–85; cities with largest number of offices of 20 leading firms

1975 City	Offices	1985 City	Offices	Change 1975–85
1 London	20	1 London	20	0
2 Birmingham	16	2 Birmingham	19	3
3 Manchester	15	3 Glasgow	17	6
4 Leeds	13	4 Leeds	16	3
5 Glasgow	11	5 Manchester	16	1
5 Liverpool	11	6 Edinburgh	15	8
5 Newcastle	11	7 Bristol	14	4
8 Bristol	10	7 Newcastle	14	3
9 Belfast	9	9 Cardiff	12	4
9 Nottingham	9	9 Liverpool	12	1
11 Cardiff	8	11 Aberdeen	11	6
11 Leicester	8	11 Belfast	11	2
13 Edinburgh	7	11 Nottingham	11	2
14 Douglas	6	14 Norwich	9	7
15 Southampton	5	14 Southampton	9	4
15 Aberdeen	5	16 Leicester	8	0
15 Sheffield	5	16 Reading	8	5
18 Bradford	4	18 Sheffield	7	2
19 Hull	3	19 Bradford	6	2
19 Reading	3	19 Douglas	6	0

(*Source:* Leyshon, Daniels and Thrift, 1987, Table 18.)

encouraged large accountancy practices to lower the generally-accepted population threshold of a town that will support the operation of an office and to begin to open offices in locations where they have no existing clients (*The Accounting Bulletin*, 1983, p.8–9). Finally, accountancy firms now have greater opportunities in the public-sector market and this development has helped to reinforce the justification of office openings in some major cities (Leyshon, Daniels and Thrift, 1987).

Although large firms within the accountancy sector have demonstrated the most vigorous expansionary growth among financial and producer service organizations, they have not been alone in extending their operations throughout the country. Commercial property firms have also steadily encroached into regional markets since the mid-1970s. These firms have also undergone substantial organizational growth as the increasing commercialization of the property market and its planned securitization have forced many firms to rethink their operational structures. A number of firms, such as Michael Laurie (now Morgan Grenfell Laurie) and Richard Ellis, have forged links with investment banks to integrate respective skills.

These pressures for organizational change have occurred at a time when commercial property firms are undergoing the beginnings of geographical expansion throughout the UK. The 20 largest general-practice firms of chartered surveyors in the UK are all headquartered in London, and the capital has long constituted the most important market for these firms. However, the period between 1976 and 1986 saw these firms begin to break out of London and during the period the number of UK offices operated by them increased from 99 to 134. By 1986 the leading firms operated in 52 locations, an increase of 15 per cent on 1976 (Leyshon, Thrift and Daniels, 1987). Nevertheless, despite this growth, most offices remained concentrated within the wider South East region, and in both 1976 and 1986 over half of all those offices operated by the leading general-practice firms were based in that region. Cities such as Edinburgh, Glasgow, Leeds and Manchester all experienced increases in their share of large firms during the period (Table 5.7). However, London remained the only city within which over half of the leading 20 firms ran an office.

Table 5.7 UK office distribution of large commercial property firms, 1975/76–1985/86

1975 City		1975 Offices	1985 City		1985 Offices	Change 1975–85
1	London	20	1	London	20	0
2	Edinburgh	6	2	Edinburgh	9	3
3	Glasgow	5	3	Glasgow	7	2
4	Birmingham	3	4	Leeds	5	3
5	Bath	2	5	Birmingham	3	0
5	Canterbury	2	5	Manchester	3	2
5	Cardiff	2				
5	Hereford	2				
5	Leeds	2				

(*Source:* Leyshon, Thrift and Daniels, 1987, Appendix 2.)

The continued predominance of London and the South East as a locational centre for leading firms of chartered surveyors can be attributed to the importance of the London commercial property market. For example, in 1985 a survey of institutional property holdings revealed that some 51 per cent of such holdings were based in London, with a further 19 per cent in the rest of the South East. There is evidence to suggest that London's pre-eminence as an outlet for property investment funds may be in decline as the property markets of other domestic centres increase in value.

A third example of a sector where firms have enjoyed considerable internal growth is that of investment (merchant) banking. UK investment banks have experienced considerable growth in the past decade as demonstrated by their burgeoning balance sheets and rising profit levels. However, unlike accountancy and commercial property firms, an analysis of the spatial expansion of their domestic office networks between 1975 and 1985 revealed that the total number of offices actually underwent a reduction of 5 per cent, despite a 140 per cent increase in the size of their overseas office networks. Moreover, an analysis of the location of the offices in Great Britain of all overseas banks between 1981 and 1986 also revealed a reduction in foreign-banking activity outside London (*The Banker*, 1981, p.113; 1986, p.74). The overall reduction in the number of domestic regional offices operated by UK investment banks and overseas banking conceals important trends towards a concentration and a transformation within banking activity in the regions. For example, Birmingham increased its share of UK investment-banking offices and remained the most important location for the offices of overseas banks outside London, while Manchester maintained its three UK investment-banking offices and experienced an increase in the number of foreign-banking offices operating there, as did cities such as Leeds, Glasgow and Liverpool. The fall in foreign bank offices in the regions was due almost entirely to radical cutbacks in the branch networks of institutions such as the Bank of Pakistan, the Habib Bank and particularly the Muslim Commercial Bank, organizations that largely provide commercial-banking facilities for ethnic segments of the banking market. Between them these organizations closed 31 offices between 1981 and 1986, predominantly in towns within the North West and Yorkshire & Humberside regions. If these banks are removed from the analysis the picture is somewhat different (Figure 5.5). Moreover, although the number of locations that contained overseas bank branch offices fell by some 23 per cent between 1981 and 1986, the number of foreign banks operating within the regions actually increased from 35 to 44. In addition, there was evidence of a change in the composition of overseas banks operating in the regions. Banks that opened regional UK offices between 1981 and 1986 included both Sumitomo Bank and Fuji Bank (in Birmingham and Manchester) who were the largest and fifth largest capitalized banks in the world in 1986 (*Euromoney*, 1987).

Therefore, large firms within the accountancy, commercial property and investment-banking sectors have experienced substantial internal growth since the mid-1970s that, for the most part, has been accompanied by a marked expansion in the domestic office networks of these firms. The cumulative locational impact of the spatial expansion of the office networks of large organizations within these three financial and producer service sectors can be assessed from Table 5.8. The table reveals those locations in Great Britain that contained the highest concentrations of 47 large accountancy firms, investment banks and commercial property firms in 1985–6 and indicates those locations where the in-migration of large multi-locational firms between 1975 and 1976, and 1985 and 1986, was strongest. The analysis clearly demonstrates the continued hegemony of London as a centre for financial and producer service activity as the only location within which all the 47 firms ran an office. The table also indicates those regional financial centres and sub-regional financial centres that were the sites of office expansion and, with the exception of Leicester, in all the provincial financial centres the number of offices operated by large financial and producer service firms increased. Among the regional centres, Edinburgh demonstrated the highest level of corporate in-migration with some 11 large producer service firms opening offices there between 1975 and 1976, and 1985 and 1986. This 70 per cent expansion in offices ensured that in 1985–6 Edinburgh contained the second highest number of large firms within the three producer service sectors. Meanwhile, the number of large firms operating in Glasgow also increased sharply, making it the third most important locational centre for such activity. Indeed, with the exception of Liverpool, the number of offices operated by the 47 large producer service firms in regional financial centres increased by at least 16 per cent.

Table 5.8 Office expansion of 47 large producer service firms in Great Britain[1], 1975/76–1985/86

City	Number of firms operating in city 1985/86	Increase 1975/76–1985/86 No.	%
London	47	0	0
Edinburgh	27	11	69
Birmingham	25	4	19
Glasgow	25	9	56
Leeds	22	6	38
Manchester	22	3	16
Bristol	15	4	36
Newcastle	15	3	25
Cardiff	14	4	40
Liverpool	13	1	8
Aberdeen	11	6	120
Nottingham	11	2	22
Norwich	10	8	400
Southampton	9	4	80
Leicester	8	0	0
Reading	8	5	167
Sheffield	8	2	33
Bradford	6	2	50

Note
1. 20 accounting firms; 20 commercial property firms; 7 UK investment banks.
(*Source*: Authors' research.)

The expansion of the domestic office networks of large producer service firms in the UK would therefore seem to correspond broadly with the pattern of employment growth in producer services in provincial financial centres outlined earlier. However, an adequate elucidation of the true nature of the relationship between multi-locational firm office growth and employment change would require access to comprehensive firm-based employment data that is not yet available. Nevertheless, the partial data that does exist would lead us to suggest that the opening of offices by large producer service firms is an important component of financial and producer service employment growth in provincial financial centres. For example, employment within large accountancy firms comprises a significant proportion of all accountancy employment within regional economies. Using both firm-based and Department of Employment data we estimate that, with the exception of East Anglia, the leading 20 accountancy firms provide at least one third of all accountancy employment within each regional economy. In the South East and Scotland the 20 largest firms provide over half of all accountancy jobs. Within the provincial centres themselves, the large accountancy firms are even more important employers. For example, four of the leading firms employed over 10 per cent of all accountancy employment in Birmingham and over 19 per cent in Glasgow. In Bristol, seven large multi-locational firms provided over 36 per cent of all accountancy employment. Although no comparable data is available, we would expect similar levels of large-firm domination to be replicated across other producer service industries.

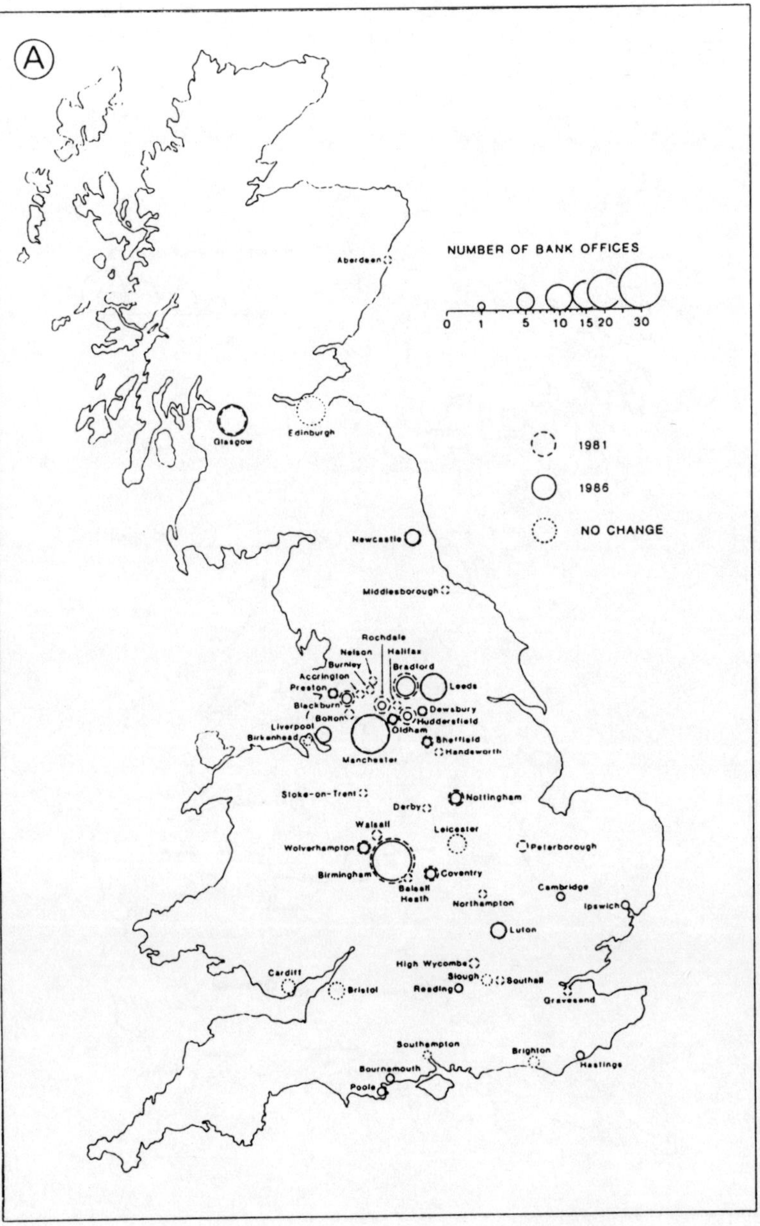

Figure 5.5 Change in the number of foreign bank offices: (a) All foreign bank offices

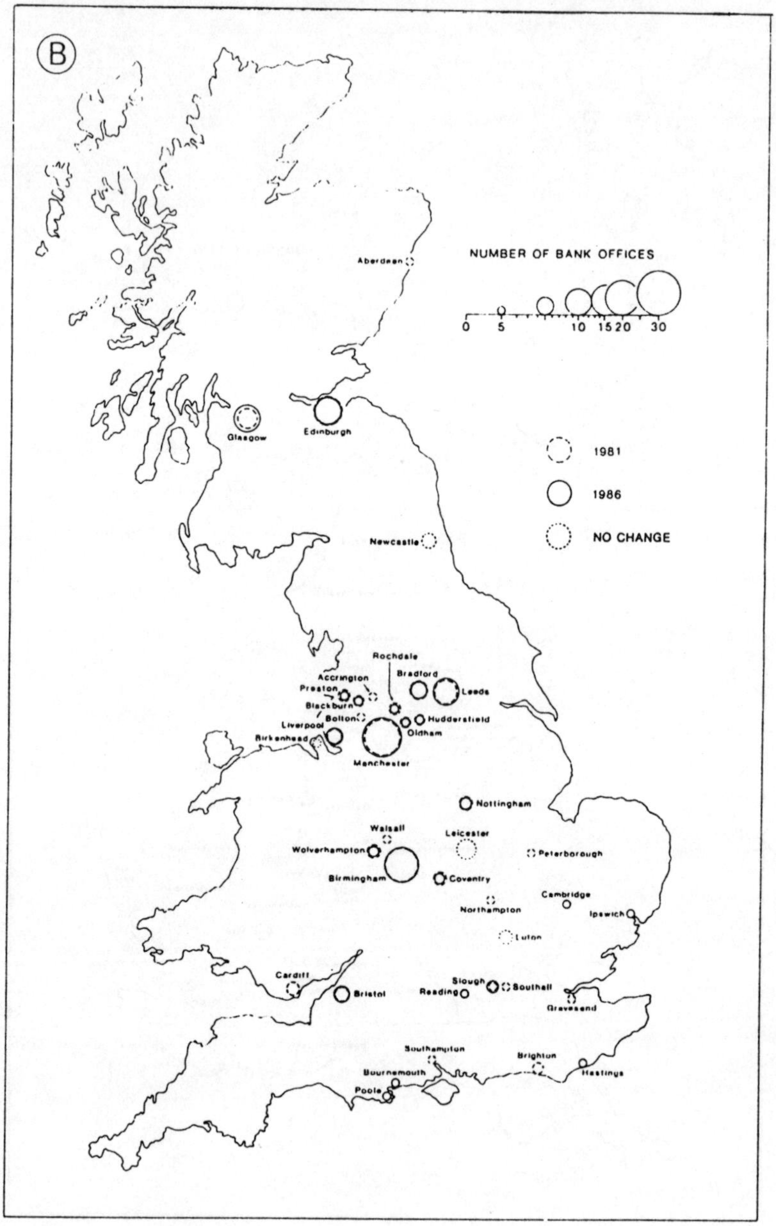

Figure 5.5 (Cont.):(b) Excluding banks catering for ethnic minorities

Both of the processes of financial and producer service employment growth discussed so far can be seen to be closely related to the local level of demand for financial and producer services within provincial centres and their hinterlands. However, in some centres employment has expanded to a level much greater than can be explained in terms of local-demand factors. For example, the regression analysis described earlier identified nine centres (Edinburgh, Bristol, Leeds, Norwich, Brighton, Reading, Southampton, Cardiff and Northampton) where financial and producer service employment was greater than would otherwise be expected given prevailing levels of local consumer and business demand. A closer examination of the financial and producer service organizations based within these centres reveals that the excess employment in many cases result from these centres possessing a functional importance that enabled them to export effectively financial and producer services beyond their regional markets. Financial and producer services are tradable over space and therefore can constitute an important source of local-income generation (Coffey and Polese, 1987; Beyers *et al.*, 1986).

The functional importance of these centres can be seen to result from a number of factors. First there are historical reasons. Edinburgh, for example, has been an important financial centre ever since the formation in the city of the Bank of Scotland and the Royal Bank, which were opened in 1695 and 1727 respectively (Draper *et al.*, 1988). The city was able to grow as a financial centre because of a separate legal system that, among other things, did not contain within it the protection afforded to the Bank of England that was enforced in the rest of Britain. Insurance companies emerged in the early 19th century to serve local markets and out of these developed the investment trusts that became of increasing importance during the late 19th century. The overseas experience of the insurance companies whose operations became international relatively early in their history, no doubt because English markets were already saturated with English insurance companies, was later highly advantageous to the investment trust groups (Draper *et al.*, 1988). The city is now one of the five most important international fund-management centres in the world, and is bracketed alongside London, Zurich, New York and Boston (*The Economist*, 1987b). Some £40 billion in funds are managed from Scotland (equivalent to 20 per cent of all British-managed money), the bulk of which is controlled by Edinburgh-based fund managers. Indeed, the financial district of Edinburgh contains what is arguably the highest concentration of investment management houses in the world (Edwards, 1988). The residual levels of financial and producer service in Norwich can also be seen to be due largely to the city exporting financial services beyond the regional market and to its historical pedigree as a financial centre. However, Norwich is a much less international centre than Edinburgh and is predominantly dependent upon one firm, the Norwich Union Insurance Company, which was established there some two-hundred years ago. Nevertheless, it is a major company and in 1987 it earned over 6 per cent of the premiums worldwide (Reeves, 1987a).

The second cause of residual levels of financial and producer service employment in centres would seem to result from certain large cities increasing their functional importance within the regional economies of which they are a part. This results both from the renaissance of local firms and from the influx of the offices of large financial and producer service organizations. For example, take the case of Leeds:

> the growing strength of the regional market is underscored by a remarkable explosion in financial and professional services in and around Leeds [which is] providing Yorkshire and Humberside with a self-sufficient financial capital city. There is almost no need for any Yorkshire company to go to London for financial service [because] almost every one of a company's professional advisors - accountants, solicitors, merchant banks, and stockbrokers - can be drawn from local ranks.
>
> (Hamilton Fazey, 1987c, p.5)

While Edinburgh is clearly the most important financial centre in Scotland, in Glasgow other producer service firms have undergone a resurgence as, for example, in the increasingly-expansionary behaviour of the corporate lawyers. In Manchester, while the level of financial and producer service overall is lower than would be expected given the prevailing level of demand, there is in fact a residual of purely financial-service employment. This residual employment results from a combination of the resurgence of local firms and of the influx of larger institutions that is helping to establish the city as the most important financial centre of the north of England:

> Finance has become a new lynchpin. The facts are readily wheeled out - over 40 different banks are represented; the Bank of England has its largest office outside London here; Henry Cooke Lumsden claims to be Britain's biggest regional stockbroker; the Manchester Stock Exchange is the settlement centre for all the northern exchanges.
>
> (Kennedy, 1988, p.54)

However, there is a group of provincial centres whose functional importance owes less to historical antecedents than to an increasing tendency of the organizations there to serve the wider regional economy. Centres such as Bristol, Reading and Brighton, for example, have benefited from becoming important destinations for office decentralizations from Central London. This has allowed these centres to engage in the export of financial services, either directly through the sale of services to the rest of the economy, or indirectly to other parts of the organization of which they are a part (Coffey and Polese, 1987).

Office decentralization from Central London

Since 1964 the process of office decentralization has transferred nearly 150,000 jobs out of Central London (Jones Lang Wootton, 1987a). Between 1979 and 1986 alone it is estimated that some 27,000 jobs were relocated from Central London in this way. Therefore, although much reduced in scale from the movements of the early-to-mid-1970s, office decentralization remains one source of mobile employment that would appear to have survived from the 'golden era' of employment redistribution in Britain that lasted from 1945 until 1973 (Morgan, 1986b). Unlike the geographical expansion of large financial and producer service firms described in the last sub-section, decentralized activities tend either to serve national markets or are key operational divisions of the organizations of which they are a part. The decentralization of financial-service firms is most commonly associated with the relocation of 'back office' activities, developments that are made possible by advances in communicative technology (Moss and Dunau, 1986; Nelson, 1986; van Dinteren, 1987). Decentralization from Central London seems to be primarily motivated by rising property costs (Jones Lang Wootton, 1987a), although labour costs may also be significantly reduced through decentralization - not only by moving out of the relatively high-wage London labour market but also by combining the move with the introduction of new technology, thereby facilitating productivity increases that enable firms to enter their new locations with reduced labour requirements (Boddy, Lovering and Bassett, 1986; Morris, 1986).

Decentralization can act as an important engine of financial-service employment growth within provincial centres, although it should be noted that only 28 per cent of all decentralizations from Central London between 1979 and 1987 involved financial and producer service firms. However, while the resurgence of local firms and the in-migration of the offices of large London-based multi-locational organizations were equally prevalent within northern and southern provincial centres, the employment benefits enjoyed by the recipient locations of office decentralization have been spatially constrained to the South East. Over 78 per cent of all decentralizations from Central London between 1979 and 1987 were directed towards locations within the South East region, with 43 per cent relocating merely within the Greater London area. Therefore, the impact of office decentralization from Central London upon financial and producer service employment growth outside the South East would seem to be limited to only certain provincial centres, given that only 22 per cent of relocations extended beyond that region.

A more detailed examination of the decentralization of offices of financial-service firms from Central London between 1983 and 1987 is illustrated in Table 5.9. The spatially constrained nature of these moves is once more clearly evident. Only four of the 26 moves listed were destined for locations outside the South East, all of which were in regions geographically contiguous to the South East. Three were destined for the South West and one for the East Midlands. It should be noted that those moves that did go beyond the South East did in fact tend to be larger - an average of 282 jobs per move compared to 239 overall - and were accompanied by a greater range of functions than were moves closer to London. Moves to Gloucester and Poole were accompanied by the entire suite of operational activities, while a firm that moved to Peterborough left behind only its investment department and two key officials. Nevertheless, such moves were relatively insignificant compared to the number of jobs transferred out of Central London and into the suburban towns of the South East.

The residual levels of financial and producer service employment identified by the earlier analysis within places such as Brighton and Reading are thus due at least in part to the locational impacts of decentralization. A clear example of the benefits that can accrue to a centre through decentralization is afforded by examination of the growth of insurance employment in Bristol. The city was the destination of a series of important insurance company decentralizations during the 1970s and early 1980s. Between 1972 and 1983, Phoenix, Sun Life, Clerical Medical and General and London Life all moved their administrative headquarters to the city, while the National Westminster Bank established its insurance subsidiary in the city during the same period (Boddy, Lovering and Bassett, 1986). Other centres in the south are increasingly benefiting from the advantages that accompany the decentralization of national administrative centres. For example, Southampton is now home to the headquarters of the Skandia Life company (Coopers & Lybrand, undated) and has been targeted as the location for the national centre of the Midland Bank's trustee division (Hampshire Development Corporation, per. comm.). Meanwhile, Brighton is the headquarters location of the Alliance & Leicester Building Society, one of the largest such organizations in Britain in 1988, and contains the administrative centre of the Legal and General Insurance Company and an operating division of American Express, the latter being decentralized in 1974 and now one of the largest ten employers within the city (SEEDS Association, 1987; Kennedy, 1988).

Although to date it has undoubtedly been provincial centres within the south that have most benefited from the injection of employment that decentralization brings, there are signs that office decentralization may indeed be creeping north and west as property prices in the south continue to rise. Therefore, provincial centres such as Northampton and Cardiff have already become the sites of financial-service administration centres. Northampton contains the Headquarters of Barclaycard, while in 1982 Chemical Bank moved its information and data-processing departments to Cardiff (Morris, 1988). However, interviews conducted by the authors with key employees in large investment banks based in the City of London in the spring and summer of 1987 did not really suggest that long-distance decentalization was a serious alternative for many of them. Most executives who were interviewed stressed that as financial markets became progressively more complex so the back-office activities also needed to become increasingly sophisticated. Many expressed a preference for keeping the back office in fairly close spatial proximity to the front-end activities so that settlement problems could more easily be ironed out, preferably by face-to-face communication. The furthest these firms seemed to be thinking of decentralizing was to Canary Wharf in the London docklands. It was clear that many whom we interviewed thought that for them even Bournemouth was somehow a wildly-eccentric location for financial services while Chemical Bank's move to Cardiff was scarcely comprehensible.

The impacts of financial and producer service growth in provincial centres

In this section we wish to consider some of the consequences of the increasing prominence of financial and producer service firms within provincial centres. The growth of these firms has had a range of impacts, of which we identify three as being of particular importance. The first is the growing importance of financial and producer service employment within the employment bases of provincial centres across the breadth of the country. Second, we wish to examine the implications of the growth of these activities upon other industrial sectors within regional economies. Third, and finally, we look at the impact of the growing importance

Table 5.9 Decentralization of financial services from Central London, 1983–7

Company	Classification	Origin	Destination	No. of jobs	Date of move
Bank of America	Bank	EC3	Bromley	350	1983
		Croydon	Croydon	350	1983
United Dominion Trust	Bank	EC3	New Barnet	200	1983
Commercial Union	Insurance	EC3	Croydon	700	1983
English & American Insurance	Insurance	EC3	Gloucester	170	1984
Lloyds Life Insurance	Insurance	EC2	Peterborough	180	1984
National Mutual Life of Australia	Insurance	EC2	Poole	180	1984
Brown & Shipley	Bank	EC3	Haywards Heath	100	N/a
Abbey National	Building society	W1	Milton Keynes	700	1985
Commercial	Insurance	EC1	Basildon	330	1985
Provident Life	Insurance	EC2	Basingstoke	250	1985
Chase Manhattan	Bank	EC2	Bournemouth	600	1986
Confederation Life	Insurance	WC2	Stevenage	250	1987
Allied Irish Banks	Bank	City	Uxbridge	1,000	N/a
Lombard North Central	Bank	WC	Redhill	350	1986
Sun Life of Canada	Insurance	SW1	Basingstoke	500	1987
Total				6,210	

Note
N/a = not available or not applicable.
(*Source*: Jones Lang Wootton, 1987a, Tables 4 and 5.)

Continued overleaf

Table 5.9 (cont.)

Type of move	Functions moved	Functions remaining	Reasons for move
Partial	Processing, servicing & admin. depts	Personnel, marketing, trading	Rationalization, consolidation
Partial	Most HQ functions	N/a	Cost reduction
Complete (small office)	All	N/a	Cost reduction
Complete (small office)	All	N/a	Cost reduction
Almost complete	All but -	Investment, MD, marketing director	Cost reduction, consolidation environmental amenity
Complete	All	N/a	Cost reduction, consolidation, environmental amenity
Partial	N/a	N/a	N/a
Almost complete	All but -	Finance, marketing	Consolidation, cost reduction
Partial	Support	HQ functions	Cost reduction
Complete (small office)	All	N/a	Cost reduction
Partial	Admin. operational	Marketing, finance	Expansion, accommodation, cost reduction, environmental
Almost complete	All but -	Investment	Cost reduction
Partial	HQ functions	N/a	N/a
Partial	HQ, banking	Deposit office	
Almost complete	All but -	Investment	Expansion

of financial and producer service employment upon the north-south dimension of the overall spatial division of labour within Britain. Much of the evidence used in this final section is anecdotal. Nevertheless, it seems to suggest that in many ways the growth engendered by the expansion of financial and producer services in provincial cities may well become self-generating.

The growing importance of financial and producer service employment within local and regional labour markets

One of the most important impacts of financial and producer service growth within the leading provincial centres of Britain has been the growing prominence of financial and producer service firms as employers. Between 1974 and 1984 the proportion of total employment that was within financial and producer service industries increased in every one of the leading financial centres in Britain. On average these industries accounted for almost 12 per cent of total employment within the leading provincial centres in 1984, compared to only 8 per cent in 1974. In 1984 financial and producer service industries were of above-average significance as employers in Bootle (26 per cent of total employment), Birmingham (20 per cent), Glasgow (18 per cent), London (16 per cent), Manchester (16 per cent), Edinburgh (15 per cent), Bristol (15 per cent), Bournemouth (14 per cent), Southend (14 per cent) and Brighton (13 per cent).

The multiplier impacts of financial and producer service employment growth within provincial centres

The growth of financial and producer service employment within provincial centres has had a wide range of beneficial impacts upon the local and regional economies in which they are based. These include the direct multiplier effects that result from increased corporate and employee spending and from the agency role that financial and producer service firms play in generating economic growth.

The increasing prominence of financial and producer service firms within provincial centres has significantly boosted the demand for ancillary services such as printing and publishing, temporary employment agencies, courier services, etc. The growing number of financial and producer service and ancillary firms in provincial centres has had a marked impact upon office rental values in provincial centres. Financial and producer service firms generate a quite specific type of demand for office space in that they prefer to occupy modern premises in central locations. The relative paucity of this type of property within provincial centres (Chesterton Research Department, 1988) has placed considerable upward pressure on rental values. Indeed, rental values are increasing to the level where the speculative funding of office developments will become increasingly economically viable within provincial centres, a phenomenon that has been of relatively little importance in provincial centres to date. This will have major beneficial impacts for the construction industry in these centres.

A further benefit to arise from the increased level of financial activity in the provincial centres derives from the multiplier effects of employee spending. The labour employed by financial and producer service firms is predominantly highly skilled and well renumerated. For example, an occupational breakdown of 18 leading accountancy firms in the UK in 1986 revealed that of the 39,500 employed, over 84 per cent were classified as 'professional staff' (*The Accountant*, 1986). Other financial and producer service firms such as corporate lawyers and commercial-property agencies similarly comprise relatively-high proportions of highly-qualified labour (Farmbrough and Jenkins, 1987; Leyshon, Thrift and Daniels, 1987). It should also be noted that the ratio of professional to support staff within the offices of multi-locational financial and producer service firms would appear not to vary spatially. This is important, for highly-qualified labour within producer service firms enjoy levels of remuneration that are much higher than average. Spending by well-renumerated, high-status staff within financial and producer service firms will have beneficial effects upon local markets of property, goods and services (for example, see Thrift, Leyshon and Daniels, 1987).

In addition to the very real impacts made by financial and producer service firms by way of corporate and employee spending, the increasing concentration of these firms within provincial centres may also be encouraging economic growth through the agency services they perform for capital. It is widely acknowledged by local financial and producer service firms that the in-migration of financial and producer service conglomerates has made a significant contribution to the increasing sophistication of many provincial financial centres. This is perceived as beneficial not only to the local firms themselves, who increasingly pick up referrals from larger firms, but it is also held to be beneficial to the wider regional economy. In northern centres this is seen to be of particular importance: 'It is not just that there is more profitable work for all of us. The fact that good professional advice and expertise is available locally helps keep the head offices and the decision-making here' (Lawyer with Yorkshire corporate legal practice, quoted in Hamilton Fazey, 1987c, p.5). The diminution of head offices and decision-making in the north (see Chapter 6) is in fact less to do with the degree of sophistication of the financial centres there than the short-term profit-seeking attitude of the large institutional investors who have actively encouraged the recent merger and acquisition boom in Britain (Scouller, 1987), and therefore also the process of capital centralization, by willingly selling their major shareholdings in British capital for the premiums offered by acquiring companies.

In another way, the increasing sophistication of the financial communities may well be bolstering the north's possession of key functions within the overall social division of production. Most venture-capital funds for new business operations in Britain are still by and large raised in the south for use by new ventures in the south (Mason, 1987). The bias towards the south holds true even for government-sponsored funding projects such as the Business Expansion Scheme (BES) (Mason and Harrison, 1987). Mason and Harrison suggest that one of the reasons for the lack of BES funds for new projects in peripheral regions may be the result of geographical biases in the risk perceptions of South-East-based fund managers, biases that discriminate against projects outside the buoyant economy of the south.

However, the burgeoning financial communities of provincial centres are rapidly developing local sources of venture funding that would overcome such a bias. Financial-service firms recognize that it is very much in their interest to encourage the growth of new firms so that sufficient management functions are retained to generate enough demand for the financial and business services they sell. Although Investors in Industry (3i) – the venture-capital organization owned by the clearing banks and the Bank of England – remains the most prominent organization of this type within Britain as a whole (Harris, 1988), it is facing increasing competition from a series of more localized venture-capital groups even within the provincial centres of the north. For example, take the case of Newcastle, where 3i's more recent competitors include 'Northern Industries, a £5m fund formed in 1984 as a private sector replacement for the government's wound-down British Technology Group, and the £5.25m Northumbria Unit Trust, one of Lazard's regional funds. Soon, the Newcastle office of Penny Easton will be launching a fund for equity deals under £50,000' (Hamilton Fazey, 1987d, p.3). This in a city that has not been noted for its entrepreneurial successes in the past. Similar examples may be found in many of the other provincial centres of the north. The development of local sources of venture capital such as these is considered to be essential for filling the 'equity gap' of under £250,000, which is below the threshold level of investment set by City of London venture-capital funds, a factor that is thought to explain the current paucity of small rapid-growth firms in the regions of the north (Mason, 1987).

In addition, the influx of the branch offices of larger financial organizations is allowing provincial centres to retain a local interest in larger financing deals that otherwise would have gone to London. For example, witness the comments of a Manchester-based director of the County NatWest investment bank:

> There comes a point when a transaction is too large for any of the locally represented investment banks to handle independently. Instead of sitting back and seeing that transaction directed to London, a number of development capitalists in Manchester get together and we now see local syndication of the large deals.
>
> (quoted in *Investors Chronicle*, 1987, p.12)

This may be particularly important in the case of large deals such as management buyouts. These deals have the added advantage for provincial financial-service firms in that they often increase the level of local decision-making within industry, a factor that is seen as crucial for the generation of future business. For example, County NatWest took advantage of the increasing sophistication of the Leeds financial community in its syndication of a £1.5 million management buyout of Holliday Dyes and Chemicals: 'It took a big risk here, buying 71 per cent of the equity itself and then selling it down to other investors. Something most observers would have thought inconceivable in an English region only a year ago' (Hamilton Fazey, 1987e, p.3).

These advances in corporate finance within provincial centres may hold out hope for an increasing level of local autonomy in industrial activity within the northern regions in particular. However, perhaps of more immediate significance for local levels of employment within such regions, the increasingly international character of the larger financial and producer service firms based in provincial cities may also be helping to attract overseas production units to the north through the agency services such firms provide to multinational capital. For example, in the four months between December 1986 and April 1987 three large overseas banks, two Japanese and one West German, opened offices in Manchester. The openings were stimulated both by a desire to penetrate local corporate finance markets and to promote foreign direct investment in the north of England (Hamilton Fazey, 1987f). The Japanese banks, especially, see Manchester as a regional financial centre within which they can act as gatekeepers to Japanese investment flowing into the north of England.

Therefore, financial and producer service firms based in provincial centres may be helping to boost employment levels, while also acting to improve the quality of such employment, by encouraging the growth of indigenous business through its corporate finance activities. Moreover, these firms may also be helping the effectiveness of industry by improving the quality of advice available in provincial centres, although of course this is an unmeasurable effect. A further point to consider in this context is the impact that the employment within financial and producer service firms actually has upon the overall spatial division of labour within Britain.

Corporate control and the spatial division of labour within financial and producer service firms

In recent years the concentration and centralization of capital within Britain has resulted in an increasing spatial polarization of social class. As the controlling functions within the overall social division of production have become increasingly concentrated within the south of the country, principally as a result of merger and acquisition activity, but also through a greater level of new-firm formation in the south, so managerial, professional and administrative occupations have become increasingly concentrated within the occupational structure of employment there (Massey, 1984; 1988). At the same time, these high-status occupations have become less important within the occupational structure of employment within northern regions. The increase in financial and producer service firms within the provincial cities of the north would seem to have had an ambiguous effect upon the general trend by which northern regions in general have lost key determining functions within the economy.

On the one hand, it is undoubtedly true that the growth of the offices of large multinational financial and producer service conglomerates within the provincial cities of the north has itself contributed to the extension of corporate control over financial and producer service activity. In this sense, the growth in the office networks of these large firms throughout the leading provincial centres can be seen as a way in which the influence of the City of London is being extended throughout the regional economies, and in this sense provincial financial centres are being increasingly integrated with national and even international financial markets. In addition, through the process of office decentralization, financial and producer service firms may even reinforce the growing spatial division of labour by relocating only the most routinized and low-wage functions within the overall work process (Boddy, Lovering and Bassett, 1986; Nelson, 1986).

However, it is also clear that an important component of financial and producer service growth has been the result of the resurgence of local firms. These firms freely acknowlege the role played by the influx of offices of larger firms in bringing a new financial 'respectability' to provincial centres that has in turn rubbed off on indigenous financial and producer service firms. Moreover, it is a notable feature of financial and producer service firms that their branch operations are endowed with levels of operational autonomy much greater than is normally the case in other sectors of the economy (Bertrand and Noyelle, 1986). This is because the success of financial services is 'increasingly dependent on product customization and individualized relationships with clients i.e. the production of a service has become far less important than its effective distribution and refinement. Tailoring sales or product development to client needs involves more autonomy, responsibility and decentralized decision-making than is typical for production' (Daniels, 1987, p.436). The relatively high degree of latitude afforded to the branch operations of financial and producer service firms has helped contribute to the growing functional cohesiveness of provincial financial centres as illustrated by the anecdotal examples presented above. The degree of operational independence does vary between sector, dependent upon the dominant form of organizational structure, with autonomy being highest where firms are organized as partnerships, as, for example, in the case of accountancy practices, while rather less independence is ceded to the branch operations of private or public limited companies, as, for example, investment banks.

Therefore, the malign local impacts that are commonly associated with the spread of the corporate economy in other sectors is not necessarily apparent within the financial and producer services sector. They pay higher than average levels of remuneration to the large numbers of professional staff they employ, which are passed into the local economy through employee spending. Furthermore, these firms possess relatively high levels of functional autonomy, enabling them to retain a greater degree of self-determination over their development than is the case for branch units within other sectors of the economy.

Conclusion

We have revealed that the leading provincial financial centres in Britain have, for the most part, enjoyed quite rapid growth in financial-service employment since the mid-1970s. Although the fastest-growing centres tended to be located in the south, northern provincial centres, too, experienced widespread employment growth within these industries. Employment growth was seen to be the result of three important processes. First, the expansion of indigenous financial and producer service firms; second, the in-migration of the offices of large multi-locational financial and producer service firms; and third, the decentralization of operating divisions of such firms from Central London. However, whereas the first two demand-led processes were of equal importance within both northern and southern centres, the third process was virtually exclusive to southern-based provincial centres. This has important implications for the creation of a spatial dichotomy between northern and southern centres in their ability to engage in the export of financial and producer services, either directly or indirectly (Coffey and Polese, 1987). Nevertheless, the growth of financial and producer service employment has meant that these industries have become increasingly important as employers, both within provincial centres and within the region in which the centres are based, and have conferred considerable economic benefits to local economies in both north and south.

We have paid particular attention to the expansion of large multi-locational financial and producer service firms into the major provincial financial centres of Britain, and this phenomenon has been an important component of producer service employment growth within such locations. The unique combination of autonomous operational behaviour linked to an ability to draw on the resources of a multinational service conglomerate has enabled these firms to penetrate regional markets successfully for financial and producer services. In doing so, the increased scale and scope of activity associated with their entry has also benefited indigenous financial and producer service firms who, where not in direct competition with the multi-locational organizations, have profited from the rising level of financial activity performed in provincial centres. There is more than a little justification in drawing a broad parallel between producer service employment growth in provincial financial centres and the growth in employment from the microelectronics industry in central Scotland: both provincial financial centres and 'Silicon Glen' have experienced employment growth through the in-migration of large multi-locational organizations. Moreover, just as Silicon Glen has reached a point of 'take-off' as an assembly point for imported components for redistribution in the international economy (Cooke, Morgan and Jackson, 1984), so the recent growth in and of provincial financial centres looks set to forge their full integration with the international financial system. However, unlike Silicon Glen, where employment is predominantly unskilled female labour working within the branch plants of US multinational corporations, the developing articulation of provincial financial centres in the world economy will be much more independent and will stimulate employment growth characteristic of the top end of the occupation hierarchy. There is increasing evidence to suggest that the influx of offices of international financial and producer service firms in provincial financial centres will soon breach London's virtual monopoly on the organization of cross-border business in financial and producer services. There will be a much greater integration of the 'local' and the 'international' in the organization of capital and informational flows, as financial and producer service firms in provincial financial centres respond to the growing international activities of regionally-based capital by allowing them direct access to the international financial system without recourse to London-based firms. The ability of financial and producer service firms directly to access the international financial system is greatly enhanced by the development and application of information-technology systems that have dramatically increased the locational flexibility of financial-service firms in particular.

However, it would be wrong to overstate the long-term role of local financial and producer service firms in this scenario. Although many local firms are currently thriving, many are doing so because of the limited geographical expansion of large London-based practices within particular sectors. The corporate lawyers are a case in point.

In addition, it is unlikely that all the leading provincial centres will continue to benefit from the growth of such activities. There is evidence to suggest that there is a process of regional centralization underway that is pushing just one centre in a region to prominence above all others. This process is most clearly evident amongst northern centres. For example, Leeds is increasingly becoming the financial centre for Yorkshire & Humberside and the Northern region and some large accountancy firms have even located national departments within the city. In this respect it is weakening the relative importance of the sub-regional centres of both Newcastle and Sheffield. Leeds is in battle with Manchester for the title of the provincial financial centre of the entire north of England. Manchester would seem to be better placed in this larger arena given its wider range of financial institutions and its ability to suck in functions from Liverpool. Liverpool seems to be in terminal decline as a regional financial centre, as it is outpaced by it larger rival. Similar examples of regional centralization can be seen elsewhere. Birmingham is growing rapidly, while Nottingham and Leicester experience relative stagnation. Bristol is the dominant centre for the West Country, and to a large extent for south Wales too. Despite the rapid growth in financial producer service employment in Cardiff (especially between 1981 and 1984), the city still lacks any important base of local financial institutions. More than any other large sub-regional centre, financial and producer service employment growth in Cardiff has been dependent upon the expansion of multi-locational organizations. The paucity of local control over financial institutions is illustrated by the fact that even the Commercial Bank of Wales is owned by the Bank of Scotland (*Euromoney*, 1988). Nevertheless, as property prices in Bristol continue to spiral, there is at least the chance that Cardiff may benefit from short-distance relocation across the Bristol Channel.

This chapter has illustrated that the common depiction of the north-south divide as an exclusively prosperous 'south' and permanently depressed 'north' is over simplistic, given that in some sectors at least northern localities have been centres of rapid employment growth and have enjoyed economic benefits such expansion brings with it. Nevertheless, as spatial centralization among northern centres proceeds, those pockets of relative economic wealth in the north will become even more concentrated around only a few, key, metropolitan areas. Moreover, it would seem likely that the future growth of financial and producer service employment will be largely concentrated within the south. This is because of the continued reluctance of decentralizing firms to move their operations out of the south and also because the most buoyant areas of new economic growth also tend to be confined to the south. In particular, the growth of new firms in 'Silicon Fen' is encouraging financial and producer services firms to move into Cambridge, especially in order to establish early client links with 'up and coming' companies, while the same motivation underlies the dramatic influx of financial and producer service firms into Swindon (Bassett, 1988; Hodson, 1988).

The continued viability of provincial financial centres throughout Britain is ultimately related to the demand for their services from their principal clients, i.e. the corporate sector. There is a clear symbiotic relationship between the level of corporate sector decision-making activity and the level of financial and producer service employment within an area, since the latter functions are in essence an extended form of the management division of labour (Gillespie and Green, 1987). As such the rate at which the processes of capital concentration and centralization are depleting northern regions of key decision-making functions would seem to be of fundamental importance for the future viability of many northern centres. Hence the enthusiasm of local financiers and professionals for local sources of venture capital. However, the prospect that new northern firms will come through at sufficient speed to counterbalance the rate at which existing firms are being absorbed by large organizations is not a hopeful one. This will inevitably cast doubt upon the ultimate long-term functional importance of the northern financial centre.

Acknowledgements

Andrew Leyshon gratefully acknowledges the bridging finance provided by Bristol University, which enabled him to remain in his post while this paper was written and researched.

Notes

1. There are necessary caveats to be attached to any analysis of the occupational data of the Census of Population. First, employees are classified purely by occupation, and cross-analysis by industry is possible only at high levels of spatial aggregation. It is important, therefore, to appreciate that what we have defined as financial and producer service occupations may not necessarily be located within financial and producer service firms. For example, certified accountants are predominantly employed within industry while chartered accountants may also be employed in industry and in public practices. 'Taxation experts', meanwhile, include not only those engaged in private practice but also civil servants employed by the Board of Inland Revenue.
2. Although other studies of financial-service employment limit the sector to banking and bill discounting, insurance and other financial institutions (for example, Draper *et al.*, 1988), we have also classified accountancy services as a 'pure' financial service since the mainstay of accountancy practice remains the adjudication of financial exchange (Leyshon, Daniels and Thrift, 1987).
3. Throughout this chapter Department of Employment data is analysed at the Amalgamated Office Employment Area (AOA) level. The exception to this rule was London. The metropolitan area was analysed in its entirety given the difficulty of separating out functionally-independent sub-areas of the city.
4. There are two main problems with the variable used to represent 'consumer demand'. First, the number of employees within the relevant TTWA may, in fact, understate the number of people using the centre for financial and producer services. A further problem arises in the use of employees in employment only. This excludes people who may in fact exercise a demand for financial services but be outside employment - for example, pensioners with investment income. The use of the 'business demand' variable is also problematic. First, the use of county-based data means that for some centres - Leeds and Bradford, Birmingham and Coventry - the values are replicated. Moreover, the county GDP figures are calculated from nation-level data and reduced geographically on a pro rata basis related to industrial structure, incomes and earnings. Even beyond this there are problems, as, for

example, in the exclusion of the demand generated by the incomes of commuters in their places of residence. These are instead apportioned to their places of work (for full details, see CSO, 1988).

REFERENCES

The Accountant (1986) 'Touche and Spicers surge in boom years for all firms', 26 June, pp. 14–16.

The Accounting Bulletin (1983) 'Big firms on the move', August, pp. 8–9.

Alexander, S. (1987) 'Lawyers on the mark', *Financial Times Survey, Bristol as a Financial Centre*, 26 November, p. 7.

The Banker (1981) 'Foreign banks with offices outside London', November, p. 113.

Bassett, K. (1988) *Economic Change in the Sun-belt Service Sector Growth and Employment Change in the Swindon Economy*, Department of Geography, University of Bristol (mimeo).

Bavishi, V.B. and Wyman, H.E. (1983) *Who Audits the World?*, School of Business Administration, University of Connecticut.

Bertrand, O. and Noyell, T.J. (1986) *Changing Technology, Skills and Skill Formation in French, German, Japanese, Swedish and US Financial Service Firms: Preliminary Findings*, Report to the Center for Educational Research and Innovation, OECD, Paris and New York.

Beyers, W.B., Tofflemeire, J.M., Stranahan, H.A. and Johnson, E.G. (1986), *The Service Economy, Understanding Growth in the Central Puget Sound Region*, Central Puget Sound Economic Development District, Seattle, Wash.

Boddy, M., Lovering, J. and Bassett, K. (1986) *Sunbelt City?: A Study of Economic Change in Britain's M4 Growth Corridor*, Clarendon Press, Oxford.

Central Statistical Office (1988) 'Regional accounts 1986, Part 2', *Economic Trends*, Vol. 410, pp. 100–5.

Champion, A., Green. A. and Owen D. (1987) 'Housing, labour mobility and unemployment', *The Planner*, Vol. 73, no. 4, pp. 11–16.

Chesterton Research Department (1988) 'The explosion in provincial office rents', *Perspectives*, February/March, pp. 8–9.

The City Directory (1984–5), Woodhead Faulkner, London.

Coffey, W.J. and Polese, M. (1987) 'Trade and location of producer services: a Canadian perspective', *Environment and Planning A*, Vol. 19, pp. 597–611.

Cooke, P., Morgan, K. and Jackson, D. (1984) 'New technology and regional development in austerity Britain: the case of the semi-conductor industry', *Regional Studies*, Vol. 18, pp. 277–89.

Coopers & Lybrand (undated) *Relocation Trends in the Financial Services Sector*, Hampshire Development Corporation, Winchester.

Crawford's Directory of City Connections (1986), Economist Publications, London.

Daniels, P. (1987) 'The geography of services', *Progress in Human Geography*, Vol. 11, pp. 333–47.

Draper, P., Smith, F., Stewart, W. and Hood, N. (1988) *The Scottish Financial Sector*, Edinburgh University Press.

Edwards, J. (1988) 'Focus on the dumb-bell', *Financial Times Weekend*, 30 April, p. 5.

Euromoney (1987) 'The power league', February, pp. 85–95.

Euromoney (1988) 'Scotland: a step ahead', *Euromoney Supplement*, April.

Farmbrough, H. and Jenkins, I. (1987) 'Big Bang starts the age of legal giants', *Financial Weekly*, 5 February, p. 7.

Fennell, E. (1987a) 'High-fliers look to the North', *The Times*, 7 May.

Fennell, E. (1987b) 'All aglow in Glasgow', *The Times*, 9 April.

Gillespie, A.B. and Green, A.E. (1987) 'The changing geography of producer services employment in Britain', *Regional Studies*, Vol. 21, pp. 397–412.

Hamilton Fazey, I. (1987a) 'Local firms thrive among the internationals', *Financial Times Survey: Sheffield*, 13 March, p. 4.

Hamilton Fazey, I. (1987b) 'Financial and professional services: centre of gravity in Manchester', *Financial Times Survey: North West England*, 29 October, p. 3.

Hamilton Fazey, I. (1987c) 'Financial and professional services: a remarkable growth of strategic importance', *Financial Times Survey: Yorkshire and Humberside*, 29 July, p. 5.

Hamilton Fazey, I. (1987d) 'Behind the nappies', *Financial Times Survey: Northern England*, 30 November, p. 3.

Hamilton Fazey, I. (1987e) 'Venture capital: many players in a growing game', *Financial Times Survey: Yorkshire and Humberside*, 29 July, p. 3.

Hamilton Fazey, I. (1987f) 'Japanese Investment: banks give a boost', *Financial Times Survey: North West England*, 29 October, p. 4.

Harris, D. (1988) 'British MBOs still thriving', *Euromoney Supplement*, April, pp. 25–6.

Hausner, V.A. (1987) (ed.) *Urban Economic Change: Five City Studies*, Clarendon Press, Oxford.

Hodson, R. (1988) 'The professionals' arrival will change the skyline', *Financial Times Survey: Swindon*, 11 May, p. 3.

Howells, J. and Green, A.E. (1988) *Technological Innovation, Structural Change and Location in UK Services*, Gower, Aldershot.

Investors Chronicle (1987) 'New merchant bank breaks the mould', *Investors Chronicle Survey: Greater Manchester*, 9 October, p. 16.

Jones Lang Wootton (1987a) *The Decentralisation of Offices from Central London*, Jones Lang Wootton Technical Paper, London.

Kennedy, C. (1988) 'Industrial journey: Manchester and Sussex', *The Director*, March, pp. 54–7.

Leyshon, A., Daniels, P. and Thrift, N. (1987) *Large Accountancy Firms in the UK: Operational Adaption and Spatial Development*, Working Papers in Producer Services no. 2, St David's University College, Lampeter, and University of Liverpool.

Leyshon, A., Thrift, N. and Daniels, P. (1987) *Large Commercial Property Firms in the UK: The Operational Development and Spatial Expansion of General Practice Firms of Chartered Surveyors*, Working Papers in Producer Services no. 5, University of Bristol and University of Liverpool.

Marshall, J.N. (ed.) (1988) *Uneven Development in the Service Economy: Understanding the Location and Role of Producer Services*, Oxford University Press.

Mason, C. (1987) 'Venture capital in the United Kingdom: a geographical perspective', *National Westminster Bank Quarterly Review*, May, pp. 47–59.

Mason, C. and Harrison, R.T. (1987) 'The regional impact of the Business Expansion Scheme', Paper presented at the Tenth National Small Firms Policy and Research Conference, Cranfield Institute of Technology, 19–21 November.

Massey, D. (1984) *Spatial Divisions of Labour: Social Structures and the Geography of Production*, Macmillan, London.

Massey, D. (1988) 'A new class of geography', *Marxism Today*, May, pp. 12–17.

Morgan, K. (1986b) 'Re-industrialisation in peripheral Britain: state policy, the space economy and industrial innovation', in R.L. Martin and R.E. Rowthorn (eds.) *The Geography of De-industrialisation*, Macmillan, London.

Morris, J. (1986) *The Internationalisation of Banking, Technological Change and Spatial Patterns: A Case Study in South Wales*, Department of Business and Economics, UWIST, Cardiff (mimeo).

Moss, M.L. and Dunau, A. (1986) *The Location of Back-offices: Emerging Trends and Development Patterns*, Sylvan Lawrence Research and Data Center, New York University, NY.

Nelson, K. (1986) 'Labour demand, labour supply and the suburbanisation of low-wage office work', in A.J. Scott and M. Slorper (eds.) *Production, Work, Territory*, The Geographical Anatomy of Industrial Capitalism, Allen & Unwin, Boston, Mass.

New Earnings Survey (1985) Department of Employment, London.

Pensions Management (1987) 'The survey: fund managers performance – surviving the squall?', *Pensions Management*, December, pp. 51–79.

Reed, H.C. (1981) *The Pre-Eminence of International Financial Centres*, Praeger, New York, NY.

Reeves, R. (1987a) 'Financial and legal services: attracting inward investment', *The Financial Times Survey: Norwich*, 9 July, p. 36.

Reeves, R. (1987b) 'Home-grown industry is expanding on all fronts', *The Financial Times Survey: Norwich*, 9 July, p. 33.

Scooder, J. (1987) 'The United Kingdom merger boom in perspective', *The NatWest Review*, April, pp. 14–30.

SEEDS Association (1987) *South-South Divide*, South East Economic Development Strategy, Stevenage.

Thrift, N. and Leyshon, A. (1988) 'The gambling propensity: banks, developing country debt exposures and the New International Financial System', *Geoforum*, Vol. 19, pp. 55–60.

Thrift, N. Leyshon, A. and Daniels, P. (1987) *Sexy Greedy: The New International Financial System, the City of London and the South East of England*, Working Papers on Producer Services no. 8. University of Bristol and University of Liverpool.

van Dinteren, J.H.J. (1987) 'The role of business-service offices in the economy of medium-sized cities', *Environment and Planning A*, Vol. 19, pp. 669–86.

Part II
Switzerland

[8]

Excerpt from Max Iklé, *Switzerland: An International Banking and Financial Center*, 3–30.

1 The Origin of the Swiss Financial Center

1. *Historical Background*

Switzerland is an Alpine country. Its development and existence is inextricably bound up with its location in the Alps. From time immemorial, populations dwelling among mountains have been inspired by a desire for freedom and independence; this was the case not only in Switzerland, but in neighboring Tyrol as well. These people do not want to be subjects, so the countries Schwyz, Uri, and Unterwalden, refused to tolerate foreign rulers as early as the thirteenth century.

With the opening of the Gotthard pass, the inhabitants of the valleys beneath this vital Alpine passageway moved into the focus of history. The strategic importance of the Alpine passages made it advisable for the potentates of Europe to be on good terms with the people dwelling at the entrance to the Gotthard, who obtained the first Charters from the German Emperors at an early time. But this did not by any means mark the beginning of peaceful development. For more than two centuries the Confederates had to defend their freedom and independence in numerous wars, and it was not until the Peace of Westphalia that their independence was definitely recognized.

Later it was in the interest of the great powers of Europe that the passes across the Alps be in the hands of an independent small nation, for if one great power had taken possession of them, it would have gained a dominant position. Thus Switzerland became the warder of the Alpine passageways, and she has continued in this role of trustee up to the present day even though the strategic importance of the passes has declined.

The Gotthard pass is protected by German-speaking inhabitants of the valleys to the north, and by Italian-speaking people dwelling in the valleys to the south. At the foot of the Great St. Bernard pass we find a French-speaking population, and around the roads leading up to the Graubuenden passes live Romansh-speaking people. A common task and common ideals brought German-speaking, French-speaking, Italian-speaking, and Romansh-speaking Swiss together, first in a loose alliance, and eventually in the Swiss Confederation. The common intellectual outlook proved stronger than the ties by which language linked them to the great cultural centers of Europe.

The bravery of the Swiss warriors was common knowledge in the Middle Ages. Even their few defeats contributed to their fame. In the late Middle Ages it was no longer necessary to defend the independence of the country by force of arms, but the warrior's spirit was still very much alive among the Swiss, and since the homeland could not provide a living for all of its sons, they emigrated in order to serve in foreign armies. At that time there were Swiss regiments on all the battlefields of Europe. The French kings, the German princes, and the Italian dukes thought it highly important to be able to hire Swiss mercenaries. The kings of France and the Popes placed themselves under the protection of Swiss guards on whose loyalty and dependability they could count. At the sack of Rome, on May 6, 1527, the Papal guards defended the Pope, suffering heavy casualties, and in the fight for the Tuileries on August 10, 1792, the Swiss guards had first to be overpowered before the French revolutionaries could lay hands on the king. The retreat of Napoleon's great army at the Berezina proceeded under the cover of Swiss battalions.

On May 20, 1815, at the Vienna Congress, the permanent neutrality of Switzerland was formally recognized as being in the interest of Europe. Up to the present day, this neutrality has been the guideline of Swiss foreign policy. It was respected by the Great Powers in both World Wars. To be sure, neutrality would have remained a dead letter had it not been protected by an efficient army. In relation to her size Switzerland has one of the strongest armies in the world. Within 48 hours an army of more than half a million men armed with modern equipment can be mobilized. Every Swiss must serve in the army. His service as a newly enlisted man lasts four months; then, over a period of eight years, he has to report each year for three weeks' routine military duty. The Swiss citizen army is firmly rooted in the minds of the people. Those who have higher education are as a rule willing to serve longer, with a view to becoming officers. After having gone through his training as a recruit, every Swiss soldier takes his rifle and military equipment to his home. Hardly ever has the weapon been misued for other purposes. This helps to make a swift mobilization possible. In the army the young soldier also gets some education toward his future life as a citizen. The fact that political life in Switzerland is more composed than in most other countries is due in no small measure to the military training the young men receive.

It was against this background that Switzerland as a financial center developed. The country, which for centuries performed the function of trustee in its capacity as a guardian of the Alpine passes, later performed the same function in other capacities. Neutrality, which the surrounding nations recognized and Switzerland protected by force of arms, secured peace for the country, although not without considerable sacrifice. The democratic tradition, which is centuries old, the successful solution of the problems of languages and national minorities, and in recent times, we may well add, the prevailing peace on the labor front, all helped create that atmosphere of confidence which is the most important prerequisite for the rise of a financial center.

2. *Geneva as Banking Center*

Geneva may well be called the oldest banking center among Swiss cities. This may be connected with the fact that in Basel and Zurich, guild laws hampered economic development. It is true that the Calvinism of Geneva did little to encourage the growth of banking activities–witness the fact that it forbade lending money at interest rates exceeding 6 2/3% at a time when the city of Geneva could raise funds only at 10%. In 1580 an attempt to establish a bank failed, characteristically, because of the objections of pastors. Thus, even in Geneva there was no trace of an autochthonous bank until the middle of the seventeenth century. In 1698 Benedict Turretini was the first to be listed as a banker in notarized records, and by 1709 we find nearly a dozen bankers whose names were to become highly famous in the financial history of Geneva–names such as Tronchin, Saladin, Caladini, Lullin and Marcet, Pictet, Boissier, Mallet, Debary, and Cramer.

During the Spanish War of Succession, Geneva as a financial center was already deeply immersed in the crosscurrents of financial events. The Allies were unable to beat France into submission, for Louis XIV managed again and again to secure the financial means for continuing the war. As suppliers of funds, Amsterdam and Geneva played a significant role. At that time government borrowing existed only in the form of loans with interest in perpetuity; short-term or medium-term financing on the market was still unknown. The banker acted as intermediary between the king and the private money lenders; in this business he operated as an independent contracting party. At the time of

Louis XIV, Samuel Bernard, in particular, was in a key position as a banker as he was in close contact with the French Minister of Finance, Chamillart. During the economic embargo of France, Jaques Henri Huguetan, a French refugee from religious persecution, came to Geneva to ensure continued contact with the Geneva bankers. Huguetan, who stayed in Geneva for two years, was able to obtain a monopolistic position as a fund-raising agent for the French Crown. He raised money at interest rates between 7 and 10%, and lent it out at 10 to 12%. But in many cases even higher profits could be reaped, for the French War Minister was willing to allow up to 35% discount whenever urgently needed funds were placed at his disposal three months earlier than had been agreed upon.

Our information is incomplete concerning the sums of money involved at that time. It has been estimated that the Spanish War of Succession cost the French King 7 million livres a month, nearly one half of which was financed through Geneva over a period of several years.

In 1709 the inevitable financial crisis took place. Bernard, for example, went bankrupt, his balance sheet showing a deficit of 38 million livres.[1] Huguetan had disappeared from Geneva even earlier.

Geneva was hard hit by the insolvency of the royal banker. The banking firm of Lullin and Marcet was the first victim. Many citizens of Geneva, through the intermediary of the firm, had bought bonds issued by Bernard and had invested their savings with the bank. In the spring of 1710 the Geneva Board of Two Hundred suspended those members unable to pay their debts. Among these were names of high standing in Geneva. Many of them subsequently moved to Paris where they thought they had a better chance to defend their claims against Bernard or the Crown. Thus in the years 1714-1716, 44 bankers from Geneva or Switzerland lived in Paris, some of them rising to great prominence later. Nearly all of them were subsequently drawn into the vortex of the John Law transactions.[2]

[1] Stelling-Michaud, Deux aspects du rôle financier de Genève pendant la Guerre de succession d'Espagne, *Bulletin de la Société d'Histoire et d'Archéologie de Genève*, Tome VI, Livraison 2.

[2] The core of John Law's "system" was the foundation of a big colonial company on the English pattern. The company issued shares that could be exchanged against government securities. In this way the whole public debt was to be converted, in due course, into shares of the Société des Indes. The operation went into the history of finance under the name of "Mississippi." At the same time a National Bank, the Banque Royale, was established. It was given the right to issue notes, to collect tax payments, and to administer the public debt. The shares of the Colonial Company were offered on the market in successive issues, first at par, then above par. Their price was driven up so effectively that on November 29, 1719, the total stock was valued on the stock exchange at 4.8 billion livres, while the nominal stock equity was 312 million livres. This could only be achieved by issuing notes in the amount of 1.2 billion livres within a single year. In 1720 when it was found necessary to

Repercussions of the "Law system" on Geneva as a financial center were manifold. Some of the Geneva bankers in Paris ran into difficulties and this had its effects on Swiss firms in Lyon. The banks, to be sure, were fairly well posted by their informers about the events in Paris, with the result that many could in time get rid of the shares of the Société des Indes. But the transfer of the profits that had accrued in Paris encountered difficulties as the value of the French livre in Geneva began to decline. Whereas in January, 1720, the exchange rate of the Geneva currency in relation to the French livre still had been in the neighborhood of 220, it rose to between 1200 and 1300 before August, with the result that book profits were wiped out.

In the years 1720-21 Geneva experienced a full-fledged liquidity crisis. Nobody had enough cash and there were a number of bankruptcies. Reputable merchants had to come to terms with their creditors.

After the Law crisis had been overcome, Geneva as a financial center developed in a satisfactory manner. Not the least important among the contributing factors were the useful contacts the bankers had established all over the world. Many of these "contacts" were Huguenots, with whom ties of family relationship existed. Correspondents, many of whom were themselves natives of Geneva, were kept at all important places. Thus Pan-Cramer wrote in 1763, "Je crois qu'il n'y a pas un coin sur la terre où l'on ne trouve un Genevois." At that time, besides the bankers in Paris, there were three bankers from Geneva in London, and two in Amsterdam, one in Marseille, and one in Lyon.

After 1770 the Geneva banks oriented themselves more and more toward France. In 1785 one could read in a bank bulletin that since 1771 nearly all capital from Geneva had been invested in France. And not all of this capital had its origin in Geneva, some of it had originated in other parts of Switzerland, or even in Germany. In 1789 a banker in Lyon expressed warnings in regard to this too large-scale, one-sided investment.[3]

As has already been mentioned, the French Crown at that time obtained its financial resources mainly by issuing rent-bearing bonds. Originally, rents in perpetuity had dominated the field. Later, rents for life, at interest rates about double those of the rents in perpetuity, came to be used more and more. At first the terms under which the rent could be purchased were made dependent on the purchaser's age; later this principle was replaced by a uniform rent based on the assumption of an average remaining life expectancy of 15 years. By an ingenious device the Geneva bankers managed to turn the obvious weaknesses of the

curb the inflation and to demand supplementary payments from the shareholders, the house of cards collapsed. Only by fleeing to Amsterdam could Law rescue himself from the Bastille, into which his collaborators disappeared. (Luethy Herbert, *La banque protestante en France*, Vol. I, p. 280ff.)

[3] Sayon André, *La banque à Genève pendant les XVIe, XVIIe, et XVIIIe siècles.*

system to their advantage. They picked 30 young girls who had survived infantile diseases and bought French rents on their names. Then they sold these rents to their customers. The healthy climate of Geneva and the hygienic conditions in the city, which were relatively good for those times, contributed to making these Geneva rents particularly attractive. In due course groups of customers who were interested in these rents formed investment partnerships with a view to spreading the risks. The banks were willing to sell the rent-bearing bonds on credit. By signing up for a share in a rent-investment partnership, it was thus theoretically possible without making any payment in cash to acquire a claim to a rent on which one could hope to start collecting actual cash after about 15 years. Around 1780 Geneva's investment in French securities was estimated at more than 100 million livres in Geneva currency, the annual claims for rents amounting to some 12 million livres. So long as one could count on a solvent government and a stable French currency, the system proved to be an excellent business arrangement. But during the American War of Independence, the French Treasury became saddled with a debt so huge that in 1788 rent payments began to slow down. Moreover, there was the decay of the currency. From 1790 to 1794 the exchange rate between the Geneva livre and the French currency unit rose, in fact, from 171 to 500. In 1793 the whole public debt of France was being consolidated into a 5% rent in perpetuity. Owing to the beginning inflation, it lost more and more of its value and, as a result, Geneva moved into a deep financial crisis. The first signs appeared in 1789. An issue in the amount of 20 million livres, which the Geneva banks had taken in as a fixed commitment, could not be sold to the public, and some less seasoned banks that lacked adequate reserves became insolvent. Everybody tried to get rid of the rent-bearing bonds at a time when a reasonable price could still be realized. To finance the rent business, some banks had incurred debt repayable in stable currency. Their clients, however, were no longer in a position to meet their obligations, and so one bank after another defaulted on its payments. The people were quite upset. A search for a culprit set in, and Michel Audéoud, believed to have been the inventor of the so-called "Geneva system," was sentenced to death.

The occupation of Geneva by France in 1798 sharply interrupted the economic development. During the 15 years of French rule, trade, industry, and banking suffered heavily. Reconstruction was not easy. Geneva was cut off from France. The German Customs Union raised new barriers; the textile industry disappeared; only clock and watch making was able to hold its own. The private banks, still the prevailing type in Geneva, financed the export of watches, and they profited from the renewed prosperity of the industry. In 1828, 140 watch manufacturers could be found in Geneva alone. New private banks came into being, many of which have survived up to the present day.[4] Soon the four most prominent banks were operating jointly conducting major business transactions. Their association was named "Quator." Alongside the private banks, other financial institutes arose, such as the Caisse d'Escompte, d'Epargne et de Dépôts in 1789, and in 1816 the Caisse d'Epargne du Canton de Genève, on the pattern of the Bernische Kantonalbank. In the revolution of 1846, James Fazy became a member of the government, and in the years that followed he shaped the fate of Geneva as a financial center. In 1848 he created the Banque de Genève as a Cantonal agency with the right to issue bank notes. Later the bank was transformed into a private institute, with the Canton as the holder of a large portion of the stock. In the same year the Caisse Hypothécaire de Genève came into being. The year 1849 saw the foundation of the Caisse d'Escompte de Genève with a 1-million franc stock equity, and in 1853 Fazy created the Banque Générale Suisse de Crédit International Mobilier et Foncier with a stock equity capital of 25 million francs (only 20% of which was paid in, however)—a universal bank of the type of the French "Banques Mobiliers." But, owing to internal difficulties this ambitiously conceived institute had to be liquidated as early as 1865.

In 1855 the Caisse d'Escompte went out of business and the Comptoir d'Escompte, organized by industrial initiative, with a stock equity capital of 1 million francs (doubled in 1861), took its place.

The Franco-German war of 1870-71 had no adverse effect on the Geneva financial center. Indeed, as a result of the foreign capital flowing into Geneva looking for secure investment opportunities, the banks of Geneva enjoyed considerable prosperity in the ten postwar years. To finance the war indemnity prescribed by the Treaty of Frankfurt, the French Government in the years 1872-73 needed about 5 billion francs. Two fifths of this amount were raised in neutral countries. Geneva was a major participant and this, inevitably, led to some rise in interest rates.

The formation of new banks as joint-stock corporations did not prevent the seasoned private banks from holding their own quite well. This was due in no small measure to the fact that they had a foreign clientele and widespread international contacts. In 1872 the Association Financière grew out of that loose association, the Quator and later, in 1890, it expanded into the Union Financière de Genève. In 1881 several private banks established the Banque Genevoise de Prêts et de Dépôts with a 10-million franc stock equity. This bank also performed the functions of a clearing house and a title search agency. In the middle of the nineteenth century the Geneva stock exchange was created and as

[4] *Histoire de la Banque de Genève*, publiée par le Comptoir d'Escompte de Genève, 1931, p. 21.

early as 1860 private banks in Geneva were advising their clients to buy American railroad shares. Side by side with these agencies, financial companies such as the "Omnium Société Civile Genevoise d'emploi de fonds," founded in 1849, appeared on the scene. The "Omnium" invested in various enterprises such as the Channel of Corinth, and in mines in Rio Tinto. The Union Financière de Genève mentioned above, in which ten major private banks had shares, grew into a full-fledged investment trust and spread its financial engagements over a wide field.

Around the turn of the century the expansion of the Comptoir d'Escompte began; as already mentioned, it had been organized in 1861 as an institute to serve the financial needs of industry. In 1898 the stock equity of the Comptoir was raised to 5 million francs. Three further raises brought the stock equity capitalization up to 15 million in 1911. The Institute had been cooperating with French banks since 1906 and at the beginning of World War I it already had the status of a large-scale bank.

3. *Swiss Bankers Abroad*

The story of the origin of the Swiss financial center would not be complete without a survey of the Swiss bankers and other men of finance who were working in Paris and elsewhere in the eighteenth and the beginning of the nineteenth century.

Bernard, the banker of Louis XIV, had only one serious competitor. That was the banking firm of the three brothers Hogguer. The Höggers, as the name was originally written, were descendants from an old family in St. Gallen. They had migrated to Lyon, where a large Swiss colony, the so-called "Nation Suisse," had settled. In Lyon the people from St. Gallen were at first engaged in the business of selling linen produced in their home town. With the conclusion of the peace treaty with Francis I, trade in linens profited more than any other product from the tariff concessions that had been negotiated in the Treaty. The three brothers Marc-Frédéric, Daniel, and Jean-Jacques, shifted their activities more and more from trade to banking and at the beginning of the eighteenth century they were the owners of a banking firm in Paris. The Höggers succeeded in establishing themselves as suppliers of funds for the King. Essentially, their business transactions consisted in importing silver and having it coined at Strasbourg, Metz, or at some other place where a mint was in operation, with a view to making the coined money available to the King. Considerable profit margins could be earned in such a business. In exchange for the delivered silver coins, the French Crown handed its bankers paper money and short-term bonds, so-called "Assignats"; but only in Paris was the paper money accepted at par value. In Lyon, a "disagio" of 25 percent had to be taken in stride, and after some time the assignats could be traded only at half their nominal value, if at all. Inevitably this created difficulties for the royal bankers who were responsible for the repayment of the funds they had raised to finance the whole business.

But the three Högger brothers were not only the bankers of the French Crown. They also lent considerable sums to Charles XII of Sweden, with the result that they were elevated to the rank of Swedish baronets. Thus we find them later as Baron de Coppet, Marquis de Garo, and Comte de Bignan, the names referring to the castles they obtained. In the financial crisis of 1709 the banking firm of Högger fared no better than Bernard, their competitor. The firm found itself caught in a labyrinth of claims and debts. To disentangle the maze, government commissions were set up. It seems that well-to-do relatives from St. Gallen helped in making the liquidation a smooth procedure. In a way it is surprising that the reputation of the Höggers suffered so little by the events, but, after all, what had brought about the collapse was the King's insolvency and not their own. The liquidation of the first Högger bank was hardly complete when Antoine, the son of Marc-Frédéric, set up a new bank which, notwithstanding the sad experience of the previous generation, again went into the business of financing the Crown. To be known as the banker of the "Roi Soleil" was valued as a supreme achievement by these Protestant republicans of Swiss descent. Antoine Högger's bank placed considerable sums at the disposal of the King, and received paper money and treasury bills in exchange. The whole thing ended in a flood of law suits and confrontations with the Crown and the creditors. Antoine Högger, who had no family, died 1767 in poverty, bitterness in his heart. He had not come to terms with the Crown.

As a young man, Antoine's cousin Jacques-Christophe, a son of Daniel, was sent to Amsterdam. In the relatively quiet climate of this city he was to learn the art of banking under his uncle Rietmann, a man from St. Gallen. In 1722 he set up a bank in Amsterdam. After his death in 1735, his widow carried on the business of the bank; later it was run by his son Daniel who brought several associates into the firm. So the bank appeared under various names, such as Horneca Hogguer, & Co., and later Hogguer, Grand & Co. The bank repeatedly extended loans to Sweden. It was also in the colonial business. After the Grands, who came from the Vaud, had joined the firm as associates, business relations with France were resumed. George Grand's brother Ferdinand, then a banker in Paris, was instrumental in re-establishing the contact. During the American War of Independence the Högger bank in Amsterdam floated loans in behalf of Benjamin Franklin and granted credits to American entrepreneurs. Repayment of these credits met with some difficulties, however. At the beginning of the nineteenth century, Paul Iwan Hogguer, scion of Daniel, attained high positions. In 1840 he became Mayor of Amsterdam and the first President of the Nederlandsche Bank.[5]

Isaac Thellusson went to Paris at an early age to join the staff of the banking firm of Tourton and Guiguer in which he swiftly rose to an executive position. When he was only 28 he was consulted, with other royal counselors, about the prospects of the Law system which was then in its beginnings. He was against Law's plans, and turned out to be one of his strongest opponents. Tourton appointed Thellusson as his sole heir, but he had to fight for his rights under this title in a law suit against Tourton's nephew. In this fight he solicited the help of Geneva, the city of his birth. In this way he once more came into contact with the Geneva authorities who appointed him as their plenipotentiary in Paris. Later François Tronchin, the son of the syndic of Geneva, became his business associate. Although Thellusson's position in the banking firm was only that of limited partner, he actually was the leading man and was held in high esteem in the financial quarters of Paris. In 1733 during the Polish War of Succession, François Tronchin and Company, like the Höggers before, became the suppliers of funds to the French army, and in the crisis year 1738 the French government assigned to Thellusson the important job of the centralized procurement of grain. He performed this job to general satisfaction. François Tronchin's brother Jean-Robert, who until then had run a banking firm in Lyon–he was Voltaire's banker–likewise moved from Lyon to Paris, where he received the highest awards for his services.

Only a few of the numerous Swiss bankers who lived in Paris during the Law period were able to stay in business: ten from Geneva, Ehinguer from Basel, and Labbard from Thurgau. The latter's bank was subsequently taken over by his son-in-law Isaac Vernet. Still later, young Jacques Necker of Geneva and Georges Tobie Thellusson became associates in this banking firm which they ran under the name Thellusson, Necker and Company. Business development was excellent and the bank was considered one of the first institutes of Paris. Necker made a large fortune and became a man of great reputation. In 1768 the city of Geneva appointed him as its representative at the Royal Court, thus making him a member of the diplomatic corps in Paris. In 1772 he retired from active business. The bank was subsequently run by Jean Girardot, Thellusson's brother-in-law, and Louis Necker, Jacques' brother. Later Louis had to take on the name Germany because Jacques Necker did not want his name to appear in the firm and in 1777 Rudolphe-Emanuel Haller, a son of the famous poet and natural scientist Albrecht von Haller, came in. The bank thereafter called itself Girardot, Haller and Company. Necker took to writing and became more and more

[5] Luethy, op. cit., Vol. I, p. 196ff., Vol. II, p. 330ff.

engaged in politics. He criticized Turgot's administration of the finances, and when Turgot had to resign, Necker was called to a post in the Ministry of Finances. The appointment of a foreign-born to such a post was an extraordinary event and a Protestant in such a position meant a challenge to the Church. Never before had a banker been made Minister of Finance. To overcome these difficulties, a stooge was appointed Minister, while Necker was given the title "Directeur Général des Finances." Although Necker succeeded in restoring general confidence in French finances, he did not remain unopposed. One of his opponents was Isaac Panchaud, the son of a Bern family born in London. He had established himself in Paris as a banker, but without great success. He had a certain standing in politics, however, and since he was a financial expert, the door to Turgot was open to him. He was the sponsor of a Caisse d'Escompte, a government agency which was actually set up in the last few weeks of Turgot's rule. The main responsibility of this institute was to be the discounting of commercial bills of exchange. The bank interests us only because on the original board of directors, which consisted of seven men, there were—apart from two government representatives—only Swiss bankers. Besides Panchaud, we find the names Pache (from Geneva), Marck (from Basel), Sellonf (Schlumpf) (from St. Gallen), and Delessert (from Cosonay and Geneva). After Necker had entered the Ministry of Finance, however, the board of directors was enlarged.

Of the other Swiss banks, which in the eighteenth century had a certain importance in Paris, we may mention the Mallet bank. The year 1723 is generally considered to have been the year of its foundation, and so the bank could celebrate its two hundredth anniversary in 1923. The institute was thus one of the oldest and most renowned private banks in Paris.[6] Another banking firm was linked with the names De la Rive, Lullin and Rillier—three old names from Geneva. Less close were the ties that linked the bankers Banquet, Chabert, and Pache to Geneva. Rougemont, a banker from Neuenburg, along with Hottinguer, represented Zurich interests for some time.

4. *Basel as Banking Center*

Whereas Basel can look back on a longer tradition of capital export than most of the other Swiss cities, banks in the present sense can be found only at relatively late date in the city on the Rhine. There were, to be sure, money changers in early medieval times but the people engaged in this business, which was not considered particularly honorable, were at first mostly Lombards. During the Council of Basel (1431-1449) many foreign money changers came to Basel. At

[6] Luethy, op. cit. Vol. II, p. 246ff.

that time even Cosimo Medici had a branch agency in Basel which took care of the money transactions of the Council. In 1533 exchange of money was made an activity reserved to the government, and a public agency was set up which in due course engaged in banking operations of all sorts but encountered strong opposition because of its monopolistic character. In 1746, in the wake of a few ill-fated credit transactions, the enterprise was discontinued.

At the turn of the eighteenth century, so-called "speculation shops"—such as, for example, the firm Merian Brothers—engaged in banking, commission business, and transactions of a speculative nature. They performed all these activities along with commodity trade. The combination of forwarding money and banking was also quite frequent. Another place where we find this combination is St. Gallen, where the private bank Wegelin and Company grew out of the forwarding agency Caspar Zyli. The firm of Merian and Speyr, which had been founded in 1816, at first also carried on banking as a sideline activity within the forwarding business. In 1824 it assumed the name Speyr & Cie and became a private bank altogether. In 1912 it was taken over by the Swiss Bank Corporation. Almost equally old is the bank La Roche, which had risen out of the firm Benedict La Roche (founded 1787).

The present banking firm Zahn and Company grew out of the firm of Bischoff, founded 1806 in St. Alben. Dreyfus Sons and Company, A.G., was founded in 1813 by Isaak Dreyfus. In 1841 J. Riggenbach established himself as a private banker. His firm was later continued in business by A. Sarasin and Company. Luescher and Company trace their existence back to 1855 and E. Gutzwiller and Company to 1886.

Even before the foundation of the Confederation in 1848 and the introduction of the Swiss franc in 1850, Basel had become an important "storehouse" of capital, not only for the rest of Switzerland but for Upper Baden as far as Karlsruhe and Stuttgart, and for eastern France as far as Besançon, Lyon, Strasbourg, and Nancy. In neighboring Alsace the Basel banks, naturally, have a particularly well-established standing; they keep up close mutual business relations with Paris, Lyon, and Frankfurt.

In the year 1862, there were 20 banks listed in the Basel official register (Ragionenbuch) but only nine of them confined themselves to banking. The others were also engaged in other business. In addition to the private banks a few other banking firms were set up in the nineteenth century, such as, in 1809, an institute that called itself "Interest-Bearing Savings," and in 1843, the Clearing and Deposits Bank (Giro-und Depositenbank) which, however, gave way only one year later to the Bank of Basel. Along with other banking activities, the last-named institute issued bank notes. In this line of business the Basel institute occupied a leading place among the banks of issue that existed in Switzerland at the time. When the Swiss National Bank was founded, the Bank of Basel was merged with the Swiss Bank Corporation.

In the middle of the nineteenth century it became evident that if Basel was to maintain its place as a banking center, the private banks would have to cooperate more closely in the issuing business and new, strong banks would have to be established. In fact two groups of private banks were formed. The first, comprising the firms Bischoff, Ehinger, Merian, Passavant, Riggenbach, and Speyr, formed a syndicate in order to spread the risks of the issuing business and to conduct major transactions for common account. The syndicate assumed the name "Bank Corporation" ("Bank-Verein"). In the second group, which was formed somewhat later, we find the names La Roche, Iselin and Staehelin, Oswald Brothers, Luescher, and Dreyfus. In 1862 this group in cooperation with commercial firms founded the first big banking house in the city, the Trade Bank of Basel ("Basler Handelsbank"), with a 20-million franc stock equity, of which 10 million were initially issued. In due course the institute set up branch offices in Geneva, Zurich, and, temporarily, in Bern. Up to the outbreak of World War I, the institute grew into one of the eight big banking houses of Switzerland.

Even after the foundation of the Trade Bank of Basel, the first-named group of banking firms continued the loose form of cooperation that had been contemplated originally. The group had no intention of setting up a new banking house. But after the war of 1870-71, when foreign financial groups made preparations for organizing a bank in Basel with international participation, the syndicate decided to take the initiative and it was a logical proposition that the new institute should be given the name "Bank Corporation of Basel" ("Basler Bankverein").[7] The stock equity was set at 50 million francs, of which 30 million were issued and taken over by the founders as a firm commitment. A bigger banking syndicate, in which foreign institutes were also represented, offered the shares on the market. As a result of the then rampant general economic crisis, the new bank suffered losses in its second year and an adjustment of the stock equity capital became necessary. In 1895 came the merger with the Bank Corporation of Zurich ("Zuercher Bankverein") and two years later the Swiss Union Bank in St. Gallen was taken over, which suggested changing the name of the firm into Swiss Bank Corporation ("Schweizerischer Bankverein"). Foreign business was taken up at an early date and in 1898 a branch opened in London. By absorbing other Swiss banks, Swiss Bank Corporation soon grew into one of the most important of the big banking houses.

The year 1890 brought suggestions from political quarters to set up a public bank. Such a step seemed plausible since in many other cantons institutes of this type were already in existence. But it was not until October 1, 1899, that the Cantonal Bank of Basel ("Basler Kantonalbank") could open its counters.

[7] A. R. Weber, *Basler Bank-und Boersenwesen* (separate reprint from "Wirtschaftsgeschichte Basel").

Besides other banking transactions, the Cantonal Bank issued bank notes during the following period up to the formation of the Swiss National Bank.

5. *Zurich as Banking Center*

As a banking center Zurich made its appearance at a relatively late date. At the beginning of the eighteenth century when Geneva was already in the thick of European financial transactions, we do not find any bank in Zurich in the full meaning of the word. The Zurich of that time was a small town of 10,000 inhabitants. To be sure, even Zurich lent money in medieval times. These money transactions were frequently connected with payments due to Swiss mercenaries. Thus we know of a loan granted by Zurich in 1570 to Charles IX, who after the peace treaty of St. Germain dismissed Swiss mercenaries but did not have the funds to pay what was still owed them. Zurich at that time granted a loan of 50,000 crowns (150,000 livres) at 5% for two years. Bern and Freiburg together made 70,000 crowns available. Frequently, also, the municipal loans were connected with the salt trade, the municipal Salt Office functioning as money lender. In the Thirty Years' War a few loans were granted to borrowers in southern Germany; private money lenders also were active in such transactions. At the end of the seventeenth century capital export from Zurich seems to have come to a standstill for quite some time. But general well-being finally increased and the municipal treasury began accumulating funds whose investment met with difficulties even in this early phase. In 1679 the city council for the first time issued an injunction against lowering the rate of interest from 5% to 4%. Nevertheless, the interest rate declined to 3%. In 1730 the idea of establishing a bank turned up for the first time. Requests for loans were flowing in from outside at an increasing rate, but the city maintained an attitude of great restraint. Unlike Geneva, Zurich did not participate in the financing of the Spanish War of Succession. Only the Salt Office granted occasional loans.

The surplus in the municipal treasury of Zurich continued piling up, however, and in 1726 investment of capital in England was contemplated for the first time. As early as 1709 Bern had invested about 1 million Taler in England and Holland. In 1727 the Council of Zurich followed this example by investing 100,000 guilders in English government securities and buying 20 shares of the South Sea Company. These foreign investments originating in Zurich amounted, however, to only 10% of those engaged in by Bern. The intermediary in these transactions was Holzhalb, a Zurich banker established in London who, however, became bankrupt soon afterwards.

In the year 1750 a commission submitted an opinion to the council expressing the view that the rate of interest could not be stabilized by government decree. In 1751 an "Interest Commission" came into being, which was assigned the business of accepting funds as deposits and investing them abroad. In 1755 the job of carrying out these transactions was delegated to a separate new organization which was given the name Leu and Company (after Mr. Leu, the city treasurer), although in actual fact it was strictly a government agency. Leu and Company issued bonds bearing 3 to 3½% interest. These bonds went into the portfolios of Zurich citizens; their value rose from 60,000 R ("Rheinische Gulden") in 1755 to 2,688,000 R in 1797. In its investment policy the commission exercised utmost care. The funds were invested in Austria and later in France. The commission did grant loans to Central and North America, and it lent money to Geneva bankers who, as we have seen, needed funds for their speculative transactions. Otherwise, however, loans raised inland were the exception.

If we disregard a short-lived attempt in 1652 to set up a municipal discount house, we cannot find a bank in Zurich until the middle of the eighteenth century. The merchants of Zurich concentrated on the textile trade without themselves engaging in the banking transactions connected with that trade. They obviously used the services of foreign banks. In the eighteenth century, however, some citizens of Zurich did begin to engage in certain credit transactions. Bonds bearing 3 to 3½% interest were in circulation. Even the craft guilds were occasionally active as money lenders. In the second half of the eighteenth century we find a few business men who could be called "merchant-bankers." The first of them may well have been H. C. Escher, who accepted funds as deposits and then invested them in securities. This enterprise collapsed, however, in 1788. There were other firms that conducted money transactions along with commodity trade. They negotiated, among other things, a loan to Copenhagen. Credits were also granted to Geneva bankers, and every now and then somebody ventured into speculative transactions with French securities.

In Zurich the first private bank in the full sense of the word is the firm Usteri, Ott, Escher and Company. It was founded in 1786 by six Zurich firms which, however, failed to endow the bank with sufficient equity capital. Operation of a branch in Paris was entrusted to the bankers Rougemont and Hottinguer. In the first few years the bank enjoyed a good rating as a financial institute; deposits came flowing in even from Basel. But the representatives in Paris were unable to escape the speculation fever that was raging there and so they ran into losses. From 1800 to 1803 one after the other of the partners got into financial difficulties. The bank had to compound with the creditors and in 1803 it was liquidated. Hottinguer, one of the guilty in the collapse, left Paris and stayed in America for some time. But after his return in 1797, he became Talleyrand's financial adviser, and during the Napoleonic era he was a banker of great standing.[8]

[8] H. C. Peyer, *Von Handel und Bank im alten Zuerich*, p. 144 ff.

But even the city treasury and the interest commission Leu and Company had to take losses on their foreign investments. Toward the end of the eighteenth century, Leu and Company were no longer in a position to pay interest on their bonds. In the autumn of 1798 a general assembly of bondholders took notice of the state of affairs and instructed the commission to liquidate, with as little loss as possible, the foreign investments. At that time only about 20% of the bonded debt, which then amounted to 2.6 million Zurich gulden, was covered by liquid assets, but it was hoped that in the course of a gradual, cautiously moving liquidation, this percentage could be raised to between 50 and 55%. The bonds were declared nonredeemable; repayment was to proceed in installments. For the time being no new bonds were issued. In 1803 the worst seemed over. Some assets could again be sold, though only at a loss. Investments abroad were reduced from 2.7 million to 700,000 gulden in 1822. From then on the business gradually shifted to the homeland. In this way Leu and Company became a private mortgage institute in Zurich.[9]

Around 1805 we find in the official register of Zurich seven firms that called themselves banks, but only two of them, H. C. Escher Son, and Tauenstein, confined themselves to banking. The others were combined enterprises of the kind that existed in other cities as well. As late as 1837, only Tobler-Stadler is listed in the newly introduced official register ("Ragionenbuch") as a bank in the strict sense, side by side with four firms that were combining banking and exchange transactions with commodity trade or silk manufacture. At that time trade in bills of exchange, including foreign bills, was the most important line of business in banking. Since the large-scale firms engaged in the silk and cotton trade were well endowed with capital and performed the money transactions connected with their business themselves, only a limited field of activity remained for the Zurich private bankers. This explains why in Zurich, contrary to what is true of Geneva and Basel, almost no really old, long-established bank can be found. Only the banking firm Rahm and Bodmer can trace its origins back to the beginning of the nineteenth century. It grew out of the firm Caspar Schulthess sel. Erben and Schinz, which existed as early as 1805.

After the Confederation had been founded, Zurich moved into the foreground as an economic and financial center. The growing industrialization and the building of railroad lines called for the setting up of financial institutes of larger size. The Swiss publisher C. Hirzel in Leipzig suggested in 1856 that a branch of the Allgemeine Deutsche Kreditanstalt be established in Zurich. This proposal, however, was not exactly welcome in Zurich. Alfred Escher, the strongest personality in economic and political life at the time, then took the initiative of founding the Swiss Credit Bank (Schweizerische Kreditanstalt) with

[9] Leu und Company, 1755-1955 (memorial).

a 15-million franc stock equity capital, and German participation, amounting to 50%, was gladly accepted. The founders reserved 3 million for themselves and offered the remaining 4½ million for public subscription. The success was extraordinary. Whereas 4½ million had been expected, subscriptions reached 218 million. Thus the young banking institute, supported by public confidence, swiftly gained in stature. Escher became the first chairman. He was also the initiator of the Gotthard railroad, an enterprise that was beyond Swiss potentialities and could only be realized with foreign participation. The Swiss Credit Bank played a leading part in the foundation of firms such as Swiss Rent Institute (Schweizerische Rentenanstalt), Swiss Reinsurance (Schweizerische Rueckversicherung), the Machinery Factory Oerlikon, and the Industrial Society for Schappe in Basel. (Schappe is a by-product of silk manufacture.) In 1890 the bank was already in the international business. By way of investment it was interested in the Bank for Oriental Railroads, in the Swiss-Argentine Mortgage Bank, and in other financial companies and in joint action with AEG (Allgemeine Elektrizitaets-Gesellschaft) it established in 1895 the Bank for Electrical Enterprises (Bank fuer elektrische Unternehmungen), known today as "Elektro-Watt."

In Winterthur, the Bank of Winterthur was formed in 1862. Leading men of the Winterthur economy were on the board of directors. The initial stock equity was 5 million; the shares, offered for public subscription, were vastly oversubscribed. The Bank of Winterthur operated predominantly as a trade bank without, however, neglecting other lines of banking. From the start it also ran a warehouse. In addition the bank was active in railroad financing; there, however, it incurred losses, as a result of which the share capital, which in the meantime had been raised to 15 million francs, had to be reduced in 1886 to the former level of 10 million. Concurrent with this measure, preferred shares were issued. After the bank had gained a foothold in various places by way of investments, it merged in 1912 with the Bank of Toggenburg, which had originated in the year 1863 and had established a good name for itself in eastern Switzerland. Out of the merger grew a new big banking house, the Union Bank of Switzerland (Schweizerische Bankgesellschaft).

In 1892 the Federal Bank (Eidgenoessische Bank) moved its headquarters to Zurich. It had been founded in 1863 on the initiative of two Paris banks, the Société Générale de Crédit Industriel et Commercial and the Société Anonyme des Dépôts et de Comptes-Courants. At that time it caused quite a stir that Jakob Staempfli, a member of the Federal council, and like Alfred Escher one of the most prominent politicians of his time, was willing to retire from the Federal council and take the post of chairman of the bank. Stock equity was set at 60 million francs, one half of which had to be subscribed at the time of foundation. Of the 60,000 shares offered at 500 francs per share, 12,000 were taken by

Swiss investors and 18,000, by the French founding banks. By public subscription 11,200 shares could be placed in Switzerland and 18,800 in France. The sum paid in amounted to 20%. In the first ten years, branches were already being set up in St. Gallen, Lausanne, Zurich, Geneva, Lucerne, Basel and La Chaux-de-Fonds. So the bank had the character of a large all-Swiss banking institute when it moved to Zurich.

After the establishment of the Zurich stock exchange in December, 1876, and the publication of the Stock Exchange Act of 1883, the private brokers, who up to that time had taken care of the trade in securities, gradually disappeared. They were replaced by "Effektenagenten" (firms admitted to the stock exchange as licensed brokers). By the Stock Exchange Act of 1886 even commercial banks could be admitted to the stock exchange as agents in this capacity. By 1896, it had 23 firms admitted—20 "Effektenagenten" and 3 joint-stock banks were active there. It was not until 1898 that the Swiss Credit Bank applied for the stock exchange license. The joint-stock company Leu and Company did so only in 1910.

6. *Times of War and Crisis*

Before the outbreak of World War I, Switzerland had already grown into an international financial center of some importance. Six big banks were in possession of a rather tightly knit network of branches all over Switzerland. The six were the Swiss Credit Bank, Swiss Bank Corporation, Union Bank of Switzerland, Trade Bank of Basel, Federal Bank, and Swiss People's Bank (Volksbank). It was no longer appropriate to speak of segregated financial centers within the country. As a financial center, Switzerland had become an integrated whole, with Zurich, Basel, and Geneva functioning as centers of gravitation and Zurich moving more and more into the foreground with four big banks—the Swiss Credit Bank, Union Bank of Switzerland, Federal Bank, and Leu and Company, A. G. The insurance business, too, was well represented in Zurich (Swiss Reinsurance Company, "Zurich" General Accident and Liability Insurance Company). Firms having their headquarters in Basel were the Swiss Bank Corporation, Trade Bank of Basel, Life Insurance Company of Basel, and the Fire Insurance Company of Basel. The Swiss People's Bank had its headquarters in Bern. In Geneva the Comptoir d'Escompte was about to grow into the dimensions of a big bank; the Geneva private bankers, with their long tradition and their international clientele, also formed an essential part of the Swiss financial center. Each year the banks floated some international loans. Thus we find the following issues in the Almanac of 1912:

4%	German Reich Loan
4%,	Prussian Consols
4%,	Italian Treasury Notes per 1917
4%,	Danish Government Loan 1912
4½%,	Gold Bonds of the City of Moscow
4½%,	Debentures, Central Mortgage Bank of Hungarian Savings Associations
4½%,	Bonds, Anatolian Railroad Company, Third Series
5%,	Gold Debentures, Chicago Rock Island and Pacific Ry. Co. 1932
7%,	Adj. Mortgage Bonds, Denver & Rio Grande R.R. Co.
5%,	Bonds, Virginian Ry. Co. 1957
4½%,	20 Year Convertible Bonds, Baltimore and Ohio R.R.
5%,	I. Mortg. Portland Railway Light and Power Co.
4½%,	Bonds, Siemens Elektrische Betriebe A.G.
5%,	I. Lien ref. Mge. Bonds, Bethlehem Steel Corporation
6%,	Notes Utah Co. per 1917
6%,	Cum. Pref. Stock Amer. Water Works Guarantee Co., Pittsburgh
7%,	Cum. Pref. Stock and Comm. Stock B.F. Goodrich Co.
7%,	I. Pref. Stock Loose Wiles Co.
7%,	Pref. Shares Emerson Brantingham Co.
7%,	Cum. Pref. Stock California Petroleum Corporation United States Motor Company Reorganization Syndicate
7%,	Pref. Stock Moline Plow Co. Common Stock M. Rumely Co.
7%,	Cum. Pref. Stock New Motor Cab Co., Ltd.

Those financial companies that were active in international business, such as Swiss Bank for Capital Investment, Swiss Company for Electric Industry, Bank for Electrical Enterprises, and others, were likewise relying on the market. Swiss banks acted as intermediaries in securing foreign titles on behalf of their customers. Since the supply of Swiss securities suitable for investment was inadequate, American stocks and bonds could be found in every major portfolio. Industry had begun to set up affiliated companies abroad and insurance companies were active in foreign markets from Russia to the United States. Important transit trade companies such as Volkart Brothers in Winterthur and the Trade Bank of Basel already had a widespread network of branches in many regions of the world, India and Africa among them.

To illustrate the degree of international interlocking of interests, we may mention the wide field in which Carl Abegg-Auer, then President of the Swiss Credit Bank, was active. Among other things, he was chairman of the Board of Directors of the Bank for Oriental Railroads (a company financing railroads in the Balkan countries); president of the Bank for Electrical Enterprises; chairman of the Board of Supervisors of the Electric Power Company of Strasbourg, of the S. A. de Filature de Schappe in Lyon, and of the Swiss-Argentine Mortgage Bank. He was a member of the Boards of Directors of the Railway Company Saloniki-Monastir, the Baghdad Railway, the Compania Barcelonesa de Electricidad, the German-Overseas Electrical Company (Deutsche-Ueberseeische Elektrizitaetzgesellschaft), the Banca Commerciale Italiana and the Dollfus, Mieg and Company, Mulhouse.

The outbreak of World War I set an abrupt end to this development. Financial and trade relations were disrupted and Switzerland was cut off from the world market. Import and export became dependent on the good will of the belligerent nations. Owing to their close connection with neighboring Germany and Austria, the financial centers Zurich and Basel were more severely affected than Geneva. The collapse of the German and Austrian currencies resulted in enormous losses to the banks and their clientele. For a long time people were unwilling to believe that the German mark was headed for an irreparable breakdown; the hope that it would recover after the war died hard. Especially hard hit were banks that had invested in mortgages in Germany, such as Leu and Company and some smaller institutes in eastern Switzerland.

The consequences of World War I were bitter. According to estimates of that time, Swiss assets abroad dwindled from 8 to 2.5 billion. The country was flooded by cheap commodities from abroad, causing the balance of trade to show a substantial deficit. The markets for short-term money, as well as the market for long-term capital, lost much of their ability to function in an efficient manner. The Confederation and a few cities found themselves in the necessity to raise loans in foreign countries. Thus Pictet and Company, jointly with Lee Higginson and Company, Boston, negotiated three loans for the Confederation: 15 million dollars at 5% for one to five years; 30 million dollars at 5½% for ten years, and 25 million dollars at 8% for 20 years. The Credit Bank jointly with Morgan and Company negotiated a medium-term loan of 20 million dollars at 5%, and one having a longer term, amounting to 30 million dollars, at 5½%. Zurich and Bern likewise raised loans in dollars.

The reparations problem, laying heavily upon Germany, prevented a rebound of her economy, and this had a crippling effect on all of Europe. When the Dawes Plan (August 1924) and the Young Plan (June 7, 1929) had gone into effect, it was believed that a solution for the difficult reparation problem had been found. This contributed to the rise of a new optimism and to a revitalizing of business.

International financial transactions were resumed. The banks granted credits to foreign commercial and industrial firms and to German banks. In connection with the stabilization of the French franc under Poincaré 1926-27, France was granted a loan, followed shortly afterwards by another loan, this time for the French State Railroad, amounting to 150 million francs at 7%. Both loans were floated by the Credit Bank; both were helpful in the stabilization of the French currency.

Even banks that formerly had not been active in international business, or had entered it only on a few occasions, now participated in it, developing a good deal of initiative. This is true of the Federal Bank, the People's Bank, the Trade Bank of Basel, and the Comptoir d'Escompte. The last-named bank continued its expansion and set up numerous branches, the aim being to become an all-Swiss bank with headquarters in Geneva.

It was not sufficiently realized how weak the foundations were on which the international financial structure and the system of currencies rested. Short-term claims in international finance totaled 55 billion dollars, and many short-term funds were sunk in long-term investments, contrary to the golden rule of banking.

The stock market crash in New York 1929 marked the beginning of the depression of the thirties. The international financial structure broke down. The project of a customs union between Germany and Austria led to withdrawals of funds from Austria. Not long after this, the Austrian Credit-Anstalt collapsed; it suspended payments on May 11, 1931. A chain reaction was thus set in motion, and the run on German banks forced the Darmstaedter and Nationalbank to close its counters on June 13, 1931. The German government decreed a bank moratorium and put the first foreign exchange restrictions into effect. Next, the spark of crisis hit Britain, whose currency after the war had been stabilized, in a somewhat too optimistic mood, at prewar parity. The pound was severed from gold and was devalued. Whereupon one European country after the other tried, by devaluing its currency, to shift to others the unemployment from which it was suffering. In 1933 even the American administration found that it had to give up the fixed parity of the currency unit. At the beginning of 1934 the dollar was devalued by 41%. The repercussions of the crisis in currencies, finance, and general economic conditions were catastrophic. The number of unemployed in Europe went up to millions. The world economy was being shackled by import and foreign exchange restrictions and capital sought refuge in those countries where the risk of devaluation was least. The currency system of the postwar period was a shambles. Hitler recruited his party members out of the armies of unemployed persons in Germany.

France, the Netherlands, and Switzerland, the last remaining members of the gold block, were still clinging to their parities. Switzerland tried in vain to lower the price level by a deflationary policy with a view to regaining her full competitive strength on the world markets. The debility from which export business was suffering could not be overcome and in the middle of the thirties the volume of Swiss exports dwindled to 800 million francs. Unemployment became rampant. The world no longer believed that the gold-block countries could successfully defend their currencies, so a withdrawal of deposits set in. In 1936 when the French government informed the Federal Council that it was under the necessity of devaluing the French franc, the Swiss government, too, though with a loaded heart and only after long deliberation, decided to take the Swiss franc off gold and to devalue it by 30%.

As a result of the devaluation foreign capitals began flowing in again and the situation on the markets for short-term and long-term funds became easier. But the time remaining until the outbreak of World War II was too short to allow the economy to regain its strength.

The international credit and currency crises placed the banks under a burden of extraordinary weight. In the postwar era financial communications with Germany had again been working well. After the experience with the inflation, German investors came to regard deposits in Switzerland as a protection in case times should get worse. Considerable sums were flowing from Germany into Switzerland. For lack of adequate investment opportunities in the homeland, the Swiss banks invested these funds in Germany. Credits to first-rate German firms, or mortgages with gold clauses on good real estate, were considered to be absolutely sound investments. So it was not at all uncommon for the German assets of a Swiss bank to attain or even to exceed the level of its stock equity capital. Hence the German bank moratorium of 1931, and the general transfer moratorium of 1933, hit the Swiss banks at a vital spot. What should be done if the German deposits with Swiss banks were withdrawn while at the same time Swiss assets in Germany were frozen? One solution, to be sure, might have come up for consideration, and was in fact recommended to the Swiss authorities a few times: Switzerland, in her turn, could have ordered a limited moratorium, thus offsetting frozen claims by frozen liabilities. But this would have been against all tradition. The Swiss banks, in fact, subsequently liquidated without fail all deposits their German customers wanted to withdraw, although the banks could no longer liquidate their own assets in Germany. This amounted to a test of strength that is hard to conceive of today. In the years 1930-36 deposits with the large banks as recorded in their balance sheets shrank from 6.6 to 3.2 billion. It is almost a miracle that the banking system could survive this bloodletting. For some banks, to be sure, financial reconstruction became inevitable. All banks that had been active in international business, with the exception of two big ones, had to reduce their stock capital. The Comptoir d'Escompte, for which financial reorganization had become necessary as early as 1931 (its name was then changed to Swiss Discount Bank), as well as the Swiss People's Bank, had to apply for financial assistance from the Federal government which shortly before had organized the Federal Loan Agency (Eidgenoessische Darlehenskasse) for such emergencies. But the Swiss Discount Bank could not be saved and the People's Bank had to undergo a second financial reconstruction. A new Banking Act was put into effect in 1935. The new act granted banks in distress the right to postpone their due dates, and numerous banks subsequently made use of this privilege. In retrospect we may perhaps say that the authorities and the banks, by choosing this difficult course, have made a significant contribution to Switzerland's reputation as a financial center. This reputation has proved its justification in a critical period.

In fact the Swiss banks and authorities did their best to safeguard financial interests in these difficult times. In September, 1931, the first standstill agreement between Swiss and German banks was concluded. After the announcement of the general transfer moratorium, which entailed heavy sacrifices for the creditors of Germany, Switzerland attempted to keep her creditor rights effective by introducing bilateral clearing with Germany. In this attempt she was in a strong position inasmuch as her commodity trade with Germany steadily produced import surpluses, so that there was enough scope, within the framework of a clearing agreement, for the accrual of interest on the Swiss claims. This brought some relief, even though capitals remained frozen.

World War II did not find Switzerland unprepared. At the peak of the crisis in 1936 the Defense Loan was issued. It was oversubscribed, despite an interest rate of 3% which of course involved a sacrifice. The Swiss people wanted thereby to enable the Federal Council to speed up armaments in view of the threatening clouds on the political horizon. Thus a reorganized and re-equipped army could occupy the frontiers of the country in 1939. The costs of national defense reached 8.2 billion francs, and during the war years the Federal debt, despite introduction of new taxes, rose from 2.3 to 8.7 billion. However, the financing of the deficit was done primarily by way of long-term loans. Credit by the bank of issue was used only quite temporarily, so that inflation could be kept within relatively narrow bounds.

Surrounded as she was by the Axis powers, Switzerland had trouble in her attempt to uphold her foreign trade. As commodity shipments from Germany declined more and more, an export surplus arose in the clearing agreement with Germany which at the end of the war reached the billion level. The country was also hard hit by the action the United States took in freezing her dollar accounts which amounted to 6 billion francs. Financial transactions with the United States thus came to a standstill. Considerations connected with the fight against inflation motivated the National Bank to accept at the official rate only those dollars originating in commodity trade. This created a "finance dollar" which at times showed a substantial disagio. An affidavit was introduced for purposes of transactions with England, the aim being to make the continuation of interest payments possible, at least to some extent.

7. *After World War II*

The second World War left a pile of rubble so vast it can hardly be imagined. The German economy was prostrate. As clearing payments came to a halt, those foreign assets of Swiss banks that were located in Germany, Austria, or in East European countries could no longer be entered as assets in the balance sheets. This forced two large banks, the Trade Bank of Basel and the Federal Bank, to transfer their Swiss assets and liabilities to stronger institutes and to carry on as "truncated banks" ("Rumpfbanken") managing only their foreign assets, which had become so problematical. It is true that the Swiss economy emerged intact out of World War II, but only a very few lines of business drew any profit from the war.

It was generally expected that the transition from the war economy to a peace economy would be accompanied by crisis and unemployment in a manner similar to what had happened after World War I. The Federal government was prepared, if necessary, to adopt a comprehensive program to create new employment opportunities. But first it tried to overcome the critical period by promoting exports. This course suggested itself all the more as there was a serious dearth of commodities in all of Europe, a dearth that could not be filled owing to the prevailing scarcity of foreign exchange. This is why so-called "Swing Credits" were provided in the trade and payment agreements of the postwar era. The purpose was to work out a setup under which the volume of exports would not depend on the volume of imports, as it had under the clearing agreements of the interwar period. France and Britain, in particular, used these credits in full; in 1948 they totaled 680 million francs. In this way the transition to a peacetime economy could be achieved without any setbacks.

The banks in their turn granted credits to foreign countries, especially France and Belgium. In part these credits financed Swiss exports, in part they helped in providing the homeland with some necessities, as did a credit to "Montecatini" in Milan and one to the "Charbonnages de France." These two credits were repaid by successive deliveries of electricity (in the first case) and of coal (in the second case). After 1947, one could again contemplate–only with hesitation at first–the floating of loans abroad, Belgium being the main borrower in the initial phase.

Following an initiative of the United States, the European countries formed the OECE (Organisation Européene de Coopération Economique), in the frame of which the European Payments Union was set up in 1950. This Union may well be called the most constructive part of the great Marshall Plan.

Various Swiss organizations, such as Swiss Help (Schweizer Hilfe) and Help for Europe (Europa-Hilfe), donated gifts, and a broad stream of food parcels flew across the frontier. The Swiss contribution to the reconstruction of Europe after the war, including the Federal credits, attained a level which, on a per head of population basis, could certainly match the American Marshall Plan.

In 1948 Germany carried out her currency reform, which was the basis for the reconstruction of the German economy. But the European currency situation was by no means settled as yet. In 1949 Britain, taking account of the depreciation the pound had experienced as a result of the war, decided to devalue her currency by 30%. Within one week, 26 other countries followed suit. Nearly all of Switzerland's most important trade partners, with the exception of the United States, devalued their currencies, most of them in the same proportion as Britain had done. What was Switzerland to do in this situation? This writer still has a vivid recollection of the decisive meeting that took place in the Department of Finances, with Mr. Nobs of the Federal government as chairman. Voices could be heard from eastern Switzerland to the effect that the textile industry would be losing its ability to compete if the existing parity were maintained. The speakers of the National Bank came out for maintenance of the existing parity, and in the Department of Finances, too, hope was expressed that it would be possible to avoid devaluation, provided this could be justified from a general economic point of view. In this debate the vote of the delegate of the Swiss Trade and Industry Association proved decisive. He forcefully emphasized that in view of the strong demand for goods that was still widespread abroad, Switzerland could stick to the existing parity. Thus a unanimous resolution, later approved by the Federal Council, was adopted. The course chosen proved to be correct. Although business activity did slow up a bit, the Swiss economy retained its competitive strength. The price level subsequently declined somewhat, and this made it possible to abolish the subsidies that had been introduced to make consumer purchases less expensive.

During the war period and in the immediate postwar era the Western powers had little understanding of Switzerland's policy of neutrality. Thus the country was put under strong American pressure in the course of the Morgenthau policy. The United States demanded that Switzerland seize the German accounts and other assets in the country in order to make the proceeds available for reparation payments. This was a serious matter for a nation that had always stood for protection of private property. The tiresome negotiations eventually led to a compromise that was acceptable even to the German owners of those assets.

Once more Switzerland had impressively asserted her role as a trustee. Nowhere in the world could the German owners of property located in other countries achieve a more favorable settlement.

Further difficult problems arose in connection with the efforts to realize Swiss claims vis-à-vis foreign countries. At the end of the war the claims of the Federal Government originating in the clearing arrangements amounted to 1 billion francs; they seemed unrecoverable. At the beginning of the fifties, an agreement about Swiss accounts could be concluded with Italy. Of the accounts representing claims of the Confederation, 60% were recognized.

After the German currency reform had been accomplished in 1948 but before termination of the regime of occupation, the Allies were interested in settling the question of the German debts. The Swiss would have preferred to tackle this difficult problem at a later time. But the timing was fixed by the Allies, who in 1952 sent out invitations to a conference in London about settlement of the German debts. Switzerland, as the third largest creditor, had to participate. The attempt to place the so-called "clearing billion" on the agenda met with great obstacles, however. The United States, Britain, and France, wished to discuss only the prewar and postwar debts. Those debts that had arisen during the war should be left aside because their inclusion in the talks would have prejudged the reparation problem. The Swiss delegates, however, were determined to settle the question of the "clearing billion" within the framework of the London conference. After long preliminary talks, the claim originating in the clearing was eventually admitted on the agenda, as the Swiss delegates would otherwise have left the conference. In subsequent negotiations in Bern, the German delegate offered a bare 50 million francs in settlement of the "clearing billion." The Swiss delegates demanded 600 million, in analogy with the result that had been worked out with Italy. After negotiations that lasted for months, 500 million francs were eventually agreed upon. For the German partner in the negotiations, acceptance of the compromise was made easier by Switzerland declaring her willingness to reinvest 100 million in the German Federal Railroads, to finance the electrification of the important connecting line Karlsruhe-Basel. Besides the "clearing billion," a number of secondary claims, amounting to 180 million francs, had to be settled. Because Switzerland's position as a negotiating party was even more difficult here, the Swiss delegates stated right at the outset that Switzerland would be willing to invest an amount to be agreed on in the German steel industry with the understanding that another agreement, to be concluded simultaneously, would provide for German deliveries of steel whenever this product became scarce. In the definitive agreement the amount was eventually set at 150 million, of which 110 million were invested in the steel industry and 40 million in the German Federal Railroads. Apart from their importance for the steel industry and the

German Railroads, these reinvestments had a positive psychological impact. The fact that Switzerland was prepared to grant credits to the German economy, which at that time was still run down, evoked great interest in and outside of Germany.

Acceptable compromises could be negotiated in London about the private claims as well. Indemnities for nationalizations were agreed on with some East European countries. Thanks to the clearing agreements concluded with these countries, the indemnities could be successively realized. Financial settlement with Eastern Germany was not achieved, however.

Within the framework of the European Payments Union, which provided for a multilateral clearing, the surplus countries had to grant to the deficit countries credits amounting, on the average, to 50% of their surplus balances. In view of the economic situation the German Federal Republic in its first few years saw fit to draw on the EPU credits to a considerable extent. As a result other countries, Switzerland among them, became creditors. The Swiss claim threatened to reach the billion level in a few years. Ways and means were therefore being sought to limit it.

When the agreement with Germany about the reinvestment of clearing balances had become known, the French State Railroad had something to say. It pointed out that the railway line Karlsruhe-Basel, which in a way was competing with French lines, was favored by the impending electrification, and the French inquired about the possibility of a Swiss credit for the electrification of French connecting lines. As the Swiss Federal Railways supported the request, the Federal Council declared its willingness to grant the credit, provided it would be handled through EPU. This meant a corresponding reduction of the Swiss creditor position within the Payment Union. The credit transaction was, in fact, carried through in this manner. Not much time passed before the Italian State Railroad, too, put out a feeler. Although the direct line leading up to the Gotthard Pass was already electrified, there were various lines on the way to the Simplon Pass which the Swiss Federal Railroads were interested in electrifying. Moreover, a large number of unsolved questions between Switzerland and Italy were still open, and these could be settled in the course of the credit negotiations. This credit, amounting to 200 million francs, was likewise handled through EPU, with a view to reducing the creditor position of Switzerland. At the end of this series of credits stood Austria, which obtained a credit of 55 million for further development of the Arlberg railroad line. In this way a network of electrified railway approaches, which greatly contributed to transit traffic through Switzerland, came into being.

Private capital export also began flowing again. From 1947 to 1955 loans to foreign borrowers, amounting to 1.7 billion, were floated on the Swiss market.

By setting up investment trusts, the Swiss banks gave a strong impetus to capital export. In ever-increasing measure foreign portfolios were entrusted to these banks, which had a long history of managing foreign property.

Foreign banks established demand deposits and time deposits with Swiss banks. As there was no domestic money market of adequate absorbing capacity, the banks reinvested these funds abroad. After convertibility had been restored in 1959, the interdependence between the Swiss banking system and foreign economies increased more and more. In the postwar period, foreign firms and financial groups decided to establish holding companies in Switzerland in order to control their European affiliated companies from there. The central location of the country, the convertibility of its currency, the fact that several languages were spoken there, all favored the development described.

Similar considerations induced foreign financial groups to set up financial companies and banks in Switzerland. In this way Switzerland grew into the role of an international financial center, although this goal had not been consciously aimed at.

The history of the Swiss financial center is very instructive in several respects. It shows, first of all, that Switzerland's role as a financial center is not an accidental result of postwar developments, but is built on an old tradition of capital export. At the same time, the historical record shows that the export of capital, viewed over this long time span, moved in waves, with many setbacks and disappointments. We have seen that there was a substantial capital export at the beginning of the eighteenth century during the Spanish War of Succession, and in another period at the end of that century until the Napoleonic era put an end to this development. In the nineteenth century Switzerland at first became a capital importing country. The construction of railways and the establishment of banks could be financed only by drawing foreign capital into the country; the growing Swiss industry absorbed to a large extent the capital that had been formed at home. It was not until after the war of 1870-71 that some capital export came to life again, and only toward the end of the century did the stream broaden. After World War I, Switzerland once more saw fit to import capital. But it would appear that capital exports exceeded imports as early as the middle of the twenties. These findings are of interest because they show that the flow of capital, unlike the flow of goods, changes direction only slowly. This is not without importance for an evaluation of the present currency situation. In the first two decades after World War II, American capital flowed into foreign countries without there being any evidence of capital imports worth speaking of. Only after the capital markets of Europe had recovered their strength did European capital once more begin to flow into the United States. This movement might help to solve the difficult balance of payments problem.

[9]

Excerpt from Benedicte Vibe Christensen, *Switzerland's Role as an International Financial Center*, iii–v, 1–40.

Switzerland's Role as an International Financial Center

By Benedicte Vibe Christensen

Contents

CONTENTS

The following symbols have been used throughout this paper:

. . . to indicate that data are not available;

— to indicate that the figure is zero or less than half the final digit shown, or that the item does not exist;

– between years or months (e.g., 1984–85 or January–June) to indicate the years or months covered, including the beginning and ending years or months;

/ between years (e.g., 1985/86) to indicate a crop or fiscal (financial) year.

"Billion" means a thousand million.

Minor discrepancies between constituent figures and totals are due to rounding.

Note: The term "country," as used in this publication, does not in all cases refer to a territorial entity that is a state understood by international law and practice; the term also covers some territorial entities that are not states but for which statistical data are maintained and provided internationally on a separate and independent basis.

Prefatory Note

This paper was prepared by Benedicte Vibe Christensen in the European Department of the International Monetary Fund under the direction of Gyorgy Szapary. It describes developments in international financial transactions conducted through the Swiss banking system until December 1985. The paper continues recent work in the Fund on capital markets in individual countries. It also supplements the annual description on developments in international capital markets prepared by the International Capital Markets Division of the Exchange and Trade Relations Department of the Fund.

The study has benefited substantially from information and assistance from the Swiss National Bank and the Federal Administration of Finance. The author also acknowledges with appreciation comments and suggestions received from John T. Boorman, David Brodsky, Eliot Kalter, Leslie Lipschitz, Duncan Ripley, Gyorgy Szapary, and C. Maxwell Watson. The author is grateful to Behrouz Guerami for research assistance and to the editor, Juanita Roushdy, of the External Relations Department. The views expressed in this paper represent those of the author and not necessarily those of the Fund.

I Introduction

Switzerland, through a long tradition of banking and finance, has developed into a major center for international financial transactions. In recent years, however, significant institutional changes in most large capital centers have challenged Switzerland's traditional role as a financial center. Deregulation of domestic banking in other countries has reduced its comparative advantage of having a universal banking system. The creation of new offshore banking facilities and the repeal of the withholding tax on interest income of nonresidents in the Federal Republic of Germany, France, and the United States in 1984 have changed the competitive environment. In addition, capital controls have been relaxed in several countries, including France and Japan, while Germany and the Netherlands have taken measures to strengthen the international competitiveness of their financial markets.

This study describes the characteristics and importance of financial transactions in Switzerland from an international perspective and the structural changes which have taken place in recent years. It also adds to the recent work in the Fund on banking and financial markets and fills a gap in the economic literature on Switzerland.[1] The significance of these transactions for the domestic economy in terms of growth and employment opportunities is not discussed. The description is mainly confined to the financial markets located in Switzerland; that is, it includes transactions by Swiss banks and foreign-owned banks within that geographical area but touches only fragmentarily on the activities of Swiss-owned banks abroad.

Section II explains the reasons why Switzerland has developed into an international financial center. Its long political stability and excellent economic performance in terms of a low rate of inflation, a strong currency and external position, a high standard of living, and sound government finances have been major factors. In addition, the existence of a universal banking system that permits banks to engage in all kinds of transactions, as well as some of the highest capital requirements in the world, has provided a sound framework for development of financial markets. Political neutrality and strict bank secrecy—preserved despite political pressure from abroad—have undoubtedly also played a crucial role.

Section III describes the banking system, including the financial institutions and bank supervision. The big three banks in Switzerland have traditionally dominated international financial business, but foreign banks established in Switzerland have increased their market share substantially in recent years, loosening the cartel-like conditions. The Swiss monetary authorities have encouraged this development to enhance competitiveness within Swiss borders.

Section IV explains the specialization of Swiss financial institutions in portfolio management, foreign exchange, and gold transactions. They have, de facto, a monopoly in bond issues in Swiss francs, as the Swiss National Bank has discouraged the emergence abroad of a Eurobond market in Swiss francs. Another characteristic of Swiss banking is off-balance-sheet fiduciary accounts which have grown rapidly in recent years and are at present of almost the same magnitude as banks' external balance sheet transactions. These accounts—characterized by anonymity and exemption from withholding tax on interest income—have attracted short-term deposits from abroad while reducing the risk of the Swiss banking system associated with international banking.

Section V focuses on three specific developments, namely (i) the relaxation of capital restrictions since 1979, (ii) the Swiss banking system in the early 1980s, and (iii) the competitiveness of Switzerland as an international financial center. First, it describes the role played by capital restrictions during the 1970s in preventing capital inflows from exerting undue upward pressure on the Swiss franc or an excessive increase in domestic liquidity. It is argued that restrictions on capital movements were largely ineffective in insulating the Swiss economy from developments abroad. Indeed, since the gradual removal of capital controls from 1979, there is no indication in terms of the difference between domestic and Euro-Swiss franc interest rates or the variability in exchange or interest

[1] Eken (1984).

rates that capital controls permitted the Swiss National Bank to pursue a more autonomous domestic policy than in the absence of controls. In addition, the removal of capital controls has not significantly increased the official reserve role of the Swiss franc.

The Swiss banking system generally performed well during the debt crisis of the early 1980s. The exposure to high-risk countries was smaller than that of many other countries, and the high capital requirement and the existence of substantial hidden reserves have provided a buffer that protected banks against losses. Swiss financial institutions appear to have benefited from the political neutrality and bank secrecy and the confidence in the Swiss banking system; for example, they have secured a marked increase in the share of deposits of some Latin American countries and Middle Eastern oil exporting countries during periods of political and economic crisis abroad.

With respect to the competitiveness of Switzerland as an international financial center, the traditional advantage of the Swiss banking system has been its universal banking system and few capital restrictions and other regulations compared with other countries. The promotion of offshore banking operations and the reduction in taxes on financial transactions in other countries have diminished this comparative advantage in recent years. Market share calculations suggest a small decline in overall market shares of balance sheet transactions in 1982 and 1983 and stagnation thereafter; the decline is partly related, however, to a reduction in assets against high-risk countries and to valuation effects in connection with the appreciation of the U.S. dollar. Moreover, in the case of Switzerland, it is particularly important to consider off-balance-sheet items, for which comparable data with other countries are not available. At present, the main policy question with respect to competitiveness is the level and structure of taxes levied on financial transactions in Switzerland and, in particular, the stamp duty, which is a major reason for the lack of both a developed domestic money market and Eurobond trading in Switzerland. The stamp duty poses a particular disadvantage for Swiss banks compared with banks in Luxembourg and the United Kingdom.

II Development as an International Financial Center

Historical Developments

Switzerland has a long tradition of capital exports. As domestic savings exceeded domestic spending, Swiss financiers and governments were already actively engaged in international finance in the eighteenth century. Net capital exports continued into the twentieth century, except during periods of the nineteenth century, when domestic credit demand increased with industrialization and the building of railroads, and for a time after World War I. The excess of domestic savings was largely a result of financially sound governments in the cantons and towns and was in marked contrast to the large financing needs of many other European governments, which resulted from continuous engagements in war. The financial performance of both the Swiss governments and the private sector was based on several factors. First, the country maintained political neutrality and thereby did not incur large war expenses. Neutrality was a consequence of the multiconfessional and multilingual character of the Confederation, the strategic location in the center of Europe, and the small size of the country.[2] Second, Switzerland was able to maintain trade with the belligerent countries and also benefited, on a large scale, from income earned from Swiss military service abroad, through treaties concluded with foreign sovereigns. Finally, in the early stage of industrialization, Swiss exports of cotton and silk products prospered because of little competition from abroad.

Although Switzerland had exported capital for centuries, it was not until the twentieth century that it became a "safe haven" for foreign funds and began to intermediate between foreign savings and credit demand. After World War I, the currencies in Austria and Germany collapsed and the financial systems were in disarray. Switzerland, having avoided hyperinflation and having been less affected by political unrest than other European countries, became attractive as a safe depository for funds during the 1920s and the 1930s, and Swiss banks received deposits on a massive scale, mainly from Germany. A new Banking Law passed in 1934, to protect depositors during the worldwide banking crisis of the 1930s, created problems for Switzerland not only with Germany during World War II but also with the United States after the war. A side product of the law was rules on bank secrecy, which prevented banks from providing information on bank accounts to outsiders. These rules precluded Switzerland from acceding to the demands of the U.S. Government to have German assets held in Swiss bank accounts and in other placements confiscated for war reparations. Despite substantial political pressure, the Swiss Government did not succumb to the demands but rather agreed to a compromise whereby only part of the German assets in Switzerland would be confiscated for war reparations.[3]

Switzerland's ability to preserve a relatively stable and strong currency increased the attractiveness of the Swiss banking system. Only once in the period from the end of World War I to 1971 was the Swiss franc devalued (in 1936). Switzerland also maintained a very low rate of inflation by international standards. During the 1950s, the increase in consumer prices averaged 1 percent a year. With the strong expansion in economic activity, prices accelerated to an annual rate of 3 percent during the 1960s and 4½–5 percent in the period 1970–85, closely following the rate of inflation in the Federal Republic of Germany, but inflation was still low compared with other industrial countries (Chart 1).

Since the early 1960s, international financial transactions have expanded strongly, with the convertibility of major currencies and liberalization of capital movements. When monetary conditions at home and abroad differed considerably, Switzerland experienced substantial inflows of foreign capital which exerted an upward pressure on the Swiss franc. During political upheavals abroad, the neutrality of Switzerland and

[2] Swiss neutrality as it exists at present developed through centuries. It was recognized formally by the European powers in the Congress of Vienna (1815).

[3] In 1952, German firms that had their assets held in Switzerland confiscated were indemnified.

Chart 1. Switzerland: Economic Indicators

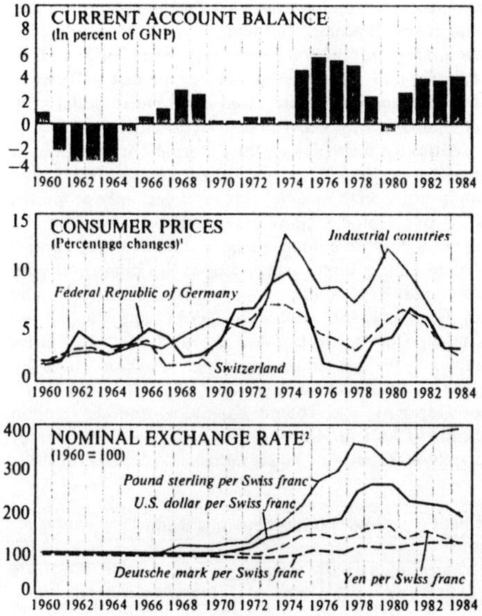

Source: International Monetary Fund, Data Fund.

¹ Compared with the same period of the preceding year.

² An increase (decrease) in the index indicates appreciation (depreciation) of the Swiss franc.

Chart 2. Nominal and Real Short-Term Interest Rates

(In percent)

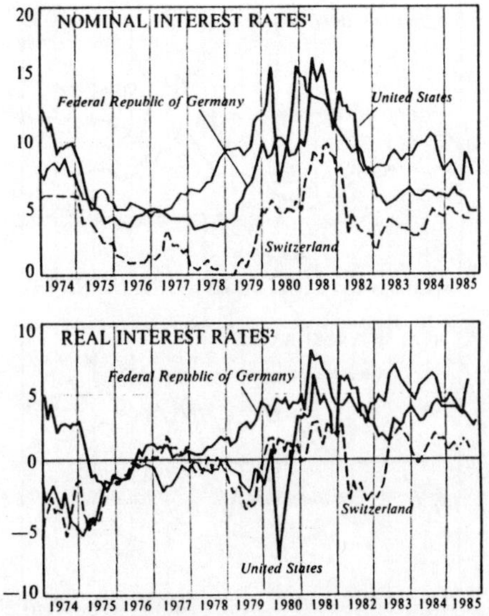

Sources: International Monetary Fund, Data Fund; and staff calculations.

¹ For the Federal Republic of Germany, three-month interbank rates; for Switzerland, three-month deposit rates with the big banks; for the United States, three-month treasury bills.

² Deflated by the increase in the consumer price index in a month compared with the same period of the preceding year.

its bank secrecy also played a role in attracting capital inflows. This was the case, for example, when Egypt's accounts in the United Kingdom and in the United States were temporarily frozen after the Suez crisis and again in the wake of the first major oil price increase in 1974 and also during the political events in the Islamic Republic of Iran in the late 1970s. Despite several attempts to discourage capital inflows, the monetary authorities frequently had difficulty in controlling domestic liquidity without allowing a sharp appreciation of the Swiss franc (Section V).

Since the early 1980s, however, international capital flows have not seriously conflicted with domestic policy aims. This is possibly explained by the sharp tightening in monetary policy in the United States and in other countries, which permitted the Swiss authorities to pursue a monetary policy aimed at securing price stability without threatening external competitiveness (Charts 2 and 3). The high return on U.S. dollar and other foreign exchange assets is possibly also the explanation why the international debt crisis in the early 1980s led to an increase in foreign exchange denominated deposits with Swiss banks (especially fiduciary deposits) rather than Swiss franc deposits, thereby leaving the exchange rate unaffected (Section V).

Conditions for Development as an International Financial Center

The history of Switzerland illustrates some of the factors which have been important for the development of its financial center. Because of its small economy, it is not a natural center for international trade and finance as are the large industrial countries (e.g., the United Kingdom and the United States). Nor has its

Chart 3. Nominal and Real Long-Term Interest Rates
(In percent)

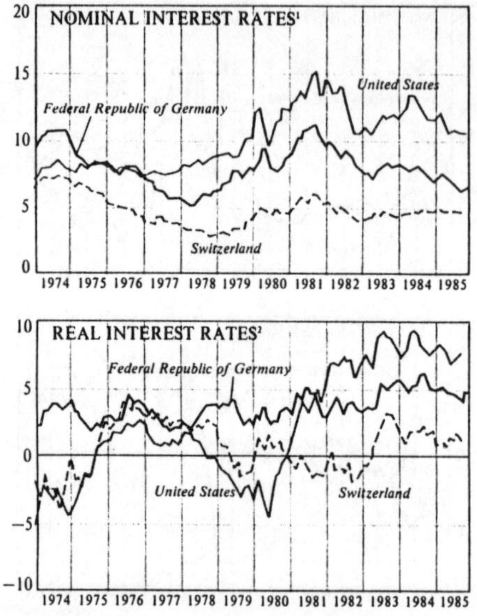

Sources: International Monetary Fund, Data Fund; and staff calculations.
[1] Public bond yields.
[2] Deflated by the increase in the consumer price index in a month compared with the same period of the preceding year.

Government promoted it through the creation of offshore facilities or special tax incentives or bank supervision as have the governments of other small economies (e.g., the Cayman Islands, Hong Kong, and Singapore). Rather, it has been a combination of fundamental political and economic factors, such as high economic growth, low inflation, external surpluses, sound government finances, political neutrality, bank secrecy, and a universal banking system, that has established confidence in its financial markets. None of these factors is unique to Switzerland. But few countries have, to the same extent, experienced so many of these conditions and maintained them over a long span of years.

Switzerland's geographic position, in the heart of Europe, also played an important role in its development as a financial center. It was no coincidence that the first Swiss banking centers emerged in Geneva and Basle close to France and the Federal Republic of Germany. In addition, the use of three main European languages (French, German, and Italian) has also facilitated international banking. The hard-working mentality of the Swiss people is no less a factor—working hours in Switzerland continue to be high by comparison with other industrial countries.

Although a surplus on the external current account is not a necessary condition for a country to become an international financial center, it certainly promotes it. Swiss capital exports developed because domestic savings exceeded domestic needs. Switzerland continues to have a high savings propensity compared with other industrial countries, such as the Federal Republic of Germany, the United Kingdom, and the United States. During the last two decades, both the gross and net savings ratios have been exceeded only by Japan's and have been substantially above the ratios of Germany, the United Kingdom, and the United States (Chart 4). Despite the relatively small size of the Swiss economy, among industrial countries in 1985,

Chart 4. Gross and Net Savings Ratios[1]

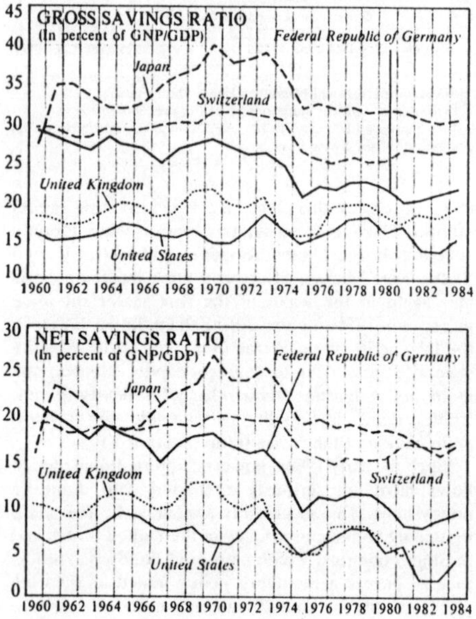

Source: Organization for Economic Cooperation and Development, *National Accounts Statistics*.
[1] Net savings equal gross savings less depreciation.

the current account surplus of Switzerland (US$4½ billion) was exceeded only by that of Japan (US$49½ billion), Germany (US$13 billion), and the Netherlands (US$5 billion). During the fixed exchange rate system that prevailed until 1973, current account surpluses and capital inflows resulted in massive exchange rate intervention by the Swiss National Bank, which led to a strong official reserve position of Switzerland. The valuation of gold plays an important role for the ranking of countries. With gold valued at SDR 35 an ounce in all countries, official reserves of Switzerland (SDR 18½ billion) were the sixth largest recorded in any country by the Fund at the end of 1985. But with gold valued at market value in all countries, official reserves of Switzerland (SDR 42 billion) were exceeded only by those of the United States (SDR 111 billion), Germany (SDR 70 billion), and France (SDR 50 billion).[4]

The existence of a universal banking system in Switzerland has given its banks a competitive advantage over countries in which specialized banking has prevailed. The federal structure of the country has made it important that banks in every canton and municipality be able to perform all kinds of banking transactions. The principle of universality was adopted in the Swiss Banking Law of 1934 at a time when a worldwide bank crisis induced other countries to impose restrictions on banking activity. For example, the 1933 Banking Act in the United States separated commercial banks from investment banks. In Europe, the Banking Law of 1935 introduced in Belgium prohibited banks from acting as both deposit banks and holding companies; in Italy, the Banking Law of 1936 drew a distinction between short-term and long-term credit institutions. In addition to Switzerland, universal banking systems exist in Denmark, the Federal Republic of Germany, Luxembourg, and the Netherlands.

The financial markets in Switzerland have benefited from the existence of bank secrecy. Bank secrecy, which protects banks' clients from misuse of confidential information relating to their financial transactions, is not unique to Switzerland. But in Switzerland, it is more protective than in most other countries.[5] It differs in two major aspects. First, the Banking Law prescribes severe penalties for breach of bank secrecy.[6] Just as with violations of official secrecy, breach of banking secrecy is prosecuted ex officio by law; while violations of other professional secrecies (e.g., medical doctors, attorneys, and priests) are prosecuted only upon request of the injured party. In most other countries, bank secrecy is protected only by civil law; in a few cases (such as Austria, France, and the Netherlands), where breaches of bank secrecy are also prosecuted under criminal law, softer sanctions apply and prosecution is not ex officio.

Second, although banks are in certain cases obliged to provide information to the public authorities on clients' accounts, such requirement applies only to cases where criminal acts as defined under Swiss law are being investigated. For violations of domestic or foreign fiscal and foreign exchange laws, bank secrecy can be lifted and international judicial assistance granted under Swiss law only when fraud is involved. This is not possible for tax evasion which, although subject to administrative sanctions, is not prosecuted at criminal level in Switzerland. The legal treatment of tax evasion, however, is to be interpreted in connection with the 35 percent witholding tax on capital earnings, which limits the scope for tax evasion.

Bank secrecy and the rules for providing information to the authorities in case of criminal offense or inheritance apply equally to "numbered" and other accounts. Numbered accounts, however, differ from other accounts in that the identity of the owner is known to fewer people within the bank. It is estimated that less than 10 percent of Swiss banking accounts are numbered accounts.[7] They are not a feature specific to the Swiss banking system but are used also, for example, in Austria, Belgium, the Cayman Islands, France, Hong Kong, Luxembourg, and Singapore. In some of these banking systems, numbered accounts are truly anonymous in the sense that the identity of the account holder is not disclosed to the bank.

In recent years, Swiss bank secrecy has come under attack from abroad in connection with "insider trading" violations. The Securities and Exchange Commission (SEC) in the United States has demanded information from Swiss banks about their customers in order to investigate cases of insider trading. According to present Swiss law, however, insider trading is not a criminal offense. Therefore, bank secrecy cannot be lifted and judicial assistance granted to foreign authorities. In retaliation, the SEC threatened to bar certain Swiss banks and their customers from the U.S. securities market. Consequently, in 1982 a

[4] International Monetary Fund, *International Financial Statistics*; foreign exchange reserves include foreign exchange from swaps with the private banks. The market price for gold in London in 1985 on average (US$317 a fine ounce) has been used to calculate the value of gold holdings at the end of 1985.

[5] Since 1981, when a new law on bank secrecy took effect in Luxembourg, the regulations concerning bank secrecy in Luxembourg and Switzerland have been almost identical. In cases of inheritance, however, Luxembourg banks are not allowed to disclose information on foreign-owned accounts to heirs, in contrast to Swiss banks.

[6] Violators may be punished by a prison term up to six months and a fine of up to SwF 50,000.

[7] Meier (1983).

compromise was reached, whereby the Swiss banks signed a Convention ("Convention XVI") that specified certain procedures to be followed. According to the Convention, a request by the SEC for information on a bank's customer in connection with insider trading investigations will be considered by a specially appointed Commission comprising Swiss citizens who are independent of banks. The banks will provide information to the Commission on the customer's transactions, and if the case fulfills certain criteria, information will be forwarded to the SEC with the possibility of blocking the accounts in question. Convention XVI is meant to be only a transitory solution. On May 1, 1985, a proposal was made by the Swiss Federal Government to Parliament concerning an amendment of the criminal law according to which insider trading would become a criminal offense. Such an amendment would enable the Swiss authorities to grant judicial assistance to foreign countries provided that the conditions mentioned in the bilateral treaties or the Federal Law concerning International Mutual Assistance in Criminal Matters are met.

III The Banking System

Financial Institutions

The Swiss banking system is characterized by the coexistence of privately and publicly owned banks. The publicly owned banks include the cantonal banks, owned by the cantons, and local savings banks, run with the capital of the municipalities. These public institutions accounted for about 16 percent of the total assets of Swiss banks at the end of 1984. The private banks are organized mainly as joint-stock corporations or as cooperatives. Although Swiss banks are organized as universal banks, their historical development has led to some specialization. Cantonal banks, regional banks, and savings and loan associations have specialized in savings deposits and long-term mortgage lending, while the so-called "big banks"[8] have concentrated on company finance and international finance. During the last two decades, however, there has been a tendency for banks to engage in a broader field of transactions; the big banks have engaged more actively in mortgage lending through proliferation of their domestic bank network, while the cantonal and regional banks have participated increasingly in portfolio management.[9]

Since World War II, a concentration has taken place in Swiss banking, as the big Swiss banks and foreign-owned banks have expanded at the expense of other banks. The main expansion occurred during the 1960s, when international operations grew strongly, but the trend has continued through the 1970s and the early 1980s. Measured on the basis of both assets and fiduciary assets,[10] the big banks increased their share in banking transactions from 42½ percent in 1974 to 47 percent in 1984 (Chart 5). During the same period, foreign-controlled banks and finance companies expanded from 14 percent to 23 percent of the total. The gains in market shares of the big banks and foreign banks relative to "other banks" mirror the much more rapid expansion in international, compared with domestic, transactions.

Most foreign banks were established during the 1960s, when Switzerland gained importance as an

Chart 5. Market Shares in Swiss Banking
(In percent)

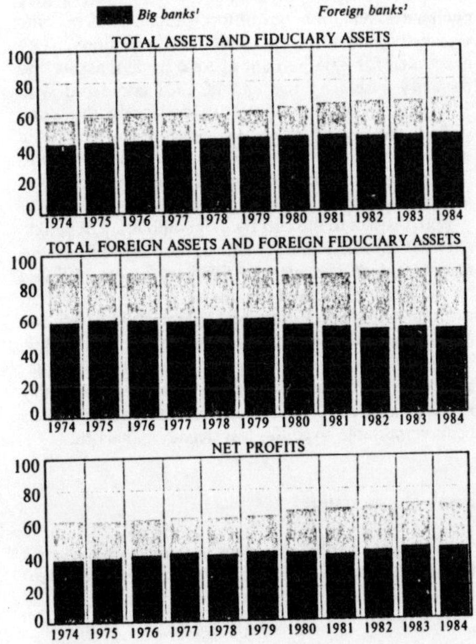

Source: Swiss National Bank, *Das schweizerische Bankwesen.*
¹ Big five banks.
² Foreign-controlled banks in Switzerland, foreign-owned finance companies, and branches of foreign banks in Switzerland.

[8] The "big banks" in Switzerland, as defined in the Swiss banking statistics, consist of five banks. Three banks (Crédit Suisse, Swiss Bank Corporation, and Union Bank of Switzerland) clearly have the character of large, universal banks, while two others (Bank Leu and Swiss Volksbank) are smaller and engage in more limited activities.

[9] Many cantonal banks are prohibited from engaging actively in international finance by cantonal laws.

[10] Fiduciary accounts are explained on pages 12–13.

international financial center. They comprise three major groups: (i) banks with more than 50 percent foreign ownership, (ii) finance companies, and (iii) branches of foreign banks in Switzerland. The establishment in Switzerland of foreign banks is permitted on a fairly liberal basis on condition that (i) the principle of reciprocity applies, that is, that Swiss banks have equal access to establishment in the country of the foreign parent bank; that (ii) the foreign banks comply with the Swiss Banking Law and rules and regulations of the central bank; and that (iii) the name of the foreign bank does not imply a Swiss character.[11] In recent years many Japanese banks have established themselves in Switzerland. This has partly occurred through opening of branches but especially through finance companies (around 20 Japanese finance companies at the end of 1984). Finance companies in Switzerland are—by contrast to similar institutions in Japan—allowed to participate in underwriting of bond issues and in portfolio management.

The increasing importance of foreign banks, finance companies, and branches of foreign banks has become especially evident in international transactions. They accounted for 37½ percent of total foreign assets and fiduciary assets by the end of 1984 compared with 31½ percent at the end of 1974. During the same period, the big Swiss banks registered a decline in market shares of foreign business, from 58 percent to 52½ percent, while the share of "other banks" was almost unchanged at 10–11 percent.

With respect to the currency denomination of banks' external transactions, at the end of 1984, 21 percent of total external assets and fiduciary assets of Swiss banks were expressed in Swiss francs, of which, external assets accounted for 17 percentage points and fiduciary accounts 4 percentage points. The remainder, 79 percent, was denominated in foreign exchange, equally divided among external assets and fiduciary assets. The Swiss franc share of external assets has been very stable over the last decade (Chart 6).

Chart 6. External Assets and Fiduciary Assets of Swiss Banks
(In percent)

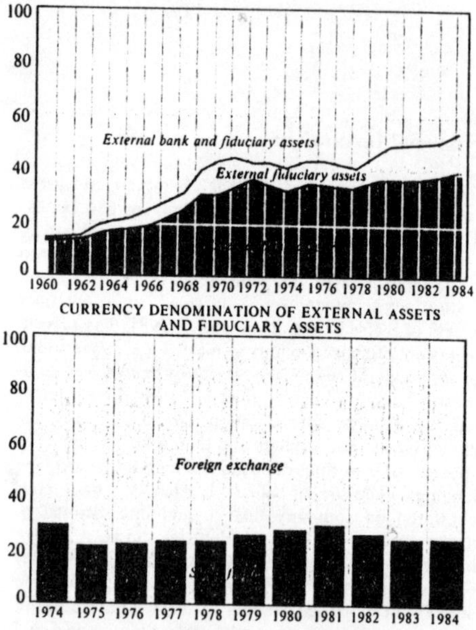

Source: Swiss National Bank, *Das schweizerische Bankwesen*.
[1] External bank and fiduciary assets in percent of total bank and fiduciary assets.
[2] External assets in percent of total bank assets.

Bank Supervision

The Swiss banking system is supervised by the Federal Banking Commission, which is independent of both the Swiss National Bank and the Federal Government.[12] A characteristic of the Swiss banking supervision is the fact that the Federal Banking Commission has delegated its authority to external auditors.[13] A few other countries apply similar systems. For instance, in Belgium, each bank appoints two external auditors, one selected by the general assembly of shareholders and the other by the Banking Commission to provide information to the Commission. In the Federal Republic of Germany, external auditors

[11] At the end of 1984, the Federal Banking Commission reported that reciprocity was guaranteed by the following countries, states, and territories: Austria, Belgium, Canada, Denmark, France, the Federal Republic of Germany, Hong Kong, Israel, Italy, Japan, Lebanon, Luxembourg, the Netherlands, Spain, the United Kingdom, and in the United States, the States of California, Connecticut, Florida, Illinois, Indiana, New York, Ohio, Pennsylvania, and Wisconsin.

[12] Separate supervisory organizations exist also in Belgium, Canada, France, the Federal Republic of Germany, and Sweden. The central bank has the responsibility for bank supervision in Italy, the Netherlands, and the United Kingdom, and in Luxembourg, the monetary institute (in the absence of a central bank) exercises supervision. In Japan, bank supervision is divided between the central bank and the Ministry of Finance, which has the formal responsibility. In the United States, bank supervision is shared between federal and state authorities, the Federal Reserve System, and special federal agencies.

[13] Eidgenössische Bankenkommission (1985).

are obligated to report irregularities to the Supervisory Office which may also insist on the appointment of a special auditor. In many other countries, however, for example, Italy, Japan, and the United States, direct inspection by the supervisory authorities is carried out with no formal contact with a bank's auditors. The United Kingdom is an exception, insofar as supervisors refrain both from inspecting directly and from relying formally on a bank's external auditors, who are under no obligation to furnish information to the supervisory body.

All banks in Switzerland are subject to supervision. Since July 1984, however, in line with recommendations of the Cooke Committee,[14] branches of foreign banks are not subject to Swiss capital requirements if the country of the parent bank exercises surveillance of the banks located in Switzerland. With respect to liquidity, however, branches of foreign banks are obliged to place at least 10 percent of their assets in Switzerland.

Bank supervision applies also to finance companies if they solicit deposits in public. In practice, only 4 of the 110 finance companies that engage in capital exports are subject to the Banking Law and banking supervision; none of the 4 is a foreign-owned company. With the rapid increase in the number of finance companies in recent years, this exception to bank supervision has gained importance.

In December 1980, the Swiss Banking Law was amended so that capital requirements would be linked more closely to the specific asset portfolio of banks. In Switzerland, the so-called weighted capital/risk asset approach is applied, which differentiates capital requirements according to the risk associated with various assets. An alternative approach is the capital/asset requirement, which relates capital requirements to the total balance sheet without regard to the difference in the riskiness of assets. In most European countries, a capital/risk asset approach is used. In the United Kingdom, a combination of both requirements is applied. In the Federal Republic of Germany a capital/asset requirement is in force. In Japan, the capital requirement does not apply to total bank assets but only to foreign assets. In the United States, a capital/asset requirement exists that varies according to the size of the bank; a capital/risk asset approach, however, is used by bank supervisors to judge the adequacy of a bank's capital.

The revision of the Banking Law in 1980 in Switzerland also introduced the principle of consolidated balance sheets for capital requirements. The consolidation encompasses all banks and subsidiaries in Switzerland or abroad in which the parent bank holds at least 50 percent of the capital or exercises a controlling influence in some other manner. The principle of consolidation also applies to the rules for maximum exposure to a single customer. Switzerland was one of the first countries which applied consolidated balance sheets to capital requirements.

Capital is defined to include (1) paid-in capital, (2) published reserves, (3) a portion of hidden reserves (if set aside on particular account), and (4) certain subordinated loans.[15] The actual capital ratios have normally exceeded the required ones. The capital ratios in Switzerland both on a capital/asset basis and a weighted capital/risk asset basis are among the highest in industrial countries. International comparisons of these ratios, however, are difficult because compositions of asset portfolios differ and the riskiness of various assets is difficult to evaluate. Moreover, the definitions of equity and reserves and the application of consolidation of balance sheets and of hidden reserves vary among other countries.[16]

The Banking Law of Switzerland provides for the creation of hidden reserves, which is beyond the practice in most other countries. Therefore, actual capital ratios for Swiss banks are probably much higher than disclosed in Table 1. While the creation and use of hidden reserves are not known to the public, the Banking Commission receives information from the banks about such transactions. Hidden reserves serve as a buffer against unexpected losses which can be absorbed without appearing in the publicized bank balances. This has the advantage of preventing a decline in a customer's confidence and—in severe cases—a run on the bank, but it also conflicts with the objective of providing an accurate picture of a bank's performance during an accounting period. In the early 1980s, the Swiss news media reported on substantial losses by specific banks, which were never reflected in the banks' balance sheets. In December 1981, however, the Banking Commission in a circular to the banks revoked the right of the banks to use hidden reserves to cover losses without limitation. Since then, the use of hidden reserves to camouflage losses of a bank has been restricted.[17]

Swiss banks are obligated to make capital provisions for certain contingent liabilities and off-balance-sheet transactions, such as open positions in foreign currency (10 percent) and precious metals (20 percent), as well as guarantees and floating rate liabilities. No provisions, however, are required for portfolio management

[14] The Cooke Committee is formally known as The Group of Ten Committee on Banking Regulations and Supervisory Practices. It meets under the auspices of the Bank for International Settlements.

[15] At the end of 1984, the composition of banks' capital was 37 percent paid-in capital, 45 percent published reserves, 13 percent hidden reserves, and 5 percent subordinated loans.

[16] Watson and others (1986).

[17] Eidgenössische Bankenkommission (1985).

Table 1. Capital Ratios for Swiss Banks[1]
(In percent of total assets)

	1981		1982		1983		1984	
	Required	Actual	Required	Actual	Required	Actual	Required	Actual
Big banks	7.0	7.4	6.7	7.3	6.7	7.1	6.8	7.1
All banks	6.4	7.5	6.2	7.5	6.2	7.3	6.3	7.4

Source: Swiss National Bank, *Das schweizerische Bankwesen.*
[1]Nonconsolidated basis.

and underwriting obligations, which also entail risks.[18] Capital requirements do not apply to fiduciary accounts. Because the Banking Law is phrased in terms of general principles rather than detailed rules, innovations in financial markets have not given rise to an immediate need for a revision of the Banking Law, as has been the case in some other countries.

The Federal Banking Commission has refrained from imposing limits on country exposure in banks' international lending. The Commission's position is that country risks should be assessed individually by the banks and that each bank should take the responsibility for its lending policy. Nevertheless, with the emergence of the international debt crisis in the early 1980s, the monitoring of country risks has increased. At the end of 1982, the Commission requested banks to provide a detailed country breakdown of their international transactions and information on their write-off practices and risk provisions for countries identified by the Banking Commission as problem countries. On this basis, it required that banks, in addition to regular capital requirements, make 20 percent provisioning for those problem countries (Section V).

[18] Lusser (1985).

IV International Capital Transactions

Short-Term Transactions

Money Market Transactions

The international money market transactions of Swiss banks serve partly as a substitute for a domestic money market and partly as a connection between the various segments of domestic and international financial transactions, including the Euro-Swiss franc market. The domestic money market is characterized by its thinness in terms of limited money market instruments and few participants. The lack of a developed money market is mainly attributable to fiscal impediments, especially the stamp duty, which amounts to 0.15 or 0.30 percent—independent of maturity—depending on whether the debtor is a resident or a nonresident.[19] This is a prime reason for the lack of short-term instruments and for the fact that existing paper is often held to maturity. The existence of the stamp duty is also one of the reasons why less than 15 percent of the marketable debt of the Federal Government consists of short-term liabilities; there is no market for treasury bills as in many other countries. In addition, Swiss banks have not issued certificates of deposits to attract funds, in part because of resistance in the past from the Swiss National Bank which has feared that this instrument would compete with savings deposits with low interest, thereby raising the overall level of banks' costs. Furthermore, Swiss industry has covered its short-term financing needs through bank credits rather than through commercial paper. Finally, export and import financing have normally not been associated with issuance of bankers' acceptances, partly due to the stamp duty but also in order to protect customer relationships.[20]

[19] This implies an annualized interest cost of, for instance, 0.6 or 1.2 percent for transactions of three months' maturity and 8.1 or 16.9 percent for transactions of one week's maturity, when the debtor is a resident or nonresident, respectively.

[20] Corti (1983).

In the absence of domestic short-term paper, Swiss banks have invested surplus funds abroad. The bulk of their interbank transactions is with foreign banks (78 percent of assets and 53 percent of liabilities, at the end of 1984). The smaller Swiss banks typically adjust their liquidity position through the big banks which, together with foreign banks in Switzerland, are the main transactors in the international money market.

Fiduciary Accounts

Fiduciary accounts constitute an increasingly important element of short-term transactions of Swiss banks and especially of external transactions.[21] They accounted for 24 percent of total assets and fiduciary assets (domestic and external) and for 44 percent of total external assets and external fiduciary assets at the end of 1984. They emerged during the 1960s at the same time as international banking picked up. They grew particularly rapidly after the second oil price rise with the emergence of sizable funds from the Organization of Petroleum Exporting Countries (OPEC). In the period between the end of 1979 and the end of 1984, foreign fiduciary assets grew by 24 percent a year in Swiss franc terms, compared with 14 percent a year of banks' external assets.

Fiduciary accounts are off-balance-sheet deposits and loans of a bank for the account of, and at the risk of, the customer with respect to the currency, transfer, and credit risk. To qualify for preferential fiscal status (exemption from withholding tax), a written contract between the bank and the customer has to exist. The maturity of deposits is normally from one to three months, but, in practice, the deposits are often rolled over so that they resemble medium-term placements.

[21] Fiduciary accounts are excluded from the reportings of Swiss banks' assets and liabilities to the international banking statistics of the Bank for International Settlements. But they are included in those of the Fund as presented in *International Financial Statistics*. In the Fund's statistics, it is assumed that fiduciary assets of Swiss banks are claims on banks abroad, while fiduciary liabilities are to nonbanks abroad.

The banks perform no maturity or currency transformation but act solely as intermediaries, especially in the international money market. Notwithstanding the fact that the customer carries the full risk of a fiduciary transaction, the customer does not always know where the funds are placed. Equally, if the funds are placed with a foreign bank that bank is usually not aware of the underlying fiduciary transaction but considers it a normal transaction with a Swiss bank.

Fiduciary accounts are mainly denominated in foreign currencies (especially U.S. dollars), and most customers are nonresidents, although Swiss residents are free to hold fiduciary assets (also without withholding tax) and receive fiduciary loans. At the end of 1984, 90 percent of all fiduciary accounts were denominated in foreign currencies (68 percent in U.S. dollars) and the remainder in Swiss francs. At the same time, 84 percent of banks' fiduciary liabilities and 99 percent of their fiduciary assets were against nonresidents.

The advantages of fiduciary deposits for the customer are (1) the exemption from the 35 percent withholding tax which applies to domestic deposits, (2) a small bank fee, (3) the discrete character of fiduciary operations compared with a direct placement in the international money market, and (4) the higher return available on Eurodeposits compared with domestic deposits. These benefits, however, have to be weighed against the risk associated with a fiduciary account compared with a bank deposit. The risks are twofold: the depositor has the full risk associated with the bank where the fiduciary deposits are redeposited abroad. In addition, the depositor has the risk with the Swiss bank where the deposit is placed, because the foreign bank which holds a liability against a Swiss bank does not distinguish the liability from any other against that bank and therefore might use it to cover outstanding claims against the Swiss bank should the Swiss bank default. For the Swiss banks, the advantages of fiduciary accounts are (1) a commission of 0.25–0.5 percent a year, (2) no risks and, consequently, (3) no liquidity or capital requirements.

From an economic point of view, the fiduciary business is close to other bank transactions, where the banks act as pure intermediaries. They affect capital movements in the same way as other bank transactions. If the Swiss banks act solely as intermediaries between two nonresidents, no net capital movements take place in Switzerland. In practice, however, Swiss residents have been providing funds for fiduciary lending to nonresidents, giving rise to capital outflows, cumulating to SwF 34 billion at the end of 1984. For the Swiss economy as a whole, the fiduciary business results in current receipts (commissions) from abroad amounting to SwF ½–1 billion a year (¼–½ of 1 percent of gross national product) (estimated by the Fund staff on the basis of outstanding fiduciary accounts at the end of 1984). To the extent that only nonresidents are involved, the fiduciary transactions imply no risk to the Swiss economy. The legal issues involved, however, are rather complex. Suppose, for instance, that Swiss banks although not legally obliged are de facto willing to cover a default connected to placements abroad. In this case, fiduciary transactions should be included in liquidity and capital requirements. There is no disclosed information about any default of a fiduciary business and the Swiss banks' response to it. Another issue which has been relevant in recent years is the treatment of fiduciary business in negotiations about "new money" to debtor countries. Swiss banks have argued that fiduciary accounts should not be included in calculations of the Swiss banks' share in package deals, despite the fact that to foreign banks there is no difference between a balance sheet transaction and a fiduciary transaction of a Swiss bank.

Medium-Term and Long-Term Transactions

General Characteristics

The comparative advantage of Swiss financial markets in international transactions has traditionally been in medium-term and long-term operations, particularly public bond and note issues.[22] The importance of Swiss markets derives, in part, from the substantial placing power of Swiss banks both with private and institutional Swiss investors associated with the high domestic savings ratio and with foreigners who rely on Swiss banks for portfolio management. For borrowers, the low nominal interest rate on Swiss franc issues, compared with issues in U.S. dollars, deutsche mark, Netherlands guilders, and pounds sterling, has also been attractive, although the exchange rate appreciation of the Swiss franc wiped out any interest rate advantage during the 1970s. A low nominal interest rate for an appreciating currency might be attractive to a borrower compared with a high nominal interest rate for a currency with a tendency to depreciate because of the reduced liquidity requirement, insofar as the appreciation of the currency is reflected in payments—other than interest—only at the time of redemption of the loan. In this respect, it resembles an indexed liability.

Bond issues denominated in Swiss francs form a significant proportion of the international bond market. In 1985, they accounted for 48 percent of all recorded

[22] The difference between notes and public foreign bond issues is explained on pages 17–19

foreign bond issues in the world, making Swiss francs the most important currency of denomination for these issues (Table 2). The share of Swiss franc issues in total international bonds, which comprise both foreign bonds and Eurobonds, amounted to 9 percent in 1985 with the Swiss franc being the second most important currency of denomination after the U.S. dollar, which accounted for 60½ percent of international bond issues. It was followed by the yen, accounting for 8 percent of total issues, and the deutsche mark, accounting for 6½ percent of total issues. The value of Swiss franc issues was roughly twice the value of issues denominated in pound sterling and in ECUs (European Currency Units). The share of the Swiss franc increased sharply from 11½ percent of international bond issues in 1974 to a peak of 25 percent in 1979. Since then, however, the share declined following the strong expansion of Eurobonds denominated in U.S. dollars in recent years.

The Swiss bond market for foreign issues is primarily confined to issues denominated in Swiss francs while Eurobond issues in other currencies are very few. The main reason for limited Eurobond activity in Switzerland is the stamp duty on every sale of securities. The stamp duty applies also to transactions of security dealers. Moreover, a large number of investors in bond issues are Swiss residents who have a preference for investments in Swiss francs rather than other currencies. There are no official data on investors in foreign bond issues on the Swiss market, but private Swiss banks estimate that more than half of public issues and about half of the notes are placed with Swiss residents. Swiss banks, however, participate actively through their foreign branches in Eurobond trading and issues abroad.[23]

That Swiss banks established in Switzerland have de facto monopoly in bond issues in Swiss francs is another feature of the Swiss bond market. The Swiss National Bank has prevented the emergence of a Eurobond market in Swiss francs for fear of uncontrolled internationalization of the Swiss franc. Legally, the Bank has not been in a position to prevent foreign banks outside Switzerland from issuing bonds denominated in Swiss francs. In practice, however, the Bank has made its position clear, both publicly and directly, to foreign banks that have considered issuing Swiss franc bonds or bonds with a Swiss franc link abroad. As long as the operations in Swiss francs remain in Switzerland, the central bank is in a position to supervise and, if necessary, to control bond issues. The nonexistence of a Eurobond market in Swiss francs has given Swiss banks a kind of monopoly that has resulted in relatively high fees and commissions for Swiss franc issues compared with issues in other currencies. For instance, the fees and commissions on an eight-year public bond issue in Swiss francs amount to about 3¼ percent, compared with about 2 percent for a Eurodollar issue with a similar maturity. This difference can probably be attributed to the absence of a Euro-Swiss franc bond market. For note issues in Swiss francs, however, the fees and commissions are similar (1⅞ percent) to public bond issues in the Eurodollar market.

Competition within the Swiss capital market seems to have increased somewhat in recent years. This is partly due to the removal of capital export regulations and the liberal implementation of the authorization practice of bond issues by the Swiss authorities, including the attitude toward swaps, which have been one of the driving forces in international capital transactions in recent years. As pointed out by the Deutsche Bundesbank in its *Monthly Report* of July 1985, the liberal authorization practice is evidenced by the fact that gross issues of Swiss franc bonds and notes of nonresident borrowers were twice as many (US$38 billion) as issues of foreign deutsche mark bonds (US$19 billion) during the period 1982–84, while Switzerland's GNP was only 15 percent of that of the Federal Republic of Germany.

Total gross medium-term and long-term capital exports, which comprise public bonds, medium-term notes, and bank credits, totaled SwF 46½ billion in 1985 (Table 3).[24] Capital exports have expanded at an annual rate of 14½ percent (measured in Swiss franc terms) during the last decade. While bank credits accounted for the strongest expansion between 1974 and 1981, public issues and notes have grown faster since 1982. This development is partly a result of the relaxation of restrictions on foreign bond issues, especially secondary market trading in notes, since 1982. In addition, the increasing importance of bond issues reflects the general trend in international lending in recent years toward securities rather than bank credits, which is, in part, related to the debt crisis of the early 1980s.

Another recent development has been the gradual disappearance of the boundaries between the various categories of capital exports. For instance, notes which used to be private placements now resemble public bond issues. Moreover, foreign bond issues comprise

[23] In 1984, Crédit Suisse First Boston, which is owned, in part, by one of the big Swiss banks, was by far the most dominant lead manager in Eurobond issues, accounting for 16½ percent of the total value of Eurobond issues. In the second and third place were a U.S. bank and a German bank accounting each for 7½ percent of total issues.

[24] The figures mentioned here and in the following sections apply to "authorized" medium-term and long-term capital exports, which comprise all transactions of SwF 10 million and above of more than 12 months' maturity.

Table 2. International Bond Issues[1]

	1974	1975	1976	1977	1978	1979	1980	1981	1982	1983	1984	1985
						(In millions of U.S. dollars)						
Eurobonds	**3,396**	**8,743**	**14,705**	**18,724**	**14,961**	**18,691**	**20,394**	**31,294**	**50,329**	**50,098**	**81,717**	**135,431**
U.S. dollar	1,991	3,379	9,390	11,573	6,767	10,360	13,649	25,761	42,228	39,205	65,334	96,482
Deutsche mark	639	2,918	2,789	5,219	6,478	5,881	3,457	1,396	3,253	4,042	4,324	9,491
Pound sterling	24	—	—	221	287	291	975	535	846	2,153	3,965	5,766
Yen	—	10	—	111	79	184	301	410	598	233	1,190	6,539
ECU	—	—	—	—	—	—	—	153	823	2,191	2,938	7,038
Other	742	2,436	2,526	1,600	1,350	1,975	2,012	3,039	2,581	2,274	3,966	10,115
Foreign bonds	**5,243**	**11,217**	**18,413**	**16,263**	**20,713**	**20,308**	**17,924**	**20,514**	**25,199**	**27,050**	**27,801**	**31,025**
U.S. dollar	3,587	6,712	10,801	7,868	6,358	4,365	2,709	6,856	6,025	4,735	4,294	4,655
Deutsche mark	—	353	1,171	1,407	1,431	2,690	4,951	1,196	2,109	2,618	2,419	1,741
Pound sterling	—	33	—	—	—	—	178	911	1,129	859	1,649	958
Swiss franc	972	3,414	5,381	4,959	7,406	9,718	7,470	8,118	11,325	13,500	13,120	14,954
Yen	—	67	226	1,276	4,388	2,671	1,543	2,723	3,317	3,851	4,873	6,379
Other	684	638	834	753	1,130	864	1,073	710	1,294	1,487	1,446	2,338
Total international bonds	**8,639**	**19,960**	**33,118**	**34,987**	**35,674**	**38,999**	**38,318**	**51,808**	**75,528**	**77,148**	**109,518**	**166,456**
						(In percent)						
Foreign bonds	**100.0**	**100.0**	**100.0**	**100.0**	**100.0**	**100.0**	**100.0**	**100.0**	**100.0**	**100.0**	**100.0**	**100.0**
U.S. dollar	68.4	59.8	58.7	48.4	30.7	21.5	15.1	33.4	23.9	17.5	15.4	15.0
Deutsche mark	—	3.1	6.4	8.7	6.9	13.2	27.6	5.8	8.4	9.7	8.7	5.6
Pound sterling	—	0.3	—	—	—	—	1.0	4.4	4.5	3.2	5.9	3.1
Swiss franc	18.5	30.4	29.2	30.5	35.8	47.9	41.7	39.6	44.9	49.9	47.2	48.2
Yen	—	0.6	1.2	7.8	21.2	13.2	8.6	13.3	13.2	14.2	17.5	20.6
Other	13.0	5.7	4.5	4.6	5.5	4.3	6.0	3.5	5.1	5.5	5.2	7.5
Total international bonds	**100.0**	**100.0**	**100.0**	**100.0**	**100.0**	**100.0**	**100.0**	**100.0**	**100.0**	**100.0**	**100.0**	**100.0**
U.S. dollar	64.6	50.6	61.0	55.6	36.8	37.8	42.7	63.0	63.9	57.0	63.6	60.7
Deutsche mark	7.4	16.4	12.0	18.9	22.2	22.0	21.9	5.0	7.1	8.6	6.2	6.7
Pound sterling	0.3	0.2	—	0.6	0.8	0.7	3.0	2.8	2.6	3.9	5.1	4.0
Swiss franc	11.3	17.1	16.2	14.2	20.8	24.9	19.5	15.7	15.0	17.5	12.0	9.0
Yen	—	0.4	0.7	4.0	12.5	7.3	4.8	5.3	4.4	5.0	5.5	8.1
ECU	—	—	—	—	—	—	—	0.3	1.1	2.8	3.6	4.2
Other	16.4	15.3	10.1	6.7	6.9	7.3	8.1	7.9	5.9	5.2	4.0	7.5

Source: Organization for Economic Cooperation and Development, *Financial Statistics*.
[1]Figures may not add up because of rounding.

an increasing share of assets portfolios of banks. The share of foreign bond issues in total foreign assets of Swiss banks has risen from 4½ percent at the end of 1974 to 7 percent at the end of 1984. Similar blurring of boundaries between traditional bank lending and capital market transactions is observed in other countries.[25]

The Swiss capital market has traditionally been accessible only to first-class borrowers. Industrial countries accounted for 79 percent of medium-term and long-term capital exports in 1985, while non-oil developing countries made up only 5 percent and state-trading countries and OPEC countries together accounted for 3½ percent (Table 3). The emergence of the debt crisis in the early 1980s prompted Swiss banks to adopt a more cautious lending policy, leading to a concentration of lending to industrial countries rather than developing countries. Indirectly, however, developing countries have benefited from the tapping of the Swiss capital market by development organizations (e.g., the World Bank, the Asian Development Bank, and the Inter-American Development Bank), which accounted for 12 percent of medium-term and long-term borrowing in 1985.

Among industrial countries, Japan has been a prominent borrower in recent years. According to the Swiss National Bank, more than half of the notes in 1983 and 1984 were issued by Japanese borrowers, implying that they accounted for at least one fourth of total medium-term and long-term capital exports.[26] This also helps explain the proliferation of Japanese-owned banks and, especially, finance companies in recent years. The bulk of the notes was issued as convertible notes, that is, with the option of conversion to equity. Frequently, these convertible notes are converted into equity six to eight weeks after the issue date and the equity is bought by Japanese investors. The early conversion practice also implies that the issues of

[25] Bank for International Settlements, *Annual Report* (1985).

[26] Swiss National Bank, *Monatsbericht*.

Table 3. Switzerland: Medium-Term and Long-Term Capital Exports (Authorized)[1]

	1974	1975	1976	1977	1978	1979	1980	1981	1982	1983	1984	1985	1974	1985
	(In millions of Swiss francs)												*(In percent)*	
By instrument:														
Public issues	1,011	2,490	3,510	3,684	4,430	5,206	5,486	7,575	9,975	10,292	11,150	16,850	20.2	36.3
Notes	2,769	7,162	10,483	9,319	8,996	11,319	9,438	11,846	17,709	20,685	19,337	18,468	41.1	41.9
Bank credits	1,876	2,482	5,167	5,263	8,464	10,345	8,398	12,784	9,849	9,205	10,137	10,089	38.7	21.7
Total	5,656	12,134	19,160	18,266	21,890	26,869	23,322	32,205	37,532	40,181	40,625	46,387	100.0	100.0
By borrower:														
Industrial countries	...	...	...	...	14,012	19,892	16,024	22,902	28,030	31,620	29,902	36,732	64.0	79.2
Non-oil developing countries	...	...	...	...	3,259	2,885	3,430	4,508	3,711	3,438	3,596	2,236	14.9	4.8
State-trading countries	...	...	...	...	745	1,473	834	1,443	539	435	916	1,654	3.4	3.6
Of which:														
Eastern Europe	...	...	...	...	*655*	*1,423*	*722*	*1,341*	*539*	*435*	*756*	*1,442*	*3.0*	*1.9*
Other	...	...	...	...	*90*	*50*	*112*	*102*	—	—	*160*	*212*	*0.4*	*0.4*
OPEC countries	...	...	...	...	662	706	434	467	127	233	386	112	3.0	1.0
Development organizations	...	...	...	...	3,213	1,914	2,600	2,885	5,125	4,456	5,826	5,653	14.7	12.2
Of which:														
World Bank, ADB, IDB[2]	...	...	...	...	*2,360*	*1,185*	*1,694*	*1,993*	*4,026*	*3,590*	*4,936*	*5,057*	*10.8*	*12.2*
Other	...	...	...	...	*855*	*729*	*907*	*892*	*1,099*	*867*	*891*	*596*	*3.9*	*2.2*
Total	5,656	12,134	19,160	18,266	21,890	26,869	23,322	32,205	37,532	40,181	40,625	46,387	100.0	100.0

Source: Swiss National Bank, *Monatsbericht*.

[1] Capital exports which are subject to authorization from the Swiss National Bank comprise public issues of at least SwF 10 million, credits or participation in credits, which amount to SwF 10 million and above and have a maturity of at least 12 months, and issues of notes amounting to SwF 3 million and above and with a maturity of 12 months and above; figures may not add up because of rounding.

[2] ADB (Asian Development Bank); and IDB (Inter-American Development Bank).

notes constitute short-term Swiss capital exports and that the statistics therefore overstate the extent of medium-term and long-term capital exports. The advantages of this "round-tripping" of Japanese borrowing via the Swiss capital market for the Japanese borrower are to secure funds at lower costs than through issues in Japan and, for the Swiss economy, to receive fees, commissions, and fiscal duties (e.g., stamp duty).

The Swiss capital market has also been attractive to international development organizations, especially the World Bank. In the World Bank's fiscal year 1985 (July 1, 1984–June 30, 1985), 25 percent of its gross borrowing (including swap transactions) was denominated in Swiss francs, followed by 20 percent in yen, 17 percent in deutsche mark, and 8 percent in U.S. dollars. Thus, Swiss franc borrowings reached the maximum limit agreed between the World Bank and the Swiss National Bank. The World Bank converts the Swiss franc proceeds with the Swiss National Bank and the latter replenishes its foreign exchange reserves through foreign exchange purchases in the market according to market conditions. In this way, the conversion requirement serves mainly to prevent disorderly conditions in the foreign exchange market resulting from large transactions.

Since 1982 the World Bank has made extensive use of currency swaps in Swiss francs because its credit rating on that market is affected by an already high amount of outstanding debt in Swiss francs.[27] The distribution between direct borrowings in Swiss francs and swaps is shown in Table 4.

In agreement with the Swiss National Bank, swap transactions have not exceeded 40 percent of total gross borrowings of the World Bank in Swiss francs.[28] The Swiss monetary authorities have generally shown a more liberal attitude than some other central banks (e.g., in the Federal Republic of Germany, Japan, and the Netherlands) to the use of swap transactions for both international development organizations and other borrowers. At the beginning of the 1980s, the Swiss authorities feared that borrowing on the Swiss market through swap transactions would increase the amount of borrowing on the market and drive up Swiss interest rates. However, as no disorderly conditions have occurred in the capital market, the official attitude has become more liberal. The Swiss authorities have recognized that they could not prevent the proceeds from loans in Swiss francs from being swapped against other currencies at some time.

Table 4. World Bank Swiss Franc Borrowing
(In millions of Swiss francs)

World Bank Fiscal Years	1981	1982	1983	1984	1985
Borrowing	1,832	3,235	2,971	3,590	4,926
Swaps	—	1,097	2,364	1,906	2,212
Total	1,832	4,332	5,335	5,496	7,138

Source: The World Bank.

Notes

Notes are medium-term bond issues and accounted for nearly half of total medium-term and long-term capital exports in 1985. The maturities range from a minimum of 18 months to a maximum of 8 years (requirements of the Swiss authorities), with 5–7 years being the normal maturity. Notes are usually paid back in full at maturity (bullet maturity), although other repayment schedules are permitted. Early redemption is allowed only after 18 months or after the expiration of half of the maturity. The restrictions have been imposed to prevent early repayments and thereby increased demand for Swiss francs in periods when the Swiss franc was appreciating. Note issues picked up strongly in 1982 after the lifting of restrictions on secondary market trading.

Until the early 1980s, notes used to be placed with a limited number of institutional investors (around 10–15) without any publicity. Similarly, they were not listed on Swiss Stock Exchanges, and no public prospectus for investors was required; however, since secondary market trading was permitted in 1982 (Section V), the character of note issues has changed, and the boundaries to public issues are disappearing. Both the amounts and the name of the borrower are now disclosed, and trading in the secondary market is very active (especially in convertible notes). Consequently, the Swiss National Bank raised the question in 1985 of whether note issues should be considered "public issues," and require a public prospectus. On the federal level, there is no supervision of the securities markets such as, for instance, the Securities and Exchange Commission in the United States. On the cantonal level, there is supervision only of stock exchanges.

The Swiss National Bank which has opposed Eurobond issues in Swiss francs has also prevented a secondary Eurofranc note market from developing

[27] A typical currency swap transaction consists of, for instance, a U.S. company borrowing in Swiss francs on the Swiss capital market and the World Bank simultaneously borrowing in U.S. dollars on the U.S. market. The World Bank and the U.S. company then swap the liability and interest payments so that the World Bank incurs a liability in Swiss francs and the U.S. firm a liability in U.S. dollars.

[28] The Swiss National Bank has requested information on swap transactions by international development organizations.

Table 5. Comparison of Notes and Public Issues

	Notes	Public Issues
Syndication	"Ad hoc" syndicate or through a single bank	Lead management by major three banks (two thirds of issues) or "ad hoc syndicates"
Amount	No limit	No limit[1]
Maturity	Swiss National Bank (SNB): min. 18 months max. 8 years Standard: 3–7 years	SNB: min. 8 years Standard: 8–12 years
Denomination	SNB: min. SwF 50,000 in bearer form	No legal requirement SwF 5,000 and SwF 100,000 in bearer form
Interest payments	Mostly annual; in case of convertibles, mostly semiannual	Mostly annual; in case of convertibles, mostly semiannual
Repayment schedule	Standard: bullet[2]	Standard: —After fifth year, borrower makes annual purchases in secondary market of up to 5 percent of issue amount if prices are at or below par. Amounts which cannot be purchased automatically become due at maturity —bullet[2]
Documentation	(a) Underwriting agreement or paying agency agreement (b) Short memorandum distributed to interested clients	(a) Underwriting agreement or paying agency agreement (b) Short prospectus published in three major newspapers (c) Full-length prospectus for investors
Listing	No listing	Zürich, Geneva, Basle, Lausanne, Bern
Secondary market	Active	Active
Investors	Private and institutional investors	Private and institutional investors
Physical delivery	SNB: not permitted; compulsory safe custody deposit account with underwriter or SEGA (Swiss Security Clearing Organization)	Possible
Withholding tax	None	None
Approvals	SNB	SNB and Admission Board of Swiss Stock Exchanges
Costs		
Underwriting commission	1½ percent for 5 years plus ⅛ of 1 percent for each additional year	2¼ percent for 8 years plus ⅛ of 1 percent for each additional year
Management fee	—	½ of 1 percent up to SwF 100 million, ¼ of 1 percent exceeding amounts
Listing commission	—	¼ of 1 percent
Taxes[3]	0.315 percent	0.315 percent
Turnover tax (paid by investor)	0.3 percent	0.3 percent
Paying agent fee	¼ of 1 percent on annual interest payments, ⅛ of 1 percent on repayment of principal	¼ of 1 percent on annual interest payments, 0.3 percent on repayment of principal
Printing costs	About SwF 20,000	About SwF 30,000
Admission and quotation fees for stock exchange listings	—	SwF 1,600 and about SwF 2,300 a year

Sources: Crédit Suisse, *Swiss Capital Market*, July 1985; and Swiss National Bank, *Monatsbericht*.
[1]On January 1, 1984, the maximum limit on public issues was raised from SwF 100 million to SwF 200 million. On May 15, 1985, the ceiling was completely lifted.
[2]Full repayment at expiration of term.
[3]Calculated on issue price less underwriting commission and management fee.

abroad. It has required that notes be held physically in custody in Switzerland with the bank of issue or (since January 1984) with the Swiss Security Clearing Organization (SEGA) from issue to maturity. The regulation seems mainly to provide information to the Swiss authorities on trading in notes and to make the notes subject to the stamp duty. While the rule may discourage secondary trading in notes among nonresidents, it does not prevent it from taking place. For instance, an investor in London is free to sell a Swiss franc note to an investor in New York. The note would physically remain in Switzerland and, in principle, the transaction would be registered in Switzerland, and be subject to the stamp duty. In practice, however, there is a market in Euro-clear and CEDEL with certificates, which replace the original notes and thereby permit secondary market trading abroad without any Swiss taxes.[29]

Public Foreign Bond Issues

Public foreign bonds comprise foreign bonds issued with a minimum maturity of 8 years and average maturities of 8–12 years. To avoid additional exchange rate pressure during currency unrest, early repayment is allowed only after 5 years. The bulk of the issues are denominated in Swiss francs, but since mid-1982 dual currency issues have appeared. Their share in total public issues rose from 4 percent in 1982 to 12 percent in 1983 and then declined to 9 percent in 1984. Typically, the principal of a dual currency issue has been expressed in U.S. dollars and interest payments in Swiss francs. They cater both to U.S. borrowers who have been able to borrow at interest rates 1–2 percentage points lower than on straight U.S. dollar issues and to Swiss investors interested in receiving interest payments in Swiss francs. Floating rate issues are allowed but remain the exception. Issues with variable interest rates are in demand especially by banks in need of matching their assets and liabilities. The bulk of investors in Swiss franc issues, however, prefer fixed interest rates. In the spring of 1985, the first zero coupon bond issue was floated in Switzerland.

Since 1980, the restrictions on public bond issues have gradually been lifted. Foreign issues are no longer subject to obligatory conversion of the Swiss franc proceeds with the Swiss National Bank.[30] Equally the queuing system has been removed effective January 1, 1984. Before then, the queuing system served to prevent the bunching of foreign bond issues and thereby erratic increases in interest rates on the bond market. De facto, this led to a quota system among market participants, insofar as bond issues were approved according to existing market shares of the various banking groups leading the issues. The system worked to the advantage of the established big banks but to the disadvantage of smaller domestic banks and foreign-owned banks.[31] The Swiss National Bank was interested in increasing the competition among banks, because banks located in Switzerland were the only issuers of Swiss franc bonds. Partly as a consequence of the elimination of the queuing system, the market share of the big banks as lead managers has declined from about three fourths, in the late 1970s and early 1980s, to about two thirds, in 1985.

Public issues by foreigners exceeding SwF 10 million still remain subject to the permission of the Swiss National Bank which, however, is granted on a liberal basis. The Swiss National Bank has also gradually eliminated the ceiling on individual public bonds. On January 1, 1984, the ceiling was raised from SwF 100 million to SwF 200 million, and in May 1985, the ceiling was eliminated altogether.[32]

[29] Euro-clear and CEDEL are international securities clearing houses formed by banks and securities dealers for the collective custody and book entry transfer of securities, notably Eurobonds.

[30] International development organizations, however, are still converting their borrowing proceeds with the Swiss National Bank.

[31] Lusser (1985).

[32] The existence of a ceiling on public issues compared with no ceiling on notes probably led to a switch from issues in public issues to note issues. The lifting of the ceiling was not expected to increase significantly the total value of foreign bond and note issues.

V Recent Developments in International Financial Markets

Relaxation of Capital Restrictions

Under a floating exchange rate system, the monetary authorities are faced with the dilemma of whether to target the growth in the money supply or the exchange rate. The dilemma is even more acute for an international financial center, where domestic residents have easy access to foreign currency deposits, which might render the demand for domestic money volatile. In addition, the demand for a reserve currency—such as the Swiss franc—reflects the portfolio choices of foreign asset holders and, therefore, might fluctuate with major shifts in world savings, for example, increases in OPEC funds in the first years following the second oil price rise and, more recently, large net savings in Japan. The demand for a reserve currency is also subject to erratic changes as a result of political events. In this respect, the Swiss franc is possibly more sensitive than other reserve currencies owing to the neutrality and bank secrecy of the country. It can also be argued that the small size of the Swiss economy and the money supply make the Swiss franc exchange rate more sensitive to capital flows than the exchange rate of major currencies, such as the deutsche mark.

During the fixed exchange rate system, capital controls were used to dampen capital inflows and the resulting increase in domestic liquidity and, thereby, in part, insulate monetary developments in Switzerland from developments abroad. With the advent of floating exchange rates, the Swiss National Bank shifted its policy target to the money supply. The setting of monetary targets began in 1975, the same year as in the Federal Republic of Germany. The shift from fixed to floating exchange rates did not resolve the conflict between exchange rate and monetary policies, as the Swiss franc appreciated strongly in real effective terms until 1978, deteriorating Swiss external competitiveness (Chart 7).[33] Therefore, during the first years of floating the Swiss National Bank continued to rely on capital restrictions to limit foreign capital inflows. But these restrictions were not effective in preventing strong capital inflows in 1978 from forcing the authorities to abandon the monetary target for that year. Consequently, from 1979, the Bank began to gradually dismantle nearly all capital restrictions and embarked on a controlled internationalization of the Swiss franc. Since 1980, the authorities have reintroduced monetary targeting as the main policy instrument to secure price stability.

The rest of this section gives a description of the background of capital restrictions and an evaluation of the effects of the removal of capital restrictions on monetary and exchange rate developments and the official reserve role of the Swiss franc. The conclusion reached is that capital controls were largely ineffective during the 1970s and their removal has not given rise to problems in monetary or exchange rate management. This outturn, however, was a crucial result of the sharp tightening in monetary policy abroad during the same period as capital restrictions were removed. Finally, the more liberal access to holdings in Swiss francs has not significantly increased the official reserve role of the Swiss franc.

Recent History of Capital Restrictions

During the 1970s, the Swiss franc was frequently exposed to strong upward pressure. In addition to reducing official interest rates and intervening in the foreign exchange market, the Swiss authorities tried to limit capital inflows through capital controls, while promoting capital exports through a liberal authorization practice. The choice of instruments, however, was greatly impaired by an almost complete lack of information on capital flows.[34]

In August 1971, when the Swiss franc came under

[33] During the same period, the deutsche mark also appreciated significantly.

[34] Swiss National Bank (1982), p. 230; see also Appendix I, Statistical Coverage.

Chart 7. Exchange Rate Developments

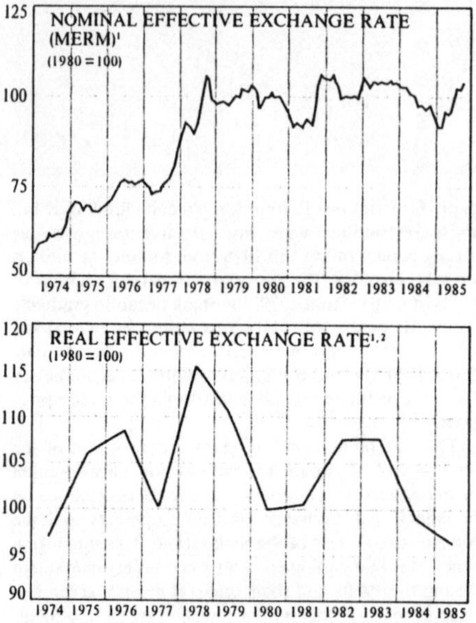

Source: International Monetary Fund, *International Financial Statistics*.

[1] An increase (decrease) in the index indicates an appreciation (depreciation) of the Swiss franc; MERM (multilateral exchange rate model).

[2] Relative unit labor cost.

strong upward pressure during the U.S. dollar crisis,[35] the Swiss National Bank ceased its intervention in the exchange market and imposed, inter alia, a 100 percent minimum reserve requirement on any increase after July 31, 1971 in banks' net liabilities to nonresidents and prohibited interest payments on any increase in Swiss franc deposits of nonresidents after July 31, 1971. When the pound sterling began floating in June 1972 and the Swiss franc again came under upward pressure, a new series of control measures was introduced. Nonresidents were not allowed to buy Swiss franc-denominated bonds or other securities or purchase real estate in Switzerland. Furthermore, foreign borrowing by Swiss nonbanks was made subject to authorization. At the same time, a penalty in the form of a commission charge of 2 percent a quarter was levied on all net increases in Swiss franc deposits of nonresidents. This so-called "negative interest rate" was temporarily suspended in October 1973.

After the floating of the Swiss franc in January 1973, the control measures were initially retained. In November 1974, when funds from oil exporters were shifted to Switzerland, the ban on interest payments and a negative interest rate of 3 percent a quarter was reintroduced. In the period from mid-1975 to mid-1977, when exchange rate pressure subsided, capital restrictions were temporarily relaxed; however, in the second half of 1977, upward pressure on the Swiss franc intensified. Consequently, in February 1978, imports of foreign bank notes were restricted, the negative interest rate on increments in nonresidents' deposits was raised to 10 percent a quarter, and the ban on interest payments was extended to deposits of foreign monetary authorities, which had hitherto been exempted. Finally, as the Swiss franc had appreciated by 26½ percent in real effective terms between the second quarter of 1977 and the third quarter of 1978 (Chart 7) the Swiss National Bank abandoned its monetary target in October 1978. Instead, the Bank announced a temporary exchange rate target against the deutsche mark, declaring its intention to intervene in the exchange markets to achieve a rate well above SwF 0.80 per deutsche mark.

The difficulty in preventing capital inflows and the appreciation of the Swiss franc gave rise to a reassessment of policies from 1979. The Swiss National Bank recognized that the main determinants of capital movements were monetary and other economic policies pursued in Switzerland and abroad. Adjustments in asset portfolios to reflect changes in economic conditions could not for a prolonged period be prevented by capital restrictions, because there was ample scope for circumvention.

As a consequence, since 1979 the Swiss National Bank has lifted practically all restrictions on capital inflows. This change was facilitated by the depreciation of the Swiss franc, stemming, in part, from a tightening of monetary policy abroad, especially in the Federal Republic of Germany and the United States. The steps in liberalization are described in detail in Appendix II. In summary, the most significant changes were permission, in January 1979, for nonresidents to buy securities denominated in Swiss francs; elimination of the limit on forward sales of Swiss francs in March 1980; gradual removal in the period to August 1980 of the ban on payment of interest and the levy of negative interest rates on increases in Swiss franc deposits of nonresidents; and removal of a license requirement for borrowing abroad by Swiss residents. The only restriction that remained on capital inflows was the requirement of approval by the cantons for real estate investment by nonresidents in Switzerland. This re-

[35] Capital controls during the period 1971–76 in Switzerland are described in greater detail in Baumgartner (1977).

striction, however, was not motivated by exchange rate considerations.

Impact of Relaxation of Capital Restrictions

The impact of the removal of capital restrictions since 1979 is discussed here in terms of (1) the monetary target, (2) the exchange rate and interest rate volatility, and (3) the official reserve role of the Swiss franc.

During the first three years of monetary targeting the annual targets were, by and large, observed (Table 6). In 1978, however, M1 expanded by 16 percent against a target of 5 percent. As mentioned earlier, the upward pressure on the Swiss franc subsided in 1979 and a monetary target was again set for 1980. In both 1980 and 1981, however, actual monetary growth fell substantially short of the targets, and the monetary base declined by 7 percent and 0.5 percent, respectively, against an announced target rate of 4 percent for each year. This was partly a result of the reversal of capital flows, but it also reflected a deliberate policy change during the target period to tighten monetary policy in the wake of the inflationary impact of the second round of oil price increases and the sharp tightening in monetary policies abroad. Since 1982, however, the targets have almost been realized, with only limited fluctuations in monetary aggregates.

From the beginning of 1979 to the end of 1985, the Swiss franc has depreciated by 22 percent against the U.S. dollar but appreciated by 5 percent against the deutsche mark. While the Swiss franc depreciated almost continuously against the U.S. dollar until the first quarter of 1985, it fluctuated against the deutsche mark (between SwF 78 and SwF 91 per deutsche mark during the same period).[36] In real effective terms (relative unit labor costs), the Swiss franc has depreciated by 15 percent from 1978 to the first half of 1985, thereby partly reversing the appreciation that took place in the earlier part of the 1970s.

Monetary and exchange rate developments since 1979 have clearly been influenced by the tightening in monetary conditions in the United States and the sharp appreciation of the U.S. dollar. As these developments have coincided with the removal of capital restrictions, it is difficult to distinguish between the effects of the separate events. However, movements in the spread between domestic interest rates and Euro-interest rates for a currency may be looked to as evidence of effective capital restrictions.[37] Changes in the spread between the two rates might indicate changes in transaction costs associated with capital restrictions or other impediments to interest rate parity. As Chart 8 shows, with the exception of 1974, there is no indication of significant changes in the difference between domestic and Euro-Swiss franc interest rates. The two rates follow each other closely, pointing to the existence of free capital movements both before and after the removal of capital controls. Statistical testing of the

Table 6. Monetary Targets in Switzerland

(Percentage change)

	M1		Monetary Base	
	Target	Actual	Target[1]	Actual
1975	6.0	4.4	...	7.4
1976	6.0	7.7	...	4.3
1977	5.0	5.5	...	2.6
1978	5.0	16.0	...	15.3
1979	...	8.4	...	6.8
1980	...	−8.1	4.0	−7.0
1981	...	−3.1	4.0	−0.5
1982	...	3.9	3.0	2.6
1983	...	7.5	3.0	3.6
1984	...	2.7	3.0	2.6
1985	...	0.4	3.0	2.2

Sources: Swiss National Bank, *Annual Reports* and *Monatsbericht*.

[1]The target for 1980 refers to the increase in the monetary base from mid-November 1979 to mid-November 1980. For the other years the target refers to annual average growth rates (average of monthly growth rates).

Chart 8. Three-Month Domestic and Euro-Swiss Franc Deposit Rates

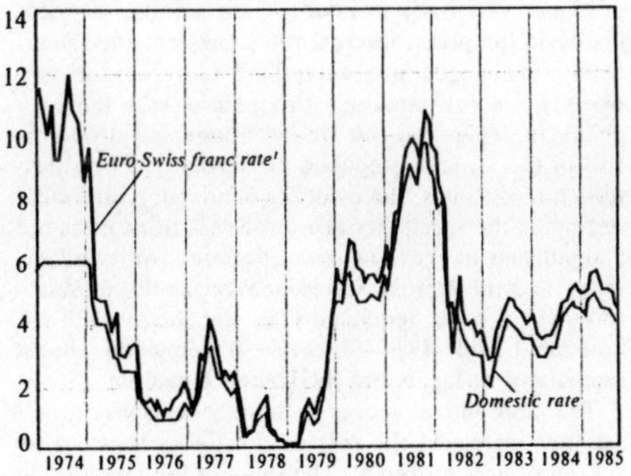

Source: Swiss National Bank, *Monatsbericht*.

[1] Three-month deposit rates in London.

[36] The bilateral exchange rate to the deutsche mark is particularly relevant for Switzerland, as the Federal Republic of Germany accounts for about 30 percent of Swiss merchandise imports and 20 percent of Swiss merchandise exports.

[37] Otani and Tiwari (1981).

two subperiods in terms of the means and standard deviations of the differences in interest rates also confirms that the difference has not diminished since the elimination of restrictions. This would seem to confirm the view that capital restrictions in place before 1979 were ineffective. A similar experience of unsuccessful application of capital controls was made in the Federal Republic of Germany, which also experienced massive capital inflows during the 1970s despite extensive administrative measures to prevent them.[38]

If capital restrictions had achieved their aim of insulating monetary developments from events abroad, it might be expected that the variability in exchange rates would be smaller during the period when capital restrictions were in force. A comparison between the period with restrictions (1974–78) and without restrictions (1979–84), however, seems rather to indicate the opposite, although firm conclusions of causality should be avoided. Since 1979, there has been a decline in the variability in the nominal effective exchange rate of the Swiss franc, while the variability in interest rates has remained unchanged. The variability in the nominal effective exchange rate (calculated using the Fund's multilateral exchange rate model (MERM)), measured as the standard deviation of changes in the natural logarithm of monthly exchange rates, declined on an annual average basis from 1974–78 to 1979–84. A similar development occurred for the deutsche mark, while the variability rose for the pound sterling, the U.S. dollar, and the yen (Table 7). The latter period, however, coincides with the introduction of the European Monetary System, which might also have reduced the variability of the exchange rate of the Swiss franc through its perceived link to the deutsche mark.

The decline in variability of the Swiss franc exchange rate does not appear to have taken place at the expense of higher variability in interest rates. Thus, the variability in long-term interest rates has remained practically unchanged in Switzerland between the two periods, notwithstanding a sharp increase in the variability in Japan and the United States and a notable rise in the Federal Republic of Germany. For short-term interest rates, the evidence is mixed, with a clear decline in the variability of Euro-Swiss franc rates but a significant increase of domestic rates. In both Germany and the United States, the variability in short-term rates rose significantly in the years 1979–84, compared with 1974–78, while it remained almost unchanged in Japan and the United Kingdom.

The more liberal access to holdings of Swiss francs has not increased the role of the Swiss franc as an official reserve currency. The share of the Swiss franc in total identified official holdings of foreign exchange—as estimated by the Fund staff—rose from 2.1 percent at the end of 1978 to a peak of 3.2 percent by the end of 1980 and subsequently declined to 2.0 percent by the end of 1984.[39] For a comparison, during the same period, the share of the yen rose almost continuously from 3.3 percent to 5.2 percent, partly reflecting an easing of capital controls in Japan. The share of "unspecified currencies," however, which especially relate to holdings of oil exporting countries, rose substantially during the same period (from 4.3 percent at the end of 1978 to 11.0 percent at the end of 1984). This implies that the overall official reserve role of the Swiss franc might be underestimated by the identified reserve holdings. The small effect on the official reserve role of the Swiss franc after the removal of restrictions is probably explained, in part, by the limited effectiveness of capital controls before 1979 in satisfying the demand of official Swiss franc holders and, therefore, avoiding pent-up demand for Swiss franc holdings and, in part, by the increase in real returns on U.S. dollar assets after 1979.

Swiss Banking System in the Early 1980s

Since 1979 there have been major shifts in world savings. In the period 1979–81, oil exporting countries experienced substantial net savings which had their counterpart in net dissavings of non-oil developing countries and industrial countries. In the years 1982–85, oil exporting countries registered external current account deficits, while the deficits of non-oil developing countries declined, and industrial countries, excluding the United States, showed growing external surpluses.

This section describes first the changes in liabilities of banks in Switzerland in the early 1980s, especially to oil exporting countries and some Latin American countries and second, the lending exposure of Swiss banks and the intensified supervision by the Federal Banking Commission. The main conclusions are that while the overall share of Swiss banks' liabilities in BIS reporting banks' liabilities declined somewhat between 1979 and 1984, a significant increase was observed in their share in deposits of the Middle Eastern oil exporting countries and Argentina and Brazil. This was probably related to the perceived stability of the Swiss banking system during the international debt crisis. On the lending side, Swiss banks have experienced less exposure to high-risk countries than banks in BIS reporting countries. The Swiss banks reduced, in time, their large exposure to Mexico.

[38] Deutsche Bundesbank (1985).

[39] International Monetary Fund (1985), Table 14.

Table 7. Variability of Nominal Effective Exchange Rates and Short-Term and Long-Term Interest Rates

	1974	1975	1976	1977	1978	1979	1980	1981	1982	1983	1984	Annual Average 1974–78	Annual Average 1979–84
Variability of nominal effective exchange rates[1]													
Germany, Fed. Rep. of	18.6	11.3	11.4	9.8	14.8	6.8	8.9	18.9	7.6	9.4	12.0	13.2	10.6
Japan	17.1	9.6	9.7	15.1	31.9	19.6	29.6	20.7	29.7	14.3	12.1	16.7	21.0
Switzerland	20.6	12.8	9.3	18.5	35.0	9.7	16.5	28.3	16.0	12.7	9.1	19.2	15.4
United Kingdom	8.1	8.8	24.1	9.4	17.6	20.8	10.5	21.8	17.5	22.6	9.5	13.6	17.1
United States	13.3	16.4	5.2	8.3	15.9	11.2	21.8	21.9	23.2	12.9	19.4	11.8	18.4
Variability of short-term interest rates[2, 3]													
Germany, Fed. Rep. of	66.7	50.0	22.1	8.6	16.8	38.6	49.6	104.3	30.2	31.7	17.7	32.8	45.4
Japan	55.0	56.7	28.0	41.1	28.8	34.0	95.0	29.8	19.2	26.0	28.3	41.9	38.7
Switzerland													
Domestic deposits	9.7	40.8	27.4	48.4	36.8	53.2	42.7	74.4	99.1	43.1	28.0	32.6	56.8
Euro-Swiss franc deposits	116.7	101.7	59.1	76.0	55.3	63.6	61.6	92.6	123.2	42.1	30.6	81.8	69.0
United Kingdom	16.3	50.8	92.4	91.6	70.6	79.2	46.0	79.3	59.2	32.5	73.0	64.3	61.5
United States	64.1	50.0	24.9	19.0	28.3	44.2	215.6	136.7	116.7	29.5	46.6	37.3	98.2
Variability of long-term interest rates[2, 4]													
Germany, Fed. Rep. of	27.6	20.5	19.0	16.1	17.3	25.0	43.7	42.3	25.4	19.6	13.5	20.1	28.3
Japan	14.7	19.5	13.4	22.8	9.5	31.0	61.0	32.5	30.7	15.9	23.3	16.0	32.4
Switzerland	16.2	14.2	15.3	21.4	8.3	14.2	21.9	27.5	18.7	10.7	7.0	15.1	16.7
United Kingdom	41.7	73.4	56.2	56.7	28.2	75.3	39.8	34.8	55.8	31.8	35.3	51.2	45.5
United States	21.7	20.8	14.4	9.7	12.9	27.4	74.8	66.4	60.6	23.8	39.9	15.9	48.8

Sources: International Monetary Fund, *International Financial Statistics*; and staff calculations.
[1] Standard deviation (multiplied by 1,000) of the change in the natural logarithm of the average monthly MERM (multilateral exchange rate model) exchange rates.
[2] Standard deviation (multiplied by 100) of changes in monthly interest rates.
[3] Domestic three-month rates, except for Japan, where call money rates have been used.
[4] Public bond yields.

Bank Liabilities

In the first half of the 1980s, total bank deposits and fiduciary deposits doubled (in Swiss franc terms) to SwF 342 billion (US$132 billion) at the end of 1984.[40] Industrial countries accounted for a declining share of total deposits, while deposits of the Caribbean rose substantially (Table 8). The balance of payments problems of Central American countries (including Mexico) resulted—as expected—in a sizable decline in deposits of those countries. By contrast, the deposits of Argentina and Brazil rose markedly at the same time as the official foreign exchange reserves dropped perceptibly in those countries. Middle Eastern oil exporting countries also increased their deposits with Swiss banks, even after several began to experience balance of payments strains from 1982. In this section, the deposits of both Middle Eastern oil exporting countries and of Argentina and Brazil with Swiss banks are compared with total deposits of those countries in BIS reporting banks.

After the second round of oil price increases, the net assets of oil exporting countries rose from US$257 billion at the end of 1979 to US$380 billion by the end of 1983, according to Bank of England estimates.[41] The financial assets of oil exporting countries were initially concentrated in liquid assets, such as bank deposits and short-term money market instruments. Subsequently, they were diversified into longer-term placements in bonds, equities, properties, and loans, often on concessional terms, to other developing countries.

By the end of 1983, about 60 percent of oil exporting countries' assets in all industrial countries was invested in the United Kingdom, the United States, and in the Federal Republic of Germany (Table 9). Most of the remaining 40 percent was probably invested in Switzerland, but a precise estimate is not possible from available data. Thus, there is no information about the amount of Swiss franc-denominated bonds bought by these countries. Equally, there are no figures on purchases of equities and properties by oil exporting countries in Switzerland. Information on oil exporting countries' placements in Switzerland is largely confined to data on bank deposits and fiduciary deposits by Middle Eastern oil exporting countries with Swiss banks.[42] Those countries—as defined in the Swiss banking statistics—include Iraq, the Islamic Republic of Iran, Jordan, Kuwait, Oman, Qatar, United Arab Emirates, Bahrain, Saudi Arabia, the Syrian Arab Republic, the People's Democratic Republic of Yemen, the Yemen Arab Republic, the Libyan Arab Jamahiriya, and Egypt.

Bank deposits of Middle Eastern oil exporting countries with Swiss banks rose from SwF 8 billion at the end of 1978 to SwF 14.9 billion by the end of 1984. The most striking development was the expansion of fiduciary deposits of oil exporting countries with Swiss banks, from SwF 6.3 billion at the end of 1978 to SwF 34.8 billion at the end of 1984 (Table 10). The increase was particularly strong between 1982 and 1984. As a large part of the fiduciary accounts is denominated in U.S. dollars, the increase in Swiss franc terms reflects, in part, the appreciation of the U.S. dollar in that period.

The Swiss banks' share of total BIS reporting banks' liabilities (including Swiss banks' fiduciary liabilities) to Middle Eastern oil exporting countries stayed at about 12 percent from the end of 1978 to the end of 1981, but in 1982 it rose to 14½ percent and in 1983 to about 17 percent. This suggests a shift of bank deposits to Swiss banks from other banks. A study made by the Bank of England[43] shows a sharp reduction in Eurocurrency deposits in the United Kingdom in both 1982 and 1983, while bank deposits in the Federal Republic of Germany declined only slightly and even rose in the United States (measured in U.S. dollar terms). Although the coverage of oil exporting countries is more comprehensive for the Bank of England data than the Swiss data, it seems plausible that oil exporting countries have shifted funds from the United Kingdom to Swiss banks and U.S. banks. In Switzerland, the increase related only to fiduciary deposits, which are mainly denominated in U.S. dollars. Therefore, there might not have been a currency switch but only a shift from Eurodollar placements in the United Kingdom to Switzerland. The increase in Swiss banks' share of oil exporting countries' deposits did not reflect an increase in the total market share of Swiss banks in liabilities of BIS reporting banks. As the increase in liabilities was largely confined to fiduciary liabilities in other currencies than the Swiss franc, the capital movements caused no problem for exchange rate and monetary policies.

In the early 1980s, as mentioned above, the deposits of Argentina and Brazil in Switzerland increased. The share of Swiss banks in total identified bank deposits of Argentina rose from 12½ percent at the end of 1979 to 33 percent at the end of 1983 (Table 11). The

[40] The country breakdown of Swiss banks' assets and liabilities comprises assets and liabilities with banks located in Switzerland, thereby including assets and liabilities with Swiss banks' branches abroad.

[41] Oil exporting countries, as defined by the Bank of England, comprise the 13 members of OPEC plus Bahrain, Brunei, Oman, and Trinidad and Tobago; Bank of England (1985).

[42] It has also been reported that an OPEC country bought promissory notes issued by the Swiss National Bank for the amount of SwF 500 million in mid-1981 at two year maturity.

[43] Bank of England, *Quarterly Bulletin* (March, 1985).

Table 8. Bank Deposits and Fiduciary Deposits of Nonresidents with Swiss Banks[1]

(End of period)

	Bank Deposits and Fiduciary Deposits							
	1979	1980	1981	1982	1983	1984	1979	1984
	(In millions of Swiss francs)						*(In percent)*	
Industrial countries[2]	98,307	130,505	154,466	161,359	164,042	168,037	58.4	49.1
France	15,723	21,584	24,961	26,674	25,815	19,621	9.3	5.7
Germany, Fed. Rep. of	8,203	10,584	12,423	12,958	13,147	12,435	4.9	3.6
Italy	14,164	18,519	23,709	22,776	23,331	23,415	8.4	6.8
United Kingdom	20,899	29,369	37,214	39,147	39,229	43,700	12.4	12.8
United States	15,256	20,101	20,055	23,754	26,095	30,507	9.1	8.9
Other	24,062	30,348	36,104	36,050	36,425	38,359	14.3	11.2
Other Western Europe	7,127	9,145	11,713	13,941	16,381	16,093	4.2	4.7
Eastern Europe	1,228	1,328	1,204	1,619	1,178	1,616	0.7	0.5
Latin America	17,214	24,100	14,815	15,882	19,279	22,091	10.2	6.5
Central America	10,977	14,998	5,207	3,401	4,558	3,063	6.5	0.9
Mexico	...	...	...	...	...	2,718	...	0.8
Argentina	1,582	2,226	2,619	4,772	5,477	6,508	0.9	1.9
Brazil	1,609	2,196	2,603	3,242	3,907	5,469	1.0	1.6
Other	3,046	4,680	4,386	4,467	5,337	7,051	1.8	2.1
Venezuela	...	...	...	...	...	2,920	...	0.9
Africa	7,057	8,679	8,973	9,896	12,451	11,982	4.2	3.5
Liberia	...	...	...	...	...	3,937	...	1.1
Nigeria	...	...	...	...	...	1,106	...	0.3
South Africa	977	987	1,041	890	1,688	1,125	0.6	0.3
Other	6,080	7,692	7,932	9,006	10,763	5,814	3.6	1.7
Middle East	23,248	33,337	36,329	44,292	50,215	57,697	13.8	16.9
Israel	1,426	1,936	2,292	2,772	3,272	3,629	0.8	1.1
Lebanon	2,335	3,305	4,224	4,702	5,576	6,346	1.4	1.9
Other	19,487	28,096	29,813	36,818	41,367	47,722	11.6	13.9
Asia	5,735	8,322	10,268	11,418	15,195	18,041	3.4	5.3
Hong Kong	...	...	...	...	...	3,584	...	1.0
India	788	862	1,069	1,247	1,586	1,937	0.5	0.6
Philippines	...	...	...	...	...	1,240	...	0.4
Singapore	527	1,008	2,264	2,420	3,608	4,131	0.3	1.2
Other	4,420	6,452	6,935	7,751	10,001	7,149	2.6	2.1
Caribbean and unallocated	8,443	8,163	25,184	34,189	43,054	46,818	5.0	13.7
Total[3]	168,360	223,578	262,948	292,593	321,792	342,375	100.0	100.0

Source: Swiss National Bank, *Das schweizerische Bankwesen*.

[1]The categories in the table have been adapted to the published statistics of the Swiss National Bank. The country breakdown of these statistics (which were published in November 1985) was increased to cover 186 countries at the end of 1984.

[2]For the industrial countries the Fund definition is used with the exception that Ireland is excluded (United States, Canada, Australia, Japan, New Zealand, Austria, Belgium, Denmark, Finland, France, Federal Republic of Germany, Iceland, Italy, Luxembourg, the Netherlands, Norway, Spain, Sweden, and the United Kingdom).

[3]Excluding Liechtenstein and gold liabilities; in the Swiss statistics, as from the end of 1984, Swiss banks' liabilities and fiduciary liabilities to Liechtenstein are considered as domestic rather than external liabilities. For comparison, these liabilities have also been excluded from total liabilities to abroad in the preceding years in this table.

in the coverage of BIS statistics. The share of deposits of Brazil has followed an almost identical development, rising from 12 percent in 1979 to nearly 30 percent in 1983, followed by a small decline in 1984. For Argentina, the jump occurred in 1982, the year of severe debt crisis and when the U.K. Government froze Argentinian assets. For Brazil, the rise was particularly large in 1980 and in 1982. For both countries, the largest increase in deposits with Swiss banks has occurred in fiduciary accounts. The increase might be related to shifts in deposits of private residents of those countries—fearing the seizure of their funds in other countries—to match banks' claims on borrowers from those countries.

Lending Exposure

Even before the debt crisis of the early 1980s, external assets of Swiss banks were composed of a

Table 9. Oil Exporting Countries' Investment in Industrial Countries

	1974	1979	1983
	(In billions of U.S. dollars)		
United Kingdom	28.3	57.5	63.1
(In percent)	(45)	(28)	(22)
United States	15.0	47.8	85.9
(In percent)	(24)	(24)	(30)
Germany, Fed. Rep. of	8.1	15.6	21.6
(In percent)	(13)	(8)	(7)
Other industrial countries	11.4	80.1	117.3
(In percent)	(18)	(40)	(41)
Total industrial countries	62.8	201.0	287.9
(In percent)	(100)	(100)	(100)

Source: Bank of England, *Quarterly Bulletin* (London, March 1985).

relatively high proportion of claims on low-risk industrial countries. At the end of 1979, 69 percent of Swiss banks' external assets (76 percent including fiduciary assets) were vis-à-vis industrial countries compared with only 56 percent for BIS reporting banks (Table 12). The difference became more marked during the early 1980s, as the share of industrial countries in Swiss banks' external assets increased to 74½ percent by the end of 1984 (81½ percent including fiduciary assets) while it remained almost constant at 56 percent for BIS reporting banks.[44]

The exposure of Swiss banks to Latin American countries, which peaked at 10½ percent of total external assets at the end of 1980, was almost as large as that of BIS reporting banks (11½ percent at the end of 1980). However, by contrast to BIS reporting banks, which maintained their relative exposure up to the end of 1984, Swiss banks reduced their lending in both nominal and relative terms, especially in 1981 and 1982, to 6 percent of external assets by the end of 1984 (Table 12). Lending to Central America (e.g., Mexico) was cut sharply in those years, but exposure to other Latin American countries, including Argentina and Brazil, was also reduced somewhat.

In line with the overall trend in BIS bank lending, Swiss exposure to Eastern European countries was halved from 3½ percent to 1½ percent of their total external assets between the end of 1979 and the end of 1984. The exposure of Swiss banks in Africa, at about 3–3½ percent of external assets, was almost the same as the exposure of BIS reporting banks. No significant change has taken place in this share in recent years.

The debt crisis of the early 1980s prompted the Federal Banking Commission to intensify its supervision of banks' country risk. In its Annual Report for 1983, the Commission described a selected survey conducted among Swiss banks at the end of 1982 on country risk measured on a consolidated basis. It concluded that Swiss banks had lower risk exposure and better capital coverage than banks in several other countries. At the end of 1982, the exposure to 60 high-risk countries amounted to SwF 23 billion (US$11½ billion at the end of 1982 exchange rate); about 60 percent of this lending was to Latin American countries. High-risk lending was concentrated in the big banks and in foreign-owned banks which were most heavily engaged in foreign lending. On average, risky lending was below banks' own capital; however, for a number of foreign-owned banks, high-risk lending exceeded substantially their own capital.

On the basis of information on the risk evaluation and provisioning of some Swiss banks with long-lasting experience in international business, the Federal Banking Commission formed a judgment on evaluating country risk by Swiss banks. In early 1983, it requested that Swiss banks make 20 percent provisioning for lending to countries which were defined as risky and that this percentage be reached in the course of two to three years for the banks which were currently below that ratio. In its Annual Report for 1984, the Commission concluded that by the end of 1984 all Swiss banks were following that recommendation.[45]

Switzerland's Competitiveness as an International Financial Center

Switzerland has never competed with other major international financial centers in terms of the overall volume of transactions. Its strength has been specialization, especially in the international bond market, in portfolio management, and in trade in precious metals. In recent years, competitiveness has increased in international banking. Capital restrictions have been reduced in the Federal Republic of Germany, France, and Japan. Deregulation in major financial centers has shifted part of international business to domestic markets, reducing Switzerland's traditional comparative advantage of having a universal banking system. The repeal of the withholding tax on interest income from securities of nonresidents in the United States in mid-1984 followed by similar moves in France and Germany

[44] The figures in this section (unless otherwise indicated) relate to exposure of banks located in Switzerland and not to Swiss banks on a consolidated basis.

[45] The fiscal authorities at both the federal and cantonal level have accepted the 20 percent provisioning as tax deductible.

Table 10. Swiss Banks' and BIS Banks' Liabilities to Oil Exporting Countries
(End of period)

	1974	1975	1976	1977	1978	1979	1980	1981	1982	1983[1] A	1983[1] B	1984[1] A	1984[1] B
Swiss banks						*(In millions of Swiss francs, unless otherwise indicated)*							
Swiss bank liabilities to Middle Eastern oil exporting countries[2]	6,311	9,394	9,115	8,990	7,951	10,582	13,991	13,740	13,090	12,420		12,890	
Of which:													
Sight deposits	*2,842*	*3,352*	*2,434*	*2,283*	*1,980*	*3,026*	*4,163*	*3,770*	*4,567*	*4,209*		. . .	
Time deposits	*3,469*	*6,042*	*6,681*	*6,707*	*5,971*	*7,556*	*9,828*	*9,970*	*8,523*	*8,211*		. . .	
Swiss banks' fiduciary liabilities to Middle Eastern oil exporting countries[2]	. . .	. . .	6,593	5,328	6,321	8,905	14,105	16,073	23,728	28,947		34,832	
Total (*in millions of Swiss francs*)	. . .	. . .	15,708	14,318	14,272	19,487	28,096	29,813	36,818	41,367		47,722	
Total (*in millions of U.S. dollars*)	. . .	. . .	6,410	7,159	8,810	12,334	15,932	16,577	18,460	18,980		18,461	
BIS reporting banks						*(In millions of U.S. dollars)*							
BIS reporting banks' liabilities to Middle Eastern oil exporting countries[2]	36,285	42,705	53,954	66,791	69,276	98,068	126,545	126,932	116,729	103,135	125,111	120,888	127,967
BIS reporting banks' liabilities plus Swiss banks' fiduciary liabilities to Middle Eastern oil exporting countries[3]	. . .	. . .	56,652	69,440	73,202	103,701	134,565	135,907	128,626	116,416	138,392	134,363	141,442
						(In percent)							
Swiss banks' share of total BIS reporting banks' liabilities to Middle Eastern oil exporting countries[3]	. . .	. . .	11.3	10.3	12.0	11.9	11.8	12.2	14.4	16.3	13.7	13.7	13.1
						(In millions of U.S. dollars)							
Memorandum items: BIS reporting banks' liabilities to OPEC countries[3]	43,503	51,494	64,292	77,915	82,876	121,003	160,678	157,662	135,307	120,336	141,884	139,938	146,952

Sources: Swiss National Bank, *Das schweizerische Bankwesen*; Bank for International Settlements, *International Banking Statistics*, 1973–83, and *International Banking Developments and Financial Market Developments.*

[1]The coverage of BIS reporting banks was substantially widened at the end of 1983, and again changed at the end of 1984, as presented in column B. Data on the old basis are presented in column A.

[2]The coverage of Middle Eastern oil exporting countries follows that of the Swiss National Bank's statistics; it includes Iraq, Islamic Republic of Iran, Jordan, Kuwait, Oman, Bahrain, United Arab Emirates, Qatar, Saudi Arabia, Syrian Arab Republic, Yemen Arab Republic, Yemen People's Democratic Republic, Libya, and Egypt.

[3]OPEC countries comprise Kuwait, Libya, Oman, Qatar, Saudi Arabia, United Arab Emirates, Algeria, Ecuador, Gabon, Indonesia, Islamic Republic of Iran, Iraq, Nigeria, and Venezuela.

Table 11. Deposits of Argentina and Brazil
(End of period)

	1979	1980	1981	1982	1983[1] A	1983[1] B	1984
			(In millions of U.S. dollars)				
Deposits with Swiss banks							
Argentina	616	626	479	719	833		949
Brazil	592	539	467	631	826		997
Fiduciary deposits with Swiss banks							
Argentina	385	639	977	1,674	1,680		1,569
Brazil	426	707	980	994	966		1,119
Total deposits with Swiss banks							
Argentina	1,001	1,262	1,456	2,393	2,513		2,518
Brazil	1,018	1,246	1,447	1,625	1,792		2,116
Deposits with BIS reporting banks							
Argentina	7,603	6,605	6,565	5,730	5,881	8,643	8,379
Brazil	8,075	4,719	4,805	4,255	5,090	11,364	17,307
Total deposits with BIS reporting banks including fiduciary deposits with Swiss banks							
Argentina	7,988	7,243	7,542	7,404	7,561	10,323	9,948
Brazil	8,501	5,426	5,785	5,249	6,056	12,330	18,426
Total deposits with Swiss banks in percent of total deposits with BIS reporting banks				*(In percent)*			
Argentina	12.5	17.4	19.3	32.3	33.2	24.3	25.3
Brazil	12.0	23.0	25.0	31.0	29.6	14.5	11.5
Memorandum items:			*(In millions of U.S. dollars)*				
Official foreign exchange reserves							
Argentina	8,858	6,057	2,586	2,406	1,172		1,242
Brazil	8,342	5,042	5,888	3,641	4,355		11,507

Sources: Swiss National Bank, *Das schweizerische Bankwesen*; Bank for International Settlements, *International Banking Statistics, 1973–83*, April 1984 and *International Banking Developments and Financial Market Developments*; and International Monetary Fund, *International Financial Statistics*.

[1]The coverage of BIS reporting banks was substantially widened at the end of 1983, which is reflected in data in column B. Data on the old basis are presented in column A.

has also reduced the competitive advantage of Switzerland as a financial center. Moreover, recent trends in international banking show a move away from expansion of balance sheet transactions toward fee- and commission-generating off-balance-sheet items, another traditional specialty of Swiss financial business. At the same time, new financial instruments have proliferated, including floating rate notes, note issuance facilities, Eurocommercial paper, and interest and currency swaps. These developments, combined with increased use of advanced telecommunications and computers, have undoubtedly exposed Swiss financial institutions to increased competitiveness.

A market share analysis for international financial transactions is only possible to a limited extent. Table 13 shows the share of Swiss banks' external assets (including fiduciary assets) in BIS reporting banks' assets. From 1974 to 1981, the share of Swiss banks' assets in BIS reporting banks' external assets remained almost unchanged at 13–14 percent, if adjustment is made for a widening in the coverage of BIS data. In 1982 and 1983, however, the Swiss market share declined by some 1½ percentage points and stayed roughly unchanged in 1984 (also corrected for changes in BIS data coverage). Is this decline to be interpreted as a deterioration in competitiveness? The figures, by nature, indicate only the magnitude not the quality of the transactions. As mentioned, Swiss banks reduced sharply their exposure to Latin American countries in 1981 and 1982 in contrast to BIS reporting banks. The decline in the market share of Swiss banks' external assets might therefore reflect withdrawal by Swiss banks from lending to high-risk countries. The period of observed decline in market share also coincides with the large appreciation of the U.S. dollar against the Swiss franc and other currencies and might therefore, in part, reflect valuation changes of external assets. In addition, these figures fail to capture the

Table 12. External Assets and Fiduciary Assets of Swiss Banks and BIS Reporting Banks[1]

(In percent)

	Swiss Banks' External Assets						Swiss Banks' External Assets and Fiduciary Assets						BIS Reporting Banks' External Assets					
	1979	1980	1981	1982	1983	1984	1979	1980	1981	1982	1983	1984	1979	1980	1981	1982	1983	1984
Industrial countries[2]	69.0	68.5	71.0	71.7	72.7	74.5	75.9	77.0	79.2	79.3	80.4	81.6	56.2	56.5	56.2	56.3	55.5	55.9
Other Western Europe[3]	4.3	4.6	4.3	4.0	4.0	2.2	3.2	3.2	3.1	3.1	2.7	1.4	2.5	2.6	2.4	2.4	2.0	2.0
Eastern Europe	3.4	3.1	2.6	2.1	1.7	1.3	2.3	1.9	1.4	1.2	1.0	0.8	5.0	4.5	3.9	3.1	2.5	2.2
Latin America	9.2	10.3	6.8	5.9	5.7	5.9	7.6	6.9	4.3	3.9	3.8	3.8	11.2	11.7	11.9	11.6	11.5	11.2
Central America	4.6	4.8	2.0	1.5	1.5	1.5	4.0	3.1	1.2	0.9	0.9	0.9	2.9	3.2	3.7	3.6	3.6	3.4
Argentina	0.9	1.4	1.2	1.1	1.1	1.1	0.7	1.0	0.8	0.9	0.8	0.8	1.2	1.4	1.5	1.3	1.3	1.2
Brazil	1.6	1.7	1.4	1.4	1.4	1.6	1.2	1.1	0.8	0.9	0.9	1.0	3.3	3.3	3.2	3.3	3.4	3.6
Other	2.1	2.4	2.2	1.9	11.7	1.7	1.7	1.7	1.5	1.2	1.2	1.2	3.7	3.7	3.5	3.4	3.3	3.0
Africa	3.3	3.0	3.5	3.4	3.5	3.2	2.6	2.3	2.3	2.2	2.1	2.0	3.4	3.1	3.0	3.1	2.8	2.5
South Africa	1.1	0.8	1.3	1.3	1.6	1.7	0.8	0.5	0.8	0.8	0.9	1.0	0.6	0.5	0.6	0.8	0.9	0.8
Other	2.2	2.3	2.2	2.1	1.9	1.5	1.8	1.8	1.6	1.4	1.2	0.9	2.8	2.6	2.4	2.3	1.9	1.7
Middle East	3.1	3.1	2.8	2.8	2.6	2.6	2.4	2.1	2.3	1.9	1.7	1.7	3.0	2.7	2.4	2.5	3.2	2.8
Asia	2.9	2.9	3.0	3.4	3.9	4.6	2.1	2.1	1.9	2.2	2.3	2.7	6.0	6.6	7.0	7.4	9.7	10.1
Singapore	0.8	0.7	1.1	1.5	1.8	2.3	0.6	0.6	0.7	0.9	1.1	1.4	1.4	1.6	2.1	2.2	2.5	2.8
Other	2.1	2.1	1.9	1.9	2.1	2.3	1.5	1.5	1.3	1.3	1.3	1.4	4.6	4.9	4.9	5.1	7.2	7.4
Caribbean[4]	4.9	4.4	6.1	6.6	5.8	5.8	4.1	4.6	5.5	6.3	6.1	1.4	12.7	12.2	13.1	13.8	12.9	13.3
Total	100.0	100.0	100.0	100.0	100.0	100.0	100.0	100.0	100.0	100.0	100.0	100.0	100.0	100.0	100.0	100.0	100.0	100.0

Sources: Bank for International Settlements, *International Banking Statistics*, 1973–83, 1984 and *International Banking Developments and Financial Market Developments*; Swiss National Bank, *Das schweizerische Bankwesen*.

[1] The categories in the table have been adapted to the published statistics of the Swiss National Bank; figures may not add up because of rounding.

[2] For the industrial countries the Fund definition is used, excluding Ireland for Swiss data but including Ireland for BIS data (United States, Canada, Australia, Japan, New Zealand, Austria, Belgium, Denmark, Finland, France, Federal Republic of Germany, Iceland, Ireland, Italy, Luxembourg, the Netherlands, Norway, Spain, Sweden, Switzerland, and the United Kingdom).

[3] From the end of 1984, Swiss banks' claims and fiduciary claims on Liechtenstein are considered as domestic rather than external assets.

[4] Caribbean includes residual for BIS statistics.

Table 13. Swiss Banks' Market Shares in BIS Reporting Banks[1]
(End of period)

	Total External Assets of BIS Reporting Banks (1)	Total External Assets and Fiduciary Assets of Swiss Banks (2)	Of which, Fiduciary Accounts (3)	BIS Reporting Banks' Liabilities to Switzerland (4)	(2) as Percent of (1)	(4) as Percent of (1)
	(In billions of U.S. dollars)				*(In percent)*	
1974	362.1	52.2	15.6	53.2	14.4	14.7
1975 A	442.6	62.5	19.6	55.0	14.1	12.4
1975 B	442.3	62.5	19.6	55.0	14.1	12.4
1976	548.0	72.5	22.7	61.6	13.2	11.2
1977 A	657.1	90.7	27.8	75.0	13.8	11.4
1977 B	689.8	90.7	27.8	76.9	13.1	11.1
1978 A	904.8	116.8	33.6	95.2	12.9	10.5
1978 B	893.2	116.8	33.6	93.5	13.1	10.5
1979	1,110.0	144.8	49.7	121.9	13.0	11.0
1980	1,321.9	176.9	67.7	144.9	13.4	11.0
1981 A	1,541.4	200.2	86.8	162.3	13.0	10.5
1981 B	1,550.2			163.0	12.9	10.5
1982	1,694.5	197.5	82.5	161.5	11.7	9.5
1983 A	1,757.1	197.7	82.7	165.9	11.3	9.4
1983 B	2,097.9			175.2	9.4	8.4
1984 A	2,151.5	200.4	88.6	183.8	9.3	8.5
1984 B	2,160.4			183.8	9.3	8.5

Sources: Bank for International Settlements, *International Banking Statistics, 1973–83*, and *International Banking Developments and Financial Market Developments*; Swiss National Bank, *Das schweizerische Bankwesen*.
[1]Two sets of figures for BIS reporting banks (A and B) refer to a break in the statistical coverage.

substantial amounts of off-balance-sheet transactions (except fiduciary accounts), which are highly important for Swiss banks and for which comparable data are not available.[46]

Swiss financial institutions have traditionally catered to portfolio management of private persons rather than institutions. In recent years, however, there has been a significant shift in savings from individuals toward institutions (e.g., social security funds) in both Switzerland and abroad. As individuals and institutional investors have different needs for portfolio management, a reorientation in the services offered by Swiss financial institutions has been required. The turnover in the portfolio of institutional investors is usually relatively high. In that case, taxes on financial transactions play a crucial role for the attractiveness of Switzerland compared with other centers.

The repeal in several countries of the withholding tax on interest income on securities held by nonresidents has fueled the debate in Switzerland on taxation of securities transactions. The taxation takes two forms: a withholding tax on interest income and a stamp duty on all securities transactions. These taxes have been introduced for fiscal reasons rather than to prevent capital inflows. The withholding tax on interest income, at 35 pecent, is high by international comparison (Appendix III) and applies to all capital earnings, including interest income on domestic bond issues (i.e., the borrower is a Swiss resident) and on bank deposits. Interest income on foreign bond issues in Switzerland (i.e., the borrower is a nonresident) and on fiduciary deposits, however, is exempt from the withholding tax.[47] The different treatment of financial transactions with respect to withholding tax has led to a shift from regular bank deposits to fiduciary deposits and presumably also to a shift in demand from domestic to foreign Swiss franc issues. However, as foreign bond issues are exempted, the shift does not cause a

[46] Off-balance-sheet transactions accounted for about 57 percent of earnings of the big banks in 1984.

[47] A Swiss peculiarity is that interbank deposits with a maturity of above 12 months are also subject to withholding tax on interest. However, the withholding tax is refunded quarterly, thereby implying an administrative cost rather than a significant tax.

competitive disadvantage for foreign bond issues in Switzerland compared with issues in other countries.

The stamp duty is a major reason for the lack of a developed money market in Switzerland (as described in Section IV). It has also prevented Swiss banks from participating actively in trading in Eurobonds in Switzerland; those transactions have been conducted via their branches and affiliates abroad. The stamp duty is a particular disadvantage compared with banks in Luxembourg and the United Kingdom, where no taxes on Eurobond trading exist. Security transactions by dealers in Switzerland are also subject to the stamp duty; in most other countries, dealer transactions are exempted from security taxes (Appendix III). The Swiss Government may consider changing the stamp duty to secure a neutral impact on federal revenue.[48] Should that happen, the Government will have to weigh the relative merits of maintaining a secure source of fiscal revenue—which, however, would impair international competitiveness of the Swiss financial market—against the possibility of reducing the stamp duty, which might attract international business to Switzerland and generate increased tax liabilities of financial institutions and private persons and would thus compensate, at least in part, for the shortfall in revenue from the stamp duty.

[48] The share of the stamp duty in total federal revenue has increased from 4.8 percent in 1980 to a projected 7.5 percent in 1985 (budget figure).

Appendix I
Statistical Coverage

The analysis of international financial transactions of Switzerland is constrained by the lack of statistics. A particular shortcoming is the nonexistence of historical data on the capital account of the balance of payments. Estimates on flows of the banking sector have been derived from the stock figures of the annual balance sheets of banks. The derived flow data give an imprecise picture because of valuation adjustments, etc. Capital flows for the nonbank sector have been derived as a residual from the estimates of the current account, changes in stock figures for banks, and changes in official reserves. Any error in these magnitudes would therefore be mirrored in the residual.

In 1983, the Swiss National Bank began publishing quarterly current account estimates. At the same time, it started the preparation of capital account statistics after the legal foundation had been established in 1980 and 1982 that permitted the Swiss National Bank to collect information on financial transactions of the private sector. The capital account of the balance of payments was published for the first time in October 1985 with data beginning from 1983.[49] The statistics have considerably improved the scope for analyzing international capital transactions. The errors and omissions, however, are still sizable (4–5 percent of GNP), suggesting that the current account surplus is underestimated or net capital inflows are underrecorded.

The main source for external capital transactions used here is the annual balance sheets of banks and finance companies, which provide a detailed breakdown of banks' foreign assets and liabilities by type of asset and, in part, maturity and currency. In addition, a country breakdown of foreign assets and liabilities as well as of fiduciary accounts is published. Another important source of information is the monthly statistics on approved medium-term and long-term capital exports comprising (a) banks' export and finance loans, (b) foreign bond issues, and (c) notes, which amount to above SwF 10 million.

[49] Kommission für Konjunkturfragen (1985).

Table 14. Balance of Payments of Switzerland
(In millions of Swiss francs)

	1979	1980	1981	1982	1983	1984
Current account balance	4.1	−0.9	5.4	8.0	8.1	8.9
(In percent of GNP)	(2.5)	(−0.5)	(2.5)	(3.9)	(3.8)	(4.0)
Capital account balance[1]	...	...	...	...	−17.4	−15.2
Of which:						
Direct investment					*−0.4*	*−1.5*
Portfolio investment					*−8.4*	*−7.0*
Banks					*−4.0*	*−3.5*
Other long-term capital					*0.8*	*0.6*
Other short-term capital					*0.1*	*−4.3*
Precious metals					*−5.5*	*0.5*
Errors and omissions					10.1	9.8
Valuation adjustment of net foreign assets of Swiss National Bank					1.0	2.7
Changes in net foreign assets of Swiss National Bank					−1.8	−6.2

Source: Swiss National Bank, *Monatsbericht* (Zürich, October 1985).
[1]Comprehensive capital account data were not compiled for the years prior to 1983.

Appendix II

Chronology of Restrictions on Capital Flows
(Position on January 1, 1979, and subsequent changes)

I. CAPITAL INFLOWS

1. Decrees of July 5, 1972 and April 16, 1973 subjecting borrowing abroad to license

Position on:

January 1, 1979:	Borrowing abroad by Swiss residents (nonbanks) is subject to license.
May 31, 1979:	Lifted.

2. Decree of July 5, 1972 (with later amendments) concerning foreign exchange positions of the banks

Position on:

January 1, 1979:	Total foreign exchange liabilities of banks has to equal the total of foreign exchange assets by the end of each day.
May 31, 1979:	Lifted.

3. Decree of November 20, 1974 (with later amendments) concerning inflow of foreign capital

a. *Ban on interest payments*

Position on:

January 1, 1979:	Bank deposits and fiduciary accounts of nonresidents (including foreign official monetary institutions) denominated in Swiss francs are not permitted to carry interest rate.
	Exception: deposits outstanding as of October 31, 1974 and new deposits up to a maximum of SwF 20,000.
February 21, 1980:	The Federal Government lifts the ban on the payment of interest on nonresidents' Swiss franc time and savings deposits (including fiduciary accounts in Swiss francs) with a maturity of at least three months. In addition the Swiss National Bank authorizes interest payments on foreign central banks' deposits with maturities of at least six months.
March 11, 1980:	The Federal Government permits the payment of interest on Swiss franc deposits of nonresidents with maturities of at least three months.
August 31, 1980:	Lifted.

b. *Negative interest rate*

Position on:

January 1, 1979:	A 10 percent negative interest rate a quarter is levied on all deposits in Swiss francs of nonresidents exceeding the balance of October 1974 plus SwF 100,000.
	Exemption: deposits below SwF 100,000 for nonbanks and SwF 250,000 for banks.
November 1, 1979:	The negative interest rate is reduced to 2.5 percent a quarter.
December 1, 1979:	The penalty is reduced to zero.
August 31, 1980:	Cancelled.

Chronology of Restrictions on Capital Flows (*continued*)

(Position on January 1, 1979, and subsequent changes)

c. *Ceiling on forward sales of Swiss francs to nonresidents*

Position on:

January 1, 1979:	The ceiling on forward sales of Swiss francs with a maturity of up to 10 days to nonresidents is 20 percent of the outstanding amounts of October 31, 1974. For forward sales with a longer maturity the ceiling is 40 percent of the amounts outstanding on October 31, 1974.
September 18, 1979:	The ceiling on forward sales of Swiss francs with a term of at least 11 days to nonresidents is raised from 40 percent to 50 percent of the amounts outstanding on October 31, 1974.
February 21, 1980:	The ceiling on forward sales of Swiss francs to nonresidents is raised from 20 percent to 40 percent of the amounts outstanding on October 31, 1974 for contracts with a term of up to 10 days and from 50 percent to 80 percent for contracts with a term of 11 days or more.
March 11, 1980:	The Swiss National Bank removes limits on the forward sale of Swiss francs to nonresidents introduced in November 1974.

4. Decree of January 22, 1975 concerning the sterilization of the proceeds from intervention on the foreign exchange market of January 22, 1975

Position on:

January 1, 1979:	The Swiss National Bank is entitled to neutralize the Swiss franc proceeds from intervention in the foreign exchange market by blocking the proceeds to the account of the selling partner without interest payment.
May 31, 1979:	The decree is lifted without ever having been used.

5. Decree of February 27, 1978 concerning imports of foreign bank notes

Position on:

January 1, 1979:	Imports of foreign bank notes of more than the equivalent of SwF 20,000 a person and a quarter is not allowed, except by special authorization of the Swiss National Bank.
January 24, 1979:	Lifted.

6. Decree of February 27, 1978 concerning foreign acquisition in domestic securities

Position on:

January 1, 1979:	Private persons or companies residing in Switzerland are not allowed to sell domestic securities to nonresidents. A nonresident is only allowed to buy domestic securities from a bank for an amount equivalent to the proceeds of sales of domestic securities.
January 24, 1979:	Lifted.

II. CAPITAL OUTFLOWS

1. Articles 7 and 8 of the Banking Law of November 8, 1939 and March 11, 1971

Position on:

January 1, 1979:	Public bond issues, notes, and bank credits to nonresidents are subject to approval by the Swiss National Bank, if the amount exceeds SwF 10 million (notes: SwF 3 million) and the maturity is one year or longer. Short-term foreign lending of banks and capital exports of Swiss nonbanks are liberalized.
	Nonresidents are allowed to buy a maximum of 50 percent of the proceeds from borrowing by other nonresidents. That half of the proceeds which is denominated in Swiss francs has to be converted to dollars at the Swiss National Bank and the other half to convertible currencies in the private market.
	A maximum of SwF 100 million a public bond issue is in force; there is no limit for notes.
January 29, 1979:	Quota regulation of placement is lifted.

APPENDIX II

Chronology of Restrictions on Capital Flows (*concluded*)

(Position on January 1, 1979, and subsequent changes)

June 8, 1979:	The obligation to convert the proceeds from borrowings in Swiss francs into other currencies is terminated.
September 1, 1980:	Conditions for capital exports are revised: rules for placement of notes are liberalized; access to the use of multicurrency clause is made easier; the permission of foreign central banks to buy notes and participate in credits is required.
January 1, 1982:	The Swiss National Bank stops making an issue program for foreign bond issues but continues coordinating the issues.
July 1, 1982:	The secondary market trading for notes is liberalized. The trading, which was confined to banks participating in issuing syndicate, is made completely free.
November 11, 1982:	Foreign investors are allowed to participate as sub-underwriters, if they are not mentioned publicly.
January 1, 1984:	The queuing system under which a limit of three issues a week was imposed on foreign bond issues is eliminated and the maximum amount of an issue is raised from SwF 100 million to SwF 200 million. The Swiss National Bank informs, on request, the leading issuing banks of the number, magnitude, and dates for approved borrowings to avoid bunching of issues.
January 18, 1984:	The deposit requirement for medium-term notes is modified. In addition to the issuing bank and the members of the issuing syndicate, SEGA (Swiss Security Clearing Organization) can now act as a custodian for notes.
May 15, 1985:	The ceiling on the amount of public bond issues (SwF 200 million) is lifted.

Appendix III

Table 15. Taxes Affecting International Portfolio Movements

	Federal Republic of Germany	Japan[1]	Switzerland	United Kingdom[2]	United States
			(In percent of interest income)		
Withholding tax for nonresidents[3]					
Shares	25	20	35	5 or 15[4]	30
Domestic bond issues	—	20	35	30[5]	—
Foreign bond issues[6]	—	20	—	30[7]	—
Bank deposits	—	20	35	30	—
Fiduciary deposits	n.a.	n.a	—[8]	n.a	n.a.
			(In percent of transaction value)		
Other taxes on transactions on securities					
Stamp/turnover tax	0.25[9]	0.01–0.55	0.15 or 0.30[10]	Bearer bonds:— (e.g., Eurobonds) Shares and registered bonds (mainly convertibles): 1[12]	—[11]

Source: National sources.

[1]Since August 9, 1984, nonresidents' interest income from Japanese corporate Euro-yen bonds has been exempt from the withholding tax.

[2]For withholding tax, the general rule is a tax rate of 30 percent, unless the borrower is exempt (e.g., development banks and the European Commission) or a double taxation treaty exists.

[3]Lower rates apply where tax conventions exist.

[4]Depends on the amount of share holdings.

[5]Some gilt-edged stocks as designated by the Treasury are free of tax to nonresidents.

[6]Foreign bond issues exclude Eurobonds.

[7]There is no withholding tax on interest from Eurobonds.

[8]The exemption from withholding tax of 35 percent requires that a written contract between the bank and the customer exists, specifying that the bank has no risk involved in the transaction.

[9]The tax does not apply to initial purchases nor does it apply to dealer transactions.

[10]Applied to issue, sale, and resale of securities of any maturity. The lower rate of 0.15 percent applies to securities where the debtor is a Swiss resident; the higher rate of 0.30 percent applies to securities where the debtor is a nonresident. The tax applies also to dealer transactions.

[11]No taxes at the federal level.

[12]Exemptions from the 1 percent tax: (i) gilt-edged stocks; (ii) collections closed within the two weeks' account period; (iii) purchases by stock exchange; others; (iv) provisions for relief for market makers over-the-counter trading.

Notation: n.a. = not applicable

APPENDIX III

Table 16. Restrictions on Foreign Bond Issues

	Federal Republic of Germany[1]	Japan	Switzerland[2]	United Kingdom[3]	United States
Unit of denomination					
National currency	n.r.	n.r.	n.r.	n.r.	n.r.
Foreign currency	n.r.	n.r.	n.r.	n.r.	n.r.
Composite units (e.g., ECU, SDR)	n.r.	n.r.	n.r.	n.r.	n.r.
Minimum required maturity					
Public bonds	5 years for DM issues	7–15 years for yen issues	8 years	5 years	n.r.
Private placements	3 years for DM issues	. . .	18 months	5 years	n.r.
Early permitted repayment					
Public bonds	n.r.	. . .	After 5 years	After 5 years	n.r.
Private placements	n.r.	. . .	After 18 months but not before half of the maturity has elapsed	After 5 years	n.r.
Maximum limit on individual issue					
Public bonds	n.r.	¥ 10–30 billion for private issues[4]	n.r.	n.r.	n.r.
Private placements	n.r.	. . .	n.r.	n.r.	n.r.
Authorization requirement	Regional and international development banks	Authorization is required	Issues at and above SwF 10 million	Sterling and Euro-sterling issues are subject to timing consent by the Bank of England	n.a.
Institutions operating in securities market					
New issues	Banks	Securities firms	Banks, finance companies, other	Banks	Investment banks
Secondary market	Banks	Securities firms	Banks, finance companies, brokers, other	Brokers, jobbers	Brokers, dealers
Futures, options, and swaps	Banks	n.a.	Banks, finance companies	Brokers, banks	

Sources: National sources.

[1]In Germany, under a "Gentlemen's Agreement" between the Bundesbank and the major banks, any bank, including German subsidiaries of foreign banks, domiciled in Germany may lead manage foreign deutsche mark bond issues and private placements. In the case of foreign currency bonds with a deutsche mark option or dual currency bonds, where interest or redemption are made in deutsche mark, it is sufficient if a German bank (including foreign bank subsidiaries) is a co-leader. However, the authorities will apply tests of reciprocity in determining whether foreign affiliated banks can lead manage new issues. This raises problems with respect to Japan, where regulations prohibit banks from engaging in new issues, which are undertaken by securities houses.

[2]In Switzerland, both Swiss-domiciled banks and branches of foreign banks in Switzerland can lead manage foreign bond issues. With respect to issues denominated in Swiss francs, the authorities make sure that the issues are kept in Switzerland. Although authorization of issues at or above SwF 10 million is required, it is given on a liberal basis. With respect to issues in foreign currencies, the Swiss authorities check that there are no objections from the foreign monetary authorities concerned.

[3]In the United Kingdom, the Bank of England will allow issues in foreign currencies only if the foreign monetary authorities have no objections. Capital market issues are administered according to the Control of Borrowing Order 1958 with guidance notes of November 1980, July 1982, and March 1985. The last of these guidance notes reduces the maturity to a one-year minimum subject to certain requirements.

[4]In Japan, there are no maximum limits on foreign issues by governments, or international organizations, or AAA private borrowers.

Notation: n.r. = no restrictions
n.a. = not applicable

Bibliography

Bank of England, *Quarterly Bulletin* (London, various issues).

Bank for International Settlements, *International Banking Developments* (Basle, various issues).

———, *Annual Reports* (Basle, various issues).

———, *International Banking Statistics, 1973–1983* (Basle, April 1984).

Baumgartner, Ulrich, "Capital Controls in Three Central European Countries" (unpublished, International Monetary Fund, February 1, 1977).

Boughton, James M., "Stable Monetary Growth and Exchange Rates as Policy Targets," *Staff Papers*, International Monetary Fund (Washington), Vol. 29 (December 1982), pp. 495–526.

Commission fédérale des banques, *Rapport de gestion 19— de la Commission fédérale des banques* (Bern, various issues).

Corti, Mario A., "Switzerland: Banking, Money, and Bond Markets," reprinted from George-Giddy, *International Finance Handbook*, Section 4.6, Vol. 1 (John Wiley & Sons, 1983), pp. 1–50.

———, *Authorization Policies and Access to the Markets: The Case of Financial Institutions Desiring To Establish Themselves in Switzerland*, panel contribution to the International Conference of Banking Supervisors, Banca d'Italia, Rome, September 13–14, 1984.

Crédit Suisse, *Swiss Capital Market: Swiss Franc Public Bond and Notes Issues for Non-Swiss Borrowers* (Zürich, July 1984).

Deutsche Bundesbank, "Freedom of Germany's Capital Transactions with Foreign Countries," *Monthly Report of the Deutsche Bundesbank* (Frankfurt), Vol. 37 (July 1985), pp. 13–23.

Eidgenössische Bankenkommission, *50 Jahre eidgenössische Bankenaufsicht* (Zürich, 1985).

Eken, Sena, "Integration of Domestic and International Financial Markets: The Japanese Experience," *Staff Papers*, International Monetary Fund (Washington), Vol. 31 (September 1984), pp. 499–548.

Emch, Urs, and Hugo Renz, *Das Schweizerische Bankgeschäft* (Basle: Ott Verlag Thun, 1984).

Föllmi, Toni, *Switzerland as a Financial Center—A Special Case on the International Monetary Scene?* (Zürich: Bank Julius Bär & Co., A.G., 1978).

Gsell, Emil, ed., *Banken und Bankgeschäfte in der Schweiz* (Bern: Paul Haupt, 1969).

Handelsbank NW (Zürich), *The Swiss Capital Market: What Makes it Tick?* a presentation by Dr. Henri B. Meier in Madrid, May 17, 1983 (Zürich, 1983).

Iklé, Max, *Switzerland: An International Banking and Finance Center* (Stroudsberg, Pennsylvania: Dawden, Hutchison & Ross, 1972).

International Monetary Fund, *Annual Report on Exchange Arrangements and Exchange Restrictions* (Washington, 1985).

———, *Annual Report of the Executive Board for the Financial Year Ended April 30, 1985* (Washington, 1985).

———, *International Financial Statistics* (Washington, various issues).

Jenny, Klaus, *Der schweizerische Geldmarkt* (Bern: Paul Haupt, 1976).

Klauser, Peter, *Das schweizerische Bankgeheimnis und seine internationale Tragweite*, Wirtschaft und Recht, Heft 1 (Zürich, 1977).

Kommission für Konjunkturfragen, *Die Zahlungsbilanz der Schweiz im Jahre 1984* (Zürich, October 1985).

Lusser, Markus, *Die Geld- und Kapitalmärkte in einer Zeit raschen Wandels*, speech presented to Schweizerische Effekten-Giro A.G. (SEGA), April 24, 1985.

Meier, Henri B., *Swiss Capital Markets* (London: Euromoney Publications 1983).

Mikdashi, Zuhayr, "Risques bancaires et créances transnationales," *Revue Economique et Sociale* (Lausanne, May 1984), pp. 152–68.

Organization for Economic Cooperation and Development, *The Capital Market, International Capital Movements, Restrictions on Capital Operations in Switzerland* (Paris, 1971).

———, *Costs and Margins in Banking: An International Survey* (Paris, 1980).

———, *The Internationalisation of Banking: The Policy Issues* (Paris, 1983).

———, *Costs and Margins in Banking: Statistical Supplement 1978–1982* (Paris, 1985).

———, *Financial Market Trends* (Paris, various issues).

Otani, Ichiro, and Siddharth Tiwari, "Capital Controls and Interest Parity: The Japanese Experience, 1978–81," *Staff Papers*, International Monetary Fund (Washington), Vol. 28 (December 1981), pp. 793–815.

Ritzmann, Franz, *Die Schweizer Banken: Geschichte, Theorie, Statistik* (Bern; Stuttgart: Paul Haupt, 1973).

Schweizerische Bankgesellschaft, *Jahresbericht 1983/84* (Basle: Schweizerische Bankiervereinigung, 1984).

Schweizerische Kartellkommission, *Die Konzentration im schweizerischen Bankgewerbe* (Zürich, 1979).

Stopper, Edwin, *Notenbank und Wirtschaft* (Bern: Paul Haupt, 1974).

BIBLIOGRAPHY

Swiss National Bank (Schweizerische Nationalbank), *75 Jahre Schweizerische Nationalbank: Die Zeit von 1957 bis 1982* (Zürich, 1982).

———, *Das schweizerische Bankwesen im Jahre 1984, Nr. 69* (Zürich, 1985).

———, *Monatsbericht* (Zürich, various issues).

———, *Quartalsbericht* (Zürich, various issues).

Switzerland, Bundesamt für Statistik, *Langfristigen Reihen der Nationalen Buchhaltung der Schweiz* (Basle, 1983).

———, *Statistisches Jahrbuch der Schweiz 1984* (Basle, 1984).

———, *Die Volkswirtschaft* (Basle, various issues).

Teeters, Nancy H., and Henry S. Terrell, "The Role of Banks in the International Financial System," *Federal Reserve Bulletin* (Washington), Vol. 69 (September 1983), pp. 663–71.

Union de Banques Suisses, Schweizerischer Bankverein, and Crédit Suisse, *Secrecy in Swiss Banking* (Switzerland, 1983).

———, *The Underwriting Business in Switzerland* (Zürich, 1984).

Watson, Maxwell, Donald Mathieson, Russell Kincaid, and Eliot Kalter, *International Capital Markets: Developments and Prospects*, Occasional Paper No. 43 (Washington: International Monetary Fund, February 1986).

Part III
European Economic Integration and European Financial Centres

[10]

European Economic Integration and the Development of a Single Financial Center for Long-Term Capital

By

Charles P. Kindleberger

Contents: I. Introduction. — II. Integration Defined. — III. Recent Experience. — IV. The Capital Market in Europe. — V. Europe and the New York Capital Market. — VI. Prospective European Financial Integration. — VII. The Emergence of a Dominant Center.

I. Introduction

This paper will deal with the definition, process and prospects of economic integration in long-term capital markets in Europe which might lead to the development of a single center for long-term capital. The subject has some heuristic value as an example of functional integration. It further raises the interesting question whether functional integration in one field — trade, taxes, agriculture, labor market, etc. — leads inevitably to parallel steps in other functions. But the integration of capital markets is not without interest in its own right. In recent years the world's major financial markets have offered a number of paradoxes:

(1) The United States, with a weak balance of payments and obliged to borrow at short term, is lending at long term; Europe, with a strong balance of payments and lending short, is borrowing long. Europe finds the explanation in the long-term rate of interest in New York which is too low; United States officials comment that the trouble lies in the restrictions on capital movements which remain in force in Europe.

(2) Europe is prepaying long-term governmental debt to the United States government but borrowing on private account. This suggests that the capital markets function differently for private and government funds.

Remark: I acknowledge with thanks the critical comments on the previous draft of Bela Balassa, James C. Ingram, Paul Meek, Robert A. Mundell, Scott Pardee, and George H. Willis.

(3) Not only do European borrowers sell securities in the New York capital market; European investors buy a sizeable portion of these securities there. In interconnected markets one would expect European capitalists either to borrow or to lend in New York, but not both. We examine this apparent anomaly for the light it throws on the question of integration.

II. Integration Defined

With some oversimplification one can establish definitions of integration of increasing rigor as:

(a) Free trade (the major element in the Tinbergen prescription)[1];

(b) The absence of all forms of discrimination (Balassa)[2] presumably going beyond merely free trade into wage, tax, and other aspects of economic policy which might impinge on trade;

(c) Factor price equalization (Myrdal)[3].

With appropriate qualification, all these definitions can amount to the same thing. Under certain limiting assumptions, free trade will bring about factor price equalization. Balassa points out that his definition presupposes an active economic intercourse, since an absence of discrimination between Iceland and New Zealand would hardly lead to economic integration in the absence of a substantial amount of foreign trade — perhaps enough to fulfill the requirements of the factor-price-equalization theorem. Equality of factor prices, which is seldom if ever achieved between trading countries, has the disability as a definition of being somewhat non-operational. It helps, however, in showing the connections among economic, social and political integration — the Negro, Jew and other minority groups can be said not to be fully integrated into the United States community until their factor rewards are identical with those of native-born Protestant whites of equal inherent capacity; and so for

[1] Tinbergen's definition is given in more general terms as "the creation of the most desirable structure of international economy" (Jan Tinbergen, *International Economic Integration*, 2nd, Completely Rev., Ed. of *International Economic Co-operation*, Amsterdam, 1954, p. 95), but in his subsequent discussion the major instrument for achieving this structure, after the establishment of national policies for full employment, etc., is the removal of quantitative restrictions and import duties (*ibid.*, p. 119).

[2] Bela Balassa, *The Theory of Economic Integration*, Homewood, Ill., and London, 1961, p. 1. — See also his "Toward a Theory of Economic Integration", *Kyklos*, Vol. XIV, Basel, 1961, pp. 1sqq., which discusses various definitions.

[3] See Gunnar Myrdal, *An International Economy, Problems and Prospects*, New York, 1956, p. 11. Myrdal puts the stress on equality of opportunity, but adds that the remuneration paid for productive services must be equal, regardless of racial, social and cultural differences. These differences, of course, are of more importance for labor than for capital.

other factors. Moreover, where factors are capable of moving, as in finance, the equality of factor returns becomes an operational definition: "Indeed, the best evidence of the complete integration of a capital market is the absence of differences in security yields according to the region where the firm issuing the security operates"[1].

The relevance of the distinction between freedom to move and movement of a sufficient degree to equalize factor returns can be illustrated from Benelux experience. Meade notes that the various steps undertaken to permit freedom of movement of workers between Belgium and the Netherlands failed to result in much movement; the Dutchman continued to emigrate, when he did, to North America or Australia rather than to Belgium[2]. In these circumstances it is inappropriate to define economic integration for labor as freedom to migrate, or the absence of discriminating regulations. The labor itself discriminates, which results in the absence of equalization of wages. Only if the Dutch and Belgians felt equally at home in each others' countries, and were willing to move freely about both countries in search of higher remuneration, could the labor markets be called integrated on the present definition. It is recognized that few national economies are integrated in this sense, but it is useful to have a standard against which various degrees of integration can be objectively compared — rather like absolute zero in chemistry which serves as a basis for measurement though it is not often achieved.

But even if we accept factor price equalization as a benchmark of integration, there may be room for finer distinctions, at least as concerns capital markets. The price of capital can be equalized between countries by the excess supply in Country A being matched against the excess demand in Country B, as in the familiar partial-equilibrium diagram shown in the following figure. Notice that with this sort of capital movement, the bulk of the demand in the capital-importing country is met from local supply, and only the excess demand is met by imported capital. But demand and supply in two geographically distinct markets can be

---

[1] Tibor Scitovsky, *Economic Theory and Western European Integration*, London, 1958, p. 88, note 2. This definition should perhaps be extended to comprehend as well the absence of differences in yield on similar securities issued in two physically separate markets by a single borrower. (See Table 1, below for the experience of the International Bank for Reconstruction and Development in this connection.) For a discussion which runs entirely in terms of movements, rather than of yields in capital markets, see Hans O. Lundström, *Capital Movements and Economic Integration, A Study of the Rôle of International Long-Term Capital Movements in International Economic Integration With Particular Reference to Europe*, European Aspects, Series B: Economics, No. 4, Leyden, 1961.

[2] James E. Meade, *Negotiations for Benelux*, Princeton Studies in International Finance, No. 6, Princeton, 1957, p. 78.

added together without regard to their geographical location[1]. The supra-marginal demander in either location may have his demand filled by an infra-marginal supplier in either location. Total demand is matched against total supply rather than excess demand against excess supply. This may be said to be an even purer form of integration than price equalization through factor movement.

Figure – *Equalization of Interest Rates Through Interconnected Markets*

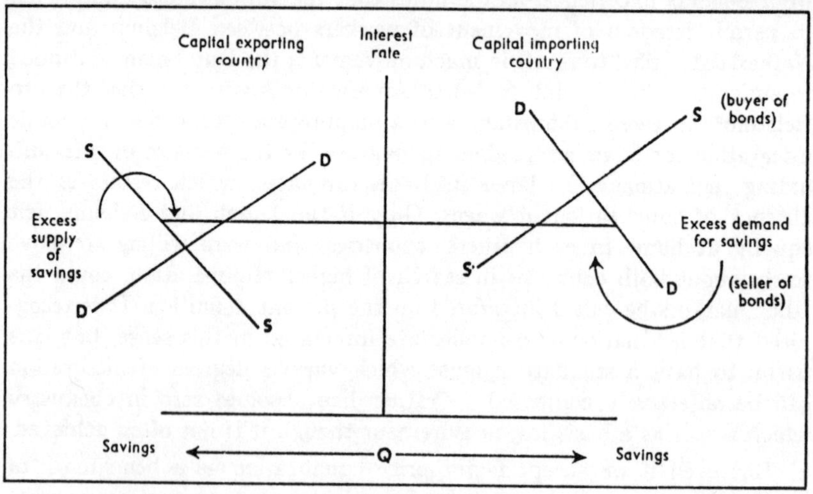

This higher form of integration may be possible only for capital and not for goods or labor because of costs of transfer. Movements of capital are virtually costless; markets for goods and labor are separated regionally and nationally by positive costs of movement[2]. In the United States

[1] See Scitovsky, *op. cit.*, p. 88 : "An integrated capital market may discriminate among borrowers according to the nature and riskiness of their business, the size of their assets, their past financial record, and other such factors, but not according to the region where they operate."

[2] The possibility of a change in the exchange rate may also be more important for goods than for long-term capital, or at least it was in the Canadian case, where long-term capital movements ignored variations in the exchange rate between 1950 and 1961, and again in trans-Atlantic movements where European capital borrowing and lending in New York appear to ignore the short-term view of the dollar. There is some opinion in the United States that the "overvaluation" has stimulated the outflow of capital, as long-term borrowers went short of the dollar. But this explanation must account for the lenders who go long. On balance, the safer hypothesis is that investors dealing in long-term bonds ignore possible changes in the exchange rate, since the mean of a probability distribution of changes in exchange rates converted to return in per cent per annum over the life of the contract is likely to be very small as compared to differences in interest rates. It is true that two-way movements in capital, and their net, might be much larger if investors entertained inelastic

"only the market for marketable securities is fully integrated, with about 80 per cent of such securities dealt in on the New York stock and curb exchanges"[1].

The technical means of integration can be the physical transfer of purchases and sales to a single location, as in New York, or the spread of the major brokers and dealers to all significant financial centers, which thereby become merged. In Switzerland, for example, it makes no difference that the Swiss Bank Corporation has its head office in Basle and the Crédit Suisse in Zurich. Zurich, Basle and Geneva are unified into a single capital market by reason of the fact that the major financial institutions are located in all of them and maintain constant and instantaneous communication among one another. An order to buy or sell placed at any single locality may be matched by another order originating in another locality without funneling all orders into, say, Zurich, as would be the case in New York. Similarly the branch banking system in Canada unifies Toronto and Montreal to such an extent that while Montreal leads as a financial center it does not dominate to the same extent as New York does in the United States.

Integration in the sense of aggregating demanders and suppliers into a single demand curve and supply curve, respectively, is not only institutionally different from matching the excess demand against the excess supply. It is different economically. Capital markets integrated in this sense demonstrate economies of scale which mean that the seller of bonds gets a higher price, and the buyer of bonds is willing to pay a higher price, than if the markets had been kept apart except for excess demand and supply. The benefit to the seller is that he faces a broader market, including investors interested in diversification of risk. The benefit to the buyer is that with a broader market his liquidity is increased. When the State of California, for example, has a large bond issue to place, it sells it in New York; and California investors go to New York to buy a sub-

---

expectations regarding the present exchange-rate structure. Despite the doubts of my critics, however, and based on the findings of Helleiner and Rhomberg in Yale doctoral dissertations examining the Canadian flexible exchange rate experience, I think the conclusion must be that while short-term capital movements respond sensitively to changes in exchange rates, long-term capital movements do not.

For a view that national demands and supplies for goods should be added into world demand and supply curves, and that the national offer curve has no operational meaning, see Frank D. Graham, *The Theory of International Values*, Princeton, 1948, p. 158: "The price of any freely traded good is unaffected by the national origin of sellers or buyers and there is, in consequence, no occasion for grouping buyers or sellers into more or less antagonistic national sectors." But this ignores transfer costs, and the possibility of exchange-rate changes.

[1] Scitovsky, *op. cit.*, p. 90.

stantial share of it. Both buyer and seller are better off than if the bonds had been sold locally — seller because of the better rate and wider placement, buyer because of the broader market with enhanced liquidity. Rather than simply adding the supply curves in the foregoing figure, integration in this sense adds them and then shifts them downward and to the right because the more liquid bond is really a different form for savings.

These economies of scale exist not only for the buyer but for the underwriter. On a larger issue in a larger market, the underwriting commission should be lower per bond. Unfortunately we have little aggregated information on the point. Meek points out that the underwriting spreads on foreign bonds issued in 1958 ranged from 1 point on shorter term issues to $3^1/_2$ points for longer ones, with the gross compensation averaging $2^3/_4$ per cent of the proceeds to the borrowers. Meek contrasts this with the bankers' spread of more than 4.5 per cent on European long-term bonds in 1915—29[1]. It has been asserted that one private United States borrower who sold bonds in Switzerland allegedly would not again go back to that source of capital because, while the coupon rate was low, the commission was high. On the other hand, borrowing in the New York market should include the expense and trouble of the Securities and Exchange Commission registration statement on the initial issue[2].

The increasing returns to scale in a financial center mean that a substantial lead achieved by one center is difficult to overcome. New York has been the dominant financial center of the United States since about 1840, when it overtook Philadelphia[3]. It is suggestive that the First Boston Corporation, one of the largest investment bankers, has its main offices in New York City[4].

---

[1] See Paul Meek, "United States Investment in Foreign Securities (Excluding Canadian and IBRD Issues)", in: *United States Private and Government Investment Abroad*, Ed. by R. F. Mikesell, Eugene, Ore., 1962, p. 253.

[2] For an interesting account of the registration process, its costs and its usefulness, see E. Nevin, "Some Reflections in the New York New Issues Market", *Oxford Economic Papers*, Vol. XIII, 1961, pp. 84 sqq.

[3] For an analysis of how New York surpassed Philadelphia, which had been the dominant financial center from about 1750, see Bray Hammond, *Banks and Politics in America From the Revolution to the Civil War*, Princeton, New Jersey, 1957, esp. pp. 149, 351 sqq. Hammond lays stress not only on New York's physical advantages — the greater commodiousness of her harbor, and the Erie Canal — but also on the energy and ingenuity of her enterprise. — See also Margaret G. Myers, *The New York Money Market*, Vol. I: *Origins and Development* New York, 1931, Chapter I.

[4] A leading contender, if never dominant, Boston suffered a setback in the hard winter of 1816 which closed Boston Harbor to shipping. This is the year known in American annals as "Eighteen-hundred and froze-to-death."

We propose to discuss the prospects for the integration of long-term capital markets in terms of this rigorous definition of integration: where buyers and sellers are assembled in a single market, located in a single center, or tightly bound by unified institutions. But first it is useful to examine the data on recent international long-term lending in the United States and Europe.

III. Recent Experience

It is not difficult to show that world long-term capital markets are not integrated, and that within the world total the capital markets of Europe are not. It is sufficient to show interest rates, as set out in Table 1.

The spread in government bond yields is wider than that in IBRD bonds: for the low-interest rate countries — the United States, Belgium and Switzerland especially — the IBRD bonds yield more than government issues; for the high-yield countries — especially the United Kingdom

Table 1 — *Bond Yields in Selected Countries,* Second Quarter of 1962 (per cent per annum)[1]

Country	Central Government Bond	IBRD Bonds	
	average yields to maturity on issues with at least 12 years' life	yields to maturity on specified issues	
		issue	yield
United States	3.89	3¼ of 1981	4.28
Canada	4.91	3½ of 1969	5.43
United Kingdom	6.18	3½ of 1974	5.50
Continental Europe			
Belgium	4.34	5 of 1969	5.30
France	5.12		
Germany	5.80[a]	5 of 1974	5.03
Italy	5.27	5 of 1976	5.31
Netherlands	4.27	3½ of 1975	4.09
Sweden	4.40		
Switzerland	3.22	3½ of 1976	3.45
Other			
Australia	4.93		
New Zealand	5.27		

[a] Covers bonds of all public authorities, including some with lives of less than 12 years.

[1] *Source:* IMF, *International Financial Statistics,* Vol. XVI, Washington, D.C., 1963, No. 2, p. 29.

and Germany — less. Canada and Italy are exceptions to this generalization in one direction; the Netherlands in the other. (Some influence may arise from differing maturities on the IBRD bonds, though its nature is not apparent.)

The IBRD has not been trying to minimize its borrowing cost, so much as to stimulate international long-term lending by borrowing on its established credit standing in a wide number of currencies. Table 2 shows that, apart from the *DM* equivalent of $ 125 million borrowed in Germany in 1960, the amounts acquired by long-term issues in markets other than New York have been small. Borrowing in Switzerland has been persistent, but generally subject to the informal Swiss restraint which limits single issues, for which permission must be sought on each occasion, to SF 60 million, or $ 11 million. I am informed by the International Bank that roughly 5 per cent of new issues placed in the United States were bought for foreign account; that subsequent open-market trading has resulted in the holding by foreigners of about 12 per cent of New York IBRD issues, apart from a number of dollar issues privately placed outside the United States[1]. The Bank observes that there has been very

Table 2 — *New Issues of 5-Year or More Maturity by the International Bank for Reconstruction and Development,* 1947—1961, *by Currency Issue* (millions of dollars)[2]

Year	All currencies	United States Dollars	Canadian Dollars	Swiss Francs	Sterling	Guilders	Deutsche Marks	Belgian Francs	Lire
1947	250.0	250.0	—	—	—	—	—	—	—
1948	4.0	—	—	4.0	—	—	—	—	—
1949	—	—	—	—	—	—	—	—	—
1950	106.6	100.0	—	6.6	—	—	—	—	—
1951	175.6	150.0	—	11.6	14.0	—	—	—	—
1952	135.2	110.0	13.6	11.6	—	—	—	—	—
1953	23.2	—	—	23.2	—	—	—	—	—
1954	208.8	150.0	22.7	11.6	14.0	10.5	—	—	—
1955	35.7	—	13.6	11.6	—	10.5	—	—	—
1956	75.0	75.0	—	—	—	—	—	—	—
1957	321.5	275.0	—	46.5	—	—	—	—	—
1958	475.0	475.0	—	—	—	—	—	—	—
1959	108.9	—	—	23.3	28.0	—	47.6	10.0	—
1960	353.2	200.2	—	28.0	—	—	125.0	—	—
1961	61.0	—	—	23.3	—	13.8	—	—	24.0
Total	2,333.8	1,785.2	49.9	201.3	56.0	34.8	172.6	10.0	24.0

[1] By private letter.

[2] *Source:* IBRD, *Annual Reports to the Board of Governors*, Washington, D.C,

little purchasing of European currency issues by foreigners outside the country of issue.

If the IBRD has other concerns than minimizing its cost of funds, there is no evidence to suggest that Australia and Norway do. These countries, including Norwegian local governments and private industry, have been avid for capital and borrowed in a wide number of capital markets. If we omit refunding on a substantial scale in London and New York, Australia started its borrowing in the Swiss market with the equivalent of $ 14 million (nominal amount) in each of 1953 and 1955, before placing two small issues in the New York market in 1956 and 1957, and borrowing on a more substantial scale in 1958. In that year the equivalent of $ 43 million was placed in London, and $ 50 million in New York. In 1959 $ 25 million more were borrowed in New York. In 1960 borrowings were Switzerland, $ 14 million; the United Kingdom, $ 34 million; the United States, $ 50 million. In 1961 the amounts were Canada, $ 20 million; Netherlands, $ 11 million; Switzerland, $ 14 million; the United States, $ 25 million. Bond sales took place in the traditional capital source — London — when this was available. Small sums were obtained from the rationed capital markets of Switzerland and Amsterdam, the latter when its prohibition of foreign lending was removed. A Commonwealth partner was approached for a limited sum; but the main borrowing, spaced out to maintain Australia's credit standing, was to New York.

Norwegian borrowing in the New York market was less extensive. If we limit ourselves to the last few years, various government and private Norwegian borrowers obtained $ 28.5 million in the United States in 1958, $ 10 million in 1960, and $ 18 million in 1961. But this experience illustrates a separate truth about international capital markets. Capital flows in channels, like irrigation ditches, rather than like sheets of water which have spilled over riverbanks. This held true in the nineteenth century, when Britain switched its lending from Europe to the Empire and the New World after the revolutions of 1848. It is true on the periphery of the world capital market today. Norway has borrowed the equivalent of $ 6.8 million in Sweden in 1957 and again in 1958 and in 1961, and $ 12 million in 1960. This is the only foreign lending Sweden has undertaken. This is partial integration of the Norwegian and Swedish capital markets, the latter of which is not well integrated with the rest of the world.

Table 3 summarizes the record of long-term new issues for new money in major international financial centers from 1947 to 1961. The table omits about $ 1,800 million of borrowing in New York on Canadian account, because of the special ties running between Canada and the United States capital market; and another $ 500 million of Israeli bonds which are sold on only quasi-commercial terms[1]. The table emphasizes the recent character of United States lending (and the exiguous German), the continuous activity in Switzerland, the sporadic behavior of Sweden and the Netherlands.

The amounts borrowed in Switzerland are not only impressive overall. They have been growing. But the business is on a different scale than that in New York. In 1959, for example, the New York figure of $ 196 million represents 8 loans as compared with 9 for the Swiss figure of half the sum. Switzerland offers a small capital market with a large proportion of foreign lending: it achieves diversification by lending to many borrowers for small amounts. New York is a large capital market with only a small interest in foreign lending: its diversification is largely domestic.

Table 3 — *Foreign Bonds Publicly Issued for New Funds in Germany, Netherlands, Sweden, Switzerland, the United Kingdom and the United States*, 1947—1961 (excluding refunding and issues in the United States for Canadian and Israeli borrowers)
(millions of dollars)[2]

Year	Total	Germany	Netherlands	Sweden	Switzerland	United Kingdom	United States
1947	97.6	—	—	13.9	13.2	50.0	20.5
1948	40.3	—	—	5.4	11.6	23.3	—
1949	45.5	—	—	—	12.4	33.1	—
1950	85.3	—	—	—	48.9	36.4	—
1951	31.6	—	—	—	—	31.6	—
1952	66.5	—	—	—	45.5	21.0	—
1953	94.4	—	—	9.7	27.3	56.0	1.4
1954	183.7	—	16.1	9.7	87.9	70.0	—
1955	220.2	—	62.9	—	81.3	28.0	48.0
1956	91.3	—	—	6.2	64.1	14.0	7.0
1957	67.3	—	5.0	6.2	3.2	—	52.9
1958	410.0	10.0	—	—	32.7	126.0	241.3
1959	356.0	33.9	—	—	95.9	30.2	196.0
1960	325.1	14.3	—	12.0	132.3	81.5	85.0
1961	613.9	3.3	146.1	6.8	217.7	112.0	128.0
Total	2,728.7	61.5	230.1	69.9	874.0	713.1	780.1

[1] The table also omits private placements of foreign bonds in New York which picked up after 1958 from very small beginnings and culminated in an $ 100 million issue for a Mexican governmental company placed with a private insurance company in 1960. For a table of such placements including $ 100 millions for European borrowers, see Meek, *op. cit.*, p. 254.

[2] *Source:* Compiled from unpublished summaries made available by the International Bank for Reconstruction and Development.

IV. The Capital Market in Europe

Eight years after the Treaty of Rome there is virtually no sign of integration of the long-term capital markets of Europe, whether in the lower form of equalized interest rates or the more advanced one of fully merged markets in a single center or through unified institutions. Individual capital markets are looking up in Germany and the Netherlands. There is a flourishing Swiss market, as we have said for individual foreign borrowers and limited amounts. But the interconnections among the various markets are thin. This is partly because of administrative obstacles in the way of new issues. Trading in outstanding securities has been relaxed and much direct investment, but not new issues[1]. In part it seems to be due to institutional obstacles and economic barriers. Investors are not particularly interested in participating in the narrow capital markets of countries other than their own. In the few cases when a number of European countries lend simultaneously to a single borrower, it is contrived rather than the result of merged market forces.

Argentina, with a weak credit standing, borrowed $ 25 million in Europe in 1961. The rate was $6^1/_2$ per cent, and interest and principal were made payable at fixed rates in seven currencies. $ 7.4 million were taken by the market in Switzerland, $ 3 million in Germany, and the rest were privately placed in Belgium, France, Italy, the Netherlands, and the United Kingdom. In 1961 a Portuguese petroleum refinery placed a $ 5 million issue: $ 0.3 million in Germany, $ 0.5 million in the Netherlands, $ 1.0 million in Switzerland, $ 2.0 million in Belgium and $ 1.2 million in Luxemburg. A *DM* 60 million ($ 14.3 million) $5^3/_4$ per cent Fonds des Routes 15-year bond, guaranteed by the Kingdom of Belgium and payable in *DM* or dollars, was sold in January 1960, but only *DM* 14 million was taken in Germany and the remainder was placed in unstated amounts in Belgium-Luxemburg, the Netherlands, Switzerland, France and elsewhere. In all these loans, the fact that national *tranches* had to be arranged by the underwriters — and for what were over-all small amounts — makes clear that a smoothly working long-term European capital market has not been realized.

V. Europe and the New York Capital Market

On the other hand, as already stated, not only the smaller European countries but the institutions of the new Europe have been selling and buying bonds in New York. We discuss the selling first, and then the buying.

[1] See: De Nederlandsche Bank, NV, *Report for the Year 1961*, Amsterdam, p. 21

The European Coal and Steel Community has placed loans of \$ 13.8 million in the Netherlands in 1961, following the sale of \$ 11.7 million in Switzerland in 1956. Its major borrowing, however, has been in New York: \$ 35 million in 1956; \$ 50 million in 1958; \$ 25 million in 1960, and \$ 25 million in 1962.

The European Investment Bank has borrowed only \$ 13.8 million (50 million guilders). This sum was obtained in the Netherlands in 1961.

The Société de Pipe-Line Sud-Européen, a private French company but European in spirit, borrowed \$ 13.8 million in the Netherlands in 1961, but placed two \$ 20 million issues in New York in 1962.

A similar private company with a European mission, Eurofima (Société Européenne pour le Financement de Matériel Ferroviaire) has placed one standard size issue in the Netherlands in 1961 (\$ 13.8 million). In August 1962 it borrowed \$ 5 million in a term loan from a New York bank; the newspaper account of the transaction[1] suggested that the firm would presently undertake to borrow larger amounts on the New York bond market.

These bonds are sold in the New York market because net rates there are below any in Europe except for the Netherlands and Switzerland, and the latter markets are rationed in amount. There is little difficulty in understanding why European organizations sell bonds in New York. The question is why they buy them.

First, it is necessary to establish the fact. Estimates differ. A. N. Overby, vice president of the First Boston Corporation, states that there are no firm estimates of the amount of foreign dollar bonds taken by foreign investors, but that in some cases the amounts have been "very large"[2]. Samuel Pizer, assistant chief of the Balance of Payments Division, Department of Commerce, has estimated that in rough terms about half of the European bonds sold in New York in 1961 and probably in the first six months of 1962 have been taken by Europeans[3]. Paul Meek, manager of the Public Information Department of the Federal Reserve Bank of New York, has written[4]: "From incomplete private and Depart-

[1] *The New York Times*, August 16, 1962, p. 35, column 6.

[2] See his address, "Investment Banking and International Finance," before the Forty-Seventh National Foreign Trade Convention, New York, November 14, 1960, p. 5 of the mimeographed version. This paper was generously communicated to me by Mr. Overby.

[3] See his testimony before the Joint Economic Committee, Congress of the United States, on August 14, 1962, in: *Hearings on the State of the Economy and Policies for Full Employment* (August 7—10, 13—17, 20, 21 and 22, 1962), p. 489. — See also the testimony of Professor Philip W. Bell on the same subject, *ibid.*, pp. 490sqq., to the effect that the movement of long-term capital to Europe is exaggerated because of the proportion of the new issues bought by Europeans.

[4] See Meek, *op. cit.*, p. 251.

ment of Commerce data it appears that foreign investors took two-thirds or more of the publicly offered and underwritten issues in 1958—59." These estimates may be high, and I have been given to understand in official Washington circles that downward revision may bring them ultimately to one-third.

A variety of reasons can be offered to explain why Europeans buy European bonds in the New York market, but as Overby indicates, it is difficult to assess their relative weight. Some of these reasons are offered to explain why European buyers are more interested in these bonds than American investors: European investors have a better appreciation of the credit standing of the borrower, more sophistication and experience in lending, and pay lower rates of income tax on bond interest than United States holders. Overby cites these three reasons why European and other non-United States investors may have a greater interest in foreign dollar bonds than the United States investor. His three other reasons are addressed to a slightly different problem: why European investors want dollar obligations rather than European bonds. This is the more relevant question for our purposes. Overby's answers (without relative weights) are interest in obtaining a dollar obligation of his own country, lack of United States withholding tax on interest paid to non-resident holders of foreign dollar bonds, and in some cases a higher return than is obtainable on bonds available in his own market[1].

Pizer's testimony before the Joint Economic Committee serves to amplify what Overby may have meant by the interest in a dollar obligation. His stress is on the marketability of the securities: "Of course, when an issuer can offer a bond to the public in the United States, the instrument becomes a much more highly marketable liquid instrument than if we had brought it out in a smaller capital market. There is that inducement of structure of the market here, even though perhaps the issuer expects only half of it to be taken in the United States market"[2].

Meek's statement on the point in the Mikesell study is terse[3]: "Foreign dollar bonds have offered to overseas investors excellent marketability, exemption from United States withholding tax on the interest paid, and strong sinking and protective call features."

In private correspondence in October, 1962, Meek has modified this statement and tentatively emphasized the rate of return. The chief European buyers of foreign dollar bonds according to his information place their orders through Belgium, the Netherlands and Switzerland,

---

[1] Overby, *op. cit.*, p. 6.

[2] Pizer, *op. cit.*, p. 489.

[3] Meek, *op. cit.*, pp. 251 sq. The statement is footnoted with a reference to Moody's Investor Service, *Bond Survey*, New York, October 27, 1958, p. 226.

countries which restrict or regulate the access of foreign borrowers to their capital markets and where rates are on the whole below those in New York. Marketability, on this showing, is not of great importance as compared with yield. The wealthy investors in Europe may even be unable to obtain foreign bond issues floated in Amsterdam and Zurich, since these are allocated to a privileged list of banks and insurance companies. In consequence, their demands spill over their national boundaries[1].

The explanation that some Europeans borrow in New York because rates are higher than in their national markets, while others sell new issues because they can obtain funds cheaper, might seem to dispose of the paradox that Europeans both buy and sell bonds here and its resolution in the face of broader markets with greater marketability. But of course it does not. It merely shifts the subject to be explained to the reluctance of the European investors to buy German bonds with rates close to 6 per cent, or French bonds at $5^1/_4$ or British at more than 6. The dollar obligations are wanted despite their lower yield than national bond issues available in Europe because of the breadth of the market and the greater marketability or liquidity of these issues.

It also suggests that the official United States view that capital market restrictions in Europe put pressure on the United States balance of payments by diverting demand for savings to New York[2] is not very compelling. Reform of the underwriting and distributing facilities for long-term capital issues in Britain, France, Italy and Germany will not alter the relative scarcity of capital in those markets[3]; eliminating the limits on new issues in the thin markets of Switzerland and the Netherlands would be virtually certain to raise yields rapidly in those markets without providing much more capital net from domestic savers. Zurich

[1] Letter from Paul Meek, October 17, 1962, paraphrased by generous permission. This explanation would apply more fully, it would seem, to Switzerland than to the Netherlands, judging by the interest yields in Table 1, and more fully to both of these than to Belgium, on the same ground and in view of Belgium's experience as a borrower on long-term bond account for new issues, rather than a lender.

[2] See Speeches of Secretary of the Treasury Dillon before the American Bankers Association at Rome, Italy, May 18, 1962 (mimeographed), p. 10; and of Deputy Under-Secretary J. Dewey Daane before the American Chamber of Commerce in the Netherlands, Scheveningen, the Netherlands, June 26, 1962 (mimeographed), p. 4. Secretary Dillon recognizes that a large proportion of the publicly floated issues in New York have been bought by Europeans but holds that the "burden is nonetheless real."

[3] Asked to comment on the Dillon speech at the Joint Economic Committee *Hearings*, F. H. Klopstock, manager, Research Department, Federal Reserve Bank of New York, combined organization of the market with its capacity without indicating their relative weights: "... to a considerable extent the motive for placing bonds in our capital market is that the absorptive capacity and the organization of the European capital market are inadequate to take care of these placements." (*Hearings, op. cit.*, p. 489.)

or Amsterdam could perhaps become a European capital center for large bond issues at reduced commissions sold to an international group of purchasers. The domestic authorities are opposed to altering the present diversification of domestic savings being placed in a number of small issues, sold by the underwriters at substantial mark-ups. The foreign borrowers, moreover, would doubtless be wary of risking a big issue on the narrow domestic market even if the official limitations were not there.

A Swiss economist suggested to the Joint Economic Committee that the United States should take a leaf out of the Swiss authorities' book and limit foreign access to the New York bond market[1]. This recommendation rests on the national view of the connection between foreign lending and the balance of payments, and overlooks the function of a financial center in providing a market for foreign lenders as well as foreign borrowers, with negligible effect on the balance.

Some interest attaches to the more intense preoccupation with liquidity in Europe than in the United States, a preoccupation which seems to inhibit the investment of excess short-term balances in long-term domestic bonds. It may be that liquidity preference, like other forms of taste, *non disputandum est* but the American official view runs to the effect that greater institutional efforts could be undertaken, by freeing markets of restrictions, providing medium-term obligations and stimulating competition among lenders, to induce European capitalists to part with their liquidity in exchange for bonds. On the other hand, it may be that the capital markets for bonds which provide too little diversification for lenders, and thereby induce them to hold cash, are narrow and unconnected by reason of investor attitudes, not official restrictions.

VI. Prospective European Financial Integration

If the financial centers of Switzerland and Amsterdam will not, and probably could not, provide the central market necessary for financial integration, what of the rest of Europe? It is the thesis of this paper that New York is the most likely center of long-term financial integration for Europe, that its head start over any potential competitor is one which cannot be overcome, and that the financial integration of the European Economic Community, with or without the adherence of the

---

[1] See the testimony of Jurg Niehans before the Joint Economic Committee, *Hearings*, *op. cit.*, pp. 387sq. Niehans describes the Swiss restrictions which apply to loans over SF 10 million, characterizes them as one of the most useful instruments of Swiss credit policy, and quotes a director of the Swiss National Bank that if the United States had had such restrictions, there would be a world dollar shortage.

United Kingdom, will be effected through the Euro-dollar for short-term funds and the dollar bond for long. Short-term integration has made great progress since the war; long-term finance much less. To the extent that the long-term capital market becomes integrated, however, it seems probable that interest rates in Frankfurt and Paris will be equalized not by direct capital movements between France and Germany, but by those through New York[1].

This is not the usual view. Representative Widnall of the Joint Economic Committee asked, "Would not the Common Market eventually provide greater ability to finance within the Common Market so that there would be no necessity to come to the United States?" to which D. D. Humphrey replied, "The British are very much hoping. If they join, they hope London will become the capital center ..."[2].

In an important study Paul Meek states[3]: "The advance of economic integration as an emerging reality in Western Europe is likely to be accompanied by a financial integration of European money and capital markets." And again[4]: "The growing integration of the European economy provides the central challenge to New York's present position. The breaking down of national economic barriers is inescapably going to be paralleled by an integration of national money and capital markets. ... If the United Kingdom joins the Common Market and London should develop as the financial center of a United Europe, New York would have a very powerful competitor indeed. And the world might then have two financial centers more nearly equal in size."

Meek recognizes the possibility that the Common Market may fail to develop a single financial center, or a completely integrated capital market united by common banking institutions like those in the Swiss market. His discussion of this possibility runs mainly in terms of the effectiveness of New York in keeping commissions low and easing the rigors of registration with the Securities and Exchange Commission[5]. There is little description of the dynamic process by which a dominant market would gain ascendancy in Europe.

[1] Note the contradiction between this view and the statement of Franz Gehrels ("Monetary Systems for the Common Market", *Journal of Finance*, Vol. XIV, Chicago, Ill., 1959, p. 313, quoted by Balassa, *Theory of Economic Integration, op. cit.*, p. 259) that "an inflow of funds from Paris to Frankfurt might be easier to bring about than one from San Francisco to Kansas City." San Francisco and Kansas City are integrated financially, of course, not by direct links between them but through the integration of each with New York. And such is likely to be the case for Paris and Frankfurt.

[2] *Hearings, op. cit.*, p. 490.

[3] Paul Meek, *New York — International Financial Center* (to be published), (mimeographed, draft of April, 1962), pp. 89sq.

[4] *Ibid.*, pp. 92sq.

[5] *Ibid.* pp. 93sqq.

VII. The Emergence of a Dominant Center

It is hard to see how the London market would acquire dominance in the long-term capital market of Europe if and when Britain joins the Common Market. London rates are high; the demand for capital in Britain is large; sources of savings have dried up. The City is no longer providing capital for the Commonwealth on a significant scale, having deferred to the Colonial Office, the IBRD and New York. The channels connecting the London capital market to European centers silted up after 1848, and there is no apparent reason to expect them to open up.

It is true that London has played a major rôle in European short-term banking, partly through the Euro-dollar market where its rôle is central[1]. Several critics of the first draft of this paper have thought that I unduly emphasize the need for London to contribute savings to an international financial center, as opposed to the institutional facilities so handy to the Continent, and that if European countries hold liquid reserves in London the practice might easily develop of centralizing purchases and sales of long-term bond issues there. This may be so. But if there are economies of scale in long-term financial markets, as I believe, a base of abundant domestic savings is needed to get started. Without this base I do not see how the first borrowers can be induced to sell issues at rates competitive with Zurich for small issues and with New York for substantial ones. With economies of scale, the problem is to achieve scale. How would London do it?

One critic, Robert Mundell, contends that London's high interest rates reflect less a relative scarcity of capital than a relatively persistent inflation. Once this inflation is cured, it follows that abundant domestic savings will lower interest rates, attract borrowers, and with broader markets, savers as well. Possible, but unlikely in my judgement, since I doubt whether the savings are really there. Income redistribution, modest profits, consumption of capital gains, middle-class dissavings and so on have undermined the bases for substantial personal savings which have not been replaced by institutional savings through insurance, pension funds, etc. But this is of course impressionistic[2].

---

[1] See O. L. Altman, "Recent Developments in Foreign Markets for Dollars and Other Currencies", in: *Factors Affecting the United States Balance of Payments*, Materials Prepared for the Subcommittee on International Exchange and Payments of the Joint Economic Committee, Congress of the United States, P. 6: *Longrun Prospects, Capital Movements, American Dollars Abroad*, Washington, 1962, pp. 483sqq.

[2] For a journalistic account which attributes significance to institutions for collecting savings, however, see Anthony Sampson, *Anatomy of Britain*, New York and Evanston, 1962, P. II, and esp. Chapter 25.

The emergence of another center — Frankfurt, Paris, Amsterdam, Brussels, Milan, or outside the EEC itself, Zurich, is possible but not likely. Switzerland and Amsterdam virtually eliminate themselves. Of the other four, there is no reason to expect financial energy to be attracted more to one than another. Perhaps Milan can be ruled out on the grounds of Italian capital needs, which leave little savings available for export. Brussels is small. Between Paris and Frankfurt, one would expect perhaps the demand for capital to fall relatively to the supply, first in Germany rather than France, but the German tradition in lending in bonds is slight — term loans to support exports have deeper roots in the foreign field. The French tradition in bonds, moreover, is one to forget.

How would one center pull ahead of the other? It would pull financial energy, as New York did in its rise ahead of Philadelphia. Benjamin Franklin was attracted from Boston to Philadelphia in 1726; Alexander Hamilton and Aaron Burr from the Antilles and Albany, in 1772 and 1783 respectively, to New York. The success of Paris in defeating the challenge of Lyon in the second half of the nineteenth century is vividly described by the biographer of the early years of the *Crédit Lyonnais*[1]. Established in Lyon in 1863, this great bank transferred its center of power to the Paris office, and with it the person of its energetic president, Henri Germain, during the 1870s. In 1881 the transfer was complete and Germain did not visit the Lyon office once during the year[2].

Another possibility would be for leading European banks and investment bankers to establish a network of branches throughout the Common Market. It is not enough for certain banks to work together for particular purposes, as is said to be the case among the *Deutsche Bank*, the *Crédit Lyonnais*, the *Banca Commerciale Italiana* and the *Morgan Guaranty Trust Company*. The interests of a syndicate may be merged for particular purposes and for periods of time, but they remain divergent in ways which those of a single institution with branches in separate portions of the market would not. The private bankers — Rothschild, Lazard Frères, Schroeder — would perhaps serve the purpose if the funds at their disposal were somewhat bigger in relation to the totals. It is worth noting that of the commercial banks it is the United States institutions — Morgan Guaranty Trust Company, Chase Manhattan, the First National City, in particular — which are represented in the several countries of the Common Market rather than European institutions.

[1] Jean Bouvier, *Le Crédit Lyonnais de 1863 à 1882, Les années de formation d'une banque de dépôts*, École pratique des hautes études, VIe Section, Centre de recherches historiques, Affaires et gens d'affaires, XXIII, Paris, 1961, T. I, Chapter IV: "Une banque bicéphale: Rôles respectifs du siège social et de la succursale de Paris."

[2] *Ibid.*, p. 275.

One further possibility for integrating the capital market is industrial firms using direct investment. In the United States, the marginal efficiencies of capital and of labor have been equalized throughout the country, in some considerable part, by the operations of national firms, borrowing in New York and investing where the marginal efficiency of capital was high and the cost of labor low. But this result only followed after an integrated capital market had been established. Stephen Hymer has asserted as a theoretical proposition which is persuasive that industrial firms are not likely to move capital more efficiently than long-term capital markets — which is why they characteristically attempt to borrow the maximum possible capital locally[1]. But in any event it is largely United States firms which have subsidiaries in several Common Market countries, and a few British[2]. As in banking, European firms typically form loose associations rather than merge or establish wholly-owned subsidiaries in one another's markets.

I conclude on the basis of this analysis that trade integration does not necessarily lead to financial integration; that long-term capital markets are now more integrated between the separate countries of Europe and the United States than among each other, with further integration likely to emerge in this direction rather than within the Common Market (with or without the British); that the same pattern is likely to be true of short-term capital markets, but to a lesser extent, with the Euro-dollar market taking the place of the New York bond market. It follows that economic integration in one field (trade) does not necessarily lead to integration in other aspects within the identical group of countries, and that the European Economic Community may continue to discriminate against outside countries in trade but be integrated with them in other respects. The flow of Dutch labor to Canada and Australia mentioned by Meade is one example. It is predicted that another will be increasingly found in capital markets.

A final point: Professor James Ingram believes that financial integration is desirable not only because of its effect on resource allocation but because it improves the efficiency of the balance-of-payments adjustment mechanism[3]. His studies, especially of the payments mechanism

[1] See Stephen Hymer, *Direct Investment and the International Operations of National Firms*, unpublished doctoral dissertation, Massachusetts Institute of Technology, 1960.

[2] British restrictions on direct investment in the little budget of July, 1961, reaffirmed in the April 9, 1962, budget, militate against the development of widespread interconnections among the European Common Market countries through British firms.

[3] See James C. Ingram, "State and Regional Payments Mechanisms", *The Quarterly Journal of Economics*, Vol. LXXIII, Cambridge, Mass., 1959, pp. 619sqq. — *Idem*, "A Proposal for Financial Integration in the Atlantic Community", in: *Factors Affecting the United*

between Puerto Rico and the United States suggest that changes in ownership of long-term assets, as well as in short-term claims and liabilities, may play an important rôle in bringing about smooth and effortless balance-of-payments adjustment of the sort so frequently found within but not between countries. This may be so, though I have doubts[1]. The present exercise is one in positive, rather than normative, economics. I am not urging financial integration within the Atlantic partnership but forecasting its emergence.

* * *

States Balance of Payments, *op. cit.*, P. 3: *The International Monetary System: Defects and Remedies*, pp. 175sqq., which suggests that the balance-of-payments disequilibrium of the United States and the need for international liquidity seen by Triffin can both be met by more effective interconnections between European and United States capital markets.

[1] See "Comment" by R. L. Pfister and Ingram's "Reply", *The Quarterly Journal of Economics*, Vol. LXXIV, 1960, pp. 641sqq. I sympathize with the Pfister position that the varying regional incidence of governmental expenditure and taxation plays a major rôle in interregional adjustment. It also seems likely to me that financial integration in short-term money markets can ease the adjustment mechanism (if it works right), though it reduces the possibility of reliance on monetary policy for internal purposes. In the one major international case where long-term capital markets were integrated — Canada and the United States — this fact did not help with adjustment.

[11]

1992-2002: The Future Evolution of Financial Markets in Europe

Professor Richard Dale, University of Southampton

The 1992 liberalisation of European financial markets is only one aspect of the global trend towards financial deregulation. Indeed, the financial restructuring that is occurring in Europe would most probably have taken place in response to internal and external competitive pressures, even in the absence of a collective liberalisation programme. Nevertheless, the effect of 1992 is to transform what would otherwise have been an evolutionary process into a more dramatic upheaval of the European financial services industry.

In looking ahead to the likely future shape of European financial markets in the decade following 1992, one rather obvious point has to be borne in mind. Much, if not most, of the financial restructuring triggered by the 1992 reforms will occur prior to 1992. After all, as we saw with "Big Bang" in the UK, the race begins with the *announcement* rather than the *implementation* of a new regulatory regime. The discussion will therefore straddle both pre- and post-1992 developments.

It is necessary to look first at the nature of the competitive process that has been set in train by the 1992 reforms; and subsequently at the kind of financial structure that might emerge from this competition.

The creation of a single European market for financial services, involving abolition of exchange controls and the right of authorised financial institutions to carry on their business anywhere in the community, is creating a competitive response at three different levels. Firstly, national regulatory authorities are introducing reforms aimed at strengthening the competitive position of the financial centres over which they preside; secondly, individual exchanges are introducing reforms designed to attract domestic and international business; and, finally, financial institutions are themselves developing strategies to enable them to compete more effectively in the new financial environment.

At an early stage it was recognised that a single European market would generate enormous competitive disparities between financial institutions if *prudential regulations*—meaning essentially capital adequacy requirements—were not broadly harmonised within the Community: hence the proposals to introduce Community-wide capital adequacy norms both for banks and securities firms. However, in those areas where national authorities retain regulatory autonomy there is bound to be a process of competitive adjustment. This is because cross-frontier liberalisation accentuates the competitive distortions caused by any remaining regulatory unevenness.

In the first place, *conduct of business rules*, which continue to be the responsibility of host authorities, will be realigned to take account of the new market realities, since any country which adopts unilaterally stringent rules in this area will simply lose business to softer European centres. As the Bank of England has recently pointed out, "although retention of host country control [of conduct of business rules] might deprive the Community of some of the advantages of mutual recognition, competition should in due course lead to more common features and closer linkages between markets".[1] To put it another way, whereas prudential rules are being formally harmonised in anticipation of 1992, conduct of business rules will eventually be *de facto* harmonised as a result of regulatory competition.

However, there are a number of difficulties with allowing regulation to find its own level in this way. The process of convergence is necessarily haphazard and may result in regulatory standards being aligned on the more permissive regimes; there is no clear dividing line between prudential and conduct of business rules in key areas such as compensation, advertising and segregation of funds; and conduct of business rules play such an important role in securities (as distinct from banking) markets that a formal EC harmonisation initiative may become necessary.

Monetary policy and regulation also remain, in theory at any rate, a matter for host authorities—but here again there is bound to be a process of competitive adjustment. Most importantly, interest-free reserve requirements imposed by national monetary authorities on banks' deposit liabilities will become a major source of competitive distortion in a unified financial market. Such requirements are equivalent in their effect to a tax on bank deposits, and to the extent that this burden varies there is an incentive for funds to be deposited in those centres with the lowest reserve requirements (and therefore the highest deposit rates). Even before the 1992 initiative was in prospect, the Bundesbank was concerned about the competitive impact of its high reserve requirements which it lowered in May 1986. More recently, the Director General of the Bank of Italy has pointed out that the high minimum reserve ratio applied to Italian banks (an average of 21 per cent in 1988) threatens to undermine their competitiveness *vis-à-vis* foreign banks.[2] In 1988 the implicit cost of reserve requirements

1. Memorandum submitted by the Bank of England, Trade and Industry Committee Fifth Report on "Financial Services and the Single European Market", p.110.

2. See "Liberalisation of Financial Services in the European Community: the Case of Italy", Address by Lamberto Dini, Director General of the Bank of Italy, Geneva, March 14 1989, pp.5-6.

(defined as the difference between the average yield on government securities and that on compulsory reserves, times the reserve ratio) was around 1 percentage point in Italy, as against 0.2 in France and 0.3 in West Germany. Under these circumstances the abolition of exchange controls in Italy would ensure the rapid emergence of a very large Euro-lira deposit market outside the Italian central bank's control. It is therefore a safe prediction that major differences in reserve requirements will not survive long beyond 1992.

Fiscal regulation will also be subject to competitive adjustment. The question here is whether and to what extent it is possible to reconcile individual countries' freedom to tax with intra-European mobility of capital. For instance, the present prospect is that differences in national taxes on savings will trigger large intra-Community flows of funds within the single market. West Germany has already experienced difficulties of this kind: when the government announced that it was imposing a 10 per cent withholding tax on interest income with effect from the beginning of 1989, the subsequent movement of funds to Luxembourg was on such a large scale as to oblige the government to withdraw the tax only six months after it had come into effect. And with European withholding tax rates varying between zero and 51 per cent the scope for destabilising tax-driven capital movements after 1992 is considerable.

In recognition of such difficulties the EC Commission early in 1989 proposed a minimum 15 per cent withholding tax on savings and bond income for all tax residents of the Community—a figure intended to be high enough to discourage tax evasion within the EC but not so high as to drive funds into tax havens outside the Community. This proposal was unacceptable to the UK and Luxembourg, in particular, given their status as international banking centres, but the fundamental policy dilemma is bound to resurface. Either withholding tax will have to be harmonised or there will have to be a mandatory system for reporting interest income accrued by EC residents. Failing such moves, there will be large intra-Community capital flows that have nothing whatever to do with the relative efficiency of competing financial markets. In particular, the European Community's UCITS Directive, which became effective last October, will encourage investment in mutual funds or investment companies located in countries such as Luxembourg where dividends are paid gross.

Withholding tax is but one example of the distortions that may arise from tax disparities within the single financial market—and the pressures that are building up to extend the process of regulatory convergence to the tax area. Another example is stamp duty where the UK and Holland are facing demands for removal of this duty on competitive grounds while West Germany has already announced its intention to abolish stamp duty with effect from January 1st 1991. Problems will also arise with VAT, corporation tax, and the tax treatment of derivative products, where the UK's futures and options markets are concerned that more favourable treatment of such instruments in European centres may drive business out of London.

In addition to prudential, conduct of business, monetary and fiscal regulation, there is finally a broad category of what might be described as anti-competitive regulation that is in the process of being dismantled in anticipation of 1992. Included under this heading are various moves to abolish price-fixing arrangements, such as fixed stock exchange commissions. The most radical review of such restrictive practices is occurring in Switzerland which, although not a member of the Community, is directly affected by the single market reforms. The Swiss Cartel Commission has recommended that the "Big Bank" cartel governing Swiss franc foreign bond issues be loosened and that agreements fixing the fees for securities broking, custodian operations and documentary credits be abolished. The Government has said that the issue of restrictive practices must be resolved in a way that safeguards Switzerland's role as a financial centre and enables the banking system to adjust to the European sinlge market. Similarly, the Swiss National Bank has warned that the Swiss banks must be ready to abandon their cartel structure if they are to remain competitive after 1992. Clearly national price-fixing arrangements cannot easily survive on the perimeter, still less within, the single European market in financial services.

Among other measures aimed at removing anti-competitive rigidities are those designed to facilitate mergers between financial institutions and to enable banks to diversify into non-bank financial activities. Proposals of this kind are contained in bills now before the Dutch and Italian parliaments. Finally a number of countries have taken steps to strengthen the competitiveness of their domestic bond markets; a notable example being West Germany's decision to allow borrowers to issue bearer bonds without seeking prior official approval.

Just as national regulatory authorities are responding to the prospect of intensified cross-border competition, so stock exchanges are seeking to strengthen their competitive position by introducing new screen-based trading systems, streamlining new issue procedures, adjusting listing and disclosure requirements and developing more efficient settlement and delivery systems. One of the more dramatic examples of this kind of competitive response is the package of capital market reforms proposed by representatives of the Dutch financial services industry, and submitted to the government in March this year, with a view to making Amsterdam "the financial gateway to Continental Europe". Less spectacular, piecemeal reforms are being proposed or implemented all over Europe.

Competition between European exchanges will in due course result in much more standardised, and certainly more efficient, securities trading arrangements throughout the Community. This will happen whether or not the International Stock Exchange's (ISE) proposal for a single European equity market comes to fruition. Indeed, the only question here, as in the regulatory field, is whether harmonisation of procedures will come about through collective initiatives, such as that of the ISE, or through the rough and tumble of competition.

At a different level, individual financial institutions are, of course, responding to the prospect of a single financial market and they are doing so in four distinct (but by no means mutually exclusive) ways: cross-border expansion or linkages; diversification into new financial services; amalgamations designed to exploit economies of scale; and financial innovation.

Cross-border activity is taking various forms, including share swaps (such as the Royal Bank of Scotland—Banco Santander link-up), asset swaps (such as proposed between Banque Nationale de Paris and Banco-Vizcaya), the establishment of new branches (such as those recently opened in Spain by NatWest under its own name), and foreign acquisitions—this last route being followed by Deutsche Bank with its bank acquisitions in Spain, Italy, Portugal, Holland and, most recently, the UK.

Financial institutions are also engaged in cross-product expansion within the Community aimed at exploiting economies of scope. The main link-up here is between insurance and banking. Such mergers have been taking place recently in West Germany, France, the Netherlands and Italy, reflecting the potential for joint marketing of banking and insurance services through retail outlets. There have also been a series of link-ups between continental banks and UK fund managers. More generally, the Second Banking Co-ordination Directive will promote universal banking throughout the Community, given the broad range of permissible financial activities which, under Article 16, host authorities will be obliged to accept.

The third kind of corporate response to 1992 is domestic expansion and consolidation aimed at exploiting economies of scale. There appears to be a firmly entrenched view, which is not confined to Western Europe, that the larger the financial institution, the better it will be able to cope with intensified competition. McKinsey, the international management consultants, have produced a report for the German Savings Bank Association recommending that the country's 584 savings banks and eleven Landesbanken (which conduct wholesale banking business for the savings banks) should establish one central wholesale banking institution to help them remain competitive after 1992. Similarly, the Bank of Italy has expressed concern over the fragmented nature of the Italian banking industry, pointing out that the four largest banks account for only 25 per cent of the total assets of the banking system, as against 40 per cent in, for instance, Belgium and France. According to its Director General, "the strategy adopted by the bank of Italy is designed to remove the obstacles to concentration while fostering competition by abolishing geographical restrictions on banking business, extending the range of permitted operations and liberalising branch networks".[3] Parallel initiatives aimed at promoting larger scale banking units are under way in a number of other European countries, notably Spain whose banking system is even more fragmented than Italy's.

Finally, financial institutions are responding to the prospect of intensified competition by introducing innovative financial techniques and services. An example here is Banco Santander's decision to offer interest-bearing current accounts—in breach of a long established understanding among the big domestic Spanish banks that has hitherto kept banks' funding costs artificially low. Such informal cartel arrangements clearly cannot survive the cross-border competition that is now developing.

Having described the competitive forces that have been released by the EEC liberalisation programme, it is possible to say something about the financial structure that might emerge after 1992. Here, it is useful to distinguish between the structure of *financial markets* and the kinds of *financial institution* which will be serving those markets.

So far as markets are concerned, the emergence of a common regulatory framework is likely to result in a significant shift in the locus of financial activity. In particular, the elimination of regulatory distortions and the standardisation of new issue procedures as well as secondary market trading arrangements, will tend to erode the external markets in European securities. In other words, the Euro-guilder and Euro-deutschmark markets (to take two of the most important external markets) may well be repatriated to Holland and West Germany. It has been estimated that about 30 per cent of the turnover of German government bonds, 50 per cent of the turnover in international DM straight issues, 80-90 per cent of the turnover of DM floating rate notes and 15-20 per cent of turnover in West German equities takes place in London.[4] When West Germany's turnover tax on securities is abolished and stock-market trading practices have been streamlined, there is no reason why such business should be conducted through London rather than Frankfurt. Similarly, it is estimated that around one half of guilder bond business is transacted in London and this activity, too, may be

3. Ibid. p.9.

4. See "London as an International Financial Centre", Bank of England Quarterly Bulletin, November 1989, p.519.

repatriated in due course. Again, around one third of all French blue chip equity trading is believed to have been conducted in London, but the abolition of fixed commissions on the Paris bourse will repatriate some of this business.

In terms of the relative status of financial centres, London and Luxembourg would have most to lose from the shrinkage of Euromarket activity. However, Luxembourg would be especially vulnerable to moves by West Germany to repatriate the Euro-deutschmark deposit market whose existence owes much to the still high level of reserve requirements imposed on West German banks.

In addition to shifting business between financial centres the regulatory and other securities market reforms that are now in prospect will have the effect of deepening financial markets in continental Europe. At the end of 1988 the UK's stock market capitalisation was equivalent to nearly 90 per cent of national income (GDP), but this ratio was only 26 per cent in Spain, 24 per cent in France, 21 per cent in West Germany and 16 per cent in Italy. In comparison with London, continental European securities markets are costly and illiquid. However, as the various stock exchange and regulatory reforms are implemented, the expectation must be that securities' financing will increase at the expense of bank lending and that continental securities markets will strengthen their position relative to London. In other words, the relative efficiency and sophistication of the London market offers less scope for reform than do the hitherto arthritic continental exchanges. The process of liberalisation must therefore favour the latter, although London's pre-eminent position will to some extent be protected by external economies of scale, ie. the mutual benefit arising from the concentration of financial firms in one location.

Nothing has been said so far about the competitive threat from outside Europe, but a Bank of England survey of UK-based financial institutions concluded that the main challenge to European firms after 1992 would come from the USA, Japan and Switzerland.[5] In this context it is worth noting that the US authorities are in a position to undermine the Eurodollar business conducted in Europe, and particularly London, by reversing the regulatory policies that have driven so much dollar business offshore. For instance, the repeal of Glass-Steagall would encourage US banks to remove their London securities business to New York, while also tending to lower underwriting commissions in the US domestic securities markets. More importantly, if the US were to compel US issuers of Eurobonds to register these securities,

5. See "The Single European Market: Survey of UK Financial Services Industry", Bank of England, May 1989.

or if there were a relaxation of SEC registration requirements for domestic security issues, the relative attractions of the Eurodollar bond market could be seriously eroded. From this standpoint the competitive threat from the US is at the regulatory level, and directed not so much at European financial institutions as at the markets they serve.

In contrast, the challenge from Tokyo arises from the enormous capital resources of Japanese banks and securities houses (the top 12 Japanese banks have a stock market capitalisation of some $500bn, which compares with a capitalisation of under $100bn for the top 50 US banks) and the growing presence of Japanese financial institutions within Europe. So far it has been the preferred policy of Japanese banks and securities firms to expand their European operations by establishing new offices—for instance the five major city banks have opened 13 offices in Europe since the beginning of last year. However, given their high stock market ratings, Japanese institutions may be tempted in future to expand via acquisitions.

Turning now to the kinds of financial institution that are likely to prosper in the post-1992 financial environment, the fundamental question is whether European financial markets are going to be dominated by giant pan-European financial conglomerates, or whether there will be a more fragmented structure based on local firms serving domestic markets. It has been suggested, for instance, that in the next ten years or so Europe will be dominated by 15 pan-European groups made up of the 22 European banks now ranked in the world's top 50.[6] Others have pointed out that outside financial services, industry market leaders typically have market shares of 10 per cent or more, whereas in insurance the European leader has 4 per cent of the market and in banking only 2 per cent.[7] This might suggest that the European financial services industry is going to become much more concentrated over the next decade.

The trend towards greater concentration is indeed already under way but there are several constraints on this process. In the first place, as the recent Bank of England survey of UK-based financial institutions suggests, the single European market has already emerged in wholesale financial services and large multinational financial institutions are expected to be among the institutions least affected by 1992 both initially and in the longer run. In other words, such economies of scale as may exist in wholesale financial services are likely to have been exploited already. This

6. See statement by Mr Rodney Schwartz, analyst with Shearson Lehman Hutton, cited in Wall Street Journal, April 5 1989, p.1.

7. See statement by Mr Daniel Lebegue, managing director of Banque Nationale de Paris, cited in Wall Street Journal, April 20 1989, p.1.

is also the conclusion of a recent study by the London Business School which states that in wholesale financial services "the European market is unified enough for most economies of scale to already have been taken up".[8]

On the other hand, retail services, where economies of scale are more likely to be achieved, will probably remain fragmented for some considerable time. In the Bank of England survey, respondent firms "considered that the majority of financial products and services (especially at the retail end) would still have to be tailored to local preferences, needs and market structures and would have to be delivered primarily through local distribution systems for some years yet".[9] Only when it is possible to devise products with genuine pan-European marketability (as is already the case with credit cards) will there be an incentive to develop pan-European corporate structures to service retail markets.

Another constraint on the emergence of multinational conglomerates is the attitude of national authorities to foreign takeovers of domestic financial institutions. In a speech delivered in October 1987 the Governor of the Bank of England said that "it runs counter to commonsense to argue that the openness of the London market must be carried to the point where control of the core of our financial system—the payments system, the supply of credit—may pass into the hands of institutions whose business aims and national interest lie elsewhere".[10] The Governor went on to say that the Bank's policy on acquisitions should therefore ensure that there is a strong and continuing British presence in the banking system of the United Kingdom. Judging from these remarks it would seem that the large UK clearing banks are forbidden territory to foreign predators, although it remains to be seen how the Bank will judge what constitutes the "core" of the UK financial system.[11] In any event, it is likely that cross-border bank mergers and takeovers within Europe will be subject to some form of political veto.

Bearing in mind the above, the prospect is that greater concentration in European banking will be achieved mainly through domestic rationalisation

8. Evan Davis and Carol Smales, "The Integration of European Financial Services", in "Myths and Realities", London Business School, 1989, p.91.

9. "Survey of the UK Financial Services Industry", op. cit. p.17.

10. Speech given at the President's Banquet of the Northern Ireland Chamber of Commerce, 13 October 1987, p.6.

11. One unanswered question in this context is how the Bank of England would view a closer relationship between the Hong Kong and Shanghai Bank and Midland Bank.

rather than by cross-border mergers and acquisitions.[12] Certainly, the scope for such rationalisation will be considerable: with a level of deposits per capita only half that of the US and 20 per cent more bank branches, Europe is arguably already "over-banked", a problem which may be aggravated by the 1992-induced expansion of banking facilities that is now taking place.

In trying to assess the structure of the European financial services industry after 1992 it is necessary to look also at the role of universal banking, since this is the model on which the Second Banking Co-ordinations Directive is based. Quite simply, will financial conglomerates displace specialist financial institutions? Certainly, the present trend is towards financial diversification, but it is as well to remember that where universal banking has worked successfully, notably in Switzerland and West Germany, it has done so in a relatively protected market environment. We will now have to see how it performs in a much more stressful market setting.

It is also the case that intellectual fashion in this area has shifted dramatically over the years. Back in 1920 the US Comptroller of the Currency stated in his annual report that the securities activities of banks "have become an element of increasing peril to the banks with which they are associated". He went on to say:

> "The business of legitimate banking is entirely separate and distinct from the kind of business conducted by many of the "securities corporations", and it would be difficult if not impossible for the same set of officers to conduct safely, soundly, and successfully the conservative business of the national bank and at the same time direct and manage the speculative returns and promotions of the ancillary institutions. These varying institutions demand a different kind of ability and experience on the part of those who manage them, and the two types of business when combined with one management are likely to be operated to the advantage of neither."[13]

Despite the Comptroller's warning US banks became increasingly involved in securities markets during the 1920s. This was largely because their conventional commercial loan business declined as companies began to

12. The consolidation of the Scandinavian banking sector over the past few months is a case in point. In Denmark two large banking groups have been formed, accounting for 60 per cent of the domestic market; in Norway two of the top three banks have merged; and three of Sweden's major banks have linked up with regional banks. The Swedish regulatory authorities have reversed their previous policy in allowing these mergers on the grounds that Swedish banks could otherwise become easy takeover targets for foreign predators.

13. Report of the Comptroller of the Currency, 1920, pp.55-56.

issue securities directly to the public. In other words there was a firm trend towards what we to-day would call "securitisation" and this was a major factor behind banks' efforts to diversify their activities.

With the onset of the 1929-33 US banking collapse there were extensive Congressional investigations into alleged abuses by banks' securities affiliates and a subcommittee of the Senate Committee on Banking and Currency reported that "the experience of the past ten years lends spectacular confirmation to the view that the more intensive participation by commercial banks in the capital market exaggerates financial and business fluctuations".[14] Many bankers appear to have shared this view. In March 1933 both National City Bank and Chase National Bank announced that they were disposing of their securities affiliates and when these announcements were made Mr Winthrop Aldrich, the chairman of Chase National Bank, issued the following statement:

> "I heartily commend the action of National City Bank in taking steps to divorce its security affiliate. . . . It is impossible to consider the events which took place during the past ten years without being forced to the conclusion that intimate connection between commercial banking and investment banking almost inevitably leads to abuses."[15]

Indeed, such was banks' disillusionment with their own securities operations that many bank securities affiliates had been voluntarily dissolved well before passage of the Glass-Steagall Act. Market forces, it seems, and not merely legal constraints, played an important part in separating banking from securities business at this time.

The purpose of this brief digression into US financial history is to suggest that universal banking should not be viewed as the inevitable consequence of liberalised financial markets after 1992. On the contrary, as the US experience shows, the universal banking model has performed least well under conditions of competitive stress. It is possible to draw similar conclusions from the UK's "Big Bang" where the Blue Arrow affair has lent topical force to the US Comptroller's warning seventy years ago about the dangers of mixing the entrepreneurial culture of investment banking with the conservative business of commercial banking.

This discussion underlines the fact that the period immediately following 1992 will be characterised by unusual risk. There are two dimensions to such

14. Cited by Edward Kelly, "Legislative History of the Glass-Steagall Act", in Ingo Walter, Ed, "Deregulating Wall Street", John Wiley, 1985, p.46.

15. Cited by Edwin Perkins, "The Divorce of Commercial and Investment Banking", The Banking Law Journal, June 1971, p.523.

potential instability. First, cross-product expansion of financial services will involve some institutions in new and possibly riskier activities. Second, and perhaps more important, is the fact that the European banking industry, starting from a position of excess capacity, is already experiencing a major restructuring, often involving expansion of banking facilities. The competitive disequilibrium created by this internal response to 1992 will be aggravated by the inward investment of Japanese (and other non-EEC) financial institutions. The Bank of England survey of 1992 prospects points to the dangers involved in this process, with a number of firms drawing parallels with Big Bang and expressing the view that "the combination of expanding financial services activity and intensified competition could increase the level of risk in financial markets".[16] It is worth emphasising, however, that whereas Big Bang was characterised by excess capacity in the securities industry, the 1992 aftermath is likely to see excess capacity in banking. The key question then is whether the process of competitive elimination could lead to financial instability or whether banks will simply contract or be absorbed by their rivals in an orderly manner.

In any event the prospect of a riskier financial environment should prompt European central banks to review their lender of last resort arrangements so as to ensure that emergency support is available wherever the need may arise. There is no evidence to suggest that the lender of last resort function has been reviewed at the European level. Yet it is essential that national authorities have a clear view of their responsibilities in this area. After all, it is no easy matter to organise financial assistance to European institutions with increasingly complex corporate structures whose problems may arise from any one of a wide range of activities conducted from anywhere within, or indeed outside, the Community. Arguably, a single financial market should be backed by a single lender of last resort, but failing that there should at the very least be close pre-emptive co-ordination between all those concerned.

In summarising the prospects for European financial markets in the decade following 1992 it is necessary to distinguish between wholesale and retail services. At wholesale level, there will clearly be further integration of capital markets but this should be viewed as a global, rather than specifically European, development. For instance, the process of regulatory convergence associated with 1992 is parallelled by global initiatives such as the Basle Accord on capital adequacy for international banks and the proposal by the International Organisation of Securities Commissions for a similar agreement covering securities firms.

16. "Survey of UK Financial Services Industry", op. cit. p.18.

The emergence of a common regulatory framework for financial markets could have adverse implications for the Euromarkets which, to an important extent, owe their existence to regulatory disparities. In the European context that could mean some shift of business from London to the continent. A much bigger issue, however, is whether regulatory developments in the US could in due course jeopardise the position of the Eurodollar bond and deposit markets.

On the retail side, markets will remain national in character for some considerable time ahead and although there will be a continuing trend towards larger banking units, particularly in Southern Europe, this is likely to be achieved mainly through domestic rationalisation rather than cross-border mergers.

It is widely assumed that the universal banking model will predominate in Europe after 1992 and that this will also become the global norm once the US and Japanese authorities permit their banks to undertake securities business at home, as they already do abroad. However, given the historical record and the less than satisfactory experience of financial diversification associated with London's Big Bang, it is far from certain that financial conglomerates will have it all their own way.

Finally, in both wholesale and retail markets—but more particularly the latter—intensified competition must mean greater risk. Managing that risk will no doubt be a major preoccupation not only of the financial services industry but of national supervisory authorities.

[12]

Europe 1992: issues and prospects for the financial markets

Vittorio Grilli
Yale University and NBER

1. Introduction

The decision to remove barriers to the flow of goods and services among the members of the European Community by 1992 will have profound consequences in many different sectors of the economy, both in Europe and the rest of the world. There is a widespread belief (almost fear) that the impact of the integration process will be particularly powerful in the capital markets. Because transformations and innovations in financial markets usually occur suddenly and rapidly, economic policy corrections may be hard to implement.

In several European countries, financial market regulation has been so extensive that the national capital markets have been isolated, almost completely protected from foreign competition. The transition to a new open environment could produce radical changes and uncertainty about what will happen is, in itself, reason for concern. Structural changes could involve shifts in the location of some of the markets and, therefore, induce a geographical redistribution of business activity, employment and income. Notwithstanding such concerns, however, there is a general enthusiasm and optimism about the benefits that the process of integration of the monetary and capital markets will bring. This sentiment is not confined to Brussels, but is shared by a large portion of the population. For example, according to a recent poll by Eurobarometer, as reported in the box below, almost 80% of Europeans list the ability freely to make payments and carry money across borders as advantages of 1992. Some 70% also list the possibility of opening bank accounts anywhere in the community.[1]

Financial support from The Council for West European Studies at Yale University is gratefully acknowledged.

[1] Table 1 also reveals considerable differences in national attitudes toward 1992.

Box. Eurobarometer survey of Spring 1988 on the advantages of the Single European Market in 1992

Question: The coming into being of the single European market by 1992 will mean the free circulation of persons, goods and property within the European Community Countries. Some people think this will mostly be an advantage. Others think it will be a disadvantage. Can you tell me, for each of this single common European market which I am going to mention, whether you personally think it will be an advantage or a disadvantage?

	E12	Blg	Dnk	Fra	Ger	Gre	Irl	Ita	Lux	Ntl	Por	Esp	UK
	% answering advantage												
Make payments	79	78	69	88	78	64	79	84	80	75	61	77	74
Carry money	79	76	61	88	82	73	79	74	77	68	68	78	79
Buy products	77	79	51	81	77	71	79	82	76	76	71	81	72
Residence	77	76	59	84	76	75	85	85	79	70	75	85	63
Work	76	73	58	81	66	67	88	88	67	72	77	85	71
Bank account	70	70	39	71	71	61	78	71	66	58	65	75	70
Buy properties	68	70	27	73	70	51	69	72	65	59	60	76	64
VAT closer	66	71	74	84	54	60	84	74	42	80	49	63	54
Border control	64	77	54	71	74	73	71	57	65	59	67	77	42
Public works	52	50	38	56	48	50	58	55	46	50	56	58	47

1. Make payments: The ability to make payments without complication within the whole European Community.
2. Carry money: The possibility to take any amount of money with you when you travel to other countries of the European Community.
3. Buy products: The possibility to buy in one's own country any product lawfully sold in other countries of the European Community.
4. Residence: The opportunity for any citizen of a country within the European Community to go and live without limitation in any country of the Community for instance to retire there or to study there.
5. Work: The opportunity for any citizen of a country within the European Community to go and work in any other country of the European Community.
6. Bank account: The possibility to open a bank account in any country of the European Community.
7. Property: The possibility to buy land or property throughout the Community.
8. VAT closer: Bringing closer together the rates of VAT applied in the various countries of the Community so that products are sold under similar cost conditions.
9. Border control: Elimination of custom controls when crossing frontiers between countries inside the European Community.
10. Public works: The possibility for a contractor from another country to be in charge of public works (for instance, building a bridge or a road) in our country if his offer is cheaper at the same level of quality.

Much of this optimism is based, at least in the professional literature, on principles borrowed from basic trade theory under the assumption of perfect competition. Current discussions start from this not so much because it is an appropriate description of how financial markets operate, but rather because of the lack of a well developed alternative. In fact, there is a paucity of theoretical and empirical analysis in the area of international financial intermediation. Neither the industrial organization literature, nor the international trade and finance literature offers many insights into the issue of what determines the structure, trade flows, and prices in these markets. Obviously, I will not attempt in this paper to fill in these gaps by formulating a complete theory of financial structures in an integrated world economy. Instead, I will illustrate how, by applying frameworks other than perfect competition, we can obtain predictions which are far less optimistic than what is often heard. I will also focus on two specific issues.

The first issue concerns the effects of liberalization on the long-run structure of international financial markets, and in particular their geographic location. Nowadays, we are familiar with the idea and existence of 'financial centres' like London, New York and Tokyo, i.e. with the clustering of different types of financial intermediaries in specific locations. Recent years have witnessed considerable changes in the relative importance of these centres, as well as the emergence of new ones like Singapore, Hong Kong and the Bahamas. How can the existence of such 'hot spots' be explained? Will the events of 1990–92 induce modifications in their relative importance, possibly leading to the emergence of new ones? The sober conclusion will be that drastic locational changes are quite unlikely. The second issue concerns the specific market for international bank deposits. One of the most debated components of the integration programme is the possibility of opening bank accounts in any member country. To what extent will this new freedom affect the international flow of bank deposits and what kind of movement should we expect in deposit interest rates? The conclusion is that most of the significant changes and gains in this area are likely to be confined to particular segments of the market, effectively bypassing a large number of depositors.

2. The effects of liberalization on the location of financial centres

'... I predict, very tentatively, that Brussels will emerge as the financial center of the European Community, for the following reasons: it serves as the headquarters for the Commission; it attracts foreign corporations and will ultimately attract foreign and European banks;

it tolerates the world intellectual medium of exchange, the English language.'
(C. Kindleberger, 'The Formation of Financial Centers: A Study in Comparative Economic History,' 1974.)

Even if Belgium (including Luxembourg) has an important role in the international banking industry, many would name London as the main European financial centre. However, even though recent developments in financial markets may prove Kindleberger's conclusion inaccurate, the question that he tried to address is now more relevant than ever. At the world level, in addition to the UK, the US and Japan host the largest financial centres. These countries' complex networks of financial markets and financial intermediaries (listed in Table 1) are not matched anywhere else in terms of manpower and volume of activity. Could the liberalization of European capital markets alter the relative importance and location of world financial markets? Will part of the business, now concentrated in these centres, move towards the newly liberalized markets thereby making the geographical distribution of financial activity more uniform? Or, instead, will the activity originated in the recently liberalized countries flow towards London, New York or Tokyo, widening the gap between the 'financially' developed areas and the rest of the world?

The real question is why financial activities tend to be highly concentrated. At the outset, it must be emphasized that we do not have a well-developed theory to answer this question. Clearly, regulations matter. 'Off-shore' centres like Nassau and the Cayman Islands, are examples of particularly favourable regulatory environments because of the absence of income, corporate, and capital gains taxes as well as because of bank secrecy. However, advantages in terms of regulation do not account for the dominance of a centre like London, where the tax structure is far less benevolent than in the off-shore centres. For such major centres the explanation is more likely to be the existence of increasing returns deriving from thick-market externalities, as described by Diamond (1982). By recognizing the dependence of a firm's productivity on the size of the market in which it operates, this approach can offer an appealing account of the growth and concentration of financial markets. The idea is simple and is formalized in Appendix A. Concentration arises whenever a firm's productivity directly benefits from the proximity of competitors or firms engaged in related activities. Each firm is more profitable, possibly larger, than if it were operating alone. On the surface, it looks as if there were economies of scale. Yet, these external economies are clearly distinct from the more traditional, internal, economies of scale.

Table 1. Principal characteristics of the main financial centres, 1987

UK (London)
Stock Exchange
60% of Eurobond Market
London Futures and Options Exchange (FOX)
London International Financial Futures Exchange (LIFFE)
London Metal Exchange
International Petroleum Exchange of London
Baltic Futures Exchange
International Freight Futures Exchange (BIFFEX)
London Grain Futures Market
London Meat Futures Exchange
London Potato Futures Market
Soya Bean Meal Futures Market
US (New York and Chicago)
New York Stock Exchange
American Stock Exchange
Commodity Exchange (COMEX)
New York Futures Exchange (NYFE)
New York Mercantile Exchange (NYMEX)
Coffee, Sugar and Cocoa Exchange
New York Cotton Exchange
Chicago Board of Trade (CBT)
Chicago Mercantile Exchange (CME)
Mid-America Commodity Exchange (Chicago)
Japan (Tokyo)
Tokyo Stock Exchange
Tokyo Commodity Exchange for Industry
Tokyo Financial Futures Exchange

This idea is well suited to describe financial centres, since they are complicated networks of various types of intermediaries and specialized firms operating and interacting in closely related markets. As these markets become larger, communication channels are more developed, the number of agents operating in the market increases, and accordingly business opportunities and commercial partners are more easily found. In addition to this improved 'matching process' on the customer side, matching on the labour input side becomes easier as well. In fact, the existence of a large market guarantees the training, and thus the availability, of a skilled labour force, which is an essential element for success in this highly specialized market. Because the productivity of the financial industry depends so crucially on the size of the market, large industrialized economies probably enjoy a comparative advantage in attracting financial firms from the rest of the world. Such thick-market externalities explain why the size of the economy matters, and why the four largest international financial centres (London, New York, Tokyo and Paris) are also the financial centres of four out of the five largest economies.[2] This idea also suggests that public incentives to create a large financial market may be hard to design. Indeed, any particular firm's incentive to move largely depends upon other firms also moving to the same location. In the end incentives may be dispensed with if many firms have moved, but initially it may be very hard, and very expensive, to trigger the change.

Even if these forms of externalities can help us understand why financial activities are not uniformly distributed in space, and why, instead, they tend to be concentrated in a few 'hot spots', several other important questions are still left unanswered. For example, why are financial intermediaries so highly concentrated in London and in New York and not in Madrid or Boston? Can the location of these centres be altered, and will European integration have such an effect?

Explaining the precise geographical location of financial centres is a difficult problem. Because the economic and institutional environments are important, policy decisions in these areas must have contributed to the configuration of today's world financial scene. Moreover, strictly geographical considerations, like the time zone to which a country belongs, are also crucial. Yet, a whole series of historical events which span over several centuries have shaped the current situation. It is probably impossible to disentangle them, as Robert Hall has recently observed:

> '. . . the distribution of economic activity is probably close to indeterminate, so the location of economic hot spots is largely a matter of historical accidents'.
> (R. Hall, 'Noise Over Space and Over Time,' 1988 Arthur Okun Memorial Lectures.)

The type of market-size externalities considered here are known to imply the possible existence of a large number of equilibria and do not provide any clue to understanding, or predicting, which one actually

[2] The fact that Germany doesn't have a centre of the same importance does not necessarily contradict the theory proposed above. Rather, the manner in which financial markets evolved in Germany after World War II is largely responsible for this absence. For obvious reasons, following World War II, Berlin ceased to be the financial capital of Germany, leaving the country without a clear dominant centre. Dusseldorf, Hamburg and Frankfurt shared a similar moderate level of status in the banking industry for almost two decades. It was only in the 1960s that Frankfurt emerged as the clear market leader and thus, until then, Germany was not characterized by the same degree of market thickness as the other major countries.

occurs. The fact that there exists more than one possible configuration indeed suggests that market locations are determined by a wide variety of factors. Thick-market externalities can also produce considerable amounts of inertia in an industry because, by itself, a firm may not be able to take advantage of a more efficient environment unless a whole number of other firms also decide to move to the new location. This is a typical example where coordination is required: unless all firms agree to move together, none will move, and there is no mechanism to trigger such a collective action. This also implies that market sizes and locations may be rather difficult to change by policy actions once an equilibrium has been reached. Quite to the contrary, we should expect that liberalization will favour countries with developed markets, so that in the medium run at least, it is very unlikely that London's supremacy will be challenged. Indeed, this would require very aggressive behaviour by the other European governments, including the adoption of off-shore types of regulations which appear to be largely incompatible with a concerted liberalization. In the whole, the existence of externalities might prevent the industry from achieving a higher level of profits, i.e. from shifting to the locations made more efficient as the result of deliberate public incentives. (Excessive market inertia is shown by Farrell and Saloner, 1986 to arise in a situation similar to that described above.)

3. The market for international bank deposits

3.1. Some stylized facts

In advanced economies, the financial sector is an important contributor to both employment and output. In Europe, the banking sector alone employs between 2.5 and 7.0% of the labour force and its value added represents between 4.2 and 6.0% of GDP (Table 2). It is, therefore, understandable that a considerable amount of attention has been directed towards the evaluation of the possible consequences of 1992 on the future of this industry. The liberalization of 1990–92 may operate through two main channels. First, liberalization will necessarily imply symmetric treatment of domestic and foreign (European) banking institutions, especially in matters like the establishment of new branches or the acquisition of existing ones. Second, the elimination of exchange controls will give individuals the freedom to choose foreign banks for their deposits or their loans. In theory, both channels could provide a way to increase competition in some of the more restricted national markets.

Several elements, however, suggest that the primary effects of 1990–92 will operate through the second channel. This is not to say that

Table 2. Importance of the financial sector, 1985

	Banking		Banking and insurance	
	Employment (% of total)	Value added (a) (% of GDP)	Employment (% of total)	Value added (% of GDP)
Belgium	3.0	4.4	3.9	5.9
France	2.5	4.9	3.4	4.5
Germany	2.7	4.6	3.7	5.5
Italy	—	6.0	2.5	5.6
Luxembourg	7.0	—	7.7	14.0 (b)
Netherlands	2.5	4.2	3.5	5.4
Spain	—	4.8	3.9	6.1
UK	2.5	4.3	3.6	12.6

Source: Price Waterhouse, *The 'Cost of Non-Europe' in Financial Services.*
Notes: (a) 1983 data; (b) 1982 data.

Table 3. Summary of restrictions in financial markets between EEC countries

	Establishment of branches	Participation and acquisition	Exchange controls
Belgium	none	none	yes
France	none	>20%	yes
Germany	none	none	none
Italy	none	none	yes
Luxembourg	none	none	yes
Netherlands	none	none	none
Spain	yes	>50%	yes
UK	none	none	none

Source: Price Waterhouse, *The 'Cost of Non-Europe' in Financial Services.*

direct foreign investment in banking will not take place, or will occur only in limited amounts. On the contrary, this phenomenon is already present and is becoming increasingly important. However, this is part of a general worldwide trend towards financial integration, and is not necessarily related to 1992. The reason is that the existing discriminatory laws against non-resident EEC financial institutions which are currently in place, and bound to become void, are not actively enforced anyway. Table 3 documents these regulations. Spain has restrictions on the number of branches that a foreign institution may open (no more than three), and restrictions on the percentage of a Spanish bank that a non-resident may acquire without prior approval (no more than 50%). These restrictions have not been too strictly enforced since in 1986 there were already 37 foreign banks operating in Spain. In France, the government has the general prerogative to cancel any foreign investment in a French company, if it exceeds a 20% share. In the specific case of banks intervention by the authorities may occur even below the 20% limit. In practice, however, the French government has been less and less inclined to intervene in these matters and, in 1983, there were already 119 foreign-controlled banks out of a total of 289. In some other European countries, foreign participation in the industry is already quite substantial, and is likely to increase in the future, but 1992 does not appear to have a major role to play in this process.

This is why we shall concentrate on the second channel, trade in international deposits. Table 3 also documents the existence of exchange controls inhibiting the flow of funds. Belgium and Luxembourg still operate under a two-tier exchange market arrangement. It is also important to notice the presence in France, Italy and Spain, of various restrictions which have prevented residents from holding bank accounts abroad. One of the most direct consequences of European liberalization on the banking sector will be the removal of these restrictions to capital flows. The market for bank deposits is a critical market, given that deposits are, by far, the most important source of funds for commercial banks, as shown in Table 4. Depending on the country, they constitute between 60 and 90% of total bank liabilities. In addition, in most of the countries surveyed, non-bank deposits (as opposed to inter-bank deposits) represent the largest share of total deposits. A different picture obtains if we consider non-resident deposits, i.e. deposits received by banks from agents resident in countries other than the one in which the bank operates; the total amount of non-resident deposits was $4,911 bn. in the second quarter of 1988, and almost 80% of these deposits are the result of international inter-bank operations. Moreover, the amount of international trade in deposits has increased considerably over the last 15 years. If we use the total output of the OECD countries as a unit of measurement, then between 1972 and 1986 inter-country bank deposits have risen from 10 to 35% of output.

In Table 5 we present the geographical distribution (as of 1988Q2) of these stocks, expressed as fractions of world totals. These tables reveal a number of interesting features. First, the UK appears to be the single favourite destination of non-resident deposits, in both the inter-bank and non-bank markets. However, grouped together the large 'off-shore' centres (the Bahamas, the Cayman Islands, Hong Kong and Singapore) have the largest share of inter-bank deposits. Second, the US and Belgium (including Luxembourg), and the UK seem to have a similar role in both the inter-bank and non-bank markets. Third, some countries seem to have become specialized in particular segments of the market. For example, Japan has established itself as the second largest

Table 4. Importance of deposits, 1985 (% of total liabilities)

	Total deposits	Interbank deposits	Non-bank deposits	Liabilities to non-residents
Austria, large commercial banks	—	79.68	50.43	29.25 33.62
Belgium, banks	87.96	63.52	24.44	63.74
Canada, banks	89.88	22.77	67.11	—
Denmark, banks	71.42	23.21	48.21	27.27
France, large commercial banks	80.35	41.33	39.02	40.48
Germany, commercial banks	76.47	27.42	49.05	24.71
Greece, large commercial banks	87.14	1.53	85.61	—
Italy, commercial banks	59.22	10.26	48.96	13.56
Japan, ordinary banks	75.85	—	—	—
Luxembourg, banks	89.72	66.70	23.02	83.56
Netherlands, banks	78.24	29.19	49.05	35.19
Portugal, banks	78.59	1.59	77.00	4.69
Spain, commercial banks	79.37	15.89	63.48	11.78
Switzerland, large commercial banks	75.20	21.95	53.25	40.70
UK, London clearing banks	91.65	—	—	—
US, large commercial banks	72.46	8.75	63.71	—

Source: OECD (1985).

market for total foreign deposits, and this position is due almost exclusively to its active role in the inter-bank market. Switzerland, on the contrary, has concentrated on the collection of deposits from non-banks.

The changes in the relative size of the most important geographical areas in the international market for bank deposits are described by Figures 1 to 3. The position of Belgium and Luxembourg has remained very stable over the years in all categories. Switzerland, on the other hand, lost almost half of its market share. The loss occurred mostly during the early 1970s, and affects particularly transactions with the non-bank sector. Part of this decline seems to have been deliberately self-inflicted with the imposition, in July 1972, of a negative interest rate on non-resident Swiss franc deposits.[3] Japan and the off-shore centres show a strong positive trend in both categories, with the exception of Japan, apparently unable, or unwilling, to attract deposits from non-banks. The UK shows a declining trend until 1978. At the time when Margaret Thatcher was elected and foreign exchange controls were removed, the decline was halted and a moderate growth in market share was observed, at least until 1985. It is worth noting that the reversal in the trend occurred earlier (1976) for deposits from non-banks. While the US share of inter-bank deposits shows a positive trend,

[3] This regulation was later removed in February 1980.

Table 5. Foreign deposits at domestic banks, 1988Q2 (% of world's total)

Non-banks' deposits		Banks' deposits		Total	
UK	20.8	UK	17.4	UK	18.5
Switzerland	14.7	Japan	16.7	Japan	13.4
Belgium–Lux.	8.8	US	12.9	US	11.9
US	7.5	Belgium–Lux. (c)	6.9	Belgium–Lux.	7.5
Cayman Islands	7.4	Hong Kong	6.3	France	5.5
France (c)	5.2	France	5.3	Hong Kong	5.0
Bahamas	5.0	Singapore	4.6	Cayman Islands (a)	4.8
Singapore	3.9	Cayman Islands (a)	3.9	Switzerland	4.6
Germany	3.4	Bahamas	2.7	Singapore	4.5
Canada (b)	2.9	Germany	2.1	Bahamas	3.2
Netherlands	2.8	Netherlands	1.9	Germany	2.5
Japan	0.7	Switzerland	1.6	Italy (b)	2.2
Italy	—	Canada (b)	0.9	Netherlands	2.1
Hong Kong	—	Italy	—	Canada (b)	1.4

Source: IMF *International Financial Statistics*.
Notes: (a) 1987Q4; (b) 1988Q1; (c) 1987Q3.

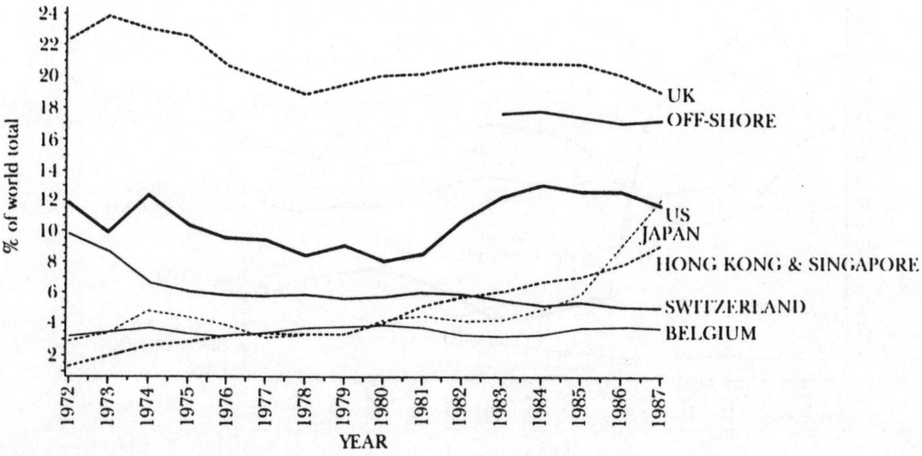

Figure 1. Total liabilities

deposits from the non-bank sector declined until 1981, and then increased substantially. It is not a coincidence that in December 1981 the international banking facilities (IBFs) were enacted. IBFs' regulations authorized US banks to operate separate books when accepting foreign Eurocurrency deposits to be lent abroad, making these funds free from reserve and insurance requirements. This allowed US-based banks to regain their competitiveness with respect to the off-shore centres, especially the Bahamas and the Cayman Islands.

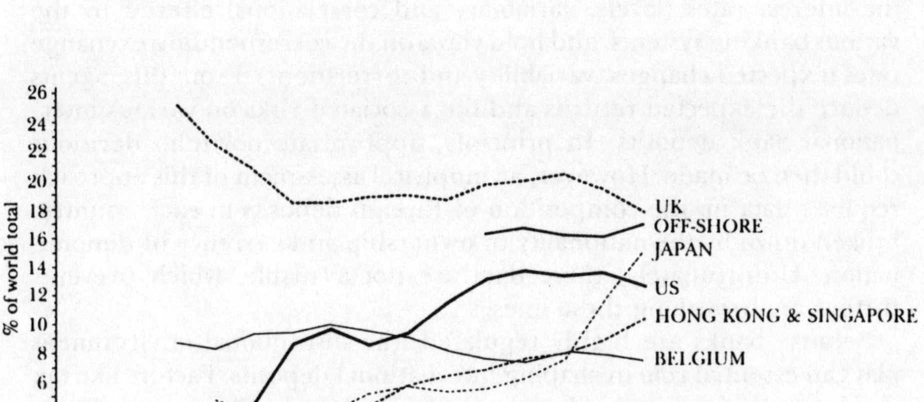

Figure 2. Inter-bank deposits

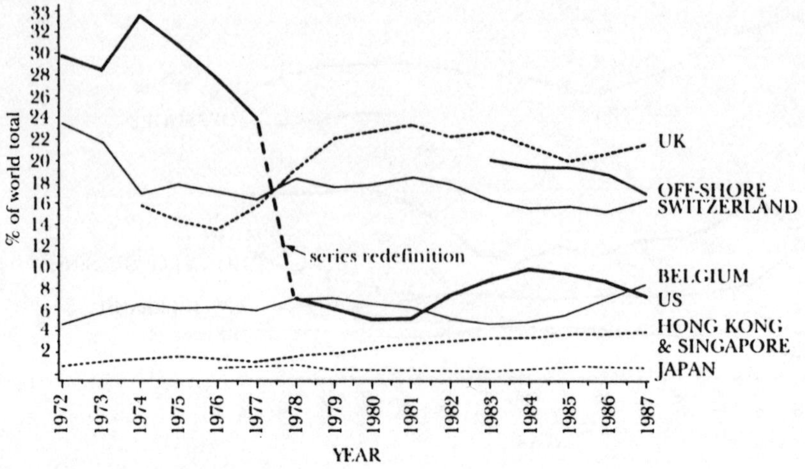

Figure 3. Non-bank deposits

3.2. The role of institutional factors in the international movements of bank deposits

As already stressed, we lack a well developed theory of international trade in banking services which could help identify the crucial elements responsible for the movements in international bank deposits described above. In principle, however, we should view the decision to deposit funds in different countries as part of a global portfolio optimization problem. Such a problem could be described as follows. Agents observe the interest rates (levels, variability and correlations) offered by the various banking systems, and hold views on the corresponding exchange rates (expected changes, variability and correlations). From this, agents deduce the expected returns and the associated risks on various international bank deposits. In principle, appropriate portfolio decisions could then be made. However, an empirical assessment of this approach requires data on the composition of foreign deposits in each country, broken down by the nationality of ownership and currency of denomination. Unfortunately, these data are not available, which prevents further analysis along these lines.

Because banks are highly regulated, the institutional environment plays an essential role in shaping international deposits. Factors like tax regulations, minimum bank reserve requirements, and secrecy laws are especially important in this context. The examples, already mentioned, of foreign exchange liberalization in the UK or the establishment of the international banking facilities in the US strongly suggest that purely regulatory factors may have strong effects on the direction of trade in bank deposits. The experiences of off-shore centres, like the Bahamas or the Cayman Islands, are other examples of the importance of such factors. Given that 1992 will operate essentially through the removal of technical barriers and the partial harmonization of regulations, it is important to determine, in more detail, the effects of these institutional elements on the performance of a country in attracting foreign deposits. Several regulations and practices may favour or frustrate the international movement of capital and, in particular, of bank deposits. In the following analysis we sort them into three different categories: capital controls, withholding taxes, and secrecy laws.

3.2.1. Capital controls. Under the generic label of capital controls, there is a large and diversified body of measures. They include the absolute legal or regulatory prohibition on making capital transactions, requirements of case-by-case authorization, restrictions on the timing of the operations, surrender requirements, prudential regulations and so on. Countries still differ considerably in this dimension. Discussions of capital controls also often implicitly refer to restrictions on capital *outflows* from a country, i.e. constraints imposed on residents' financial decisions. Indeed, countries like Italy and France have had very restrictive legislation of this kind throughout the 1970s and the 1980s. Others, like the UK and Japan, removed such restrictions at the end of the 1970s. At the same time, other countries like Germany and Switzerland have always had a very permissive attitude toward capital outflows but, from time to time, have limited the amount of capital inflows in order to maintain close control over monetary aggregates:

> '... restrictions have from time to time been imposed to ward off speculative inflows of foreign exchange and create greater room for maneuvers for monetary and fiscal policy at home. In 1972–3, for example, capital imports into the Federal Republic of Germany were restricted by a number of administrative measures.'
> (*Deutsche Bundesbank Special Series* No. 7., p.70.)

Some of these administrative measures have involved the imposition of particularly high reserve requirements on liabilities to non-residents. At one time, in 1978, the reserve requirement was virtually 100%. Another example, already mentioned, is the temporary imposition, in Switzerland, of a negative interest rate on non-resident Swiss franc deposits. In general, all types of restrictions on capital movement tend to isolate the domestic financial market and delay its development, thereby discouraging the inflow of deposits.

3.2.2. Withholding taxes. Another regulatory element that is crucial in international deposit decisions is the extent to which interest on bank

Table 6. Withholding taxes, 1988 (%)

	Bank deposits		Dividend income non-residents (d)
	Residents	Non-residents	
Belgium	25	25	25
Denmark	0	0	—
France	45	46 (a)	25
Germany	0	0 (b)	25
Greece	0	0	—
Ireland	35	0	—
Italy	30	30 (c)	32
Luxembourg	0	0	—
Netherlands	0	0	25
Portugal	15	15	—
Spain	20	20	—
UK	variable	0	0
Austria	0	0	—
Finland	0	0	—
Japan	20	35	35
Sweden	0	0	—
Switzerland	35	35	35
US	0	0	30

Source: Bank deposits: Banca d'Italia, *La Tassazione delle Rendite Finanziarie nella CEE alla Luce della Liberalizzazione Valutaria*; Dividend income: *Business International Money Report, Business Europe, International Tax Summaries.*

Notes: Special bilateral conventions to avoid double taxation may reduce the above rates for specific countries. For example, for Italian residents the withholding tax in Spain is 12%, instead of 20%; (a) checking accounts and special saving accounts are not subject to withholding tax; (b) starting 1-1-89 is 10%; (c) not subject to withholding tax if in foreign currency; (d) 1987.

deposits is subject to withholding taxes. As reported in Table 6, which describes the current situation on the matter, there are considerable differences in tax regulations regarding the treatment of non-resident deposits. In some countries, like Germany, Luxembourg, the Netherlands and the UK, deposits owned by non-residents are not subject to any withholding tax. Other countries, like Italy, Japan and Switzerland, apply heavy withholding taxes. The rates reported in Table 6 should be used with caution because special bilateral conventions can substantially reduce the tax rate applicable to the residents of the signatories. The rates in Table 6 apply in absence of a treaty. The difference between these statutory rates and special treaty rates can be quite substantial.

The location of deposits is obviously related to the net rate of return available in the various centres but also depends on net rates available on other assets into which bank deposits can be easily converted. Indeed, it is likely that foreign bank deposits are also used as convenient temporary parking for funds to be invested in other assets abroad. It is, therefore, important also to consider how income from other assets is taxed. Interestingly, countries which do not levy any withholding tax on bank deposits, like Germany or the US, instead impose high tax rates on dividend income.

3.2.3. Secrecy. Banking secrecy takes various forms, depending on the history, legal framework and customs of a country. Adherence to banking secrecy is analogous to the exercise of professional discretion which is typical of lawyers or doctors. This type of professional confidentiality does not legally extend to banks in all countries. When it does, bank secrecy is enforced to varying degrees. In some countries it is limited to the dissemination of information to other private citizens and institutions, in others it also extends to public authorities, either domestic or foreign. The demand for secret or hidden assets is believed to be quite substantial. It arises from different motivations, both legal and illegal. Walter (1985) offers five reasons underlying the demand for secrecy: personal confidentiality, business confidentiality, capital flight motivated by political reasons when secrecy is needed to preserve the safety of the owner, tax evasion and criminal activities.

Switzerland has the longest tradition of banking secrecy and the strictest legislation. Actually the legal basis of the Swiss banking secrecy can be found in its Constitution and Civil Code. Violations of bank confidentiality are met with severe punishment. Penalties include not only administrative and financial measures, but also criminal sanctions. In 1977, a Convention of Diligence was signed by all the major Swiss banks. The purpose of this action was to limit the role of banking secrecy in illegal activities. Though somewhat weakened by the Convention, bank secrecy is consistently maintained in Switzerland. In 1981, Luxembourg also passed strict bank secrecy laws, thereby becoming the EC country with the most protective legislation in this area. None of the other main industrialized countries has extensive secrecy laws. In some countries, like the UK and Germany, the principle of secrecy is recognized and applied to a certain (though limited) extent. Yet in others, like France and Italy, banks are 'required by law to be informers' (Chambost, 1983).

In order to investigate the influence of these various regulations on international bank deposits we use data from 10 countries (Belgium–Luxembourg, Canada, France, Germany, Italy, Japan, the Netherlands, Switzerland, the UK and the US) covering 16 years (1972-87). The previous discussion suggests the following relationship:

$$D_{it} = \alpha_0 + \alpha_1 TaxI_{it} + \alpha_2 TaxD_{it} + \alpha_3 CapitalIn_{it} + \alpha_4 CapitalOut_{it} + \alpha_5 Secrecy_{it} + \alpha_6 GNP_{it} + \alpha_7 Time_t + \varepsilon_{it} \quad (1)$$

where D_{it} is the stock of non-resident deposits in banks of country i at time t; *TaxI* is the withholding tax on non-resident bank deposits; *TaxD* is the withholding tax on non-resident dividend income; *CapitalIn* is a dummy variable representing restrictions on capital inflows; *CapitalOut* is a dummy variable representing restrictions on capital outflows; and *Secrecy* is a dummy representing the extent of banking secrecy. The exact values of the dummies are described in Appendix B, which also provides bibliographical references. *GNP* is the country's contribution to total OECD output: it is meant to capture thick-market externalities which, we argued in Section 2, are likely to be related to the relative size of the country. Finally, given the strong growth of trade in deposits, a time trend is also included. Table 7 reports the results of estimating (1) for *inter-bank* and *non-bank* foreign deposits separately. The distinction between inter-bank and non-bank deposits is very important since they seem to respond to very different incentives. Only controls on the inflow of capital appears to have a significant effect on both. Otherwise, inter-bank deposits are affected by the tax treatment of dividends and by the size of the economy. Non-bank deposits, on the other hand, respond to the withholding tax on bank accounts and to secrecy protection.

These results provide some interesting insights into what really motivates international bank deposits. For individual investors (non-banks), tax avoidance is probably the main motivation: this would explain why they seek bank secrecy and low levels of withholding taxes. By contrast, institutional investors (banks), while considering taxes, attach most importance to the dimension and development of the financial markets, at least if we accept that the GNP variable reflects the existence of thick-market externalities. Finally, we note the highly significant and negative effect that the withholding tax on dividends exerts on inter-bank deposits. This suggests that bank deposits are not made simply to earn interest income but are also used by banks as 'parking' in between other financial market transactions.

What are the implications of these results for the liberalization of 1990? By eliminating the existing restrictions on the free movement of capital, liberalization will definitely have an effect on the location of deposits. However, the tax treatment of interest and dividend incomes may play an even more powerful role in shaping the geography of bank deposits. Undoubtedly, the abolition of capital controls will favour

Table 7. Regression results (Panel data: 10 countries, 1972–87)

	Non-banks' deposits ($\bar{R}^2=0.53$)	Inter-bank deposits ($\bar{R}^2=0.68$)
Constant	1.69	3.96
	(3.40)	(11.86)
Interest tax	−4.04	−0.61
	(−4.97)	(−1.10)
Dividend tax	−1.01	−5.09
	(−1.01)	(−7.49)
Capital inflow	−1.22	−0.45
	(−3.70)	(−2.02)
Capital outflow	−0.30	0.19
	(−1.40)	(1.33)
Secrecy and offshore	0.66	0.10
	(8.64)	(1.97)
GNP	−0.11	0.22
	(−1.31)	(3.82)
Time trend	0.68	0.98
	(4.96)	(10.50)

Notes: *t*-statistics in brackets. The 10 countries are: Belgium–Luxembourg, Canada, France, Germany, Italy, Japan, the Netherlands, Switzerland, the UK and the US.

countries with low withholding tax rates. This problem is widely recognized but, to date, no decision regarding withholding tax levels has been agreed upon. Although EC governments are negotiating about some form of tax rate harmonization, there is still much discord and disagreement. As a result, it is difficult to predict the ultimate effects that liberalization will have through this channel. Similar arguments hold for the issue of bank secrecy. In this case, the possibility of harmonization may be even smaller. In fact, the revision or elimination of banking secrecy may involve changes in the fundamental structure of a country's legal system and is thus very difficult to implement.

4. Imperfect competition, switching costs and bank deposits

The evidence offered in the previous section supports the view that international bank deposits respond strongly to the institutional structure of national markets and various forms of controls and regulations. Other factors are likely to be important too, although difficult to capture empirically. Certainly, we expect that the relative efficiency of different national banking sectors has a role to play. Liberalization, by eliminating capital controls, will put banking systems with different levels of cost efficiency and quality of service in direct competition. This is why this section focuses on the differences in microeconomic factors, abstracting from the institutional environment. A prerequisite to pursuing this line of investigation is to agree on the proper way of characterizing the market structure of the banking sector. If it were a perfectly competitive market, and if depositors were intrinsically indifferent between using domestic or foreign financial intermediaries, then immediately following liberalization we should observe a massive flow of deposits toward the lower cost countries. The process would continue until prices were equalized through a general reduction towards the lowest levels in the Community. The less efficient, high cost intermediaries would either reshape or disappear. This characterization is quite extreme.

In what follows, we show that price convergence following liberalization will be limited and that the gains are not going to be uniformly shared by the whole population. In particular, if price reductions occur, they are likely to be confined to limited segments of depositors, while remaining consumers will be unaffected, or even harmed, by liberalization. The reason behind this assessment is essentially that the markets for bank deposits are characterized by segmentation and frictions that substantially reduce the extent of competition. Evidence that the banking industry is not perfectly competitive is provided by the casual observation that product differentiation is an important dimension of bank competition. Within the same country, where the institutional and regulatory environments are relatively homogeneous, the terms of a deposit contract vary substantially from bank to bank. Even within the same bank similar types of deposits are frequently remunerated differently, suggesting that banks have the ability to discriminate across customers (and the size of their deposits). Hence, banks have some market power stemming from product differentiation and it is preferable to describe the market for deposits as oligopolistic. Of course, the scope for product differentiation and price discrimination arises from the diversity of depositors. In particular, depositors are likely to respond very differently to interest rate incentives (technically, they differ in the interest rate elasticity of their demand for deposits). Such heterogeneity most probably arises because different customers have different levels of information about alternative forms of investment and they face different costs of acquiring, updating and processing such information. Not only does the cost of searching for better opportunities vary, but the cost of managing 'international' portfolios differs substantially among individuals as well. It is reasonable, at least for expository purposes, to assume that large depositors are more sensitive to deposit yields.

In this type of market, the best strategy for a bank is to price-discriminate among customers, offering low prices (e.g. high deposit

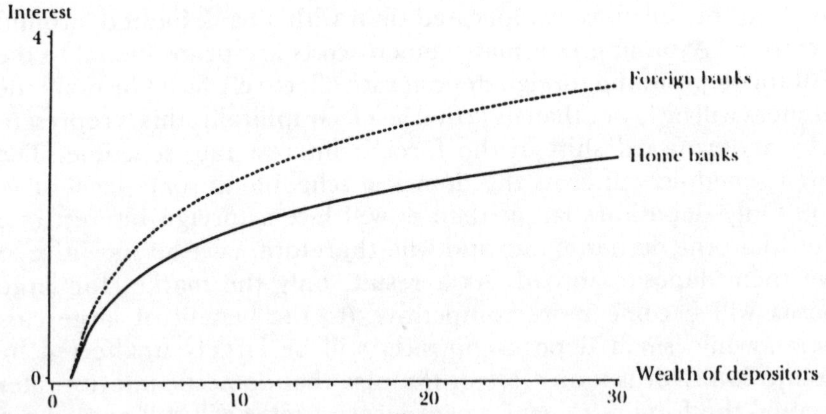

Figure 4. Interest offered and size of deposit

rates) to the more sensitive customers (e.g. the large depositors), and high prices (low deposit rates) to the less sensitive customers (small depositors). (Appendix A presents formally the implications of a departure from the assumption of perfect competition). This effect is described graphically in Figure 4, where customers are differentiated by their wealth (w), wealthier consumers being more sensitive to deposit yields. The interest rate schedules are upward sloping because banks offer better rates to larger customers.[4] Now suppose that the country opens its commercial banking market to foreign competition and that the country is small enough so that foreign banks do not change their strategies, i.e. they maintain their interest rate schedule unchanged. If the foreign banking system is more competitive and/or more efficient than the domestic one, it will be characterized by a higher deposit interest rate schedule. In the absence of any other market friction, capital market liberalization will lead to an outflow of deposits which will lead either to a global increase in the domestic interest rate, or to the failure of the domestic intermediaries.

However, if market imperfections exist and are important, the effects of capital market integration may be far less extensive. As mentioned above, collecting and updating information about alternative banking systems is costly and, even if we ignore the burden of this searching process, we still have to consider the costs, both monetary and non-monetary, of switching between domestic and foreign bank accounts. Moreover, maintaining a business relationship with a bank located

[4] The precise shape of the curve depends on the specific characteristics of the demand for deposits. In the case of Figure 4, we assume that the elasticity of demand increases with the size of the depositor, and does so at a decreasing rate.

abroad can be far more complicated than with a bank located 'around the corner'. Assuming that management costs are proportional to the size of the deposit, the foreign deposit rate effectively faced by domestic customers will be lower than its actual level. Graphically, this is represented by a downward shift in the foreign interest rate schedule. The foreign schedule will cross the domestic schedule at some level of w, say $\bar{w}$. Only depositors larger than $\bar{w}$ will face a foreign interest rate higher than the domestic rate and will, therefore, have an incentive to move their deposits abroad. As a result, only the market for large deposits will become more competitive (to the benefit of large customers), while small deposit contracts will be largely unaffected by liberalization. Nor is it any longer the case that domestic interest rates will equal the foreign rates. Foreign interest rates will still exceed the corresponding domestic rates. (These basic conclusions are not altered, under the alternative assumption that the 'switching costs' are fixed. In this case the shift of the foreign interest rate schedule will now be greater at a lower level of deposit size and it is, therefore, possible that the cut-off level $\bar{w}$ will be larger than in the previous analysis.)

It is even conceivable that small depositors could actually be worse off and face declining yields on their bank deposits. So far it has been implicitly assumed that the banking sector was characterized by fixed marginal costs. In this case, increased competition for large deposits will not have spill-over effects on smaller deposits. However, if the banking industry were characterized by decreasing marginal costs (internal economies of scale), negative spill-over effects would arise. Because the loss of market share to the foreign competitors would reduce the scale of operation of the domestic banks, their marginal cost would increase and they would lower the interest rate on those deposits which are smaller than $\bar{w}$.[5] Whether this last effect is likely to occur is an open question. Evidence from the US suggests that constant or increasing marginal costs are the norm (Benston, Hanweck and Humphrey, 1982, and Murray and White, 1983). However, it is interesting to notice what happened in the UK equity market after deregulation in October 1986. The Price Waterhouse (1988) report on the 'Cost of Non-Europe' shows that the commission costs for *large transactions* decreased after October 1986 while commission costs have actually increased for *small bargain* values (Table 8). To be sure the apparent existence of the negative spill-over effect may be related to other reasons

[5] In the opposite case, in which the banking industry is characterized by increasing marginal costs, the spill-over effects will be positive. Increased competition in the large deposit tier will tend to raise interest rates for small deposits as well.

Table 8. Commission rates on equities in the London stock exchange

Bargain values (pounds)	Pre-deregulation (%)	Post-deregulation (%)
1,000	1.53	1.63
5,000	1.26	1.60
10,000	1.02	1.25
20,000	0.60	0.63
50,000	0.53	0.34
100,000	0.39	0.28
5000,000	0.31	0.25
1,000,000	0.22	0.22

Source: Price Waterhouse, *The 'Cost of Non-Europe' in Financial Services.*

than decreasing marginal costs; it could be the result of cross-subsidization of larger deposits by small deposits. Yet, if the British experiment is a front-runner to EC-wide deregulation, there is some indication that small deposits may end up at the losing end.

So far we have assumed that the foreign banking sector did not change its interest rate schedule in response to the opening of the home market. It is possible, however, that in order to attract new depositors from the home country, foreign banks decide to raise their rates in order to capture a larger share of the domestic market (lower $\bar{w}$ in Figure 5). Of course such a strategy would reduce profits from the already established clientele. Therefore, the smaller the size of the domestic market, the smaller the potential gain in depositors and,

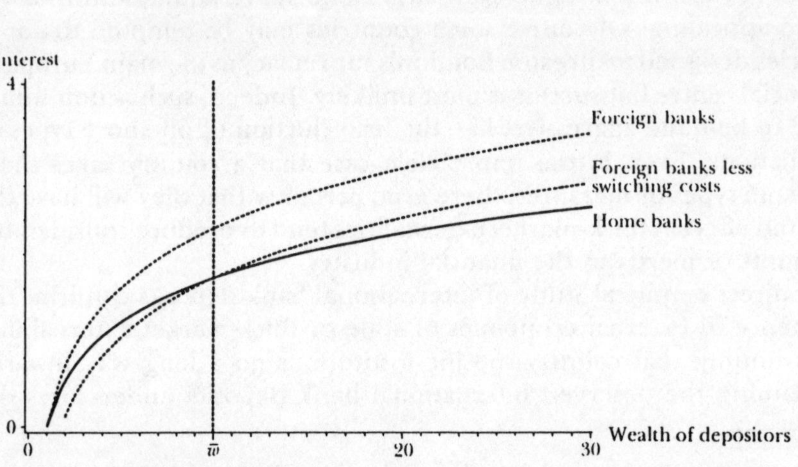

Figure 5. The determination of $\bar{w}$

therefore, the less likely it is that foreign banks will alter their pricing behaviour.[6] A related point was recently raised by Klemperer (1987), analysing the impact of switching costs on the strategic behaviour of firms. Because the existence of switching costs makes the demand for deposits less responsive to price changes, the best strategy for a bank would be to increase the deposit rate only temporarily. Then, after having increased its market share, they could exploit the fact that customers are partially 'locked-in' by the existence of switching costs and decrease the interest rate back to its original level. Thus, while on impact, the liberalization could produce considerable price adjustments, in the longer run these effects may tend to disappear. When most of the movements of deposits have taken place, and the market shares are firmly established, the banks could find it optimal to decrease the interest rates towards pre-liberalization levels. However, if depositors anticipate this type of behaviour, they may decide to limit the extent to which they reallocate their deposits. In this case, the liberalization will only produce an apparent price competition among financial intermediaries, without affecting much the cross-country movements of deposits.

5. Conclusions

Three main conclusions emerge from this article. The first concerns the geographical location of the main financial markets, the so-called 'hot spots'. It seems highly likely that the liberalization process will strengthen the already existing dominant markets, namely London and possibly New York. As residents of countries with relatively small financial markets find it more attractive to operate in developed centres, these markets will become even larger and more liquid, and thus yet more appealing. Of course some countries may be tempted to adopt policies designed to threaten London's supremacy as the main European financial centre but success is most unlikely. Indeed, such action would have to be quite aggressive, like the introduction of off-shore types of regulations. Even in the improbable case that a country takes these extreme types of measures, there is no certainty that they will have the desired effect as thick-market externalities tend to produce considerable amounts of inertia in the financial industry.

A direct empirical study of international bank deposits confirms the existence of external economies of scale or thick-market externalities. The finding that country-specific institutions go a long way towards explaining the observed international bank deposits underscores the

[6] Notice, however, that the rest of the analysis would still be valid even if the foreign banks were to increase their interest rate schedule. The only difference is that $\bar{w}$ would be smaller.

importance of the liberalization move for the industry. Of particular interest is the result that the inter-bank deposit market responds to a different set of regulations than the general public deposit market: both markets are of course quite sensitive to capital controls, but inter-bank deposits seem driven above all by the size of the economy – a measure of thick-market externalities – while non-bank deposits respond primarily to the tax treatment and to the extent of banking secrecy. These results imply that the wholesale market (inter-bank deposits) should follow the same trend as the 'hot spots'. While there is some scope for movement in the retail market (non-bank deposits) if countries try to change the regulatory environment, switching costs once again may frustrate these efforts. This is why the third main conclusion is that the increase in competition induced by the European integration will primarily affect the market for large deposits. Small deposit contracts will probably remain unaffected, at least in the short run. It cannot even be ruled out that the increased competition in the larger deposit market will have adverse spill-over effects on smaller bank customers.

Discussion

Charles Bean
London School of Economics

There is a school of thought according to which 1992 will have more profound implications in financial markets than in goods markets, which are already fairly integrated. The removal of remaining capital controls and restrictions on the location of banking activities will affect both the structure of financial markets and the functioning of macroeconomic policies such as the EMS. Much has been written on the latter topic, but little on the former, with the exception of the European Commission's 'Costs of non-Europe' exercise. Grilli has drawn welcome attention to some debatable assumptions in the Commission's report – particularly that of perfect competition.

In the first part of the paper, Grilli addresses the question why financial activity locates where it does and, therefore, whether financial liberalization will lead to a more homogeneous distribution of financial services throughout the Community. He points to economies of scale arising from 'thick-market externalities' as the main reason for the agglomeration of financial activity in a few centres. The focus is very much on physical externalities, such as those due to communication networks. However, a non-tangible externality in the form of a centre's general reputation for excellence may be equally important. Unlike physical externalities, such a reputation can be destroyed quite quickly by one or two financial scandals (Guinness?). It should also be said that these externalities need not always be beneficial. Congestion externalities may be important, as in the bidding-up of the salaries of a small number of financial experts with specialist expertise.

This line of argument predicts that the present pattern of financial 'hot spots' is unlikely to be affected by 1992. An individual firm will not relocate in pursuit of small internal cost reductions, because of the loss of the external benefits of staying where it is. Only if all firms move together is a relocation likely to occur. Governments may provide financial incentives to encourage such co-ordinated movement, but Community regulations will limit the extent of such action. So, is London's hegemony assured? Probably. But the current British attitude to the EMS and the process of monetary unification raises the prospect that the UK will be left on the sidelines as the rest of the Community forges a common currency area and a system of central banks to administer it. The resulting shift in focus away from London could be exactly the push needed to ensure that financial firms centre their activities in Paris or Frankfurt.

The rest of the paper looks at the market for bank deposits. Grilli argues, probably correctly, that 1992 will not lead to major changes in banks' direct investment, since foreign participation in the banking sector is already widespread. The evidence presented suggests that, while capital controls are important, the tax regime and the level of bank secrecy are equally important, so the degree of harmonization in these fields may be important in determining the reallocation of bank deposits in the Single Market.

This analysis ignores difference in the efficiency of banks in different countries. Price Waterhouse took the view in the Commission's report that deposits would flow towards the most efficient financial intermediaries who could offer the most attractive terms to depositors. Grilli argues that this will occur only for large deposits, since the market for small deposits is subject to significant segmentation and frictions. While I think this judgment is correct, the evidence is not entirely persuasive. Deposit accounts and other instruments are typically bundles of characteristics. A cheque account may or may not have associated overdraft facilities; a building society deposit account may make it easier to get a loan, and so on. There may also be fixed costs or other non-linearities in the costs of servicing an account: the apparent variation in the terms offered (e.g. in Table 8) may reflect these features rather than a lack of competitive behaviour *per se*.

Grilli also draws attention to switching costs that lock in existing customers. It is worth emphasizing that these do not imply the absence of competition, but rather that such competition occurs when customers first open accounts. This is evident in the UK where there is intense competition between the banks for student accounts through introductory offers.

Though I have considerable sympathy with the paper's general arguments, let me close by noting two shortcomings. First, I was disappointed that, having dismissed the analysis in the Commission's study as simplistic, Grilli did not attempt to furnish alternative estimates of the microeconomic gains from financial market integration. Are the issues discussed in the paper important or are they just second-order effects? Second, there is no discussion of the asset side of banks' balance sheets. Financial market integration could be just as important for the cost and supply of bank loans as in the market for deposits.

Jean-Pierre Danthine
University of Lausanne and CEPR

'There is a paucity of theoretical and empirical analysis in the area of international financial intermediation. Neither the industrial organization literature, nor the international trade and finance literature offers many insights into the issue of what determines the structure, trade flows, and prices in these markets.' This observation by the author gives the paper the right outlook. 1992 will indeed be as much of a challenge for the economics profession as it is likely to be for the European economies themselves. This paper squarely faces important issues that have not previously been addressed. It shows us how poorly prepared we are, as a profession, to produce convincing and insightful answers to the questions raised by the occurrence of a significant shock such as the completion of the internal market.

The paper tackles three issues. First, it argues that the supremacy of London as the dominant financial centre in Europe is likely to be unchallenged. It is on this point that Grilli's contribution is most convincing. The model he provides is useful to organize thoughts. Its prediction looks like a fairly safe bet, elegantly supported by the concept of thick-market externalities: even if Paris were to develop into an objectively more efficient financial centre than London, coordination problems could well prevent the emergence of the most efficient geographical distribution of activities and indeed would favour the status quo.

The second issue that the paper addresses relates to the institutional determinants of foreign bank deposits. Here Grilli's main conclusion is that the factors explaining inter-bank deposits (the level of the dividend tax, the existence of capital controls and the size of the economy) are quite different from the factors explaining non-bank deposits (the level of the interest tax, the presence of controls on capital outflows and the extent of banking secrecy and offshore facilities). While this is a plausible result, one should use the usual dose of caution in interpreting econometric estimates, such as these, derived outside a fully specified economic model. (In the absence of appropriate data, the economic determinants of international movements of deposits are not part of the regressions). Furthermore, the values given to some of the explanatory variables, notably the secrecy dummy, would deserve further discussion and a sensitivity analysis. The ranking of countries on the secrecy issue is debatable, as is, *a fortiori*, the index of secrecy ranging from −1 (for France) to +5 (for Switzerland).

Third, pursuing the question of international competition for deposits, Grilli develops a model suggesting that the assumption of perfect competition used in computing the gains from integration in financial markets is likely to lead to an overvaluation of these gains. Assuming an oligopolistic market structure with depositors differentiated by their interest rate elasticity, he obtains the result that an increased degree of competition between banks will favourably affect only the largest depositors. The small depositors could be left unaffected or could even be hurt if the loss in market share to foreign competitors reduces the scale of operations of domestic banks and increases their marginal cost.

I wonder about the significance of bank deposits in the context of 1992. Competition in international banking focuses less and less on deposits and increasingly on the range of services that the banks can offer to corporations. Yet the general message conveyed on this issue is undeniably important: let us be cautious about the benefits of the internal market when they have been computed on the basis of perfect competition models (even if we are not really in a position to produce comparable data under more realistic hypotheses). As to the specific conclusion that the biggest share of the benefits from financial deregulation and integration in Europe is going to accrue to the largest players in the markets, it conforms with the strategy of the large international banks; apparently they do not expect to make profits from small customers in foreign markets.

General discussion

Luigi Spaventa wondered whether the demand for deposits was determined on a portfolio basis. The main reason for holding deposits abroad was to facilitate investment in other assets: Belgium and Luxembourg were good countries in which to do so because of the absence of withholding taxes. Several other speakers pointed to the significance of arbitrage induced by differences in regulatory regimes. Denis Richard stressed the distinction between the liberalization of capital movements by 1990, which would not make a great difference since there was considerable movement of capital already, and the establishment by 1992 of the freedom to supply services, which could lead to a major shake-up of the regulatory environment and competition via product innovation.

This led to a discussion of whether the gains from 1992 in the financial sector had been exaggerated in the Cecchini Report. Victor Norman was puzzled by the magnitude of the estimated gains in relation to gains in the real economy. 1992 was not just about coordinating regulation but also about lowering transaction costs more generally. But these were already low in financial markets. Jacques Melitz thought the Report had attached too much significance to apparent price differentials for service products. Many banking services were joint products so that pricing decisions for any one product were largely arbitrary. He also pointed out that reserve requirements would not be unified. Damien Neven said that domestic and international banking were very different: the Price Waterhouse study of prices had included many products that were not internationally traded. Colin Mayer thought that many of the existing price differentials were exacerbated by informational problems faced by consumers. 1992 was about diminishing these problems, especially through the development of common regulatory standards. It would be important to know how much freedom of access financial institutions enjoyed in each other's markets. Jean-Pierre Lambert was worried by the effects of 1992 on concentration in the industry.

Mayer also said he was unconvinced by the arguments that London's preeminent position in Europe was secure. Two reasons why markets might move could be major differences in regulatory costs, and differences in the efficiency of the settlement process. Paris was already on the way to establishing a much more efficient settlement process than that in London, and it would take London some time to catch up.

Appendix A. The theoretical models

A1. Thick-market externalities, 'hot-spots' and financial centres inertia

Assume that the production function of a typical financial intermediary is given by:

$$y = \beta x^{\alpha} \qquad \alpha < 1 \tag{A1}$$

where y is the amount of financial services produced, and x is the amount of input. The financial firm is assumed to maximize profits:

$$\max \Pi = y - px \tag{A2}$$

where p is the price of input in terms of output. In the absence of any thick-market externalities, firms in different locations will have similar production decisions given by:

$$x = \left(\frac{\alpha\beta}{p}\right)^{1/(1-\alpha)} \tag{A3}$$

If we abstract from possible differences in the relative price of inputs at different locations, financial intermediaries in different countries will make similar decisions, i.e. they will be producing the same amount of services, and they will have the same level of profits.

Thick-market externalities mean that the productivity of a firm is positively affected by the size of the market in which it operates so that the production function of a financial firm in country i is given by:

$$y_i = \beta x_i^{\alpha} Y_i^{\gamma} \qquad \gamma > 0;\ (\alpha + \gamma) < 1 \tag{A4}$$

where Y_i is the total amount of financial services produced in country i. The larger the size of the market, the larger the firm's production for a given use of inputs. Let $Y_i = n_i y_i$, i.e. the product of the number of banks in country i multiplied by the amount of services offered by each firm. Therefore,

$$y_i = \beta^{1/(1-\gamma)} x_i^{\alpha/(1-\gamma)} n_i^{\gamma/(1-\gamma)} \tag{A5}$$

The production decision of the typical firm in country i is given by:

$$y_i = \left(n_i^{\gamma} \beta \left(\frac{\alpha}{(1-\gamma)p} \right)^{\alpha/(1-\gamma)} \right)^{1/(1-(\alpha+\gamma))} \tag{A6}$$

In the presence of thick-market externalities output and profits are affected by the size of the market. In a large economy, with a large number of firms, output and profit for each bank are greater than those in a small economy. If the various national markets become integrated, firms located in smaller markets will have an incentive to move towards larger markets.

The government can reduce the incentive for domestic financial intermediaries to relocate part of their activities abroad by acting as a market maker, i.e. by trying to broaden the dimension of the domestic market before the opening of frontiers. Even if there are initially only a few operators in a particular financial market, the government could substantially increase the degree of liquidity by actively participating in the market. A natural example would be futures and options markets for government securities. Let then $Y_i = g_i n_i y_i$, where g_i is an indicator of the participation of the government in the market. Now the output of the firm in the domestic market will be given by:

$$y_i = \left(g^{\gamma} n_i^{\gamma} \beta \left(\frac{\alpha}{(1-\gamma)p} \right)^{\alpha/(1-\gamma)} \right)^{1/(1-(\alpha+\gamma))} \tag{A7}$$

so that government intervention can compensate for the initially small size of the domestic market, and reduce the incentive for domestic firms to move abroad.

The model can also illustrate the potential inertia of markets characterized by agglomeration externalities. Suppose that a country, say France, introduces new measures which increase the efficiency of its domestic financial market. This is captured by an increase in the β coefficient in the production function. Firms which decide to locate in Paris will face a production function given by:

$$y_p = \beta^1 x_p^{\alpha} (n_p y_p)^{\gamma} \tag{A8}$$

where $\beta^1 = k\beta$, with $k > 1$, and the subscript p indicates the location 'Paris'. It is clear that if the whole market moved to Paris, the productivity of the sector could increase. However, whether this move will happen is an open question. Consider the case of a bank located in the current leading centre, say London, which is evaluating the possibility of a switch to Paris. The effects of the decision on bank productivity and profits depend on the actions of the other firms. Suppose that nobody else decides to move to Paris. It can be shown that the output (profits) of the switching firm will be greater than if it remained in London only if:

$$k > \left(\frac{n_L}{n_p} \right)^{\gamma} \tag{A9}$$

where n_L and n_p are the size of the London and Paris markets, respectively. The increase in productivity must be large enough to compensate for the differential in liquidity in the two markets. If this is the case, the move is always profitable, independent of the other firms' decisions, and the market will unquestionably move to Paris. However, if (A9) does not hold, a firm will decide to move to Paris only if it thinks that a large enough number of firms are doing the same. The outcome, therefore, depends on market expectations which, in this case, will be self-fulfilling. It is quite possible that the market will remain in London, despite the potential advantage of moving to Paris.

A2. Monopolistic competition in the market for deposits: an example

Suppose, for the moment, that marginal costs are constant and identical across firms. Potential depositors have different elasticities of demand for deposits. This difference derives from different levels of a characteristic variable, w, with which individuals are endowed. For convenience, we refer to this variable as wealth. There are N banks in the market, supplying a homogeneous product (deposit) to customers with identical characteristics. Therefore, they will offer the same interest rate to everyone in the same class of depositors. Finally, we make the standard Cournot assumption that firms compete by choosing a level of deposits and we look for a non-cooperative Nash equilibrium. With fixed marginal costs, banks will decide on the level of deposits for each class of customers, independently of other classes. Routine calculations yield the equilibrium level of interest rate for the customer class w, as:

$$r_d(w) = \left(\frac{N\varepsilon(w)}{1+N\varepsilon(w)}\right)(\bar{r}_L - c) \tag{A10}$$

where c is the level of the marginal cost, $\bar{r}_L$ is the (exogenously given) rate on bank assets and $\varepsilon(w)$ is the interest rate elasticity of the demand for deposits of customers with wealth w.

First, notice that more competitive markets, i.e. markets with larger numbers of banks, will be characterized by a higher deposit interest rate, for all classes of customers. Second, the higher the marginal cost, the lower the interest rate. Given the opposite effects of competition and cost efficiency, it is possible that high cost banking systems can nonetheless offer high interest rates if they are characterized by a high degree of competition (i.e. large N). Finally, note the existence of price discrimination across customers: different classes of depositors will face different deposit rates. Under the reasonable assumption that larger depositors (high w individuals) have larger elasticities of demand, i.e. $\varepsilon' > 0$, they will be offered higher rates than small depositors.

A3. Monopolistic competition, switching costs and international trade in deposits

Suppose that the banking system of the rest of the world is completely identical to the domestic one, except for a lower (constant) marginal cost. In this case, it is easy to show that:

$$r_D^*(w) = r_D(w) + \left(\frac{N\varepsilon(w)}{1+N\varepsilon(w)}\right)(c - c^*) \tag{A11}$$

where $r_D^*(w)$ is the foreign interest rate on deposits and c^* is the foreign marginal cost, and $c > c^*$. Therefore, the foreign interest rate is always higher than the domestic one, for all classes of deposits. Moreover, since $\varepsilon' > 0$, the difference between domestic and foreign rates is increasing in w. This is described in Figure 4. Now suppose that, for domestic residents, there is a positive cost of switching to a foreign bank and of managing foreign bank accounts. We represent these costs by assuming that the foreign interest rate effectively faced by domestic customers ($i_D^*(w)$) is given by:

$$i_D^*(w) = r_D^*(w) - s \tag{A12}$$

where s is the 'switching cost'. The $i_D^*(w)$ and $r_D(w)$ schedules intersect at a level of wealth $\bar{w}$ implicitly defined by

$$s = \left(\frac{N\varepsilon(\bar{w})}{1 + N\varepsilon(\bar{w})}\right)(c - c^*) \tag{A13}$$

Consequently, domestic customers who are smaller than $\bar{w}$ will face foreign effective rates which are below the domestic ones (Figure 5 in the text). The positive effects of liberalization are further reduced under the plausible assumption that smaller depositors face larger 'switching costs', i.e. if $s = s(w)$ and $s' < 0$. In this case, in fact, the intersection between $i_D^*(w)$ and $r_D(w)$ will occur at a higher level of w.

Finally, consider the case in which the marginal cost is not constant. It could be shown that in this case the interest rate equation would be given by:[7]

$$r_D(w) = \left(\frac{N\varepsilon(w)}{1 + N\varepsilon(w)}\right)(\bar{r}_L - c'(\tau)) \tag{A14}$$

where τ is the total amount of deposits sold to all classes of customers. If, because of foreign competition τ decreases, the marginal cost $c'(\tau)$ increases thus generating a decrease in $r_D(w)$, for $w < \bar{w}$.

Appendix B. Dummy variables used in the regression

Table B1. Restrictions on capital outflows

	72	73	74	75	76	77	78	79	80	81	82	83	84	85	86	87
Belgium	0	0	0	0	0	0	0	0	0	0	0	0	0	0	0	0
France	1	1	1	1	1	1	1	1	1	1	1	1	1	1	1	1
Germany	0	0	0	0	0	0	0	0	0	0	0	0	0	0	0	0
Italy	1	1	1	1	1	1	1	1	1	1	1	1	0	0	0	1
Netherlands	1	1	1	1	0	0	0	0	0	0	0	0	0	0	0	0
UK	1	1	1	1	1	1	1	1	0	0	0	0	0	0	0	0
Canada	0	0	0	0	0	0	0	0	0	0	0	0	0	0	0	0
Japan	1	1	1	1	1	1	1	1	0	0	0	0	0	0	0	0
Switzerland	0	0	0	0	0	0	0	0	0	0	0	0	0	0	0	0
US	1	1	0	0	0	0	0	0	0	0	0	0	0	0	0	0

Source: IMF *Exchange Arrangements & Exchange Restrictions*, Summary Table (restrictions on payments in respect of capital transactions); OECD *Controls on International Capital Movements.*

[7] For simplicity, we now assume that $N = 1$.

Table B2. Restrictions on capital inflows

	72	73	74	75	76	77	78	79	80	81	82	83	84	85	86	87
Belgium	0	0	0	0	0	0	0	0	0	0	0	0	0	0	0	0
France	0	0	0	0	0	0	0	0	0	0	0	0	0	0	0	0
Germany	1	1	0.7	0.5	0.5	1	1	0.5	0.5	0.5	0.2	0.2	0	0	0	0
Italy	0	0	0	1	0	0	0	0	0	0	0	0	1	1	0	0
Netherlands	1	1	0	0	0	0	0	0	0	0	0	0	0	0	0	0
UK	0	0	0	0	0	0	0	0	0	0	0	0	0	0	0	0
Canada	0	0	0	0	0	0	0	0	0	0	0	0	0	0	0	0
Japan	0	0	0	0	0	0	1	1	0	0	0	0	0	0	0	0
Switzerland	1	1	1	1	1	1	1	1	0	0	0	0	0	0	0	0
US	0	0	0	0	0	0	0	0	0	0	0	0	0	0	0	0

Source: Sarver (1987); OECD, *Controls on International Capital Movements.*

Table B3. Secrecy laws

	72	73	74	75	76	77	78	79	80	81	82	83	84	85	86	87
Belgium	0	0	0	0	0	0	0	0	0	1	1	1	1	1	1	1
France	−1	−1	−1	−1	−1	−1	−1	−1	−1	−1	−1	−1	−1	−1	−1	−1
Germany	0.5	0.5	0.5	0.5	0.5	0.5	0.5	0.5	0.5	0.5	0.5	0.5	0.5	0.5	0.5	0.5
Italy	−1	−1	−1	−1	−1	−1	−1	−1	−1	−1	−1	−1	−1	−1	−1	−1
Netherlands	0	0	0	0	0	0	0	0	0	0	0	0	0	0	0	0
UK	1	1	1	1	1	1	1	1	1	1	1	1	1	1	1	1
Canada	0	0	0	0	0	0	0	0	0	0	0	0	0	0	0	0
Japan	0.5	0.5	0.5	0.5	0.5	0.5	0.5	0.5	0.5	0.5	0.5	0.5	0.5	0.5	0.5	0.5
Switzerland	5	5	5	5	5	5	5	4	4	4	4	4	4	4	4	4
US	0	0	0	0	0	0	0	0	0	0	0	0	0	0	0	0

Source: Blum (1984); Chambost (1983); Sarver (1987); Walter (1985).

References

Banca d'Italia (1989). 'La Tassazione delle Rendite Finanziarie nella CEE alla Luce della Liberalizzazione Valutaria', *Temi di Discussione.*

Benston, G., G. Hanweck and D. Humphrey (1982). 'Scale Economies in Banking. A Restructuring and Reassessment', *Journal of Money, Credit, and Banking.*

Blum, R. (1984). *Offshore Haven Banks, Trusts, and Companies.* Praeger. *Business International Money Report*, various issues.

Chambost, E. (1983). *Bank Accounts. A World Guide to Confidentiality.* John Wiley & Sons.

Diamond, P. (1982). 'Aggregate Demand Management in Search Equilibrium', *Journal of Political Economy.*

Farrell, J. and G. Saloner (1986). 'Installed Base and Compatibility: Innovation, Product Preannouncements, and Predation', *American Economic Review.*

Hall, R. (1988). 'Noise Over Space and Over Time', in the Okun Memorial Lecture, Yale University, September.

International Tax Summaries, John Wiley, various issues.

Kindleberger, C. (1974). 'The Formation of Financial Centers: A study in Comparative Economic History', *Princeton Studies in International Finance.*

Klemperer, P. (1987). 'The Competitiveness of Markets with Switching Costs', *Rand Journal of Economics.*
Murray, J. and R. White (1983). 'Economies of Scale and Economies of Scope in Multiproduct Financial Institutions: A Study of British Columbia Credit Unions', *The Journal of Finance.*
OECD (1978). *Regulation Affecting International Banking Operations.* Paris.
—— (1980). *Controls on International Capital Movements.* Paris.
—— (1981). *Regulation Affecting International Banking Operations.* Paris.
—— (1984). *International Trade in Services: Banking.* Paris.
—— (1985). *Bank Profitability.* Paris.
—— (1987). *International Tax Avoidance and Evasion.* Paris.
Price Waterhouse (1988). 'The Cost of Non-Europe in Financial Services', in *Research of the Cost of Non-Europe,* Commission of the European Communities, volume 9.
Sarver, E. (1987). *The Eurocurrency Market Handbook.* Prentice-Hall.
Walter, I. (1985). *Secret Money.* Lexington Books.

Part IV
North America

[13]

U.S. West Coast as an International Financial Center

Hang-Sheng Cheng

The study of regional international financial centers is a long-neglected subject. In the literature on international finance, it is customary to consider the world as consisting of separate national money and capital markets, linked together by international capital flows, with each national market assumed to be a uniform, homogeneous entity. Alternatively, the entire world is regarded as a single market in which competition for national funds takes place through various institutional channels such as banks, international bond markets, etc. By and large, these analytical approaches have served their purposes well. But, with their emphasis on national and international developments, they do not take into consideration the rise in the last decade or so of regional international financial centers such as Singapore, Panama, and the U.S. West Coast. These new regional centers have contributed importantly to the growth of international finance by being both competitive with, and complementary to, old-established centers such as London, New York, Frankfurt, and Zurich.

A number of studies have now appeared on various regional financial centers, both old and new, but none as yet on the rise of the U.S. West Coast as an international financial center. The purpose of this study is to fill that gap.

Economic Factors

Despite these recent contributions, a conceptual framework for the study of regional financial centers is still lacking. Regional economics, with its sophisticated theoretical models of locational distribution of industry and intra-urban land use,[2] rarely concerns itself with the location of finance. There appears to be no obvious way to apply the factor-endowment approach (Heckscher-Ohlin) or the distance-from-center approach (von Thunen) used in regional economics to the explanation of regional financial centers. On the other hand, a growing literature on the pivotal role of money and capital markets in economic development[3] leaves largely unexplored the question of the location of financial centers and the functional links among these centers.

It is beyond the scope of this study to develop a rigorous theoretical framework for analyzing the factors underlying the rise and fall of regional international financial centers. Nevertheless, it would be useful to consider briefly a few relevant hypotheses in economic literature that might throw light on the subject.

First, we may consider the portfolio-balance theory of finance, as used in the analysis of international diversification of asset-holdings and international capital flows.[4] In essence, it states that an asset-holder (say, a bank) that desires maximum return from his investment portfolio with minimum risk can improve his welfare through international diversification of his asset holdings, and that his gains are the larger the less (algebraically) the returns from the various assets are correlated with one another. This paper contains partial evidence suggesting that, in the 1973-74 environment, an internationally diversified portfolio apparently assisted a number of West Coast banks in improving their overall earnings.

Second, we may consider economies of scale. The portfolio-balance theory, while accounting for banks' desire for international asset diversification, can not tell us why, at one particular juncture in the early 1970's, so many West Coast banks initiated or expanded international activities. Obviously, overseas branching is costly, requiring a certain minimum scale of operations to undertake. In this respect, it may be pertinent to note that loans and investments of all commercial banks in the San Francisco Federal Reserve District nearly doubled from $51 billion in 1967 to $101 billion in 1974, increasing at an average rate of 10 percent per year.[5] Presumably, during this period a number of West Coast banks must have attained a size sufficiently large for them to initiate profitable international operations.

Third, growth of international banking is related to that of international trade. Between 1967 and 1974, the total value of West Coast foreign trade (exports plus imports) rose three and a half times to $37 billion[6]—at an average growth rate of 24 percent per year. About two-thirds of this trade was conducted with the booming economies of the countries located around the Pacific Basin.[7]

Fourth, insights obtained from studies of industrial structure might throw some additional light on the subject. Among the West Coast banks now active in international banking, by far the largest are California banks. Besides its substantial economic base, California is also noted for a liberal banking law that permits statewide branching. Presumably, the resultant sharp competition among banks may have driven profits from domestic operations down to a level that provided a strong incentive for expansion in areas where competitive conditions were less severe, as in the less-developed areas of the world.

Keeping these factors in mind, we may now turn to an examination of the rise of the West Coast as an international financial center during the 1970's. Following a quick overview, we will look into the various components of the growth process: the overseas expansion of West Coast banks, the activities of Edge Act corporations on the West Coast, and the activities of foreign banks in the region. One section analyzes the experience of West Coast banks during the turbulent 1974-75 period, and another the profitability of international operations. Finally, some preliminary conclusions are drawn concerning the future of the West Coast as an international financial center.

Overview of Growth, 1969-75

Table 1 summarizes the growth of West Coast international banking from 1969 to 1975. Not all the series are available for the entire period, but the overall impression of rapid growth is unmistakable.

Between 1969 and 1974, total foreign assets of West Coast banks increased from $7 billion to $32 billion.[8] Moreover, there was a broad participation of West Coast banks in this rapid expansion. In 1969, only five West Coast banks had more than $100 million in foreign assets;[9] by 1974, the number has increased to eleven.[10] Five of these banks—Bank of America, Security Pacific, United California, Wells Fargo, and Crocker—each had more than $1 billion in foreign assets; together the five accounted for $30 billion of the $32 billion of total foreign assets of all West Coast banks in 1974.

The number of banks having branches abroad increased from nine in 1969 to twenty in 1975. The number of branches rose from 102 to 138, and the number of representative offices from 28 to 61, while foreign-branch assets jumped from $5.6 billion to $35.7 billion.

Table 1

Growth of West Coast International Banking 1969-75[a]

	1969	1975
Total foreign assets of West Coast banks (billions of dollars)	7.0	32.0
Overseas Branches		
Number of West Coast banks	9	20
Number of branches	102	138
Branch assets (billions of dollars)	5.6	35.7
Number of representative offices abroad	28	61
Edge Act Corporations		
Number of Edge corporations	7	23
Total assets (millions of dollars)	80	930
Foreign Banks		
Number of agencies and branches	16	50
Agency assets (billions of dollars)	0.7	9.0
Number of subsidiary banks	7	15
Subsidiary bank assets (billions of dollars)	0.9	4.5

[a]Data for total foreign assets are as of end-1969 and end-1974; overseas branch data, end-1969 and end-1975; Edge corporation data, end-1969 and mid-1975; and foreign bank data, mid-1969 and mid-1975.

Sources: Based on subsequent tables.

Increased activities of Edge Act corporations also testified to the growth of international banking in the region. The number of such corporations increased from 7 in 1969 to 23 in 1975, while their total assets increased more than 11 times from $80 million in 1969 to $930 million in 1975.

Another measure was the expansion of foreign banks' activities on the West Coast. Agencies and branches of foreign banks increased from 16 in 1969 to 50 in 1975, and foreign-owned state-chartered banks increased from 7 to 15. The total assets of these foreign banking offices increased from $1.6 billion in 1969 to $13.5 billion in 1975.

The growth phenomenon was also reflected in a substantially enlarged volume of international capital flows reported by West Coast banking institutions. Over the 1974-75 period, U.S. capital outflows reported by West Coast banks (measured by changes in U.S. foreign assets) averaged $3.2 billion per year, or about 18 times the average rate of the 1969-70 period. Foreign capital inflows reported by West Coast banks (measured by changes in U.S. foreign liabilities) averaged $740 million per year during the 1975-75 period, or about three times the average 1969-70 rate. U.S. capital outflows through West Coast banks accounted for 20 percent, and foreign capital inflows 6 percent, of the respective total flows reported by all U.S. banks during the 1974-75 period. By coincidence, these percentages were almost the same as the West Coast banks' shares at the end of 1975 in the total U.S. claims on foreigners and liabilities to foreigners reported by banks—20 percent and 7 percent, respectively.[11]

Overseas Branch Activities

West Coast banks were relatively late starters in overseas banking. As late as 1968, Bank of America was the only West Coast bank with branches abroad, although a few others—Bank of California, Crocker, United California, Wells Fargo, Security Pacific, and National Bank of Commerce of Seattle (now Rainier)—maintained representative offices and interests in joint ventures in a handful of foreign countries.[12]

Bank of America opened its first foreign branch in 1931, but did not add another until 1947. It added a total of 21 foreign branches in the 1947-63 period. But then, in a burst of expansion covering the 1964-68 period, it opened another 64 branches—more than one new overseas branch a month on the average. Despite a

Table 2

Growth in Overseas Operations of Individual Banks
1969-1974
(Deposit and loan volume in millions of dollars)*

		1969	1974	Ratio: 1974/1969
Bank of America				
Deposits:	Total	21,509	45,348	2.11
	Overseas	5,040	18,110	3.59
	Percent Overseas	23%	40%	
Loans:	Total	13,842	27,649	1.99
	Overseas	2,402	8,459	3.52
	Percent Overseas	17%	31%	
Security Pacific				
Deposits:	Total	4,474	10,047	2.25
	Overseas	20	2,276	113.80
	Percent Overseas	0%	23%	
Loans:	Total	3,873	8,612	2.22
	Overseas	36	1,068	29.67
	Percent Overseas	1%	12%	
United California				
Deposits:	Total	3,934	7,098	1.80
	Overseas	270	1,799	6.66
	Percent Overseas	7%	25%	
Loans:	Total	2,709**	5,114	1.89†
	Overseas	87**	598	6.87†
	Percent Overseas	3%	12%	
Wells Fargo				
Deposits:	Total	4,542	9,065	2.00
	Overseas	101	1,670	16.53
	Percent Overseas	2%	18%	
Loans:	Total	3,386	7,336	2.17
	Overseas	29	941	32.45
	Percent Overseas	1%	13%	
Crocker				
Deposits:	Total	4,169	7,896	1.89
	Overseas	283	1,431	5.06
	Percent Overseas	7%	18%	
Seattle First				
Deposits:	Total	1,612	3,118	1.93
	Overseas	2	354	177.00
	Percent Overseas	0%	11%	
Loans:	Total	1,187	2,317	1.95
	Overseas	3	117	39.00
	Percent Overseas	0%	5%	
Rainier††				
Deposits:	Total	1,078	1,861	1.72
	Overseas	90	298	3.31
	Percent Overseas	8%	16%	
Loans:	Total	683	1,271	1.86
	Overseas	11	130	11.82
	Percent Overseas	2%	10%	

*Daily or weekly average balances.
**1970
†Ratio, 1974/1970.
††Excluding Edge Act subsidiaries.
Sources: 1974 Annual Reports of the respective banks.

later slowdown in the expansion pace, it maintained at the end of 1975 a network of 107 overseas branches and 13 foreign representative offices, with $33 billion in weekly average assets in the bank's World Banking division—about 54 percent of the bank's total average assets.[13]

Other West Coast banks started overseas branching in 1968, with the opening of a London branch by National Bank of Commerce of Seattle. As shown in Table 1, by the end of 1969 there were nine West Coast banks with overseas branches,[14] with total branch assets amounting to $5.6 billion. However, aside from Bank of America branches, all were located in either London, the Bahamas, or Luxembourg. During the six years 1970-75, 11 other West Coast banks opened branches abroad.[15] The combined assets of the foreign branches of all West Coast banks increased to $35.7 billion at the end of 1975.[16] During this period, they undertook extensive branching activities in Japan and other countries in the Far East.

These aggregate data reveal little about the operations of individual banks. However, seven individual banks report considerable detail in their annual reports to stockholders (Table 2). Over the 1970-74 period, total loans and deposits of each of seven major West Coast banks about doubled; but in all cases, their overseas loans and deposits grew at a much faster pace. Overseas operations more than tripled for Bank of America, an established international-banking institution, and jumped over a hundred-fold for such newcomers as Seattle First and Security Pacific. As a result, overseas loans and deposits were by 1974 a substantial portion of portfolios for all these institutions—from a high of 40 percent for Bank of America to between 10 and 20 percent at other banks.

Table 3

Total Assets of Foreign Branches of West Coast Banks, by Region December 31, 1975

Region	Total Assets	Share of Total
	(Millions of Dollars)	(Percent)
Europe*	23,188	65
Caribbean	5,619	16
Pacific Basin[1]	6,863	19
Total	35,670	100

[1]Japan, Korea, Taiwan, Hong Kong, Philippines, Malaysia, Singapore, Thailand, and Indonesia.

Source: Based on data reported by banks to the Federal Reserve System.

Overseas operations have remained heavily concentrated in Europe and the Caribbean (Table 3), reflecting the importance of Eurodollar operations. The only other measurable activity was in Pacific Basin countries—almost entirely in Japan, Singapore, and Hong Kong.[17]

Besides overseas branches, West Coast banks also have invested large sums in foreign affiliates which are engaged in all sorts of banking or near-banking activities. These activities include merchant banking, investment banking, finance companies, leasing, mortgage, trust, factoring, etc. Data on the amounts involved, however, are lacking.[18]

Edge Act Corporations on the West Coast

Edge Act Corporations are wholly-owned subsidiaries of U.S. banks set up under Section 25(a) of the Federal Reserve Act to facilitate international banking activities. They may be established in states outside their parent banks' home states, and therefore represent an exception to the usual barriers against interstate branching by U.S. banks. This provision enables banks which are located outside major financial centers to engage in international banking in such centers; on the other hand, it also permits banks which are located in one major financial center to participate in international banking in other centers. The establishment of a large number of out-of-state Edge corporations in a region is, therefore, a good sign of the region's growing importance as an international financial center.

In addition to their international banking activities, Edge corporations may also make equity investments in foreign corporations which do not transact business in the United States—an activity which their parent banks are prohibited by law from doing. Hence, many banks which are located in an international financial center may set up Edge corporations in the same locale, often on the same premises, for conducting international equity-investment businesses. These Edge corporations are commonly referred to as "investment Edges," in contrast to the "banking Edges" described above.

Edge activity on the West Coast was quite modest until recently. As late as 1965, there were only three such corporations: a banking Edge in Seattle (International Bank of Commerce) and two investment Edges in San Francisco (Crocker International and Bank of California International). In 1967, First National City Bank of New York opened a banking Edge in San Francisco—the first representative from outside the region—and then five West Coast banks (Security Pacific, Bank of America, U.S. National of Oregon, Seattle First, and Union) established investment Edges. By the end of 1969, seven Edge corporations were operating on the West Coast, but with total assets of only $80 million.

The big wave hit the West Coast in 1973 and 1974, when ten new Edge corporations were established—mostly from outside the region—raising the total number to 23 and their aggregate assets to $1 billion. The wave then appears to have subsided, as the total assets fell to $930 million by mid-1975,[19] and the number dropped to 22 with the merger of two investment-Edge subsidiaries of Crocker in August 1975. Today, there are 13 banking Edges—8 from New York, 3 from Chicago, and 1 each from Boston and Seattle—along with 9 investment Edges which all represent West Coast institutions.

Measured by asset size, the banking Edges are far more important than investment Edges. At mid-1975, banking Edges had total assets of $841 million, compared to only $88 million for all investment Edges. Activity is largely concentrated in San Francisco ($418 million in assets) and Los Angeles ($500 million), with the balance about equally distributed between Portland and Seattle.

Foreign Banks on the West Coast

Most foreign banks on the West Coast use the agency form, rather than the branch form of organization.[20] The latter is effectively barred from California, because the state requires all domestic deposits to be insured by the FDIC, and the FDIC insures only U.S.-chartered banks. A similar situation exists in Oregon, although the branches of two foreign banks—Bank of Tokyo and Canadian Imperial—have "grandfather" privileges there. The state of Washington permits branches of foreign banks, but with domestic deposits severely limited by law, the branches in effect act much like agencies. The most effective arrangement has evolved in California, where foreign banks have established both agencies and full-service state-chartered subsidiary banks, in an attempt to obtain flexibility in both lending limits and deposit-accepting capabilities.[21] In fact, each of the 15 foreign banking subsidiaries in California, except for Lloyds, operates in tandem with an agency of the same parent bank.

Foreign banks came early to the West Coast. Canadian Imperial Bank of Commerce opened an agency in San Francisco in 1902, and Bank of Montreal established a subsidiary bank in San Francisco in 1918 and an agency there in 1934. Other Canadian and Far Eastern banks followed in the 1930s and after the Second World War. Yet by mid-1969, there were only seven foreign subsidiary banks and sixteen agencies and branches of foreign banks on the West Coast, with assets totaling about $1.5 billion.

The pace of expansion was relatively slow until mid-1971. But within the next four years, 29 new agencies and 8 banking subsidiaries opened in California and 4 new branches opened in Seattle. At mid-1975, agency and branch assets totaled $9.0 billion and subsidiary-bank assets $4.5 billion—13 times and 9 times their respective sizes only six years earlier. Within the same period, their share of all commercial-bank assets within the San Francisco Federal Reserve District increased from 2.1 percent to 9.8 percent.

Foreign banks prefer California to any other state (except New York) as a place to conduct business. As of last September, 66 branches and agencies were located in New York, 43 in California, and 35 elsewhere; while 16 subsidiary banks were in New York, 15 in California, and only 2 elsewhere. New York accounted for 68 percent, California 26 percent, and other regions only 6 percent, of the $56.5 billion total assets of all the foreign banking offices in the United States.[22]

Banks from thirteen foreign countries in Asia, Europe, and the Americas are now represented on the West Coast. The Japanese banks account for a full two-thirds of the $13.5 billion total assets of all foreign banking offices in California; four British banks account for 15 percent; six Canadian banks for 9 percent; and seventeen other foreign banks for the other 9 percent.[23]

Foreign banks bring to a region financial expertise and special ties with foreign business partners which local banks do not possess. Their comparative advantage in this respect enables them to overcome the cultural and business barriers of entry into a (for them) foreign environment. Being complementary to the indigenous banks, foreign banks help to broaden and strengthen a region's institutional base as an international financial center. In addition, as they become established in the new market, they help to enhance competition by offering local savers and borrowers a greater choice of financial services.

Recent Developments

Nineteen seventy-four was a particularly turbulent period for international banking. The lifting of U.S. capital controls in January 1974 coincided with the liberalization of controls over international capital flows by other major industrial countries. This coordinated shift in policy occurred just as the world's major banks were called upon to help manage the huge flows of international oil payments. At the time, there was widespread concern over the banks' ability to handle such flows and to bear the risks involved. Then in May, 1974, came the Franklin National failure, followed soon after by the Herstatt debacle and a series of other international banking failures and near-failures. On top of it all, inflation became rampant worldwide, causing interest rates to soar and the world bond market to decline during a time of large international-payments imbalances. From late 1974 on, a spreading business recession engulfed the world, with declining export markets, falling commodity prices, and continually rising import costs seriously undermining the payments positions of a number of developing nations and forcing them to seek substantial loans from the banking system. Through it all, international banking underwent considerable strains while offering unprecedented opportunities as well.

How did West Coast banks manage through that period of perils and opportunities? In response to the lifting of capital controls and to the world-wide demand for the financing of oil deficits, West Coast banks stepped up their foreign lending very sharply during the second quarter of 1974, both at their head offices and through their foreign branches, as shown in Table 4. Following the Herstatt debacle, they drastically reduced their lending activities, leading to a substantial net liquidation of head-office loans during the third quarter and of foreign branch loans in the fourth quarter of 1974. Subsequently, however, foreign lending recovered momentum, and head-office lending even surpassed the 1973-74 pace.

Thus, in fact, West Coast banks did not undergo as much of a "consolidation and retrench-

Table 4
International Activities of West Coast Banks and Their Foreign Branches Quarterly, 1974-75
(Millions of dollars)

Period		West Coast Banks: Change in Foreign Assets	West Coast Banks: Change in Foreign Liabilities	Foreign Branches: Change in Total Assets
1973[1]		515	173	1,944
1974	I	537	260	1,199
	II	2,138	186	4,458
	III	− 705	766	1,887
	IV	487	391	− 191
1975	I	1,123	68	394
	II	587	− 143	528
	III	780	− 88	458
	IV	1,529	41	2,403

[1]Quarterly average.

Source: Based on data reported by banks to the Federal Reserve System and the U.S. Treasury.

ment" in 1974 as was alleged in the financial press. Reports of "an age of expansion in international banking coming to an end" were unfounded. Measured by banks' foreign claims, any retrenchment was quite brief—lasting no more than one quarter of a year. Foreign lending resumed growth at both head offices and foreign branches in 1975, although the foreign-branch expansion was at a slower pace than previously.

Profitability of International Operations

The feature attracting banks to international operations must be their profitability. Indeed, a recent industry study shows that the international earnings of a group of nine major U.S. banks increased at a 37-percent annual rate over the 1970-74 period, compared to only a 3-percent rate of gain for domestic earnings.[24] Comparable data for West Coast banks are not available for that period, but scattered data for 1973 and 1974 show the same type of upsurge in overseas earnings (Table 5). In the three cases shown, earnings from international operations grew considerably faster than domestic earnings between those two years. Thus Bank of Amer-

Table 5
Assets and Earnings of Selected Individual Banks 1973 and 1974
(Millions of dollars)

	Assets 1973	Assets 1974	Assets Changes	Earnings 1973	Earnings 1974	Earnings Change
Bank of America						
Total	49,400	60,400	+22%	219	257	+17%
International	18,000	25,000	+39%	70	100	+43%
Domestic	31,400	35,400	+13%	149	157	+ 5%
Security Pacific						
Total	9,756	12,069	+24%	60.0	56.0	− 7%
International	808	1,068	+32%	5.4	6.7	+24%
Domestic	8,948	11,001	+23%	54.6	49.3	−10%
Seattle First						
Total	3,595	4,190	+17%	25.5	29.5	+16%
International	89	117	+31%	1.5	3.4	+127%
Domestic	3,506	4,073	+16%	24.0	26.1	+ 9%

Source: Estimated on basis of data in 1974 Annual Reports

ica's international earnings increased 43 percent, compared to only 5 percent for domestic earnings; those of Seattle First increased by 127 percent, compared to only 9 percent for domestic earnings; and those of Security Pacific by 24 percent, compared to an 11 percent decrease in domestic earnings.

To a large extent, the faster increase in international earnings can be attributed to a greater growth rate in international assets than in domestic assets. Indeed, between 1973 and 1974, Bank of America's international assets grew by 39 percent, compared to 13 percent for domestic assets; while the comparable figures were 31 to 16 percent for Seattle First and 32 to 23 percent for Security Pacific.

If the average rate of return is measured by the ratio of earnings to assets, then changes in the profitability of an operation can be measured by the difference between the earning-growth rates and asset-growth rates. Thus, on the basis of the data in Table 5, the profitability of Bank of America's international operations appears to have improved slightly between 1973 and 1974; while Seattle First's improved enormously, and Security Pacific's declined somewhat. In contrast, the three banks' domestic profitability all declined sharply, apparently as a result of the U.S. recession in 1974. Thus, in two of the three cases examined, increased profitability in international operations provided a cushion against the decline in profitability of domestic operations. Even in the third case, where international profitability also declined, the absolute increase in such earnings helped to offset the decline in domestic earnings.

A similar picture is presented by recently published 1975 data for Bank of America (Table 6). Clearly, the 23-percent growth in its international earnings in 1975 remained considerably above its 12-percent growth of domestic earnings. (The comparable growth figures for 1974 were 43 percent and 5 percent, respectively.) When deflated by the respective growth rates in earning assets, the bank's international profitability continued to improve, and its domestic profitability to deteriorate in 1975.

Table 6
BankAmerica Corporation
Growth in Earnings and Assets
International and Domestic
1974-1975

	Average Earnings			Average Earning Assets		
	1974	1975	Increase	1974	1975	Increase
	(Million $)		(Percent)	(Billion $)		(Percent)
Total	257	302	17.5	43.5	49.3	13.3
International[1]	136	167	22.8	23.9	27.1	13.4
Domestic	121	135	11.6	19.6	22.2	13.3

[1]World Banking Division. Data differ from the corresponding figures presented in Table 5, because of "profit center changes, changes in international allocation of overhead expenses and risk changes and improvements in building block system."

Source: BankAmerica Corporation, *Annual Report 1975*, p. 50.

Conclusion

As stated at the outset, the rise of regional financial centers has been one of the most interesting developments of the past decade in international finance. These newly-developed centers both complement and compete with old-established centers in the allocation of the world's financial resources. To the extent that these centers have provided closer contacts between international and regional sources and users of funds, they have enhanced the efficiency of international financial markets. Moreover, they have undoubtedly added to the prosperity and economic growth of the regions in which the centers are located.[25]

This paper has traced the rise of the U.S. West Coast as an international financial center. The rise has been remarkably rapid since 1969. In terms of both the volume of capital flows and the worldwide financial interests represented, the West Coast has become today a significant factor in international finance.

Economic theory has largely ignored the phenomenon of regional financial centers. Yet, for both regional economics and development economics, it should be a topic of considerable interest. Recent contributions to economic analysis have emphasized the central role of financial markets in promoting economic growth. To a large extent, the analysis should be applicable to both developed and developing economies. Regional financial centers have evolved in both types of economies to provide important links between national money and capital markets on the one hand and broader world markets (such as the Euro-currency market) on the other. Further, the regional clustering of international banking institutions suggests that the optimal geographic size of financial markets is perhaps smaller than a large country (such as the United States) and larger than most small countries.

At the present stage of knowledge, this paper is more concerned with *what* has occurred than with *why*. Nevertheless, the brief discussion of economic factors suggests that as commercial banking expanded on the West Coast, a growing number of banks in the past decade attained a size sufficiently large to reap the benefits of international portfolio diversification. Available profits data appear to reinforce the impression that banks were indeed able to reap such benefits by balancing declining domestic loan demand (due to the U.S. recession) with increased international loan demand (due to large payments deficits abroad).

Another key factor has been the rapid growth of West Coast international trade, which has attracted many Edge corporations and foreign banks to the region while inducing domestic banks to start or expand their own international operations. In 1975, the growth of trade slowed down considerably as a result of the worldwide recession. Nevertheless, as many as seven new agencies and branches of foreign banks were opened on the West Coast, and nine new branches of West Coast banks were established abroad. Thus, it appears that the banking industry's interest in international banking on the West Coast remained undaunted by the recession. Both domestic and foreign banks apparently saw the need to maintain their present stake in the market, and thus set the groundwork for further profitable operations in the years ahead.

FOOTNOTES

1. Charles P. Kindleberger, **The Formation of Financial Centers: A Study in Comparative Economic History,** Massachusetts Institute of Technology, Department of Economics, Working Paper No. 114 (August 1973). Harry G. Johnson, "Panama as a Regional Financial Center," **Economic Development and Cultural Change,** (January 1976), pp. 261-286. Robert F. Emery, **The Asian Dollar Market,** Board of Governors of the Federal Reserve System, International Finance Discussion Papers, No. 71 (November 1975). The older literature includes Margaret C. Myers, **The New York Money Market** (New York: Columbia University Press, 1931); Frank Tamagna, "New York as an International Money Market," **Banca Nazionale del Lavoro Quarterly Review,** (June 1959), pp. 201-234; Sidney M. Robbins and Nestor E. Terleckyj, **Money Metropolis** (Cambridge: Harvard University Press, 1960).
2. A useful survey of the literature on the subject is Gerard S. Goldstein and Leon N. Moses, " A Survey of Urban Economics," **Journal of Economic Literature,** (1973), pp. 471-515.
3. Raymond W. Goldsmith, **Financial Structure and Development** (New Haven: Yale University Press, 1969); Arnold W. Sametz, editor, **Financial Development and Economic Growth** (New York: New York University Press, 1972); Ronald I. McKinnon, **Money and Capital in Economic Development,** (Washington, D.C.: Brookings Institution, 1973); Edward S. Shaw, **Financial Deepening in Economic Development** (New York: Oxford University Press, 1973).
4. Herbert G. Grubel, "Internationally Diversified Portfolios: Welfare Gains and Capital Flows," **American Economic Review,** (December 1968), pp. 1299-1314.
5. Federal Reserve Bank of San Francisco, **Western Economic Indicators,** January/February 1976, p. E-4.
6. Ibid., p. A-8.
7. Raymond Jallow, "World Trade in the West," **California Business,** (May 16, 1974), p. 2.
8. By convention, a bank's total foreign assets equal the difference between its **global** consolidated total assets and its **domestic** assets. Global-asset data are published annually in **Rand McNally International Bankers Directory** (Chicago: Rand McNally & Co.). Domestic asset data are reported weekly by large commercial banks to the Federal Reserve System.
9. The five were: Bank of America, United California, Crocker, Wells Fargo, and National Bank of Commerce of Seattle (now Rainier).
10. The newcomers were: Security Pacific, Seattle First, Bank of California, Bank of Tokyo of California (now California First), U.S. National of Oregon, and Sumitomo Bank of California.
11. At the end of 1975, the claims on foreigners reported by West Coast banks amounted to $12.0 billion, and the liabilities to foreigners $6.4 billion.
12. **American Banker,** February 29, 1968.
13. BankAmerica Corporation, **Annual Report,** 1969, and **Annual Report,** 1975.
14. The nine banks were Bank of America, Bank of California, Crocker, First Western, Security Pacific, Union, United California, Wells Fargo, and National Bank of Commerce of Seattle. **American Banker,** February 27, 1970.
15. The eleven were Arizona Bank, First of Arizona, Valley National, Lloyds of California, Tokyo of California, Sumitomo of California, Barclay of California, First of Oregon, U.S. National of Oregon, Seattle First, and First of Hawaii. **American Banker,** February 27, 1976.
16. Data reported by banks to the Federal Reserve System.
17. However, the data do not include assets of a) European branches whose total liabilities payable in U.S. dollars amount to less than $10 million, and b) those elsewhere (except Bahamas) whose total liabilities payable in U.S. dollars are less than $30 million. Such foreign branches are exempted from reporting their monthly assets and liability positions on FR 502.
18. For a listing of these activities at the end of 1974, see **American Banker,** February 28, 1975.
19. Data on total assets understate the Edge corporations' operations. Since their loan limits are tied to the size of their capital, it is common practice for Edge corporations to generate loans and then sell them or pass them on to their parent banks. There may have been about $425 million outstanding in such loans at West Coast banking Edges in 1975.
20. The differences between the various types of organizations are discussed elsewhere in this issue. Robert Johnston, "Proposals for Federal Control of Foreign Banks."
21. U.S. Department of Commerce, **Foreign Direct Investment in the United States,** Interim Report to Congress (October 1975), Volume 2, Appendix VIII: "Foreign Banking in the United States," esp. pp. VIII 5-10.
22. George W. Mitchell, Vice Chairman, Board of Governors of the Federal Reserve System, **Statement Before the Subcommittee on Financial Institutions of the Senate Banking Committee,** January 28, 1976, Appendix, Tables 1-6.
23. Two banks each from France, Italy, Switzerland, Brazil, Mexico, and Hong Kong; and one each from Germany, the Netherlands, Korea, and the Philippines; plus a multinational bank, the European American Banking Corporation.
24. Cited in C. Frederic Wiegold, "Overseas Earnings in Sharp 5-Year Rise," **American Banker,** October 20, 1975, page 1.
25. See Harry G. Johnson, **op. cit.,** for an attempt at measuring the welfare gains from the rise of a regional financial center.

Chicago: city of the big straddles

Paul L. Kasriel and Randall C. Merris

Chicago is a full-service financial center. In assessing the city's role in the national and international marketplace, it is useful to delineate two broad classes of financial services. One class contains those financial services of which Chicago is *a* major supplier and *a* market participant; the other, those services of which Chicago is *the* major supplier and *the* market maker.

Chicago has retained its historical prominence as a financial center through its continuing ability to meet the investment and credit demands of a large segment of the local market and to compete in the national and international marketplace (See Box). And Chicago in recent years has developed a unique niche—as the birthplace of financial futures and exchange-based options trading.

This article focuses primarily on Chicago as *the* national and international center for futures and options trading. In addition to describing current activity in these markets, some explanations are offered for Chicago's emergence as the capital of financial futures and options. Some assessment also is made concerning Chicago's prospects for retaining its leadership in futures and options and for remaining a prominent supplier of banking and other financial services.

Futures trading today

In 1981, the three Chicago futures exchanges—the Chicago Board of Trade (CBT), the Chicago Mercantile Exchange (CME) including its International Monetary Market (IMM) division, and the MidAmerica Commodity Exchange—accounted for about 77 percent of the total contract volume of all organized futures trading in the U.S. In October 1982 the dollar value of the CBT's and CME's combined open interest (i.e., the number of contracts still outstanding) is $48.8 billion, or 80 percent of the dollar value of total U.S. futures open interest. The Chicago Board Options Exchange (CBOE) in 1981 accounted for about 53 percent of all exchange-traded options contract volume in the U.S. In 1980, the market value of contracts on the CBOE was $27.9 billion or about 61 percent of the total market value of exchange-traded U.S. options.

In 1976, the combined CBT and CME volume was about 25 million contracts. By 1981, their combined volume had skyrocketed to more than 73 million contracts traded—a 192 percent increase over those six years. A significant portion of this phenomenal growth can be attributed to continued development of financial futures—i.e., foreign currency and interest rate futures. In 1976, financial futures accounted for about 2 percent of CBT-CME volume. In 1981, this had risen to almost 39 percent.

Currently, the CBT's Treasury bond futures contract is the most actively traded futures contract in the United States. In 1981, the average daily dollar volume (at par value) in the CBT's Treasury bond futures contract and the CME's 90-day T-bill futures contract was $27.7 billion. This was $3 billion more than the daily average of transactions in the cash market in all maturities of U.S. government securities of the 36 reporting dealers. So, not only is Chicago the dominant center in futures trading, but in a sense, the dominant center in U.S. government securities trading.

Chicago's past in futures

That Chicago became the dominant center of futures trading in general was to a large extent a matter of geography. The 1848 completion of a canal joined Lake Michigan to the inland tributaries of the Mississippi River. This canal provided inexpensive water transportation for corn from the interior to Chicago. But corn harvested in late fall and early winter could not be moved from the interior on frozen waterways and thus,

Paul L. Kasriel is a senior economist, and Randall C. Merris is a research economist in the Research Department of the Federal Reserve Bank of Chicago. This article is adapted from a paper presented at the Illinois Economic Association meetings, Chicago, November 1982.

had to be stored at river grain elevators until the spring thaws. As a result, river elevator operators were subject to considerable price risk over the winter. To hedge this risk, grain elevator operators began to sell corn in the late fall at a firm price for May, or forward, delivery in Chicago.

The Chicago Board of Trade was organized in 1848 for the purpose of trading these forward, or time, contracts in corn. Over time, rules were promulgated that dealt with trading conduct and delivery grade standards. The Chicago Board of Trade became a full-fledged futures exchange in 1865 when a clearinghouse was established.

The Chicago Mercantile Exchange traces its ancestry back to the Chicago Produce Exchange, formed in 1874. This exchange served as a cash market for butter, eggs, poultry, and other perishable agricultural products. In 1898, the butter and egg dealers withdrew from this exchange to form the Chicago Butter and Egg Board.

Later, as the exchange's cash business in butter and eggs waned, its membership looked for additional lines of business to revive it. Because there was a considerable amount of forward contracting in eggs and, perhaps, because the neighboring CBT had been trading futures for years, the membership decided to trade futures in butter and eggs. Trading began in 1919, and the exchange became known as the Chicago Mercantile Exchange.

More than half-a-century later, a major breakthrough occurred in futures trading when the newly-formed International Monetary Market division of the Chicago Mercantile Exchange began trading foreign currency futures in 1972. This innovation pioneered the concept of trad-

Some financial dimensions

Chicago is home to some of the largest financial institutions in the nation, including

- 2 of the 10, and 5 of the 100, largest commercial banks ranked by total assets;
- 2 of the 10, and 4 of the 50, largest savings and loan associations ranked by total deposits.

The Chicago SMSA is home to 10 of the 100 largest finance companies ranked by total capital and to some of the largest insurance companies, investment banking houses, and brokers and dealers in bonds and equities.

Chicago is a major supplier of retail and wholesale banking services in local, national and international markets. Some figures:

- The 404 insured domestic commercial banks in the Chicago SMSA hold approximately $97 billion* in domestic assets, accounting for 5.6 percent of such assets of all insured U.S. banks.
- The 95 domestic banks located in Chicago have domestic assets of about $76 billion.
- The 95 domestic Chicago banks have about $18 billion of domestic assets exposure to non-U.S. residents, representing about 9 percent of such foreign lending of all U.S. domestic banks.
- Two Chicago banks rank among the nation's 10 largest holders, and 3 more are among the top 25 holders, of interbank demand deposits.
- Domestic Chicago banks own 8 Edge corporations—5 in Chicago and 3 elsewhere—engaged strictly in international banking operations.
- Chicago banks and Chicago offices of foreign banks own about 20 branches of Edge corporations in U.S. locations outside of Chicago.
- Domestic banks headquartered outside of Chicago own more than a dozen Chicago offices of their Edge corporations.
- Foreign banks have established 42 Chicago branches since 1973 when foreign bank branches were permitted under Illinois law.
- Foreign banks are majority owners of 2 domestic Chicago banks and 4 Chicago offices of Edge corporations.
- The 48 Chicago offices of foreign banks have total assets of about $10 billion, representing about 4 percent of the total assets of all U.S. offices of foreign banks.
- Eight Chicago banks have over 60 foreign branches with total asset exposure to non-U.S. residents of about $40 billion.
- Chicago banks and Chicago offices of foreign banks have established about 25 International Banking Facilities since December 1981 when these in-house foreign depository-lending facilities were authorized by Federal Reserve regulation.

*Dollar amounts are as of June 30, 1982.

ing futures in something other than a physical commodity.[1] Soon, interest rate futures appeared—GNMA futures (October 1975, CBT), 90-day T-bill futures (January 1976, IMM), and Treasury bond futures (August 1977, CBT). Contracts in other maturities of government securities, and commercial paper, domestic CDs, and Eurodollar time deposits have since been introduced. The Eurodollar contract also represented a breakthrough by introducing cash settlements for open expired contracts rather than actual delivery of the "commodity."

The acceptance of cash settlement has spawned the development of stock market index futures. Futures on the S&P 500 stock index began trading at the IMM in April 1982. In just six months, the daily volume of trading in this contract rivaled that of 90-day T-bill futures, the IMM's most successful previous financial futures contract. The CBT introduced options on financial futures in October 1982.

In 1973, Chicago was the site of another financial innovation—exchange-traded options on equities at the newly-created Chicago Board Options Exchange. When the CBOE opened, it listed call options in 16 stocks and put options in none. At year-end 1981, calls had grown to 120 and options to 119. The CBOE also introduced options trading on U.S. government securities.

It is understandable that Chicago became a dominant center in futures trading for agricultural products, given its location and transportation facilities. But how did it come to be dominant in the trading of futures and options on financial instruments? By all rights, New York City, the U.S. center of equities and fixed-income securities, also ought to lead in the trading of their derivative instruments. The reason for Chicago's dominance in these instruments has to do with economies of scale and that nonquantifiable variable, entrepreneurial spirit.

Working's hypothesis

A good part of futures market "infrastructure" was in place in Chicago at the beginning of the 1970s. The physical plant and management already existed. Moreover, there already existed a group of well-capitalized and experienced local floor traders who could provide the requisite liquidity to the markets so as to attract public participants—hedgers as well as speculators. Stanford University's Holbrook Working, a distinguished student of the futures markets, highlights the importance of this infrastructure:

> An exchange that conducts futures trading in a number of different commodities can provide a more uniformly fluid market for any one of them than could an exchange dealing only in that one commodity. That is especially true for a commodity in which trading is light. To maintain a highly fluid market, scalpers must operate on an almost infinitesimally small profit margin, and a professional floor trader can afford to do that only if he does a great volume of business. That is not possible on a single-commodity exchange with a small volume of trading; but it is possible in a small futures market operating on a multi-commodity exchange, where a floor trader is not restricted to dealing only in that one commodity. Futures markets that are individually small can prosper modestly on a multi-commodity exchange whereas attempt *(sic)* to operate them separately would fail, for much the same reason that retail trade in a small and isolated town must be conducted in a "general store" rather than a number of specialty shops.[2]

Working's hypothesis may partially explain why New York City's futures exchanges have failed to capture a larger market share of financial futures trading. In September 1978, the American Commodity Exchange (ACE), a subsidiary of the American Stock Exchange, began trading GNMA futures. ACE added 90-day T-bill futures and Treasury bond futures to its menu in June 1979 and November 1979, respectively. By September 1980, however, ACE volume was so low that it was acquired by the newly-organized New York Futures Exchange (NYFE), a subsidiary of the New York Stock Exchange.

[1]While this was a milestone for futures trading, it should be noted that there was already a well-established interbank forward market in foreign currencies.

[2]Holbrook Working, "Economic Functions of Futures Markets," in *Selected Writings of Holbrook Working*," compiled by Anne E. Peck, Board of Trade of the City of Chicago, 1977, p. 284.

ACE's demise could have been predicted from Working's hypothesis. It was a new exchange trying to trade low-volume contracts. It lacked a significant group of experienced and well-capitalized local floor traders to provide the necessary liquidity. Moreover, the exchange did not offer a diversified set of contracts or any high volume contracts to support the traders. And all of the ACE contracts were already being traded relatively successfully on the Chicago exchanges. NYFE, until recently, seemed destined to meet with the same fate as its acquisition. NYFE was also trading duplicates of futures contracts traded at the Chicago exchanges. Recently, however, volume on the NYFE has picked up because of its new and exclusive futures contract on the New York Stock Exchange index.

Another New York exchange, the Commodity Exchange (COMEX) also has ventured into financial futures. COMEX, unlike ACE and NYFE, is an established exchange and the leader in metals (gold, silver, and copper) futures trading. With established and high volume contracts, COMEX might have been expected to generate more than minimal volume in financial futures. But again, COMEX's financial futures contracts are essentially duplications of established Chicago contracts.

A somewhat different outcome has occurred with regard to options trading. The CBOE began trading call options on equities in April 1973. Unlike the Chicago exchanges' experience with financial futures, CBOE's dominance in equity options trading has diminished, with competition coming from options trading on the American Stock Exchange (January 1975), the Philadelphia Stock Exchange (June 1975), and the Pacific Stock Exchange (March 1976). Despite this competition, the CBOE retained over 50 percent of the options contract volume in 1981.

Chicago's financial future

The outlook for Chicago to continue as the financial center in futures and options trading is good indeed. The use of financial futures by institutions is still in its infancy. In this new era of increased interest rate volatility and deregulation of our financial system, depository institutions will be forced to manage their assets and liabilities more actively if they are to survive. Financial futures and options are additional tools that can be employed to this end.

Recently, large banks have begun to establish financial futures units either in-bank or in holding-company subsidiaries to provide consulting and brokerage services to the public. Given their correspondent relationships with smaller banks and other financial institutions, these large-bank financial futures units can be expected to generate increased institutional participation in the futures markets. Stock index futures, options on futures, and options on fixed-income securities have started trading only in recent months. The industry believes that these new instruments will match the success of the IMM's S&P 500 index futures contract.

The outlook for Chicago's share of the market of other financial services may not be quite so sanguine due to secular production and population trends. The composition of U.S. output appears to be moving more toward the services and light manufacturing industries, and away from capital goods and heavy manufacturing in which the Midwest has specialized. A possible offset may be the entrance of traditionally nonfinancial businesses into the financial services industry. Sears Roebuck and Company is an obvious example. Sears, with such subsidiaries as Allstate Insurance, Dean Witter Reynolds, and Coldwell Banker, along with its mammoth consumer credit card operations, may become a major provider of retail financial services. This potential is enhanced by Sears' relative lack of regulatory impediments.

With regard to banking, the current move toward deregulation and, to a limited degree, decreased taxation should help Chicago banks compete locally, nationally, and globally. In December 1981, the Federal Reserve authorized the opening of International Banking Facilities (IBFs). Through their IBFs, U.S. banking offices may accept deposits from and make loans to foreign residents, including foreign banks, without being subject to Regulations Q and D or to FDIC insurance coverage and assessments. Moreover, Illinois has granted favorable tax treatment under state law for IBF operations.

Illinois state law prohibits statewide commercial bank branching. This regulation has surely put Chicago banks at a disadvantage to their New York and California counterparts. If it were not for well-developed federal funds and large negotiable CD markets devoid of Reg Q ceilings, Chicago banks would be at an even greater disadvantage. A minor crack in the Illinois law was made in 1981, effective 1982, when multibank holding companies were permitted on a limited basis in contiguous counties.

To develop a specific plan for local business and political leaders to follow in order to enhance Chicago's financial role would be very difficult. However, actions that would tend to diminish Chicago's role readily come to mind.

In the mid-1970s an existing stock transfer tax in New York City was increased and a new bond transfer tax was imposed. In response, many securities firms threatened to move and, in some cases, actually relocated. Securities exchanges also gave thought to relocating. In reaction to the actual and threatened exodus of the securities industry from New York City, the bond transfer tax was repealed, and in 1976 the burden of the stock transfer tax was reduced. By June 1981, the collection of the New York City stock transfer tax had been phased out.

Increased taxation and/or regulation of financial production in which Chicago specializes would, all else the same, detract from the city's role as a provider of these products.[3] The worst case for Chicago would be to tax the futures and options industries sufficiently to induce them to move elsewhere. A step along that "worst case" path was nearly taken in 1973 when a local revenue proposal emerged that would have imposed a transfer tax on transactions consummated on organized financial exchanges located in Chicago. In response to this proposal, the CBT and CME began investigating relocation sites outside the Chicago city limits. The transfer tax proposal was withdrawn.

At the national level, amendments to the Futures Trading Act of 1982 were introduced that would have empowered the Commodity Futures Trading Commission (CFTC)—the Federal agency with regulatory jurisdiction over U.S. futures trading—to impose a transaction fee or tax on all futures trades in order to defray some of the Commission's expenses. These amendments were defeated. However, the final form of the Futures Trading Act of 1982 passed by Congress and signed by the President authorizes the CFTC to charge appropriate fees for services rendered and activities performed incidental to its regulatory responsibilities. User fees may not be as onerous as a transaction tax *per se*, but they still represent an increase in the cost of conducting futures trading. Increased taxation or regulation at the national level could be just the boost needed to get a proposed Bermuda-based futures exchange or the London International Financial Futures Exchange, which opened its doors and floors in September 1982, off and running. If the notion of driving our futures business offshore appears to be farfetched, consider what has happened in banking. Many analysts would agree that Regulations Q and D have played a significant role in the growth of the London and Caribbean Eurodollar markets.

Chicago has truly come of age as an international financial center and, in many areas, as an unrivaled financial innovator. In his poem "Chicago," Carl Sandburg characterizes the city as "Stormy, husky, brawling." To observe the trading in the pits of Chicago's exchanges is to understand his description. Writing today, Sandburg might say:

> Frozen pork belly trader of the world,
> International market maker, stacker of
> wheat futures,
> Player with stock options, financial
> futures,
> And, now, options on futures;
> Stormy, husky, brawling,
> City of the big straddles.

[3]This discussion is focused on the impact of increased taxation and regulation of financial products on Chicago as a provider of these services. It does not address the issue of whether the public interest is better served by such taxation or regulation.

[15]

Excerpt from Richard McGahey, Mary Malloy, Katherine Kazanas and Michael P. Jacobs, *Financial Services, Financial Centers*, 183–228.

5

Front Office Competition Among U.S. Financial Centers

The competitive forces unleashed by the transformation of financial services activities have weakened the grip on markets, firms, and jobs once held by traditional financial centers. Convergence, globalization, liberalization of regulatory regimes, and technology all have loosened traditional bonds, forcing financial institutions to develop new competitive strategies. These strategies often have meant the expansion or relocation of activities outside of traditional financial centers.

The next two chapters address the economic implications of the financial services revolution and firms' responses to the new competitive climate by examining New York, America's historical financial center, and its rivalry with other domestic locations. While it is true that global financial markets are emerging, competition for employment and economic development benefits is still mainly domestic from the point of view of U.S. locations. New York may lose market activities to London or Tokyo, but a much greater threat to New York's employment base comes from New Jersey or Delaware. Other U.S. cities, especially Chicago and Los Angeles, are becoming significant players in the emerging global marketplace and threaten to take jobs away from New York.

This chapter begins with a profile of New York, America's historic financial center, in order to identify the present basis for its leadership in domestic financial activities and the factors which will tend to heighten competitive pressures in the future. After comparing various domestic locations along key dimensions of competitiveness, the chapter examines competition for front office activity by contrasting the rise of two major financial centers, Los Angeles and Chicago.

Chapter 6 then considers the dimensions of competitiveness influencing the location of back office and data processing centers by profiling northeastern New Jersey and Delaware, two of New York's chief competitor locations for these activities. The chapter concludes by identifying a number of issues which point to the likelihood of intensifying competition among domestic centers in the future and the implications for traditional financial centers like New York, setting the stage for consideration of public policy options.

New York: America's Historic Financial Center

New York City is America's historic financial center. While its story is interesting in its own right, it is more important as an illustration of how changing markets, firm strategies, and resulting employment patterns have challenged its historic dominance.

New York's financial leadership is based in large part on its role as the economic center of gravity of a leading region in the U.S. — the world's largest, most developed, and now most indebted economy. In this role, New York has developed dense concentrations of borrowers, investors, financial intermediaries, and businesses providing essential support services. In many banking and securities activities, New York-based institutions are consistent leaders, providing most of the major financial innovations that have transformed the industry in recent years. For years, the large commercial banks and investment houses of Wall Street have provided borrowers, investors, and other financial intermediaries with sophisticated products and services and new techniques.

Convergence and globalization in financial markets now are forcing a redefinition of New York's position in relation to other domestic and international financial centers. Heightened competition and the new alignment of domestic and global economic growth are diminishing New York's former near-oligopolistic control over financial services. Rather than the sole source of energy, New York's position in the future constellation of financial centers is likely to be as a bright star, perhaps the brightest, among others.

New York's historic financial leadership was linked to its dynamic regional economy, the strength of its industrial and commercial base, and its position in the U.S. economy. The New York metropolitan area still is the largest, most populous metropolitan economy in the nation, and is also the hub of a state economy whose gross product in 1986 was 8.5 percent of America's total GNP, second only to California's 12.5 percent.[1] This scale of economic activity and concentration of population provides a strong market for financial services in New York.

But, starting in the mid-1970s, New York's financial services leadership became less directly tied to the fortunes of regional industry and commerce and more attuned to developments in the larger domestic and international arenas.

Between 1979 and 1988, New York City lost significant employment in manufacturing, transportation, and wholesale trade. Nearly 30 percent, over 140,000, of its manufacturing jobs vanished, a decline worse than anywhere else in the nation.[2] While still boasting the highest concentration of Fortune 500 industrial firms, employment in the administrative centers of New York-based manufacturing firms fell by 47 percent in these years.[3]

What remained were many of the largest corporate administrative centers, treasury operations, and insurance and institutional fund managers, who together formed one of the world's deepest concentrations of capital suppliers. As Table 4.8 shows, in 1986 New York City's financial institutions held 21 percent ($911 billion) of the world's assets invested by the 130 largest global institutional investors worldwide, a third of the U.S. total.

This enormous pool of capital is supported by the strongest concentration of large financial intermediaries in the nation, if not the world. Of the world's 25 largest securities firms in 1988, ten are New York-based, with over 44 percent ($33 billion) of the total capital held by the leading firms.[4] Salomon Brothers, Merrill Lynch, Shearson Lehman Hutton, Goldman Sachs, Drexel Burnham Lambert, Morgan Stanley, First Boston, Paine Webber, Bear Stearns, and Smith Barney have consistently led the industry with innovative financial products and techniques.

New York also has nine of the 50 largest U.S. domestic life insurers and 16 of the top diversified financial firms, with one-third and nearly one-half of the total assets of these industry leaders, respectively.[5] These include such giants as Metropolitan Life, The Equitable, New York Life, Teachers Insurance and Annuity Association, and American Express.

New York also is first among U.S. banking centers with seven of the ten largest commercial bank holding companies (see Table 5.1), holding approximately one-third ($628.4 billion) of the total assets of America's top 100 bank holding companies. Citicorp, a New York bank with more than twice the assets of its nearest competitor, is in a class by itself among American banks.

Through their retail and wholesale networks, New York commercial banks book large shares of the market in domestic consumer and business loans. Seventeen percent of the total consumer loans held by the 100 leading domestic banks at the end of 1987 were issued by New York firms, including strong shares of the bank credit card and home equity loan markets.[6] At that time, the seven New York money center banks also led with 20 percent ($55.2 billion) of the total in domestic business loans issued by the top 100 domestic commercial banks.[7]

In recent years, Citicorp, J.P. Morgan, Bankers Trust, Manufacturers Hanover, Chase, and Chemical Bank also have dominated the growing market for large syndicated loans. The resurgence of loan syndication reflects the importance of the loan market for financing domestic corporate restructurings. The large New York banks also are leaders in the sale of loans originated, which enables a much greater turnover of capital and potential earnings in lending operations. And by mediating a substantial share of domestic lending activity, New York banks provide their clients access to the international capital markets, where New York banks and their subsidiaries lead in a growing range of lending and securities activities.

New York serves as an important link between foreign and domestic loan activity. As Table 5.2 shows, it has the largest domestic

TABLE 5.1 Top Ten Domestic Bank Holding Companies, 1988

Rank		Total Assets ($billions)
1	Citicorp, New York	207.7
2	Chase Manhattan Corp., New York	97.5
3	BankAmerica Corp., San Francisco	94.6
4	J.P. Morgan & Co., New York	83.9
5	Security Pacific Corp., Los Angeles	77.9
6	Chemical Banking Corp., New York	67.3
7	Manufacturers Hanover Corp., New York	66.7
8	First Interstate Bancorp, Los Angeles	58.2
9	Bankers Trust New York Corp., New York	57.9
10	Bank of New York Co., New York*	47.4

* Doubled its assets by acquiring Irving Bank Corp. in 1988.
Source: *American Banker*, January 24, 1989, p.2. Reprinted by permission.

concentration of foreign bank offices of any U.S. city. With 454 foreign bank offices in mid-1988, New York hosts nearly half of all U.S. offices of foreign banks. These banks hold almost two-thirds of the total assets, almost three-fourths of total deposits, and over half of all C&I loans booked by all the U.S. offices of foreign banks. Los Angeles, despite its rapidly growing Asian investment, remains a distant second.

New York's large banks also hold the deposits of other domestic and foreign banks needed to complete servicing of claims and settlements. Taken together, Citibank, Chase, Bankers Trust, Manufacturers Hanover, Bank of New York, and Morgan Guaranty and Trust hold one-third of the total correspondent balances of the leading 240 banks in the U.S.[8] Because of their size and strategic location at the hub of U.S. domestic and international financial transactions, these banks traditionally have formed the upper stratum of the domestic banking system.

But as some of the strongest expansion opportunities emerge elsewhere in the U.S, New York's commercial banks face formidable competitive pressures from strong regional banks. As noted in Chapter 3, regional banking compacts in the U.S. were designed in

TABLE 5.2 U.S. Cities With the Largest Foreign Bank Presence Ranked by Number of Offices

	Total Number of Offices			Assets ($billions)		C&I Loans ($billions)	
	1988	1985	1981	1988	1985	1988	1985
New York	454	405	342	412.1	250.8	96.6	58.4
Los Angeles	123	111	101	77.2	51.9	24.3	13.2
Chicago	84	79	69	44.3	24.2	18.1	7.9
Houston	76	70	58	2.2	*	1.3	—
San Francisco	67	69	64	36.4	50.3	8.9	11.3
Miami	53	55	43	10.2	6.6	1.2	2.3
Atlanta	25	22	17	5.3	3.6	3.5	2.0
Washington, D.C.	15	16	9	0.3	*	0.03	—
Dallas	15	13	—	0.2	—	0.06	—
Seattle	13	13	11	2.8	1.7	1.2	0.7
Total Top 10	925	853	NA	591.0		155.2	
Total All US Offices	1,037	NA	NA				

* Insignificant.

Source: "Foreign Banks in the United States: 1988 Roundup," *American Banker*, March 6, 1989, p. 4A; "Foreign Banking in the U.S.," *American Banker*, February 14, 1986, p. 2A; "Foreign Banking in the U.S.," *American Banker*, February 12, 1982, p. 2A. Reprinted by permission.

large part to impede the entry of New York money center banks. This, along with strong economic growth in many states, nurtured the rise of superregional institutions, which now have strong and deepening roots in their respective markets. Some of these superregionals are now developing the presence and expertise in international markets to compete with New York firms.

With its significant concentrations of large investors and financial intermediaries, New York remains the center of gravity for domestic capital markets. The total domestic market for new issues of U.S. corporate debt and equity reached $307.7 billion in 1989,[9] and the greatest share of this market was held by New York financial firms. As Table 5.3 shows, in the first quarter of 1989, Merrill Lynch,

TABLE 5.3 Top Underwriters of U.S. Debt and Equity, First Quarter, 1989

Manager	Value ($millions)	Market Share (%)
Merrill Lynch Capital Markets	13,758.4	19.7
Goldman, Sachs	10,113.9	14.5
First Boston	9,934.4	14.2
Salomon Brothers	6,229.1	8.9
Shearson Lehman Hutton	5,269.0	7.5
Morgan Stanley	4,671.6	6.7
Drexel Burnham Lambert	3,573.0	5.1
Bear, Stearns	3,342.8	4.8
Prudential Bache Capital Funding	2,725.0	3.9
Kidder, Peabody	2,282.9	3.3
Union Bank of Switzerland	1,443.0	2.1
Dean Witter Capital Markets	1,062.0	1.5
Paine Webber	1,016.1	1.5
L.F. Rothschild	744.0	1.1
Citicorp	488.8	0.7
Subtotals	66,664.0	95.4
Industry Totals	69,888.3	100.0

Source: Matthew Winkler, "Merrill Remains No. 1 Underwriter as Securities Industry is Squeezed," *Wall Street Journal*, April 3, 1989, p. C1. Reprinted by permission of *Wall Street Journal*, Copyright © Dow Jones & Company, Inc. (1989). All rights reserved worldwide.

Goldman Sachs, and First Boston headed the list of the top 15 underwriters of U.S. debt and equity, where all but one are New York-based, managing 93 percent of the total market.

New York firms lead in other major segments of the domestic capital markets. In new issues of mortgage- and other asset-backed securities, nine of the top ten underwriters are New York-based institutions.[10] High-yield or "junk bond" financing is completely dominated by New York investment houses, as is the municipal bond market.[11]

Paradoxically, New York firms' leadership in financial markets exposes them to emerging competitive and structural trends. As the mortgage securities market slumped and the lowest volume of new equity issues in six years unfolded in 1988-89, fees from underwriting stocks and bonds shrank. Ten of the largest New York securities firms saw underwriting fees for the first quarter of 1989 fall by over 30 percent from the previous year's level.[12]

This narrowing of revenues and profits in traditional strongholds has pushed firms to concentrate on more lucrative, fee-generating activities. Merchant banking and corporate mergers and acquisitions (M&A) have been increasingly important and extremely profitable activities for several well-capitalized, highly skilled New York investment houses.

The corporate shake-out triggered by the recession of the early 1980s contributed to a vast expansion in demand for corporate restructuring and financial engineering, especially in the U.S. Here again, New York firms led in arranging some of the most spectacular corporate takeovers and leveraged buyouts of the boom years. Table 5.4 shows that nine of the top ten domestic M&A advisors in the first half of 1988 were New York-based firms.

The fees generated by M&A activities are largely based on the value of the deal, and the intense corporate restructuring activity of the 1980s made financial consulting a very profitable line of business.

The 50 largest deals (not counting the record-breaking RJRNabisco leveraged buyout for $25 billion) were worth a total of $111.8 billion in 1988, with dealmakers earning a record estimated $687 million in advisory fees beyond commissions on related financing.[13] As Table 5.5 indicates, some of the larger transactions can mean fees of as much as $25-30 million for individual advisors.

In addition to banking and nonbank private capital markets, New York also is the nation's leading primary and secondary market for U.S. government securities. With the ballooning of the federal budget deficit in the 1980s, and the high degree of liquidity and interest of U.S. government securities, demand has risen dramatically in recent years. In dealing government securities, New York financial firms have an historic special relationship with the Federal Reserve Bank, where the dealer market is comprised of institutions recognized by the Federal Reserve Bank of New York. Of the nation's 42 recognized primary dealers, 25 are New York-based firms.[14] Dealers maintain

TABLE 5.4 Top Ten Advisors in Domestic Mergers and Acquisitions

Rank	Company	Total Value of Deals ($millions)
1	Morgan Stanley	36,255
2	Shearson Lehman Hutton	32,972
3	Salomon Brothers	23,508
4	First Boston	20,122
5	Drexel Burnham Lambert	13,733
6	Schroder Group	11,294
7	Wasserstein Perella	10,430
8	Dillon, Read	10,360
9	Kidder Peabody	8,978
10	SG Warburg	5,935

Source: "Global Financing Guide," *Euromoney*, September 1988, p. 221. Reprinted by permission.

inventories of various issues for themselves but their activity increasingly has been in secondary market trading where volume has been fueled by foreign purchases, especially by Japanese investors.

The concentration of investors and the domestic capital markets in New York may be best reflected in the value and volume of trades on the area's stock exchanges, which are unparalleled anywhere else in the country and second only to Japan among international centers. On the New York Stock Exchange alone, a total market value of $1.4 trillion (over 44 billion shares) in U.S. corporate equities and options were traded in 1988, 80 percent of the total trades on all U.S. securities exchanges.[15] The American Stock Exchange (AMEX) ranks third among the nation's exchanges with close to 5 percent of domestic trading volume.[16] In recent years, AMEX has developed the capacity to trade in equity options, attracting a third of total trades in the domestic market and rising to a close second to the Chicago Board Options Exchange.[17] If accomplished, the proposed merger of the Philadelphia Stock Exchange with AMEX would make the New York exchange at least Chicago's equal in trading volume.

One of the most significant developments to emerge from the New

TABLE 5.5 Fees Generated by Corporate Restructuring: Top Five Deals of 1988

Companies	Value ($billions)	Financial Intermediaries	Fees ($millions)
1. Philip Morris acquires Kraft	12.9	Wasserstein Perella	12.0
		Goldman, Sachs	30.0
		Lazard Freres	3.5
2. Campeau acquires Federated Department Stores	6.52	First Boston	18.9
		Wasserstein Perella	10.0
		Goldman, Sachs	17.9
		Hellman & Friedman	16.2
		Shearson Lehman Hutton	19.8
3. BAT Industries acquires Farmers Group	5.1	Conning & Co.	4.1
		Goldman, Sachs	12.4
		Shearson Lehman Hutton	2.0
		First Boston	10.7
		Morgan Stanley	9.8
4. Eastman Kodak acquires Sterling Drugs	5.1	Shearson Lehman Hutton	8.0
		Morgan Stanley	28.5
5. Santa Fe Southern Pacific (special dividend)	4.7	Goldman, Sachs	12.5
		Salomon Brothers	12.5

Source: Ronald Henkoff, "Deals of the Year," *Fortune*, January 30, 1989, p. 163. Reprinted by permission.

York exchanges was the growth of over-the-counter (OTC) trading on the National Association of Securities Dealers Automated Quotation system (NASDAQ), a fully automated on-screen market. OTC shares are usually those of newer, smaller, and riskier companies who are less able to list on the larger domestic exchanges. From its inception in 1971, NASDAQ grew to be the third largest stock "exchange" in the world by 1985.[18]

New York's development of automated trading networks has demonstrated the ability to link traders around the nation or the world into a highly efficient and liquid market. Paradoxically, this has sown the seeds of competition for New York. Fully automated networks pose a serious challenge to floor brokers and exchange trading, threatening to move huge volumes of equities trading off the floor and making them, like foreign exchange and money market activities, less captive to New York.

New York's technological edge as a financial center is tied to the development and sophistication of technologies for payments settlement. The New York Clearing House Association, the first and largest bank clearing house in the U.S., operates the New York Automated Clearing House (NYACH) and the Clearing House Interbank Payments System (CHIPS), handling payments settlements for regional member institutions and international settlements, respectively. NYACH's volume of transactions has increased annually between 25 and 40 percent since its inception in 1975, with average monthly processing of over eight million items.[19] Since 1970, CHIPS has been the foremost means of settling U.S. dollar payments among international banks, handling as much as 90 percent of total transactions and an average daily volume of 146,000 items.[20] The continuous development of processing speed, security, and capacity in each system has contributed to New York's leadership.

Another of New York's historic competitive advantages has been its concentration of expertise in financial dealing. Many of the new instruments and products that helped to transform finance emerged from New York's financial institutions. New York remains the place where domestic and international financial firms send trainees to learn the most sophisticated skills and the latest techniques. For example, in 1987 Shearson Lehman Hutton entered into a $538 million investment agreement with the Nippon Life Insurance Company which included an elaborate program of intensive classroom training and on-the-job apprenticeships for Nippon Life employees in such areas as swaps and bond analysis.[21]

By buying into established Wall Street firms, others, particularly the large Japanese banks and securities houses, can develop U.S. contacts and learn the trade. Sumitomo Bank's 12.5 percent passive ownership share in Goldman, Sachs allows the U.S. house access to important Japanese customers and capital, while Sumitomo receives a share of profits and access to skills in securities dealing.[22] Similarly, in 1988, Nomura Securities paid $100 million for a 20 percent share in the takeover specialist firm of Wasserstein, Perella.[23] Nomura provides capital needed by Wasserstein, Perella for full merchant banking and gets in return important lessons in M&As involving U.S. corporations, a lesson which cannot be learned in Tokyo.

Some observers suggest that by exchanging skills for access to foreign markets and short-term profits, New York financial firms may be making a devil's bargain, subverting one of their most important competitive advantages.[24] However, regardless of training programs and buy-ins, diffusion of knowledge and techniques in financial services, as in any other industry, often is a matter of time. For New York as a location, this fact redoubles the pressure to help its firms remain on the cutting edge of financial innovations.

Another of New York's attributes which supports its role as a financial center is its business support services sector, perhaps the world's most sophisticated. Between 1979 and 1987, the growth of New York's business support services matched that of financial services, underscoring the significant linkage in their respective development. As Table 5.6 shows, combined employment growth in these two sectors contributed over two-thirds of the overall net increase in total jobs in New York. As financial services become more complex, support services including accounting, law, management consulting, computer software, advertising, and specialized printing have developed in parallel. In many of these fields, New York firms are recognized world-class leaders, often called upon to devise strategies for the most intricate financial transactions.[25]

The deepening expertise of New York's financial and business support services sectors will contribute to New York's competitiveness as a financial center for some time to come. But some observers believe that these advantages will erode. As market opportunities continue to draw New York firms into other regional domestic and international centers, the concentration of expertise will become more dispersed and less dependent on New York as a location for these activities. As expertise develops in the regional or foreign offices of Wall Street financial and business services firms, or in foreign firms, fewer deals will have to be arranged, approved, or tied to New York-based activities.

TABLE 5.6 Financial and Business Services Employment in New York City, 1979 and 1987 (in thousands)

		1979	1987
SIC 60	Commercial Banking	144.0	172.0
SIC 62	Securities	76.1	156.6
SIC 63	Insurance Carriers	75.7	65.1
SIC 64	Insurance Agents & Brokers	26.4	29.1
SIC 61, 66, 67	Savings & Loan & Other Financial Sectors	23.4	28.1
SIC 73	Business Services*	228.8	298.0
SIC 81	Legal Services	42.9	68.9
SIC 89	Accounting, Architecture, Engineering	57.0	63.7
Total Finance		345.6	450.9
Total Business, Legal & Accounting Services		328.7	430.6
Total Non-Agricultural Employment		3,278.8	3,584.9
Net Increase in Finance, 1979-87		105.3 (34.4%)	
Net Increase in Business & Other Services, 1979-87		101.9 (33.3%)	
Net Increase, All Sectors, 1979-87		306.1 (100.0%)	

*Including advertising, consulting, software, and others.

Source: U.S. Department of Labor, Bureau of Labor Statistics, New York Regional Office; in Thierry Noyelle, "New York's Competitiveness," in Thierry Noyelle (ed.), *New York's Financial Markets: The Challenges of Globalization* (Boulder, Colo.: Westview Press, 1989), p. 110. Reprinted by permission.

Indeed, the very concentration of sophisticated activities in New York may be having the paradoxical effect of encouraging dispersion. As employment is skewed more and more to higher-skill levels inadvanced services, there is progressively less need for lower skill workers. And, as general skill levels in financial services are driven upward with new technologies in clerical and data processing operations, the problem of finding sufficient numbers of adequately trained clerical workers will become a major barrier to growth. This pattern of development could have serious long-term consequences for the local and regional economy and may encourage the migration of back office and data processing operations out of New York.

With all its advantages of scale, depth, and concentration of markets and market players, New York will certainly remain a key financial center in the more integrated network of domestic and international centers. Many of these activities are high-cost and highly profitable. Lower-profit or support activities will be harder to maintain in New York.

In addition, other factors are diminishing New York's historic influence in financial services. Shifting regional growth patterns within the U.S. economy and the rise of regional financial centers in Los Angeles, Atlanta, Charlotte, Dallas, Pittsburgh, and Boston, have dispersed activities. Meanwhile, rising costs and growing competitive pressures on firms to rationalize, restructure, and sometimes downsize operations often requires relocation of front and back offices. The application of advanced telecommunications and computing technologies enables markets to be dispersed while requiring the upgrading and generalization of skills. And the development of whole new markets altogether outside of New York, such as the risk management instruments arising from the Chicago futures pits or the expansion of Japanese investment on the West Coast, will further encourage dispersion.

New York and Its Rivals: Key Competitive Dimensions

The outlook for U.S. financial centers is premised on several factors: historical strength, the dynamism of firms headquartered there, and their relative mix of cost advantage, labor force adequacy, technology, and regulatory posture. New York, in part because of its historic concentrations of firms, capital, and expertise, will continue to be a major U.S. center. The size and importance of institutions like the New York Stock Exchange, the privileged position of the New York District Bank within the Federal Reserve system, and the traditional and present leadership of New York's financial institutions and markets all indicate that for the foreseeable future, New York will remain home to much of the nation's financial services activity and a primary center in international financial markets.

But New York's predominance will not go unchallenged, as indicated by recent dynamic growth of financial services activity and employment in numerous other U.S. cities and states. Table 5.7 shows the growth of the Finance, Insurance, and Real Estate (FIRE) sector employment, which was especially strong between 1983 and 1988 in emerging regional centers. Cities like Chicago, Los Angeles, Charlotte, Dallas, and Boston were attracting front office expansions and relocations, while areas like Wilmington, Delaware and Jersey City, New Jersey, attracted more back office activity.

By comparison, New York showed relatively modest growth over the boom years. Yet, with the exception of San Francisco, in all of these cities the FIRE sector grew at a greater rate than overall employment. Employment in the financial services sector now represents a significant portion of total nonfarm employment in these locations. (See Table 5.8.) Over 15 percent of New York's workforce is employed directly in the FIRE sector, with substantial proportions found in San Francisco, Dallas, Boston, and other regional locations. Given this significance of the FIRE sector in the context of overall economic activity, the new competitive environment and changes which influence the location decisions of financial firms have a direct and profound effect on the future growth of these centers.

Before profiling major rivals to New York for financial services activity and employment, it is useful to compare various domestic competitor locations on key competitive dimensions, especially those relating to costs. Many cost and non-cost attributes contribute advantages to locations for financial services employment and activity. These various attributes undergird a location's competitive position. While lower costs contribute greatly to the success of New Jersey, Delaware, and other areas in competing for back offices, non-cost dimensions are of equal or greater importance in determining attractiveness for front office activity.

A comparison of various domestic locations demonstrates a wide range of variation in both cost and non-cost dimensions of competitiveness. For example, while New York rates favorably on

TABLE 5.7 Growth of FIRE Sector Employment in Selected U.S. Financial Centers,* 1983-1988

	FIRE Sector Growth (%)	Overall Growth(%)
Wilmington	81.8	20.8
Jersey City	61.4	15.8
Charlotte, N.C.	44.7	26.2
Atlanta	33.5	29.3
Boston	31.8	14.8
Dallas	25.1	17.7
Los Angeles	20.0	15.5
Chicago	19.3	16.6
New York City	10.1	7.4
Pittsburgh	8.7	4.5
San Francisco	-0.1	8.1

* Metropolitan areas, except New York City.

Source: *Employment and Earnings*, U.S. Department of Labor, Bureau of Labor Statistics, May issues, 1984 to 1989.

TABLE 5.8 FIRE Sector Employment as a Percent of Total Employment in Selected U.S. Financial Centers, Annual Average 1988

New York City	15.1%
San Francisco	11.8
Dallas	9.6
Wilmington	9.2
Boston	8.8
Chicago	8.7
Atlanta	7.3
Los Angeles/Long Beach	7.0
Charlotte	6.3
Pittsburgh	6.0
Jersey City	5.3

Source: *Employment and Earnings*, U.S. Department of Labor, Bureau of Labor Statistics, May 1989.

several non-cost dimensions, it remains a high-cost location relative to other financial centers. But the attractiveness of any location for a particular financial firm depends upon both the location's qualities and that firm's ranking of locational criteria.

Cushman and Wakefield's Business America Real Estate Monitor, an annual survey of chief executive officers from all sectors of U.S. industry, shows how business leaders compare major U.S. cities along the criteria that these leaders deem most important for location decisions. These criteria include: access to domestic markets and clients; access to international markets; cost and availability of labor; the quality of life; cost and availability of office space; tax and regulatory business climate; and economic development packages offered by localities.[26]

Table 5.9 compares New York and seven other domestic financial centers, indicating the percent of respondents rating each location excellent along the criteria, and each location's ranking in the 31-city survey. Whereas the major financial centers of New York, Los Angeles, and Chicago rank favorably on some criteria but unfavorably on others, the smaller regional centers of Atlanta and Dallas/Ft. Worth rate consistently higher in the rankings.

The cost dimension of competitiveness where New York compares most poorly with other domestic locations is office rents. Table 5.10 presents average office rents for the second quarter of 1989 in several domestic financial centers. With average rents in midtown and downtown Manhattan of $39.90 and $34.89 per square foot, respectively, New York is rivalled only by Boston, where the average is $39.15 per square foot. Los Angeles, the next most expensive city among financial services competitor locations, has an average rent of $28.46, between 20 and 30 percent less than New York's. Several regional financial centers — Charlotte, Wilmington, Atlanta, Dallas, and Pittsburgh — have rents that are much less than the central business districts of New York and Boston, ranging from one-third to over one-half less.

Electricity costs to commercial users are another important variable for financial services, especially in operations that use substantial power for computers. Table 5.11 shows utility rates for commercial users. New York's rate, 10.5 cents per kilowatt-hour, is approximately one-third higher than Boston's, the next most expensive city listed,

TABLE 5.9 Locations Rated "Excellent" for Office Facilities[1]

Criterion[2]	Atl.	Bos.	Chi.	Dls./F.W.	L.A.	N.Y.	Pitts.	S.F.
Domestic Markets	39 (2)	26 (6)	43 (1)	27 (5)	35 (4)	38 (3)	9 (28)	23 (8)
International Markets	16 (9)	20 (7)	22 (6)	10 (14)	39 (2)	53 (1)	3 (20)	32 (3)
Labor	22 (2)	8 (22)	11 (13)	19 (3)	9 (18)	9 (19)	7 (23)	5 (29)
Quality of Life	37 (2)	18 (12)	13 (17)	16 (13)	9 (9)	7 (26)	9 (22)	20 (9)
Office Space	16 (5)	1 (31)	7 (16)	36 (2)	2 (30)	6 (23)	6 (20)	3 (28)
Taxes and Regulations	17 (1)	3 (26)	4 (22)	10 (5)	5 (17)	2 (30)	8 (7)	5 (18)
Incentives	7 (3)	1 (26)	2 (22)	8 (2)	[3] (30)	1 (28)	2 (20)	2 (23)

[1] Numbers on top line indicate the percent of respondents rating city "excellent." Numbers in parentheses indicate the city's ranking for that criterion among the 31 cities surveyed.

[2] For reasons of space, criteria listed have been shortened from the following: Access to Domestic Markets and Clients; Access to International Markets and Clients; Cost and Availability of Labor; Quality of Life for Employees; Cost and Availability of Office Space; State and Local Government Tax and Regulatory Business Climate; and Economic Development Packages Offered.

[3] Less than 0.5 percent.

Source: "Best Business Cities," *Business America Real Estate Monitor*, Study No. 881006, Cushman and Wakefield, Inc., New York, May-June 1988, pp. 21-27. Reprinted by permission.

and almost two-thirds higher than Chicago's. Northeast New Jersey's rate is also about 25 percent lower than that of New York, making New Jersey a lower-cost option for the back offices, data processing center and other operations of firms that need not be located with company headquarters.

TABLE 5.10 Average Office Rents in Domestic Locations, 1989[1]

New York, Midtown	$39.90
Boston	39.15
New York, Downtown	34.89
Los Angeles	28.46
Chicago	28.23
San Francisco	24.55
Dallas	23.70
Atlanta	21.30
Pittsburgh	20.86
Northern New Jersey[2]	20.05
Wilmington[3]	19.50
Charlotte, N.C.	18.60

[1] Office rents are per square foot of "Class A" space in central business districts, second quarter of 1989, except where noted.

[2] Northern New Jersey figure includes both "Class A" and "Class B" space in non-central business district areas.

[3] Wilmington figure is for New Castle County, Delaware.

Source: Cushman and Wakefield, Inc., Market Research Department, New York; and Cushman and Wakefield of Pennsylvania, Inc., Philadelphia. Reprinted by permission.

TABLE 5.11 Electricity Costs to Commercial Users, Without Incentives

New York (metro area)	10.50 cents/kwh
Boston	7.88
Northern New Jersey	7.84
San Francisco	7.61
Atlanta	7.24
Chicago	7.07
Los Angeles	7.05
Pittsburgh	6.67
Wilmington	6.45
Dallas	5.35

Source: "Ranking of Electricity Prices to Commercial Users," *Energy User News*, April 18, 1988, p. 6.

Surprisingly, labor costs are one area where centers are more equal. Table 5.12 compares the relative pay levels in 1987 for office

TABLE 5.12 Wage Indices[1] for Office Workers in Nonmanufacturing Industries, 1987

	Office Clerical	Electronic Data Processing
New York City/ Northeast N.J.	107	111
San Francisco	120[2]	119
Los Angeles/Long Beach	117	114
Newark	103	105
Chicago	102	103
Atlanta	101	105
Boston	101	102
Dallas/Fort Worth	101	98
Pittsburgh	98	96
Charlotte	95	93
Wilmington	92	99

[1] Average pay levels for each occupational group in 326 metropolitan areas equals 100.

[2] San Francisco office clerical pay level for all industries.

Source: "Wage Differences Among Metropolitan Areas, 1987," U.S. Department of Labor, Bureau of Labor Statistics, July 1988.

clerical and electronic data processing personnel in non-manufacturing industries in various cities. While New York wages for office clerical and electronic data processing are 107 percent and 111 percent, respectively, of the national average, they are lower than those in both Los Angeles and San Francisco. Pay levels for clerical and data processing personnel in Chicago, Atlanta, and Boston also are above the national average, and within 5.6 percent to 8.9 percent of New York's. Personnel in the New York suburbs of Nassau and Suffolk Counties and in Newark, New Jersey, make from 3.7 percent to 7.2 percent less than New York clerical and data processing workers, also above the national average. Pay levels in the Dallas/Ft. Worth, Charlotte, Pittsburgh, and Wilmington areas are below the national average. Even so, the greatest differences between any of the cities reported here are Wilmington's wages for clerical help, which are 14 percent less than New York's, and Charlotte's wages for electronic data processing, which are 16.2 percent lower than New York's.[27]

But although the money wages and salaries paid to employees in some financial centers are not widely out of line with each other, the real purchasing power of those wages may not be as great as elsewhere because of a higher cost of living. Table 5.13 shows the percentage growth in recent years of the Bureau of Labor Statistics' Consumer Price Index (CPI) across various metropolitan areas. From 1982 to 1988, the increase in the CPI was 29.8 percent in the New York area (which includes northeastern New Jersey), a percentage increase greater than all other areas except Boston. The inflation rate in New York was over 40 percent greater than the comparable change in Dallas/Ft. Worth and almost 17 percent greater than that of the Los Angeles area.

In May 1988, Runzheimer also surveyed the average cost of a 2,100-square-foot suburban house in various metropolitan locations around the country. The average cost of such a house was well over $300,000 in the New York City suburbs of Westchester County and Fairfield County, Connecticut, and over $250,000 in the Long Island and northern New Jersey suburbs. Other than in New York's suburbs, only in Boston was the cost of this model house over $250,000. In comparison, the model house cost under $250,000 in Los Angeles and under $175,000 in Wilmington. Runzheimer also reported that the average price of the house in the New York suburbs climbed over 107 percent between 1980 and 1987, compared to only a 53 percent increase in Atlanta. [28]

A more recent relative cost measure, Runzheimer's multi-city analysis of living costs for a homeowning family of four with a $55,000 annual income, reflects recent economic trends in different regions of the country. Table 5.14 indicates that while New York is over 28 percent more costly than the median of 100 communities surveyed, both San Francisco and Los Angeles are even more expensive. In comparison, San Francisco is nearly 40 percent above the national median. With the exception of Dallas, other financial centers also are more costly than the national average, but none except Boston and San Francisco approach New York in the cost of living.

As an indirect cost of doing business, a high cost of living puts financial centers at a competitive disadvantage because of the pressure on wages that firms must pay to attract and hold qualified personnel.

TABLE 5.13 Percent Change in Consumer Price Index for All Urban Consumers, Selected Locations, 1982-1988

New York City/Northeast N.J.	29.8
Boston	30.0
Los Angeles/Long Beach	25.5
Atlanta	25.4
Chicago	23.7
San Francisco	23.5
Pittsburgh	21.7
Dallas/Ft. Worth	20.9
All Cities Average	22.6

Source: *CPI Detailed Report*, U.S. Department of Labor, Bureau of Labor Statistics, January issues, 1983 to 1989.

TABLE 5.14 Cost of Living Indices, Selected Locations*

San Francisco	139.4
Los Angeles	128.7
New York	128.1
Boston	121.4
Chicago	107.8
Atlanta	106.8
Pittsburgh	101.5
Dallas	95.2

* The cost-of-living analysis conducted by Runzheimer International, a management consulting firm, compares transportation, tax, goods and services, and housing costs for a home-owning family of four with an annual income of $55,000. The median of living costs in 100 representative U.S. cities is given a value of 100.

Source: Runzheimer International, Rochester, Wis. Reprinted by permission.

Firms in other locations can offer lower wages and salaries that still yield greater purchasing power to their employees. This results in both a cost advantage and perhaps an advantage in attracting relatively more skilled labor with lower turnover rates.

Taxation is another important cost dimension of competitiveness that varies by location. High personal income and general sales taxes raise the cost of living in a location, eroding real purchasing power and indirectly increasing labor costs. A high corporate income tax burden more directly adds to the cost of doing business in a location.

Table 5.15 summarizes personal income, general sales and corporate income tax rates for financial institutions along with other information for selected states.[29] Local taxes also must be considered in assessing tax burdens. This is especially important when analyzing the relative competitiveness of New York City. Despite comparable tax rates between New York and its neighboring states, the combined burden of State and local income and sales taxes on firms located in New York City is a disincentive. State and local general sales taxes amount to 8.25 percent in New York City, one of the highest rates in the country.[30] The New York City commercial rent tax of 6 percent is perhaps the most noted example of a burdensome local tax.

Finally, locations can be compared in terms of telecommunications attributes. Figure 4.1 presented the findings of New York Telephone's analysis of the telecommunications infrastructure of New York City and seven other domestic and international competitor locations. Rating each area's infrastructure along five different dimensions, the analysis found New York's to be slightly less favorable on balance than New Jersey and Chicago, and on a par with that of Los Angeles. New York also compares less favorably to its foreign financial center rivals, with the possible exception of London.

According to New York Telephone, the use of modern technology in telecommunications and the responsiveness of local phone companies to the needs of large business customers is relatively higher in New York. But New York compares unfavorably to other domestic centers in terms of the governmental and regulatory climate that influences the quality and levels of investment in telecommunications, and in terms of cost. In turn, all the U.S. centers rate less favorably than foreign centers on levels of investments being made to upgrade the existing telecommunications structure. Measured by ratios such as investment dollars per access line or investment dollars as a percent of sales, investment levels provide an indication of future technological capacity.

TABLE 5.15 State Tax Rates, Selected Locations

(a) Financial Institution Income Taxes

Calif.	For financial institutions, the income tax rate on net income is the corporate tax rate of 9.6% plus the ratio of personal property taxes and business license taxes paid by corporate taxpayers to the sum of net income, personal property taxes and business license taxes. Minimum tax: $300.
Del.	For banks and trust companies, the tax rate is 8.7% on the first $20,000,000 net earnings; 6.7% on the next $5,000,000; 4.7% on the next $5,000,000; and 2.7% on net earnings over $30,000,000.
Ill.	Tax rate for corporations and financial institutions is 8% of federal taxable income, with adjustments, plus $10. The minimum tax is $20.
N.J.	The tax rate is 9% of allocated net income. A 7-1/4% direct net income tax is imposed on the entire net income of corporations not subject to the business (income) tax. For savings banks, savings and loan, and building and loan associations, the tax rate is 3% of federal taxable income with adjustments.
N.Y.	Banks and financial institutions are taxed the greater of (a) 9% of federal taxable income with adjustments, or (b) 3% of alternative net income, or (c) 0.1 mill per dollar of taxable assets or (d) $250. Other rates may apply depending on net worth ratio and if 33% or more of total assets are comprised of mortgages.

(b) Personal Income Taxes

	Lowest Bracket		Highest Bracket		Personal Exemptions		
	Rate %	Up to Net Income of	Rate %	Net Income Over	Married	Single	Dependent
Calif.	1	$3,818	9.3	$25,052	$104	$52	$52
Del.	0	2,000	7.7	40,000	2,000	1,000	1,000
Ill.	2.5	All			2,000	1,000	1,000
N.J.	2	20,000	3.5	50,000	2,000	1,000	1,000
N.Y.*	3	6,000	8.375	34,000	0	0	1,000

*Rates for New York are for married persons filing joint returns.

(c) General Sales Tax Rates

Calif.	4.75%
Del.	None
Ill.	5%
N.J.	6%
N.Y.	4%

Sources: CCH Tax Law Editors, *State Tax Handbook* (Chicago: Commerce Clearing House, 1988), pp. 670-681; and The Tax Foundation, *Facts and Figures on Government Finance* (Baltimore: Johns Hopkins University Press, 1988), Tables E23, E27, and E29.

Domestic Competition for Front Offices

Across the United States, competitors for financial services vary widely in their attributes and attractions, and they draw a variety of financial services activities for different reasons. For example, wholesale-oriented firms are attracted to areas with an agglomeration of institutional investors and borrowers. But retail-oriented firms will be attracted to areas with a healthy economy and a growing, yet underserved, population. Location choices are different for firms seeking to invest globally and serve international customers than for firms whose activities are limited to domestic or regional spheres. Finally, the strategic considerations of firms in locating front offices and complex strategic activities are in general less sensitive to costs than those considerations in locating back offices.

In the last several years, domestic competitors for wholesale and international financial services across the United States have challenged New York's historic leadership. Economic centers of gravity have increasingly shifted from the Atlantic to the Pacific rim, and from large corporations to the small- and middle-corporate sectors. New products and technologies have loosened the bonds tying markets to particular locations. In several ways, advantages are shifting away from New York to other locations elsewhere.

Competition is growing for both front and back office activities, but among different locations. The growth of Los Angeles and Chicago as major domestic contenders for front office international and wholesale financial services will be profiled here, while financial center competition for the location of back office activities will be profiled in the following chapter. In general, competition for these activities responds to different competitive pressures and locational advantages.

Of all the domestic locations competing with New York for front office activities, Los Angeles and Chicago pose the greatest challenge. Some of the reasons are obvious. Demographically, Los Angeles and Chicago are principal population centers, ranking second and third respectively next to New York, a fact which attracts regional retail financial services. They also are the key centers of their regional economies with significant concentrations of business and investment activity. As such, they offer a strong attraction to wholesale banking and securities activities.

But their more important challenge to New York lies in their growing strength in key financial markets and activities, and the extent to which they have become integral links in domestic and international finance. The rise of Los Angeles and Chicago and their attendant advantages illustrates the potential for greater dispersion of front office activity which had for so long been concentrated in New York and the eastern United States. This dispersion has been driven by macroeconomic shifts and major new product developments. The challenge New York faces is one of gaining position and expanding its own importance in these new markets.

Los Angeles: California and the Rise of the Pacific Rim

In recent years, a number of economic and demographic factors have combined to propel the West Coast, and Southern California in particular, to the forefront in terms of growth and economic potential. Southern California's privileged location on the Pacific Rim, its own economic health and diversity, and its strong population growth all contribute to attractiveness for financial services activities and the expansion and relocation of financial firms. Los Angeles has now emerged as the region's undisputed economic and financial center, eclipsing San Francisco in its traditional regional leadership position and challenging New York's preeminence as a domestic and international center.

Los Angeles enjoys a natural locational advantage in its key position on the Pacific Rim. The spectacular growth of the East Asian economies over the past 15 years, coupled with the weakened dollar, has led to a vast expansion of East-West trade, industrial growth, and financial activity concentrated in the Los Angeles area. U.S. trade with the countries of the Pacific Basin is now one-third greater than U.S. trans-Atlantic trade, and fully 60 percent of it, valued at over $88 billion, passes through the Los Angeles customs district.[31] The port of Los Angeles/Long Beach accounts for over half of the tonnage handled by all West Coast ports,[32] and is the nation's largest and fastest growing in value terms. Since 1980, total trade handled in Los Angeles rose 150 percent, compared to second-place New York, which rose by only 37 percent.[33]

Export-oriented activity has been a major component of southern California's boom, with foreign trade accounting for one in ten jobs in the Los Angeles area.[34] Trade has also stimulated significant flows of foreign direct investment. Eight of the nine Japanese auto makers have their U.S. headquarters in the Los Angeles area while 1,500 other Japanese commercial and manufacturing companies have located there.[35] Consequently, the growth of trade-related investment activity has been a powerful impetus to financial services firms.

Another factor in Los Angeles' growth as a leading financial center is the strength and diversity of regional economic growth. Greater Los Angeles has a gross regional product of $228 billion, making it the second largest metropolitan economy in the country after New York.[36] As compared to the gross national product of the world's economies, the Los Angeles region is the 11th largest. Unlike New York, whose employment growth has become increasingly dependent upon its financial and business services, or Boston on its high-tech industries, or Northern California on Silicon Valley, Los Angeles boasts a highly diversified economic base, including agriculture, aerospace, biotechnology, films and entertainment, apparel, high-tech electronics, and finance, insurance, and real estate. This diversity has enabled the Los Angeles area to withstand the more damaging effects of cyclical downturns.

Beyond diversity, however, what is most striking about Los Angeles' economic growth is that it has occurred mainly among small- and middle-sized businesses. The overall business formation rate for Los Angeles County between 1984 and 1988 was one-fifth higher than that of New York, while small business birth rates for Los Angeles and New York were 3.5 and 2.6 per one thousand in population respectively.[37] Eighteen of the Fortune 500 companies are headquartered in the Los Angeles area, while 95 percent of its firms have fewer than 50 workers.[38] By contrast, New York's economic base has seen a steady erosion in its small- and middle-sized corporate sector since the late 1970's. Between 1978 and 1986, small businesses accounted for only 20 percent of new private sector jobs in New York, as compared to the nationwide rate of over 65 percent.[39]

This orientation toward high-growth small- and middle-sized business has fostered the image of Southern California as a hotbed for the small entrepreneur, and helped trigger an influx of venture capital into the area. With roughly 30 venture capital firms present, Orange and Los Angeles counties now account for over 7 percent of the nation's pool of venture capital, making it the largest in the country next to New York, [40] but perhaps the fastest growing.

The region's population growth also contributes to an expanding potential retail financial services market. Between 1980 and 1986, population grew in Los Angeles County by almost 11 percent, with a projected growth rate to 2010 at a striking 20.6 percent.[41] By comparison, New York City's population growth rate between 1980 and 1986 was 2.4 percent with a projected growth of only 2.6 percent.[42] By 1986, 60 percent of California's $100 billion in consumer deposits were located in Southern California.[43] This growth and market expansion was instrumental in shifting the financial center of gravity away from San Francisco to Los Angeles in recent years, and will continue to support financial services business for the foreseeable future.

Los Angeles' growing regional and international importance as a financial center is reflected in its growing strength and number of domestic and foreign financial institutions. Particularly since the end of the last recession in 1982, Los Angeles has experienced a rapid rise to the position of "second city" among U.S. financial centers, and is now a major second-tier location for international finance. Despite evidence of some recent slowing in the growth of the regional economy, Los Angeles could still continue to ride the tide into what some observers have called the "Pacific Century," attracting significant financial services activity for some time to come.

Los Angeles is the headquarters location of two of the nation's top ten bank holding companies, measured by asset size. Security Pacific and First Interstate are ranked fifth and eighth largest respectively.[44] Even though they are San Francisco-based, two others in the top ten,

BankAmerica and Wells Fargo, have established a major presence in Los Angeles.

With the exception of Security Pacific, the large commercial banks of these holding companies were once major players in Third World lending. In recent years, however, they have sharply reduced their presence in international markets and concentrated on building strong superregional wholesale and retail networks.

In fact, it was the near collapse of Bank of America in the early to mid-1980's that gave Security Pacific, First Interstate, and Wells Fargo unprecedented opportunities to expand. Once the nation's largest and most aggressive bank through the 1960s and 1970s, Bank of America had over-extended its reach both domestically and internationally and accumulated a massive portfolio of non-performing assets, including Third World, energy, agricultural, real estate, and other loans. Meanwhile, its competitors took up the market shares that Bank of America was forced to shed. Bank of America's problems helped shift California's financial focus to Los Angeles.

Wells Fargo was among the first of the large California banks to close most of its foreign offices, sell off non-performing loans, and focus on becoming a healthy superregional bank with strong footholds in middle and retail markets. Currently, at least 75 percent of Wells Fargo's loans are made to borrowers within the state, and acquisitions allowed Wells Fargo to expand its retail network and cut its operating costs, enabling it to emerge as the state's lowest-cost producer of retail financial services.[45]

By pursuing a similar reorganization, First Interstate now has half of its business in retail and middle-market banking.[46] It is a major issuer of credit cards, ranking eighth in the nation in credit card loans outstanding. In addition, it has pursued an aggressive strategy to penetrate consumer lending markets through the acquisition of smaller banks and thrifts elsewhere in California and in neighboring states like Arizona, Washington, Colorado, Nevada, Utah, and Idaho.[47]

In contrast, Security Pacific has pursued a vigorous expansion of both domestic retail services and wholesale activities at home and in international capital markets. By acquiring banks and thrifts all along the West Coast and throughout the Southwest as well as in California,

Security Pacific is building and consolidating a strong regional retail services network. Building on the region's growing internationalization, Security Pacific also has become a major player in global capital markets, as evidenced by its 1986 acquisition of Hoare Govett, a London-based brokerage, to better participate in the Euromarkets. By 1988, Security Pacific was rated the best house overall in the swap market by over 100 of the largest users of swaps internationally,[48] ranking with Citicorp and Bankers Trust. In internationally syndicated loans, Security Pacific ranked 19th among the top 50 arrangers in 1988, up from 25th the year before.[49]

Like Citicorp in New York, Security Pacific is committed to the vision of providing all products to all customers. And the prospect of nationwide banking in 1991 is pressing major Los Angeles banks to build their regional strengths in anticipation of full competition from money center banks. Citicorp and Chase Manhattan already are in Los Angeles, providing limited services and using their West Coast locations to serve Asian clients, to compete with California banks, and to wait for the barriers to fall.

Los Angeles is also the headquarters of several of the largest thrifts in the U.S., and of three of the nation's top 50 diversified financial companies.[50] Four of the top 50 life insurers also are located in Los Angeles.[51]

Because of the growing internationalization of its economy, its strategic location, and the size of its market, Los Angeles has a large and growing foreign bank presence. Although Los Angeles ranks a distant second to New York in the total number of foreign bank offices, these offices expanded by 22 percent between 1981 and 1988, as was shown in Table 5.2. Every other U.S. location with a major foreign bank presence, including New York, showed a declining rate of growth between 1985 and 1988. Of the total offices of foreign banks in the U.S., Los Angeles presently has 12 percent, compared to New York's share of 44 percent.

Table 5.2 also indicated that in June 1988, Los Angeles' foreign bank offices held $77.2 billion in U.S. assets, almost 50 percent higher than in 1985. Of these assets, $24.3 billion were commercial and industrial (C&I) loans. Between 1985 and 1988, the C&I loan portfolios of foreign banks in Los Angeles rose by 84 percent, in large part reflecting the purchase of these assets from other U.S. banks that originated them.

Most of the foreign bank activity in the Los Angeles area is Japanese. Japanese banks now hold roughly 15 percent of California bank deposits.[52] Their share of the California loan market has grown considerably over the past decade, rising from 2 to 22 percent largely through acquisition.[53]

One of the largest Japanese investments in the U.S. financial industry was the 1988 purchase by a Bank of Tokyo subsidiary of California's fifth largest bank, Los Angeles-based Union Bank, previously owned by Britain's Standard Chartered. This acquisition added another $9.1 billion of assets to Bank of Tokyo's existing $1.3 billion pool, and made them the fourth largest in the state, just behind First Interstate.[54] In the past five years, Barclays and Midland Banks also have moved out of California, selling out to either the Japanese or to the four large California banks. Mitsubishi Bank, Sanwa Bank, and Sumitomo Bank all have moved in to fill the vacuum and now dominate middle-tier banking in the state.[55]

However, despite their growing presence in most retail markets, most foreign bank business in Los Angeles is trade- and manufacture-related finance, servicing corporate clients in the U.S. and international markets. Some observers feel that Japanese banks in Los Angeles have not provided either the benefits of scale economies or special expertise to their customers and currently pose no serious threat to the "big four" Los Angeles banks.[56]

But foreign bank inroads into the Los Angeles markets will undoubtedly intensify the competition to come in 1991, when barriers to nationwide banking are removed. Money center banks eager to offer full services in Los Angeles will face formidable superregionals and foreign banks as competitors. Penetrating these markets will not be easy or cheap. Superregional banks like Security Pacific and First Interstate have pursued cost-cutting strategies to improve profitability and market capitalization, making them resistant to acquisition attempts. This may slow the pace of westward migration by the New York banks despite the competitive necessity to establish and maintain a presence in such a strategic location.

Until recently, financial activity in the Los Angeles area was mainly the province of the region's commercial banks. If Los Angeles corporations and large investors needed the services of investment bankers, they usually went east to Wall Street. But, especially since the early 1980's, many New York-based securities and investment houses have gone west to enter the growing markets there.

Largely shut out of the Silicon Valley boom of the 1970s that was dominated by the San Francisco-based regional securities firms, New York investment houses migrated in full force to Los Angeles to tap its regional development and its strategic location. Merrill Lynch and First Boston were drawn by the growing computer industry, the expanding manufacturing base, and mortgage and real estate financing. The possibilities of extending their client base and trading day on the West Coast was a powerful incentive to locate there.[57]

Morgan Stanley, while drawn to the same possibilities, also saw tax-exempt financing as a major market in Southern California. In 1985, California issued over 10 percent of the nation's tax-exempt securities, more than $20 billion, of which Los Angeles issued roughly a third.[58] Drexel Burnham's Michael Milken developed a highly successful corporate finance unit that dominated the junk bond market in Beverly Hills. Joining these firms are E.F. Hutton, Paine Webber, and Bear, Stearns. The concentration of these regional headquarters of the major New York-based securities firms has earned Los Angeles the title of "Wall Street West."

A few large regional securities firms in Los Angeles face stiff competition from the New York houses who, somewhat uncharacteristically, have sought out business from the middle-sized corporate sector in the region. Los Angeles-based regionals like Jeffries and Company, Bateman Eichler, and Montgomery Securities have seen their traditional markets challenged by New York firms who have been more willing to handle smaller issues while building up large corporate and institutional accounts.[59]

Most of the Los Angeles-based regionals like Morgan Olmstead, Wredbush Securities, and Great Western Financial have a heavy retail market orientation. Here, despite their size, the large national full-line firms like Merrill Lynch, Paine Webber, and E.F. Hutton do not have a decisive advantage over the regionals. As the Securities Industry Association has observed, the profitability of regional securities firms, while poor in recent years, has surpassed that of the national full-line firms.[60] Despite the attractions of the large retail market in the Los Angeles area, the slowed activity in retail securities markets since the October 1987 market crash has generally forced many Wall Street firms to rationalize costs and slow future expansion plans.

In terms of efficiency and strategic importance, the Pacific Stock Exchange (PSE), with trading floors located in both Los Angeles and San Francisco, is one of the most successful and significant regional exchanges in the nation.[61] The PSE is the only exchange located west of the Mississippi River, and thus enjoys an advantage in its time-zone location over other domestic and international exchanges.

In fact, in 1985 the prospect of extending trading hours and linking the East and West Coasts with the London and Tokyo markets was so attractive that the New York Stock Exchange (NYSE) explored a possible merger with the PSE. But the idea of passing unfilled orders on to PSE traders and specialists at the end of the trading day in New York did not appeal to New York market makers.[62]

Trading volume on the PSE remains small relative to volume on the New York exchange: the Pacific handles roughly 9 percent of the total volume of NYSE-listed stocks compared to New York's share of over 80 percent.[63] But since 1985, the PSE has invited a number of large New York brokerages like Merrill Lynch, Paine Webber, and Donaldson, Lufkin & Jenrette to become specialists. These New York houses now send considerably more orders to the West Coast than before.[64]

There are two reasons for the PSE's growing importance as a major link in a national market: leadership in the application of advanced technology to order routing, execution, and pricing, and a solid reputation as a highly liquid and efficient market for smaller-lot trades. In 1969, the Exchange introduced the country's first automated order execution system, which evolved a decade later into SCOREX (Securities Communications Order Routing and Execution).[65] SCOREX executes orders of up to 1,099 shares in 15 seconds or less for roughly 1,100 securities nationally. By comparison, the NYSE will not guarantee trades in less than three minutes. This speed and efficiency contributes to a very active market, and automatic trades now represent nearly 65 percent of all orders on the PSE.[66]

In addition, the PSE is a strong participant in the Intermarket Trading System (ITS) that links all seven domestic exchanges and the National Association of Securities Dealers to create one continuous auction market. This network allows brokers and dealers complete interaction in all eight markets and practically guarantees the best available price nationally within 45 seconds.[67] The PSE has averaged roughly 20 percent of ITS trading each year since 1979.[68]

As the primary and secondary securities markets continue to evolve, the West Coast, and Los Angeles in particular, is becoming highly significant in linking domestic and international markets. The competitive challenge to historic centers like New York will be to maintain its key position relative to the growing importance of regional centers. This becomes even more important as the need to participate in a continuous trading market deepens. For now, Los Angeles, through its position on the Pacific Rim and through the extension of its ties to Asian markets, holds a distinct advantage over New York.

In the past few years, regional economic growth in the Los Angeles area has begun to slow, in part due to cuts in military spending and its effects on related industries, as well as to the strains which rapid growth has placed on land use, building costs, infrastructure, and pollution control.[69] These factors and the region's efforts to control its growth may lead to a slowing in the pace with which others seek to migrate there. Despite this, however, Los Angeles will continue to be a frontier for both retail and wholesale financial services activities, attracting the front office expansions and relocations of firms from other domestic and international centers.

Chicago: Developing Unique Markets

Chicago's emergence as a prominent domestic and international financial center has less to do with regional economic growth, or the strength of its regional financial firms, or its strategic location than with its origination and dominance of key financial markets. Despite some resurgence of industrial production in the nation's "rust belt," triggered in part by the weakened dollar, Chicago's importance as a financial center is due primarily to the spectacular growth of its financial futures and options markets.

Since the early 1970s, and especially since 1982, the Chicago exchanges have consistently led in the development of new futures and options products, which have become indispensable tools in risk management strategies and as sources of arbitrage profits used by domestic and global investors. As these products grow in importance, and as the markets for futures and options become further integrated with global and domestic equities, government securities, and currency markets, Chicago may continue to draw these activities. However, competition in these markets is strong and growing. Recent regulatory changes since the October 1987 crash, along with product innovations and technological advances, may erode Chicago's dominance in these activities, and shift more business to New York and other domestic and international centers.

Chicago's emergence as a key financial center is a relatively recent phenomenon. For most of this century, Chicago's growth was fueled by an economy highly geared to supporting heavy industry and agriculture. The city's central geographic location in the country's manufacturing and agricultural heartland led many firms to establish their domestic and international headquarters there. Even today, despite large-scale disinvestment and the loss of well over a quarter of its manufacturing employment, Chicago still is the headquarters location of 43 of the Fortune 500 industrial firms, a concentration second only to New York's.[70]

Although the Chicago area ranks third in the nation in corporate R&D spending, boasts the country's fifth largest concentration of electronics firms (DuPage County is known as "Silicon Prairie"), and manages a large share of the nation's pool of venture capital, none of the newer high-tech industries that have spawned growth elsewhere has filled the gap left by a shrinking manufacturing base.[71] As in New York, Chicago's service sector, especially financial and related business and legal services, has been the engine of growth in the last boom.

Within its financial services sector, several Chicago-based firms are among the nation's largest. Ranking among the top 50 domestic life insurers and diversified financial companies are such firms as Continental Assurance, Allstate Life, Kemper, and Household International.[72]

In banking, decade-long problems in Illinois forced a massive restructuring of Chicago's leading lending institutions. Bad loans to the Third World and to the agriculture and energy sectors forced major banks and thrifts like Continental Illinois, First Federal Savings and Loan (acquired by Citicorp), and Talman Home Federal Savings and Loan to the brink.[73] They survived only after acquisition and reorganization or government bailout, including the then-largest bank rescue of Continental Illinois in 1984, worth $4.5 billion. Among Chicago's largest banks, American National was acquired by First Chicago, LaSalle National by Algemene Bank Nederland, and Harris Bank by the Bank of Montreal.[74]

Such restructurings and continuing erosion of the former strength of the industry has underscored the vulnerability of Chicago area banks to economic swings and possible acquisition by relatively stronger out-of-state superregionals like BancOne of Columbus, Ohio or NBD Bancorp of Detroit. As one bank executive put it, "Banks in Chicago don't control their destinies like they once did."[75]

Through the turmoil, both Continental Illinois and First Chicago have continued as two of the nation's largest money center banks, ranking tenth and eleventh in assets.[76] Continental Illinois has shifted out of retail banking, now modelling itself after Bankers Trust and J.P. Morgan as a "business bank," developing its client base among Chicago's corporate middle-market and large multinationals. It now ranks sixth in the nation in business lending.[77]

Meanwhile, First Chicago continues to expand in both the retail and corporate middle markets. By acquiring retail branches and expanding credit card operations, First Chicago has become the nation's fourth largest in bank credit card lending and is a major securitizer of credit card receivables.[78] And by buying up a 35 percent share in Wood Gundy, a Canadian brokerage, First Chicago is pursuing primary and secondary markets in securities as well as venture capital operations.[79]

Perhaps more significantly, Chicago area banks have become closely tied to the clearing operations of the city's financial exchanges. The settlement of trades on the futures exchanges alone averages $4 billion to $5 billion per night, and such daily capital needs provide a huge market for banks. Realizing this, Continental Illinois acquired First Options Corp, one of the country's largest clearing houses, which uses a total of 15 banks (11 of them outside of Chicago) in its clearing operations.[80]

But Chicago's banking sector, despite some recent improvement in profitability, is not the central element in the city's rise to prominence. By far the most important development in making Chicago a leading financial center is the growth of financial futures and options traded on the city's major exchanges: the Chicago Board of Trade, the Chicago Mercantile Exchange, the Chicago Board Options Exchange, and the Midwest Stock Exchange.

Chicago has always led the market in futures, based on its historic role as the major link to Midwestern agriculture. The Chicago Board of Trade (CBOT) established the world's first commodities futures exchange in 1848, trading contracts in grain futures. Likewise, the Chicago Mercantile Exchange (CME or "Merc") began trading livestock futures at the beginning of this century.

Financial futures markets were launched with the introduction of floating international exchange rates in the early 1970s. In 1972, CME special counsel Leo Melamed founded the International Monetary Market to trade foreign currencies. The following year, the Chicago Board Options Exchange (CBOE) was created by the CBOT as the world's largest options exchange. Ten years later, the Merc began trading stock index futures and options on futures, which quickly grew to dominate total trading volume.[81]

Today, the CBOT and the CME offer a full line of futures products which include contracts on U.S. government securities, foreign currency, and stock indexes (S&P 500, S&P 100, and the Major Market Index). Together, the two exchanges account for almost 80 percent of the domestic and 60 percent of the global futures market.[82] Both exchanges have aggressively sought to extend their links to international investors. The CME has had a mutual offset agreement to trade futures on the Singapore Monetary Exchange since 1982, and has obtained from the Japanese government exclusive rights in North America and in Asia (outside of Japan) to create a market in futures for the Nikkei 225 blue chip stock index.[83] In 1987, in a move to capture the Japanese futures market ahead of the Tokyo Stock Exchange, the CBOT was the first to offer a three-hour evening session, Sunday through Thursday, in U.S. government securities futures and options to coincide with the opening of the bond markets in Asia.[84]

The CBOE is the only domestic exchange that specializes in trading options, and dominates the domestic and international markets with a 60 percent share. Its strongest competitor, New York's AMEX, holds a 24 percent share of options trades in the U.S., while the New York Mercantile Exchange accounts for only a 7 percent share of domestic trades.[85] Despite its huge share of the world's markets in options on equities and stock indexes, the CBOE continues to seek leadership with such moves as initiating early morning trading sessions that coincide with the opening of European markets.[86]

Chicago's leadership in the financial futures and options markets has been built not only on successes in product innovation, but in the development and application of advanced computer and telecommunications technologies, which make high trading volumes and sophisticated markets possible. Nearly every major product development in futures and options originated in the Chicago pits. The latest in a long series of innovations comes from the Merc — the "Euro-Rate Differential" contract (or DIFF), which may be the most significant hedging instrument to appear since the swap, particularly for international banks.

To promote these new products and instruments, Chicago has been committed to expanding computer links to all major futures and options markets around the world. In a joint venture with Reuters, the Merc is developing Globex, a completely computerized trading system for financial futures contracts, scheduled to begin in October 1989. Globex is a continuous auction market where orders of any size are matched with the best price possible and recorded within 1/100th of a second with automatic confirmation.[87] Such speed and efficiency is indispensable to the fast-paced currency and bond markets.

However, as in many other examples, such technology is a double-edged sword. While Globex makes increased trading volumes in Chicago possible, 24-hour screen trading also loosens the bonds of time and geographic location. Futures and options activities can now more easily shift to where the underlying markets are more active.

This is certainly the basis of the perceived threat to Chicago's exchanges from Tokyo. Since 1985, the Tokyo Stock Exchange has offered futures on Japanese government bonds. These futures now are the most actively traded in the world. In 1989, futures on U.S. Treasury bonds will be traded alongside these on the Tokyo exchange.[88] Coupled with the explosive turnover of foreign exchange in the Tokyo market, these developments may challenge Chicago's current dominance in financial futures and options in the years to come.

Whether other cities such as New York can benefit from the growth of financial futures and options activities depends upon a number of factors. The New York Mercantile Exchange should gain in trading activity with its decision to join the Globex network. In futures, the relatively late entry of the NYSE has forced them to mimic basket trading techniques developed in Chicago. This includes designing a system for one-day clearing of trades, offering its own "basket contract" as an alternative to the stock index future, and possibly reducing the role of floor "specialists," whose jealously guarded control over trading individual stocks cuts against the concept of an auction.[89]

But unless this kind of transition is made, New York is likely to continue to remain on the fringe of these important markets. As it is, investors increasingly are using financial futures and options not just as insurance to complement their equity portfolios. Soaring trading volumes indicate that these instruments have become substitutes for

FIGURE 5.1 Average Daily Value of Trading: Stock Index Futures vs. Stocks

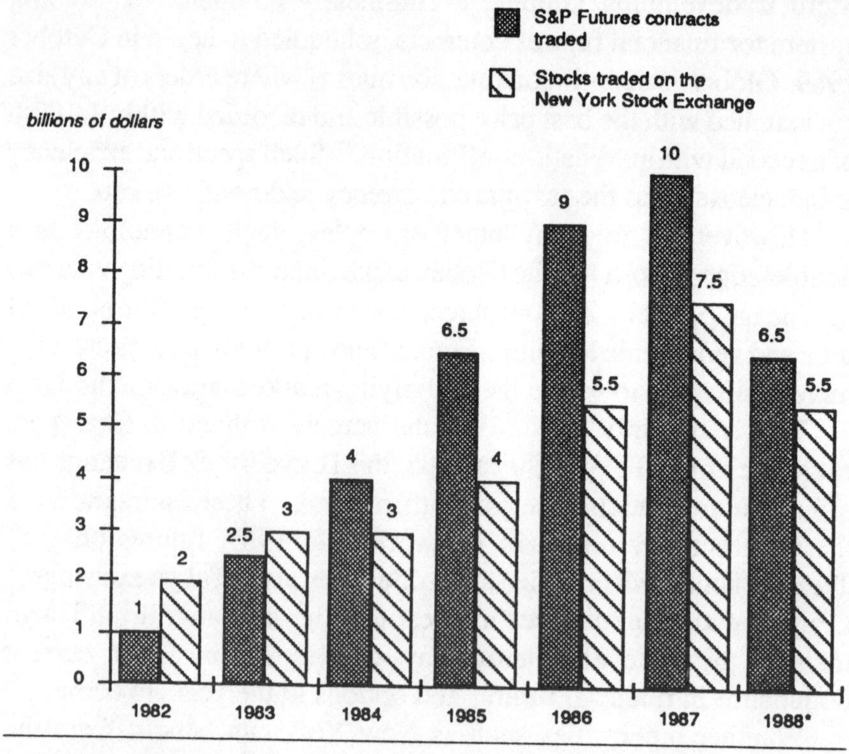

* Through May.

Source: James Sterngold, "John Phelan's New Game Plan," *New York Times*, Sunday, June 26, 1988, sec. 3, p. 10. Copyright © The New York Times Company. Reprinted by permission.

stocks themselves, in part because of the leverage that can be applied. Options on futures of the S&P 500 cost much less than purchases of the underlying equities in the index. As Figure 5.1 shows, trading volume in the S&P 500 stock index futures contract has been consistently higher than the volume of stocks traded on the NYSE since 1984.

Recent developments may help place other financial centers in a more competitive position in the equity options market. Under a new rule adopted by the S.E.C., multiple exchanges would be allowed to trade an equity option, unlike the present arrangement where each option is allotted to a particular exchange, usually the originating exchange.[90] Industry observers feel that this rule will threaten the small regional options exchanges with loss of market share to such giants as the CBOE, and will trigger mergers such as that proposed between the Philadelphia Stock Exchange and the AMEX.[91]

One possible arrangement under discussion would be to move the entire options business (which includes equities, currency, and index options) from Philadelphia to AMEX in New York. This would make AMEX, which is presently ranked second to the CBOE, equal in options trading volume.[92] As the futures and options markets become less tied by necessity to Chicago, New York could benefit to the extent that it can make the necessary changes in products and trading practices.

The Future of Front Office Competition

Financial institutions and markets in New York, Los Angeles, and Chicago do not exhaust the range of front office activities in the United States. Growing regional economies and protective interstate banking compacts have helped to support the growth of superregional banks in North Carolina, Pennsylvania, New England, and elsewhere. These banks are unencumbered by Third World debt, and have grown significantly through expanded services to their regional economies, and through mergers and acquisitions. When measured by market capitalization, their size challenges that of many money center banks, and several of them are entering into larger and more complex financial markets.

However, merely combining size and traditional lines of business may not be adequate for future competition. Convergence means that other nonbank competitors will continue to invade niches that traditionally belonged only to banks. And globalization will make it increasingly difficult to insulate regional and local economies from national and global pressures on sources of funds or opportunities for profitable investment. Analysts at McKinsey and Company have suggested that by the time competition in American banking plays itself out, there will be only two or three truly national banks, and perhaps 15 to 25 "dominant superregionals."[93]

Front office centers have two basic needs: a critical mass of economic and/or financial activity and an adequate pool of professional talent, which is both supported by and, in turn, encourages financial services growth. Because of this, the emergence of key financial centers as locations of front office activities is not simply a matter of increased size or scale. New York maintains much of its leadership in the face of high operating costs and other problems because of its concentrations of talent and support business services. Los Angeles is growing because of the strong California economy and the global importance of the Pacific Rim. And Chicago's global role is based largely on market and product innovation, which has helped to develop its critical mass. Duplicating such factors would be very difficult, if not impossible, in many other U.S. or overseas locations.

But front office competition is not the only form of competition among locations for firms, activity, and employment. In fact, several states and cities are profiting as locations for back office and data processing jobs that increasingly can be disconnected from the front office. In the future, competition for these jobs may be more intense than front office competition, because more locations can feasibly position themselves as viable back office or data processing locations rather than as front office centers. The next chapter discusses this competition in more detail, with special attention to two successful competitors — northeastern New Jersey and Delaware.

NOTES

1. Robert D. Hershey, Jr., "Three Coasts Gain in 'Superstates,'" *New York Times*, August 6, 1988, p. 35.
2. *News*, U.S. Department of Labor, Bureau of Labor Statistics, Middle Atlantic Regional Office, March 14, 1989, p. 6.
3. Ibid., p. 9.
4. "Global Finance," *Wall Street Journal*, September 23, 1988, p. 22R.
5. "The Service 500," *Fortune*, June 6, 1988, pp. D19 and D25.
6. *American Banker Top Numbers 1989* (New York: American Banker/ Bond Buyer, 1989), p. 47.

7. Ibid., p. 42.

8. Total correspondent balances include the demand deposits booked by U.S. banks and thrifts, foreign banks, foreign governments and official institutions, and the clearing balances of Edge Bank subsidiaries. Ibid., p. 71.

9. Matthew Winkler, "Underwriting Profits Skidded in '89," *Wall Street Journal*, January 2, 1990, p. R26.

10. Matthew Winkler, "Surging Short-Term Rates Give Corporate Bonds a Lift," *Wall Street Journal*, April 3, 1989, p. C13.

11. Matthew Winkler, "Is Drexel Still King of the Junk Heap?" *Wall Street Journal*, April 3, 1989, p. C12; and Matthew Winkler, "New Stock Offers Hit 6-Year Low as Hangover from Crash Lingers," *Wall Street Journal*, April 3, 1989, pp. C12 and C13.

12. Matthew Winkler, "Fees from Underwriting Tumbled as Market for New Issues Dried Up," *Wall Street Journal*, April 3, 1989, p. C12.

13. Ronald Henkoff, "Deals of the Year," *Fortune*, January 30, 1989, p. 162.

14. Federal Reserve Bank of New York, Market Reports Division, memorandum, July 10, 1989.

15. *SEC Monthly Statistical Review*, U.S. Securities and Exchange Commission, February 1989, Table A-120.

16. Ibid.

17. Ibid.

18. Adrian Hamilton, *The Financial Revolution* (New York: The Free Press, 1986), p. 43.

19. "The New York Automated Clearing House," brochure, The New York Clearing House Association, p. 8; and data provided by the New York Clearing House Association.

20. "The New York Automated Clearing House," p. 14; and data provided by the New York Clearing House Association.

21. Michael Miller, "Foreign Exchange Students," *Wall Street Journal*, September 23, 1988, p. 14R.

22. William Glasgall, et al., "Japan on Wall Street," *Business Week*, September 7, 1987, p. 86.

23. "Big Wheels, Small Deals," *The Economist*, July 30, 1988, p. 78.

24. Miller, "Foreign Exchange Students," p. 14R.

25. Thierry Noyelle, "New York's Competitiveness," in Thierry Noyelle (ed.), *New York's Financial Markets: The Challenges of Globalization* (Boulder, Colo.: Westview Press, 1989), p. 109.

26. "Best Business Cities," *Business America Real Estate Monitor*, Study No. 881006, Cushman and Wakefield, Inc., New York, May-June 1988, p. 16.

27. "Wage Differences Among Metropolitan Areas, 1987," U.S. Department of Labor, Bureau of Labor Statistics, July 1988.

28. Iver Petersen, "More Resisting Transfers to New York," *New York Times*, Sunday, May 29, 1988, sec. 10, p. 5.

29. As discussed in Chapter 2, proper measurement and comparison of the

effective tax burden must consider other factors along with tax rates, such as tax bases, credits, deductions, attribution rules, and other special features. For example, while New Jersey's top income tax rate is lower than New York's, its tax base is much broader, thus offsetting in part the two states' tax rate differential. Also, the rate and methods of taxation may or may not be uniform for all types of financial institutions within a state.

30. The Tax Foundation, *Facts and Figures on Government Finance* (Baltimore: Johns Hopkins Press, 1988), Table F18.

31. "America Learns to Love L.A.," *The Economist*, December 24, 1988, p. 82.

32. Marie D'Amico, "L.A.: The Future is Now," *Venture*, January 1989, p. 28.

33. "America Learns to Love L.A.," p. 82.

34. "Los Angeles: The New Global Crossroads," *Forbes*, October 24, 1988, p. A5.

35. Ibid.

36. D'Amico, "L.A.: The Future is Now," p. 26.

37. Joel Kotkin, "I Love L.A.," *Inc.*, March 1989, p. 99; and John Tepper Marlin, *Cities of Opportunity* (New York: Master Media, Ltd., 1988), pp. 29-30.

38. "America Learns to Love L.A.," p. 81.

39. Kotkin, "I Love L.A.," p. 99.

40. D'Amico, "L.A.: The Future is Now," p. 29.

41. Marlin, *Cities of Opportunity*, pp. 219 and 254; and Kotkin, "I Love L.A.," p. 99.

42. Ibid.

43. "B of A Boosts Rise in Los Angeles Prominence: Southern California Finance," *Euromoney* (Supplement), September 1986, p. 6.

44. *American Banker*, January 24, 1989, p. 2.

45. Bill Emmott, "International Banking: Survival of the Fittest," *The Economist*, March 26, 1988, p. 33.

46. Ibid.

47. *Top Numbers 1989*, p. 54.

48. "Global Financing Guide," *Euromoney*, September 1988, p. 216.

49. "Annual Financing Report," *Euromoney*, March 1989, p. 28.

50. "The Service 500," p. D19.

51. Ibid., p. D25.

52. Emmott, "International Banking," p. 34.

53. Nina Easton, "This Takeover Could Open California Banks to All Comers," *Business Week*, February 29, 1988, p. 31.

54. Ibid.

55. Ibid.

56. Ibid.

57. "Investment Bankers Tap California's Opportunities," *Euromoney* (Supplement), September 1986, p. 12.

58. Ibid.

59. Ibid.

60 "Observations on the Regional Firm," *Trends*, Securities Industry Association, New York, April 14, 1989, p. 7.

61. The other six domestic securities exchanges registered with the SEC are the American, Boston, Cincinnati, Midwest, New York, and Philadelphia Stock Exchanges.

62. Michelle Bekey, "Trading Places," *Los Angeles Magazine*, November 1986, p. 51.

63. Ibid., and "The Pacific Edge," The Pacific Stock Exchange, Inc., Los Angeles and San Francisco, 1989, p. 1.

64. Bekey, "Trading Places," p. 59.

65. "The Pacific Edge," p. 10.

66. Ibid.

67. Ibid., p 7.

68. Ibid.

69. Richard W. Stevenson, "California's 6-Year Boom May Be Over," *New York Times*, January 11, 1989, p. D1; and Brian O'Reilly, "The War Against Growth Heats Up," *Fortune*, December 5, 1988, p. 124.

70. "The Fortune 500 Largest U.S. Industrial Companies," *Fortune*, April 24, 1989.

71. David Moberg, "Can Chicago Be Saved?" *Inc.*, March 1988, pp. 86 and 88.

72. "The Service 500," pp. D19 and D25.

73. George Palmer, "High Hopes in the Windy City," *The Banker*, October 1988, p. 109.

74. Bob Tamarkin, "Chicago: 150 Years of Financial Innovation," *Fortune*, Fall 1987.

75. Ibid.

76. *Top Numbers 1989*, p. 16.

77. "Single-Track Strategy," *The Banker*, October 1988, p. 110; and *Top Numbers 1989*, p. 40.

78. *Top Numbers 1989*, p. 54; and Michael Quint, "Chase and Morgan Report Declines," *New York Times*, July 18, 1989, p. D6.

79. Tamarkin, "Chicago: 150 Years."

80. Ibid.

81. "Chicago's Financial Exchange Community: A Report on its Economic Contribution to the City of Chicago," The Commercial Club of Chicago, 1987, p. 18.

82. Ibid., p. 13.

83. John N. Frank, "The Japanese are Elbowing Into Chicago's Futures Pits," *Business Week*, June 1, 1987, p. 107.

84. Ibid.

85. Margaret E. Kriz, "First City of Futures," *National Journal*, June 25, 1988, p. 1671.

86. Tamarkin, "Chicago: 150 Years."

87. Floyd Norris, "Computers for the Futures Pits," *New York Times*, February 13, 1989, pp. D1 and D6.

88. Neil Osborn, "Running Scared in Windy City," *Euromoney*, February 1989, p. 41.

89. James Sterngold, "John Phelan's New Game Plan," *New York Times*, Sunday, June 26, 1988, sec. 3, p. 11; and Lisa Kartus, "Market Wars," *Chicago*, September 1988, p. 28.

90. Kurt Eichenwald, "Amex Studying a Merger with Philadelphia Exchange," *New York Times*, July 18, 1989, p. D1.

91 Ibid.

92 Ibid., p. D2

93. Lowell Bryan and Paul Allen, "Geographic Strategies for the 1990s," *The McKinsey Quarterly*, Winter 1988, p. 63.

The editor gratefully thanks Runzheimer for their permission to reprint table 5.14 and would like to draw the reader's attention to the more recent values based on 1993 data as follows: San Francisco 139.6; Los Angeles 126.6; New York 123.4; Boston 114.6; Chicago 109.7; Atlanta 105.8; Pittsburg 106.0; Dallas 97.9. The annual income of a home-owning family of four has also changed from the above figure of $55,000 to $60,000.

Corporate Spatial Links With Financial Institutions: The Role of the Metropolitan Hierarchy

James O. Wheeler

Department of Geography, University of Georgia, Athens, Georgia 30602

Abstract. This study focuses on the spatial linkages between major U.S. corporations and financial institutions. The results support the hypothesis that corporations reach up the metropolitan hierarchy for banking services, i.e., they are more strongly linked with higher-order centers than with lower-order metropolitan areas. A second hypothesis, also confirmed, is that larger corporations are more strongly tied to the upper end of the metropolitan hierarchy than are smaller firms. Although some elements of banking are located in the same metropolitan area as the corporate headquarters that use their services, a significant component of banking services—especially investment and foreign banking—involves intermetropolitan linkages. These linkages are national rather than regional and do not follow the traditional distance-decay model.

Key Words: corporate headquarters, banking, metropolitan hierarchy, producer services.

THE spatial and functional connections between corporations and banks have been longstanding and strong. The basis for these connections lies in the nature of banking and the requirements of corporations for banking services. Only the largest of banks can accommodate the financial needs of large corporations. Although all metropolitan areas offer commercial banking services, commercial banking—measured by deposits—is highly concentrated in only a small number of the very largest metropolitan areas (Wheeler and Dillon 1985).[1] In general, the larger the metropolitan area, the disproportionately higher will be its banking deposits, with New York serving as the highest-order center in the United States. The reason for this highly concentrated pattern has to do with economies of scale associated with specialized, high-quality information services. Only the largest banks can provide such services, which extend far beyond the normal level of business services and in fact become a part of day-to-day corporate decision making (Marcus 1975). Large commercial banks can thrive only in the information-rich environment of high-order metropolitan areas. In effect, it is not metropolitan size per se that attracts high-level banking services; size is a result of function. Large metropolitan areas contain the largest scale, most specialized group of activities and share information and risk. Therefore, the greater a corporation's need for sophisticated banking services, the greater the likelihood the corporation will turn to a large metropolitan area that both creates information that is crucial for high-level business decisions and creates a demand for this information (Meyer 1980).

Although there is a strong tendency for corporations to use local banking services, when corporate needs lie beyond the local area, corporations will look up the metropolitan hierarchy to meet nonlocal needs. The larger the corporation, the greater the need for these nonlocal ties. "The structure of the accounting, legal, banking, and investment banking professions [has evolved into] a division of labor whereby only a few firms [offer] the most sophisticated skills and strategic information" (Cohen 1977, 215).

Even more concentrated geographically than commercial banks are investment banks, highly concentrated in New York. Corporations are thus forced to go up the metropolitan hierarchy to meet investment banking needs to an even greater extent than they are with commercial banks. Likewise, foreign banking services are limited to a small number of banks in only a few of the largest metropolitan areas, and in many instances banks located in foreign countries are

Annals of the Association of American Geographers, 76(2), 1986, pp. 262–274

used by large U.S. corporations (Hayes, Spence, and Marks 1983).

Both corporate headquarters and banking institutions have long been concentrated in the largest metropolitan areas (Slaven and Aldcroft 1982). An important factor in explaining the concentration of economic activities in metropolitan areas stems from the interplay between industrial, commercial, and service corporations and banking services (Coakley and Harris 1983). Evidence suggests that "bankers have re-emerged, after a period of partial eclipse during the Great Depression and World War II, as the major group that controls large corporations" (Kotz 1978, ix). This close association is "restricted to a small number of giant, well-established banks, principally in New York City, and secondarily in Pittsburgh, Chicago, Cleveland, and a few other major cities (Kotz 1978, ix).

One aspect of the interrelationships between corporations and banking is that of interlocking directorates. Research on interlocking directorates, mainly aspatial in nature, has established unusually close ties between corporate and banking directorates (Fennema 1982; Mizruchi 1982). Based on data for the 1960s, Mintz and Schwartz (1983) found that commercial banks were more "central" within the interlocking directorates than any other firms. Using the same method of analysis for the period 1904 to 1974, Mizruchi (1983, 178) reported that there was a "continuously high centrality of commercial banks during the entire period" and that "a small group of New York banks consistently held the most central positions from 1904 through 1974." Kindleberger (1983), in tracing the history of banking and industrial expansion, found a close relationship between the relative growth of these two sectors. Spatial treatment of interlocking directorates (Green and Semple 1981; Green 1983) has not focused specifically on the banking component.

The purpose of this study is to examine the geographical linkages between large corporations and financial institutions among metropolitan areas in the U.S. To which metropolitan areas do large corporations turn for their major commercial banking services, investment banking, and foreign bank connections? Do these spatial linkages follow any identifiable pattern from one metropolitan area to another? To what extent do corporations bank within the metropolitan area in which they are headquartered and to what extent do they follow the metropolitan banking hierarchy? Are there identifiable regional banking linkages, such as within the U.S. South?

This study sets forth the hypothesis that corporations seeking major banking relationships tend to go up the metropolitan hierarchy, i.e., to seek out banks in higher-order metropolitan areas rather than banks in lower-order centers. Figure 1 illustrates this hypothesized relationship, which is that a metropolitan area at any level of the hierarchy will be more strongly linked with centers of higher order. The higher the order, the stronger the linkage. For all metropolitan areas, the most intense banking links will be with the highest-order (national) center. The next strongest linkages will be with major regional centers, and so on down the hierarchy. A second and related hypothesis is that larger corporations, here measured in assets, will fit the first hypothesis better than will smaller corporations. The larger corporations are expected to link to a greater degree with the upper end of the metropolitan hierarchy.

Context of Study

This study may be viewed within the context of four interdependent conceptual developments in urban geography. The first is the emerging literature on quaternary place studies (Semple

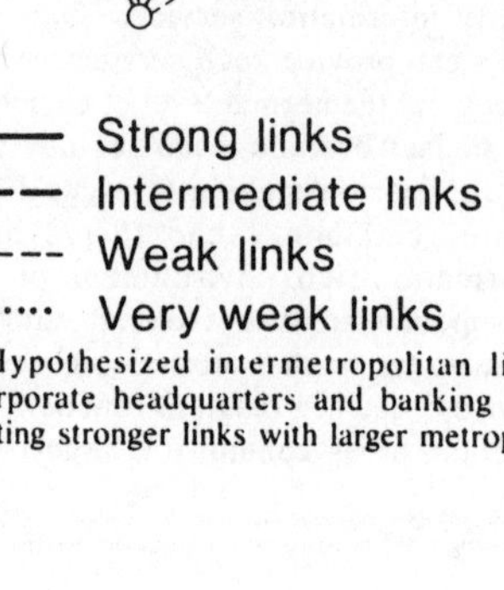

Figure 1. Hypothesized intermetropolitan links between corporate headquarters and banking services, reflecting stronger links with larger metropolitan areas.

1985), which seeks to explain the location of corporate decision making and the spatial linkages of control points with the rest of the economic system (Borchert 1978; Pred 1977). Although issues of external control have been studied largely in industrial geography (Dicken and Lloyd 1978; Watts 1981; Wheeler and Park 1984), the issues are of equal if not greater importance in the service sector where the most jobs are now found. Although most service jobs are low wage and unskilled, the higher paying jobs are associated with the producer services and are growing especially rapidly in large metropolitan areas that act as headquarters for major corporations. Thus, the decision-making role of the largest corporations is increasingly being recognized as central to an understanding of urban and economic change (Simmie 1983).

Second, this research may be seen within the framework of the so-called Stanback hypothesis (Stanback et al. 1981; Stanback and Noyelle 1982; Hanson 1983). Stanback, in explaining the role of the new service economy in metropolitan viability, has argued for the strong functional and spatial linkages between corporate headquarters and producer services, such as planning and management, advertising, legal counsel, marketing, consulting, and financial services. Metropolitan areas with a large number of major corporate headquarters will be economically healthy because the corporations will generate the need for an array of these producer services. Thus, corporate headquarters and the associated producer services provide an export base for the metropolitan area, much as manufacturing specialization was earlier a basic activity. Whereas the findings of the present research are largely consistent with the Stanback hypothesis, the pattern of spatial linkages with major banks hypothesized here suggest that—at least for the banking component of producer services—not all such services will be locally based.

The systems of cities concept provides a third context for this research (Berry 1973; Conzen 1977, 1981; Pred 1977; Meyer 1980). Two kinds of linkages mediate the metropolitan system of cities: control and coordination links and physical links (commodities and business travel (Meyer 1984, 349)). Corporate spatial links with financial institutions are examples of the former. Based on data on bank correspondent linkages from 1880 to 1910, Conzen (1977) outlined the spatial maturation of the U.S. urban system. Focusing on interdependence among cities, his analyses traced the emergence and continued dominance of New York banks in the U.S. metropolitan economy and the subsequent emergence of banks in other centers, such as Boston, Philadelphia, Chicago. Conzen "documented the evolution of a multilevel, regionally organized, and nationally integrated banking system during the last quarter of the nineteenth century" (1977, 105). New York achieved early primacy and grew with the expanding space economy: "New York's banking hinterland grew from 486 counties in 1881 to 943 in 1910" (Conzen 1977, 105). In general, subregional data show a hierarchy of urban regions, with New York as the national center for banking and smaller banking hinterlands existing at the regional and subregional (lower-order) levels. Although the present research does not depart conceptually in major ways from Conzen's article, the results of the two analyses (Conzen's based on nineteenth-century data and this one based on 1983 data) do differ, raising the issue of whether the spatial pattern of financial linkages in the post-industrial U.S. diverges significantly from the pattern in an earlier industrial U.S.

Another study of bank correspondent linkages focused on the U.S. South invites some comparison with the present research (Meyer 1984; see also Eberstein and Galle 1984). Meyer (1984, 349) found that "although national links are important, interurban links that include the regional metropolis and its hinterland cities remain a major factor in the system of cities even in a society that is often characterized as shifting from a local/regional to a national orientation." Unlike the present study, which identifies national metropolitan linkages, Meyer (1984, 359) found little support for "the suggestion . . . that national metropolitan linkages now exceed intraregional linkages."

The final context in which to view this study is the classical concept of metropolitan dominance (McKenzie 1925, 1927). Metropolitan dominance holds that small centers dominate or control small surrounding areas, and as metropolitan size increases the territory under the control of that metropolitan area correspondingly grows such that we have local centers, subregional centers, and regional centers. Although urban dominance has been demonstrated for many kinds of flows, based on the process of distance decay, this paper argues that the metropolitan-dominance–distance-decay theme is inappropriate for describing corporate spatial linkages with major banks. The hypothesis advanced suggests size, not distance, is the major factor underlying the linkage patterns.

Data

Data for this study were compiled from *The Corporate Finance Bluebook, 1983* (Zehring 1983), published for the first time in 1983. This data source lists, for the 2,000 largest U.S. corporations, the names and addresses of the financial institutions with which each corporation does business. By aggregating corporate headquarters by metropolitan areas and correspondingly aggregating banking connections by metropolitan areas, one can construct a matrix showing metropolitan corporate concentration and banking services. These data were compiled for the 16 largest metropolitan areas in the U.S., and include all corporations in the U.S. South, a study region chosen in particular to test the first hypothesis above. Data were compiled for each corporation in each of the metropolitan areas in terms of major commercial bank(s), investment banks(s), major foreign banking relationships, auditors, pension managers, as well as legal counsel. A bank link is defined in the Zehring (1983) questionnaire as the bank or banks with which a corporation has a "major banking relationship(s)."

Findings

As a first step in examining the hypothesis that corporations reach up the metropolitan hierarchy to satisfy their major banking needs, a series of maps was compiled showing the major commercial banking links of corporations headquartered in individual metropolitan areas (Figs. 2–4). Several features are apparent from these figures. First, it is clear, as hypothesized, that corporations link upward in the metropolitan hierarchy for major banking relationships. New York, at the apex of the banking hierarchy, is linked with corporations headquartered in metropolitan areas throughout the country. Other national-level banking centers (Chicago, Los

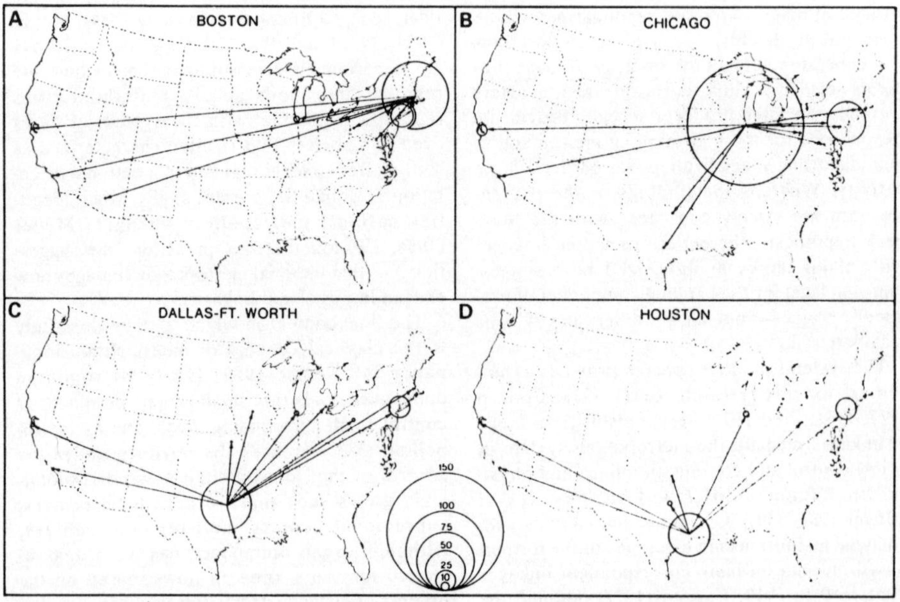

Figure 2. Actual links between corporations headquartered in Boston, Chicago, Dallas-Ft. Worth, and Houston and the commercial banking services they utilized. Size of circle is proportional to the number of banking links.

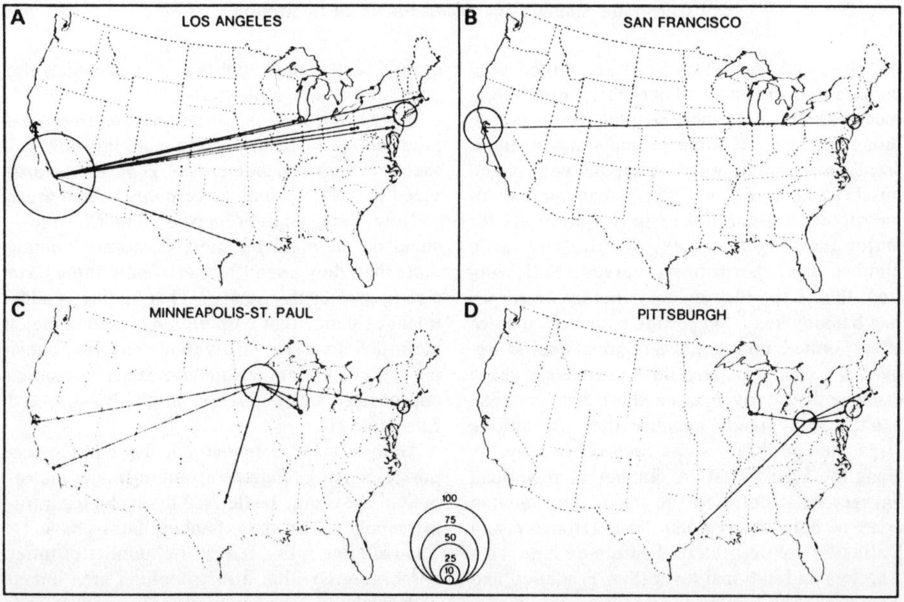

Figure 3. Actual links between corporations headquartered in Los Angeles, San Francisco, Minneapolis-St. Paul, and Pittsburgh and the commercial banking services they utilize. Size of circle is proportional to the number of banking links.

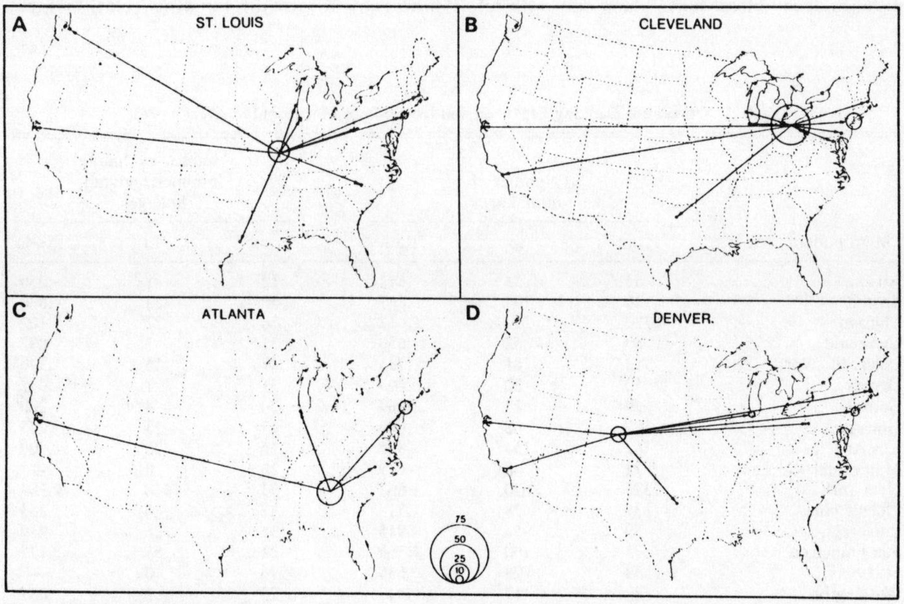

Figure 4. Actual links between corporations headquartered in St. Louis, Cleveland, Atlanta, and Denver and the commercial banking services they utilize. Size of circle is proportional to the number of banking links.

Angeles, and San Francisco) are linked with corporations in almost all of the larger metropolitan areas. It is extremely rare to observe corporations seeking out banks in small- and medium-sized metropolitan areas. A second and related observation is the relatively small number of metropolitan areas linked to corporations for major banking services, despite the large number of corporations involved. Following from this is the long-distance nature of corporate banking links, suggesting a national pattern of corporate banking, not a regional one. Moreover, the spatial pattern does not have a sharp distance decay. Even when short-distance links exist, it is typically because they are among large metropolitan areas located nearby, as along the East Coast. A number of reciprocal linkages exist between the major metropolitan areas at both the regional level (Houston and Dallas-Ft. Worth; San Francisco and Los Angeles) and national level (San Francisco and New York; San Francisco and Chicago). Finally, as suggested by Stanback, the dominant role of the headquarters city must be noted, as these centers invariably have concentrations of major corporations and banking services. An obvious distance-decay effect takes place only with reference to the metropolitan area in which the corporation is headquartered.

Insight into how major selected metropolitan areas differ in terms of the banking linkages their corporate headquarters generate is provided in Table 1. Only three metropolitan areas —New York, San Francisco, and Chicago— stand out as receiving more corporate banking links than they "send" (that is, only three have a ratio greater than unity). This finding is additional evidence that corporations, even in major metropolitan areas, link with higher-order banking centers. Other metropolitan areas with ratios approaching unity are Pittsburgh, Boston, and Los Angeles.

An even more meaningful measure of the corporate-banking relationship among major metropolitan areas may be derived by excluding intrametropolitan corporate banking links (Table 1). The resulting ratios reflect the number of times corporations within a metropolitan area linked with banks in other metropolitan areas. It may be argued that the higher the ratio, the higher the metropolitan area lies in the metropolitan banking hierarchy. The evidence here is even more conclusive that corporations reach up the hierarchy for major banking relationships.

Table 1. Corporate Banking Links[a] to and from Major Metropolitan Areas, 1983

	Number of all linkages			Number excluding intrametropolitan linkages		
Metropolitan area	From	To	Ratio	From	To	Ratio
Atlanta	53	34	.642	20	1	.050
Boston	120	104	.867	39	23	.590
Chicago	222	229	1.032	70	77	1.100
Cleveland	80	52	.650	31	3	.097
Dallas-Ft. Worth	112	81	.723	47	16	.340
Denver	50	20	.400	31	1	.032
Detroit	39	23	.589	20	4	.200
Houston	102	68	.666	47	13	.277
Los Angeles	162	134	.827	56	28	.500
Minneapolis-St. Paul	74	48	.649	26	0	—
New York	373	620	1.662	73	320	4.384
Philadelphia	39	28	.718	17	6	.353
Pittsburgh	59	54	.915	31	26	.839
San Francisco	73	100	1.369	24	51	2.125
St. Louis	44	28	.636	16	0	—
Washington	38	17	.447	23	2	.087
Total	1640	1640	1.000	571	571	1.000

Source: Compiled by author from Zehring 1983.

[a] Corporate banking links were defined by corporations as their "major banking relationship(s)" on the Zehring (1983) questionnaire.

Again, New York, San Francisco, and Chicago are the only centers having ratios greater than unity, with New York especially dominant. Smaller places such as Atlanta, Cleveland, Denver, Minneapolis-St. Paul, St. Louis, and Washington are headquarters for corporations that look to other metropolitan areas for banking but attract little or no banking business from corporations elsewhere, at least from those located in the major metropolitan areas selected here.

Further evidence of New York City's dominance is presented in Table 2. When intrametropolitan banking links are excluded, New York is, for all 16 of the major metropolitan areas selected, the leading banking center. Almost 80 percent of all major banking links of corporations headquartered in New York are with New York banks. Among the other metropolitan areas, the percentage varies from 18.5 percent (Los Angeles) to 40 percent (Detroit). No other metropolitan area has percentages remotely approaching these magnitudes. Ample evidence exists, therefore, that corporate banking linkages are overwhelmingly with the highest levels of the metropolitan banking hierarchy.

To evaluate the hypothesis of hierarchical linkages further, the 46 largest (in terms of population) metropolitan areas in 13 states of the U.S. South were examined in greater detail.[2] These metropolitan areas were placed into three categories (large, medium, and small) on the basis of the number of corporate banking links originating there. Those in the *large* category include the dominant banking centers of Dallas-Ft. Worth, Houston, and Atlanta, which together account for 44.4 percent of the total corporate banking links originating in the South. The *medium*-sized category includes 8 metropolitan areas, each having between 15 and 30 corporate banking links: Charlotte-Gastonia, Greensboro-Winston-Salem-High Point, Louisville, Miami, Oklahoma City, Richmond, San Antonio, and Tampa-St. Petersburg. The remaining 35 metropolitan areas constitute the *small* category, and have fewer than 15 corporate banking links each. These classes were constructed to compare the spatial pattern of banking links among the size categories to test for hierarchical linkages.

Table 3 shows the percentage of each category's banking linkages with each of the other size categories. Linkages originating in each of the three categories were calculated for six classes of corporate banking destinations. Four classes are intraregional, i.e., within the South.

Table 2. Percentage of Banking Links of Corporations in Major Metropolitan Areas With Classes of Metropolitan Areas, 1983

Metropolitan area	Intrametropolitan	New York	National centers[a]	Major centers[b]	Other centers
New York	—	78.5	8.6	10.7	0.01
Chicago	67.6	23.1	6.2	2.2	0.08
Los Angeles	65.4	18.5	10.5	5.6	0.00
San Francisco	66.2	24.3	8.1	0.0	1.35
National Centers[c]	66.6	21.7	8.0	3.0	0.07
Atlanta	61.1	29.6	7.4	0.0	1.85
Boston	66.9	19.8	8.3	4.1	0.08
Cleveland	60.0	24.4	6.1	8.5	1.22
Dallas-Ft. Worth	56.5	23.5	9.6	7.8	2.61
Denver	37.3	19.6	29.4	11.8	1.96
Detroit	47.5	40.0	10.0	0.0	2.50
Houston	52.9	26.9	10.6	7.7	1.92
Minneapolis-St. Paul	69.6	23.2	13.0	1.4	1.45
Philadelphia	56.4	38.5	5.1	0.0	0.00
Pittsburgh	47.5	38.9	8.5	5.1	0.00
St. Louis	59.6	19.1	8.5	8.5	4.26
Washington	34.1	36.4	13.6	4.5	11.36
Major Centers	55.6	26.5	10.3	5.4	2.17

Source: Compiled by author from Zehring 1983.
[a] New York, Chicago, Los Angeles, and San Francisco.
[b] The 12 SMSAs, excluding national centers, listed in this table.
[c] Excluding New York.

Table 3. Banking Links of Corporations in Small, Medium, and Large Metropolitan Areas in the U.S. South, 1983

	Intraregional						
Metropolitan categories[a]	Small	Medium	Large	Intrametropolitan	Extraregional	New York	Total
Small	6.59	9.89	10.99	24.18	16.48	31.87	100.0
Medium	3.75	2.50	5.63	41.25	16.25	30.62	100.0
Large	0.73	0.37	3.30[c]	56.04	13.55	26.01	100.0

Source: Compiled by author from Zehring 1983.
[a] *Small* metropolitan areas have fewer than 15 banking links; *medium* have between 15 and 30 banking links; and cities in the *large* category are Atlanta, Dallas-Ft. Worth, and Houston with 54, 115, and 104 banking links, respectively.
[b] Excluding New York.
[c] Excluding intrametropolitan links.

Of these, one includes banking links within the same metropolitan area, and three represent the three size categories noted above. Two extraregional classes were used, one being links with New York and the other being links with other extraregional metropolitan areas.

Corporations in all three of the metropolitan size categories reach up the metropolitan hierarchy for commercial banking services, and corporations in all size categories of metropolitan areas are most strongly linked with New York. As the size of the metropolitan category increases, so too does the proportion of intrametropolitan banking linkages. Corporations in the *large* category have almost no banking linkages with medium- and small-sized metropolitan areas (1.1 percent). It is only corporations in the small centers that have noticeable banking ties with other small metropolitan areas (6.59 percent). The percentages of intraregional links increase with the increasing size categories. This evidence from the U.S. South, therefore, supports the hypothesis of hierarchical linkages. When intrametropolitan banking links are excluded, smaller centers have almost 21 percent of their total banking ties with higher-order centers within the region compared to just over 1 percent of the links of the largest metropolitan areas being with small and medium centers. This finding that corporations in the small centers substitute regional banking links for intrametropolitan linkages is the only evidence of any sort of a distance-decay relationship.[3] Corporations in smaller metropolitan areas also have strong banking links, however, with extraregional banks and with New York banks, which are attractive for corporations in all sizes of metropolitan areas in the South. The difference is that the larger the southern metropolitan area, the higher the probability that a corporation in that center will be involved in a major intrametropolitan banking linkage.

The second hypothesis argues that larger corporations are more likely to be linked in major banking relationships with the highest levels of the metropolitan banking hierarchy than with smaller, lower-order metropolitan areas. The basis for this notion is that larger corporations have a greater need for the types of banking services that can be provided only by the largest banks, which are located in metropolitan areas at the upper end of the hierarchy. To test the hypothesis regarding corporate size and banking linkages, corporations in 13 large metropolitan areas were classified as *large* if they had more than $1 billion in assets and *small* if their assets were less than $1 billion.[4] (Three metropolitan areas could not be used because they did not have enough links in the two size categories.) For each metropolitan area, a 2 × 2 contingency table was constructed relating corporate size (above or below $1 billion in assets) with whether the major banking relationship was with New York, representing the highest level in the hierarchy, or with a bank within the particular metropolitan area (Fig. 5). The hypothesis suggests a higher frequency of banking links with New York banks for the larger corporations, with the $1 billion asset level being an arbitrary but hopefully meaningful division. Chi-square was used to test this hypothesis.

Of the 13 metropolitan areas, 9 yielded a chi-square value significant at $p \leq 0.05$ (Table 4). Of the 4 for which a statistically significant relationship was not found, 3—San Francisco, Pittsburgh, and Boston—have already been

	Corporate Size < $1 Billion	Corporate Size > $1 Billion
New York	low	high
Intrametropolitan	high	low

Figure 5. Hypothesized relationship between corporate size and the likelihood of obtaining banking services locally or in New York.

identified as important banking centers in their own right. In every instance, including St. Louis, for which the relationship was not statistically significant, the percentage of banking links with New York was higher among corporations with over $1 billion than for corporations having assets less than $1 billion. Further, when all banking links are summed over all 13 metropolitan areas, a chi-square value significant at the 0.001 level is the result. This evidence suggests that larger corporations are indeed more strongly linked to the upper end of the metropolitan banking hierarchy.

It might be assumed that the greater regional banking focus of corporations in smaller metropolitan areas noted above is simply the result of the fact that these smaller centers have fewer large corporations. Using the $1 billion asset level again as the definition of a large corporation, it was found that 35.2 percent of all corporations headquartered in New York had assets over $1 billion (Table 5). For the three national centers of Chicago, Los Angeles, and San Francisco, 26.3 percent of all corporations headquartered in these centers had over $1 billion in assets. For nine other major metropolitan areas (listed in Table 6), large corporations made up only 20.3 percent of all corporations. Thus, at the upper end of the metropolitan hierarchy, the larger the size of the center, the higher the percentage of large compared to small corporations. When one examines the metropolitan size categories in the U.S. South, however, no such relationship is observed. In fact, the centers with the fewest banking links have the highest percentage of large corporations.

Investment banking links show overwhelming evidence of corporations looking directly to New York (Table 6). Approximately 80 percent of corporations in the 20 largest metropolitan areas turn to investment banks in New York, 15 percent obtain investment banking services within the metropolitan area in which they are headquartered, and less than 5 percent seek such banking services in a metropolitan area other than New York.

For foreign banking relationships, corporations in large U.S. metropolitan areas use banks in foreign countries nearly one-half of the time (Table 6). New York banks are used for foreign banking 23 percent of the time, and banks in the same metropolitan area as the corporation are utilized about 17 percent of the time, leaving approximately 12 percent of corporate links with other U.S. metropolitan areas. Thus, foreign banking services are highly concentrated, though not as concentrated as is investment banking.

The Stanback hypothesis suggesting the close functional and spatial links between the headquarters location of corporations and producer services is given strong support in terms of auditors and legal counsel (Table 7). Among the 20 metropolitan areas with the largest numbers of corporate headquarters, 94 percent of the auditors used by those corporations are located within the same metropolitan area, though these auditors may be branches of accounting firms headquartered in New York. The percentage for legal counsel is 84 percent. Forty percent of the pension managers used are located within the same metropolitan area.

Conclusions and Implications

Corporate links to banking services tend to proceed up the metropolitan hierarchy. Larger corporations, because of greater need for more sophisticated banking services, are linked more strongly with New York (by far the dominant center for large-scale banking in the U.S.) than they are with local banking services. This relationship is strongest for investment banking, somewhat less strong for foreign banking, and least strong for major commercial banking relationships. Furthermore, large corporations are more strongly involved in the upward hierarchical links than are small corporations.

Three major implications of these findings deserve to be highlighted. The first is the Stanback hypothesis, which holds that a close spatial

Table 4. Chi-Square Tests for Banking Links with New York for Largest Corporations, 1983

Metropolitan area	χ^2	*N*	Percentage of links with New York: Corporations > $1 billion assets	Corporations < $1 billion assets
Atlanta	18.80[a]	49	78.6	14.2
Boston	2.59	105	44.4	20.8
Chicago	20.89[a]	204	43.0	14.4
Cleveland	18.30[a]	69	73.3	16.7
Dallas-Ft. Worth	3.99[c]	92	50.0	25.0
Detroit	17.72[a]	35	86.7	15.0
Houston	9.52[b]	83	58.3	23.7
Los Angeles	17.36[a]	136	45.0	12.5
Minneapolis-St. Paul	7.24[b]	64	53.8	17.6
Philadelphia	6.16[c]	39	85.7	34.4
Pittsburgh	2.84	51	62.5	37.1
San Francisco	0.65	67	33.3	23.9
St. Louis	2.66	37	37.5	14.3
Total	60.62[a]	975	52.3	18.7

[a] Significant at the .001 level.
[b] Significant at the .01 level.
[c] Significant at the .05 level.

and functional association exists between major corporations and producer services. Metropolitan areas that are headquarters for major corporations will generate a local need for these high-level services, which in turn will set up an urban multiplier effect. The findings here, relating to high-level financial institutions, call the Stanback hypothesis into question. Whereas corporations seek out local producer services for legal counsel, auditors, and perhaps for planning and management consulting, marketing, or advertising (though the latter lie beyond the present study), a significant proportion of high-level financial transactions involve intermetropolitan links, and these almost invariably are up the hierarchy. Almost half of the commercial banking links, 83 percent of foreign banking ties, and 85 percent of investment banking links extend beyond the metropolitan area in which the corporate headquarters are located—a finding that runs counter to what would be expected from the Stanback hypothesis.

By extension, the second implication relates to the export orientation of high-order financial services. The conventional (Christallerian) view is that services are local and not "city building." The finding here, consistent with a small but growing literature on this subject, contradicts the traditional view and sees high-order commercial banks, investment banks, and foreign banking as an important new export base of cities, especially for the very largest cities. The traditional viewpoint has recognized manufacturing as exporting commodities and thereby bringing dollar flows to the producing metropolis. But high-order financial institutions also export highly specialized information, expertise, and service to corporations in distant metropolitan areas in return for dollar flows to the financial headquarters. Here we must recognize the different role of high-order and low-order services.

Finally, what are the implications for industrial decentralization and for service expansion, especially in the Sunbelt economy? Population, manufacturing, and retailing showed the early signs of decentralization from the northeastern U.S. to the South and West, and yet high-order

Table 5. Percentage of Corporations by Metropolitan Area Class With Assets Greater than $1 Billion

	%	*N*
New York	35.23	176
Chicago, Los Angeles, San Francisco	26.34	262
9 Leading SMSAs[a]	20.27	296
South (Large)	20.60	165
(Medium)	22.08	77
(Small)	29.11	79
Total	25.12	1055

Source: Compiled by author from Zehring 1983.
[a] Atlanta, Boston, Cleveland, Dallas-Ft. Worth, Detroit, Houston, Minneapolis, Philadelphia, and Pittsburgh.

Table 6. Percentage of Corporate Banking Links by Metropolitan Area

Metropolitan area	Investment banking: Intrametropolitan	Investment banking: New York	Investment banking: Other domestic	Major foreign banking: Intrametropolitan	Major foreign banking: New York	Major foreign banking: Other domestic	Major foreign banking: Foreign
New York	96.8	—	3.2	65.6	—	4.7	29.7
Chicago	17.5	80.4	2.1	47.1	19.1	0.0	33.8
Los Angeles	15.6	77.8	6.6	12.3	17.5	22.8	47.4
San Francisco	11.1	88.9	0.0	38.7	25.8	3.2	32.3
Boston	9.4	81.2	9.4	11.6	39.5	4.7	44.2
Pittsburgh	0.0	91.2	8.8	0.0	52.6	0.0	47.4
Minneapolis	44.6	51.8	3.6	3.5	10.7	42.9	42.9
Cleveland	20.6	76.5	2.9	10.5	5.3	21.0	63.2
Atlanta	22.2	72.2	5.6	0.0	50.0	0.0	50.0
Dallas-Ft. Worth	13.2	83.0	3.8	0.0	21.1	26.3	52.6
Houston	9.3	86.7	4.0	10.3	6.9	10.3	72.4
Detroit	0.0	100.0	0.0	0.0	4.0	16.0	60.0
Philadelphia	5.6	77.8	16.6	0.0	33.3	0.0	66.7
12 large SMSAs[a]	15.4	79.8	4.8	17.3	23.0	12.3	47.4

Source: Compiled by author from Zehring 1983.
[a] Excluding New York.

financial institutions have remained concentrated. The post-World War II industrial decentralization was, to a large extent, achieved through establishing branch plants in peripheral regions of the country while corporate control was maintained in the U.S. Northeast. Recent evidence (Wheeler and Brown 1985) indicates that headquarters location shows evidence of decentralization to peripheral regions by the growth of indigenous firms, mergers, and by relocation of corporate headquarters, in that order of importance. As industrial and headquarters decentralization continues, the question is whether high-order financial institutions will likewise decentralize. The financial infrastructure of a place like New York is not readily

Table 7. Percentage of Auditors, Legal Counsel, and Pension Managers Used by Corporations Located in the Same Metropolitan Area

	Auditors	Legal counsel	Pension managers
New York	95.1	98.4	64.3
Los Angeles	94.1	81.3	30.5
Minneapolis-St. Paul	98.3	95.7	44.6
San Francisco	82.1	82.1	29.7
Chicago	95.7	88.2	32.3
Atlanta	92.6	85.7	29.8
Miami	85.7	61.5	0.0
Philadelphia	89.5	76.3	29.1
Kansas City	100.0	100.0	27.6
Detroit	100.0	72.7	20.4
Washington, D.C.	75.0	50.0	19.5
Baltimore	83.3	90.9	54.2
Tampa-St. Petersburg	87.5	57.1	0.0
Dallas-Ft. Worth	93.8	75.0	48.7
Houston	97.3	82.2	51.4
St. Louis	90.9	60.0	31.3
Boston	91.9	86.4	58.4
Cleveland	100.0	94.1	35.1
Denver	96.1	75.9	33.3
Pittsburgh	97.1	84.6	21.6
Total	93.9	84.4	40.5

Source: Compiled by author from Zehring 1983.

re-created elsewhere, leading one to expect an infinitely slower decentralization of financial institutions.

As noted earlier, the present findings and those of Conzen (1977, 1981) differ in that Conzen found greater evidence of regional linkages with correspondent banking. (A correspondent banking relationship allows a bank in a small center to maintain a deposit account with a bank in a larger center and to utilize various services of the bank in the larger center.) Are these spatial patterns of financial linkages attributable to the change from an industrializing U.S. to a post-industrial U.S.? Conzen found hierarchical banking links, with New York the national center and with the emergence between 1881 and 1910 of regional and subregional banking links. He thus found evidence of distance-constrained bank links, whereas the present study has emphasized a lack of distance decay, or regional and subregional links. Although Conzen focused on linkages among banks themselves and the present study has examined links between large corporations and banks, one might wonder whether post-industrial financial linkages will evolve to parallel the "mature" conditions identified by Conzen for 1910, i.e., into a more detailed pattern. Although it is not within the scope of this paper to forecast or document change empirically, it is tempting to see certain parallels between future change and Conzen's maturation of the urban system as the new service economy surges ahead, especially in the Sunbelt. Whereas New York will continue as the national banking capital, growing regional centers such as Atlanta, Dallas-Ft. Worth, Houston, Miami, and Phoenix will grow in significance as centers for banking. Changes in regulation of intrastate, and even interstate, banking will have an important effect for future financial centers.

Acknowledgments

I wish to thank David R. Meyer and an anonymous reviewer for helpful comments on an earlier draft of this paper. Thanks also to Ling Bian for her assistance in compiling data and to Audrey Hawkins for typing the manuscript.

Notes

1. A commercial bank refers to all banks except investment banks and savings and loan institutions. Commercial banks offer the normal range of checking and savings deposit services and loans, whereas investment banks not only supply capital "but intelligence necessary to maximize the profits on that capital . . . a total range of financial services that embraces every aspect of corporate operation as it relates to capital (Marcus 1975, 172).
2. These states include Alabama, Arkansas, Florida, Georgia, Kentucky, Louisiana, Mississippi, North Carolina, Oklahoma, South Carolina, Tennessee, Texas, and Virginia.
3. The chi-square value calculated on the frequencies on which the percentages in Table 3 are based was highly significant ($\chi^2 = 78.2$; $p \leq 0.001$).
4. The $1 billion dividing point was selected as a convenient figure to ensure a representative number of firms in both the large and small size categories.

References

Berry, B. J. L. 1973. *Growth centers in the American urban system*. Vol. 1. Cambridge, Mass.: Ballinger.

Borchert, J. R. 1978. Major control points in American economic geography. *Annals of the Association of American Geographers* 68:214–32.

Coakley, J., and Harris, L. 1983. *The city of capital: London's role as a financial center*. Oxford: Basil Blackwell.

Cohen, R. B. 1977. Multinational corporations, international finance, and the Sunbelt. In *The rise of the Sunbelt cities*, ed. D. C. Perry and A. J. Watkins, pp. 211–26. Beverly Hills: Sage Publications.

Conzen, M. P. 1977. The maturing urban system in the United States, 1840–1910. *Annals of the Association of American Geographers* 67:88–108.

———. 1981. The American urban system in the nineteenth century. In *Geography and the urban environment*, vol. 4, ed. D. T. Herbert and R. J. Johnston, pp. 295–347. New York: John Wiley and Sons.

Dicken, P., and Lloyd, P. E. 1978. Inner metropolitan industrial change, enterprise structure and study of external control and regional development. *Regional Studies* 10:401–12.

Eberstein, I. W., and Galle, O. R. 1984. The metropolitan system in the South: Functional differentiation and trade patterns. *Social Forces* 62:926–40.

Fennema, M. 1982. *International networks of banks and industry*. The Hague: Martinus Nijhoff.

Green, M. B. 1983. The interurban corporate interlocking directorate network of Canada and the United States: A spatial perspective. *Urban Geography* 4:338–54.

Green, M. B., and Semple, R. K. 1981. The corporate interlocking directorate as an urban spatial information network. *Urban Geography* 2:148–60.

Hanson, R., ed. 1983. *Rethinking urban policy: Urban development in an advanced economy*. Washington, D.C.: National Academy Press.

Hayes, S. L., III; Spence, A. M.; and Marks, D. V. P. 1983. *Competition in the investment banking* *industry*. Cambridge, Mass.: Harvard University Press.

Kindleberger, C. P. 1983. International banks as leaders or followers of international business. *Journal of Banking and Finance* 7:583–95.

Kotz, D. M. 1978. *Bank control of large corporations in the United States*. Berkeley: University of California Press.

McKenzie, R. D. 1925. The ecological approach to the study of the human community. In *The city*, ed. R. E. Park, E. W. Burgess, and R. D. McKenzie, pp. 63–79. Chicago: University of Chicago Press.

———. 1927. Spatial distance and community organization patterns. *Social Forces* 5:623–38.

Marcus, B. W. 1975. *Competing for capital: A financial relations approach*. New York: John Wiley and Sons.

Meyer, D. R. 1980. A dynamic model of the integration of frontier urban places into the United States system of cities. *Economic Geography* 56:120–40.

———. 1984. Control and coordination links in the metropolitan system of cities: The South as case study. *Social Forces* 62:349–62.

Mintz, B., and Schwartz, M. 1983. Financial interest groups and interlocking directorates. *Social Science History* 7:183–204.

Mizruchi, M. S. 1982. *The American corporate network, 1904–1974*. Beverly Hills: Sage Publications.

———. 1983. Relations among large American corporations, 1904–1974. *Social Science History* 7:165–82.

Pred, A. 1977. *City-systems in advanced economies*. New York: John Wiley and Sons.

Semple, R. K. 1985. Quaternary place theory: An introduction. *Urban Geography* 6:285–96.

Simmie, J. M. 1983. Beyond the industrial city? *Journal of the American Planning Association* 49:59–76.

Slaven, A., and Aldcroft, D. H., eds. 1982. *Business, banking and urban history*. Edinburgh: John Donald Publisher.

Stanback, T. M., Jr.; Bearse, P.; Noyelle, T. J.; and Karasek, R. 1981. *Services: The new economy*. Totowa, N.J.: Allanheld, Osmun and Co.

Stanback, T. M., Jr., and Noyelle, T. J. 1982. *Cities in transition*. Totowa, N.J.: Allanheld, Osmun and Co.

Watts, H. D. 1981. *The branch plant economy: A study of external control*. London: Longman.

Wheeler, J. O., and Brown, C. L. 1985. The metropolitan corporate hierarchy in the U.S. South, 1960–1980. *Economic Geography* 61:66–78.

Wheeler, J. O., and Dillon, P. M. 1985. The wealth of the nation: The United States metropolitan banking hierarchy, 1970–1980. *Urban Geography* 6:297–315.

Wheeler, J. O., and Park, S. O. 1984. External ownership and control: The impact of industrial organization on the regional economy. *Geoforum* 15:243–52.

Zehring, K. 1983. *The corporate finance bluebook, 1983*. New York: Zehring Publishing.

[17]

The Location of International Financial Activity: An Interregional Analysis

MICHAEL A. GOLDBERG, ROBERT W. HELSLEY and MAURICE D. LEVI
Faculty of Commerce and Business Administration, University of British Columbia, Vancouver, BC, V6T IY8, Canada.

(Received October 1987; in revised form August 1988)

GOLDBERG M. A., HELSLEY R. W. and LEVI M. D. (1989) The location of international financial activity: an interregional analysis, *Reg. Studies* **23,** 1–7. This paper examines the determinants of the spatial distribution of financial activity. The determinants of the sizes of the financial services sector are estimated using data for a sample of US states. Although our analysis is limited by the availability of data, the results are strong and clear. The level of international financial activity is positively and significantly related to per capita income, the level of imports, and the number of corporate headquarters. The results indicate that international trade is intensive in its use of financial services and that financial services tends to be exported along with goods.

International financial activity   Spatial   US states   Bank deposits   Location

GOLDBERG M. A., HELSLEY R. W. et LEVI M. D. (1989) La localisation des opérations financières internationales: une analyse interrégionale, *Reg. Studies* **23,** 1–7. Cet article examine les déterminants de la distribution géographique des opérations financières. A partir des données relatives à un échantillonnage des états aux E-U on évalue les déterminants de l'importance du secteur des services financiers. Bien que l'analyse soit limitée en fonction des données disponibles, les résultats sont puissants et clairs. L'ampleur des opérations financières internationales se rapporte de façon positive et sensible au revenu par tête, à l'importance des importations et au nombre de sièges, les résultats laissent supposer que le commerce international nécessite une utilisation intensive des services financiers, et que les opérations financières ont tendance à être exportées aussi bien que les biens d'exportation.

Opérations financières internationales
Géographique   États aux E-U
Dépôts bancaires   Localisation

GOLDBERG M. A., HELSLEY R. W. und LEVI M. D. (1989) Standorte internationaler Tätigkeit auf finanziellem Gebiet: eine interregionale Analyse, *Reg. Studies* **23,** 1–7 Dieser Aufsatz untersucht die bestimmenden Faktoren der räumlichen Verteilung der Tätigkeit auf finanziellem Gebiet. Die bestimmenden Faktoren der Grössen des finanziellen Dienstleistungssektors werden mit Hilfe von Daten einer Auswahl von Staaten der USA geschätzt. Obwohl unsere Analyse durch die Verfügbarkeit von Daten beschränkt ist, treten die Ergebnisse doch kräftig und klar heraus. Der Umfang internationaler Tätigkeit auf finanziellem Gebiet steht in positiver und bedeutsamer Beziehung zum Einkommen pro Kopf, dem Umfang der Einfuhren und der Anzahl der Hauptgeschäftsstellen von Unternehmen. Die Ergebnisse weisen darauf hin, dass der internationale Handel sich intensiv finanzieller Dienstleistungen bedient, und dass Güterausfuhr meist vom Export finanzieller Tätigkeit begleitet wird.

Internationale Tätigkeit auf finanziellem Gebiet
Räumlich   Staaten der USA   Bankeinlagen
Standort

INTRODUCTION

With the pace of international financial activity expanding at an extraordinary rate,[1] and with so much income and employment generated by this activity, it is perhaps surprising that economists have paid so little attention to the factors affecting the development of centres of international finance. Indeed, after noting that, 'it is a curious fact that the formation of financial centres is no longer studied in economics', KINDLEBERGER, 1974, hypothesized that this is due to the issue falling between two areas of investigation: urban and regional economics, which is concerned with locational matters, but which concentrates on industry, housing and transportation rather than finance; and monetary and financial economics, which has little interest in geographic location.

KINDLEBERGER, 1974, in a paper that sparked renewed interest in financial centres, tried to fill the void by tracing the events that led to the emergence of national banking and centres of financial activity in Europe and North America. However, his comparative historical account is, in his own words 'qualitative rather than quantitative', (p. 68), an attribute which 'derives from the limitation of the writer, the magnitude of the task of deriving comparable data from a wide number of countries, and an interest more in process than in detailed outcome'. In his classic studies of financial activity in the United States, GOLDSMITH, 1958, 1965, 1968, 1969, documented many aspects of the regional distribution of banking and financial activity. However, perhaps because of the heavy data requirements to which Kindleberger alluded, Goldsmith did not analyse the determinants of the spatial distribution of financial activity. More recently, REED'S, 1981, ambitious study of the evolution of a hierarchy of centres of international finance uses cluster analysis to delineate the common characteristics of centres of international finance. Unfortunately, Reed's analysis sheds little light on the economic forces underlying the location of financial activity.

The purpose of this paper is to build on the work of these authors by empirically estimating the importance of a few basic economic forces affecting the 'geography of finance' as it was described by KERR, 1965. Specifically, we present cross-section results on the determinants of the level of national and international financial activity in thirty US states and the District of Columbia in 1984.[2] We show that a large portion of the spatial variation in the level of financial activity in the US can be explained by surprisingly few variables.

SPECIFICATION AND MEASUREMENT OF THE RELEVANT VARIABLES

There exist no equilibrium models of the development of financial centres or the regional location of financial activity. Indeed, the only conceptual idea that appears repeatedly in the meagre literature on financial centres is that there are economies inherent in banking and finance that encourage financial firms to concentrate geographically.[3] However, models from international finance of the size of the financial sector in a country may be combined with basic concepts from location theory to uncover the factors that are likely to influence financial location across regions of a country.

We adopt several measures of the level of financial activity in US states, the dependent variable in the study. These are: (1) total assets and deposits in domestic banks located in the state; (2) total assets and deposits in foreign banks located in the state; and (3) total state employment in finance, insurance, and real estate.[4] Assets and deposits in foreign banks are crude measures of the amount of international financial activity occurring in a state.

Conceptual models of the size of the financial sector in a country suggest a number of potentially relevant explanatory variables.[5] In general, theory suggests that a country will contain more banking and financial activity the greater is the level of economic development there. On the supply side, savings and the supply of loanable funds tend to rise with the level of economic activity. On the demand side, the demand for goods and services, including financial goods and services, tends to rise with the level of economic activity. We conjecture that these effects are also present at the regional or local level. To capture regional variations in the level of economic development, we include state personal income as an explanatory variable.[6]

International financial theory also suggests that the amount of banking and financial activity in a country should vary positively with the volume of international trade. This occurs because international transactions utilize financial services more intensively than domestic transactions. We expect variations around the level of financial activity attributable to a state's personal income to result from variations in the level of international trade in that state. The level of international trade is captured by including the total dollar value of imports and exports booked through the state's custom office as an explanatory variable. The availability of export and import data limits our sample to the thirty states (and the District of Columbia) containing US customs offices. It is important to note that the import data used in our analysis pertain to the point of unlading, rather than the point at which the merchandise first enters the US.[7] Imports and exports are entered as separate explanatory variables, since there are reasons to suspect they generate different demands for financial services, and hence different effects on bank location. For example, the access to importers may be especially important to banks, because importers are often required to guarantee payment with a letter of credit.

REED'S 1981, study of the hierarchical structure of international financial centres suggests that a disproportionate share of banking will occur in those states in which large companies maintain their head offices. He concludes (p. 74) that, 'prominent international financial centres are also prominent communication and management centres'. Many financial decisions and transactions are initiated in corporate headquarters, where decision-making authority is concentrated. To the degree that banking and financial services are purchased locally, this will lead to a positive relationship between financial activity and headquarters location. Alternatively, the presence of a large number of corporate headquarters may reflect the presence of the institutional infrastructure which confers cost advantages on banks and other businesses through agglomeration economies. We include several measures of the number of corporations in a state as explanatory variables. These are: (1) the number of US multinational corporation headquarters in a state; (2) the number of foreign corporations in a state; and (3) the total number of corporations in a state. The number of foreign corporations is included to examine the relationship between foreign corporate activity and international financial activity in a state.

Finally, the average corporate state income tax rate was included in early regressions to control for regional variations in tax burdens. Location decisions of both financial institutions and the businesses they serve could be affected by tax rates, and there is significant variation across the states in this regard. However, consistent with most studies of business location, this fiscal variable did not add explanatory power and was never statistically significant. It is not included in the regressions reported in this paper.

To summarize, the following regression equation was estimated using ordinary least squares for the thirty states containing US customs offices and the District of Columbia for 1984:

$$\text{Financial activity} = \beta_0 + \beta_1 \text{ income} + \beta_2 \text{ imports} + \beta_3 \text{ exports} + \beta_4 \text{ corporations} + \mu$$

The first explanatory variable, state personal income, controls for variations in the level of economic development. The second and third explanatory variables, the dollar value of imports and exports cleared through the customs office in a state, capture the effects of international trade. The fourth explanatory variable accounts for the impact of the number of corporations located in a state. *A priori*, we expect the coefficients on all the explanatory variables to be positive.

RESULTS

The results using the different measures of financial activity are summarized in Tables 1–3. The first observation that can be made is that the models account for a very high fraction of the variation in the dependent variable: the adjusted R^2 lies between 0·90 and 0·99 in all regressions. The models using employment in finance, insurance, and real estate as the dependent variable consistently have the highest R^2 and those using foreign assets or deposits the lowest. In general, it appears that the most important variables have been included.

As expected, total domestic assets are positively related to the level of economic development as measured by total personal income in each state (Table 1, row a). However, when the number of foreign corporation employees (*FCORP*) or the total number of corporations (*CORPS*) is added, the income variable is no longer significant in the domestic asset equations. The insignificance of personal income in the domestic asset equations when *FCORPS* or *CORPS* are included could represent a multicollinearity problem. The simple correlations between personal income and *CORPS* and *FCORPS* are slightly higher than that between personal income and domestic deposits.

However, personal income is positively and significantly related to deposits in domestic banks, independent of the measurement of corporate activity (Table 1, rows f–j). The income variable appears to

Table 1. The determinants of the level of domestic financial activity in thirty-one states in 1984

	Constant	Income	Imports	Exports	*USMN*	*FCORPS*	*CORPS*	R^2
Assets in domestic banks[1]								
(a)	−101·97	0·271*	2·63*	−1·25	316·97*			0·96
	(−0·026)	(4·09)	(2·83)	(−1·04)	(3·31)			
(b)	−3333·9	0·152	5·41*	−4·65*		40·56**		0·96
	(−0·744)	(1·44)	(7·43)	(−4·20)		(2·63)		
(c)	−1794·0	0·134	4·51*	−3·66*			0·328**	0·96
	(−0·403)	(1·09)	(6·23)	(−3·48)			(2·31)	
(d)	−4443·0	0·016	3·14*	−2·30**	327·50*	41·79**	0·026**	0·98
	(−1·24)	(0·157)	(3·90)	(−2·19)	(3·84)	(2·83)	(0·189)	
(e)	−4414·5	0·025	3·15*	−2·30**	332·53*	43·32*		0·97
	(−1·25)	(0·282)	(4·01)	(−2·23)	(4·19)	(3·59)		
Deposits in domestic banks[1]								
(f)	−865·7	0·359*	0·885	−0·169	123·10***			0·97
	(−0·332)	(3·27)	(1·45)	(−0·216)	(1·97)			
(g)	3147·41	0·254*	2·12*	−1·77*		26·16*		0·97
	(−1·23)	(4·22)	(5·08)	(−2·80)		(2·97)		
(h)	−1552·50	0·303*	1·61*	−1·11			0·131	0·96
	(−0·563)	(3·98)	(3·59)	(−1·70)			(1·49)	
(i)	−3510·36	0·224*	1·24**	−0·820*	144·69*	30·80*	−0·060	0·98
	(−1·48)	(3·35)	(2·33)	(−1·18)	(2·57)	(3·17)	(0·670)	
(j)	−3579·25	0·204*	1·21**	−0·829*	132·89**	27·26*		0·98
	(−1·53)	(3·47)	(2·31)	(−1·21)	(2·51)	(3·39)		

Notes: 1. Dependent variables: *t*-ratios in parentheses
* significant at the 1% level
** significant at the 5% level
*** significant at the 10% level

explain the largest component of the variation in domestic deposits. The fact that the relationship between income and deposits is stronger than that between income and assets is consistent with the financial intermediation function of banking.

When employment in finance, insurance, and real estate is used to measure financial activity, personal income is positive and significant in all cases, and it seems to explain the largest component of the variation in the dependent variable. The strength of the income variable's performance in both the deposit and employment equations lends credence to the suspicion that multicollinearity is partly responsible for the income variable's poorer performance in the asset equations.

The most puzzling results occur when foreign assets or deposits are used to measure financial activity. In these cases personal income is significantly negatively related to the dependent variable (Table 2). Income appears to explain somewhat less of the total variation in foreign banking than imports, but the negative coefficient for the income variable is unexpected. In terms of total explained variation the 'foreign' equations perform less well than domestic models.

Imports have a positive impact on financial activity; the estimated coefficient is significant in all but one of the twenty-five equations. While imports account for somewhat less of the variation in domestic financial activity than is accounted for by personal income, they appear to be the most important explanation for foreign assets and deposits. Generally the magnitude of the estimated coefficients for imports is greater in the asset equations (foreign and domestic) than the deposit equations, while the opposite was true for the income variable. The inference is that imports are more fundamental to the distribution of assets, while personal income is more important for deposits.

What might at first glance seem surprising is that exports were found to have a negative impact on the level of financial activity in all cases (Tables 1, 2 and 3).[8] The estimated coefficients are generally significant except when financial development is measured by domestic deposits. Like imports, exports seem to be more fundamental to the explanation of foreign than domestic financial activity, judging from the size of the respective *t*-statistics. In all of the estimated equations the absolute value of the coefficient for imports is greater than that for exports, indicating that the balanced trade multiplier for financial services is positive, as expected. Thus international trade appears to have an incremental impact on financial activity beyond a simple addition to overall aggregate economic activity.

While the significantly negative coefficient on exports might seem strange at first, a little reflection reveals it to be the mirror image of the positive coefficient on exports. To see this, imagine for a moment that the coefficients on imports and exports

Table 2. The determinants of the level of foreign financial activity in twenty-six states in 1984

	Constant	Income	Imports	Exports	*USMN*	*FCORPS*	*CORPS*	R^2
Assets in Foreign Banks[1]								
(a)	−1863·4	0·245*	3·97*	−2·68*	206·22**			0·92
	(−0·450)	(−4·17)	(4·72)	(−2·53)	(2·43)			
(b)	−1011·2	−0·240**	5·61*	−4·50*		9·62		0·90
	(−0·212)	(−2·42)	(8·28)	(−4·42)		(0·684)		
(c)	−2996·7	−0·394*	5·15*	−4·31*			0·288**	0·92
	(−0·716)	(−4·07)	(8·86)	(−5·17)			(2·57)	
(d)	−3699·7	−0·396	3·94*	−2·95*	162·16***	−4·60	0·263***	0·94
	(−0·910)	(−4·06)	(4·88)	(−2·85)	(1·95)	(0·325)	(2·01)	
(e)	−2963·3	−0·308*	4·11*	−2·96**	209·96**	11·17		0·93
	(−0·681)	(−3·30)	(4·77)	(−2·66)	(2·46)	(0·882)		
Deposits in Foreign Banks[1]								
(f)	−1377·9	−0·220*	3·46*	−2·29**	191·26**			0·93
	(−0·399)	(−4·39)	(4·80)	(−2·52)	(2·63)			
(g)	−827·2	−0·222**	5·00*	−4·02*		10·14		0·90
	(−2·06)	(−2·60)	(8·54)	(−4·57)		(0·834)		
(h)	−2376·0	−0·351*	4·57*	−3·80*			0·257**	0·93
	(−0·673)	(−4·19)	(9·06)	(−5·27)			(2·65)	
(i)	−3078·4	−0·359*	3·46*	−2·57*	154·92*	[−1·63]	0·220***	0·94
	(−0·908)	(−4·32)	(5·02)	(−2·90)	(2·18)	(−0·134)	(1·96)	
(j)	−2497·54	−0·286*	3·60*	−2·57**	195·03**	11·54		0·93
	(−0·694)	(−3·62)	(4·93)	(−2·73)	(2·69)	(1·07)		

Notes: 1. Dependent variables: *t*-ratios in parentheses. (Maine, Montana, North Dakota, and Vermont have no foreign assets or deposits; South Carolina has no foreign assets).
* significant at the 1% level
** significant at the 5% level
*** significant at the 10% level

Table 3. The determinants of the level of financial employment in thirty-one states in 1984[1]

	Constant	Income	Imports	Exports	*USMN*	*FCORPS*	*CORPS*	R^2
(a)	−89·02	1·32*	3·25**	−1·94	462·79*			0·99
	(−0·017)	(14·17)	(2·60)	(−1·21)	(3·61)			
(b)	−5640·8	1·09*	7·43*	−7·13*		67·66*		0·99
	(−0·976)	(8·04)	(7·91)	(−5·00)		(3·40)		
(c)	−2331·40	1·14*	6·02*	−5·45*			0·448**	0·98
	(−0·380)	(6·72)	(6·02)	(−3·76)			(2·29)	
(d)	−7147·7	0·931*	4·13*	−3·66*	502·38*	78·93*	−0·070	0·99
	(−1·75)	(8·06)	(4·51)	(−3·05)	(5·16)	(4·51)	(−0·454)	
(e)	−7228·0	0·907*	4·10*	−3·68*	488·55*	71·72*		0·99
	(−1·79)	(9·00)	(4·56)	(−3·11)	(5·37)	(5·19)		

Notes: 1. Dependent variable: = employment in finance, insurance and real estate: *t*-ratios in parentheses.
* significant at the 1% level
** significant at the 5% level

have opposite signs, but are equal in absolute value. This would indicate that international trade has no net effect on financial activity: a state containing a large amount of balanced international trade (large and equal quantities of imports and exports) would have a level of financial activity equal to that dictated by other forces, say the level of income or the number of corporations within its boundaries. Now imagine that there are two states in a country, a net import region and a net export region, but maintain the assumption that trade is balanced in the aggregate. The net importing state will have a higher level of financial activity than could be accounted for by its other characteristics, and the net exporting state a correspondingly lower level of activity. Thus, trade shifts the location of financial activity away from regions dependent on exports toward regions dependent on imports.

There are sound economic reasons for expecting this type of shifting to occur. First, as discussed earlier, it may be more important for banks to have access to importers since the importer is the one who frequently finances the trade and applies for letters of credit. If important attributes of the importer, for example, his credit worthiness, are only revealed through local experience, then banks may concentrate in areas where imports constitute a larger fraction of international trade. Further, it may be just as important for banks to be near importers to obtain access to their demands for credit.

Second, exporters may have an incentive to conduct financial transactions in the countries containing their major export markets. By denominating their debt in the importer's currency, exporters can match the currency of payables and receivables, thereby reducing their foreign exchange exposure.[9] This can often be done most expendiently by using banks or financial markets in the importer's country. This may lead fewer banks to concentrate in areas where exports constitute a larger fraction of international trade.

The number of US multinational companies (*USMN*) headquartered in a state is positively and significantly related to state financial activity in all the models we estimated. In all cases replacing *USMN* with *FCORP* increases the proportion of variation explained by the trade variables (equations (a) and (b), all tables). While *FCORP* is significant on its own in the domestic equations, this is not the case in the foreign assets or deposits equations. When all three measures of business concentration are included (equations (d), all tables), *FCORP* performs satisfactorily except in the foreign equations where the sign is opposite to that expected, although it is not significant. This is consistent with the argument outlined above: just as US exporters may use foreign banks (i.e. banks in the importer's country) to hedge foreign exchange risk, foreign corporations in the US may favour American banks over 'their own', for similar reasons.

The total number of corporations in a state is not a superior measure of the impact of business concentration on financial development. If it is true that multinational and foreign corporations are more likely to be involved in international trade, the poorer performance of the *CORPS* variable (versus *USMN*, *FCORPS*) underscores the importance of trade in explaining the variation in the distribution of financial activity between states.

All the models in Tables 1–3 were initially estimated with a corporate tax variable. The variable was never significant, and removing it had almost no impact on the coefficients of the remaining variables.

CONCLUSION

While there are limitations imposed by the availability of data, it is possible to examine empirically the relevance of different factors which influence the growth of financial centres. The simple models described in this paper explain at least 90% of the variation in financial activity across US states.

Our results suggest that financial activity is closely related to the overall level of economic activity in a state, which is hardly surprising. Any theory of the development of centres of financial activity needs to take into account income levels and the location of corporate headquarters. Of course, there is a great deal of simultaneity in these relationships. Banking and financial markets are as much a cause as a consequence of economic development (GOROSTIAGA, 1984; FENNEMA, 1982). KINDLEBERGER, 1974, argues that financial intermediaries are crucial in providing effective means of commercial payments, enabling the expansion of trade and general economic activity.

Our results also suggest that any theory of the development of centres of financial activity should take into account international trade and the distinct effects of imports and exports on financial activity. Our results indicate that international trade is intensive in its use of financial services and that financial activity tends to be exported along with goods. Only a theory which implies a positive influence of imports and a negative influence of exports would appear to fit the empirical facts.

Acknowledgements—The authors extend their thanks to two anonymous referees for helpful comments. The generous financial support of the British Columbia Ministry of Finance and Corporate Relations is gratefully acknowledged. Doug McLean and Reagan Pratt provided research assistance. The authors are solely responsible for the views expressed and for any errors that remain.

NOTES

1. The explosion in international financial services has been documented and studied at length in recent years. For details of the growth of the international financial sector see MAYER, 1985; HAMILTON, 1986; and FERRIS, 1984. For critical commentary on the growth of international debt and international finance see KAUFMAN, 1986, and WACHTEL, 1986.
2. GOLDBERG, HELSLEY and LEVI, 1988, examine the geography of international finance using national data rather than data for regions within a country. Where comparisons between the studies are feasible, the results are remarkably similar to those reported here.
3. REED, 1981, p. 4, discusses these 'eminence theories'.
4. Details about the data and their sources are provided in the appendix.
5. These models include: ALIBER, 1980, 1984; BALL and TSCHOEGL, 1982; DEAN and GRUBEL, 1979; GRAY and GRAY, 1981, FIELEKE, 1977; GRUBEL, 1977; and MONTI, 1982.
6. The international finance literature also suggests that variations in savings rates and financial regulations (for example, reserve requirements) should affect the level of financial activity in a country. Since regional variations in the former are unmeasurable, and regional variations in the latter do not exist, these factors are excluded from our analysis.
7. The Commerce Department's *Guide to Foreign Trade Statistics* states (p. 11), 'the Customs district shown is the district of unlading, i.e., the district at which the merchandise is unloaded from the importing vessel or aircraft. The district of unlading may not be the same as the district of entry'.
8. This result also occurs in our time series and cross section studies of the determinants of the level of financial activity across nations, see GOLDBERG, HELSLEY, and LEVI, 1988.
9. LEVI, 1987, establishes the tendency of exporting firms to hedge foreign exchange risk by borrowing in the currency of their receivables.

APPENDIX

Data descriptions and sources

Five different measures of financial activity were used as dependent variables. The *Annual Statistical Digest* published by the US Department of Commerce provides information on total assets and deposits in each state. Both figures can be disaggregated into domestic (US) and foreign bank assets (deposits). *The Statistical Abstract of the United States* provides statistics on the number of persons employed in finance, insurance or real estate in each state. Although there is reason to expect employment to behave differently from the other measures of financial activity, the simple correlations between financial employment and domestic assets (deposits) are 0·90 (0·98) and between foreign assets (deposits) 0·75 (0·76).

The measure of overall economic activity in each state is total personal income as published in the *Statistical Abstract of the United States*. Simple correlations between this variable and domestic assets (deposits) are 0·90 (0·96) but are only on the order of 0·59 for foreign assets and deposits.

Data on the value of international trade measured by imports and exports by state is contained in *The Statistical Abstract of the United States*. This data measures the value of goods booked through Federal Customs Offices in the thirty states (plus the District of Columbia) with these offices. The states included in our study are: Alabama, Alaska, Arizona, California, Connecticut, Florida, Georgia, Hawaii, Illinois, Louisiana, Maine, Massachusetts, Maryland, Michigan, Missouri, Minnesota, Montana, New York, North Carolina, North Dakota, Ohio, Oregon, Pennsylvania, South Carolina, Virginia, Vermont, Wisconsin, Rhode Island, Texas, and Washington. As noted in the text, this data pertains to the point of unlading, which may not correspond to the point at which the merchandise first entered the US. The simple correlation between exports and imports in our sample is 0·96.

The locations of the headquarters of US multinationals were derived from the addresses shown in *Who Owns Who: North America* published by Dun and Bradstreet. The number of foreign corporations (non financial) in each state is available in *Foreign Direct Investment in the United States: Operations of U.S. Affiliates–1983 Estimates* published by the US Department of Commerce, Bureau of Economic Analysis. Our figure for the number of corporations in each state is the total number located in each state who filed federal tax returns, which is contained in *Commissioner of Internal Revenue, Annual Report*, published by the US Department of Treasury.

The average corporate tax rate used in early regressions was calculated by dividing corporate taxes paid by corporate profits as published in *Tax Capacity of the Fifty States*, US Department of Commerce, Bureau of the Census.

REFERENCES

ALIBER R. (1980) The integration of off-shore and domestic banking systems, *J. Mon. Econ.* **6,** 509–26.

ALIBER R. (1984) International banking: a survey, *J. Mon. Cred. Bank.* **16,** 661–78.

BALL C. and TSCHOEGL A. (1982) The decision to establish a foreign bank branch or subsidiary: an application of binary classification procedures, *J. Fin. and Quant. Analysis* **17,** 411–24.

CHAPMAN S. (1984) *The Rise of Merchant Banking.* George Allen & Unwin, Hemel Hempstead, Herts.

DEAN J. and HERBERT G. (1979) Regulatory issues and the theory of multinational banking, in EDWARDS F. R. (Ed.) *Issues in Financial Regulation,* McGraw-Hill, New York.

DUN and BRADSTREET (1986) *Who Owns Who: North America.* Dun and Bradstreet, New York.

FENNEMA M. (1982) *International Networks of Banks and Industry.* Martinus Nijhoff, Boston.

FERRIS P. (1984) *The Master Bankers.* New American Library, New York.

FIELEKE N. S. (1977) The growth of US banking abroad: an analytical survey, in *Key Issues in International Banking,* pp. 9–40. Conference Series 18, Federal Reserve Bank of Boston, Boston.

FREEDMAN C. (1974) The foreign currency business of Canadian banks: an economic study, bank of Canada Staff Research Studies, Ottawa.

GOLDBERG L. and SAUNDERS A. (1980) The causes of US bank expansion overseas: the case of Great Britain, *J. Mon. Cred. Bank.* **12,** 630–43.

GOLDBERG L. and SAUNDERS A. (1981a) The determinants of foreign banking activity in the United States, *J. Bank. Finance* **5,** 17–32.

GOLDBERG L. and SAUNDERS A. (1981b) The growth of organizational forms of foreign banks in the US, *J. Mon. Cred. Bank.* **13,** 365–74.

GOLDBERG M. A., HELSLEY R. W. and LEVI M. D. (1988) Factors influencing the development of financial centers, Research Papers in International Business, Trade and Finance, University of British Columbia.

GOLDSMITH R. W. (1958) *Financial Intermediaries in the American Economy Since 1900.* Princeton University Press, Princeton, NJ.

GOLDSMITH R. W. (1965) *The Flow of Capital Funds in the Post-War Economy.* National Bureau of Economic Research, New York.

GOLDSMITH R. W. (1968) *Financial Institutions.* Random House, New York.

GOLDSMITH R. W. (1969) *Financial Structure and Development.* Yale University Press, New Haven.

GOROSTIAGA X. (1984) *The Role of International Financial Centres in Underdeveloped Countries.* Croom Helm, London.

GRAY J. M. and GRAY H. P. (1981) The multinational bank: a financial MNC? *J. Bank. Finance* **5,** 33–63.

GRUBEL H. (1977) A theory of multinational banking, *Banca Nazionele del Lavoro Quart. Rev.* **1–3,** 349–63.

HAMILTON A. (1986) *The Financial Revolution.* The Free Press, New York.

ILKE M. (1972) *Switzerland: An International Banking and Financial Center.* Dowden, Hutchinson, and Ross, Strodsburg, PA.

KAUFMAN H. (1986) *Interest Rates, the Markets, and the New Financial World.* Times Books, New York.

KERR D. (1965) Some aspects of the geography of finance in Canada, *Can. Geogr.* **9,** 175–92.

KINDLEBERGER C. (1974) The formation of financial centers: a study in comparative economic history, Princeton Studies in International Finance No. 36, Princeton University Press, Princeton, NJ.

KINDLEBERGER C. (1985) The functioning of financial centers: Britain in the 19th century, the United States since 1945, in FEATHER W. and MARSTON R. (Eds.) *International Financial Markets and Capital Movements,* Princeton University Press, Princeton, NJ.

LANDES D. S. (1958) *Bankers and Pashas.* Heinemann, London.

LEES F. *Foreign Banking and Investment in the United States: Issues and Alternatives.* Wiley, New York.

LEVI M. D. (1987) Exchange rates and the value of the firm: the theory and evidence, Research Papers in International Business, Trade and Finance, University of British Columbia.

LOGAN M. I. and DALY M. T. (1984) *The International Finance System and Economic Development.* Department of Geography, University of Sydney.

MAYER M. (1985) *The Money Bazaars: Understanding the Banking Revolution Around Us.* New American Library, New York.

MONTI A. (1982) Recent trends in international banking, *J. Bank. Finance* **6,** 389–99.

REED H. (1981) *The Preeminence of International Financial Centers.* Praeger, New York.

TERRELL H. and SYDNEY K. (1977) The growth of foreign banking in the United States: an analytical survey, in *Key Issues in International Banking Conference Series 18,* pp. 54–86. Federal Reserve Bank of Boston, Boston.

US DEPARTMENT OF COMMERCE (1983) *Guide to Foreign Trade Statistics.* US Government Printing Office, Washington, DC.

US DEPARTMENT OF COMMERCE, BUREAU OF THE CENSUS (1985) *Foreign Direct Investment in the United States: Operations of US Affiliates—1983 Estimates.* US Government Printing Office, Washington, DC.

US DEPARTMENT OF COMMERCE, BUREAU OF THE CENSUS (1986a) *Annual Statistical Digest.* US Government Printing Office, Washington, DC.

US DEPARTMENT OF COMMERCE, BUREAU OF THE CENSUS (1986b) *Statistical Abstract of the United States.* US Government Printing Office, Washington, DC.

US DEPARTMENT OF COMMERCE, BUREAU OF THE CENSUS (1986c) *Tax Capacity of the Fifty States.* US Government Printing Office, Washington, DC.

US DEPARTMENT OF TREASURY, COMMISSIONER OF INTERNAL REVENUE (1984) *Annual Report.* US Government Printing Office, Washington, DC.

WACHTEL H. (1986) *The Money Mandarins: The Making of a Supranational Economic Order.* Pantheon Books, New York.

[18]

SOME ASPECTS OF THE GEOGRAPHY OF FINANCE IN CANADA

DONALD KERR
University of Toronto

URBAN geographers engaged in diverse tasks have virtually ignored finance as an urban economic activity. It is obvious that financial activity ranks high in some cities and not in others, but little attempt has been made to measure its magnitude and to study its functional organization. A major aim of this article is to select and employ a variety of statistical and non-statistical criteria to describe spatial variations of financial activity in Canada, and thereby, it is hoped, to cast some light on the broader problems of measurement and definition. Particularly in any attempt to define the financial centre, it seems necessary to distinguish between volume of financial activity and financial functions. This article seeks also, in a preliminary way, to show the significance of the hinterland concept in offering explanation for the rise and fall of financial centres; and to make brief reference to their connectivity. It should be noted that financial systems, although basically similar in broad structure in all capitalistic countries, do differ in detail, and therefore conclusions reached may or may not have relevance in the United States and other nations.

MEASUREMENT AND DEFINITION

Finance is varied and complex, and the problems of securing data to measure its magnitude and character spatially are formidable. Little can be gained by comparisons with other economic activities, for there is in finance no over-all total figure of value and, consequently, no possibility of abstracting "value added" (which has proved to be so meaningful in studies of manufacturing). Furthermore, it is unlikely that an aggregate figure, if one were available, would have much meaning; broadly speaking, finance is not part of the productive process as are agriculture and manufacturing, but, on the other hand, it is not entirely a service industry.

Unquestionably, the most accessible body of statistical data is that of employment in finance, and, indeed, such figures have been used by Harris, Bogue, and others in systems of classification and analysis.[1] But, at least in Canada, other types of statistical data may also be assembled. If the focus is changed from employment to financial institutions, it is possible to reveal a somewhat different geographic pattern. For this reason assets of financial institutions, according to head office locations, have been tabulated and mapped. Thirdly, the selection of one important financial activity—the movement of cheques through clearing houses—allows yet another regional pattern to be identified. All these criteria have serious limitations, however, and, in terms of defining the financial centre, one must pay attention to selected financial functions.

CANADIAN GEOGRAPHER, IX, 4, 1965

Employment

No record of employment in finance is kept by census areas. However, by making the broad assumption that the labour force in finance is approximately the same as employment in numbers and location, it is possible to measure variations in the number of people engaged in financial. activity from one urban centre to another.[2]

Two very obvious characteristics of finance and the labour force can be listed: employment in finance is quite small (only 3.5 per cent of the Canadian total in 1961), and it is concentrated to a greater extent than any other economic activity in large cities. Whereas wholesaling, manufacturing, and retailing, on the basis of employment, are rather widely dispersed throughout the urban hierarchy, finance is very much concentrated in Toronto and Montreal (41 per cent) and in all major urban centres having a population over 100,000 (74 per cent) (Table I). It is not surprising that the spatial distribution of financial activity (Figure 1) mirrors that of major urban centres. Toronto and Montreal stand out, the radii of the circles for

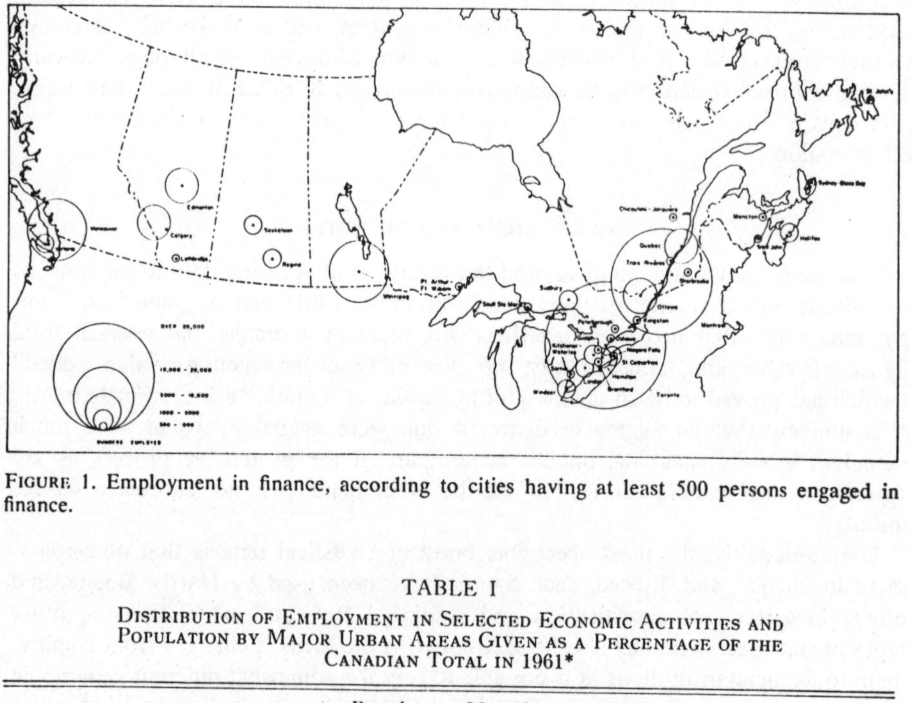

FIGURE 1. Employment in finance, according to cities having at least 500 persons engaged in finance.

TABLE I

DISTRIBUTION OF EMPLOYMENT IN SELECTED ECONOMIC ACTIVITIES AND POPULATION BY MAJOR URBAN AREAS GIVEN AS A PERCENTAGE OF THE CANADIAN TOTAL IN 1961*

	Population	Manufacturing	Wholesale trade	Retail trade	Finance
Urban areas with population greater than 1,000,000 (Montreal and Toronto)	21	35	31	26	41
Urban areas with population 100,000 to 1,000,000	24	24	33	29	33
All others (rural and urban areas)	55	41	36	45	26

*SOURCE: *Census of Canada 1961*, vols. 1 and 3.

Winnipeg and Vancouver not reaching half the values of the two eastern cities. Southern Ontario contains the largest number of centres that have an employment in finance over 500, while southern Quebec, in spite of a relatively large population, supports only Quebec City, Trois Rivières, Sherbrooke, and Chicoutimi outside of Montreal. The pattern on the prairies shows the dominance of Winnipeg; in the maritimes the absence of a large centre of financial activity is noteworthy.

Table II provides more detailed information by ranking the cities according to employment in finance; thus Toronto stands first over Montreal, and Calgary outranks Edmonton. By also giving employment data for sub-group 704 (investment companies and security dealers, see reference 2), Table II further emphasizes the concentration of finance in Montreal and Toronto, where indeed approximately 60 per cent find employment. To single out this category has merit, because many of its employees are involved in all aspects of the capital market and are in fact specialists in financial transactions. It is revealing that Vancouver, Winnipeg, and Calgary are the only other cities, besides the aforementioned, in which a substantial number are employed in this category.

In order to refine descriptions of financial activity, it is possible to manipulate statistical data on employment in a number of ways[3]; but in view of the over-all aims of this article only one very simple exercise is presented, that is, the relating of employment in finance to total employment. The calculation of these ratios gives insight into the relative importance of finance in the total structure of various cities. The arithmetical mean for all urban areas over 100,000 population is 4.4 per cent, which, as Table II shows, is exceeded only by Toronto, London, Regina, Vancouver, Winnipeg, Montreal, Calgary, Kitchener-Waterloo, and Ottawa, in that order. In fact, on the basis of this ratio, with modifications, Toronto stands fourth among the large cities in North America, exceeded by Dallas, San Francisco, and New York; Montreal is seventh, exceded by Minneapolis and Atlanta.[4]

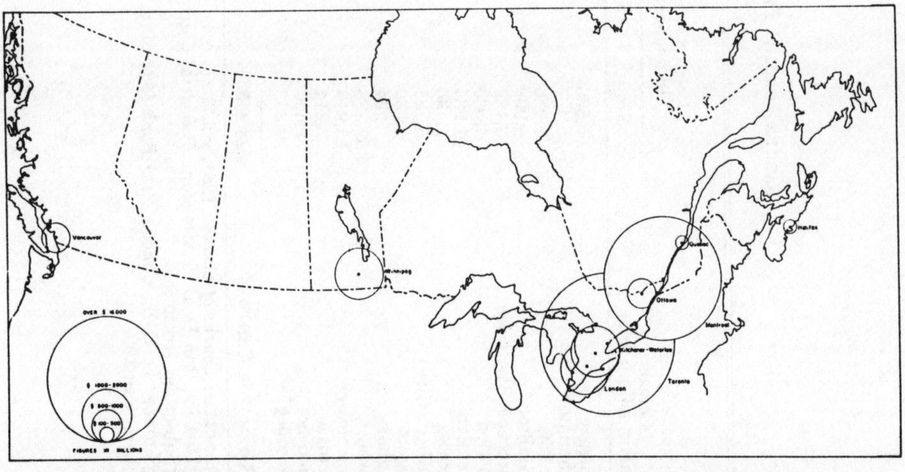

FIGURE 2. Total assets (exceeding 100 million dollars) of financial institutions according to head office location (based on an average 1959–1963). Only a few Canadian cities show a concentration of head offices of financial institutions.

TABLE II

LABOUR FORCE IN FINANCE AND CHEQUES CASHED AT CLEARING HOUSES FOR SELECTED CENSUS METROPOLITAN AREAS (OVER 100,000) IN 1961*

Census metropolitan area	Labour force in finance†		Ratio of labour force in finance to total labour force		Labour force in investment companies and security dealers‡		Cheques cashed§	
	No.	Rank	Ratio	Rank	No.	Rank	$000,000	Rank
Calgary	5,566	6	5.0	7	445	5	10,300	5
Edmonton	5,467	7	4.1	11	328	6	6,700	7
Halifax	2,988	12	4.1	10	137	13	2,800	12
Hamilton	4,969	9	3.3	15	213	7	6,000	8
Kitchener-Waterloo	3,152	11	4.8	8		15	1,300	15
London	4,580	10	6.2	2	163‖	10	3,700	11
Montreal	41,984	2	5.2	6	3,649	2	78,600	2
Ottawa	7,480	5	4.4	9	205	9	5,900	9
Quebec (City)	5,127	8	4.0	12	211	8	7,900	6
Regina	2,530	14	5.4	3	113	14	4,900	10
Sudbury	994	16	2.5	16		16	700	—
Toronto	52,338	1	6.6	1	5,703‖	1	109,600	1
Vancouver	15,918	3	5.4	4	1,165	3	17,800	4
Victoria	2,244	15	4.0	13	143	11	2,700	13
Windsor	2,690	13	3.9	14	155	12	2,400	14
Winnipeg	10,252	4	5.3	5	830	4	20,900	3
TOTAL FOR CANADA	228,905		3.5		15,459		293,784	

*SOURCE: *Census of Canada 1961*, vol. 3.
†Division 9 in D. B. S., *Standard Industrial Classification Manual* (Ottawa, 1960), p. 42.
‡Sub-group 704 in *ibid.*
§SOURCE: D. B. S., *Canada Year Book 1962* (Ottawa, 1962), p. 1105.
‖Less than 100.

TABLE III

ASSETS OF FINANCIAL INSTITUTIONS (MILLIONS OF DOLLARS) ACCORDING TO HEAD OFFICE LOCATION FOR SELECTED CENTRES*
(BASED ON AN AVERAGE 1959–1963)

	Montreal	Toronto	Vancouver	Winnipeg	London	Ottawa	Kitchener-Waterloo	Halifax
Chartered banks	10,300	9,000	nil	nil†	nil	nil‡	nil	nil§
Insurance (life, property, and casualty)	3,500	4,500	50	950	850	850	900	30
Trust and loan companies	2,100	1,900	‖	10	540	nil	100	270
Others (finance companies, investment funds, etc.)	500	2,100	350	440	210	nil	nil	‖
TOTAL	16,400	17,500	400	1,400	1,600	850	1,000	300

*SOURCES: *Financial Post Survey of Industrials* (Toronto, annually); *Report of the Superintendent of Insurance for Canada* (Ottawa, annually).
†Bank of Western Canada has not yet been established.
‡Bank of Canada not included.
§It has been assumed that the executive head office of the Bank of Nova Scotia is in Toronto.
‖Less than 10.

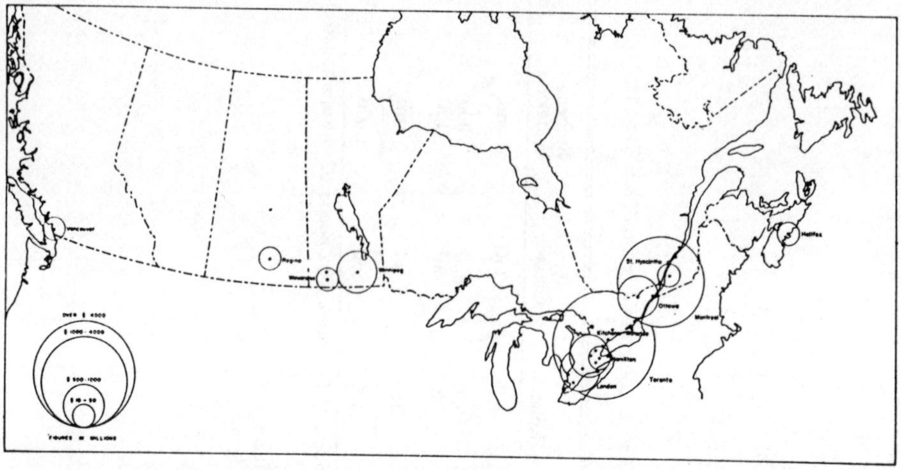

FIGURE 3. Total assets (exceeding 10 million dollars) of insurance companies according to head office location (based on an average 1959–1963). Life insurance companies comprise by far the largest share of the assets.

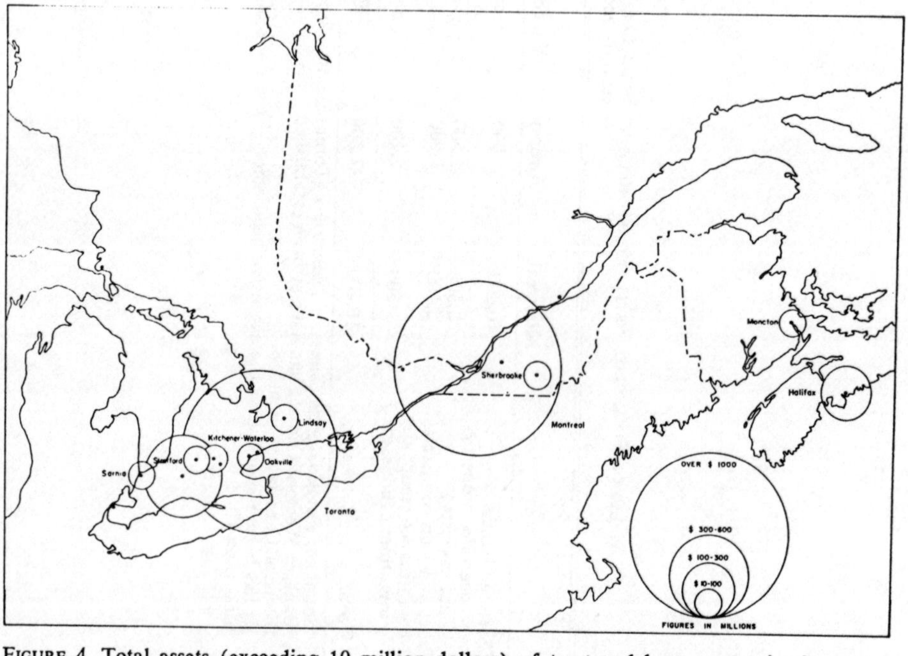

FIGURE 4. Total assets (exceeding 10 million dollars) of trust and loan companies in eastern Canada; only Winnipeg in western Canada has assets over 10 million dollars (based on an average 1959–1963). This pattern has important historical ramifications.

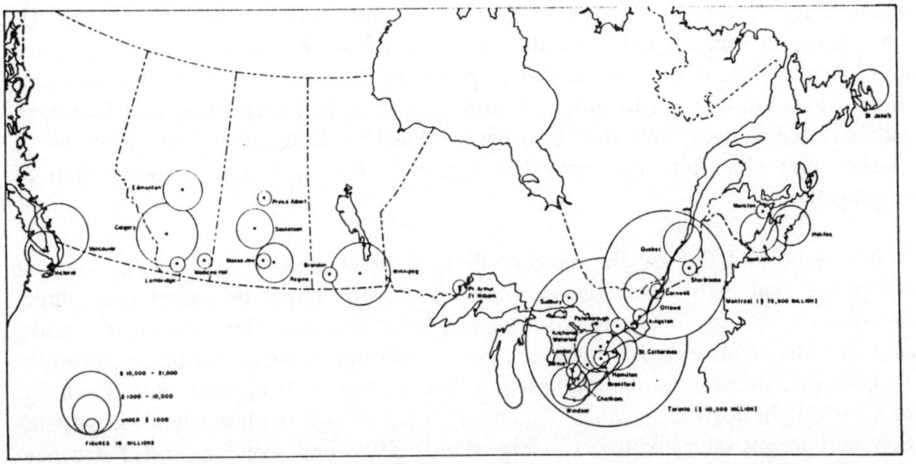

FIGURE 5. Cheques cashed at clearing houses 1961. Apart from Montreal and Toronto where almost two-thirds of all cheques are cashed (by value), the pattern reflects quite well nodal points in the distribution of population.

Assets of Financial Institutions

A tabulation of assets of all financial institutions according to head office location gives some measure of the geographical concentration of finance in Canada, at least for an average of the five-year period 1959 to 1963[5] (Table III). Quite arbitrarily, a decision was made to include only private financial institutions (non-government), namely, chartered banks, life, casualty, and fire insurance companies and societies, trust and loan companies, instalment finance and small loan companies, and investment trusts. Montreal and Toronto dominate the financial structure of Canada by accounting for 85 per cent of all assets (Figure 2), although Winnipeg, London, Kitchener-Waterloo, and Ottawa rank reasonably high mainly because of the wealth of large insurance companies. Western cities (other than Winnipeg) have spawned very few financial institutions, and even Vancouver, ranking third on the basis of employment, drops to seventh place.

When total financial assets are separated into categories (Table III), the dominance of Toronto and Montreal is again apparent. Both cities show a concentration of chartered banks[6]; indeed, when compared with American cities, Montreal ranks third behind New York and San Francisco, and Toronto fifth behind Chicago. Insurance companies and trust and loan companies are somewhat more widely dispersed, but mainly through eastern Canada (see also Figures 3 and 4). None the less, the concentrations in Toronto and Montreal are very striking; in all of North America these two cities are exceeded in assets of insurance companies only by New York, Hartford, Boston, and Milwaukee.

Cheques Cashed at Clearing Houses

A record of the value of cheques charged to customer accounts in all bank offices in major clearing house centres gives some insight into the amount of banking activity in various cities,[7] and, as such, it is an index of a very common financial transaction. The relevant data for Canadian cities appears in Table II, from which a ranking has been drawn up (see also Figure 5). Again, Toronto and Montreal are dominant, having respectively 37.2 per cent and 26.7 per cent of the Canadian total, or together, almost two-thirds. It is interesting that Winnipeg outranks Vancouver, and that Calgary is ahead of Edmonton. The positions of Quebec and Hamilton are somewhat higher in this system of ranking than in employment.

It may be said that on the basis of these three criteria—employment, assets of companies, and bank clearings—a measure of what might be called the volume of financial activity in Canadian cities has been achieved. Toronto clearly ranks first and Montreal second, a reversal of their rankings in almost all other categories (population, manufacturing, wholesaling, and so forth). It appears that Winnipeg, to a very slight degree, outranks Vancouver, even though the latter leads in population and industrial rankings. Calgary stands fifth, and London and Kitchener-Waterloo show up strongly on the basis of assets.[8]

Clearly there are limitations in the use of these data. Total employment in finance embraces a great variety of occupations, ranging from real estate agents through bank messengers, trust officers, investment analysts, and bank presidents. Certainly, the meaningfulness of an aggregate figure is a problem and must be questioned, but it is always such in a summing of the values of disparate categories.

The problem of emphasizing assets of financial institutions, of course, focuses on the function of the head office and invites the question of whether it is realistic to attribute so much importance to a single location within the system of a large financial company. No simple answer can be made, but clearly this is a major limitation in the use of these aggregates of assets. Even more serious is the fact that accounting procedures between firms are not always uniform and disparities may arise in the tabulation of assets.[9] However, although double counting is a distinct possibility in manufacturing concerns in which physical as well as monetary assets are included, it is less likely to occur in financial institutions.

In many ways bank clearings are more indicative of the amount of economic activity within a city than of a specific financial activity. It can be argued that most of the population is very much involved in the process of writing cheques and that therefore bank clearings measure this energy rather than financial transactions *per se*.

Despite the above and other limitations, these three criteria do portray impressions of the amount of financial activity by urban areas, although they give little, if any, insight into the concentration or dispersal of certain financial functions.

SELECTED FINANCIAL FUNCTIONS

Although financial activity is extremely complex, it is possible for the purposes of this article to identify three major functions: the collection and accumulation of funds, their disbursement or investment, and trade in financial instruments.[10] Some of these activities are nation-wide in the sense that they take place in towns or even villages, but unquestionably there is a concentration of substantial transactions in large centres.

It is not difficult to envisage the neighbourhood bank performing the task of collecting, accumulating, disbursing, and lending money within a fairly well-defined trade area. Nor is it unusual that a large life insurance company will direct all of its collections through its head office, at which point large sums accumulate to be disbursed through payment or invested in mortgages or securities. The former activity is in a sense ubiquitous, the latter centralized. The third function, trade, is highly concentrated, and its importance in the workings of what might be called the capital market cannot be minimized.[11] Such trade makes provision for liquidity of non-monetary financial assets or, in short, for the shift in ownership of outstanding liabilities. For a number of reasons, largely of historical significance but focusing to a great extent on the notion of economies of scale, this trade goes on only in a few centres. It may be carried on through the facilities of an organized market such as the stock exchange, or in a less formal way such as "over-the-counter" bond sales.

It is indeed unfortunate that the statistical data to measure the regional variations of these different facets of finance are fragmentary or entirely lacking. For this reason, and partly because of the great complexity of financial systems, the commentary which follows deals only with underwriting and trade in stocks and bonds. Although the discussion is of necessity restricted, the significance of the financial centre is underlined, and indeed some progress is made towards its definition.

Underwriting

One important way in which capital can be raised is through the process of underwriting, that is, by making new security issues available for sale by one or more investment bankers. It is not the purpose of this article to review the various aspects of underwriting; a comprehensive and informative description has been provided by Fullerton, especially with reference to Canadian conditions.[12] What can be emphasized, however, is that a new issue is organized by an investment dealer or, more commonly, by a syndicate, which is simply a collection of investment dealers. An advertisement describing the securities to be sold and listing the investment dealer, or dealers, handling the sale appears in a financial newspaper. No record of these sales is made available; consequently it is impossible to compare the amount of underwriting in one city with that in another. All that can be said is that Montreal- and Toronto-based investment firms appear most frequently in advertisements,[13] and it is not unusual for a syndicate to comprise several different firms from both cities.

There are 181 investment firms in Canada, of which fourteen, without any question, have national significance.[14] Of these, seven have head offices in Toronto, five in Montreal, and one each in Winnipeg and London. It is not meant to imply that *all* new issues emanate from the Toronto and Montreal markets, for a significant number of provincial and municipal bonds are floated in local markets, the sales of which are helped along by local laws and prejudices.[15] Also, conditions may make it desirable for governments, or even private companies, to borrow money in New York. Nevertheless, it is not an exaggeration to state that practically all corporate and most governmental issues arise in either the Toronto or the Montreal markets, or both. On the basis of interviews with a number of investment dealers, selected at random, it can be noted that there is at present a somewhat greater volume of underwriting in Toronto than in Montreal.

A number of specialists engage in underwriting. Investment dealers perform the specific tasks of underwriting but bankers, investment counsellors for insurance companies, corporation lawyers, chartered accountants, geologists, and others help to prepare and support such ventures. The propinquity of these specialists within the financial district of the financial centre is noteworthy. In Canada such concentrations are to be found almost entirely in Montreal and Toronto, where as previously noted 60 per cent of the employment in sub-group 704 (investment companies and investment dealers, Table II, reference 2) is found. It may be added that this concentration of the machinery for underwriting often makes it necessary for a company or a business venture, when contemplating the raising of money through underwriting, to proceed directly to either Toronto or Montreal. There is little possibility that a manufacturing company in Moose Jaw, for example, would be able to arrange for the issue of new securities in Regina, or for that matter in Winnipeg, and would of necessity have to deal with investment bankers in either Toronto or Montreal.

Trade in Bonds and Stocks

It has been indicated that provision must be made for the liquidity of non-monetary financial assets in a capitalistic economy. Through the course of history, markets have grown up in various centres where securities may be traded. These markets form an integral part of the larger capital market and are, in fact, essential to its proper functioning. New York and London contain the largest number of both organized and less formal financial markets.

Some measure of the magnitude of this trade can be gained by tabulating stock market transactions on organized stock exchanges. In Canada, five such exchanges handle on the average 3.5 billion dollars of trade annually (Table IV). Toronto clearly dominates, and in North America stands second to New York; the Montreal exchanges account for over a quarter of all trade, and Vancouver less than one-twentieth; Calgary and Winnipeg are quite insignificant.

Typically, the stock exchange building occupies a central position within the financial district around which investment dealers and other financial institutions are grouped. Very often the street on which it is located, such as Bay Street in Toronto, St. James in Montreal, and Howe in Vancouver, has become synonymous with the whole financial community and carries a connotation into the hinterland analogous to that of Wall Street in the United States.

Trade in bonds and debentures outranks that of the stock market in value, but in view of the fact that all transactions are "over-the-counter" no record is published. The trading system is rather intricate and is based on the connectivity of investment firms by private telephone lines and teletype services; in fact, some investment firms have as many as ninety direct telephone lines, making it possible to sell and buy bonds very quickly. Banks and some insurance companies are also linked by

TABLE IV

AVERAGE ANNUAL VALUE OF STOCK MARKET TRANSACTIONS ON STOCK EXCHANGES IN CANADA, 1962–64*

City	Value in millions of dollars	% of total Canadian
Toronto	2,420	68.8
Montreal†	939	26.7
Vancouver	153	4.3
Calgary	3	0.1
Winnipeg	3	0.1
TOTAL	3,518	100.0

*SOURCES: *Toronto Stock Exchange Year End Review*, 1962–64; *Statistical Summary Montreal and Canadian Stock Exchanges*, 1962–64; *Vancouver Stock Exchange*, 1962–64; *Calgary Stock Exchange Official Yearly Summary*, 1962–64; *Winnipeg Stock Exchange Official Yearly Summary*, 1962–64.

†Figures for the Montreal and Canadian stock exchanges have been combined. The latter is also located in Montreal and has emerged from the old Curb Market.

wires in the trading system. Most trading goes on within Toronto and/or Montreal and between the two centres. Connections are also maintained with New York, and in Canada with major centres such as Winnipeg and Vancouver.

It is obvious that underwriting and trade in bonds and stocks, among other activities, are highly concentrated in a few places, and indeed help to define the nature of the financial centre. The implication is one of primary functions stimulating the flow of funds not only in the financial centre but also over a wide area which may be regional, national, or even international in scope. The substance of the financial centre is to be seen in the composition of the financial district within the central business district. The buildings comprise not only the offices of investment dealers, headquarters of banks, and the stock exchange, but also a great variety of other establishments including legal firms and chartered accountants specializing in underwriting and investment in general, consulting geologists, investment analysts, and financial newspapers and magazines. In short, employment in finance in a financial district may be distinguished from that in other cities by a retinue of specialists in financial affairs.[17]

CLASSIFICATION

The preceding discussion on measurement criteria suggests that, in any classification of cities based at least in part on finance, functional organization must be recognized. Clearly, employment measures only the volume of activity; thus employees performing certain services in finance (bank tellers and insurance agents) are found in all urban places regardless of size. It is not difficult to define the trade area of a bank around a village or suburban shopping plaza, or that of an agency of a life insurance company in larger context. These service functions in finance are therefore widespread and would find closest correlation with population density and income levels.

Other activities in finance are very much tied up with certain specific workings of the capital market, most of which, as have been noted, take place in only a few centres. Thus the financial centre has been defined as that place in which markets are provided for financial trading and in which facilities are available for large-scale borrowing and lending. It can therefore be distinguished from other urban places, regardless of size, in which these activities do not take place. A hierarchy can be envisaged in which, on a world-wide scale, New York and London would rank at the top. The question of which cities among Tokyo, Amsterdam, Paris, Milan, Toronto, San Francisco, and so forth would occupy successively lower strata is challenging, but impossible at present to answer.

With respect to non-financial centres further research is needed to designate sub-classes. Does the regional city (for example, Saskatoon) function in any way that is different from the small town (such as North Battleford), with its branch banks and insurance offices? It may be that in this class there is no hierarchy at all but rather a continuum. Also, provision should be made for the city which lacks the trappings of a financial centre but houses the head offices of financial institutions. In Canada London and Kitchener-Waterloo may be identified (Table II), and in the United States Hartford, Connecticut, stands out.[18] Accordingly, such a city does not function as a financial centre but, on the other hand, the contribution of its financial institutions to the economic structure of the city—providing employment, paying taxes, and demanding office space—is significant.

According to the definition given above, only Montreal, Toronto, Vancouver, Winnipeg, and Calgary qualify as financial centres in Canada. It is rather obvious that the first two stand out as national and even international centres and have first rank; the others are important regional centres and are of second rank. Worthy subjects as well for further research are those cities such as London, Halifax, Quebec, Regina, and Kitchener-Waterloo which do not rank as financial centres but nevertheless carry out important financial activities.

THE HINTERLAND CONCEPT

The classification and ranking of Canadian cities according to financial functions and activity raise a number of questions on spatial distribution, some of which have historical relevance. Whereas in most countries of the world one city clearly dominates as financial capital, in Canada two share primary functions. Furthermore, the present growth of Vancouver and Calgary, the slow and long decline of Halifax, and the vigorous growth of Winnipeg just before and during World War I are noteworthy. Obviously, to lay bare the rationale of the changing significance of various centres is beyond the scope of this article; in fact, much is central to fundamental problems in Canadian economic history and historical geography. But it may be fruitful to comment briefly on the hinterland concept and illustrate with reference to Toronto and its relationships with the Canadian Shield.

According to Gras, the emergence of financial centres fulfills the fourth and final stage in the development of a metropolitan economy, especially with reference to the control that the metropolis exerts in financing the hinterland: "from the nature of things the metropolis will develop financial resources to the limit to care for both the extended and the hinterland trade, the inter-metropolitan and intra-metropolitan commerce."[19] It follows that not only does the financial centre play a vital role in the development of the hinterland, but in turn that that very development profoundly influences the financial centre. By way of illustration, the development of inter-relationships between Toronto and the Canadian Shield can be briefly, if somewhat superficially, examined.[20] Of necessity, discussion will be very limited and will refer only to the financing of mineral resources.

There is little question that the ability of some segments of the financial community to wrest control of mineral developments on the Shield has brought great wealth to the city and laid the basis for vigorous growth of the stock exchange, particularly since the late 1940's. That part of the Shield which has fallen under the dominance of Toronto includes a broad belt from Rouyn and Noranda in Western Quebec to the Northwest Territories; the eastern Shield has, to a large extent, and especially in recent years, come under the control of Montreal interests. Quite obviously the tentacles of New York, but no longer those of London, also extend through the whole Shield but those of Toronto are dominant. It need only be reiterated that the great wealth of mineral resources has proved to be a remarkable attraction to mining companies, investors, speculators, and the like.[21]

The roots of Toronto's conquest of the Shield may be traced to the building of the Ontario Northland Railway in the early years of the twentieth century. Intended to stimulate agricultural developments on the Clay Belt, this railroad directly and indirectly resulted in the discovery and development of mineral resources. Although it was later extended into western Quebec, giving Toronto an advantage over Montreal in trade[22] and accessibility,[23] it has been supplemented increasingly by highway facilities and airline services.

The historical record indicates that Toronto groups were interested in promoting mining properties in British Columbia[24] and on the Shield as early as the 1880's. The formation of two small mining exchanges, later to merge in 1898 to form the Toronto Standard Stock and Mining Exchange, facilitated the promotion of mining ventures which the more conservative Montreal and Toronto Stock Exchanges did not wish to handle.[25] Clearly, some of the techniques, facilities, and energies for financing mineral properties had taken hold in Toronto before the discovery of very rich deposits of silver at Cobalt in 1903, and of gold at Porcupine in 1911 and Kirkland Lake in 1912 had made the Shield so attractive. On the basis of very scanty evidence it appears that similar traditions had not developed to any extent in Montreal; nor did there seem to be much desire to build them up until a later date. Some capital for development came from varied interests in Montreal, New York, Buffalo, and other cities as well as Toronto, but the mining exchange became a focus of a great deal of speculation, and increasingly mining activities centred on Toronto.

Thus, the financing of the hinterland revolved around the nature of the resources (rich minerals), the initial advantage of transportation links, and the traditions of the financial community, and increasingly in the early twentieth century evolved inter-relationships between the Shield and Toronto which have had a profound influence on subsequent developments. In the 1930's, in an otherwise depressed market, gold issues became buoyant following an increase in the price of gold, and activity increased on the Toronto market. Following the crash of 1929, the Montreal Stock Market remained weak, and the volume of trade on the Toronto exchange in the early 1930's, although relatively small, exceeded that of Montreal for the first time. A merger of the old Standard Stock and Mining Exchange with the Toronto Stock Exchange in 1934 was followed by more stringent regulations in speculation, and as the financing of mining issues became more sophisticated other segments of corporate and governmental financing increased in Toronto at the expense of Montreal. The post-war period brought forth great activity in mining issues (uranium, copper, oil, and so forth), which, when combined with the improvement of trading facilities (high-speed electronic equipment and data processing centre) and the accelerated establishment of branches of Toronto brokerage houses throughout Canada, led to a further acquisition of the market in industrials. In short, it is suggested that the prominence of the Toronto financial market at present may be traced to earlier developments of mining properties on the Shield which, in turn, strengthened the financial community and made Toronto a somewhat more attractive trading centre than Montreal during and, in particular, after the depression.

Such broad assertions are based on scanty evidence but even so suggest the relevance of the hinterland concept in any analysis of the growth of financial centres. Only part, however, and a very small part, of the nature and significance of the rivalry of the Montreal and Toronto financial communities comes to light from the previous discussion.

Quite briefly and superficially, the relationship of other cities to their hinterlands can be reviewed. At the time of World War I Winnipeg was on the verge of becoming a metropolitan centre, in a financial sense, but, the lack of variety and substance in its hinterland economy, so overwhelmingly dominated by grain, made this leap impossible. Can the decline of Halifax, so well endowed with fiancial institutions in the nineteenth century, be attributed to the poverty of its hinterland? To what extent may the rise of financial power in Calgary and Vancouver be attributed to their abilities to capture extensive hinterlands?

It may be that, if attention is directed to the relationship of the financial centre to the hinterland—a geographical approach of long standing—while at the same time colleagues in other fields write histories of financial institutions and of the men who directed their destinies, further progress can be made towards understanding the evolution of financial centres in Canada.

SPATIAL INTERACTION AND FINANCIAL CENTRES

Financial centres grew up, if not entirely independent one of the other, at least largely so. As communications improved, however, and as financial capitalism grew more important,[26] interactions between financial centres increased. The questions may now be asked how closely are financial centres linked and, therefore, how inter-dependent are they, and to what extent do they still function as independent entities? Some comments can be made with reference to Montreal and Toronto.

Spatial interaction[27] between Toronto and Montreal in commodities, people, information, and so forth, is the most intense in Canada. There is some evidence to support the view that the interaction of these two financial communities is such that they tend to participate, at least in some activities, as one large financial centre (as defined in this article) and are not necesarily the custodians of two separate financial markets. For example, it is not unusual for a Toronto-based investment firm to arrange the underwriting of new securities for an industrial company which has its head office in Montreal; nor is it so for a Montreal investment firm to handle the financing of a Toronto industry. The syndicates referred to earlier comprise investment dealers in both cities, and it has been emphasized that Montreal and Toronto are intimately connected by all sorts of electronic communications equipment which allow instantaneous trade in bonds or stocks between a desk in one city and that in another. Fullerton comments that with reference to the bond market the rivalry of the two centres is, in some respects, academic.[28] Furthermore, Walter and Williamson state that, among other factors, because there is a large amount of inter-listing of stocks on the Toronto and Montreal exchanges and because the large brokerage houses have memberships on both exchanges, the interaction between the two exchanges is significant.[29] From time to time there is even discussion about the possibility of merging the stock exchanges in Canada to form a national one, an initiative, however, which comes entirely from Toronto circles. Most Montreal interests are vigorously opposed, and the fact that they have moved into a new stock exchange building and have plans for a vigorous publicity campaign suggest that the independence of the two centres and indeed their rivalry have by no means disappeared. None the less, it is not entirely unrealistic to view these two historic centres as being increasingly drawn together and in some spheres of financial activity functioning as one.

CONCLUSION

It is of relevance geographically to distinguish between general services in finance and primary financial functions. The former, epitomized best in the workings of the neighbourhood branch bank or local insurance agent, are found in all urban centres; the latter, comprising mainly trade in financial instruments and large-scale borrowing and lending, are highly concentrated, notably in Montreal and Toronto, and to a certain extent in Vancouver, Winnipeg, and Calgary. However, the distinction between these two types of activities is by no means sharp, for such cities as London, Kitchener-Waterloo, Halifax, and Ottawa house the head offices of one or two large financial institutions or a number of small to medium-sized ones. Clearly these cities do not function as financial centres, but they do nevertheless carry out important financial activities. Furthermore, research is needed to discover the significance of divisional or regional offices of financial institutions in the Canadian financial system and thus to define more precisely financial functions in such cities as Winnipeg, Calgary, Vancouver, Halifax, and Quebec City. Particularly, the role of Regina, which has among all cities the third highest ratio of employment in finance to total employment, might be discovered.

To answer why two large financial centres should have emerged in Canada instead of a single dominant one as is the case in nearly all countries would be to engage in a long and complex historical discussion beyond the scope of this article. It is obvious that the status of a financial centre may change through time; noteworthy has been the striking rise of Toronto in recent decades to exceed Montreal in value of trade and in underwriting. At present, considerable evidence suggests that Vancouver may be on the threshold of becoming a primary financial centre, thus to compete more vigorously with its eastern counterparts.

In conclusion, it is apparent that varied and more substantial research is suggested by this article. Investigations into the changing spatial organization of financial institutions from the nineteenth century to the present should be made to define the changing status of cities and to cast light on urban growth processes. In what way does a concentration of financial wealth and power affect the growth of a city? Clearly the whole question of agglomeration theory is very much at issue. What is the threshold at which the grouping of financial institutions affects, and is in fact interrelated to, other decision-making units of the economy such as industrial corporations? Finally, it appears that a vigorous and expanding financial community exerts a profound influence on the sturcture of the central business district. In fact, the vitality or decline of central areas of the city may, in large measure, be related to the nature and volume of financial activity.

ACKNOWLEDGMENTS

Parts of the first and second drafts of this article were improved by the comments of colleagues in political economy—Professors Neufeld and Currie; in geography—Professors Gentilcore, Spelt, and Birch.

REFERENCES

1. HARRIS, C. D., "A Functional Classification of Cities in the United States," *Geog. Rev.*, XXXIII (1943), 86–89; BOGUE, D. J., *The Structure of the Metropolitan Community* (Ann Arbor, 1950).
2. Employment in finance is tabulated under two broad headings: (1) financial institutions, and (2) insurance and real estate industries. Five sub-groups have been recognized: no. 702, savings and credit institutions; no. 704, investment companies and security dealers under group (1); no. 731, insurance carriers; no. 735, insurance and real estate agencies; no. 737, real estate operations under group (2).
   For a detailed description of the types of employment see DOMINION BUREAU OF STATISTICS, *Standard Industrial Classification Manual*, no. 12-501 (Ottawa, 1960).
   For the purposes of this article, and despite obvious drawbacks, the labour force and employment in finance are considered to be one and the same. All data on the labour force have been taken from *Census of Canada 1961*, vol. 3, no. 2, "Labour Force for Industries by Metropolitan Areas."
3. One paper can be cited: MORRISSETT, IRVING, "The Economic Structure of American Cities," *Papers and Proc. Regional Sci. Assoc.*, IV (1958), 239–52. See also FLORENCE, P. S., *Investment, Location and Size of Plant* (Cambridge, 1948), for a review of statistical procedures to be used in describing the location of industry.
4. In order that the Canadian figures would be more comparable with those of the United

States, employment in real estate was deleted from the total figures for Toronto and Montreal. See ROBBINS, S. M., and N. E. TERLECKYJ, *Money Metropolis* (Cambridge, Mass., 1960), p. 277.

5. *Financial Post Survey of Industries* (McLean Hunter Co., Toronto, annually) and *Report of the Superintendent of Insurance, Department of Finance* (Queen's Printer, Ottawa, annually). From these two publications it was possible to identify all non-governmental financial institutions. The assets for each insurance company, finance company, bank, etc., were compiled for a five-year period (1959–63) and averaged. The resulting value for each company was then inserted in the column of the appropriate city as determined by the location of the head office. Total assets for each major category of finance, and for finance as a whole, were summed for each city.
6. Branch banking developed in Canada from the outset. Amalgamations, mergers, and bankruptcies characterized the period of the late nineteenth and early twentieth centuries, and now only a few very large banks dominate chartered banking in Canada. The merger movement also affected other financial institutions. See JAMIESON, A. B., *Chartered Banking in Canada* (Toronto, 1955). At present the federal government, for the first time in several years, is considering applications for the formation of three new banks: the Bank of Western Canada, the Bank of British Columbia, and the Laurentide Bank.
7. D. B. S., *Canada Year Book 1962* (Ottawa, 1962), p. 1105.
8. Because of the thinness of the statistical data, it was impossible to apply any sophisticated statistical techniques to achieve a formal ranking of cities.
9. For a useful discussion see PORTER, JOHN, *The Vertical Mosaic* (Toronto, 1965), Appendix II, p. 570.
10. For a discussion of various functions in Canada, see HOOD, W. C., *Financing Economic Activity in Canada*, vol. XXIV of Report of Royal Commission on Canada's Economic Prospects (the Gordon Commission) (Ottawa, 1958), and ASHLEY, C. A., *Corporation Finance* (Toronto, 1949).
11. Unquestionably the Bank of Canada which controls currency in Canada is an integral part of the market. Other government bodies such as Central Mortgage and Housing Corporation and the Industrial Development Bank play a much less significant role in the workings of the capital market.
12. FULLERTON, D. H., *The Bond Market in Canada* (Toronto, 1962), pp. 138–55.
13. Each week the *Financial Post* (Toronto) lists the new issues and the participating dealers, and each January a list of the year's underwriting by months appears in an early edition.
14. A firm having national significance is arbitrarily defined in this paper as one with at least ten branch offices scattered in at least five provinces. For an inventory of all firms see *Membership List of the Investment Dealers' Association of Canada on December 31, 1964* (Toronto, 1965).
15. FULLERTON, *The Bond Market in Canada*, p. 91.
16. *Ibid.*, pp. 164–66.
17. For a description of Toronto's financial district see KERR, D., and J. SPELT, *The Changing Face of Toronto: A Study in Urban Geography* (Geog. Branch, Dept. of Mines and Tech. Surveys, mem. no. 11, Ottawa, 1965), pp. 153–57. For a description of the money market and New York's financial community see ROBBINS and TERLECKYJ, *Money Metropolis*, chap. 2.
18. GOODWIN, W., "The Management Center in the United States," *Geog. Rev.*, LV (Jan. 1965), 12.
19. GRAS, N. S. B., *An Introduction to Economic History* (New York, 1922), p. 243.
20. KERR and SPELT, *The Changing Face of Toronto*, pp. 83–85.
21. For a useful analysis and review see CURRIE, A. W., *Canadian Economic Development* (Toronto, 1963), pp. 222–43.
22. FIELD, F. W., *The Resources and Trade Prospects of Northern Ontario* (Board of Trade pub., Toronto, 1911), p. 73.
23. The influence of Toronto on Cobalt, the leading mining centre in the first decade of mining developments, may be measured by examining advertising in copies of the *Daily Nugget* of Cobalt, an incomplete set of which is available in the Provincial Archives, Toronto. For example, in advertising by law firms and stockbrockers of Toronto and Montreal origin, the number from the first exceeded that from the second city by a ratio of 3:1.

24. INNIS, H. A., *Settlement and the Mining Frontier* (Toronto, 1936), p. 281.
25. "The Stock Market in Canada," *Monthly Review* (Bank of Nova Scotia, Sept. 1960).
26. GRAS, N. S. B., *Business and Capitalism* (New York, 1946), pp. 246–59.
27. ULLMAN, E. L., "The Role of Transportation and the Bases for Interaction," in THOMAS, W. L. (ed.), *Man's Role in Changing the Face of the Earth* (Chicago, 1956), pp. 862–80.
28. FULLERTON, *The Bond Market in Canada*, p. 90.
29. WALTER, J. E., and J. P. WILLIAMSON, "Organized Securities Exchanges in Canada," *J. of Finance*, XV, no. 3 (Sept. 1960), 311, 313.

RÉSUMÉ

Les données statistiques sur les réserves des institutions financières, le nombre des employés et des chèques déposés en banque permet à mésurer les variations spaciaux dans le volume d'activité financière au Canada. Deux fonctions importantes dans la finance, l'assurance et le commerce en valeurs mobilières, aident à définer la caractère du centre financier.

Il est conclu que Montréal et Toronto dominent la vie financière du Canada, et en plus grand mésure qu'elles dominent aucune autre activité économique, l'industrie et le commerce en gros inclus. Sur la base de tous critéria, ces centres sont plus importantes que Vancouver, Winnipeg et Calgary. L'accroissement impressive de Toronto, surtout pendant les décades recentes, à excéder le volume de commerce de Montréal, est particulièrement intéressante. Pourtant, l'evidence suggère que quelques segments de leur communautés financières respectives fonctionnent comme une unité à travers les opérations du marché financièr. L'intense rapport entre les deux communautés financières reflète non seulement ceci, mais, le fait possible.

[19]

xcerpt from L. Rasminsky and R.W. Lawson, *Canada as an International Banking Centre*, 1–19, –4.

A. The Nature of International Banking and of International Banking Centres

The world's banks provide many services that cross national boundaries, and in some contexts all of them are considered to be international banking. But as used in the term "international banking centres", international banking has a much narrower meaning which excludes many of the cross-border services provided by banks. It excludes, for example, virtually all the services that are related directly to the individual payments and receipts and foreign-exchange operations arising from the international trade of the country in which the bank is operating. While such services constitute much the greater part of the work of the international departments of banks they are not international banking in the narrower sense.

The international banking done by international banking centres is principally the channelling of flows of capital between countries. It is the intermediation by banks in the world's capital market.

In this role of providing channels for the international flow of capital, the operations of the world's banks have changed dramatically in recent years. Historically those channels were primarily bilateral, capital flowing between the banks of an international financial centre – first London and then increasingly New York – and the banks of other countries. The world system was rather like a wheel with the channels radiating from the financial centre of the world's major international currency. This tended to be the case whether the capital that flowed was generated in the hub-country or elsewhere, and whether the capital flowed through banks or through bond and equity markets.

In the mid-1950s that system began to change, at first slowly but then rapidly. Although the U.S. dollar had become the world's major international currency, the world's banks *found* that the circumstances of the time enabled them to be competitive in doing international business in U.S. dollars from offices outside the United States. By the 1970s, when the international movements of capital were massive and were denominated mainly in U.S. dollars, a very large part of them did not go through the United States. They flowed through channels that had become known as the Euro-dollar market.

The Euro-dollar market provided a new way for the world's banks to intermediate in the flow of capital across national borders. The new way is extra-national, and its activities are not directly subject to national regulation. Through it the world's banks compete for deposit balances in all parts of the world, including countries that are themselves net borrowers on international account, and use the funds to make loans and acquire other assets in all parts of the world, including countries that are themselves net lenders on international account.

A number of factors contributed to the development of the Euro-dollar market. Some early role appears to have been played by the desire of the Soviet authorities during a period of tension to hold their U.S. dollar balances with banks outside the United States and thus outside U.S. control. Another element was that the postwar weakness of sterling limited its use by the highly-sophisticated international financial market that existed in London, and the London market turned to using the U.S. dollar. Banking regulation in the United States (involving the cost of reserve requirements and the restraint of interest-rate ceilings) played a role by making it difficult for banks to compete effectively in the Euro-dollar market if they operated from within the United States. During the 1970s the market's growth was greatly stimulated by the huge imbalances in international payments that were generated by the increases in the price of crude oil; the Euro-dollar market played a major role in recycling the large dollar surpluses of the oil-producing countries, making them available to many oil-importing countries through lending operations.

All the world's larger banks participate in the Euro-dollar market, with U.S. banks operating (until recently) mainly from offices outside the United States. While the market still works very largely (80 per cent) in U.S. dollars, enough use is made of other currencies, mainly the D-mark and the Swiss franc, that it is now usually called the Euro-currency market. The market has now spread from Europe to other regions. A peculiar feature of this activity is that most of it is carried on by banks operating from outside the country whose currency is being used.

It is this Euro-currency activity that we shall have in mind when we refer in this Report to international banking. Though it is in principle quite separate from the other international services that banks provide to their customers it is usually not physically separate. The fact that the world's larger banks use as bases for their Euro-currency activities the facilities that they already had around the world means that it is virtually impossible in practice to distinguish between the facilities that are required for Euro-banking and those that are required for other purposes.

The Euro-currency market is now very large indeed. The usual way of measuring its size is by totalling the foreign currency assets or liabilities recorded in the banking offices in as many countries as possible. The estimates available differ in their coverage, but they indicate that the size of the market is now approaching U.S. $2,500 billion (as compared with about $450 billion 10 years ago and about $110 billion in 1970). Well over half of the current total is inter-bank business because it is the practice of the banks to re-deposit with other banks a considerable proportion of the Euro-currency deposits that they receive. If inter-bank deposits are netted out, the size of the market is not far short of U.S. $1,000 billion. This is well over five times the size of the Canadian-dollar business of the Canadian banking system.

Because of the parlous external-debt situation of a number of countries, the Euro-currency market is unlikely to grow nearly as rapidly in the foreseeable future as it did in the 1970s, but it seems very likely to remain large.

While banks from many countries are active in the Euro-currency market, figures recently released by the Bank for International Settlements indicate that banks from eight countries accounted for about 85 per cent of the market as at the end of 1984. U.S. and Japanese banks together accounted for about 50 per cent, and the banks of France, United Kingdom, Switzerland, Germany, Canada and Italy together accounted for a further 35 per cent. Canadian banks make up about 4 to 5 per cent of the total market.

The business that the Euro-currency market does can be negotiated wherever around the world those involved find it convenient to meet. In practice that is mainly in the world's larger financial centres, notably London and New York, but it is frequently elsewhere. Hong Kong and Singapore are important centres for Asian business. When the business is arranged, the participating banks usually have a fair amount of latitude as to where it is entered on the books of one of their branches or subsidiary companies. Banking considerations will normally point to a suitable place to book (place or domicile) the business, but decisions about where to book are often influenced by non-banking considerations, notably by government regulations and taxation. The result is that, though there are a small number of places in the world where a lot of international banking business is negotiated (and often also booked), there are many more places where a lot of business is booked but little is negotiated. There are few international banking centres but many international booking centres.

The locations of either banking centres or booking centres have virtually nothing to do with the source or use of the capital which flows through them. The centres are places for the negotiation, recording and subsequent administration of the business of a genuinely international market, and the countries in which they are located have, by virtue of that location, no more access to the funds which flow through the Euro-currency markets than they would if the centres were located elsewhere. The benefits to the countries in which such centres are located consist in the employment and income of those who do the centres' work.

Since Euro-currency business is very much a wholesale business, with very large individual transactions, a great deal of it (in money terms) can be done by relatively few people. It involves only a small fraction of the employment that would be involved in a comparable dollar volume of retail banking business. Of those involved, the great majority of the more-skilled people are employed in head offices of the participating banks and in the few banking centres. Employment in international banking in the booking centres is small relative to the magnitude of the portfolios being managed, and is mainly of a routine nature.

B. The Determinants of the Geographical Distribution of the Activity Involved in International Banking

In this section we shall comment on the main forces that contribute to the present distribution around the world of the activity (work) involved in international banking, grouping them under four headings – operating efficiency, customer preferences, regulation, and taxation.

The forces are the same for all banks participating in Euro-currency banking, but their relative importance in explaining the outcome varies from country to country because the regulatory and taxation arrangements in countries differ. We have concentrated on how these forces affect the decisions of Canadian banks rather than those of banks in other countries, but we have enquired into the experience with the International Banking Facilities (IBFs) established in the United States in 1981 and a note on IBFs is attached as Appendix A to this Report.

Operating Efficiency

The Euro-currency markets are highly competitive, and to do well in them a bank must be energetic and efficient. Business must be pursued, and when it is won the client must be well serviced. The objective of the participating banks is to provide good service at the minimum cost.

To compete effectively a bank must be well represented in the main places where international business is done. Only by having a competent presence in the active markets can it keep well informed on developments and make good decisions on what kind of business to seek, and where and how to seek it. International banking goes on around the clock, and a major bank cannot operate efficiently from one time zone; it must at the very least have adequate offices in Europe, in the Western Hemisphere, and in Asia. To service its customers, it may need offices in many other places as well. Effective participation in a world-wide banking system requires offices world-wide.

While the existing distribution of activity in international banking is determined primarily by the views of the participating banks on where the business can be done most efficiently, that distribution is considerably different from what it would be if the banks were not exposed to other influences that affect their decisions. It is the effect of these other influences on the distribution of activity that is the centre of interest in this Report.

It is mainly the distribution of the business of the banks with customers other than banks that is affected by these other influences. We have already noted that the inter-bank activity of the Euro-currency banks is large, but its nature is such that we believe its distribution to be determined almost entirely by banking considerations. It is done primarily for reasons of liquidity, and it is done at such small margins that it is not an important source of bank profits and is thus little exposed to being influenced by tax considerations.

Customer Preferences

The preferences of customers that are most likely to affect the locations at which their transactions are booked have to do with banking secrecy and country risk.

Sometimes the interest of customers in banking secrecy arises from the fact that they are trying to hide funds that were obtained through illegal activity. Most banks do not like to be used in that way, and they try to know enough about their customers to avoid that role.

There are, however, other reasons why customers may want the privacy of their banking transactions to be as well protected as possible. Customers attaching particular importance to privacy will want their business booked in countries that they think give high priority to such privacy. Banks can do business with such customers only by having regard to where they want the business booked.

Like privacy, country risk is relevant mainly to the location of booking of the liability or deposit side of the banks' business. The claim of a depositor on a bank is exposed to the law and the legal processes of the country in which the deposit is booked, and it is also exposed to possible intervention by the government of that country in a way that might reduce the usefulness of the deposit, as, for example, by the imposition of foreign exchange control. If a depositor is uneasy about a country on any of these scores, he will not want his deposit booked there. Canada's reputation in this regard is an advantage in attracting Euro-currency deposit business to Canada.

Regulation

Government regulations affecting banking, including the reserve requirements of the monetary authorities, have had a major effect on the location of the activity involved in international banking. The regulations of the United States making the deposit liabilities of banks to non-residents (as well as residents) subject to reserve requirements and to interest-rate ceilings were a major factor in the development of the Euro-dollar market. Until the U.S. authorities made arrangements in 1981 for International Banking Facilities, it was very difficult for U.S. banks to be competitive in the Euro-dollar market if they operated from inside the United States. For the same reasons foreign banks could not be competitive if they did such business from their U.S. offices.

By contrast, regulation has not had a major influence on the location of the activity in international banking of the Canadian banks. In their operations in foreign currencies, the Canadian banks are largely free of specific regulatory restraints, the only exception of consequence being that their foreign currency liabilities to residents booked in Canada attract a reserve requirement of 3 per cent. This requirement was imposed in 1980 in order to make their treatment comparable to that of Canadian dollar deposits.

Another regulatory factor that has had some influence in increasing the external activity of Canadian banks is that the powers of banks with respect to the security market are greater in some other countries than they are in Canada. Some of the business in securities that the Canadian banks do in London, for example, would not be possible in Canada under the provisions of the Bank Act.

The requirements in Canada for reserves on Canadian dollar deposits put the Canadian banks at a competitive disadvantage against foreign banks if they book in Canada international business denominated in Canadian dollars or issue fully-transferable certificates of deposit denominated in Canadian dollars because such transactions attract reserves in Canada.

Taxation

Just as regulation provides a good deal of the explanation of the development of the Euro-currency market, so taxation explains a good deal of the curious distribution of the booking of the business generated by that market. Much of the business is booked in locations that are not large as financial centres in other respects, and their use as booking centres is mainly due to the fact that there is a tax advantage in placing the business there.

It is normal for banks doing Euro-currency business to analyze the difference in taxation that would result from doing it in different ways. In order to be competitive they have to take account of tax factors in deciding what business to do and how to do it.

The tax benefits to be had from the selective placing of international banking business are of various types, and they depend on the interrelationship between the taxation arrangements in the bank's home country and the country in which the business is placed. What may be involved is a lesser rate of (or no) profits tax, a lesser rate of (or no) business, capital or other relevant tax, less exposure to withholding taxes, lower licensing fees or other charges, or a more favourable system of foreign tax credits.

The tax factors that lead the Canadian banks to book international business abroad are discussed in the next section.

C. How Taxation Affects the Location of the Activity of the Canadian Banks in International Banking

The following table presents a broad picture of the places where the foreign currency business of the Canadian banks appears on their books or on those of their subsidiaries. It shows:

1. Of the total inter-bank business (assets plus liabilities), about 45 per cent is booked in Canada, about 10 per cent is booked in what in the table are called offshore centres, and the rest is booked elsewhere, presumably mainly in London and New York. (The countries treated as offshore centres in the table are listed in a footnote to it; they are mainly Caribbean countries, Hong Kong and Singapore.)

2. Of the claims on non-residents other than banks, a little under 10 per cent is booked in Canada, about 35 per cent is booked in the offshore centres, and the rest is booked elsewhere, again presumably mainly London and New York.

3. Of the liabilities to non-residents other than banks, nearly one-half is booked in Canada, about 15 per cent is booked in the offshore centres, and the rest is booked elsewhere.

4. Of the business with residents other than banks, nearly all of the claims are booked in Canada and about 40 per cent of the deposits are. The rest of the deposits are booked largely in New York and London.

All the determinants mentioned in the preceding section contribute to this result. Nearly all of the distribution of the inter-bank business and a good deal of that with non-banks is explained by ordinary banking considerations, and customer preferences and reserve requirements explain some. But a lot of the booking abroad, and particularly that of claims on non-banks (loans and securities) in the so-called offshore centres, has something to do with taxation.

The features of the Canadian tax system that are relevant are quite different if the international business in question is booked abroad in a branch of the bank or in a subsidiary. We shall look first at the case of a branch and then at that of a subsidiary.

Where the booking is in a branch, the rate of corporation profits tax in Canada is not of itself a great inducement to book business abroad. The reason is that all the branches of a bank, foreign and domestic, are consolidated for tax purposes. The Government of Canada applies a tax rate of 46 per cent to that part of a bank's

Place of Booking of Foreign Currency Business of Canadian Banks at June 1984

Place of Booking		Assets: Deposits with Banks[1]	Assets: Loans and Securities	Assets: Total	Deposit Liabilities: To Banks[1]	Deposit Liabilities: To Others	Deposit Liabilities: Total
		(in billions of U.S. dollars)					
Vis-à-vis Non-Residents							
Canada		17.0	6.0	23.0	24.2	22.7	47.0
Offshore centres[2]		2.7	22.8	25.5	7.6	6.9	14.5
Elsewhere:	of which	14.4	36.6	51.0	28.6	17.1	45.8
	United States	n/a		20.4	n/a		15.1
	United Kingdom			20.8			23.5
	Other			9.8			7.2
Total		34.1	65.5	99.6	60.4	46.8	107.2
Vis-à-vis Residents							
Canada		3.0	22.4	25.4	3.1	5.8	8.8
Offshore centres[2]		.1	.1	.3	.5	.7	1.2
Elsewhere:	of which	.7	.8	1.5	1.0	8.7	9.7
	United States	n/a		.7	n/a		5.9
	United Kingdom			.6			3.7
	Other			.2			.1
Total		3.8	23.3	27.1	4.6	15.2	19.8
Total							
Canada		20.0	28.3	48.4	27.3	28.5	55.8
Offshore centres[2]		2.8	23.0	25.8	8.1	7.6	15.7
Elsewhere:	of which	15.1	37.4	52.5	29.7	25.8	55.5
	United States	n/a		21.1	n/a		21.0
	United Kingdom			21.4			27.2
	Other			10.0			7.3
Total		37.9	88.8	126.7	65.0	61.9	127.0

(1) Includes official monetary institutions.

(2) Countries included are the Bahamas, Bahrain, Barbados, Bermuda, the Cayman Islands, Hong Kong, Lebanon, Liberia, the Netherlands Antilles, Vanuatu (New Hebrides), Panama, Singapore, the Virgin Islands and the West Indies.

Source: Bank of Canada

profits that are deemed to have been earned abroad, and the same rate with a 10 point abatement in favour of the provinces (i.e. a rate of 36 per cent) is applied on profits earned in Canada. In nearly all cases the provincial profits taxes exceed the abatement, and several provinces also impose capital taxes and other relevant taxes. (Information on taxes imposed by the provinces appears in Appendix B to this Report.) To the extent that the burden of the relevant taxes in a province exceeds the relief provided by the federal tax abatement there is a tax inducement to the banks to book business abroad rather than in that province.

For business booked in bank branches, a strong inducement to use branches abroad rather than at home arises from two differences in the way that the federal profits-tax liability is calculated. These differences have to do with foreign tax credits arising from withholding tax and with the distinction made between "business" and "non-business" foreign income.

It is quite common for governments to collect withholding tax on income paid abroad, including interest paid to banks, by private-sector entities. The rate of withholding tax on income flows between pairs of countries is often agreed in tax treaties between them, but many countries, including some who are large borrowers in Euro-currency markets, do not have any tax treaties and determine their withholding tax practices unilaterally. In the treaties that Canada has signed there is typically provision for withholding tax at the rate of 15 per cent on interest paid abroad by private borrowers. Rates of this order or higher are often applied to interest paid to Canadian banks by private-sector borrowers in countries with which Canada has no tax treaty.

A bank making a Euro-currency loan cannot afford to absorb a tax of this magnitude. Profit in banking arises from the spread between what a bank has to pay on the deposits that it attracts and what it can earn by lending the funds, and competition in international banking keeps that difference small on loans to customers who have a good credit rating. At current interest rates a withholding-tax deduction at 15 per cent would normally exceed the pre-tax profit to a bank from an international loan, and no bank would make the loan if it had to absorb any significant part of the tax.

This can be illustrated as follows: Suppose a bank were to lend at 12 per cent per annum $1,000,000 that cost the bank 10 1/2 per cent to borrow, and that interest on the loan were subject to a 15 per cent withholding tax. The annual withholding-tax deduction would be 15 per cent of $120,000, or $18,000, leaving the bank with $102,000 to cover its own interest cost of $105,000. If the bank had to absorb the withholding tax it would lose $3,000 per year plus the non-interest costs of the transaction.

There are nevertheless various circumstances in which a loan normally subject to withholding tax can be profitable to a lending bank. It may be that the bank has a lending office in the country of the borrower, in which case it can lend from that office and avoid the tax. It may be that there is a country outside the borrowing country in which the bank can, by virtue of a tax treaty between that country and the borrowing country, book a loan without attracting withholding tax. In some cases the borrower may agree to pay a sufficiently high rate of interest to offset the withholding tax, perhaps receiving from his own government a rebate of some or all of the withholding tax that it levies on his loan. But the usual way for the lending banks to escape the incidence of withholding tax is to receive credit for it against profit taxes that they would otherwise have to pay to their home country. The relevant national taxing authorities have arrangements for giving credit for foreign taxes paid as part of their systems for minimizing double taxation.

It is the practice in Canada to give to Canadian corporations operating abroad credit on a country-by-country basis for foreign taxes that they have paid, that is, credit is given for taxes paid to a particular country against taxes otherwise payable in Canada on profits earned in that country. Under this arrangement full credit for withholding tax paid will be available only if there is a suitable fit by country of profits earned and taxes paid. In the case of bank branches abroad, however, all the income of a branch and all the taxes paid (other than to Canada) by the branch are attributed to the country in which the branch is located. This allows an aggregating of profits and foreign taxes paid, and makes it very much easier for a bank to get full credit against Canadian profits tax for withholding taxes paid on loans which are booked abroad than on loans which are booked at home. Full credit can be obtained in a branch abroad if the profits of the branch from all sources generate a Canadian tax liability equal to or greater than the total of its foreign tax credits. One way of ensuring enough profit for that purpose in a particular branch abroad is to book there sufficient loans that do not attract withholding tax, that is, loans to governments.

The other Canadian tax practice that offers banks an inducement to book international business in a branch abroad rather than at home is the distinction made between foreign tax credits in respect of "business" foreign income and those in respect of "non-business" foreign income in accordance with whether the taxes for which credit is being given are related to the income of a business operation carried on abroad (business foreign income) or at home (non-business foreign income). Unused foreign tax credits in respect of business foreign income can be carried forward for seven years or back for three, while those in respect of non-business foreign income are lost if they cannot be used in the year in which they are earned. In their international business the Canadian banks make many loans to borrowers in countries in which the banks do not have business establishments, and if such loans are booked in Canada any foreign tax credits that may arise (e.g. from withholding taxes) are generally treated as being in respect of non-business foreign income. But if such loans are booked in a foreign branch, any foreign tax credits that arise are generally treated as being in respect of business foreign income. There is thus an incentive to the banks to gain flexibility in tax matters by booking abroad any business that would give rise to foreign tax credits on non-business foreign income if it were booked in Canada.

So far in this section we have been looking at the incentives that flow from the tax system for the Canadian banks to book their Euro-currency business at foreign branches rather than at home. The tax system provides quite different incentives to place that business in foreign subsidiaries rather than at home.

It is the Canadian practice not to tax the profits of foreign subsidiaries of Canadian corporations unless and until the profits are brought to Canada. When they are brought to Canada they normally become subject to corporate income tax unless they come from tax-treaty countries. If they come from tax-treaty countries they are not taxed in Canada in accordance with a provision in the tax treaties that Canada has signed that limits the taxation of corporate profits to the country in which they are earned.

These circumstances offer a strong inducement to banks to place international business in subsidiaries in countries where the rate of profits tax is appreciably below that in Canada. Even though the profits are exposed to Canadian taxes if and when they are remitted to Canada, the attraction of a host country with a zero or low rate of profits tax is great because the banks can reasonably expect to have opportunities to use the funds abroad rather than to bring them to Canada, and in any event the payment of the taxes is delayed. In the case of tax-treaty countries there is the additional advantage that the profits after local tax may be brought to Canada without attracting tax in Canada. Canada's tax treaties are mainly with countries that have corporate tax rates broadly similar to those in Canada, but in a few cases, e.g. Singapore and Barbados, there are arrangements that provide a low rate of local tax on profits from international business.

D. International Banking in Canada by Foreign Banks

In this Report we have used the terms international banking centre and Euro-currency centre as virtually synonymous, both meaning those places where the world's banks tend to congregate to do international business. The larger home-banks of a country in which a centre is located can be expected to be important participants in the business done there, but a principal feature of such centres is the large share of the business done in them by foreign banks.

The international banking business done in Canada by foreign banks is that done by their subsidiaries in Canada, the Schedule B banks. The Schedule B banks are, of course, legally Canadian banks but they are foreign owned, and it is foreign-owned banks that we have in mind when we talk about foreign banks in the context of international banking.

The Schedule B banks do international banking in amounts that are significant for them in some cases but that are small relative to amounts done by the Schedule A banks. The parents of a number of the Schedule B banks are among the largest participants in Euro-currency banking, but they make very limited use of their Canadian offices in that regard.

The Canadian regulations governing the operations of foreign banks in Canada are primarily concerned with defining the terms on which such banks can participate in the domestic banking business in Canada. While they do not prevent the Schedule B banks from doing international banking, the fact that the regulations do not permit the foreign parent banks to operate branches in Canada does not encourage it since a branch is the best instrument for competing for Euro-currency deposits.

E. Comments on Some Means of Attracting to Canada More of the Activity Involved in International Banking

By virtue of the relatively large role that the Canadian-owned banks play in international banking, a considerable amount of activity in that business now occurs in Canada. Most of it is in the banks' international departments and in the branches that handle the international business that is booked in Canada.

At the same time, a good deal of the activity of the Canadian-owned banks in international banking occurs outside of Canada, and there is very little international banking activity by foreign banks in Canada.

If the consequences of any initiatives taken to attract to Canada more of the activity involved in international banking were largely limited to more booking here of the Euro-currency business that the Canadian-owned banks do, the benefits in terms of employment would not be large. Even though the amount of business that moved to Canada might look huge in money terms, the amount of additional employment generated here would be small. The reason is that the amount of on-site employment involved in administering even a large portfolio of Euro-currency assets and liabilities is not great. The efficiency of the Canadian banks would be somewhat greater if they could book more of their international business in Canada because they would be able to make better use of their facilities here, and their communications and control would be made easier; as a result the increase in employment in Canada would probably be less than the reduction in employment abroad.

The limited size of the benefits that could flow from booking more international banking business in Canada necessarily puts a limit on the cost that would be warranted to achieve them. It does not, however, preclude all initiatives, and there are some that we think merit consideration.

One important inducement to the Canadian banks to book business abroad has been the difference referred to in the previous section between the treatment of domestic and foreign branches in respect of tax credits arising out of withholding tax and the distinction between business and non-business foreign income.

If this difference were eliminated by extending these aspects of the tax treatment of domestic branches to the foreign branches, the result would be to make it more difficult for the Canadian banks to make international loans that attract withholding tax. Our banks would become less competitive in that type of lending and would do less of it.

If the difference were eliminated by extending these aspects of the tax treatment of foreign branches to the domestic branches, the result would be an increase in international assets booked in Canada.

We understand that the reluctance of the tax authorities to eliminate the difference in the latter way stems from a desire to preserve a country-by-country approach to foreign tax credits and a distinction between business and non-business foreign income for application to non-financial institutions.

If it is desired to preserve these principles for general use, there seems to us to be merit in exploring the feasibility of some special arrangement that would respond to the banking situation by making available offshore tax treatment for international portfolios held onshore. We believe that it would be possible to define and administer an arrangement that would permit the banks to set up in Canada international banking accounts into which they could put eligible international assets and liabilities and which would be treated as foreign branches for the aspects of profits tax that we have been discussing. The business that would be made eligible to be held in such accounts would be Euro-currency business with non-residents.

One problem that would arise in setting up this arrangement would be how to fit it into the provisions for tax sharing between the federal and provincial governments. Should the international banking accounts be regarded as offshore or onshore in that context? Most of the business that would be eligible for them is now booked abroad, and profits arising from it are not taxed by the provinces. On the other hand, a good deal of business now booked in Canada would be eligible to be held by such accounts, and the profits on that business are now taxed by the provinces. There would thus be arguments for and against the extension by the federal government of the 10-point tax abatement to the profits of such accounts.

If the international banking accounts were treated as offshore in the context of tax sharing, i.e. taxed at the 46 per cent rate by the federal authorities and not taxed by the provinces, the result would be that the Canadian tax arrangements would be neutral as between foreign and domestic branches. We believe that the banks would then show, for operating reasons, a preference for booking in Canada rather than in foreign branches, and more international business would be booked here.

If the international accounts were treated as onshore for purposes of tax sharing, i.e. a 10-point abatement extended to the provinces, then the outcome as regards booking would depend essentially on what the provinces did. At one end of the spectrum, if the host provinces did not give them some tax concession there would remain a tax inducement to the banks to leave abroad their business booked in foreign branches because the relief provided by the 10-point abatement would be exceeded by the burden of provincial taxes (see Appendix B). At the other end of the spectrum, if, in addition to the 10-point abatement, the host provinces exempted them from profits and capital taxes, great encouragement would be given to book business in the new international banking accounts in Canada rather than in foreign branches. Thus the assessment by interested provinces of the possible advantages to them of the international banking accounts would be crucial; without the strong support of some provinces little could be achieved. The April 1985 Budget of the Government of Quebec indicates that that province is disposed to give strong support to measures to attract international financial operations to Quebec.

It would not be realistic to expect that the banks would respond to even a strongly-provincially-supported system of international banking accounts of the kind discussed above by more than a partial shift from the foreign booking of claims on non-banks to the domestic booking of such claims. There are both banking and tax reasons that would lead them to continue to book many such claims abroad. The banking reasons include access to regional economic information, access to their customers, and time-zone considerations. The principal tax reason is the tax advantage that we have already noted from placing international banking business in subsidiary companies in low-tax countries.

There are important legal differences between a foreign branch and a foreign subsidiary but in the context of international banking their similarities have tended to be emphasized. A branch, being an integral part of the bank, automatically engages the full resources of the bank, and this engagement is an essential element in winning and holding the confidence of customers. Even though the legal position may be that a foreign subsidiary stands on its own feet, it is generally assumed that in case of need the foreign subsidiaries of Canadian banks would have the same access to the parent banks' resources as branches, and this has helped them to operate like branches in Euro-currency markets. This assumption has tended to become more explicit in recent years as the risk of losses in international banking has received greater attention. It is not now uncommon for parent banks to enter into formal arrangements, in exchange for a fee, to guarantee or insure their own subsidiaries against loss on their assets.

Up to this point we have been discussing action that might be taken to affect the place of booking of the international assets of the Canadian-owned banks and bring more of this booking to Canada. There remains to be considered the possibility of much stronger action which would have as its objective to make Canada a truly important international banking centre by providing conditions which would encourage foreign banks to carry on a large part of their international banking business from this country. Those who urge this objective appear to believe that if Canada and the provinces were to exempt the profits on international business by banks in Canada from taxation (either wholly or substantially), this would bring to Canada a great deal of international financial activity which would provide employment for many skilled persons and would over time have a major general economic fall-out. (In some cases the proposal is that the tax concessions, and consequently the economic effects, should be restricted to one or two cities. This is essentially a political question on which we do not comment.)

These proposals recognize the vital fact that it is indeed the nature of a real international banking centre that foreign banks should have an important presence there. This is the case in London, in New York, in Hong Kong and in Singapore.

We have already noted that the regulation of the activities of foreign banks in Canada has not so far been designed to encourage them to do international banking here.

There can be no doubt that the exemption of the profits on international banking transactions from taxation would attract more of this business to Canada. The same can be said of tax exemption for any other business. A decision to offer it to international banking would require the support of evidence that the ratio of benefits to costs would be particularly favorable in that field.

It does not seem to us likely that Canada could win more than modest benefits from aggressive tax competition to attract international banking activity, and the extent of these would be uncertain. We recognize that Canada has important advantages as a base for supplying financial services to the world market – political stability, a good legal system, free and well-developed financial markets, large and highly-regarded banks – but several other countries have similar advantages. The competition that Canada would face in developing as an international banking centre would be intense. Canada would be most competitive in the Western Hemisphere time zones, and there we would face the competition of New York and other U.S. cities in our time zones. In Europe, London is well established and is vigorously seeking to maintain its position. Whatever the longer-term prospects of Hong Kong, it remains at present an important financial centre. If the Japanese authorities permit it, Tokyo seems very likely to emerge as the major international banking centre in Asia. Finally, it has to be borne in mind that, while the Euro-currency market will no doubt remain large, it is most unlikely to show the remarkable growth rates of the 1970s in the foreseeable future.

None of the other countries with Canada's advantages has tried to win a competitive edge in international banking through major tax concessions. No one knows how our competitors would react. London and New York did not achieve their predominance in that way, and the rates of profits tax there and in other comparable centres are not greatly different from those in Canada. The positions of London and New York have been buttressed by the increasing freedom that their countries have given to foreign banks to operate in them.

It should not be supposed that such benefits as Canada could obtain from major tax concessions to attract international banking business would be costless on the ground that the tax concessions would apply only to business that is not here now. Any reasonable definition of international banking activity would include a good deal of business that is now done in Canada and that now contributes to the tax base. The potential tax-revenue loss would not be insignificant. Moreover, a large differential between the tax rates on bank profits earned in international business (however defined) and in other business would necessitate a careful, difficult and costly allocation of bank costs and revenues. There would also be the non-measurable but real cost to public policy of major tax discrimination in favour of a particular activity.

The conclusion that we reach is that the benefits to be derived from major tax concessions designed to make Canada a truly important international banking centre would not be worth the cost. Our fear is that these concessions would have as their main result to make us an important international booking centre, with little important economic fall-out.

F. Summary and Concluding Comments

We have enquired into the business of international banking from the point of view of the distribution around the world of the employment involved in it to see if we would find room for initiatives that would be in Canada's interest to change that distribution.

By the business of international banking we mean the handling of the international capital flows that go through the world's Euro-currency markets. Though these channels are relatively new, they are now very large and seem likely to continue to be large. The Canadian banks are major participants in this business, accounting for 4 to 5 per cent of the total.

The principal determinant of the geographical distribution of the activity involved in international banking is the operating needs of the participating banks. The business is highly competitive, and the banks have to be suitably represented wherever in the world they can best do business and best serve their customers. A large proportion of the business is arranged in a few important banking centres, notably London and New York, where the participating banks find it efficient to have establishments for that purpose.

In order to be competitive, the Euro-currency banks have to minimize the costs imposed on them by banking regulations and by taxation, and this frequently obliges them to record their business on the books of their branches or subsidiary companies in countries that they would not otherwise have chosen. Thus a good deal of international business is booked in low-tax countries which are not otherwise financial centres. These are often referred to as booking centres.

Some features of the Canadian tax system provide a strong inducement to the Canadian banks to book their international business outside of Canada. International business booked at branches abroad rather than at home receives more favorable treatment in respect of foreign tax credits arising from withholding tax and in respect of a distinction made by the tax system between business and non-business foreign income. International business placed with foreign subsidiaries receives more favorable treatment than at home in that profits are not taxed by Canada until they are brought to Canada, and if they come from a country with which Canada has a tax treaty they are not taxed then.

We think that it would be reasonable, and advantageous for Canada, to give no less favorable tax treatment to the profits from international business booked in Canada than is now given when it is booked at branches abroad. We have outlined for consideration an arrangement that could help to achieve this result. It involves permitting the Canadian banks to set up international banking accounts in Canada in which they could book international business with non-residents and have it treated in respect of foreign tax credits and the distinction between business and non-business foreign income as though it were booked in a foreign branch. How much influence this arrangement would have on place-of-booking decisions would depend to a considerable extent on how it was fitted into the system of federal-provincial tax sharing, and how much support the provinces thought that it warranted.

The benefit to Canada of an initiative of this kind would be that some, though by no means all, of the business now booked abroad by the Canadian banks would be booked in Canada. There would remain both banking and other tax reasons for a good deal of international business to continue to be booked abroad. While the amount of business that would move to Canada over time might be large in money terms, the increase in employment in Canada would not be large because the administration of even large Euro-currency portfolios takes relatively little on-site work. Neither the costs nor the benefits of an initiative of this kind would be great.

We have noted that proposals have on occasion been made by others for very strong action to attract activity in international banking to Canada. These have involved the total (or substantial) exemption of such activity from both federal and provincial taxes.

Proponents of major tax concessions foresee substantial economic benefits to Canada from them, in part from the booking and management in Canada of a much larger part of the international business now done by the Canadian-owned banks but mainly from the attraction to Canada of an appreciable part of the Euro-market activity of foreign banks.

We recognize that Canada has some natural advantages as a supplier of financial services to the world, and we also recognize that it is only by attracting a lot of Euro-market activity of foreign banks – by becoming a real and important international banking centre – that there could be more than a modest increase in employment in Canada in the international banking field. We believe, however, that Canadian efforts to develop into an international banking centre would meet intense competition from the existing centres and from other places with a potential as great as ours, and that it would be unwise to force the issue by vigorous tax competition. If the view is taken that rich priority should be given to increasing Canada's role in international financial affairs, it is our opinion that the way to pursue that goal is to take care that the tax arrangements in Canada are no less favorable than they are in the major international banking centres and that foreign banks in Canada are given as much flexibility for their international operations as they are given in those centres.

Appendix A

International Banking Facilities in the United States

The introduction of International Banking Facilities (IBFs) in the United States in 1981 is an interesting example of an initiative taken to change the geographical distribution of international banking activity.

Before the introduction of IBFs it was difficult for banks to compete effectively in the Euro-currency market from offices in the United States. The reasons included both regulatory and tax elements.

From the point of view of banking regulation the situation of the United States was unlike that of other countries in that the currency being used abroad was its domestic currency. U.S. banking regulations imposed reserve requirements (and had earlier imposed interest-rate ceilings) on the liabilities of banks in the United States to non-residents as well as to residents. Since banks operating in other countries were not subject to similar costs and constraints in doing business in U.S. dollars, banks operating in the United States were at a competitive disadvantage. The U.S. banks thus did their Euro-currency business mainly from offices outside the United States.

The tax element was state and local taxes. The federal profits tax was not seen by the banks as an obstacle to onshore banking because the method of calculating the tax, that of consolidating the profits of domestic and foreign branches, meant that the tax was not avoided by going offshore. Moreover, the federal rate of profits tax was not out of line with those in the home countries of the banks with whom the U.S. banks were competing. State and local taxes, however, tended to be high, particularly in New York State and New York City, and these could be avoided by doing international business abroad.

The fact that relatively little international business was booked in New York did not mean that that city was not a very important international banking centre. It is the world's largest financial centre, and much of the international business of both U.S. and foreign banks was arranged there. Much of the business of U.S. banks abroad was directed from there. But the final stage of the international banking transactions, the recording and on-site administration of them, was usually done elsewhere.

The constraint of the regulatory arrangements on the international operations of U.S. banks had long been recognized, but there had been concern that any significant easing of them would erode the effectiveness of monetary control. This concern was reinforced on the occasions in the 1960s and 1970s when the U.S.

authorities felt it necessary to take special measures to strengthen the international payments position of the country. While they lasted, these measures reduced the availability of capital from the United States and thereby stimulated the growth of the Euro-dollar market as an alternative source of U.S. dollar credit. U.S. banks participated actively in the Euro-dollar market but on an offshore basis, attracting the funds that they loaned from outside the United States.

In the late 1970s there was growing interest in the United States in searching for an acceptable way that would allow U.S. banks to participate in the Euro-dollar market from within the country. New York State played a leading role, and offered to exempt international banking transactions from state and local taxes if the other steps necessary to accommodate them onshore were taken. After much discussion the IBFs were agreed upon and introduced. The argument for them was that they would, without eroding monetary control, increase employment and improve banking surveillance and banking efficiency at very little cost in that the reserve and tax concessions involved were already available to the banks through operating offshore. On a more global level it was argued that a U.S. initiative of this kind would be a constructive step towards more intergovernmental cooperation in the management of the international financial system.

The IBFs are systems of separate accounts kept by deposit-accepting institutions for business which is eligible, that being business with non-residents of the United States that is wholly external to the United States. The deposits in IBFs are free from reserve requirements, from interest-rate limitations, and from deposit insurance coverage and assessments. IBFs are available to any U.S. bank and to any foreign bank operating in the United States. IBFs have been given no concessions from U.S. federal income tax, but they have been given major concessions from state and local income taxes in a number of states.

Although the regulations governing the IBFs permit them to be used for many kinds of international business, there are still some constraints imposed for reasons of monetary control. IBFs cannot accept overnight deposits from non-financial sources, they cannot issue instruments in negotiable or bearer form, and they cannot do individual transactions with non-bank customers of less than $100,000. Nor can they do business with residents of the United States (except other IBFs), or with foreign affiliates of U.S. corporations to finance U.S. activities.

As of April 24, 1985, 159 institutions had IBF assets or liabilities of at least $300 million, and 51 of these were U.S. institutions and 108 were U.S. agencies or branches of foreign banks. They reported liabilities other than to their own U.S. offices of $231 billion, $89 billion for U.S. institutions and $142 billion for foreign institutions. Of the 159 institutions, 98 were in the State of New York, with liabilities of $179 billion, and 75 of these were the U.S. agencies or branches of foreign banks, with liabilities of $116 billion. Less current statistics indicate that nearly all the other IBFs were in the states of California, Florida, Illinois and Texas.

The extent of the use of IBFs by foreign banks has been surprising. It appears to reflect in considerable part their use for Western Hemisphere business by Japanese banks, and to a lesser extent Italian banks, these banks having made little use of booking offices in the Caribbean. Several Canadian banks have established IBFs but their use of them does not seem to have been great.

It is still too early to judge what the impact of IBFs on the distribution of international banking activity will eventually be. Some large U.S. banks have moved substantial amounts of business to the United States from their Caribbean offices but others have tended to put only new business into IBFs. The use of IBFs in the State of New York has been constrained by uncertainty about how the new tax regulations of that state will be interpreted. There seems to be a considerable range of opinion among U.S. bankers about the longer-term effects of the limitations on IBFs compared with offshore operations, and there has been disappointment that Euro-dollar depositors have not shown the preference that some bankers expected for deposits booked in IBFs over deposits booked elsewhere.

It has become clear, however, that the IBFs are not going to generate the large increase in employment in New York or elsewhere in the United States that some earlier advocated. Suggestions that they would create, directly or indirectly, 5,000 to 6,000 new jobs have turned out to be substantial overestimates. The experience has been that moving even large amounts of Euro-dollar business from the books of one bank office to another involves very little movement of staff. That is particularly the case when business is moved to the head office, where large and specialized staffs and facilities are available to absorb the extra work.

Appendix B

Some Provincial Tax Rates Relevant for Banks[1]
(as at end 1984)

	Corporation income	Corporation capital
	(per cent)	
British Columbia	16	0.8/2.0[2]
Alberta	11	nil
Saskatchewan	16	0.8
Manitoba	16	1.9
Ontario	15	0.8
Quebec	05.5	0.9
New Brunswick	15	nil
Nova Scotia	15	nil
Prince Edward Island	10	nil
Newfoundland	16	1.5

(1) Other provincial taxes that affect the operating costs of banks are also relevant. In Quebec, for example, a levy on corporations of 3 per cent of payroll for health insurance, and relatively high rates of personal income tax, are relevant. The April 1985 Quebec budget proposes a number of tax reductions in order to attract international financial operations to Quebec.

(2) 0.8 per cent where the amount taxable is $500 million or less, and 2 per cent where it is in excess of $500 million.

Part V
Hong Kong and Singapore

[20]

Excerpt from Leung Chi-keung, J.W. Cushman and Wang Gungwu (eds), *Hong Kong Dilemmas of Growth*, 161–94.

HONG KONG AS A REGIONAL FINANCIAL CENTRE: EVOLUTION AND PROSPECTS*

Y.C. JAO

Hong Kong's post-war transformation from an entrepot into an industrial economy based largely on the export of labour-intensive manufactured goods has already been well documented. Since about 1969, Hong Kong has also been fast emerging as a major financial centre for the Asian-Pacific region. Perhaps because of the very recent origin of this phenomenon, there have been relatively few serious studies of its economic significance.[1]

The purpose of this paper is to provide a broad survey of Hong Kong's financial sector as at the end of 1979, against the backdrop of the evolving financial scene since the late sixties.

* * * *

The term 'financial centre' has often been used indiscriminately without specifying its geographical and functional coverage. Some international financial centres, such as London, New York and Zurich, are also simultaneously national and regional centres, but the same is not true the other way round: most major cities of the world are obviously national centres only. Since Hong Kong is a city-state, to describe it as a national financial centre is evidently meaningless. But Hong Kong is also not of the same class as the leading international centres. From the functional point of view, Hong Kong, unlike the traditional centres such as London and New York, did not begin its career as a net exporter of capital. At the same time, unlike many other newly emergent centres, it does not confine its activities to entrepot financial services or offshore banking, since the domestic market is also highly dynamic.[2] The most appropriate appellation is therefore 'regional financial centre'. As the designation implies, it is a focal point for the flow of funds across national boundaries in the Asian-Pacific area. What then are the salient features of Hong Kong's financial growth during the past decade?

The first readily observable feature is the presence of a large and still increasing number of international banking institutions and other non-bank financial intermediaries. A comparison between the end of 1969 and 1979, as given in Table 1, is revealing.

A brief explanation of the table is in order. Under Hong Kong's banking law, only incorporated entities holding government-issued licences are allowed to transact the whole gamut of banking business, both retail and wholesale. The number of institutions holding such licences increased from seventy-three to seventy-four only from the end of 1969 to mid-March

---

*The present paper is an up-dated, expanded, and thoroughly revised version of an earlier one that has appeared in the July 1979 issue of *Asian Survey* under the title 'The Rise of Hong Kong as a Financial Centre'.

TABLE 1

Number of Financial Institutions in Hong Kong

	31 December 1969	31 December 1979
Licensed Banks:		
Number of main offices	73	105
Number of total offices, including branches	362	1,011
Representative Offices of Foreign Banks	21	114
Registered Deposit-taking Companies*	nil	269
Insurance Companies		
Life	51	109**
General	156	334**

* including merchant banks and finance companies
** as of 31 March 1979
Source: Banking Commissioner's Office and Registrar-General's Department

1978, due to a moratorium on new bank licences imposed in 1966 after the 1965 banking crisis.[3] On 15 March 1978 the moratorium was relaxed for foreign banks that met certain regulatory and capital criteria.[4] This gave rise, however, to such an avalanche of new entrants that the moratorium had to be re-imposed on 7 August 1979 for a period of six months. During the seventeen-month interval, no less than forty-one licences had been issued to foreign banks, thirty-one of which had started operation as of 31 December 1979. Even before this new influx, however, the branch network of the existing licensed banks within Hong Kong had been expanding rapidly so that the number of their total bank offices more than doubled during the period under review. Other financial institutions expanded even more spectacularly: representative offices more than quintupled, while registered, deposit-taking companies (DTCs), which were non-existent before 1970, proliferated to 269.[5] Concomitantly, life insurance companies and general insurance companies also more than doubled in number.

The international flavour of this large congregation is conveyed by an impressive presence of non-indigenous institutions. Of the 105 licensed banks now operating, for example, 71 are foreign banks incorporated outside Hong Kong. The representative offices are by definition of foreign origin. Of the 269 registered DTCs, about half are subsidiaries or joint ventures set up by foreign commercial banks, merchant banks and investment houses. My own investigation reveals that, of the top 100 commercial banks in the world, some 69 are now operating in Hong Kong in one form or another.[6] According to another estimate by the Banking Commissioner before the relaxation of the bank licence moratorium, there were in early 1978 about 188 foreign banks transacting banking business through fully licensed branches, representative offices, or registered deposit-taking subsidiaries.[7] The number could be magnified by another 30 or so if partners in some of the consortium banks represented in Hong Kong were also included. This would make Hong Kong probably next only to London and New York in having the largest number of foreign banking and near-banking institutions. The same pattern of foreign presence is visible in the insurance sector: 60 of the 109 life insurances companies and 174 of the 334 general insurance companies are incorporated overseas. In terms of sheer number, there can be little doubt that Hong Kong is the leading insurance centre in the Asian-Pacific region.

The presence of a large number of international financial institutions is however only a necessary, but not sufficient condition, for turning a city into a regional financial centre. The essence of such a centre is that non-domestic financial intermediaries assemble not only to transact business in the host city's or host country's domestic financial markets, but also to engage actively in the channelling of funds to and from third countries. Even before 1969, Hong Kong could boast of a cosmopolitan banking structure where, with the exception of the Soviet bloc and the poorer Third World countries, all the major trading nations were represented, including of course the People's Republic of China (PRC). But most foreign banks then were content to confine their activities to financing Hong Kong's external trade and domestic economic activities. There was little thought of using Hong Kong as a regional base for conducting offshore banking business. Notwithstanding its earlier roots, the growing internationalization of banking operations and financial activities has become evident only in the past ten years. This may be seen by comparing the consolidated balance sheet of the licensed banking sector between the end of 1969 and the end of 1979, as in Table 2.

In interpreting the balance sheet, our attention is focussed on the extent to which the various items reflect the international orientation of the banking system. Starting from the liabilities side, the seven-fold increase in bank deposits in itself cannot be taken as an unambiguous indicator of Hong Kong's rise as a financial centre. This is because in the absence of exchange control, the banking system does not distinguish between resident and non-resident accounts, so that it is impossible to ascertain how much of this deposit growth is externally generated. Nevertheless, Hong Kong has always been regarded as a safe haven for capital funds in the area, particularly by the fourteen million *huaqiao* (overseas Chinese) living in various parts of Southeast Asia. It is believed in banking circles that a substantial proportion of such deposits - perhaps between a quarter and a third - is held by overseas Chinese and other nationals. It is also likely that the proportion of savings and time deposits held by non-residents is higher than that of demand deposits.[8]

The most notable feature on the liabilities side is, however, the phenomenal growth of the item 'amount due to banks abroad', which in absolute terms increased by thirty-nine times, or at an annual rate of 44.5 per cent during the ten years ended 31 December 1979. The relative share of this item rose from only 11.2 per cent of total liabilities at the end of 1969 to 39.6 per cent at the end of 1979. The significance of this change lies in the fact that it reflects not only Hong Kong's importance

TABLE 2

Consolidated Balance Sheet of the Licensed Banks

(million HK dollars)

	31 December 1969	31 December 1979
LIABILITIES		
Deposits:		
Demand	3,714	20,472
Savings	3,367	33,258
Time	5,216	34,284
	12,297	88,014
Amount due to banks abroad	1,845	73,685
Other liabilities	2,385	24,159
Total	$16,527	$185,858
ASSETS		
Cash	333	1,495
Amount due from bank abroad	5,299	66,435
Loans and advances:		
Hong Kong	7,680	73,690
Abroad	204	20,778
Investments:		
Hong Kong	659	5,462
Abroad	10	180
Other Assets	2,342	17,818
Total	$16,527	$185,858

Source: Banking Commissioner's Office

as a financial centre, but also the banking system's evolving method of managing its source of funds. Foreign banks in Hong Kong with insufficient local currency deposit base but faced with a strong loan demand have tended to borrow heavily from their head offices or other sources, principally the Euro-dollar market and Asian-dollar market, in order to fund their local or offshore lendings in or emanating from Hong Kong. The proximate counterpart of this item on the assets side is therefore loans and advances within and outside Hong Kong. This is a good illustration of the now familiar concept of 'liability management' developed originally in the early sixties by some large American banks.[9] Consistent with this interpretation was the decline of the relative share of total deposits in total liabilities from 74.4 to 47.4 per cent during the same period, which shows that the banking system has become less dependent on the traditional cash-flow from domestic depositors as their source of funds. It is unfortunate that there is no breakdown in the item 'other liabilities', but from accounting identity we know that they must consist of (a) net inter-bank balances within Hong Kong; (b) fiduciary issue of the two note-issuing banks; and (c) net worth of the banking system. Since (a) and (b) are known to be very small, the whole item can be treated as an approximate surrogate for the net worth of the banking system.[10] During 1969-79, such liabilities increased ten-fold, or at an annual rate of 26 per cent. Their relative share however declined from 14.4 to 13 per cent, implying a higher leverage for the capital structure of the banking system. This trend is consistent with the experience of other advanced countries.

On the assets side, total assets increased more than ten-fold, or at an annual rate of 27.4 per cent. One feature that underlies quite dramatically Hong Kong's rapid rise as a financial centre has been the phenomenal growth of 'loans and advances abraod' from $204 million to $20,778 million, representing an annual growth rate of 58.8 per cent. This compares with the annual growth rate of 25.4 per cent for loans and advances within Hong Kong. According to the latest available geographical breakdown, the largest borrowers as of 31 December 1979, were, in order of importance, Liberia, Indonesia, South Korea, Taiwan, Malaysia, Japan, Australia, Panama, Philippines, Thailand, India and New Zealand.[11] The inclusion of Liberia and Panama is, however, suspect, for the well-known reason that most Hong Kong-owned shipping companies, flying 'flags of convenience', are incorporated there. Thus in our judgment these two countries should not be classified as overseas borrowers. The remaining leading borrowers, as we can see, were all in the Asian-Pacific region, but there were substantial borrowers from Latin America (Brazil and Mexico) and Europe (Ireland) as well. It is to be noted that the borrowers are defined as non-bank customers ranging from private corporations to central or local governments. The combined total of domestic and offshore loans grew at an annual rate of 28.2 per cent, which was 6.4 per cent higher than the growth rate of total deposits. This explains the need for 'liability management' mentioned earlier. Another item that has expanded rapidly is 'amount due from banks abroad', consisting of demand and time deposits with banks in other financial centres. Growing at an annual rate of 28.6 per cent, its relative share in total assets increased from 32.1 to 35.7 per cent, reflecting the banking system's increasing use of foreign balances both as earning assets and secondary reserves. The consistently rapid growth and rising relative shares of external assets and liabilities provide an unmistakable indicator of Hong Kong's increasingly important role as a financial entrepot. Specifically, in 1969 about 11.2 per cent of total liabilities and 41.9 per cent of total assets were external. At the end of 1979, however, 39.6 per cent of total liabilities and 51.5 per cent of total assets were external, reflecting the greater international orientation of Hong Kong's banking operations.

The same trend towards internationalization can be discerned in the financial markets. Thus on the short-term money market, activities are no longer confined to inter-bank dealings in Hong Kong dollars: 'currency swaps', under which multinational merchant banks sell US dollars to local licensed banks for Hong Kong dollars with an agreement to repurchase them at a future date, have become extremely important.[12] As there is no exchange control of any kind, access to offshore money markets such as the Euro-currency markets and the Asian-dollar market based in Singapore is totally unimpeded to financial and non-financial entities and individuals. It may be noted that banks in Hong Kong can offer deposits of various maturities in foreign currencies, and one interesting example is that banks controlled by the People's Republic of China offer deposit facilities denominated in China's currency, *renminbi*.[13] On the capital market, since the late sixties there have been a number of listings of foreign stocks and bonds on the local stock exchanges, followed by similar listings of top-grade Hong Kong stocks and bonds on the London stock exchange. Together with Singapore, Hong Kong is now one of the twin centres for the issue and trading of Asian-dollar bonds. An offshore Hong Kong dollar bond sector was created in May 1977, whereby two first class Hong Kong companies and a province in Canada floated bonds from Europe denominated in Hong Kong dollars.[14]

This international orientation in banking operations and financial activities in turn gives rise to a need for specialist services, and it is no mere coincidence that during the past decade many well-known international money brokers, securities houses and exchange dealers, have opened offices in Hong Kong.

Hong Kong's financial growth has been accompanied by structural changes in the financial sector and the economy as a whole. With respect to the financial sector, two important changes may be noted. One is the emergence of depository financial institutions other than the licensed commercial banks. Prior to 1970, the licensed commercial banks were overwhelmingly dominant, with other non-bank financial intermediaries playing only a marginal role - a situation which the present writer has characterized elsewhere as a lack of 'institutional diversification and functional specialization'.[15] In 1970, however, a couple of merchant banks burst upon the scene, and were soon followed by a host of similar institutions ranging from multinational giants to small local finance companies. As mentioned earlier, the portmanteau title of 'deposit-taking companies' has been given by regulatory authorities to all these institutions. One common characteristic that distinguishes them from the licensed commercial banks is their exclusion from the retail end of banking business - they are not allowed to operate chequing accounts and savings deposits repayable within three months, or to take time deposits of less than HK$50,000. They are also not permitted to use the word 'bank' in their titles. Apart from these disabilities, however, they are free to transact every conceivable wholesale banking business. Some functional specialization within these depository institutions can however be detected. Generally speaking, the large multinational merchant banks tend to specialize in loan syndication, foreign exchange/money market operations, underwriting, corporate advice, project finance, and investment management. Loan syndication is a particularly important activity. An outstanding recent example is the Euro-dollar credit facility totalling US$600 million for the Korea Development Bank syndicated in Hong Kong in July 1979. This is the single largest loan syndication ever packaged in Hong Kong, reflecting the territory's growing stature as a financial centre, as in the past such 'jumbo loans' have been as a rule put together in London or New York. Altogether fifty-nine major banks, representing a broad spectrum of national origins, are participating in the loan, with two international merchant banks, BA Asia Ltd and BT Asia Ltd, acting as lead-managers. The smaller local finance companies, on the other hand, lacking capital resources, international connections and managerial expertise, tend to specialize in local stock market, mortgage and consumer loans.

The aggressive actions of these newly emergent intermediaries have sharpened competition and tended to undermine the entrenched positions of the established commercial banks. Some of the merchant banks, it is true, are themselves wholly or partly owned by the commercial banks, but collectively the merchant banks do compete vigorously with the licensed banks, particularly in the more specialized areas of offshore loans and foreign exchange.

According to an analysis by the then Assistant Banking Commissioner of the 188 DTCs registered at the end of May 1977, only 31, or 16.5 per cent of the total, were controlled by licensed banks in Hong Kong. Branches, subsidiaries and associated companies of foreign banks not licensed in Hong Kong, many of which are multinational giants, numbered no less than 58 or 30.9 per cent of the total. Moreover, of the 10 largest DTCs, 7 were either branches or subsidiaries of international banks not licensed in Hong Kong.[16] In short, the appearance of major merchant banks, backed by their huge parent organizations, has introduced a new factor into the Hong Kong banking scene.

Statistical time series on the DTCs, being very recently compiled and published, start from the end of 1978 only. Table 3 presents their consolidated balance sheet at the end of 1978 and 1979.

As the time series is too short, no meaningful historical comparison can be made, though a few comparative comments on DTCs and the licensed banks may be noted. At the end of 1979, the size of the balance sheet of the DTCs as a whole was about 42 per cent of that of the licensed banks. However, the external orientation of the DTCs appeared to be more pronounced than that of the licensed banks. Thus, 40.2 per cent of their liabilities and 53.2 per cent of their assets were external, reflecting no doubt the influence of the multinational merchant banks. As further evidence of this, the DTCs actually granted more offshore loans than the licensed banks. The latest geographical breakdown at the end of 1979 shows that the largest borrowers, in order of their importance, were Liberia, South Korea, Philippines, Panama, Indonesia, Thailand, Japan, Netherland Antilles, Malaysia, Brazil, Taiwan, Mexico and Greece. Again for the same reason mentioned earlier, Liberia and Panama should be deleted from the list, while Netherland Antilles, as a tax haven, probably serves as a 'booking centre' only. The other major borrowers included not only countries in the Asian-Pacific region, but also Brazil, Greece and Mexico. In general, the merchant banks' syndicated loans seem to have a much wider geographical coverage. Thus other significant borrowers included United Kingdom, Italy, Sweden and Spain. Several East European countries including East Germany, Hungary, Poland, and Soviet Union, were

TABLE 3

Consolidated Balance Sheet of Deposit-taking Companies

(million HK dollars)

	31 December 1978	31 December 1979
LIABILITIES		
Deposits	10,447	24,495
Amount due to banks in Hong Kong	6,386	11,463
Amount due to banks abroad	27,398	31,160
Other liabilities	8,121	10,347
Total	$52,352	$77,465
ASSETS		
Cash	5	4
Amount due from banks in Hong Kong	6,760	20,029
Amount due from banks abroad	8,943	13,559
Loans and advances:		
Hong Kong	10,139	13,566
Abroad	21,165	24,778
Investments:		
Hong Kong	1,062	1,157
Abroad	842	997
Other Assets:		
Hong Kong	1,644	1,459
Abroad	1,792	1,916
Total	$52,352	$77,465

Source: Banking Commissioner's Office

also among the borrowers. Another point to note is that the widely held belief that the DTCs rely heavily on the licensed banks in Hong Kong for support is not borne out by statistical evidence. Thus Table 3 shows that the net claims of the DTCs on banks in Hong Kong increased from $374 million to $8,566 million during the year ended 30 June 1979. The DTCs did, however, borrow heavily from banks abroad: their net liabilities to banks abroad decreased from $18,455 million to $17,601 million, but the outstanding net indebtedness was still a very considerable one. This net debtor position is consistent with our earlier comment on 'liability management' practised by international financial institutions.

The second change is the trend towards greater banking concentration, which manifests itself chiefly in the acquisitions of local Chinese banks by foreign banks or financial concerns. The origin of this trend can be traced back to the 1965 banking crisis. On the one hand, the moratorium on bank licences imposed after the crisis meant that foreign banks have had to use acquisition as the principal means of gaining a foothold in the Hong Kong market; on the other hand, those local banks that were dangerously exposed during the crisis naturally welcomed new injections of capital and managerial expertise. As shown in Table 4, some twenty-two licensed banks have sold equity interests of varying percentages to banks and financial institutions all but two of which are incorporated outside Hong Kong.[17] However, three of the acquired banks have subsequently repurchased their stocks. The latest situation at the time of writing is that of the thirty-four locally incorporated licensed banks, only fifteen are independent of foreign participation or control.

Structural changes in the economy as a result of Hong Kong's financial growth may be gauged by the changing percentage contribution of the financial sector (comprising banks, other financial institutions and insurance companies) to gross domestic product (GDP). According to International Standard Industrial Classification (ISIC), the financial sector is grouped together with real estate and business services under major division 8. As shown in Table 5, the percentage contribution of major division 8 increased from 14.6 to 18.8 per cent during the period 1970-76. Unfortunately, there is no detailed breakdown within this division, so that it is not possible to isolate the percentage contribution of the financial sector. However, in an earlier official estimate for the fiscal years 1960-61 and 1961-62 based on tax returns, there is such a breakdown, which shows that the financial sector on average accounted for about 64 per cent of major division 8. Assuming that this relationship is stable and can be extrapolated to 1970-76, one may conclude that the share of the financial sector in GDP probably increased from 9.3 per cent in 1970 to 12 per cent in 1976. Although these numbers should be treated with caution, there can be little doubt that over the long run, the financial sector has steadily grown in terms of its relative share in GDP: the corresponding figures for fiscal years 1960-61 and 1961-62 were 6.1 and 7 per cent respectively. It is also noticeable that during 1970-76, the combined share of service industries (major division 6 through 9) rose from 60.7 to 64.6 per cent, while the shares of manufacturing and other sectors (except construction) all declined. Hong Kong's experience in this respect is generally consistent with the well-known observation that as the economy becomes more affluent and mature, the tertiary sector tends to gain at the expense of the primary and secondary sectors.[18]

The growth of the financial sector, in both absolute and relative terms, can also be demonstrated by employment statistics. Since detailed data are not available for earlier years, Table 6 covers the period 1975-79 only.

As can be seen from Table 6, total employment in the financial sector increased by 43.5 per cent in 1975-79. Expressed as a percentage of

TABLE 4

Bank Acquisitions in Hong Kong

Name of bank acquired	Controlled by/affiliated with	Equity acquired (per cent)
1. Hang Seng Bank Ltd	Hong Kong and Shanghai Banking Corporation, Hong Kong	61
2. Far East Bank Ltd	Citibank N.A., USA	76
3. Shanghai Commercial Bank Ltd	Wells Fargo Bank, USA	10
4. Ka Wah Bank Ltd	Yu Chuan Finance Ltd, Malaysia	74
5. Dao Heng Bank Ltd	Grindlays Bank, UK	100
6. Bank of Canton Ltd	Security Pacific National Bank, USA	72
7. Commercial Bank of Hong Kong Ltd	Tokai Bank, Japan	10
8. Chekiang First Bank Ltd	Dai-Ichi Kangyo Bank, Japan	33
9. Overseas Trust Bank Ltd	Toronto Dominion Bank, Canada*	60
10. Kwong On Bank Ltd	Fuji Bank, Japan	55
11. Wing Lung Bank Ltd	Chartered Bank Ltd, UK	13.3
12. Wing Hang Bank Ltd	Irving Trust Co, USA	51
13. Hang Lung Bank Ltd	Toronto Dominion Bank, Canada*	50
14. Hong Kong Industrial and Commercial Bank Ltd	Toronto Dominion Bank, Canada*	10
15. Liu Chong Hing Bank Ltd	The Mitsubishi Bank, Japan	25
16. Hong Kong Metropolitan Bank Ltd	BCCI Holdings, Luxembourg	43.64
17. Underwriters Bank	Continental Illinois Bank, USA	60
18. Nanyang Commercial Bank Ltd	Bank of China, PRC	unknown
19. Po Sang Bank Ltd	Bank of China, PRC	unknown
20. Chiyu Banking Corporation	Bank of China, PRC	unknown
21. Hua Chiao Commercial Bank Ltd	Bank of China, PRC	unknown
22. Hong Kong Industrial and Commercial Bank Ltd	Overseas Trust Bank, Hong Kong	94.34

Source: Y.C. Jao, *Banking and Currency in Hong Kong* and current press announcements.

*Divested in late 1977

TABLE 5

Gross Domestic Product by Industrial Origin 1970-76
(at current prices, million HK dollars)

ISIC Major Division	1970 Amount	1970 %	1976 Amount	1976 %
1. Agriculture and fishing	377	2.2	645	1.6
2. Mining and quarrying	27	0.2	28	0.1
3. Manufacturing	5,448	31.1	11,165	27.4
4. Electricity, gas and water	334	1.9	716	1.8
5. Construction	572	3.3	1,683	4.1
6. Wholesale and retail trade and restaurants and hotels	3,809	21.8	9,674	23.8
7. Transport, storage and communication	1,299	7.4	2,475	6.1
8. Financing, insurance, real estate and business services	2,561	14.6	7,668	18.8
9. Community, social and personal services	2,959	16.9	6,496	15.9
10. Activities not adequately defined	110	0.6	163	0.4
All industries (GDP at factor cost)	17,496	100.0	40,713	100.0

Source: Census and Statistics Department, *Estimates of Gross Domestic Product* (Hong Kong, 1979).

TABLE 6

Employment in the Financial Sector

	November 1975	November 1976	May 1979
Monetary Institutions	26,522	28,582	35,549
Other Financial Institutions	8,384	8,838	14,357
Financial Services	585	579	654
Insurance	3,940	4,131	6,035
Total	39,431	42,130	56,595
As percentage of labour force	2.19	2.30	2.70

Source: *Hong Kong Monthly Digest of Statistics*.

labour force, the share of financial sector rose steadily from 2.19 to 2.70 per cent.

The growth process of financial institutions and markets is also reflected in 'financial deepening', a notion pioneered by Shaw and McKinnon to emphasize the interactions between financial and real variables in economic development.[19] Although the concept is not directly related to the emergence of financial centres as such, it is clearly relevant to our understanding of Hong Kong's dynamic growth, particularly during the past decade. A wide range of indicators can be used to evaluate financial deepening, depending on data availability. Unfortunately, financial data, particularly with respect to wealth and non-bank assets, are generally incomplete, and Hong Kong is no exception. Table 7 therefore lists some leading indicators constructed on the basis of available and reasonably reliable raw data suitably adjusted for our purpose.

One widely accepted measure of financial deepening is the accumulation and diversification of financial assets over time adjusted for population and price changes. In Hong Kong, data on financial assets or wealth other than monetary assets are virtually non-existent, and for this reason, only real balances of the two versions of money are given. These holdings of monetary assets have been adjusted by the consumer price index and GDP deflator, since the two measures of inflation may differ considerably. Furthermore, the initial and terminal dates may differ from one indicator to another, depending on whether the data in question are available. Another important indicator of financial deepening is the ratio of financial stocks to national income. However, again due to the same reason, we have to use the ratios of the two versions of money to gross domestic product as proxies, in rows 5 and 6 of the table. Financial deepening may also be gauged by banking density, since both the absolute level of savings and the propensity to save may be relatively elastic to the existence and development of financial institutions. Two definitions of density are given in rows 7 and 8. Finally, financial deepening may be captured by structural shifts in the economy in favour of the financial sector. Rows 9 and 10 present two such indicators, the relative shares of financial sector in GDP and labour force.

It is abundantly clear from Table 7 that all the ten indicators have shown a positive growth trend, the annual rate of growth ranging from 1.4 to 9.7 per cent, with a mean of 6.3 per cent, during different periods for which data are available. Apart from the impressive rates of growth, however, certain indicators are remarkable in terms of their absolute magnitude. Thus, the ratio of M_2 to GDP not only is extremely high for a developing country, but also compares favourably with those of advanced industrialized countries.[20]

Finally, Hong Kong's status as a regional financial centre has been further strengthened recently by the complementary development of gold and commodity markets. Since the ban on the import and export of gold was lifted in 1974, Hong Kong's gold market has developed into one of the four largest in the world besides London, New York and Zurich.[21] In May 1977 a Commodity Exchange was established to provide future trading facilities initially for cotton and sugar, but eventually for metals and other commodities as well. Trading in silver, suspended in 1935 when Hong

TABLE 7

Indicators of Financial Deepening

	Initial Date	Terminal Date	Annual Growth
1. Per capita real balances of M_1, adjusted for consumer price changes	HK$1,162 (end of 1971)	HK$1,985 (end of 1978)	8.0%
2. Per capita real balances of M_1, adjusted by GDP deflator	HK$1,235 (end of 1971)	HK$2,207 (end of 1978)	8.6%
3. Per capita real balances of M_2, adjusted for consumer price changes	HK$701 (end of 1954)	HK$6,374 (end of 1978)	9.7%
4. Per capita real balances of M_2, adjusted by GDP deflator	HK$2,764 (end of 1966)	HK$7,272 (end of 1978)	8.1%
5. Ratio of M_1 to GDP	31.8% (end of 1971	35.0% (end of 1978)	1.4%
6. Ratio of M_2 to GDP	47.3% (end of 1954)	115.3% (end of 1978)	3.8%
7. Banking density, narrowly defined	0.42 (end of 1954)	2.02 (end of 1979)	6.5%
8. Banking density, broadly defined	2.32 (end of 1976)	2.78 (end of 1979)	6.2%
9. Relative share of financial sector in GDP	6.1% (end of March 1961)	12% (end of 1976)	4.4%
10. Relative share of financial sector in total labour force	2.19% (Nov. 1975)	2.7% (May 1979)	6.2%

Notes: M_1 = the sum of currency in the hands of non-bank public and demand deposits

M_2 = the sum of M_1 and savings and time deposits

GDP = gross domestic product at factor cost

Banking density narrowly defined = Number of offices of licensed banks per 10,000 population

Banking density broadly defined = The sum of offices of licensed banks, representative offices, and registered deposit-taking companies per 10,000 population

Financial sector = monetary institutions, other financial institutions, financial services and insurance companies

Source: Census and Statistics Department, for various issues of *Hong Kong Monthly Digest of Statistics, Economic Background*, and *Estimates of Gross Domestic Product; Hong Kong Government Gazette; Hong Kong Statistics, 1947-1967*.

Kong followed China in abandoning the silver standard, was reactivated in 1978.

* * * *

The factual and statistical evidence cited in the previous section should leave one in no doubt that Hong Kong is now firmly established as a financial centre in the Asian-Pacific region. What needs to be explained are the reasons for Hong Kong's rise as a money metropolis during the seventies.

Economists and economic historians have long been aware of the vital role of banking and finance in economic development.[22] Their attention, however, has been focused primarily on the facilitating or retarding effects of the financial sector on economic growth, given its widely varying institutional features in different countries. Only very recently have economists begun to show interest in the history and theory of the formation of financial centres.[23] It is beyond the scope of this paper to review this burgeoning literature or to discuss the issue in any depth. For our purpose a highly simplified conceptual framework would suffice.

This framework concerns itself largely with the demand-supply relationships governing financial services and urban facilities. Since a financial centre is by definition a place where international or multinational banks and other non-bank intermediaries assemble, a convenient starting point is the demand-supply perspectives from the point of view of such intermediaries, typically a bank of fairly large size.

The pertinent question to ask is: what comparative advantage an international or multinational bank enjoys that is denied to its domestic counterparts in the financial centres, since the latter are presumably more familiar with local laws and customs and have better ties with domestic governments and clients? The very formulation of this question precludes those banks that are relatively small. Only when a bank has grown to a certain size can it begin to exploit the familiar economies of scale in expanding a network of branches, offices and subsidiaries abroad. In other words, its superior capital resources, knowledge and technology enable it to offer a wide range of financial services at lower marginal costs, particularly in specialized areas such as loan syndication, foreign exchange and corporate financial advice.

This ability to expand abroad must be coupled with the urge to do so. The inner dynamics of international banking ensure that this will be the case. Multinational banking is the financial analogue of direct foreign investment by multinational corporations, which during the post-war era has grown at a rapid pace. The large, and often oligopolistic banks have no choice but to follow their multinational clients abroad to service their needs, if only as a defensive measure. For quite obvious reasons, the US banks took the lead in expansion abroad, but they were soon followed by the European, Japanese and Canadian banks. In 1960, there were only 8 US banks operating 131 branches and agencies overseas with total assets of US$3.5 billion, but by September 1978, there were already 132 US banks operating some 796 branches and offices abroad with total assets of US$207.4 billion. The United States itself is not immune to invasion by foreign banks. As late as 1965, a congressional study shows that foreign banks altogether had only 85 agencies, branches and subsidiaries in the United States with total assets of about US$7 billion. By the end of 1978, foreign banks had some 300 branches, agencies and subsidiaries with total assets of US$116 billion.[24]

Even without this pressure to follow clients abroad, the multinational banks themselves are compelled to follow a strategy of international diversification to open up new horizons of business opportunities and sources of income and thus as least maintain their growth and market shares. It is also well known that large and highly diversified banks have much more stable earnings records. It has been estimated that the major US banks now derive 30-60 per cent of their net annual earnings from foreign sources.[25]

The spread of multinational banking has also been greatly facilitated by the emergence and rapid rise of the Xeno-currency markets, particularly the Euro-dollar market, which may be broadly defined as the markets for funds denominated in any currency other than that of the host country. This important innovation in international financial mechanism, made possible at the end of 1958 by the multilateral currency convertibility which signalled the end of the post-war dollar shortage and the beginning of dollar glut, has enabled multinational banks without a large local currency deposit base to draw huge balances originating in many parts of the world into the financing of international trade and investment. The offshore money markets have been particularly important to American banks which at one time or another have been subject to onerous domestic constraints with respect to reserve requirements, compulsory deposit insurance, interest rate ceilings and foreign lending. Because the Euro-dollar market provides depth, flexibility and freedom from government control to an extent unknown to any other form of financial market, access to it has enabled multinational banks to supply longer-term loan facilities, typically at maturities within the five-to-ten year range, in contrast to the conventional short-term lending provided by domestic commercial banks.

In short, a typical multinational bank is both able and willing to supply a menu of extraordinarily rich and varied financial services through its world-wide network of branches, offices and subsidiaries. There must be of course a corresponding demand for such services if the supplier is to stay in business. Again, the internationalization of trade and production, the rise of multinational corporations, and the increasing integration of world financial markets ensure that such a demand will be forthcoming. Large manufacturing and commercial concerns stationed abroad naturally prefer to deal with banks of their own national origins since mutual trust built over a period of years can cut information and transaction costs to a minimum. Even wealthy individuals and corporations in the host cities or countries may also prefer large and prestigious international banks for security and other reasons (such as easy transfer of funds abroad). Generally speaking, however, the demand for specialized wholesale banking services is likely to be greater than that for retail banking services, since the latter is an area where indigenous banks may enjoy greater comparative advantage, quite apart from the fact that national governments often exclude foreign banks from domestic retail banking or at least severely restrict their scope of business therein. This explains why multinational banks tend to be much more successful in such activities as underwriting, loan syndication, consortium banking, corporate advice, project finance, and foreign exchange and money market operations.

The demand for and supply of financial services which can best be handled by multinational banks pave the way for the emergence of financial centres. But we still have to explain why certain cities succeed in becoming regional or international financial centres while others do not. Again the demand-supply framework is a handy device, but the focus is now on the demand for and supply of urban facilities. From the point of view of multinational banks there is obviously no point in choosing some backwood villages as the situs for their overseas activities: the focal points must not only be cities, but cities that possess certain desirable locational and physical attributes such as a central geographical position with a modern network of transportation and communications, and a time zone situation that permits maximum contacts with other centres during a working day. It also follows that cities that are already established commercial and industrial centres, or are backed up by a hinterland of national or regional economies with promising growth potential, will be in strong demand as financial centres. More important, the host government must provide a reasonably hospitable environment for multinational banks to operate. Political or legal entry barriers against foreign banks explain for example why no regional or international financial centres of any real significance exist in Communist-ruled countries. Ideally, there should be no discrimination of any kind against foreign banks, but some discrimination is acceptable as long as foreign banks are allowed at least to operate in the offshore sector without undue governmental interference, especially in the form of onerous exchange control and taxation. One can go on to list other relevant variables, suffice it to say that any well-defined demand function for urban centres must contain the major determinants already described. Clearly, cities that can supply the kind of business environment, locational and physical attributes, and other facilities that match the demand requirements stand a good chance of emerging and prospering as financial centres. It is true that the supply of certain services and amenities (such as the supply of legal and accounting expertise) may itself change in response to demand. However, there must be a minimum supply of desired attributes and services in the first place before multinational banks can be attracted *en masse*.

We have used the multinational banks as the core of our analysis, but the same analytical framework can be applied to other non-bank financial intermediaries. Moreover, it is a widely observed fact that the convergence of multinational banks is invariably followed or accompanied by a similar convergence of non-bank financial intermediaries, and complementary or supportive service personnel like lawyers, accountants, brokers and so forth. Financial transactions require many face-to-face contacts. The agglomeration of financial institutions and related entities can generate further economies of scale.

In the light of this admittedly simple framework, which nevertheless draws its inspiration from several branches of economics, including money and banking, industrial organization, and urban economics, one can readily see why Hong Kong has been emerging so swiftly during the seventies as a major money metropolis. The demand for 'total banking', a package of integrated retail service and wholesale banking, and other complementary or ancillary financial services, has been in existence for some time in Hong Kong and the Asian-Pacific region as their economies become more industrialized and affluent. These banking and financial services are more sophisticated and complex than can be handled entirely by indigenous financial institutions. Multinational banks and other financial intermediaries are well poised to fill this need. At the same time, Hong Kong possesses nearly all the ingredients of a viable financial centre which cannot fail to attract a host of international banking and non-bank financial intermediaries.

In terms of locational and physical attributes, Hong Kong's advantages are well known: the city is centrally situated in the Asian-Pacific area, supported by a network of excellent transport and telecommunication facilities. Its time-zone position and flexible working hours enable it to engage in arbitrage operations between the Atlantic and Pacific seaboard centres. Its proximity to mainland China acts as a magnet for multinational firms, both financial and non-financial, that have an eye on the vast China market.

Financially, Hong Kong is blessed with a free exchange market, and a prudent fiscal system with low tax rates and simple tax structure. One need hardly belabour the importance of free convertibility: capital funds will converge towards a centre only in the secure knowledge that in the absence of exchange control they can be quickly repatriated or transferred elsewhere.[26] Tax incentives of course constitute another important impetus to the growth of financial activities. While Hong Kong is by no means a tax haven, its tax rates, despite some upward adjustments during the post-war period, are substantially lower than those in most other countries: the standard rate on profits and income now stands at only 15 per cent, with a 2 per cent surcharge on corporation profits. Equally attractive to international financial institutions is the simplicity of the city-state's tax structure, particularly its adherence to the 'territorial source' principle under which only income arising in or derived from domestic transactions is chargeable to tax.[27]

Economically, Hong Kong has during the post-war years built up a solid reputation as a major commercial, manufacturing and shipping centre in the Far East. In the more recent period of 1961-78, for which official national income estimates are available, the economy grew at an average annual rate of 9.1 per cent in real terms. Hong Kong's per capita gross domestic product (GDP) at constant 1966 prices increased from HK$2,091 in 1961 to HK$6,309 in 1978. Expressed in terms of current prices and exchange rates, the per capita GDP increased from HK$1,910 (approximately US$335) to HK$13,826 (approximately US$2,870) during the same period.[28] This seven-fold increase in money income per head was achieved despite the fact that total population also increased from 3.2 million to 4.7 million, or by 47 per cent. A mere dot on the world map, Hong Kong nevertheless ranked nineteenth in the world's leading trading nations in terms of total external trade in 1977.[29] A city-state of nearly 5 million people with such a proven record of dynamic growth can hardly be ignored by multinational financial institutions. Moreover, Hong Kong is only part of a region with vast human and natural resources where several individual countries, such as Japan, South Korea and Taiwan, can also boast of a brilliant record of economic development.[30]

Liberal government policy towards the private sector is another strong point in respect of which Hong Kong has few rivals. The city-state has often been depicted as one of the world's last bastions of *laissez-faire*, but while this label was perhaps not inappropriate thirty years ago, it has become less and less so in recent years, in view of the government's increasing role in housing, education and social welfare.[31] What remains true however is the policy of not interfering with the market mechanism unless absolutely necessary. In the financial sphere this policy manifests itself in the absence of onerous regulations and discrimination against or undue restrictions on foreign financial institutions.[32] It also shows up in the absence of any rigid rules concerning the employment of expatriates. This is of some importance, as the formation of a financial centre, especially at its early stages, may require substantial recruitment of foreign specialists.

Except for a brief interlude in 1967, Hong Kong has been remarkably free from internal social and political unrest. Since the end of the Cultural Revolution, relations between the People's Republic of China on the one hand, and the United Kingdom and Hong Kong on the other, have steadily improved to a point where it is possible to say that they are not only correct, but even cordial. Indeed, whatever the long-term uncertainty about Hong Kong's future, the colony's current *status quo* is virtually underwritten by China.

There are other relatively minor factors, which may nevertheless influence the decisions of multinational financial institutions. One is that English, the language of world commerce and finance, is also the official language in Hong Kong. Second, the legal system of Hong Kong, which is based on English law, provides a framework for enforcing contracts and settling disputes easily intelligible to international financial institutions and other non-financial entities. Implicit in such a system is a guarantee against arbitrary expropriation of private property and foreign interests without compensation.

Finally, one should also briefly explain why the emergence of Hong Kong as a financial centre began circa 1969-70 and not earlier. The answer lies in the concurrence of a number of favourable circumstances. Multinational banks whose post-war expansion concentrated mainly in America and Europe started to turn their attention to the Asian-Pacific region.[33] The extension of the Euro-currency market to Asia also took shape at the end of the sixties. The simultaneous stock market boom in the major cities of the area provided an initial impetus, in the form of lucrative underwriting, to the proliferation of merchant banks which were often subsidiaries or joint ventures of large multinational banks. Basically however the time was ripe for the provision of more sophisticated and internationally oriented financial services to the area. China, jolted by its border clashes with the Soviet Union, was groping at about the same time towards a rapprochement with the West. This had an immediate stabilizing effect on Hong Kong and the whole area. Thus, even though the Vietnam war was still going on, it became clear to the multinational entities that the region as a whole was poised for a new era of economic development in a relatively peaceful environment. In such a setting, the choice of Hong Kong as the regional headquarters for both financial and non-financial multinational firms was hardly surprising.

* * * *

The attainment of a financial centre status may bring both benefits and costs to the host economy. Traditionally, the benefits are analyzed primarily in terms of the invisible earnings which the financial centre generates. The classic example is the City of London, whose contributions to Great Britain's balance of payments are well documented.[34] For Hong Kong, such an exercise is unfortunately impossible because of the total lack of an external sector accounting system and hence balance of payment data. However, some major benefits to the Hong Kong economy can be briefly identified.

One obvious benefit is the greater opportunity for employment provided by the financial sector. A rather short time series with complete coverage of the financial sector has already been given in Table 6. A longer time series, with less complete coverage, shows that the number of persons engaged in banks, money exchanges and insurance companies more than doubled from 18,233 in 1969 to 39,098 in 1978.[35] As is well known, such an increase in employment gives rise to multiplier effects on national income, particularly as the average wage level in the financial sector is comparatively high according to census statistics. Moreover, as Tables 5 and 6 have shown, the relative weight of the financial sector has steadily gained over the years, a trend consistent with Hong Kong's aim to achieve a more diversified and balanced economic structure. The relative productivity of Major Division 8, comprising financing, insurance, real estate and business, was also the highest in 1976, according to a recent estimate.[36] It is important, however, not to exaggerate the significance of this benefit. Being one of the most open economies of the world, Hong Kong is highly dependent on the export-oriented manufacturing industries for its survival and growth. Despite its relative decline in recent years, the manufacturing sector still accounted for about 26 per cent of total net output and 44 per cent of total labour force in 1978. In the immediate future one can see no viable substitute for the secondary industries, of which manufacturing is the most important, as the key sector and propellant of growth. The financial sector's role is to serve as their lubricant.

Another obvious benefit is the ready availability of finance at competitive terms for large-scale capital-intensive projects. A prime example is Hong Kong's multi-billion mass transit railway system, the construction of which began in 1975. Had the system been launched ten years earlier, the banking system and capital market then could hardly have coped with the financing problem. In the mid-seventies, however, this problem became a matter of routine for the galaxy of international financial institutions.[37]

A more important benefit is, in the present writer's view, the on-going financial innovations that must characterize a viable financial centre. Hong Kong is not good at original inventions, but it is highly receptive to foreign ideas and technology. In the seventies alone, new financial techniques, instruments and services that appeared in Hong Kong included loan syndication, project finance and term lending, currency swaps, leasing, factoring, corporate advice (especially on mergers and acquisitions), certificates of deposit , credit cards, offshore bond issues, auto-pay, cash dispenser, bank-administered Central Provident Fund, Hong Kong dollar-denominated travellers cheques, automatic telephone answering service for exchange rates, etc. Other major innovations in earlier periods included hire-purchase finance for residential units and consumer durables in the fifties, and export credit insurance, electronic data processing, and underwriting in the sixties. In organizational forms, the monolithic structure of commercial banking on the British model has in recent years been enriched by the emergence of merchant banks, consortium banks, and finance companies that are often joint ventures of banks, trading firms and security houses. Virtually all these innovations have been borrowed from, or directly introduced by, overseas institutions. Moreover, Hong Kong's open-door policy on expatriate employment means not only that foreign specialists are free to work in the city, but also that they can be used to train local talent or impart their skills and knowledge to their local counterparts. This is an example of international transfer of technology, even though its primary effects are on the financial sector. While exact quantitative information is hard to come by, there can be little doubt that the net result of these innovations has been to provide a wider range of better financial services at lower costs to users and borrowers, thereby raising the overall level of efficiency and welfare.

As against these benefits, multinational banks and other financial intermediaries may give rise to what the economists call 'negative externalities'. They are often accused of undermining national monetary sovereignty, complicating the task of monetary management and purdential supervision of banking and depository institutions, and contributing to the acceleration of world inflation through the multiple expansion of deposits in the Xeno-currency markets. To what extent are these alleged costs also valid for Hong Kong?

The question has to be answered in the context of a deteriorating record of monetary management since 1977. The Hong Kong dollar, which used to have a solid reputation as a hard currency, has during the past two years become one of the weaker currencies in the world, as measured by a trade-weighted exchange rate index.[38] Hong Kong's annual inflation rate has also doubled during the same period to around 12 per cent, mainly, though not exclusively, due to an accelerating and explosive growth of money supply and bank credit.[39] The fact that the period 1977-79 also saw the lifting of the bank licence moratorium and a large influx of multinational banks into Hong Kong would seem to lend credence to the charge that their presence has somehow contributed to the current difficulties. It is not easy, however, to substantiate this by statistical evidence. The Banking Commissioner's Office has steadfastly refused to grant outside investigators access to the monthly statutory returns submitted by banks and DTCs on the grounds of confidentiality. This means that the published banking statistics are aggregates only, without identifying the individual banks or types/groups of banks responsible for the changes in the consolidated balance sheet items. Furthermore, the absence of exchange control and the lack of an external accounting system also means that there are no realiable data on capital flows. Thus it is impossible to ascertain quantitatively the role of multinational banks and DTCs in domestic credit expansion or capital flows that affect the rate of monetary growth and the stability of the exchange rate.

Nevertheless, on *a priori* grounds, it is not unreasonable to infer that domestic monetary policy works much less effectively than it would in the absence of multinational banks. The reason is that these banks, with their world-wide network of branches, offices, and easy access to international money markets, are adept at 'liability management', internal 'back-to-back' arrangements, and a variety of window-dressing techniques that can circumvent the host country's controls on money and credit. As an illustration, the Hong Kong Government in its 1979-80 budget introduced for the first time certain measures to restrict the creation of bank credit. The measures were concerned with Government balances at the banking system and the appropriate definition of liquidity requirement. The relevant section of the existing Banking Ordinance (Section 18) has been revised so that the short-term balances of the Exchange Fund - now the sole repository of the Government's monetary assets - with the local banking system are deemed to be deposits from a bank and thus subject to 100 per cent liquidity requirement, as comparied to the usual 25 per cent for deposits from a non-bank customer. This differential treatment arises from a stipulation in the Banking Ordinance that inter-bank short-term liabilities must be fully deducted from inter-bank assets in order for such liquid assets to be freed for general reserve-backing purposes. The Government's aim is of course to 'freeze' its balances with the banking system - effectively the two note-issuing banks - so that they will not form the basis for multiple credit creation. What it has overlooked, however, is an important loophole. The relevant section in the Banking Ordinance applies to domestic inter-bank balances only, and not to balances with banks outside Hong Kong. Thus it is open to a foreign bank in Hong Kong, if it so wishes, to make a 'back-to-back' arrangement whereby it borrows from its head-office or affiliate outside Hong Kong in the form of sight deposit liabilities and immediately redeposits the same fund back to the overseas office. Since under the present banking law, banks need not hold liquid assets against balances due to banks abroad, while balances at call or on demand with banks outside Hong Kong count fully as 'specified liquid assets', the book entry 'assets' can be created out of thin air and made to support multiple credit creation. The assets, for example, can be used as reserve backing for borrowing Hong Kong dollars from the inter-bank market for on-lending to non-bank customers. With Hong Kong now established as a financial centre, there is a host of local branches of international banks with a small local dollar deposit base which rely heavily on the inter-bank market for funding their local lending operations, and these banks will be only too glad to exploit the existing loophole. We have commented earlier on the rapid growth of the balance sheet items 'amount due to banks abroad' and 'amount due from banks abroad', the variations of which are highly manipulable by the multinational banks. The lack of success so far of the Government's credit squeeze is therefore hardly surprising. The hasty decision to re-impose a bank licensing moratorium on 7 August 1979 for a further period of six months implicitly acknowledged the potentially disequilibrating role of the multinational banks.[40]

Multinational banks may also complicate the task of prudential supervision of banking and despository institutions, but in the case of Hong Kong the problem arises more from the proliferation of financial intermediaries in general rather than multinational entities as such. The first Banking Ordinance enacted in 1948 did little more than define 'banking business' and stipulate a licensing requirement. It was not until after bank runs occurred in 1961 that the Banking Ordinance was replaced by a new one and a Banking Commissioner's Office was formally set up in 1964 to strengthen prudential control in the form of minimum capital and liquidity requirements, monthly returns of assets and liabilities, and other stautory obligations. These came too late to prevent the outbreak of a serious crisis that shook the banking system to its foundation in 1965. Subsequently the 1964 Ordinance was extensively revised in 1967 in the light of further problems uncovered by the crisis.[41] The provisions of the Banking Ordinance, however, apply to domestic and foreign banks alike: the only concession to foreign banks is the exemption from compulsory publication of financial accounts. In the seventies, the initial attitude of the authorities towards the proliferation of merchant banks and finance companies which operated outside the purview of the Banking Ordinance was fairly relaxed: the official policy was that self-policing by an association of these institutions was preferable to any formal control. The collapse of the stock market in 1973-74, however, gave rise to widespread concern about the soundness of the smaller finance companies.[42] Experience elsewhere, such as the crisis of 'fringe banks' in Great Britain, and the runs on building societies and finance companies in Australia, fortified the concern about unregulated financial institutions. Consequently a Depost-taking Companies Ordinance was enacted in 1976, under which all depository institutions other than the licensed banks are required to register with the Commissioner of Deposit-taking Companies and have a minimum issued capital of HK$5 million. They may not use the word 'bank' in their titles, and are allowed only to take time deposits of not less than HK$50,000 from the public. This is a rather devious way of protecting the small depositor: because he is assumed to possess less cash than the stipulated amount, he can only put his money into the more stringently regulated licensed banks. However, apart from this provision, the DTCs were not subject to other detailed regulations applicable to the licensed banks. This differential treatment had understandably given rise to much criticism from the licensed banking sector. In 1978-79, concern had also been expressed about the deep involvement of some DTCs in the speculative boom of the property market, a situation reminiscent of the early sixties, when similar involvement on the part of some licensed banks triggered off a serious liquidity crisis. Towards the end of 1979, therefore, liquidity and other prudential regulations along the lines of the Banking Ordinance were extended to the DTCs. Specifically, the DTCs are now required to observe a 15 per cent liquidity ratio against their long-term deposit liabilities, and a 30 per cent ratio against their short-term ones. In general, the events of recent years have made the Government more aware of the need of protecting Hong Kong's reputation as a financial centre.[43] The city-state's image, for example, has been seriously tarnished by the stock market excesses of 1972-74, in which both domestic and multinational financial institutions took part.

The question whether multinational financial institutions are responsible for the acceleration of inflation in Hong Kong or on a world-wide basis hinges on the fundamental issue of how inflation is determined. This is not the place for reviewing the on-going controversy between the monetarist, Keynesian, Scandinavian and other interpretations of the inflationary process. For Hong Kong, it has been shown that the inflation rate, as proxied by the annual change in various consumer price indices, cannot be explained entirely by prior changes in the money stock, however defined. For a fairly long historical period, 1961-78, the 'imported' type of inflation played a significant role, though during 1977-79 the explosive growth of money supply may well have been of preponderant influence.[44] Even if one subscribes wholly to the monetarist view, the precise role of multinational banks in causing the accelerated growth of money and credit remains to be verified as explained earlier. It is also possible that domestic credit expansion attributable to the multinational banks impinges primarily on asset prices and only secondarily on consumer prices. On a world-wide basis, the controversy regarding multinational banks seems to have narrowed down to an empirical test of whether there is a multiple credit creation process in the Xeno-currency markets - the natural habitat of multinational banks and other financial intermediaries. Conflicting results have been obtained, but the majority view appears to be that, while there is a definite multiple credit creation in such markets, the numerical value of the multiplier is not very large.[45] In the words of McKinnon, 'the "uncontrolled" Eurocurrency system is not now directly an engine of inflation - of excess liquidity creation - as is often posited'.[46] The relevance of this issue is that, being a highly open economy, Hong Kong will be affected by an inflationary impulse originating anywhere in the world, whatever its causes.

The debate about multinational banks and other financial intermediaries is only part of a much wider issue concerning the pros and cons of multinational enterprises (MNEs) to the host country, particularly a less developed one. The extensive literature on MNEs used to be couched in highly emotional language, but fortunately there has been a recent trend for rhetoric to be replaced by rigorous economic analysis.[47] Confining our attention to the multinational financial institutions again, their benefits and costs to Hong Kong are difficult to quantify, given the present gaps in financial statistics and other relevant information. Furthermore, the benefit-cost calculus is not independent of the 'objective function' or 'value judgment' of the society. If, for example, higher priority is accorded to economic growth, full employment, structural diversification, and technological transfer, then there can be little doubt that the benefits of being a financial centre will far exceed their costs. If, on the other hand, greater weight is attached to price stability and monetary equilibrium, the verdict will be much less certain. The prevailing climate of opinion, however, appears to favour the former set of goals, from which it is natural to conclude that Hong Kong's development into a major financial centre is consistent with its long-term interests.[48]

Turning to Hong Kong's future prospects, our analysis has shown that it possesses all the ingredients of a viable financial centre. This is not to suggest that other cities in the region do not possess one or more of the desirable characteristics, but very few can claim that they possess *all* of them. Tokyo, for example, is the financial centre of an economic super-power, but it is somewhat out of the way, and is still hemmed in by a maze of exchange controls and restrictive barriers against foreign financial institutions. For a variety of reasons, mainly connected also with entry barriers and exchange controls, cities like Melbourne, Seoul and Taipei do not figure as regional financial centres, even though they may be national financial centres of resource-rich or fast-growing economies. Manila has allowed offshore banking units (OBUs) to operate only since 1977.[49]

The only city in the region that can compete seriously with Hong Kong as a financial centre is Singapore. The Singapore Government has always pursued a much more activist and conscious policy in promoting the city-state as a regional centre since its independence in 1965. By contrast, the Hong Kong Government has preferred to take a permissive or accommodating posture: it merely aims to provide a stable framework for the development of the city as a financial centre, but does not, however, offer specific concessions or incentives to encourage such a trend. A case in point is Singapore's readiness and Hong Kong's reluctance to abolish the withholding interest tax on offshore deposits. As a result, Singapore rather than Hong Kong succeeded in hosting the Asian-dollar market - which in essence is an extension of the Euro-currency market - in the late sixties.[50] This initial success of Singapore has not, however, prevented Hong Kong from emerging rapidly as a leading financialy centre. Indeed, there are signs that Singapore is lagging behind Hong Kong in some areas such as syndication of offshore currency loans, placement of Asian-dollar bond issues, fund management, and equity market devleopment. Thus, published data show that, of the ninety-eight major offshore loans in the region from July 1976 to June 1978, fifty-one were arranged and syndicated from Hong Kong, while only fourteen were syndicated from Singapore. It is also believed that over half of Asian-dollar bond issues, even those lead-managed out of Singapore, are placed by Hong Kong underwriters.[51] The reasons for this are not merely that there are more multinational banks and financial intermediaries in Hong Kong, but also that Hong Kong's business environment is generally considered to be more congenial.

Conscious of this deteriorating position, the Singapore Government has introduced a series of financial measures some of which were clearly designed to regain the city-republic's lost ground against Hong Kong. In the 1978-79 budget, a package of tax-cuts, including further liberalization of the tax on Asian-dollar operations, was unveiled.[52] Subsequently, the Singapore Government also announced the abolition of all exchange controls with effect from 1 June 1978. A wide-ranging study has also been conducted with a view to internationalizing its capital market.[53] Paradoxically, while the Singapore Government has been trying to use tax incentives to attract more offshore banking business, the Hong Kong Government has sought to plug some tax loopholes in the same area. In his budget speech on 1 March 1978, the Financial Secretary of Hong Kong, C.P. Haddon-Cave, announced that he had accepted a tax reform committee's recommendation to bring within the ambit of the profits tax earnings from offshore banking business obtained 'without the substantial intervention of a branch elsewhere'.[54] This proposal aroused strong opposition from the banking sector in Hong Kong but was greeted with undisguised glee by Singapore. However, the expected exodus of international banks from Hong Kong to Singapore did not materialize, and although offshore loans declined for a while immediately after the announcement of the new tax, they resumed their uptrend again in 1979. Multinational banks have soon discovered that Singapore's nominal 10 per cent tax on offshore banking profit is in reality not appreciably lower than Hong Kong's 17 per cent counterpart, whereas Singapore's standard corporation tax at 40 per cent is more than double Hong Kong's. Singapore is, however, well ahead of Hong Kong in establishing primary and secondary markets in fixed and floating rate US dollar certificates of deposit.

One advantage of Hong Kong which Singapore is unable to match is of course Hong Kong's proximity to China and its intermediary role in financing China's modernization programme. In line with the pragmatic reorientation of China's economic policy, there has also been a dramatic change in China's attitude towards foreign credit and investment. Whereas as late as mid-1978 China was prepared to accept only deferred payment schemes, supplier's credit and reciprocal deposits with international banks, its position has now become so flexible that it is willing to consider all forms of foreign credit, including government-to-government loans, on their respective merits. It is true that Beijing can always negotiate direct with the head-offices of international banks outside China, but the facilities offered by Hong Kong, where fact-to-face contacts between PRC banks and international banks can be arranged on a daily routine basis, are simply too convenient to be ignored. This is particularly so since it will be some time before China allows foreign banks to open full branches or offices inside its territory. As an example, on 10 May 1979 the Hong Kong branch of the Bank of China (BOC) - whose status has recently been upgraded under a reorganization whereby it will henceforth report direct to the State Council rather than the People's Bank of China - participated in a consortium of major world banks in a US$42 million syndicated loan to Gloxin, a subsidiary of a leading Hong Kong finance company, the Sun Hung Kai Securities Ltd.[56] The deal was intriguing in at least two respects: it marked the debut of a PRC bank as a lender in the international money market, and second, the fact that the loan was intended for a Hong Kong company can be taken as a sign of Beijing's continued interest in the city's growth and prosperity. Other publicized loan agreements, in which the Bank of China has appeared as the borrower, have been ostensibly arranged elsewhere but it is almost certain that Hong Kong has played, and will continue to play, an important intermediary role. Thus, the latest statistical returns show that, as of 31 December 1979, licensed banks and DTCs in Hong Kong had liabilities to, and claims on, banks in China totalling HK$205 million and HK$5,837 million respectively.[56]

Hong Kong's importance to China can also be gauged by China's substantial stake in the city's financial sector. There are thirteen PRC banks with a network of 151 branches in Hong Kong. Apart from the traditional activities such as financing China's foreign trade, handling remittances and foreign exchange, and negotiating financial deals on behalf of China, these banks during the past two years have also been aggressively expanding their banking business in Hong Kong itself. Their stepped-up activities have included competitive bidding for deposits denominated in both *renminbi* and Hong Kong dollars, increased lending to industry, property, the stock market and other such activities. To achieve these ends, the PRC banks have also recently installed a centralized computer system, acquired more premises, and set up deposit-taking subsidiaries. The dynamism of the Hong Kong economy has clearly convinced Beijing of the need to maintain a strong presence in the tiny British colony. Thus, even if Beijing eventually does allow foreign banks to open branches inside China, Hong Kong's stature as a financial centre will not necessarily diminish. As long as Hong Kong continues to be the focal point for servicing the financial needs of the vast Chinese hinterland, its position as the region's leading financial centre will be extremely difficult to dislodge indeed.

It would be wrong, however, to exaggerate the rivalry, real or imagined, between Hong Kong and Singapore. The consensus of most bankers is that Hong Kong, because of its more central geographical position, being closer to China, Japan, South Korea and Taiwan, and greater representation of multinational banks, is emerging as a more important loan syndication centre, and to a lesser extent, an underwriting and fund management base. Singapore, on the other hand, has remained principally an interbank funding centre. In many respects the two centres are complementary to each other. Syndicated loans packaged in Hong Kong are often funded, for example, from Singapore. Thus at the end of 1979, banks and DTCs in Hong Kong had net liabilities to banks in Singapore totalling HK$16,502 million.[57] Both cities serve, however, as offshore booking centres, deposit centres, currency centres, and arranging centres in varying degrees. Provided that the whole Asian-Pacific region can maintain its growth momentum, and that Tokyo does not go out of its way to compete on the financial front, there is no reason why both city-states cannot prosper together as financial centres.[58]

Despite its undoubted growth in the seventies, the financial sector of Hong Kong is still characterized by many lacunae and deficiencies. Thus, although the appearance of merchant banks and finance companies has enriched the financial structure, there is still a lack of specialist institutions like a development bank or an industrial bank that concentrate on the long-term financing of infrastructural and industrial development, and financial intermediaries that cater to the special needs of small business. The certificates of deposit market is in its early stage of development, and its long-term viability is still hindered by the lack of a strong secondary market. The equity market has not yet outlived its dubious fame as a casino, and the fact that there is no full disclosure requirement for listed companies, no effective check against insider trading, and no uniform set of rules for the four stock exchanges does not exactly inspire confidence on the part of the genuine investor.[59] In the insurance sector, prudential supervision is still too lax and regulatory legislation woefully out of date. More important, the absence of a formal lender of resort and built-in stabilizer like a deposit-insurance scheme implies that any chain reaction from the failure of even a small number of banking and depository institutions could be highly damaging to the whole financial structure and economy. Thus, even though prospects over the near to intermediate term remain bright for Hong Kong, its reputation as a financial centre depends to a large extent on how effectively the existing lacunae and deficiencies can be remedied.

The longer term outlook is necessarily more cloudy due to the uncertainty over Hong Kong's status: more specifically, the uncertainty over the lease of the New Territories which is due to expire in 1997. The conventional wisdom about Hong Kong is that long before the due date, capital funds will leave Hong Kong, financial markets will collapse and foreign banks will close their offices, if no explicit agreement on the lease that will allow Hong Kong to carry on under British administration is reached. How likely is this scenario?

In a way the very formulation of the question reflects a culture-bound attitude. Western bankers and investors, brought up in the tradition of contractual rights, are naturally worried about the possible non-renewal of the lease which could imply the cessation of British rule. The Chinese, however, do not look at the matter in this way. To them neither the 1842 Treaty of Nanking nor the 1898 Convention of Peking has any legal validity since they are both 'unequal treaties'. It follows that the lease and its expiry date also have no real meaning. The People's Republic has always held that Hong Kong is a part of China, but pending a final settlement in the unspecified future, the present *status quo* should be maintained. The pragmatic leadership in Beijing, however, realizes that some form of an assurance will have to be given if the *status quo* is to be viable and mutually beneficial. Since the downfall of the 'gang of four', there have been indeed a series of statements and concrete deeds designed to bolster confidence in Hong Kong. These range from Vice-Premier Deng Xiaoping's message to investors in Hong Kong that they should 'put their hearts at ease', to increased investment activities on the part of Beijing-controlled or affiliated banks and trading bodies in the city.[61] Short of an explicit undertaking to renew the lease, these gestures probably represent as far as China can go in hinting that Hong Kong's present institutional framework might survive 1997.

This willingness to leave Hong Kong alone has often been explained in terms of economic advantages which China derives from the city. In 1978 China's net visible trade surplus against Hong Kong alone amounted to some US$2.18 billion. There is no reliable estimate of invisible earnings such as remittances, tourism, banking services, and investment profits, but an educated guess is that China probably obtained foreign exchange worth US$3.7 billion from Hong Kong in 1978. Apart from this, Hong Kong also serves as a trans-shipment centre for Chinese exports, a laboratory for testing consumer products, and an outpost for acquiring market information and foreign technology. Hong Kong's entrepreneurs have also been very actively investing in China in the form of 'compensation trade' or joint ventures. In the course of China's modernization programme, which may take decades to achieve, Hong Kong can be expected to play a vital facilitating and intermediating role.

But these economic benefits, well-known as they are, do not exhaust Hong Kong's usefulness to China. A less appreciated aspect is its strategic importance to China should hostilities break out between China and the Soviet Union. Given the obsession of the Chinese leaders with the Soviet threat - and the Sino-Vietnamese border war in early 1979 and the Soviet occupation of Afghanistan in late 1979 have only served to strengthen their conviction that the Soviets are engaged in a grand design of encircling and ultimately subjugating China - it is essential that the free port of Hong Kong be kept open and administered by a friendly power so as to ensure China's access to the outside world.

In the end, therefore, what determines Hong Kong's future is not a piece of paper on which China signed under duress in the nineteenth century, but China's evolving Realpolitik in which many wider and more urgent issues are involved.

NOTES

[1]My own work on money and banking in Hong Kong was written in the early seventies and was not able to cover the rapid developments since 1974. See Y.C. Jao, *Banking and Currency in Hong: A Study of Postwar Financial Development* (London, 1974). For earlier studies before Hong Kong evolved into a major financial centre, see F.H.H. King, *Money in British East Asia* (London, 1957); Y.M. Lin, *Hsiang-kang Yin-hang Wen-ti* (Hong Kong, 1962); C.H. Yao, *Hsiang-kang Chin-yung* (1962); D. Stammer, 'Money and Finance in Hong Kong' (Ph.D. diss., Australian National University, 1968); T.B. Lin, *Das monetäre System und das monetäre Verhalten in Hong Kong* (Freiburg, 1970); K. Chang, *Hsiang-kang T'sai-cheng* (Taipei, 1970); T.B. Lin, *Monetary Behavior under the Sterling Exchange Standard: Hong Kong as a Case Study* (Hong Kong, 1971).

[2]For a discussion of the functional roles of a financial centre, see G. Dufey and I.H. Giddy, *The International Money Market* (New Jersey, 1978), Appendix 2.

[3]The only exception was the issue of a licence to Barclays Bank International in 1972.

[4]The criteria are firstly, that the applicant banks are incorporated in countries whose monetary authorities exercise effective supervision and have, where necessary, approved the establishment of a branch in Hong Kong; secondly, that the applicant banks have total assets, net of contra items, exceeding US$3 billion; and thirdly, that some form of reciprocity is available in the applicant's country of incorporation to Hong Kong banks. Financial Secretary's statement to the Legislative Council, *Official Report of the Proceedings of Hong Kong Legislative Council*, 15 March 1978, pp.621-25.

[5]Under the Deposit-taking Companies Ordinance of 1976, any financial institution other than licensed banks that takes deposits from the public must register with the authorities, but is not allowed to use the word 'bank' in its title. The term 'deposit-taking companies', therefore, covers a wide range of financial intermediaries, principally merchant banks and finance companies. However, these intermediaries appeared on the scene well before 1976, and during the stock market boom of 1972-73 as many as two thousand were said to be in operation. The simple requirement of registration in the 1976 ordinance has apparently weeded out a large number of fly-by-night operators.

[6]These 100 banks are taken from the list of the top 300 commercial banks of the world published in *The Banker* (June 1979), pp.87-149.

[7]The actual figure quoted was 212 banks from which one must deduct 34 locally incorporated licensed banks. Speech by the Banking Commissioner, Anthony Ockenden, as reported in *South China Morning Post*, 9 February 1978.

[8]In this connection, it is interesting to note that the structure of total bank deposits has changed considerably over the years. In 1954, the first year for which banking statistics are available, demand deposits accounted for no less than 82 per cent of total deposits, while savings and time deposits accounted for the remaining 18 per cent. By 31 December 1979, the relative proportions had changed to 23.3 per cent and 76.7 per cent respectively. Since demand deposits are a more volatile, while savings and time deposits are a more stable form of bank deposits, this structural shift may reflect, among other things, the growing confidence of both residents and non-residents in Hong Kong, not just as a temporary abode, but as a semi-permanent or even permanent haven for their monetary assets.

[9]'Liability management' denotes the technique whereby a bank actively tries to influence the size and composition of its liabilities through selling debt instruments, borrowing from international money markets, and other forms of incurring debt, in order to accommodate credit demands. The concept began with the innovation of negotiable certificates of deposit (NCDs) and the phenomenal growth of the Euro-dollar market. For a lucid discussion, see S.A. Schweitzer, 'Bank Liability Management: For Better or Worse', *Federal Reserve Bank of Philadelphia Business Review* (December 1974), pp.3-12.

[10]Before 1976, balances due to and due from banks in Hong Kong were separately entered on both sides of the consolidated balance sheet of the banking system. But this practice has been discontinued since 1976. In 1978, the fiduciary issue amounted to HK$95 million only, or 0.7 per cent of 'other liabilities'.

[11]'External Liabilities and Claims of Financial Institutions in Hong Kong', for the quarter ended 31 December 1979, Banking Commissioner's Office.

[12]For a description of the mechanics, see H.P. Schobert, 'How Hong Kong's Money Market Works', *Asian Money Manager*, no.12 (August 1977), pp.12-16.

[13]Technically, all banks accepting foreign currency deposits do so as agents for foreign banks outside Hong Kong. PRC banks in Hong Kong offering *renminbi* deposits, for example, act as agents of the head office of the Bank of China in Beijing. Under Hong Kong's tax law, interest on such deposits is tax-exempt.

[14]These were Hong Kong Land International HK$300 million 7¼ per cent bonds due 1985, Jardine Matheson International HK$200 million 7¼ per cent bonds due 1985, and Province of Manitoba HK$150 million 6.875 per cent notes due 1982.

[15]Y.C. Jao, op.cit., p.69.

[16]Colin Martin, 'Deposit-taking Companies Find Their Place in Hong Kong's Financial System', *South China Morning Post Finance and Investment Review* (July 1977), pp.10-15.

[17]The two exceptions among the acquiring banks are The Hongkong and Shanghai Banking Corporation, and The Overseas Trust Bank, both incorporated in Hong Kong. However, because the former is predominantly owned and managed by British nationals, it is generally regarded as a foreign bank, and is classified as such in the licensed banks' interest rate cartel arrangement.

[18]However, Hong Kong's growth process did not conform entirely to the stylized sequence of economic development in that it never has had any primary sector of any real significance. Prior to the industrialization in the fifties, the entrepot economy was highly geared to the provision of mercantile services, so that there was a period when manufacturing industries gained in relative terms at the expense of tertiary rather than primary industries. For an earlier official estimate of national income for fiscal years 1960-61 and 1961-62 based on tax returns, see *Report on the National Income Survey of Hong Kong* (Hong Kong, 1969).

[19]E.S. Shaw, *Financial Deepending in Economic Development* (New York, 1973); R.I. McKinnon, *Money and Capital in Economic Development* (Washington, 1973).

[20]In 1977, Hong Kong's ratio of M_2 to GDP was 107.4 per cent. This compares with 44.9 per cent for the United States, 33.8 per cent for the United Kingdom, 84 per cent for Japan, 65 per cent for Germany, and 53.4 per cent for France. (For United Kingdom, the numerator used is M_3.)

[21]See *Asian Finance*, 15 June 1977, pp.24-25; S. Au, 'How to Make Money by Trading Gold', *Asian Money Manager* (June 1979), pp.11-13.

[22]The outstanding examples are J.A. Schumpeter, *Theorie der wirtschaftlichen Entwicklung* (Berlin, 1911); A. Gerschenkron, *Economic Backwardness in Historical Perspective* (Cambridge, Mass., 1962); R. Cameron (ed.),

Banking in the Early States of Industrialization (New York, 1967), and *Banking and Economic Development* (New York, 1972); R.W. Goldsmith, *Financial Structure and Development* (New Haven, 1969); R.I. McKinnon, op. cit; E.S. Shaw, op.cit.

[23]See F.H. Klopstock, 'A New Stage in the Evolution of International Banking', *Revue Internationale d'Histoire de la Banque*, 6 (1972), 1-22; H.G. Johnson, 'Panama as a Regional Financial Center: A Preliminary Analysis of Development Contribution', *Economic Development and Cultural Change* (January 1976), pp.261-86; C.P. Kindleberger, *The Formation of Financial Centers: A Study in Comparative Economic History* (Princeton, 1974); R.Z. Aliber, 'Toward a Theory of International Banking', *Federal Reserve Bank of San Francisco Economic Review* (Spring 1976), pp.5-8; H.G. Grubel, 'A Theory of Multinational Banking', *Banca Nazionale del Lavoro Quarterly Review* (December 1977), pp.349-64.

[24]See R. Johnston, 'International Banking, Risk, and U.S. Regulatory Policies', *Federal Reserve Bank of San Francisco Economic Review* (Fall, 1977), pp.36-38; K.J. Auerback, 'International Banking: Where Do We Go From Here?', Federal Reserve Bank of Minneapolis Staff Report No.10 (1976); 'International Banking', *The Economist*, 31 March 1979, pp.11-22.

[25]See F. Edwards, 'International Banking: An Overview', *Columbia Journal of World Business* (Winter 1975), p.7; W.E. Moskowitz, 'Global Asset and Liability Management at Commercial Banks', *Federal Reserve Bank of New York Quarterly Review* (Spring 1979), pp.42-48.

[26]Formal exchange control came to an end in Hong Kong after it was excluded from the Sterling Area in July 1972 following the floating of sterling. However, even before then an uncontrolled free market in US dollar and other convertible currencies was allowed to exist side by side with a controlled market in sterling. See Y.C. Jao, op.cit., pp.88-94.

[27]The 'territorial source' principle has been recently modified, in the case of offshore banking profits that are earned without the substantial intervention of a branch elsewhere. For an explanation, see Y.C. Jao, 'Tax Reform and Fiscal Policy in Hong Kong', *Bulletin for International Fiscal Documentation* (April 1977), pp.175-84, and 'Hong Kong's New Tax on Offshore Banking Profits', *Bulletin for International Fiscal Documentation* (January 1979), pp.15-18. For a comprehensive study of Hong Kong's fiscal system, see H.C.Y. Ho, *The Fiscal System of Hong Kong* (London, 1979).

[28]Census and Statistics Department, *Estimates of Gross Domestic Product 1961-74* (Hong Kong, 1976) and *Estimates of Gross Domestic Product 1966 to 1977* (Hong Kong, 1979); Hong Kong Government, *The 1979-80 Budget: Economic Background* (Hong Kong, 1979).

[29]The ranking is based on underlying data from International Monetary Fund, *International Financial Statistics*, December 1978. China and the Soviet-bloc countries are excluded.

[30] For a recent study of rapid growth in the these countries, see E.K.Y. Chen, *Hyper-Growth in Asian Economies: A Comparative Study of Hong Kong, Japan, Korea, Singapore and Taiwan* (London, 1979).

[31] For example, since 1955 the Hong Kong Government has been involved directly in a huge public housing programme for low-income groups. The low-cost housing estates now accommodate 1.9 million people, or 41 per cent of total population. The expansion of the programme is an on-going one, and it is estimated that by the mid-eighties, more than 3 million people, or some 55 per cent of the projected population, will have been accommodated in subsidized public housing estates.

[32] It is true that during 1966-78 there was a moratorium on bank licences, but this applied to both domestic and foreign banks. The relexation of moratorium in March 1978 was offered to foreign banks only, though new licences could only operate one office each. However, existing licensed banks, whether domestic or foreign, are treated on the same footing. Indeed, there is a concession to foreign banks in that they are not required to publish their financial statements.

[33] See M. Eng, *U.S. Overseas Banking: Its Past, Present and Future* (New York, 1970); F.A. Lees, *International Banking and Finance* (New York, 1974); and F.H. Klopstock, loc.cit.

[34] See, for example, B.J. Cohen, *The Reform of Sterling* (Princeton, 1969), and *The Future of Sterling as an International Currency* (London, 1971). For two recent surveys, see the symposia on the City of London in *The Banker* (February 1978), pp.61-98 and *Euromoney* (January 1978), pp.69-87.

[35] I am indebted to the Labour Department and the Census and Statistics Department for this unpublished information.

[36] See Report of the Advisory Committee on Diversification 1979, Annex 7. Relative productivity is defined as the ratio of the output share for an industry to its corresponding employment share.

[37] For more details, see J. Trueman, 'Financing Hong Kong's Mass Transit System', *The Banker* (September 1977), pp.51-54.

[38] A trade-weighted exchange rate index for the Hong Kong dollar, based on its exchange rates against fifteen other major currencies, has been compiled and released daily. The base is the date of the Smithsonian Agreement (18 December 1971 = 100). After reaching its peak of 115.5 in mid-March 1977, the index then showed a consistent downtrend until 26 July 1979, when it dropped to a low of 87.2. Since then the index has recovered somewhat, and at the end of January 1980 stood at 95.0.

[39] The annual growth rates of M_1 and M_2 rose from 7.1 per cent and 20 per cent respectively in the first quarter of 1977 to 24.6 per cent and 29.8 per cent respectively at the end of 1979. The growth rate of domestic loans increased from 18.1 per cent to 39.5 per cent during the same period.

[40]In a circular letter to all licensed banks dated 5 July 1979, the Secretary for Monetary Affairs, D.W.A. Blye, pointed out that 'certain groups of banks appear to have paid less heed to the Government's wish to restrain banking lending in Hong Kong than other groups'. In November the Deputy Secretary for Monetary Affairs, Peter Allsopp, publicly accused the US banks for lending at a much higher rate than other banks.

[41]Y.C. Jao, op.cit., Appendix B.

[42]The Hang Seng Index of stock prices (31 July 1964 = 100) reached its peak of 1,774.96 on 9 March 1973 after a year of frantic speculation. Then it began to fall sharply, hastened subsequently by rising interest rates, the oil crisis and the world-wide recession. By 12 December 1974, the index had fallen to 150.11. Over a period of only twenty-one months, the market had decined by 91.5 per cent. The fall was much sharper and speedier than the Wall Street crash of 1929-32.

[43]See C.P. Haddon-Cave, 'Government and the Financial Services Sector', paper read to the Hong Kong Society of Accountants on 4 November 1977.

[44]A more detailed analysis is contained in Y.C. Jao, 'Financial Structure and Monetary Policy in Hong Kong', unpublished working paper, 1979.

[45]See, *inter alia*, Karl Keinath, *Geldschöpfung auf dem Euro-dollar Markt* (Tübingen, 1973); F.H. Klopstock, *The Euro-dollar Market: Some Unresolved Issues* (Princeton, 1968); B.E. Lee, 'The Euro-dollar Multiplier', *Journal of Finance* (September 1973), pp.867-74; J. Hewson and E. Sakakibara, 'The Euro-dollar Deposit Multiplier: A Portfolio Approach', *IMF Staff Papers* (July 1975), pp.307-28; and D.T. Llewellyn, 'The Eurocurrency Markets and World Credit', *The Banker* (January 1979), pp.61-69.

[46]R.I. McKinnon, *The Eurocurrency Market* (Princeton, 1977), p.34.

[47]For an excellent and concise recent review of the issues, see Paul Streeton, 'Multinationals Revisited', *Finance and Development* (June 1979), pp.39-42.

[48]This seems to be the rationale behind the Report of the Advisory Committee on Diversification 1979. See especially chapter 8.

[49]See Abby Tan, 'The Philippines: New Window on the World', *The Banker* (December 1978), pp.61-65.

[50]For a discussion of the origins and operations of the Asian-dollar Market, see S.Y. Lee, 'The Asian-dollar Market in Singapore', *Malayan Economic Review* (April 1971), pp.46-56; S.A. Pandit, 'The Asian Dollar and Free Gold Markets in Singapore', *Finance and Development* (June 1971), pp.32-36; R.F. Emery, 'The Asian Dollar Market', Federal Reserve Board discussion paper (November 1975).

[51]*Euromoney* (July 1977), pp.88-97; (July 1978), pp.44-45.

[52]'Focus on Achievement and Growth', Budget Speech by Hon Sui Sen, Minister for Finance, Singapore, 27 February 1978 (Singapore, 1978), pp.12-16.

[53]S. Awanohara, 'On the Road to Internationalization' and A. Rowley, 'Building a Financial Supermarket', *Far Eastern Economic Review*, 25 January 1980, pp.44-47.

[54]This has been claimed by the Government to be consistent with Hong Kong's 'territorial source' principle, which has been reaffirmed. See *The 1978-79 Budget*, 1 March 1978, pp.83-84.

[55]Melinda Liu, 'China Comes in from the Cold', *Far Eastern Economic Review*, 1 June 1979, pp.42-45. Since then the Bank of China has participated in several more syndicated loans for both local and foreign companies

[56]I am indebted to the Banking Commissioner's Office for this information.

[57]I am indebted to the Banking Commissioner's Office for this information.

[58]According to a Hong Kong delegation that visited Tokyo in 1978, the Japanese Government is reluctant to allow Tokyo to perform its natural role as the financial centre in the Far East, mainly because of its insistence on maintaining strict control over the monetary system and preventing the yen from becoming an international reserve currency. See the Report of the Advisory Committee on Diversification, 1979, para.324-25.

[59]In October 1977 the Government set up an Insider Trading Tribunal to investigate cases of insider trading. However, since the tribunal can only issue censure but not mete out punishment, its effectiveness is open to doubt. Talks about a merger of the four stock exchanges have been dragging on for years without any tangible progress. In early 1979 the Government announced that legislation would be introduced to bring about compulsory unification.

[60]Vice-Premier Deng's message was conveyed to Sir Murray MacLehose, Governor of Hong Kong, when the latter visited Beijing in March 1979. China's increased investment activities in Hong Kong have included expansion of oil depots and gas stations, establishment of a machine-tool plant and a shipyard, more aggressive lending by PRC banks, and a joint venture with Hong Kong and American interests for setting up a HK$1 billion cement plant.

[21]

Excerpt from *The Asian NIEs: Success and Challenge*, 39–82.

HONG KONG AS AN INTERNATIONAL FINANCIAL CENTRE: EVOLUTION AND PROSPECTS

Y.C. JAO

As one of the NIEs in the Asia-Pacific Region, Hong Kong is noted for two economic achievements during the post-World War II era. One is its transformation from a small, low-income entrepot into a high-income export-oriented industrial economy.[(1)] The other is its emergence as a major financial centre in the region, and perhaps also as a potential global financial centre. The first achievement has been extensively studied and documented elsewhere. The second achievement is the object of this chapter. Readers will appreciate however that these two developments, one of the real economy and another of the financial sector - are not independent of each other. Indeed, it can be argued that the two processes are mutually interactive and reinforcing. The limited scope of this discussion is dicated therefore only by considerations of space and specialization.

The Typology of Financial Centres

Some 17 years ago, Kindleberger (1974) lamented the fact that "the formation of financial centres is no longer studied in economics". He sought to remedy this by sketching, on a broad historial canvas, the development of national financial centres in Europe and North America. Since then, a burgeoning literature on financial centres in general, and individual centres, many of which are located outside Europe and North America, has appeared.[(2)] As a result, there is now much better

---

(1) Hong Kong's per capita GDP in 1990 is estimated at HK$94,138 (US$12,060). See Census and Statistics Department, Estimates of Gross Domestic Product 1966 to 1990, Hong Kong March 1991. The World Bank has therefore included Hong Kong among the "high-income economies". See the World Bank, World Development Report 1990, Table 1, p. 179.

(2) See inter alia, Aliber (1976, 1980), Bryant (1985, 1986), Choi, Tschoegl and Yu (1986), Christensen (1986), Dufey and Giddy (1978), Gerakis and Roncesvalles (1983), Gorostiaga (1984), Grubel (1977), Ho (1989, 1991), Hadjera (1978), Jao (1979, 1980, 1988), Johnson (1976), McCarthy (1979), Lee (1971, 1984), Lee and Jao (1982), Lessard and Tschoegl (1988), Park (1982), and Reed (1980).

understanding why certain cities or metropolises have become financial centres, while others have not. Certainly it can no longer be claimed that financial centres are of no interest to economists.

This is not the place for a detailed review of the literature. It would be useful and relevant, however, to discuss briefly the typology of financial centres which could provide a conceptual framework for comparative analysis.

From a teleological point of view, McCarthy (1979) makes a useful distinction between a "paper" centre and a "functional" centre. A "paper" centre acts as a location for recording financial transactions only, but otherwise little or no actual banking or financial business is carried out there. Many transnational financial institutions find it convenient, for example, to keep "shell" offices in places where taxes and prudential regulations are non-existent or minimal, in order to minimize their overall costs. Among this category are Anguilla, Bahamas, Bahrain, Cayman Islands, Jersey, Netherlands, Antilles etc. For this reason, they are also called "brass plate" centers. A "functional" centre, on the other hand, is one where financial services and transactions of all kinds, notably deposit-taking, lending, forex dealings, and buying and selling of securities, are actually provided and executed, thereby generating both income and employment for the host country.

Within the category of "functional" centre, Jao (1980, 1988) distinguishes between an "integrated centre" and a "segregated centre". By an "integrated centre" is meant one where no artificial barriers exist between the "onshore market" and the "offshore market", so that once a financial institution is established, it can engage in both onshore and offshore business, whether denominated in home or foreign currencies, without restriction. By contrast, a "segregated centre" is one where the authorities make clear distinctions between the "onshore market" and "offshore market", or between domestic currency-denominated and foreign currency-denominated business. Non-domestic institutions are mostly confined to the offshore sector: they are either barred from, or severely restricted in, the onshore sector. Some financial centres, however, combine the features of both, so that only a certain number of authorized institutions can engage fully in both onshore and offshore business.

Dufey and Giddy (1978, pp. 35-46) classify financial centres into three major types according to their services provided and stages of development. The first is the traditional centre which serves as a net creditor to the world through bank lending, and securities market activities such as flotation, underwriting, and placements.(3) The classic examples are London before the Second World War and New York after the Second World War, though in recent years Tokyo has increasingly been playing this role. The second is the financial entrepot. It is defined as a centre that offers the services of its domestic financial institutions, money markets and securities markets to both domestic and foreign residents. It is not, however, a net capital exporter. London since the end of the Second World War, and especially since the rise of the Euro-currency market in the late fifties, and New York since the late seventies, are again prime examples. The third is the offshore banking centre. It is a centre where financial intermediation is performed primarily for non-resident borrowers and depositors. Although there can occasionally be some domestic resident participation in the offshore sector, typically the domestic financial sector is insulated from the offshore sector by an array of controls or restrictions. Dufey and Giddy include Luxembourg, Singapore, Hong Kong, Bahamas, Cayman Islands, and Panama under this category.

From a geographical standpoint, financial centres can be classified according to the scope, or at least the main focus, of their activities. Proceeding from the small to the large, the first category is obviously "domestic centre" or "national centre". Once a financial centre outgrows its national boundary, it then becomes a "regional centre". Some well-defined geographical regions readily come to mind: Europe, America, Middle East, Asia-Pacific, the Caribbean etc. The apex is, of course, the "global centre", whose activities extend all over the globe. It should be noted that the concept "international financial centre" encompasses both "regional financial centre" and "global financial centre", though the geographical domain of the latter is, of course, the largest.

The purely domestic or national centre is not of interest here, for the simple reason that practically all countries, except perhaps the poorest, can boast of a city which they regard as their national financial

(3) The capital-exporting financial centre should not be confused with capital-exporting countries such as the larger oil-producing countries.

centre, no matter how primitive it may be by international standards. At the same time, there are some metropolises which serve simultaneously as domestic, regional, and global financial centres. The best current examples are London, New York and Tokyo.

Park (1982) combines the functional and geographical criteria and classifies offshore financial centres into four types: primary, booking, funding, and collection. A "primary centre" is one whose sources and uses of funds are world-wide: London and New York are his examples. A "booking centre", which corresponds to McCarthy's "paper centre", is only a location for booking Euro-currency deposits and loans. Nassau (Bahamas) and Cayman Islands are the representatives. A "funding centre" plays the role of inward financial intermediation, channelling offshore funds from abroad towards local uses. He gives (somewhat questionably in my opinion) Singapore and Panama as examples. By contrast, a "collection centre" engages in outward intermediation by channelling excess domestic funds to external users. The sole example given is Bahrain.

Finally, from a historical and neo-Marxist perspective, Gorositiaga (1984) distinguishes between the "traditional international financial centres" and the "new international financial centres". The former category denotes the established financial metropolises of advanced capitalist countries (London, New York, Frankfurt, Zurich etc.) whose currencies are also international trading or reserve currencies. The colonies and protectorates of these countries, as well as other small countries, often depend on such centres as the principal sources of external financing. The latter category includes all financial centres on the periphery of the capitalist system that have emerged since the mid-sixties. According to Gorositiaga, "these lack financial autonomy and are normally intermediate regional centres, geographical extensions of the traditional centres operating in different time zones" (p.1). Although there is some truth in this classification, as far as the historical sequence of development is concerned, the world financial scene has been changing rapidly during the past two decades, so that this bi-polar typology can no longer do full justice to the increasingly sophisticated global system. For instance, Tokyo, as generally agreed, is a newcomer as a global financial centre. Yet no one can seriously claim that Tokyo is on the "periphery of the capitalist system". Similarly, no one can seriously argue that Hong Kong and Singapore "lack financial autonomy", despite their common colonial background. Therefore, the terms "traditional centres" and newly emergent centres" are used here without any neo-Marxist connotation.

What Kind of a Financial Centre is Hong Kong?

The above typology can now be used to characterize Hong Kong as a financial centre.

First, although Hong Kong is noted for its low rate of taxation and simple tax system, it is definitely not a tax haven. Hence, it is also definitely not a "paper centre" or "booking centre". It is a genuine "functional centre" where the financial sector generates substantial income and employment.

Hong Kong is also an "integrated centre" in the sense that the onshore financial sector is not artificially insulated from the offshore sector: once a bank or financial institution is licensed or authorized to operate in Hong Kong, it can engage in both onshore and offshore business, whether denominated in local or foreign currencies. The only restriction is that foreign banks licensed after March 1978 can open only one office, i.e., effectively it can only transact wholesale banking business. This however does not pose any problem to international banks. First, foreign banks licensed before 1978 are not affected: they can engage in both retail and wholesale business. Second, international banks themselves are not keen to conduct retail banking because of the high cost involved. Even if they are interested, they can do so in a more cost-effective way by acquiring interests in locally incorporated banks. Third, since 1965, only one new licence has been granted to a locally incorporated bank, but that bank has subsequently been taken over by foreign interests.[(4)] Indeed, foreign banks are exempt from certain prudential regulations (such as publication of financial statements, and capital adequacy ratios). In short, foreign banks do not suffer any adverse "national treatment."

For this reason, the widespread practice overseas of describing Hong Kong as an "offshore centre" is incorrect, because it implies either the onshore sector is closed to foreign institutions, or that it is small and negligible. In fact neither is true. The appellation "financial entrepot"

---

(4) This was the Sun Hung Kai Bank, later renamed the International Bank of Asia Ltd. after it was taken over by the Arab Banking Corporation.

is closer to the truth, but because there is as yet no official balance of payments accounting system, it is impossible to determine precisely whether Hong Kong is a net capital exporter or not.[5] Consequently, it is also difficult to determine whether Hong Kong is strictly a financial entrepot. Since Hong Kong conducts both inward and outward financial intermediation, it seems the best label is still an "integrated centre".

It is easier to describe the geographical attributes. Although Hong Kong now transacts financial business with all the principal continents and areas in the world, the core remains the Asia-Pacific region, or the Pacific Basin. Hong Kong is not in the same league with London, New York, Tokyo in terms of the scale and scope of financial activities. At the same time, Hong Kong's financial activities are clearly not confined within its territorial limits. Therefore the most appropriate appellation is "regional financial centre". Within the Asia-Pacific region itself, Hong Kong is without doubt the financial entrepot for South China, Taiwan and Macau. Indeed, the Hong Kong dollar has served as both a medium of exchange and store of value in South China and Macau for a long time, a point to which will be returned to later.

Given that sovereignty is to revert to China in 1997, one wonders whether Hong Kong could also be regarded as a "national financial centre" of China. While Hong Kong is certainly qualified, the problem is that China forbids Hong Kong's financial institutions, except for a handful of China-owned institutions, to engage in Renminbi-denominated financial transactions. Moreover, China is keen to restore Shanghai's former status as a financial centre, at least in the domestic sense. On the other hand, it would not be misleading to treat Hong Kong as China's "offshore centre" after 1997 if the territory is indeed allowed to retain its separate currency and financial system, as promised in the Joint Declaration and the Basic Law.

Finally, from the point of view of historical evolution, Hong Kong is of course a newly-emergent financial centre. Although exact dating is difficult, it is generally agreed that Hong Kong's rise as a financial centre has occurred largely during the past two decades. While Hong

[5] However, during 1984-89, Hong Kong enjoyed a surplus on the trade account. It has been inferred therefore that during that period, Hong Kong was probably a net capital exporter. See "Capital Flows in Hong Kong", The Hongkong Economic Report, April 1990.

Kong probably started as an extension of the Euro-currency market, it soon gained momentum as a financial centre in its own right. In other words, Hong Kong is not just an appendage of either London, or New York, or Tokyo.

Evolution and Indicators

Dufey and Giddy (1978, p.35) defines a financial centre as "a metropolitan area that has a high concentration of financial institutions and where the financial transactions of a given country or region are centralized". Despite the proliferation of financial institutions, it is generally agreed that commercial banks remain their core. Seen in this light, Hong Kong's rise as a regional financial centre can be dated from the turn of the century. According to Reed (1980), during the period 1900-50, Hong Kong consistently ranked among the top 2 or 3 cities in Asia with the largest number of domestic and international banks. This early eminence was due as much to Hong Kong's role as a commercial entrepot, as well as its traditional laissez faire policy.

However, it was not until the seventies that Hong Kong began to take off as a financial centre. In the late sixties, transnational banks started to search for a major Asian city that would host the Asian Dollar Market - the logical extension of the rapidly growing Eurodollar market to a different time zone. Because Tokyo at that time was still extremely inward-looking, Hong Kong and Singapore became the natural contenders. The Hong Kong Government at that time was unwilling to waive the 15% withholding tax on interest income from foreign currency deposits, while the Singapore Government, which right from the beginning has taken a dirigiste approach to the formation of financial centre, was more than willing to oblige. The method adopted was to give favoured regulatory and tax conditions to international banks that established separate departments, known as Asian Currency Units (ACUs), to handle financial transactions for non-residents.[6] Thus the Asian Dollar Market (ADM) was born in Singapore in 1968.

Although Singapore scored an important initial success, it was not able to pre-empt the field completely. The fact was that the size of its economy was too small to absorb all the offshore deposit, mainly

[6] See Hodjera (1978), Lee (1971, 1986), and Bryant (1985, 1986).

denominated in US dollar, for domestic use. Much of them had in fact been channelled elsewhere, including Hong Kong, and on-lent to ultimate borrowers. Indeed, Hong Kong enjoyed comparative advantage in arranging syndicated loans for both corporate and sovereign borrowers in Japan, Taiwan, South Korea, and Hong Kong itself. For a time therefore Hong Kong was able to grow as a syndication centre pari passu with Singapore as a funding centre.

By the late seventies, however, Hong Kong's further progress as a financial centre had met with two major impediments. One was the withholding tax already mentioned above. The other was the moratorium on the granting of full-service licences to foreign banks which the authorities imposed after the outbreak of a serious banking crisis in 1965. It was true that during the period 1966-78, foreign banks which wished to enter the Hong Kong banking market could still do so by either establishing subsidiary deposit-taking companies (DTCs), or acquiring interests in locally-incorporated banks. Nevertheless, international banks had become increasingly frustrated by their inability to open full-service branches in Hong Kong.

Confronted by the growing pressure from international banks and competition from Singapore, the Hong Kong Government announced in March 1978 that it was ready to issue bank licences to foreign banks again, provided they met certain regulatory criteria. They were, firstly, that the applicant banks were incorporated in jurisdictions where the monetary authorities exercised effective supervision; secondly, that the applicants had total assets, net of contra items, exceeding US$3 billion (subsequently raised to US$14 billion by several steps); and thirdly, that some reciprocity was available to Hong Kong banks in the jurisdictions concerned.[7] The effect of this measure has been dramatic: before 1978, there were 40 foreign-incorporated licensed banks, but this number increased steadily over the years to 135 at the end of 1990.

Other measures of liberalization also followed. In February 1982 the interest withholding tax on foreign currency deposits was lifted, though the same tax on Hong Kong dollar deposits was only reduced

[7] The moratorium was briefly reimposed in 1979-80, to enable the authorities to review the situation.

to 10%, and was not abolished until October 1983.[8] In 1989, however, all interest tax, including that paid by non-financial institutions to depositors/lenders, was abolished; at the same time, lending and

Table 1

Number of Financial Institutions in Hong Kong

Types	End of 1969	End of 1990
I. Licensed banks	73	166
a. domestic	20	15
b. foreign	53	151
c. total no. of offices	362	1,399
II. Representative offices of foreign banks	21	155
III. Restricted licence banks	0	46
a. domestic	0	3
b. foreign	0	43
IV. Deposit-taking companies	0	219
a. domestic	0	191
b. foreign	0	28
V. Insurance companies	214	258
a. incorporated in Hong Kong	58*	121
b. incorporated overseas	156*	137
VI. Unit trusts and mutual funds	n.a.	882
a. incorporated in Hong Kong	n.a.	151
b. incorporated overseas	n.a.	731

Note: n.a. = not available
*as at March 1971

Source: Office of the Commissioner of Banking; Registrar-General's Department; and Securities and Furture Commission.

[8] This discriminatory tax treatment led to substantial portfolio shifts in 1982-3, and was one of the causes of the 1983 currency crisis. See Jao (1985).

borrowing of share scripts for settlement purposes was also exempted from stamp duty.

Since one major feature of a financial centre is the concentration of financial institutions, both domestic and foreign, Hong Kong's progress in this respect during the past two decades is shown in Table 1.

Several points about Table 1 may be noted. The first is, with the exception of insurance companies, the large increase in the number of financial institutions, especially of foreign-owned or incorporated institutions. Note that, in the case of licensed banks, restricted licence banks, and deposit-taking companies, data are available for determining whether they are domestic or foreign-owned. The dividing line is more than 50% of beneficial ownership. In the case of insurance companies, unit trusts and mutual funds, we have only information as to whether they are incorporated locally or abroad. This information may understate foreign presence, since locally incorporated institutions may be owned by overseas entities, while the reverse is generally not true, or extremely rare. The second point is that a new three-tier structure of depository institutions has come into effect from February 1990. The first tier, licensed banks, can take deposits of any amount and any type from the public. Locally incorporated licensed banks must have a minimum paid-up capital of HK$150 million. The second tier, comprising restricted licence banks, replaces the previous one of "licensed deposit-taking companies". These institutions can now call themselves "banks", but can only take time deposits of not less than HK$500,000. They also must have a minimum paid-up capital of HK$100 million. The third tier, comprising deposit-taking companies, replaces the former "registered deposit-taking companies". These companies can only take time deposits of not less than HK$100,000 with an original term to maturity of not less than three months. Their minimum paid-up capital is HK$25 million.[9] The new three-tier system is more indicative of Hong Kong's status as an international financial centre in that the former "licensed deposit-taking companies", which were in effect merchant or investment banks, can now include the word "bank" in their names, thus facilitating their participation in international transactions. In any case, the international flavour of financial institutions is quite apparent: with the exception of Soviet Union, Eastern Europe, and Africa, practically all major countries/regions are represented.

The quality of banks and depository institutions is indicated by Table 2, which shows the presence of the world's largest 500 commercial banks. Note that a bank may be present in Hong Kong in different forms: licensed bank, restricted licensed bank, registered deposit-taking company, and representative office. Thus the number of forms which a bank may assume ranges from one to four. To eliminate overlapping, we use the concept of "standardized unit" to quantify a bank's presence. This is calculated by dividing the number of forms which a bank assumes by 4. Thus, if a bank is present in Hong Kong in all four forms, its "standardized unit" of presence is 4/4, or 1. If, on the other hand, it operates here only as a licensed bank, then its "standandized unit" of presence is 1/4. On this calculation, the total number of "standardized units" is about 220, or about 220 of the largest 500 commercial banks of the world are present in Hong Kong in one form or another.

Table 2
Presence of World's Largest 500 Banks in Hong Kong, 1987-90

World Ranking[1]	Licensed overseas banks in Hong Kong	Restricted licence banks owned by overseas banks	Deposit-taking companies owned by overseas banks	Local representative offices
	87 88 89 90	87 88 89 90	87 88 89 90	87 88 89 90
1 - 20	18 19 19 18	3 3 6 9	18 18 17 14	1 0 0 0
21 - 50	25 25 26 26	5 4 2 3	21 18 16 17	3 3 0 1
51 - 100	33 31 32 32	4 4 4 4	22 21 22 20	6 9 7 7
101 - 200	15 21 24 29	1 1 1 2	16 14 19 24	29 21 24 27
201 - 500	11 12 16 20	5 5 4 6	22 21 23 24	41 49 50 48
others	18 17 17 13	2 2 3 9	34 33 31 30	63 70 79 72
	120 125 134 138	20 19 20 33	134 125 128 129	143 152 160 155

Source: Commissioner of Banking Annual Report for 1989.

Top 500 banks/banking groups in the world ranked by total assests less contra items. Figures are extracted from The Banker, July 1987, 1988, 1989 and 1990 issues.

Table 3
Simplified Consolidated Balance Sheet of Hong Kong's Depository Institutions (HK$mn.)

	End of 1969	End of 1990
Liabilities:		
Notes in circulation	2,116	40,886
Demand, savings and time deposits	12,297	1,231,271
Amount due to authorized institutions in Hong Kong	1,239	560,721
Amount due to banks abroad	1,845	3,129,323
Certificates of deposits outstanding	0	36,228
Other liabilities	2,296	235,613
Total liabilities	19,794	5,234,042
Assets:		
Cash	333	5,568
Amount due from authorized institutions in Hong Kong	1,290	550,803
Amount due from banks abroad	5,644	2,482,561
Loans and advances to customers:		
Hong Kong	7,644	828,375
Overseas	240	960,234
Certificates of deposits held	0	28,744
Portfolio investments	669	237,321
Other assests	3,895	140,526
Total assets	19,794	5,234,042

*For end of 1969, the only existing depository institutions were licensed banks; for end of 1990, they included licensed banks, restricted licence banks, and deposit-taking companies.

Source: *Hong Kong Monthly Digest of Statistics*

The congregation of a large number of financial institutions is only one of the many indicators or symbols of a major financial centre. Even more important is the scale of business or volume of transactions, particularly cross-border and cross-currency transactions. Reasonably adequate time series data exist only, however, for banks and other deposit-taking institutions (collectively labelled "authorized institutions" under the Banking Ordinance).

Table 3 presents a simplified consolidated balance sheet of the banking system, which comprises all "authorized institutions". Owing to space constraint, we select two years for comparison: end-1969 and end-1990. In so doing, we have had to omit many items or sub-headings which are not available for the initial year.

However simple the table may be, it does show the tremendous growth and transformation of the Hong Kong banking system during 1969-90. For example, the balance sheet size of the banking sector increased by 263 times to HK$5,234 billion (US$671 billion), while customers' deposits increased by 100 times to HK$1,231 billion (US$158 billion). This clearly indicates that, despite the banking crisis of 1983-86, the banking sector as a whole was still able to expand enormously. Particularly impressive are those items that reflect cross-currency transactions. Thus, the amount due to banks abroad increased by 1,695 times, the amount due from banks abroad increased by 433 times, while loans and advances abroad increased by 4,000 times. These are, of course, unmistakable signs of Hong Kong's metamorphosis into an international financial centre.

Even more meaningful indicators are given by annual (compound) growth rates of the principal banking variables. They are presented in Table 4 below.

As may be seen, both nominal and real growth rates are shown, the latter being derived by making use of the implicit GDP deflator.[10] During the same period, the annual growth rate of real GDP was 8.1%. But the real growth rates of all banking variables were much higher than that, indicating that the banking sector grew at a much more rapid

(10) The implicit GDP deflator grew at an annual rate of 9.07% during 1969-90. See Census and Statistics Department, Estimates of Gross Domestic Product 1966 to 1990, March 1991.

Table 4
Annual Growth Rates of Banking Variables, 1969-90
(percent per annum)

Variables	Nominal Growth Rate	Real Growth Rate
Balance sheet size	32.0	22.9
Customers' deposits	24.5	15.4
Amount due to banks abroad	42.5	33.4
Amount due from banks abroad	33.5	24.4
Loans and advances:		
local	25.0	15.9
abroad	48.4	39.3
Amount due to authorized institutions in Hong Kong	33.8	24.7
Amount due from authorized institutions in Hong Kong	33.4	24.3

Source: underlying data from *Hong Kong Monthly Digest of* Statist*ics*, various issues.

rate than the real sector.

Structural changes of the banking system's consolidated balance sheet may also indicate Hong Kong's rise as a financial cente. Table 5 shows that external claims of Hong Kong's depository institutions increased from 40% to 65.3% of total claims during 1969-90, while their external liabilities increased from 15.1% to 56.2% of total liabilities during the same period. However, external liabilities in that table are understated, because while there is an item called "claims on non-bank customers outside Hong Kong" in the official statistics, there is no counterpart on the liabilities side. One reason for this may be that neither the monetary authorities nor the banking system require depositors/lenders to reveal their resident status. Another important indicator is the proportion of claims and liabilities denominated in foreign currencies. Detailed breakdowns by currency denomination in the banking statistics date only from 1980, hence they are unavailable for 1969. As shown in the table, at the end of 1990, over 80% of the banking system's assests and liabilities were denominated in foreign currencies. In respect of customers' deposits, some 63.3% were denominated in foreign currencies. One cautionary note should however be sounded at this point. Both government officials and bankers often like to cite the extremely high proportion of foreign currency denomination as evidence of Hong Kong's stature as an international financial centre. Such an unqualified claim is, however misleading, since the high proportion of foreign currency denomination, especially of deposits, may be a result of portfolio shift or currency subsitution, as domestic residents continually switch from Hong Kong dollar deposits to foreign currency deposits as a hedge against future uncertainty. Unfortunately, as there is no breakdown as regards residents and non-residents in the banking and financial statistics, and also no separate ACUs as in

Table 5
Balance Sheet Structure of Hong Kong's Depository Institutions (percent of total)

Items	End of 1969	1990
External claims	40.0	65.3 (end of June)
External liabilities	15.1	56.2 (end of June)
Claims denominated in foreign currencies	n.a.	80.9 (end of December)
Liabilities denominated foreign currencies	n.a.	82.1 (end of December)

Source: underlying data in *Hong Kong Monthly Digest of Statistics*

Singapore, it is impossible to ascertain precisely to what extent the high proportion of foreign currency denomination reflects Hong Kong's ascent as an international financial centre.

Another indicator of structural change in the banking system's balance sheet is the appearance of new financial instruments. Thus, negotiable certificates of deposits (CDs) were unknown in 1969, but by the end of 1990, they appeared on both sides of the consolidated balance sheet, as depository institutions may issue their own CDs as well as purchase CDs issued by others. Other new instruments which have appeared in recent years include bank acceptances, floating rate notes, commercial papers etc. For simplication they are lumped together under "portfolio investments" in Table 3 (see before). At the end of 1990, such instruments, largely unavailable in 1969, totalled HK$116 billion. In any case, the proliferation and growth of financial innovation is another hallmark of an increasingly sophisticated financial centre.

Table 6 presents the claims and liabilities of Hong Kong's depository institutions against banks abroad, by geographical distribution. As explained earlier, there are data on claims on non-bank customers, but not liabilities to non-bank customers, outside Hong Kong. The table is confined therefore to transactions with banks abroad, in order not to over-state the external claims of Hong Kong's banking system. The data show that Asia and Pacific is the core of the banking system's

Table 6
Claims and Liabilities of Hong Kong's Depository Institution vs Banks Abroad
(June 30, 1990, HK$mn.)

Regions	Liabilities	Claims	Net Liabilities(-) or Claims(+)
Asia and Pacific	1,895,457	1,639,372	-256,085
Africa	751	1,316	+565
North America	80,472	90,813	+10,341
Latin America	69	1,911	+1,842
Caribbean	54,985	106,732	+51,747
Middle East	37,827	6,688	-31,139
Western Europe	423,542	242,289	181,253
Eastern Europe	4,283	10,107	+5,824
	2,497,386	2,099,228	-398,158

Source: underlying data in *Hong Kong Monthly Disgest of Statistics* external inter-bank transactions, accounting for 75.9% of external claims and 78.1 of liabilities. This finding is entirely consistent with our characterization, in the previous section, of Hong Kong as a regional financial centre. Other regions, in order of their importance in terms of inter-bank transactions, are Western Europe, North America, Caribbean, Middle East, Eastern Europe, Africa, and Latin America. Thus, Hong Kong conducts banking transactions with all regions of the world. With respect to individual regions, Hong Kong is a net debtor to Asia and Pacific, Middle East, and Western Europe, but a net creditor to all other regions. Overall, Hong Kong is a net debtor to the tune of HK$398 billion (US$51 billion) as at June 30, 1990. While this is not the place for a detailed discussion of individual countries, it is worthy of note that on the same date, Hong Kong had liabilities to China amounting to HK$95.3 billion, and claims amounting to HK$61.2 billion, hence net liabilities to China amounting to HK$34.1 billion (US$4.4 billion). Chinese banks, in other words, kept substantial net balances with depository institutions in Hong Kong.

Because of space considerations, we can only be very brief regarding financial markets. Hong Kong's foreign exchange market ranked sixth in the world (behind United Kingdom, United States, Japan, Switzerland, and Singapore) in terms of daily turnover, estimated US$49 billion in 1989.(11) Together with London, New York, and Zurich, Hong Kong is one of the world's four largest gold markets.(12) Hong Kong's securities market (comprising both the equity and bond segments) ranked sixth in the Asia-Pacific region (behind Japan, Australia, Singapore, Taiwan and South Korea) in terms of capitalization, and fourth (behind Japan, Australia, and Taiwan) in terms of annual trading value.(13) The inter-bank market, being closely connected with the banking system, has grown rapidly in recent years, its total size

(11)See Bank for International Settlements, *Survey of Foreign Exchange Market Activity*, Basle, Feb. 1990.

(12)The Hong Kong gold market consists of two sectors: one sector is operated by the Chinese Gold and Silver Exchange Society, and another by the loco-London market. In the former, gold traded is of 99 per cent fineness, weighed in taels (1 tael = 1.2 troy ounces), and quoted in Hong Kong dollars. Turnover totalled 59 million taels in 1988 and 51 million taels in 1989. In the latter, gold of 99.95 per cent fineness is traded, quoted in US dollars per troy ounce, and delivered in London. The main participants are banks, major international bullion houses, and gold trading companies. No statistics on trading volume are however available.

(13)See Asian Perspectives: Statistical Supplement, Sept, 1989, Vol. 6, No. 5 The data are for 1987.

having increased from HK$134 billion at the end of 1981 to HK$545 billion at the end of September 1990, of which some 52% was denominated in foreign currencies.[14] This is a wholesale market, with minimum transactions of HK$1 million, used by licensed banks, restricted licence banks, and deposit-taking companies for largely short-term lending and borrowing among themselves, from overnight up to six months for Hong Kong dollars, and up to 12 months for US dollars. Hong Kong's futures market was established in 1977, one of the earliest in the region. It initially traded in cotton, sugar, soybean, and gold, but cotton was suspended in 1981. Trading in financial futures, in the form of Hang Seng stock index futures, commenced in May 1986. Unfortunately, the futures market nearly went bankrupt during the worldwide crash of October 1987, and had to be rescued by the authorities.[15] Since then it has not yet recovered to the pre-crash level of activity.

In the last section it is argued that Hong Kong is a functional financial centre that generates income and employment for the residents. This is strongly supported by statistical evidence. As shown in Table 7, total employment in the financial sector tripled between 1975

Table 7
Employment in the Financial Sector, Selected Years

	End-1975	End-1980	End-1985	End-June 1990
Financial Institutions	35,491	65,344	78,400	107,371
Insurance	3,940	6,728	9,283	18,479
	39,431	72,072	87,683	125,850
As percentage of labour force	2.2	3.1	3.3	4.5

Source: *Hong Kong Annual Digest of Statistics*

(14) Underlying data in Hong Kong Monthly Digest of Statistics, various issues.

(15) For details, see Securities Review Committee, The Operations and Regulation of the Hong Kong Securities Industry, Hong Kong, May 1988.

— the first year for which sectoral employment satistics are available — and 1990. Expressed as a percentage of total labour force, employment in the financial sector doubled to 4.5% during the same period.

In recent years, the government has also prepared and published production-based value-added statistics of the major economic sectors, beginning from 1980. As shown in Table 8, the financial sector's share of total value-added rose from 7.5% in 1980 to 8.1% in 1982, then dropped sharply to 6.8% in 1985 before recovering somewhat, only to drop again to 7.2% in 1988. The disappointing performance of the value-added since 1983 has probably been caused by the banking crisis of 1983-86 and the securities market crisis of 1987. However, the fact that the financial sector's share in total labour force has steadily increased, while that of the total value-added has remained stagnant, suggests that labour productivity in the whole sector may have declined, possibly due to continuing brain drain and high labour turnover.

Table 8

Value Added of the Financial Sector, 1980-88, Year End

	1980	1981	1982	1983	1984	1985	1986	1987	1988
Financial institutions (HK$mn.)	8,803	11,533	12,982	13,181	14,265	14,368	18,362	23,767	26,057
Insurance (HK$mn.)	868	1,278	1,347	1,525	1,629	2,001	2,221	2,820	3,551
(HK$mn.)	9,671	12,813	14,329	14,706	15,894	16,369	20,583	26,587	29,608
As percentage of total value-added	7.5	8.1	8.1	7.6	6.9	6.8	7.3	7.6	7.2

Source: Census and Statistics Department, *Estimates of Gross Domestic Product 1966-1990*

However, the financial sector's performance in the importing and exporting of financial services has remained impressive. Table 9 shows that during 1980-89, both imports and exports showed a consistent uptrend. Moreover, Hong Kong enjoyed consistently a surplus in exports, the net exports of financial services having increased more than 14 times during that period.

One remaining question is the role of Hong Kong dollar, given Hong Kong's prominent position as a financial centre. The Hong Kong

Table 9
Hong Kong's Imports and Exports of Financial Services
(HK$mn)

	1980	1981	1982	1983	1984	1985	1986	1987	1988	1989
Imports:										
Insurance	653	598	704	823	1,147	1,293	1,328	1,580	1,606	1,807
Banking services	232	340	406	454	655	777	809	861	996	1,031
Financial assets dealing and broking	—	—	219	378	438	559	1,246	1,364	1,350	1,614
Exports:										
Insurance	594	573	612	749	893	889	778	1,172	1,032	1,080
Banking services	500	751	806	1,088	1,506	1,798	2,200	2,409	2,608	3,164
dealing and broking	—	—	450	677	909	96	1,970	2,500	2,533	3,194
Total imports and exports	1,979	2,262	3,197	4,169	5,548	6,278	8,331	9,886	10,125	11,890
Net imports (-) or exports (+)	+209	+386	+539	+859	+1,608	+1,020	+1,565	+2,276	+2,221	+2,986

Source: Census and Statistics Department, *Estimates of Gross Domestic Product 1966 to 1990*

dollar is not an international currency, of course, comparable to the US dollar, Japanese yen, or pound sterling. It is not well known outside Asia. However, it has had a long history of circulating in South China and Macau. According to King (1990), the Hongkong and Shanghai Banking Corporation estimated in the 1920s that some 70% of its Hong Kong issued notes were actually circulating across the border. When the Communists came to power in 1949, circulation of the Hong Kong dollar was prohibited, and private holdings of the currency had to be surrendered to the authorities at the official exchange rate. After China began its open policy, however, the circulation of Hong Kong has reappeared. Indeed, in the Special Economic Zones of Guangdong and Fujian, the Hong Kong dollar is both the preferred means of payment and store of value (Jao, 1986). Greenwood (1990) estimates that, at the end of 1989, about HK$6.3 billion circulated in South China and about HK$0.88 billion in Macau. Together they accounted for about 18% of total Hong Kong dollar issue. Thus, the Hong Kong dollar can be regarded as a regional currency, which is consistent with its status as a major financial centre in the Asia-Pacific region. The Hong Kong dollar's own crisis in 1982-83 has not affected its preeminence in South China and Macau for two reasons. First, the implementation of the linked exchange rate system in October 1983 has been highly effective in stabilizing the external value of the Hong Kong dollar. Second, people in South China realize that whatever the problem of the Hong Kong dollar, it is still superior to the renminbi in terms of stability and convertibility. To a lesser extent this attitude also prevails in Macau.

To sum up this section, Hong Kong is a major and newly emergent financial centre of Asia and Pacific. Unlike New York, Tokyo, and London, which have large national economies as their hinterlands, and smaller domestic centres as their satellites, Hong Kong is only a city by itself – unless China can transform itself into a prosperous market economy, a prospect most unlikely in the foreseeable future. As a financial centre, Hong Kong is strong in banking, fund management, insurance, and gold trading, but is relatively weak in securities market, especially bond market, activity. Hong Kong is also a functional centre in the sense that the financial sector generates considerable income and employment for the local population, though in the past decade, employment growth has outstripped value-added growth.

Causal Factors

These facts and statistics should leave one in no doubt that Hong Kong is now firmly established as a financial centre. What needs to be explained are the causal factors for Hong Kong's rise as a money metropolis in the Asia-Pacific region during the past two decades.

Dufey and Giddy (1978) list four necessary conditions for the development of an international entrepot centre: economic and political stability, an efficient and experienced financial community, good communications and supportive services, and an offical regulatory climate favourable to the financial industry, in the sense that it protects investors without unduly restricting financial institutions. These conditions are also applicable to functional financial centres in general. But they are not the only conditions necessary for a major international financial centre. Moreover, stated at such a general level, they cannot explain why, of the many cities which seem to satisfy the minimum conditions, only a few have managed to attain the status of leading financial centre.

The causal factors can be illuminated by using a simple conceptual framework that deals with the demand-supply relationships governing financial services and urban facilities. Since an international financial centre is by definition a metropolitan area where transnational and domestic banks and other non-bank financial intermediaries assemble, a convenient starting pointing is the demand-supply perspectives from the point of view of such intermediaries, typically a bank of large size.

The pertinent question to ask is: what is the comparative advantage a multinational bank enjoys that is denied to a domestic bank in the host country, since the latter is presumably more familiar with local laws and customs, and has better ties with domestic authorities and clients? The very formulation of this question precludes those banks that are relatively small. Only when a bank has grown to a certain size can it begin to exploit the economies of scale in establishing a network of branches, offices and subsidiaries abroad. In other words, a transnational bank's superior resources, skills, experience and technology enable it to offer a wide range of financial products and services at lower marginal costs, particularly in specialized areas such as loan syndication, foreign exchange, securitization, and corporate financial advice.

This ability to expand abroad must be coupled with the urge to do so. The inner dynamics of international banking ensure that this will be be the case. Transnational banking is the financial analogue of direct foreign investment by transnational corporations, which during the post-war era has grown at a rapid pace. The large, and often oligopolistic banks have no choice but to follow their clients abroad, if only as a defensive measure against their rivals. US banks initially took the lead in the sixties in expansion abroad, but they were soon followed by European, Japanese and Canadian banks. The US itself was not immune to invasion by foreign banks.

Even without this pressure to follow clients abroad, the transnational banks themselves are compelled to follow a strategy of international diversification to open up new markets and sources of income. Hong Kong's own Hongkong and Shanghai Banking Corporation — the only locally incorporated bank that qualifies as a transnational bank — provides a good example of this strategy. Bryan (1986) shows that during the period 1964-1985, net international bank credit grew at an annual compound rate of 25.8%, compared to 10.4% for world GDP (excluding the Soviet bloc) and 12.4% for world trade (again excluding the Soviet bloc) at current prices and exchange rates.

Despite the Third World debt crisis, BIS statistics show that net international bank credit doubled between 1985-90 to US$3,100 billion.[16]

The spread of transnational banking has also been greatly facilitated by the phenomenal growth of the xeno-currency markets (popularly known as the Euro-currency markets), which may be broadly defined as the markets for funds denominated in any currency other than that of the host country. This important innovation in international finance, made possible by multilateral currency convertibility in 1958, has enabled transnational banks without a large local currency deposit base to draw huge balances originating in many parts of the world into the financing of international trade and investment. This market has been particularly important to US banks, which at least before the Depository Institutions Deregulation and Monetary Control Act of 1980, had been subject to onerous domestic regulations and restrictions. Because the Euro-currency market provides depth, flexibility and freedom from government regulations and restrictions to an extent unknown to any other form of financial market, access to it has enabled transnational banks to supply longer and multi-currency term loan facilities, and securitized lending such as Euro-notes.

In short, a typical transnational bank is both able and willing to supply a menu of rich and varied financial services and products through its global network of branches, offices and subsidiaries. There must be of course a corresponding demand for such services and products if the supplier is to stay in business. Again, the internationalization of trade and production, the rise of transnational corporations, and the increasing integration of world economies and financial markets ensure that such a demand will be forthcoming. Large manufacturing and commercial concerns stationed abroad naturally prefer to deal with banks of their own national origins. Wealthy individuals and corporations in the host cities or countries may also prefer large and prestigious transnational banks for security and other reasons (such as easy transfer of funds abroad). Governments and government-owned corporations also often turn to transnational banks for their financial needs. Generally speaking, however, the demand for the transnational banks specialized, wholesale services and products is likely to be

(16) See Bank for International Settlements, International Banking and Financial Market Developments, Basle, Feb. 1991. Net international bank credit is defined as total international claims of reporting banks minus inter-bank double-countries.

greater than that for retail banking services and products, since retail banking is an area where indigenous banks may enjoy greater comparative advantage, quite apart from the fact that national governments often exclude foreign banks from the retail market, or severely restrict their scope of activities therein. This explains why transnational banks tend to be much more successful in such activities as underwriting, syndication, securitization, corporate advice, project finance, certificates of deposits, and forex and money market operations.

The demand for and supply of financial services and products which can best be handled by large transnational banks pave the way for the emergence of financial centres. But there must be an explanation why certain cities succeed in becoming international financial centres while others do not. Again the demand-supply framework is a useful device, but this time the focus in on the demand for supply of urban facilities. From the perspective of a transnational bank, there is obviously no point in choosing an obscure small town or village: the centres must not only be cities, but cities that possess certain desirable locational and physical attributes such as a central or accessible geographical position, a modern network of transportation and communications, and a time zone situation that permits maximum contacts with other centres during a working day. It also follows that cities that are already established commercial or industrial centres, or are backed up by a hinterland of national or regional economies with promising growth potential, will be in strong demand as financial centres. More important, the host government must provide a reasonably hospitable environment for transnational banks to operate. Political or legal entry barriers against foreign banks explain, for example, why no international financial centre has ever existed in Communist-ruled countries. Ideally, there should be no discrimination of any kind against foreign banks, but some discrimination is acceptable as long as foreign banks are allowed to operate at least in the offshore sector without undue interference from the authorities. One can go on to list other relevant variables, suffice it to say that any well-defined demand function for urban facilities must contain the major determinants already mentioned. Clearly, cities that can supply the kind of business environment, locational and physical attributes, and other facilities that match the demand requirements stand a good chance of emerging and prospering as financial centres. It is true that the supply of certain services and amenities (such as the supply of legal and accounting expertise) may itself change in response to demand. But there must be a critical mass of desirable attributes and characteristics in the first place before transnational banks can be attracted *en masse*.

The transnational banks have been used as the core of this analysis, but the same analytical framwork can be applied to other non-bank financial intermediaries. It is a widely observed fact that the presence of a sufficient number of banks in a city is followed or accompanied by a similar influx of other non-bank financial intermediaries, and supportive professional personnel like lawyers, accountants, brokers, economists etc., apart from the executives and employees of the financial institutions themselves. The aggolmeration of financial institutions and related entities in turn make the creation and functioning of a variety of financial markets possible. Advances in telecommunications have lessened, but not eliminated, the need for face-to-face contacts in financial transactions. Hence the agglomeration of financial institutions and markets may generate further economies of scale.

With the aid of this admittedly simple conceptual framework, which nevertheless draws its inspiration from several branches of economics – monetary economics, international finance, industrial organization, and urban economics – one can readily see why Hong Kong has emerged so swiftly during the past two decades as a major financial centre in the Asian-Pacific region. As the economies of Hong Kong and other countries in the region become more industrialized and affluent, the demand for banking and financial services has grown enormously. These services and products are more sophisticated and complex than can be handled entirely by indiginous financial institutions. Transnational banks and other financial intermediaries are well poised to fill this need. At the same time, Hong Kong possesses all the ingredients of a successful financial centre which cannot fail to attract a host of financial intermediaries, ranging from depository institutions to unit trust and mutual funds.

In terms of locational and physical attributes, Hong Kong's advantages are well-known: the city is centrally situated in the Asia-Pacific region, and supported by an excellent transport and telecommunications network. Its time-zone position enables it to fill the gaps between the US West Coast and Europe, thus ensuring the existence of a global 24-hour trading in financial markets. Its proximity to mainland China acts as a magnet for transnational firms, both financial and non-financial, that have an eye on the vast China market. According to a recent government survey, at the end of March 1990, there were 572 overseas companies using Hong Kong as their regional headquarters for Asia and Pacific, of which 252 were US companies.(17)

Financially, Hong Kong is blessed with a free exchange market, and a prudent fiscal system with low tax rates and simple tax structure. One need hardly belabour the importance of free convertibility: financial institutions and capital funds will converge towards a centre only in the secure knowledge that money can be repatriated or transferred elsewhere without hindrance.(18) While Hong Kong is by no means a tax haven, its tax rates, despite some upward adjustments during the post-war period, are substantially lower than those in most other countries: the standard rate on profits and income now stands at 15%, with a 1.5% surcharge on corporation profits.(19) Equally important is the relative simplicity of the tax structure, especially the adherence to the "source principle" under which only income arising in or derived from domestic transactions is chargeable to tax. For financial institutions that engage only in offshore or entrepot activities, this feature is of course most attractive.(20)

Economically, Hong Kong during the post-war period had built up a solid reputation as a major commercial, manufacturing and shipping centre even before it became a financial centre. In the more recent period of 1966-90, for which official national income statistics are available, the economy grew at an average annual rate of nearly 8% in real terms. Expressed in terms of current prices and exchange rates, the *per capita* gross domestic product increased from HK$3,758 (US$626)

(17) See Industry Department, Hong Kong Government, *Report on the Survey of Regional Headquarters of Overseas Companies in Hong Kong,* August 1990.

(18) Formal exchange control came to an end in Hong Kong after it was excluded from the sterling area in 1972. However, even before then an uncontrolled free market in US dollar and other convertible currencies was allowed to exist alongside the controlled market in sterling.

(19) The standard tax rate was gradually raised from 10% in 1945 to 17% in 1984, with a 1.5% surcharge on corporation profit tax from 1977. During 1987-89, these were lowered again to 15% and 16.5% respectively.

(20) The "source principle" was modified in 1978 in respect of banking profits that are earned without the substantial intervention of a branch abroad. See Jao (1979b) for an explanation. However, in a recent court case involving a major bank, the Privy Council of the United Kingdom has reaffirmed the "source principle". See Harris (1991).

in 1966 to HK$94,138 (US$12,069) in 1990, even though the population increased by 57% to 5.8 million during the same period.[(21)] A mere dot on the world map, Hong Kong nevertheless ranked 10th in the world's leading exporters in 1988.[(22)] A city of 5.8 million with such a proven record of dynamic performance can hardly be ignored by international financial institutions. Moreover, Hong Kong is only part of a region whose average rate of economic growth has been consistently higher than others.[(23)]

Liberal, non-interventionist government policy towards the private sector is another strong point conducive to the formation and development of a financial centre. Hong Kong has often been depicted as a last bastion of *laissez-faire*. While this label was not inappropriate forty years ago, it has become less and less so in recent years, because of the government's role in housing, education and social welfare. What remains true, however, is the policy of not interfering with the workings of the market mechanism unless there is a patent case of "market failure"– a policy which the Hong Kong authorities have described as "positive non-interventionism". Moreover, this liberal policy is applied equally to both domestic and foreign firms, i.e., the principle of "national treatment" is well oberved. In recent years, especially after the banking crisis of 1983-86 and the securities market crisis of 1987, the regulatory framwork for the financial sector has visibly tightened. There are critics who claim that this stricter regulatory policy is not only inconsistent with Hong Kong's traditonal *laissez faire* policy, but also with the worldwide trend of deregulation. This is however a profound misunderstanding. The tightening of the regulatory policy since 1986 seems to be severe because the previous one was too lax. Moreover, the crises of 1983-87 have exposed many cases of mismanagement, imprudence or even fraud, which constitute clear evidence of "market failure". As a result of the regulatory reform during the past 5 years, the banking system has improved very considerably in terms of safety and soundness. One concrete result is that Hong Kong's depository institutions have over-fulfilled the Basle Committee's minimum capital adequacy ratio of 8% two years ahead of schedule, at a time when many other countries - notably the United States and Japan – are still struggling to attain the recommended

(21)Census and Statistics Department, *Estimates of Gross Domestic Product* 1986 to 1990.
(22)Census and Statistics Department, *Hong Kong Review of Overseas Trade in 1989*, 1990.
(23)See World Bank, *World Development Report, 1990*, Table 2, pp. 180-1

minimum ratio.[(24)] At the same time, measures of financial liberalization, such as the total abolition of interest tax and the reduction of stamp duty, have continued to be made, also during the past 5 years. Thus there is nothing inconsistent with the declared policy of "positive non-interventionism". The authorities have rightly recognized that "competition by laxity" is a poor way of promoting Hong Kong as a financial centre, being destabilizing and destructive to the financial sector in the long run.

Except for a brief period in 1967, when China's Cultural Revolution spilled over into Hong Kong in the form of disturbances organized by ultra-leftists, Hong Kong has been remarkably free from political and social unrest. Since 1982, when China declared its intention of regaining sovereignty over Hong Kong, uncertainty over the post-1997 future has given rise to a widespread malaise. This malaise has manifested itself in peaceful emigration, capital flight, or portfolio shift, but not in violent social or political unrest. It can hardly be over-emphasized that over half of Hong Kong's population consists of first or second generation refugees from mainland China. While there is little or no democracy in Hong Kong, individual liberty, human rights and property rights are well respected and protected. People therefore realize that violent political struggle and civil strife can only destroy Hong Kong's survival. This realization, plus the common refugee background, perhaps also explains why industrial relations have remained relatively good by international standards, despite the fact that trade unions have become more assertive in recent years. In any case, the experience of Beirut – the classic example of a financial centre destroying itself by civil war – is a sharp and vivid lesson for Hong Kong.

Last but not least, the rule of law is also an essential causal factor. The legal system of Hong Kong, which is based on English law, provides a framwork for enforcing contracts and settling disputes highly congenial to international financial institutions and other non-financial enties. The judiciary is fully independent. Implicit in such a system is a guarantee against arbitrary actions against any individual without due process of law, or against arbitary expropriation of private properties and foreign interests without compensation. Associated

[(24)] The Commissioner of Banking, *Annual Report 1989*, p.11

with this is another factor (though of secondary importance), that English, the language of world commerce and finance, is also an official language of Hong Kong.

It may be argued that the causative factors listed above, while no doubt important and valid, are not the monopoly of Hong Kong: many other cities in the region also share such desirable attributes or characteristics. It is true that Hong Kong is not the only international financial centre in the region. In explaining Hong Kong's past success, however, it is worth enphasising two points. First, Hong Kong satisfies all the essential conditions for an international centre, an achievement only a few other cities can match. Second, Hong Kong is nonpareil in at least two respects. The first is Hong Kong's liberal and non-interventionist ethos and policy. Even though it is not pure laissez faire, as explained earlier, Hong Kong still imposes the least restrictions, as far as the Asia-Pacific region is concerned, not only on financial institutions and markets, but also on the private sector in general. The second is Hong Kong's fine record of "national treatment". The concept of "national treatment" forms part of the principle of "non-discrimination", one of the main pillars of the General Agreement Tariffs and Trade (GATT) codified in 1947. As enshrined in Articles I and III of GATT, the "most favoured nation" (MFN) clause requires that, subject to certain exceptions, imports from all sources should face identical barriers, while "national treatment" requires that, once through the customs, foreign goods are subject to no taxes or regulations more onerous than those on equivalent domestic goods (Winters, 1990). Since then the concept has been extended to direct investment and the financial sector.

A previous study (Jao, 1988, pp.20-1) shows that Hong Kong had the best record of "national treatment" in Asia and Pacific in 1986. A recent report by the U.S. Treasury has reconfirmed this finding. This

Table 10

Complaints on Barriers to Foreign Financial Institutions (as of June 1990)

Country	Complaints
1.Australia	While deregulation has continued, only lim-

	ited progress towards full national treatment. Additional trading bank licences are not expected to be offered to foreign entities, though limited licences are available.
2.China	Significant denials of national treatment to banks and other financial institutions. Foreign banks can only open branches in the 5 special economic zones and the Pudong areal of Shanghai. They may not take local currency deposits or grant local currency loans. Foreign banks may open representive offices in other areas, but cannot engage in profit-making business.
3.India	Significant denials of national treatment to both foreign banks and securities firms in respect of entry, expansion and business operation. No progress seen.
4.Indonesia	Significant improvement towards national treatment in banking and securities market following recent reforms, though denials remain.
5.Japan	Despite efforts at liberalization, foreign banks and securities firms are still placed at a competitive disadvantage vs domestic counterparts. Factors cited include regulated interest rates, restrictive operating regulations, strong ties among related domestic firms (*keiretsu*), excessive compartmentializations of financial markets, lack of transparency in regulatory process, and *de facto* prohibition of innovative products and services and services offered by foreign entities.
6.Philippines	Significant denials of national treatment, especially with regard to entry, remain with no improvement.

7.Singapore	Though national treatment is accorded in the offshore banking market, significant denials of national treatment continue to exist in the domestic banking market in respect of entry, expansion, and banking business. Despite some liberalization, the foreign share of new joint ventures with local brokerages is still limited to 49 percent.
8.South Korea	Significant denials of national treatment to both foreign banks and securities firms in respect of entry, branching, expansion, local currency funding, and business operations in general.
9.Taiwan	Despite some improvements, significant denials of national treatment to foreign banks and securities firms exist in respect of entry, branching, local currency deposit-taking and funding, investment in local securities, ownership of local brokerage, underwriting etc.
10.Thailand	Significant denials of national treatment in respect of entry, branching, AAATM network.

Source: US Treasury, *The 1990 Report on Foreign Treatment of U.S. Financial Institutions*, Washington, 1990.

report contains complaints against 27 countries or regions for failing to accord full "national treatment" to foreign banks and financial institutions, but none against Hong Kong. Table 10 gives summary of such complaints against countries in Asia and Pacific, because they are more relevant to Hong Kong.

The fact that Hong Kong performs best in respect of "national treatment" is fully consistent with the view that Hong Kong is an integrated financial centre in the sense that once a foreign bank or financial institution is admitted, it can engage in the whole range of banking and financial business, whether onshore or offshore, and whether denominated in domestic or foreign currencies. There is also no restriction on foreign ownership of domestic forms, whether financial of non-financial. The only barrier, as noted earlier, is that foreign banks licensed after 1978 can only operate one branch, but this has not caused any concern to foreign banks, as also explained before. Indeed, in certain respects, such as the exemption from publishing financial statements, and exemption from the capital adequacy ratio, it may even be argued that better than "national treatment" is accorded to foreign banks.

Prospects

The evolution of Hong Kong as a international financial centre, and its causative factors, have been analyzed in some detail in the previous pages. Past success, no matter how brilliant, does not guarantee future success. Can Hong Kong continue to be a leading financial centre beyond 1997? This is a matter of considerable concern, not only to Hong Kong, but also to China and the whole Asia-Pacific region.

One general, and rather obvious answer to this question would be:if Hong Kong can preserve and maintain permanently the various conditions and factors that have been identified as being responsible for and conductive to its rise as a financial centre in the past two decades, then there is no reason why it cannot continue to be a leading financial centre in the Asia-Pacific region in the future. Such an answer will not be meaningful however if one does not examine in depth whether the various conditions and factors can in fact be preserved and maintained permanently in a rapidly changing environment.

Hong Kong is perhaps unique in that it is confronted with a fundamental change in its political and constitutional status in the near future: the return to Chinese rule in 1997 after 156 years as a British colony. Normally, decolonization should be an event for joyous celebration. In Hong Kong, however, 1997 is anticipated at best with resignation, and at worst with apprehension, or even despair. For the new metropolitan power is a Communist-ruled country whose institutions and values are diametrically opposed to those of Hong Kong.

Even concentrating on the financial sector alone, pessimists about Hong Kong's future can cite the undeniable fact that, since the the Bolsheviks seized power in Russia in 1917, no financial centre has ever existed, or has been allowed to exist, in all Communist-ruled countries. Indeed, until very recently, certain necessary conditions for a financial centre, such as freedom of capital movements, free conversion of currency, financial institutions and markets owned and operated by the private sector, and liberal policy towards foreign financial institituions, were regarded as heresies by Marxist ideologues and Party bureaucrats.

China has a two-fold answer to this powerful charge. Firstly, Hong Kong's capitalist system and financial centre status are to be preserved unchanged for 50 years after 1997 under the "one country, two system" formula. Second, China itself has been pursuing a new economic policy of reform and an opening up to the world since 1979.

Concerning China's first point, it may be acknowledged that, from the purely de jure point of view, the minimum conditions for an international financial centre appear to have been met. Thus, in the Basic Law promulgated in April 1990, the preservation of the capitalist system and protection of private property are laid down in Chapter I on "General Principles"; more detailed provisions regarding an independent fiscal system, separate and fully concertible currency, freedom of capital movement, continuation of free port status and free trade policy, separate customs etc. are given in Chapter V on "Economy". Article 109 specifies that "The Government of the Hong Kong Special Administrative Region shall provide an appropriate economic and legal environment for the maintenance of the status of Hong Kong as an international financial centre."

A law is only as good as its actual implementation. Since the power to interpret and amend the Basic Law is vested in China's National People's Congress – a body completely dominated by the Communist Party – there is widespread fear in Hong Kong that the Basic Law may not provide adequate safeguards for a truly autonomous territory. China's domestic record during the past four decades in respect of human rights and property rights is, to putis very mildly, not one that can inspire confidence. Since a substantial proportion of the Hong Kong population has a refugee background, and even the non-refugees have ties with the mainland, the widespread sense of anxiety and apprehension is well justified. The military crackdown on Tiananmen Square in June 1989 has only served to aggravate this malaise. The credit standings of both China and Hong Kong have been lowered by international credit agencies.[(25)] In general, Hong Kong's "country risk" and "sovereign risk" will increase as 1997 draws nearer.

Thus, even though the "Economy" chapter appears to be reasonable, it has failed to dispel doubt in the business community. A dramatic recent example is the decision by the Hongkong and Shanghai Banking Corporation (HSBC) – the largest commercial bank which also carries out certain central banking functions - to shift its legal domicile from Hong Kong to London in November 1990. Another long-established British conglomerate, Jardine Holdings, had moved its legal domicile to Bermuda as long ago as 1984. Not satisfied with this, Jardine now intends to shift the primary listing of its shares also to London. It is true that both HSBC and Jardine have continued to maintain their presence here, because Hong Kong remains their principal profit centre. They are however only two conspicuous examples: there must be hundreds of other firms which have quietly moved their legal domicles elsewhere over the years. Changing legal domicle means that the ultimate control of assets lies outside Hong Kong. It reflects therefore a deep distrust of the post-1997 regime.

As regards China's second point, the reform and "open door" policy since 1979 has indeed brought about considerable progress. China's economy grew at an annual rate of nearly 9% in real terms in 1979-90. Significant gains have been made in agriculture, after the replacement of the commune system by the "household responsibility system", and in international trade, after the normalization of relations with the West. In the field of financial reform, China has also scored success in rejoining the world financial community, and in restoring, or creating, financial institutions and markets. Further progress has been checked, however, by the tragic events of June 1989. Moreover, China has failed to achieve comprehensive price reform and other institutional reforms, and to solve the perennial fiscal deficit problem. It has not succeeded in installing a market-based macroeconomic stabilization mechanism. The reduction of the inflation rate to the single-digit range

---

[(25)]Since the Tiananmen massacre, Hong Kong's credit standing has been lowered twice. In the latest adjustment, Standard and Poor's downgraded the Hong Kong Government's implicit long-term rating from Single-A-1-plus-i to Single-A-A-i, while the short-term rating was lowered from A-1-plus-i to A-1-i. See Eva To, "Territory's rating cut for second time in four months", *South China Morning Post Business Post*, Feb. 14, 1990.

in 1990 was made by administrative and coercive means, at the heavy price of high umemployment. The measured inflation rate may also merely indicate the repressed inflation rate and not the true inflation rate. Finally, despite a good growth record, China's *per capita* GDP, measured at current prices and exchange rates, amounted to only US$293 in 1990, as compared to US$12,060 for Hong Kong.(26) Even after purchasing power parity adjustments, China's per capita GDP is unlikely to be more than one-twentieth of Hong Kong's. This wide income gap has already give rise to one of Hong Kong's most intractable problems, namely, illegal immigration from the mainland, which is likely to get worse after 1997.

One encouraging aspect of the China Dimension (which should be broadly defined to include not only mainland China, but also Taiwan) in recent years has been the growing signs of *detente* between the two sides of the Taiwan Straits. The residents of Taiwan, including civil servants, are now allowed to visit the mainland. Although direct investment in, and trade with the mainland are still forbidden by the authorities in Taiwan, business is soaring mainly through the intermediation of Hong Kong. Most significantly, at the time of writing, Taiwan is planning to repeal the Communist Rebellion Act, a legacy of the Nationalist era in mainland China. If this is done, a new page will be turned in the relationship between mainland China and Taiwan, which can only benefit Hong Kong. One major obstacle remains however: China's unwillingness to publicly and openly renounce the use of force in achieving reunification with Taiwan, which inevitably still casts a long shadow over the Taiwan Straits. This is a great pity, for with the renunciation of force, economic coorperation within "Greater China" (comprising mainland China, Taiwan, and Hong Kong) will become a much more practicable and meaningful concept.

Be that as it may, the triangular relationship may also give some insight into Hong Kong's future. Given that Beijing's ultimate aim is to reunify Taiwan, it is in China's own interests to preserve Hong Kong's stability and property, if only as a "demonstration effect" on Taiwan. Apart from this, China itself has a considerable stake in the Hong Kong

(26)China's GDP is given in State Statistical Bureau, Bulletin on National Economy and Social Development for 1990, the full text of which is published in Renmin Ribao, Feb. 23, 1991. The per capita GDP is then calculated and converted at the current exchange rate. For Hong Kong's per capita GDP, see Note 1.

economy. Hong Kong accounts for about 25-30% of China's foreign exchange earnings, and about 80% of direct foreign investment inside China. China's own investment in Hong Kong is large and growing, though there is no precise quantitative estimate.(27) However, in the banking sector alone, China owns or controls 32 depository institutions, which accounted for HK$254 billion of deposits, or 20.6% of total deposits, and HK$397 billion of assets, or 7.6% of total assests, of the banking system.(28) Hong Kong also serves as a vital entrepot as well as an export market for Chinese goods, and plays a key role in the collection of market intelligence and transmission of modern managerial know-how to China. Seen in this light, the Sino-British Joint Declaration and the Basic Law do have a restraining influence on China, since they provide the constitutional framwork within which Hong Kong can continue to function as a dynamic market economy and international financial centre.

Competition from other financial centres is often cited as another factor affecting Hong Kong's prospects as a financial centre. The prevailing consensus is that Tokyo, Hong Kong and Singapore are the three leading financial centres of the Asia-Pacific region. Tokyo, being backed by an economic superpower, is both a global and regional financial centre, which neither Hong Kong and Singapore can match in terms of growth potential and the scale of banking operations and financial transactions. Tokyo's degulation and liberalization has taken place much later and at a slower pace than Hong Kong and Singapore's and English is not an official language there. Although the offshore banking market since its inauguration in December 1986 has grown rapidly, foreign financial institutions still find it difficult to penetrate the domestic banking and financial markets. Hong Kong and Singapore are more similar in background, and competition between them as regional financial centres has always been a favourite topic for economists and journalists. Detailed comparison cannot be attempted here, but the situation at present is roughly that Hong Kong lags behind Singapore in the size and activity of forex market, bond market, and futures market. As mentioned earlier, Singapore is the host to the Asian

(27)However, according to Mr. Anthony Russell, Head of the HSBC's China division, Chinese state-owned corporations have invested nearly US$10 billion in Hong Kong. See G. Crothall, "Investment in HK by Chinese corporations close to US$10b", *South China Morning Post Business Post*, April 22, 1991.

(28)The Commissioner of Banking, *Annual Report 1990*, Table 2.6 and 2.7.

Dollar Market, but since Hong Kong's banking market is fully integrated, and there are no separate ACUs, it is impossible to ascertain which has the larger offshore banking market. However, Hong Kong has definitely a larger domestic banking market, reflecting the fact that its economy is more than twice Singapore's. Hong Kong has more foreign financial institutions of all kinds, and is ahead of Singapore in loan syndication, fund management, gold trading, and equity market turnover. Hong Kong used to have a distinct tax advantage over Singapore, but this is being whittled away, especially in respect of offshore transactions, by Singapore's aggressive tax incentives in recent years.(29) It is a stated policy of the Singaporean Government to promote the city-state as a premier financial centre in the region.(30)

A potential newly emergent financial centre is Taipei. Taiwan's postwar economic miracle has been well-documented and widely praised, but its financial sector has generally lagged behind its real sector. In recent years, measures of liberalization and privatization have been taken in the financial sector, partly because of pressures by the United States. In 1984, an offshore banking centre was established to allow domestic and foreign banks to operate "offshore banking units" broadly modelled after Singapore's ACUs (Sun, 1984). The total assets of OBUs had increased nearly five-fold from US$4.3 billion in 1984 to US$20 billion in January 1991.(31) Other measures include interest rate deregulation, liberalization of commercial banks, relaxation of exchange controls, relaxation of restrictions on domestic banks to set up branches abroad, establishment of the Taipei foreign currency call loan market in 1989 etc. (Shea, 1990). Recent press reports suggest that Taiwan is keen to develop Taipei into a regional financial centre, perhaps with an eye to the uncertainty over Hong Kong's post-1997 future.(32) With an external reserve of nearly US$80 billion,(33) reput-

(29) For details, see Monetary Authority of Singapore (1989), pp. 78-88.

(30) See Ministry of Trade & Industry, Republic of Singapore (1986), Part 5, section 19.

(31) See the Central Bank of China, Financial Statistics Monthly: Taiwan District, The Republic of China, Feb. 1991.

(32) See Cynthia Owens, "Taiwan is fueling competition in banking", Asian Wall Street Journal, May 24, 1990; Jeremy Mark, "Taiwan opens its stock market to foreigners", *Asian Wall Street Journal*, Dec. 28-29, 1990; "Taipei's 8-point plan for a financial centre", Hong Kong Economic Journal, Jan 2, 1991; "On planning for an international financial centre", Taiwan Independent Evening Post, Jan. 10, 1991.

(33) At the end of 1991, Taiwan had forex reserves of US$72.4 billion. In addition, it had a gold stock worth some US$5.6 billion. See The Central Bank of China, Financial Statistics: Taiwan District, The Republic of China, Jan. 1991.

edly the largest in the world, a proven record of dynamic economic growth, a favourable time-zone location, and a huge infrastructural modernization programme, Taiwan is well poised to develop its capital into a new financial centre. What is needed is more liberalization, privatization, and better "national treatment".

Competititon *per se* from other financial centres, however, should not be of too much concern to Hong Kong for several reasons. First, Hong Kong has a good record of resilience and flexibility in the face of keen competition, as the experience of the past four decades, not just in the financial sphere, has amply demonstrated. Second, Hong Kong is still unrivalled in respect of its liberal non-interventionist policy and fine record of "national treatment". Third, financial centres are not a "zero-sum" game in the sense that one centre's gain must mean another's loss. While competition certainly exists, there is another aspect of the inter-relationship between financial centres, namely, their complementarity. We have already noted how Singapore's initial success of hosting the Asian Dollar Market did not prevent Hong Kong's parallel rise as a financial centre in the seventies. A very recent example is Tokyo's offshore banking market. When it was first established in December 1986, there was considerable consternation in both Hong Kong and Singapore that it would take business away from the two centres. Developments since then have shown that such fears are unfounded (H0, 1989). As also noted in a previous study, in international finance, as in international trade, there is a "trade diversion effect" (business taken away by a competitor) and a "trade creation effect" (business created by a larger market). If the "trade creation effect" dominates, then all will benefit. (Jao, 1988, p.228). Thus, liberalization and internationalization of other centres may well generate more business in the forex and securities markets in the form of, for example, arbitrage activity. It may also lead to increased entry of banks and other financial institutions into all the centres on a reciprocal basis. Already there are reports of several leading banks in Taiwan planning to set up offices or branches in Hong Kong. In short, provided that the whole Asia-Pacific region can continue to maintain its better-than-average growth, and that there is no retrogression into protectionism in the financial sphere, then there is no reason why financial centres cannot grow and prosper together.

If however after 1997, the provisions of the Joint Declaration and Basic Law are violated to an extent that foreign banks and other financial institutions can no longer operate profitably, then there is no doubt that they will leave for other centres in the region. This is Hong Kong's real worry. But this is related to the change in Hong Kong's political and constitutional status rather than the competitive pull of other centres. Nonetheless, even ruling out the above scenario, it is still important for Hong Kong to maintain its competitive edge all the time.

Last but not least, the continuing brain drain also poses a serious problem for Hong Kong's prospects as a financial centre. There are two aspects to this problem: one is the general problem of emigration, which affects all sectors of the economy, and the other is the industry-specific one of high turnover in the financial services sector. Regrading the first aspect, emigration is, of course, not a new phenomenon. But whereas before the establishment of the People's Republic of China in 1949, emigration from Hong Kong was predominantly influenced by economic considerations, after 1949, non-economic factors have increasingly become more dominant. One confidence-shattering event occurred in 1967, when the Cultural Revolution spilled over into Hong Kong in the form of violent disturbances organized by Maoists. Many people began to realize that emigration was not just a matter of seeking a higher standard of living, but one of seeking permanent refuge from the deprivation of human rights and property rights. China's announcement in 1982 that it would resume sovereighty over the whole Hong Kong area, and the brutal military suppression of the pro-democracy movement in June 1989, have further strengthened the non-economic determinants of emigration. A government manpower survey estimates that between 1989-96, total net emigration will reach 425,664 persons.(34) For 1990 alone, net emigration is estimated at 62,000, up 13% on the previous year.(35) A pilot study shows that most of the emigrants were fairly young, with 77% between the ages of 26 and 39; in terms of occupational nature and organizational grades, they were largely from the professional (13%), technical (15%), managerial (24%), supervisory (19%), and clerical grades (18%) (Kirbride and Chan, 1988). A banking industry survey shows that, for the year ended November 1988, the turnover rate within the banking industry was a high as 27%. Of those employees who left, about 8% gave emigration

(34) See Fanny Wong, "425,664 to leave in eight years", South China Morning Post, Sept. 4, 1990.

(35) Fanny Wong, "Brain drain estimate up 13 per cent", "South China Morning Post, Sept. 4, 1990.

as their reason.[36] The high turnover rate reflects of course the general phenomenon of labour shortage, but the emigration of skilled personnel does pose a serious problem for the financial services industry as a whole. For example, the loss of experienced forex dealers has been cited as a cause of the fact that the daily turnover in Singapore's forex market is now higher than that of Hong Kong's.[37]

To counter the growing exodus of talent, the Hong Kong Government has announced an ambitious programme of doubling first-degree places in tertiary institutions by 1994-5. The government-financed Banking Trainging Board of the Vocational Training Council provides on-job training courses to employees of banks and other financial institutions. The banking industry's own Chartered Institute of Bankers conducts similar courses and examinations. While this accelerated educational and training programme may alleviate the brain drain to some extent, it cannot solve the problem itself if confidence in Hong Kong's future remains less than robust.

The brain drain is only part of what one might call the "1997 syndrome". This syndrome manifests itself in various forms such as emigration, capital flight, portfolio shift, currency substitution, change of legal domicile etc. In its most acute form, the syndrome gave rise to the currency crisis and collapse of the asset markets in 1982-83. The danger is that, at some critical juncture, the syndrome might once again degenerate into a *sauve qui peut* situation with incalculable consequences to the financial system and the economy.

From these discussions it is clear that all the major issues affecting Hong Kong's prospects as a financial centre are either directly or indirectly related to the impending change in Hong Kong's political and constitutional status.

While the establishment of the linked exchange rate system in October 1983 and other stabilization measures taken by the Hong Kong authorities (e.g. the abolition of the withholding interest tax on Hong Kong dollar deposit, the "accounting arrangements" between the

(36) See Banking Training Board (1989).

(37) Eva To, "HK slips as Asia's second forex centre", South China Morning Post Business Post, Sept. 14, 1989.

Exchange Fund and the HSBC etc.) have strengthened Hong Kong's defences against a recurrence of the 1982-83 currency crisis, the Joint Declaration and the Basic Law have failed to allay people's fears and concerns about future. The burden of proof that the concept of "one country, two system" can work must therefore rest on its originator.

Conclusion

In conclusion, although Hong Kong cannot be described as a global financial centre, it can be considered a major financial centre in the Asia-Pacific region. In contrast to other centres in the region, Hong Kong is an integrated functional centre which accords full "national treatment". As regards its long-term future, there are cross currents in the underlying political and economic situation, which no doubt both optimists and pessimists can cite in support of their views. However, all would presumably agree that Hong Kong's long-term future as a regional financial centre depends on whether those conditions and factors responsible for Hong Kong's success in the past can be preserved and maintained on a permanent basis. This in turn depends, in the last analysis, on China's good will and rational behaviour. These are, however, variables which no one can predict with any certainty, and are in any case beyond Hong Kong's control. If pressed for a less agnostic conclusion, we can only say: *Dieu aidant*, Hong Kong may still survive as a financial centre, provided that there is no political catastrophe that renders the Joint Declaration and the Basic Law inoperative. However, given that other centres do not suffer from the "1997 syndrome", it will become increasingly difficult for Hong Kong to maintain its present position as as the second largest financial centre in the Asia-Pacific region.

References

Aliber, R.Z. (1976). "Toward a theory of international banking", Federal Reserve Bank of *San Francisco Economic Review*, Spring, pp. 5-8.

——— (1980). "The integration of the offshore and domestic banking system", *Journal of Monetary Economics*, Vol. 6, pp. 509-26.

Banking Training Board (1989). *1988 Manpower Survey Report on the Banking Industry*, (Hong Kong: Vocational Training Council).

Bryant, R.C. (1985). "Financial structure and international banking in Singapore", Brooking Discussion Papers in International Economics, No. 29, May.

——— (1986a). "The Evolution of Singapore as a financial center", Brookings Discussion Papers in International Economics, April.

——— (1986b). "The Internationalization of financial intermediation: an empirical survey", Brookings Papers in International Economics, September.

Choi, S.R., Tschoegl, A.E., and Yu, C.M. (1986). "Banks and the world's major financial centres, 1970-1980", *Weltwirtschaftliches Archiv*, Vol. 122, No. 1, pp. 48-64.

Christensen, B.V. (1986). "Switzerland's role as an international financial center", IMF Occasional Paper No. 45, July.

Dufey, G. and Giddy, I.H. (1978). *The International Money Market* (Englewood Cliffs, N.J.: Prentice-Hall Inc.).

Gerakis, A.S. and Roncesvalles, O. (1983). "Bahrain's offshore banking center", *Economic Development and Cultural Change*, Vol. 31, pp. 349-64.

Gorostiaga, X. (1984). *The Role of the International Financial Centres in Underdeveloped Countries* (London: Croom Helm).

Greenwood, J.G. (1990). "An estimate of HK$ currency circulating in Guangdong Province", *Asian Monetary Monitor*, July-August, pp. 37-44.

Grubel, H.G. (1977). "A theory of multinational banking", *Banca Nazionale del Lavoro Quarterly Review*, No. 121, pp. 349-64.

——— (1982). "Towards a theory of free economic zones", *Weltwirtschaftliches Archiv*, Vol. 118, No. 1, pp. 39-61.

Harris, I.W. (1991). "Hong Kong's source principle established by the Privy Council ", *Bulletin for International Fiscal Documentation*, Vol. 45, No. 2, pp. 67-70.

Ho, Y.C. (1989). "Hong Kong, Singapore and Taiwan as new financial centres", paper presented to the Conference on the Future of Asia-Pacific Economics, 8-10 November, 1989, Bangkok.

——— (1991). "Hong Kong as an international financial centre", in Ho, Scott and Wong op. cit., pp. 381-405.

Ho, Y.K., Scott, R. and Wong K.A. (eds.) (1991). *The Hong Kong Financial System* (Hong Kong: Oxford University Press).

Hodjera, Z. (1978). "The Asian Currency Market: Singapore as a regional financial center", *IMF Staff Papers*, Vol. 25, No. 2, pp. 221-53.

Jao, Y.C. (1979a). "The rise of Hong Kong as a financial centre", *Asian Survey*, Vol. XIX, July, pp. 674-94.

——— (1979b). "Hong Kong's new tax on offshore banking profits", *Bulletin for International Fiscal Documentation*, Vol. 33, No. 4, Jan. pp. 15-8.

——— (1980). "Hong Kong as a regional financial centre: evolution and prospects", in C.K. Leung, J.W. Cushman, and Wang Gungwu (eds.), *Hong Kong: Dilemmas of Growth* (Canberra: Australian National University Press), pp. 161-194.

——— (1985). "The 1997 issue and Hong Kong's financial crisis", *Journal of Chinese Studies*, Vol. 2, No. 1, April, pp. 113-54.

——— (1986). "Banking and currency in the special economic zones", in Y.C. Jao and C.K. Leung (eds.), *China's Special Economic Zones: Policies, Problems and Prsopects* (Hong Kong: Oxford University Press), pp. 160-83.

——— (1988). (ed.) *Hong Kong's Banking System in Transition: Problems, Prospects and Policies* (Hong Kong: Chinese Banks Association).

Jao, Y.C. and King, F.H.H. (1990). *Money in Hong Kong: Historical Perspective and Contemporary Analysis* (Hong Kong: Centre of Asian Studies, University of Hong Kong).

Johnson, H.G. (1976). "Panama as a regional financial center: a prelminary analysis of development contribution", *Economic Development and Cultural Change*, Vol. 24, pp. 261-86.

Kindleberger, C.P. (1974). *The Formation of Financial Centers: A Study in Comparative Economic History* (Princeton: Princeton University).

King, F.H.H. (1990). "The extraordinary survival of Hong Kong's private note issue", in Jao and King, *op. cit.*, pp. 3-74.

Kirbride, P.S. and Chan E. (1988). "Emigration from Hong Kong: the interim results of an organizational survey", *Human Resources Journal*, Vol. 4, No. 2, pp. 5-17.

Lee, S.Y. (1971). "The Asian Dollar Market in Singapore", *Malayan Economic Review*, Vo. 16, April, pp. 46-56.

———— (1984). "Developing Asian financial centres", paper presented to the 14th Pacific Trade and Development Conference, June 18-21.

———— (1986). *The Monetary and Banking Development of Singapore and Malaysia*, 2nd edition, (Singapore: Singapore University Press).

Lee, S.Y. and Jao, Y.C. (1982). *Financial Structure and Monetary Policies in Southeast Asia* (London: Macmillan Press).

Lessard, D.R. and Tschoegl, A.E. (1988). "Panama's international banking center: the direct employment effects", *Journal of Banking and Finance*, Vol. 12, pp. 43-50.

McCarthy, I. (1979). "Offshore banking centers: benefits and costs", *Finance and Development*, Vol. 16, No. 4, pp. 45-8.

Ministry of Trade & Industry, Republic of Singapore, (1986). *Report of the Economic Committee: The Singapore Economy: New Directions* (Singapore: Singapore National Printers).

Monetary Authority of Singapore, (1989). *The Financial Structure of Singapore, 3rd edition*, (Singapore: Singapore National Printers).

Park, Y.S. (1982). "The economics of offshore financial centers", *Columbia Journal of World Business*, Vol. XVII, No. 4, Winter, pp. 31-5.

Reed, H.C. (1980). "The ascent of Tokyo as an international financial center", *Journal of International Business Studies*, Vol. 11, No. 3, Winter, pp. 19-35.

Shea, J.D. (1990). "Financial development in Taiwan: a macro analysis", May, mimeo.

Sun, I.S. (1984). "Prospects of the Taipei offshore banking center", *Bulletin for International Fiscal Documentation*, Vol. 38, No. 6, pp. 259-60.

Winters, L.A. (1990). "The road to Uruguay", "*Economic Journal*, Vol. 100, No. 403, Dec., pp. 1288-1303.

[22]

Excerpt from Richard Yan-Ki Ho, Robert Haney Scott and Kie Ann Wong (eds), *The Hong Kong Financial System*, 381–405.

17. Hong Kong as an International Financial Centre

RICHARD YAN-KI HO

Introduction

Hong Kong is continually referred to as an important international financial centre. What actually is a financial centre? Every person on the street seems to have a pretty good idea of what it is. They would probably say that a financial centre should have many banks, especially multinational banks; a very active foreign exchange market; a very large equity market; and a variety of other financial institutions and markets. They can keep adding to the list but they have just described the many characteristics of a financial centre, which is a generic term like 'business centre' or 'trade centre'. In a broad sense, a financial centre is a place where financial intermediation services are provided.

In Chapter 1 we discussed the evolution of financial institutions in intermediating funds between fund surplus units and fund deficit units. People with excess funds go to banks to deposit their money, while people in need of funds go to banks to borrow. The bank is thus a location, a focal point or a 'centre', where people use intermediation services. This basic concept also applies to a financial centre.

Within a country, fund surplus units and fund deficit units may not be geographically evenly distributed. Some surplus units may be concentrated in one location and some deficit units may be concentrated in another. The evolution of a financial centre requires that the fund surplus units and the fund deficit units be located in different areas. Funds are thus flowing from one area to another, that is, from fund surplus areas to fund deficit areas. Such a flow of funds across different geographical areas is intermediated through banks in one or a few locations. Thus, the bulk of the funds that are channelled within a country must go through certain areas where most of the big banks are located and where people have the most sophisticated financial know-how. Such locations are called 'financial centres' — examples are New York and San Francisco in the United States. Since they provide intermediation services for people within a country, such centres are usually referred to as domestic financial centres and the funds involved are usually demoninated in local currency.

The concept of domestic financial intermediation can be extended to the international context. In many countries or regions, some borrowers or investors may choose to go overseas to fulfil their financial needs because of insufficient domestic demand for or supply of funds (and hence too high or too low interest rates), inefficient financial markets, or stringent government regulations. Their needs have to be accommodated through financial institutions and markets located elsewhere. Some cities have thus emerged to provide intermediation services for other countries. In this sense, financial centres link different domestic financial markets and institutions. In these centres, people wishing to purchase or issue foreign securities need to purchase or sell foreign currencies, and the foreign exchange market becomes the important link. However, in some cases the participants are really supranational in that they may not need to go through the foreign currency market, for example, a British borrower may borrow United States dollars in order to make payment in United States dollars.

There may be many reasons that a certain area or city evolves into a financial centre in general, or into an international financial centre in particular. Such reasons include:

1. Foreign Exchange Control. A large amount of foreign exchange flows in and out of an international financial centre. Governments that impose foreign exchange control may greatly impede the functioning of the centre.

2. Supply of Funds. The country in which the centre is located may have a huge supply of funds, such as Switzerland or Japan. Although the existence of a trade surplus on the external current account is not a necessary condition for becoming an international financial centre, it will facilitate its formation. In the case of Switzerland, Swiss capital exports developed partly because domestic savings exceeded domestic needs and Switzerland continues to have a very high saving propensity compared with other industrial countries, such as Germany, the United Kingdom, and the United States. Tokyo, Japan, which also has a very high propensity to save, will also naturally evolve into a major international financial centre.

3. Financial Executives. The centre has highly efficient, trained, and experienced financial executives.

4. Environment. The political and economic environment is stable.

5. Communication Systems. There exists an efficient communications system and good air transportation to neighbouring countries.

6. Time Zone and Geographical Location. The centre is located in an appropriate time zone for it to enable certain financial markets, for example, the foreign exchange market or the gold market, to continue trading when the other markets are closed. Physical location is also important. Proximity to potential borrowers is essential for bankers to market their loans and to negotiate with borrowers. Thus, it would be beneficial to the development of a financial centre to be near to countries that have a very high growth rate, are industralizing very rapidly, and have a huge demand for funds.

7. Regulations. Regulations and prudential supervision of the banking system are not unduly stringent, especially to foreign financial institutions.

8. Number of Financial Institutions. There exists a sufficient number of banking and financial institutions to provide a critical mass

for the provision of services to international clients in a highly effective and efficient way. Moreover, most of the syndication loans volume is huge and the sharing of risk among different banks is thus crucial.

9. Inter-bank Money Market. There exists an active inter-bank money market to facilitate an efficient flow of funds among financial institutions within the centre and between centres. Such a market also provides an opportunity for efficiency with minimal amount of risk.

10. Universal Banking Practice. The practice of universal banking, as in the Swiss system, may help in the functioning of a financial centre because banks, under such a system, are able to perform all kinds of banking transactions.

Some Terminology of Financial Centres

As mentioned earlier, the term 'financial centre' is a generic term. There are a number of other terms that need further clarification.

1. Domestic Financial Centres. Domestic financial centres provide intermediation services for local residents in local currency. Good examples include San Francisco in the United States, and Shanghai in China.

2. Global Financial Centres. Global financial centres provide intermediation services for people within their region and also for people outside of their region. The host country of the centre may also have a huge supply of funds. Examples may include London in the United Kingdom and New York in the United States.

3. Regional Financial Centres. Regional financial centres may only provide financial intermediation services for people who live within their region.

4. Offshore Financial Centre. 'Offshore' financial centre is probably the most widely used term. Fig. 17.1 illustrates the difference between a domestic financial centre and an offshore financial centre. An offshore financial centre usually has two features: (1) it usually deals with overseas clients, that is, neither the borrowers (users of funds) nor the lenders (sources of funds) are residents of the country where the financial centre is located, and (2) the transactions are usually denominated in foreign currencies.

London is referred to as one of the most important offshore centres or, in banking terms, one of the most important *Eurocurrency Centres.* The term 'Eurocurrency' is not specific to London. A Eurocurrency transaction is one that is denominated in a currency other than the domestic currency of the place where the transaction is executed. Thus, a United States dollar transaction carried out in London is called a 'Eurodollar deal.' If it is denominated in Japanese yen, it is called 'Euroyen'. One the reasons for the evolution of London into a Eurocurrency centre is the Cold War of the 1950s, which made Russia think that the United States Government would impound its United States dollar holdings in banks in the United States. Russia therefore

Fig. 17.1 Schematic View of Transactions in an International Financial Centre

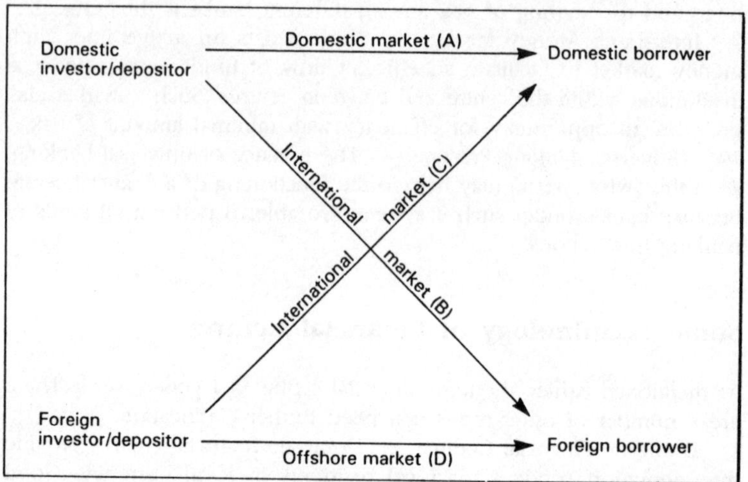

Source: David K. Eiteman and Arthur I. Stonehill, *Multinational Business Finance*, 5th ed. (Reading, Mass., Addison-Wesley, 1989), p. 253. Reprinted by permission of the publisher.

began to deposit its dollars in London, starting the Eurodollar market. Another reason is that, because of the stringent government regulations of the United States banking sector, many United States dollars were transferred to London in the 1950s, making London the most important Eurodollar centre in the world.

Within the family of offshore financial centres, Professor Y. S. Park (1982) delineates four types: primary centres, booking centres, funding centres, and collection centres. A primary centre serves world-wide clients, but the most important uses and sources of funds are within its major market area. These clients both supply funds to and withdraw funds from the centre. Good examples of primary centres are the global centres, that is, London and New York. A booking centre is usually a tax haven. It serves as a centre for booking both Eurocurrency deposits and international loans, but the actual operations and executions are not done there. Such a centre is just used for accounting entries, to capture favourable tax treatment. Nassau and Cayman Island are examples of booking centres. A funding centre plays the role of an inward financial intermediary, channelling funds from outside its market area toward regional uses. Hong Kong and Singapore fall into this category because they usually collect funds from London and lend them to other Asian countries. A collection centre such as Bahrain performs outward financial intermediation functions. There are excess savings generated from the region and the centre collects the funds and invests them efficiently.

Features and Development in International Financial Markets in the 1970s and 1980s

Since banking is the major activity carried out by international financial centres, we highlight here some features of international banking. One of the commonly used measurements of international banking activity is the size of the external claims of the Bank for International Settlements (BIS) reporting banks.[1]

Table 17.1 shows the total cross-border claims of reporting banks. These claims increased from US$1,671.4 billion in 1982 to US$4,485.3

Table 17.1 International Banking Activities (US$ billion)

Year	Total Cross-border Claims	Inside Area Inter-bank Claims	Total Net International Bank Credit
1982	1,671.4	931.8	1,015.0
1983	1,753.9	1,007.3	1,085.0
1984	2,153.5	1,268.5	1,265.0
1985	2,512.7	1,504.9	1,480.0
1986	3,221.1	2,063.3	1,770.0
1987	4,157.2	2,780.2	2,220.0
1988	4,485.3	3,068.1	2,390.0

Source: ***International Banking and Financial Market Development***, Bank for International Settlements, various issues.

Fig. 17.2 International Banking Activities

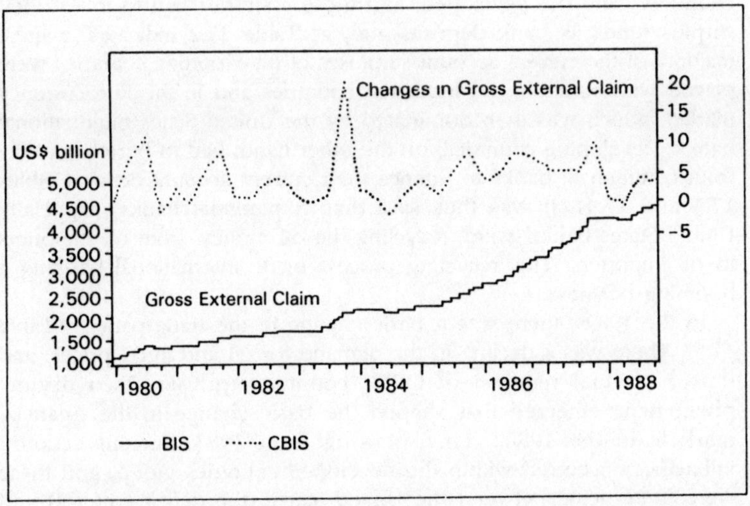

billion in 1988. One of the most striking features is that inter-bank assets within the reporting area contribute a significant share of the total assets, and the share rose from 55.7 per cent in 1982 to 68.4 per cent in 1988. Claims on countries outside the reporting area contribute only about 20 per cent of the share.

Fig. 17.2 shows the gross external assets of the reporting banks from the fourth quarter of 1979 to the fourth quarter of 1988. On the whole, the growth rate was relatively rapid with a compound annual growth rate of 17.2 per cent. However, the growth path was not that smooth. The years 1980 to 1982 and late 1983 to early 1985 were periods of relatively slow growth, but the growth rate picked up in 1985 to late 1987. However, activities began to level off in the first quarter of 1988. While international banking activities moved broadly in line with economic fluctuations, there were some basic structural changes in the international financial market which deserve further elaboration.

Structural Changes in the International Financial Markets

International banking enjoyed tremendous growth during the 1970s. This was due mainly to the two oil crises that occurred during that time. The oil crises created huge surpluses on the part of the oil-exporting countries, that is, the OPEC countries. The developing countries, especially those in Latin America and Asia, also had a huge demand for funds to finance their current account deficit. A concentration of funds in the hands of a few oil exporters initiated the demand for investment opportunities. Financial markets in those OPEC countries were not developed, and those countries had to invest their surplus funds as bank deposits and, as Table 17.2 indicates, a great majority of the current account surpluses of oil-exporting countries were placed with banks in the industrial countries and in the Eurocurrency market, which was then dominated by the United States multinational banks. Developing countries, on the other hand, had to borrow heavily from commercial banks to finance their current account deficit (Tables 17.3 and 17.4). It was thus said that commercial banks, especially United States banks, were 'recycling the oil money' from oil exporters to oil importers. This recycling process made international banking a booming business.

In the 1980s, there was a basic change in the trade pattern (Table 17.5). There was a decline in the demand for oil and in oil prices, and thus a gradual removal of OPEC country surpluses. Two distinct phenomena emerged that shaped the basic change in the financial markets in the 1980s. First, starting from 1983, current account imbalances occurred within the developed countries group, and these were more acute between the United States (the deficit country) and Japan (the surplus country). Second, there was a rapid decline in the

Table 17.2 Oil-exporting Countries: Estimated Disposition of Current Account Surplus, 1974–1983 (US$ billion)

	1974	1975	1976	1977	1978	1979	1980	1981	1982	1983	Total 1974–1983
Current Account Surplus	69	35	39	29	6	63	111	53	–12	–16	377
Plus: Oil sector capital transactions (outflow –)[1]	–12	1	–6	–1	2	–9	–2	3	6	3	–15
Net borrowing[2]	2	3	9	11	16	10	7	7	15	16	96
Equals: Cash surplus available for disposition	59	39	42	39	24	64	116	63	9	3	458
Disposition of Cash Surplus											
International Monetary Fund (IMF) and World Bank[3]	4	3	2	—	–1	–1	1	3	3	6	20
Loans and grants to non-oil-exporting, developing countries[4]	5	7	7	8	9	9	11	10	8	7	81
Bank deposits in industrial countries (net)[5]	30	11	13	13	5	40	42	2	–16	–15	125
Direct placement	7	2	1	2	2	8	6	—	4	—	32
Eurocurrency deposits	23	9	12	11	3	32	36	2	–20	–15	93
Other placements[6]	20	18	20	18	11	16	62	48	14	5	232

Notes:
1. Mainly changes in accounts receivable from oil exports.
2. Total net increase in external liabilities of public and private sectors (including banks). Includes a small amount of money in official transfer, inward non-oil direct investment capital, and miscellaneous capital items. Excludes borrowing from other oil-exporting countries.
3. Includes lending to the IMF, other changes in the reserve position in the IMF, and direct purchases of World Bank bonds.
4. Includes contributions and capital subscriptions to multilateral development agencies (other than the World Bank). Estimates are based on highly uncertain information.
5. Includes deposits in Eurocurrency markets.
6. Includes net acquisitions of government securities, corporate stocks and bonds, bilateral lending (except to non-oil-exporting, developing countries), real estate and other direct investments, and prepayments for imports. Also includes unidentified placements and statistical discrepancies.

Source: International Monetary Fund, *World Economic Outlook*, various issues.

Table 17.3 Non-oil-exporting, Developing Countries: Financing of Current Account Deficits and Reserve Accretions, 1977–1984 (US$ billion)

	1977	1978	1979	1980	1981	1982	1983	1984
Current Account Deficit	30.4	42.3	62.0	87.7	109.1	82.2	56.4	50.0
Increase in official reserves	11.5	16.3	11.8	6.8	5.4	–3.8	6.1	13.3
Total	41.9	58.6	73.8	94.5	114.5	78.4	62.5	63.3
Financed by								
Non-debt-creating flows, net	14.1	17.0	23.7	24.1	27.2	23.9	21.3	23.0
Long-term borrowing from official creditors, net	13.1	13.8	17.0	20.0	22.6	21.6	22.6	23.1
Borrowing from private creditors, net	18.4	32.8	36.5	60.6	70.5	36.2	20.2	21.2
Reserve-related liabilities	2.9	2.0	–0.5	5.3	9.8	15.4	8.4	1.0
Errors and omissions	–6.5	–6.9	–3.0	–15.4	–15.5	–18.8	–10.0	–5.0
				(In Per cent)				
Distribution of Financing Flows								
Non-debt-creating flows, net	33.6	28.9	32.2	25.5	23.8	30.6	34.1	36.3
Long-term borrowing from official creditors, net	31.3	23.5	23.0	21.1	19.7	27.5	36.1	36.5
Borrowing from private creditors, net	43.8	55.9	49.5	64.1	61.6	46.2	32.3	33.5
Reserve-related liabilities	6.9	3.4	–0.6	5.7	8.5	19.6	13.4	1.6
Errors and omissions	–15.5	–11.8	–4.1	–16.3	–13.6	–24.0	–15.9	–7.9

Note: Figures are rounded to the nearest tenth.

Source: International Monetary Fund, *World Economic Outlook*, various issues.

Table 17.4 Developing Countries: External Debt Outstanding, 1977–1984 (US$ billion)

	1977	1978	1979	1980	1981	1982	1983	1984
Total External Debt*	329.3	398.2	472.0	559.9	646.5	724.8	767.6	812.4
Short-term debt	51.7	63.7	75.8	106.5	128.1	148.2	126.2	97.6
Long-term debt	277.7	334.5	396.3	453.4	518.4	576.6	641.4	714.8
By Type of Creditor								
Official creditors	111.0	130.6	148.5	169.1	186.0	205.4	229.6	254.4
Governments	79.1	91.8	102.2	114.3	123.6	134.9	150.8	166.4
International institutions	31.9	38.8	46.4	54.8	62.4	70.5	78.9	88.0
Private Creditors	166.7	203.9	247.7	284.3	332.4	371.2	411.8	460.4
Unguaranteed debt	55.1	56.6	67.8	81.0	100.8	108.4	110.5	112.3
Guaranteed debt	111.6	147.3	179.9	203.2	231.6	262.8	301.3	348.1
Financial institutions	78.9	107.4	137.5	160.0	185.5	212.4	250.0	296.3
Other private creditors	32.7	39.9	42.4	43.2	46.1	50.4	51.3	51.8

Note: *Figures are rounded to the nearest tenth.

Source: International Monetary Fund, *World Economic Outlook*, various issues.

Table 17.5 Summary of Payment Balances on Current Account, 1979–1988* (US$ billion)

	1979	1980	1981	1982	1983	1984	1985	1986	1987	1988
Industrial Countries	–23.1	–60.5	–18.7	–22.3	–19.5	–58.5	–51.4	–18.1	–38.9	–44.2
United States	–1.0	1.9	6.9	–8.7	–46.3	–107.0	–116.4	–141.4	–152.1	–140.6
Other industrial countries	–22.1	–62.4	–25.6	–13.6	26.7	48.5	64.9	123.3	113.2	96.4
Japan	–8.8	–10.7	4.8	6.9	20.8	35.0	49.3	85.8	85.1	83.2
Germany, Fed. Rep. of	–6.0	–15.7	–5.2	4.1	4.2	8.4	15.2	37.2	40.7	32.5
Developing Countries	6.4	30.4	–48.5	–87.1	–64.2	–33.8	–23.9	–47.0	–19.6	–19.3
Africa	–3.4	–1.9	–22.4	–21.5	–12.3	–8.0	–0.1	–9.4	–7.5	–6.1
Asia	–9.7	–14.4	–19.0	–17.4	–14.9	–4.2	–14.0	4.9	15.3	10.0
Europe	–13.6	–15.6	–14.3	–8.7	–5.9	–3.2	–3.3	–1.7	–2.3	–2.5
Middle East	54.2	92.5	50.0	3.0	–20.1	–15.8	–2.2	–23.3	–12.1	–7.0
Western Hemisphere	–21.1	–30.2	–42.7	–42.5	–10.9	–2.6	–4.3	–17.5	–13.1	–13.8

Notes: * Includes official transfers.
Figures are rounded to the nearest tenth.

Source: International Monetary Fund, *World Economic Outlook*, various issues.

current account deficit in developing countries, and the Asian developing countries (especially Hong Kong, Singapore, Taiwan, and Korea) actually enjoyed a current account surplus starting from 1986, indicating that there was a corresponding decrease in fund demand. Since both the major deficit and surplus countries were developed countries where matured financial markets existed, the 'recycling of trade money' did not have to be carried out by commercial banks alone. Indeed, because of the expertise that the surplus countries had in portfolio investment, they could directly buy securities, that is, bonds, stocks, commercial paper, and various notes issued directly by the deficit countries. Thus, the Japanese have been a major buyer of United States securities, bringing life to the direct securities market in the 1980s.

As shown in Table 17.6, international bond issues increased from US$34 billion in 1976 to a peak of US$227 billion in 1986 (net international bond issues also increased from US$26 billion to US$87 billion). During the same period, net international lending (net of redepositing) increased from US$70 billion in 1976, peaked at US$165 billion in 1981, then declined to a low of US$90 billion in 1984 but recovered to US$165 billion in 1986. Thus, the ratio of bond issues to imports decreased from 2.8 per cent in 1976 to a historical low of 1.0 per cent in 1980, but then picked up rapidly to reach 4.1 per cent in 1986. The ratio of bond issues to bank lending followed roughly the same trend, but the ratio peaked in 1985 and declined in 1986, showing a recovery in the international lending market. However, a slow-down occurred in 1987, especially after the stock-market crash in October of that year.

There were three factors affecting the development of the international bond market during the past few years. The first is the rise in the market interest rate, which affected the fixed-rate securities market the most. The weakness of the United States dollar and the expectation of further depreciation also dampened the issue of United States dollar denominated bonds. Before the 1987 October Crash, one of the driving forces behind the activity in equity-related issues, mostly in the form of equity warrants, was the buoyancy of the stock-market. Such equity-related issues declined tremendously during the fourth quarter of 1987. Moreover, the collapse of the perpetual Floating-rate Notes (FRNs) market in late 1986 also affected 1987 activities. Since their first appearance in 1984 up to 1986, the total perpetual FRNs issued was US$18 billion, and US$7.4 billion was issued in 1986. In late 1986, it was perceived that such perpetual FRNs were severely underpriced and in December 1986 no investors wanted to purchase any perpetual FRNs and the price dropped sharply. Because of a drop in the bond market activities, 1987 saw a rapid recovery in the syndication loan market, the volume of which increased from US$24.8 billion in 1986 to US$53.2 billion in 1987. In early 1988, the international bond market staged a strong recovery owing to a stable interest rate and exchange rate environment.

Table 17.6 Size of International Financial Markets, 1976–1986 (US$ billion)

	1976	1977	1978	1979	1980	1981	1982	1983	1984	1985	1986
Total gross international bond issues	34	36	36	39	38	52	76	77	110	168	227
International bond issues (net)[1]	26	27	24	23	19	29	49	46	62	77	87
International bank lending (net of redepositing)	70	68	90	125	160	165	95	85	90	105	165
International bond issues (net) deflated by U.S. GNP deflator	24	24	20	17	13	18	29	26	34	41	45.2
International bank lending (net) deflated by U.S. GNP deflator	66	60	74	94	111	105	56	49	50	56	86
					(In Per cent)						
Bond issues as ratio to world imports (in U.S. dollars)	2.8	2.5	1.9	1.5	1.0	1.5	2.7	2.6	3.3	4.0	4.1
International bank lending (net) as ratio to world imports (in U.S. dollars)	7.5	4.6	7.2	7.8	8.6	8.7	5.2	4.9	4.9	5.6	7.8
International bond issues (net) as ratio to international bank lending (net)	37.1	39.7	26.7	18.4	11.9	17.6	51.6	54.1	68.9	73.3	52.7

Note: 1. New international bond issues less redemptions, repurchases, and bank purchases of bonds.

Sources: International Monetary Fund, *World Economic Outlook* and *International Financial Statistics*, Organization for Economic Co-operation and Development, *Financial Market Trends*; and Bank for International Settlements.

Table 17.7 The Presence of the World's 500 Largest Banks in Hong Kong

World Ranking[1]	Licensed Overseas Banks in Hong Kong		Licensed Deposit-taking Companies Owned by Overseas Banks[2]		Registered Deposit-taking Companies Owned by Overseas Banks[2]		Local Representative Offices	
	1987	1989	1987	1989	1987	1989	1987	1989
1–20	18	19	3	6	18	17	1	0
21–50	25	26	5	2	21	16	3	0
51–100	33	32	4	4	22	22	6	7
101–200	15	24	1	1	16	19	29	24
201–500	11	16	5	4	22	23	41	50
Others	18	17	2	3	34	31	63	79
Total	120	134	20	20	133	128	143	160

Notes: 1. Top 500 banks/banking groups in the world ranked by total assets less contra items.
2. Figures in these columns represent the number of deposit-taking companies which are branches or subsidiaries of overseas banks, classified in accordance with the world ranking of these overseas banks.

Sources: Figures for 1987 and 1989 are extracted from *The Banker*, July 1987 and 1989 issues.

The Position of Hong Kong in the World Financial Market

People like to call Hong Kong the third largest financial centre in the world. Does Hong Kong really qualify for the third rank in the world financial scene? This is a very difficult question, and the rank will change under different criteria. According to an estimate by Jao (1988a), by world standards Hong Kong is the fourth largest loan syndication centre, the fifth largest foreign exchange trading centre, the fourth largest foreign bank centre (in terms of number), and the eleventh largest centre in terms of external assets of banks.[2]

Indeed, Hong Kong is an international banking centre. As indicated in Table 17.7, there was an increase in the representation of the world's largest banks in Hong Kong. Nineteen of the twenty largest banks in the world maintained a full-fledged licensed bank in Hong Kong in 1989. It is natural that most of these banks come from Japan and the United States. However, there was no increase in representation in the form of licensed DTCs, and there was even a decrease in the number of registered DTCs owned by overseas banks, while there was an increase in branches of foreign banks. This indicates that DTCs, especially registered DTCs, have limited usefulness to overseas financial institutions.

Table 17.8 shows the amount of foreign currency deposits in the Hong Kong banking system (including licensed banks and DTCs) which is another indication of the development of Hong Kong as a financial centre. There was an increase in foreign currency deposits from 1980 to 1989 and the share of foreign currency deposits in total deposits increased from 12.2 per cent to 60.1 per cent. The most dramatic rise occurred in 1982 when the Hong Kong Government abolished the

Table 17.8 Customer Foreign Currency Deposit

Year	Amount (HK$ million)	Per cent in Total Deposits
1980	10,621	12.2
1981	18,588	17.8
1982	82,384	43.3
1983	115,200	48.0
1984	138,099	46.6
1985	193,104	52.6
1986	278,016	56.6
1987	363,192	56.6
1988	498,766	59.0
1989	620,017	61.5

Note: These figures include deposits of both licensed banks and DTCs.

Source: *Hong Kong Monthly Digest of Statistics* (Hong Kong, Census and Statistics Department), various issues.

withholding tax on the interest earned from foreign currency deposits. Of course, due to the depreciating Hong Kong currency, the increase in the shares during the period of 1980 to 1983 was partly due to the exchange rate valuation effect. However, since the linked exchange rate was established in late 1983, such a currency valuation effect was minimal.[3]

Functions Performed by the Hong Kong Financial Centre

As a financial centre or an international banking centre, Hong Kong performs three main functions: financial intermediation, clearing, and maturity transformation.

Financial Intermediation

Table 17.9 gives the total net claim position (total assets minus total liabilities) of the Hong Kong banking system (including licensed banks, LDTCs, and RDTCs) *vis-à-vis* other countries or regions. Some of the most salient features of the net position from 1979 to 1988 are described here. Please note that a positive net claim means that Hong Kong is a net creditor to other countries or regions, while a negative net claim means that Hong Kong is a net debtor to other countries or regions.

On the whole, Hong Kong is a net creditor to the rest of the world. In 1979, Hong Kong had a net claim of US$3,872 million *vis-à-vis* the rest of the world and this net claim increased very rapidly to US$40,218 million in 1988 with a compound annual growth of 29.7 per cent. This indicates that Hong Kong also provides funds to the rest of the world. Hong Kong was also a net creditor to the rest of the Asia Pacific region and there was a consistent increase in the net position, from US$5.7 billion in 1979 to US$42.0 billion in 1988, an annual increase of 24.8 per cent. In the Asia Pacific region, the major net debtor countries are Japan, China, Taiwan, South Korea, and Australia. China used to be a net creditor *vis-à-vis* Hong Kong, from 1982 to 1984, but started to take a net debtor position in 1985. This net debt increased to US$5.2 billion in 1988. This was mainly due to the need for financing China's trade deficit and its huge modernization programme. South Korea used to be Hong Kong's largest net debtor, as demonstrated by the fact that Korea's net debt reached a high of US$7.1 billion in 1986, but due to an improvement in its current account, its net debt was gradually reduced to US$4.1 billion, indicating that South Korea was retiring some of its debt.

The increase in net claims of Hong Kong on both Japan and Taiwan was also very rapid (47.5 per cent for Japan and 21.6 per cent for Taiwan), but such an increase did not seem to relate to their trade deficit financing because both these countries have enjoyed huge trade surpluses over the years. There is a general trend for Taiwan to borrow

Table 17.9 Net Claims of the Hong Kong Financial System *vis-à-vis* Other Countries (US$ million)

	1979	1980	1981	1982	1983	1984	1985	1986	1987	1988
International Organizations	0	0	0	0	0	0	0	135	143	313
Asia Pacific	5,741	5,101	1,946	6,353	8,269	11,135	12,121	28,083	42,010	41,972
Australia	197	183	443	733	1,166	1,224	1,122	1,663	1,651	3,430
Bangladesh	0	6	5	12	8	12	25	23	54	25
Brunei	−2	0	1	7	27	30	16	−18	−71	−75
Burma	−59	21	9	9	5	2	−14	0	13	0
China	1,156	1,297	346	−838	−1,178	−1,366	1,098	1,921	2,235	5,237
Taiwan	727	1,167	1,026	972	1,244	432	53	1,833	4,379	4,219
Fiji	8	4	11	12	14	16	−3	3	4	−2
French Polynesia	0	0	0	0	0	0	−1	4	11	−1
India	119	102	73	111	227	344	748	629	916	1,343
Indonesia	955	831	441	1,008	1,139	948	820	1,202	970	1,159
Japan	693	187	537	1,591	356	2,947	2,589	14,291	26,514	22,938
Kampuchea	0	0	0	0	0	0	0	0	−1	−1
Laos	0	0	0	0	0	0	−1	0	−1	0
Macau	−226	−464	−390	−209	−95	84	172	269	472	−141
Malaysia	237	295	616	651	1,513	888	800	813	754	655
Nepal	11	12	8	−1	0	−2	0	2	−3	−1
New Zealand	165	276	310	558	510	536	436	467	1,200	2,466
North Korea	2	62	−6	4	8	1	12	41	−45	−11
Pakistan	8	9	20	24	44	40	86	109	34	77
Papua New Guinea	−13	31	99	137	163	188	187	139	123	84
Philippines	1,033	1,722	2,001	2,255	2,365	2,224	2,289	2,182	2,351	1,765
Singapore	−3,227	−4,686	−6,437	−5,082	−4,610	−3,882	−5,701	−6,021	−5,170	−5,101
Solomon Islands	0	0	3	−3	−5	75	227	329	−18	−6
South Korea	1,858	2,307	3,324	4,480	5,538	6,131	6,924	7,135	5,757	4,148
Sri Lanka	−17	6	22	163	146	188	102	201	70	59
Thailand	518	670	1,282	1,150	1,245	1,402	1,428	1,182	1,535	1,748
Vanuatu	1,475	1,180	−960	−1,113	−1,058	−935	−956	−1,258	−1,570	−1,911
Vietnam	80	57	48	37	28	26	33	30	27	22
Others	42	−171	−889	−317	−530	−418	−369	−594	−210	−155
Africa	1,691	1,929	1,958	1,752	1,607	1,829	1,851	1,859	2,087	2,034
North America	−995	−243	−44	−1,851	−2,207	−2,085	323	194	1,782	2,170
Latin America	630	805	1,139	1,111	1,170	1,149	1,108	923	942	791
Caribbean	198	−261	1,841	1,468	1,104	3,169	4,330	5,341	5,893	4,052
Middle East	−732	−805	−938	−571	−519	−1,111	−1,888	−2,330	−2,435	−2,616
Western Europe	−2,893	−5,009	−5,269	−4,543	−1,837	−1,558	−317	−3,749	14,519	−9,452
Eastern Europe	191	283	282	341	306	268	245	383	507	941
Unallocated	0	0	0	0	0	0	0	70	53	89
Total	3,872	1,924	959	4,103	7,953	12,834	17,867	29,466	36,462	40,216

Source: *Hong Kong Monthly Digest of Statistics* (Hong Kong, Census and Statistics Department), various issues.

in the international financial market because of the expected appreciation of the New Taiwan dollar.[4]

Between 1979 and 1988 Hong Kong consistently remained a net debtor *vis-à-vis* western Europe and the Middle East, indicating that these two regions were net suppliers of funds to the Hong Kong financial centre. Within western Europe, the great bulk of funds were supplied through the London centre. North America used to be another net fund supplier up until 1984 but turned into a net debtor *vis-à-vis* Hong Kong in 1985, and this net debt has increased tremendously since, at an annual rate of 88.7 per cent. Obviously, this is consistent with the world trend that the United States has also turned into a net debtor *vis-à-vis* the rest of the world in view of its rapidly increasing trade and budget deficits.

Inter-bank Activities[5]

Inter-bank borrowing and lending are an integral part of the international financial intermediation process. Indeed, in the offshore markets, wholesale inter-bank activities tend to dominate. The international inter-bank market is basically an informal market for banks lending to each other. The amount of transactions is usually very large (at least US$1 million) and of relatively short maturity (usually shorter than six months). All transactions are done through telecommunication networks between the banks' dealers or through money brokers. The major currency for international inter-bank deals is United States dollars, but other currencies such as the Deutschemark, Swiss franc, and Japanese yen are gaining importance. Since inter-bank loans are unsecured, banks participating in the market have to have good credit ranking. Banks with different credit standings are granted different credit limits, and their borrowings are also priced differently.

There are several reasons for the use of the inter-bank market:

1. Balancing Uses and Sources of Funds. At a certain point in time, some banks may find that they have more deposits than they can use, while other banks may find themselves in the opposite position. Thus, the inter-bank market serves as a central market for banks to handle their surpluses and deficits. Non-bank depositors and end-users of funds can be matched more efficiently, though indirectly, through such a market. In the international arena, the picture is more complicated because some banks may have more expertise in dealing in certain currencies and with certain regions or countries. Thus, some banks may need to go through the inter-bank market to deal in currencies or regions and countries that are not familiar to them.
2. Risk Management. The inter-bank market can also be used to manage interest rate risk and exchange rate risk by lending or borrowing funds with similar maturities or currencies.
3. Profit Making. Banks may use the inter-bank market to generate profit, a transaction that may not be related to the ultimate needs of their customers. Banks, for example, may borrow three-month funds

and place them for six months when the yield curve is positive and the banks are expecting a fall in the interest rate. The banks are thus trying to generate profit by taking additional risk. Transactions such as interest rate arbitrage and currency swaps also provide sources of income.

Table 17.10 shows the external claims of the Hong Kong financial system (including banks and DTCs) *vis-à-vis* banks and non-banks. It shows that claims on banks account for 64.5 per cent of total external assets and claims on non-banks account for 35.5 per cent of the total in 1979. However, in recent years, (from 1985 to 1988), claims on banks usually account for more than 80 per cent of the total external claims. No corresponding data exist on the liability side. However, the external position of the BIS reporting banks *vis-à-vis* Hong Kong is available, and Table 17.11 indicates that the contribution of inter-bank transactions between Hong Kong and the BIS reporting countries is even more pronounced. In both 1987 and 1988, inter-bank transactions are shown to account for more than 90 per cent of the transactions. In both cases, the trend for inter-bank activities is generally upward, indicating the increasing dominance of wholesale business in the financial centre of Hong Kong.

Maturity Transformation

Banks are usually said to implement maturity transformation by borrowing short and lending long. Thus, banks can be said to manufacture liquidity, which is important in the functioning of the economy. This is because borrowers can have access to a stable source of funds while holders of funds can invest in highly liquid assets.

Since there are no published data on the maturity structure of the asset and liability items of the Hong Kong banking system, it is impossible to demonstrate the maturity transformation process of the Hong Kong centre. However, Hong Kong and Singapore are very similar, and it may be useful to look at the maturity distribution of the Singapore Asian dollar market (Table 17.12). It is obvious that the Asian dollar market has a larger proportion of short-term liabilities and a relatively larger proportion of long-term assets. It is believed that in the late 1960s and early 1970s, the Asian dollar market served as a conduit of funds from the Asian region to Europe and North America because of the higher interest rates and the lack of investment opportunities in the Southeast Asia region. At that time, the main borrowers were banks. Thus, the maturities of assets and liabilities of banks in the Asian dollar market were carefully matched. Starting in the mid-1970s, funds began to flow from Europe and the United States back to the developing countries in Asia (especially South-east Asia). This has changed the maturity structure of assets and liabilities in the market, with relatively longer term assets and shorter term liabilities. Thus, the function of maturity transformation has been carried out more effectively since the mid-1970s.[6]

Table 17.10 External Claims *vis-à-vis* Banks and Non-banks of the Hong Kong Financial System (US$ million)

Year	Bank		Non-Bank		Total Claims
1979	16,124	(64.5)	8,865	(35.5)	24,990
1980	23,303	(67.5)	11,215	(32.5)	34,518
1981	32,335	(69.8)	13,968	(30.2)	46,193
1982	42,443	(72.9)	15,783	(27.1)	58,225
1983	50,345	(74.3)	17,404	(25.7)	67,749
1984	59,869	(75.8)	19,062	(24.2)	78,931
1985	81,670	(80.6)	19,617	(19.4)	101,288
1986	132,678	(85.4)	22,596	(14.6)	155,274
1987	217,696	(82.2)	47,163	(17.8)	264,859
1988	252,808	(81.5)	57,370	(18.5)	310,178

Note: Figures in parentheses are proportions (in percentage) of the total.

Source: *Hong Kong Monthly Digest of Statistics* (Hong Kong, Census and Statistics Department), various issues.

Table 17.11 External Position of Banks in Twelve Reporting Countries *vis-à-vis* Hong Kong (US$ million)

	Assets			Liabilities		
	Bank	Non-Bank	Total	Bank	Non-Bank	Total
1982	23,948 (84.5)	4,393 (15.5)	28,341	16,802 (71.0)	6,876 (29.0)	23,678
1983	30,443 (85.4)	5,200 (14.6)	35,643	22,922 (74.2)	7,974 (25.8)	30,896
1984	54,273 (90.0)	6,049 (10.0)	60,322	52,127 (82.5)	11,062 (17.5)	63,189
1985	70,307 (90.3)	7,550 (9.7)	77,857	69,179 (84.1)	13,114 (15.9)	82,293
1986	110,697 (92.1)	9,452 (7.9)	120,149	115,599 (88.4)	15,153 (11.6)	130,752
1987	216,647 (95.9)	9,305 (4.1)	225,952	208,119 (92.3)	17,271 (7.7)	225,390
1988	249,643 (96.2)	9,771 (3.8)	259,414	243,024 (92.5)	19,626 (7.5)	262,650

Note: Figures in parentheses are proportions (in percentage) of the total.

Source: Bank for International Settlements, *International Banking Developments*, various issues.

Table 17.12 Maturity Structure of Assets and Liabilities of the Singapore Asian Dollar Market (in percentages)

	1976		1980		1984		1988	
	Assets	Liabilities	Assets	Liabilities	Assets	Liabilities	Assets	Liabilities
≤ 1 month	35.1	49.2	32.6	44.4	35.6	46.1	42.8	54.8
> 1–3 months	27.3	28.0	26.8	30.1	23.9	30.0	24.3	22.8
> 3–12 months	20.9	19.4	21.6	20.5	20.4	21.1	17.4	16.1
> 1–3 years	3.2	1.6	5.5	3.0	4.1	1.3	4.4	2.0
> 3 years	13.5	1.9	13.5	2.0	16.0	1.6	10.9	4.3

Source: Monetary Authority of Singapore, *Monthly Statistical Bulletin*, various issues.

Prospects and Problems[7]

There are now five offshore banking centres in Asia.[7] They are Hong Kong, Manila, Taipei, Singapore, and Tokyo. However, the development of Manila's Offshore Banking Units is not very successful because its telecommunication system is underdeveloped, its inter-bank market is inactive, and its political environment is very unstable. The Taiwan Offshore Banking Units were set up in 1984. However, the Taiwan banking system is less sophisticated and more heavily regulated than that of Hong Kong. Thus, Hong Kong's real competitors seem to be Singapore and Tokyo.

Jao (1988a) provides a detailed comparison of these three centres in his book, which is summarized briefly here.

Hong Kong Versus Singapore

Advantages

(a) Hong Kong is an integrated financial centre in that foreign banks as well as DTCs can engage in offshore and domestic business.
(b) The policy of the Hong Kong Government is more liberal than that of Singapore, and financial regulations are more lenient.
(c) The tax rate is very low and the tax system is very simple.[8] Moreover, overseas income is generally exempt from taxation.
(d) Hong Kong has a longer tradition of being a syndication and fund management centre than does Singapore.
(e) Hong Kong's economy is bigger than Singapore's. Thus, both business and financial transactions are more active in Hong Kong than in Singapore.
(f) The gold and equity markets in Hong Kong are much larger and more active than those of Singapore, and this is more attractive to foreign investors and fund managers.
(g) Because of its proximity to and traditional ties with China, Hong Kong is likely to benefit from the positive effects of the China's open door policy especially in terms of financing China trade and China's financial needs.

Disadvantages

(a) Because of the political uncertainty surrounding the resumption of sovereignty by China in 1997, the political risk of Hong Kong is higher than that of Singapore.
(b) Hong Kong seems to be less stable financially as demonstrated by the frequency of banking or financial crises.
(c) Hong Kong seems to lag behind Singapore in developing financial markets and instruments. Obvious examples include the Asian dollar market, the Asian bond market, the financial futures market (the Simex), and the discount houses.
(d) The Hong Kong Government does not have a long-term and

consciously formulated plan to foster the development of Hong Kong as a financial centre.

Hong Kong Versus Tokyo

Advantages

(a) Again, Hong Kong is an integrated financial centre while the Tokyo Offshore Banking Units are segregated from the domestic market.
(b) The policy of the Hong Kong Government is more liberal and financial regulations are more lenient than Tokyo's.
(c) The Hong Kong tax rate is very low, the tax system is simple, and overseas income is exempt.
(d) The Hong Kong legal system is based on that of the United Kingdom, and English is more widely used than in Tokyo.
(e) The cost of operating an office in Hong Kong is cheaper than it is in Tokyo.
(f) Again, proximity to China may also benefit Hong Kong.

Disadvantages

(a) The Hong Kong political risk may be higher than that of Tokyo, again because of the problem posed by the political changes of 1997.
(b) Hong Kong may be more unstable financially than Tokyo, as seen by its record of financial crises.
(c) The size of the Hong Kong economy is much smaller than that of Japan and Hong Kong itself cannot generate as many funds (and denominated in a stable and strong currency) as Japan.
(d) The capital market of Hong Kong is much less developed than that of Tokyo.

Discussion

In addition to their competitive relationship, the Hong Kong, Singapore, and Tokyo centres complement each other. It has long been recognized that Singapore is a funding centre while Hong Kong is a lending centre, because the countries surrounding Singapore, for example, Malaysia and Indonesia, are not able to absorb all the funds in the Asian dollar market. Hong Kong can thus serve as a conduit of funds from the Asian dollar market to South Korea, Taiwan, Australia, China, and Hong Kong itself.

The establishment of the Offshore Banking Units in Tokyo has not diverted business from Hong Kong. Hong Kong may, in fact, benefit from Japan's financial liberalization because more business is generated in foreign exchange and securities dealings. Moreover, the nature of the two markets is different. The Tokyo market is more efficient in long-term financing, while the Hong Kong market (and the Singapore one) are more efficient in short- to medium-term financing.

Indeed, in a survey done by this author in late 1986 on ten major Japanese banks in Hong Kong, it was confirmed that the prospect for Hong Kong as a centre for short- to medium-term financing as well as a place for arranging China-related financing packages was very good. In the survey, 60 per cent of the respondents believed that the prospects of Hong Kong remaining a market for medium-term syndication loans and a market for arranging short- to medium-term financial instruments (including certificates of deposit, commercial paper, note-issuing facilities, and revolving underwriting facilities) in the next ten years was 'very good' to 'extremely good'. Seventy per cent of the respondents believed that the prospects of Hong Kong remaining a market for arranging China financing packages in the next ten years were 'very good' to 'extremely good'. However, the prospects for being a market for long-term financing does not seem to be as promising as short- to medium-term financing.

Until May 1989, the China factor seemed to be working in favour of Hong Kong's development. However, the political turmoil in China in May to June of 1989 shook the confidence of Hong Kong people very badly. The Hang Seng Index dropped from the post-crash high of 3,310 points (on 15 May 1989) to a low of 2,094 points (on 5 June 1989). In August 1989, the dust seemed to settle. Activities in the property market started to pick up, and the Hang Seng Index recovered very rapidly and reached a level of around 2,900 by the end of 1989.

After the June 4th events, many multilateral lenders such as the World Bank and the ADB and foreign commercial banks suspended new loans to China. Hong Kong may be affected by such movements because China has become one of Hong Kong's major borrowers, and also one of Asia's biggest borrowers, since the mid-1980s. Hong Kong would definitely earn less on fees and interest by arranging loans to China. However, according to a report published in the *Asian Wall Street Journal*, China would have no difficulties in meeting scheduled repayments for its debt and China's debt service ratio is still considered to be low by world standards.[9] Thus, given that China can contain its economic problems of quickening inflation and a widening trade deficit, China's credit ranking would remain fairly good. If a go-ahead is given by both the World Bank and the ADB, the commercial banks would still continue to lend money to China. Moreover, Australia and other rapidly industrializing Asian countries, such as Thailand and Malaysia, still have a great demand for funds. In the future, we can see Tokyo develop into a global financial centre of the same status as New York and London. Hong Kong and Singapore will perform the functions of 'satellite' centres, complementary to the Tokyo one, which also functions as a fund-supplying centre. Although Singapore has been trying very hard to promote its fund management business, Hong Kong remains superior because of its excellent telecommunications system and financial expertise. There is no doubt that Singapore would capitalize on the growth potential of countries such as Indonesia, Malaysia, and Thailand, but such countries may not be able to absorb all the funds deposited in Singapore. Hong Kong would remain a natural centre for absorbing Singapore's excess funds. Moreover, although Taiwan has also been promoting its role as a financial centre by establishing the Offshore Banking Units in 1984, its financial markets are still underdeveloped. This author envisages that Taiwan would still require the financial intermediation services provided by the Hong Kong centre. All these elements together with the recovery of China's relationship with western countries would further strengthen the role of Hong Kong as an international financial centre.

Notes

1. The BIS reporting banks include banks in the group of ten countries (Belgium, Canada, France, Germany, Italy, Japan, the Netherlands, Sweden, the United Kingdom, and the United States) plus Luxemburg, Austria, Denmark, Finland, Ireland, Norway, and Spain, as well as banks engaged in international business in the Bahamas, the Cayman Islands, Hong Kong, and Singapore, all offshore units in Bahrain, all offshore banks operating in the Netherlands Antilles, and the branches of United States banks in Panama.
2. Y. C. Jao (ed.), *Hong Kong's Banking System in Transition: Problems, Prospects, and Policies*, (Hong Kong, Chinese Banks Association Ltd., 1988).
3. However, due to the rapid depreciating United States dollar *vis-à-vis* other currencies, there was a rapid increase in other non-United States dollar foreign currency deposits in Hong Kong in 1987 and 1988 (notably the Australian dollar and the New Zealand dollar). Thus, the exchange rate movement has affected the share of foreign currency deposits in these two years.
4. See 'International Banking and Financial Developments', Bank for International Settlements, May 1988.
5. This section is partly taken from 'The International Interbank Market: A Descriptive Study', *BIS Economic Papers*, No. 8, July 1983.
6. This is the observation made by Kenneth Bernauer, 'The Asian Dollar Market', *Economic Review*, No. 1, FRB-San Francisco, Winter 1983.
7. This section draws heavily from Y. C. Jao (ed.), *Hong Kong's Banking System in Transition: Problems, Prospects, and Policies*, (Hong Kong, Chinese Banks Association Ltd., 1988).
8. The current tax rate for personal income is 15 per cent and the current profit tax is 16.5 per cent.
9. See Christopher Hunt, 'China's Rising Debt Isn't Yet a Problem', *Asian Wall Street Journal*, 14–15 July 1989.

References

Bank for International Settlements, 'The International Interbank Market, a Descriptive Study, *BIS Economic Papers*, No. 8, July 1983.

—— *International Banking Developments*, various issues.

Bernauer, Kenneth, 'The Asian Dollar Market', *Economic Review*, No. 1, FRB-San Francisco, Winter 1983.

Ho, Y. K., 'The Role of Hong Kong and Singapore in the International Financial Intermediation Process', paper presented at the *Conference on Research in International Finance*, Centre HEC-ISA, Jouy-en-Josas, France, June 19–20, 1986.

Jao, Y. C., *Banking and Currency in Hong Kong*, (London, Macmillan Press, 1974).

—— 'Financial Structure and Monetary Policy in Hong Kong', in S. Y. Lee and

Y. C. Jao (eds.), *Financial Structures and Monetary Policies in Southeast Asia*, (London, Macmillan Press, 1982).

—— 'The Rise of Hong Kong as a Regional Financial Centre', *Asian Survey*, July 1979, pp. 674–94.

—— 'Hong Kong as a Regional Financial Centre: Evolution and Prospects', in C. K. Leung, J. W. Cushman, and Wang Gungwu (eds.), *Hong Kong: Dilemmas of Growth*, (Canberra, Australian National University Press, 1980), pp. 161–94.

—— (ed.), *Hong Kong's Banking System in Transition: Problems, Prospects, and Policies*, (Hong Kong, Chinese Banks Association, 1988a).

—— 'Monetary System and Banking Structure', in H. C. Y. Ho and L. C. Chau (eds.), *The Economic System of Hong Kong*, (Hong Kong, Asian Research Service, 1988b).

Park, Y. S., 'The Economics of Offshore Financial Centres', *Columbia Journal of World Business*, Winter 1982, pp. 31–5.

Scott, R. H., Wong K. A., and Ho Y. K. (eds.), *Hong Kong's Financial Institutions and Markets*, (Hong Kong, Oxford University Press, 1986).

[23]

Excerpt from Phillip D. Grub, Tan Chwee Huat, Kwan Kuen-Chor and George H. Rott (eds), *East Asia Dimensions of International Business*, 21–8.

3 A Comparison of Hong Kong and Singapore as Asian Financial Centres

Prof. Yoon S. Park

Dr Yoon Sik Park is an Associate Professor of International Finance and Banking at The George Washington University. He has had extensive background in the finance and banking areas as Senior Economist at the World Bank and at the International Finance Corporation.

Role of International Financial Centres

Since the late 1960s, a number of international financial centres have emerged in Asia. These include Singapore, Hong Kong, Tokyo and Manila. The rapid economic development of many Asian countries in the 1970s has attracted international banks to Asia. On the surface, Tokyo seemed the idea place as 'the' financial centre for Asia, with Japan's prosperous and dynamic economy, her huge trade surpluses, and the excellent service facilities in Tokyo. However, the Japanese Government has maintained rather strict controls on banking and foreign exchange operations, and this has discouraged development of a truly international financial centre in Tokyo.

Manila also has failed to attract much international business, mainly because of the Philippines' relatively lacklustre economy and her political and social instability. In contrast, Hong Kong and Singapore have developed into the two most important financial centres of Asia. This paper will evaluate the advantages of these two cities as international financial centres and compare their respective contributions as the Asian financial centres.

International financial centres are a natural response by bankers to benefit from the economy of scale in their international operations. For example, it would be very costly to set up an elaborate infrastructure of international banking in each country to service just one market. By locating most international banking and financial infrastructure in one central place, banks can spread their overhead cost in servicing clients in various countries.

Modern international financial centres required sophisticated and costly infrastructure to support them, such as telecommunications, air transportation, accounting and legal professions, and other service industries. Also a sufficient number of banking and financial institutions have to be located in one financial centre to provide the critical mass needed to service the international clientele effectively and efficiently. Modern international banking requires both financial expertise and up-to-date market information. Such knowledge cannot be generated in a vacuum; it needs constant innovations and cross-fertilization of ideas among bankers and other finance professionals. An accurate and up-to-date sense of the financial market can be obtained only with the existence of an active market right there in the financial centre.

Further, modern international banking frequently requires teamwork among many banks in loan syndication and other credit transactions. The amount of money involved is often huge, and no one bank can prudently handle such transactions single-handedly. International banking syndication necessitates close co-ordination and smooth working relationships among banks. Familiarity with other's interest and strengths in a banking community facilitates such co-ordination and teamwork. A financial centre provides the environment for frequent interaction among bankers and other finance professionals.

Apart from syndication and risk sharing, a cluster of international banking institutions in one place is helpful for funding and investment operations. Existence of active inter-bank money markets leads to efficient channelling of financial resources. Banks invest their surplus funds in the inter-bank market, while other banks obtain funding from there to finance their international lending operations. Such a market is possible only where a large number of banking institutions are clustered together in one place. Attractive international financial centres serve not only as a location for an international banking and financial community serving clients in a number of countries, but also as a haven for international savings and pools of liquidity seeking profitable investments free from the monetary and exchange control restrictions. Efficient inter-bank markets provide the opportunity to invest these surplus funds easily and with minimum risk.

Location economics is important for international banking. Financial centres should be easily accessible in terms of geography and time zone to both investors and borrowers. Especially, contacts with potential borrowers are essential to bankers for marketing purposes and for packaging and negotiating appropriate loans for their customers. Location economics in international banking implies that a financial centre should be in or near the countries whose economies are dynamic and industrializing fast, requiring extensive foreign borrowings. Also the development stage of their economy should be relatively high enough to assure reasonable credit risk for banks.

Availability of good air transportation links to neighbouring countries is also essential for a financial centre as well as telephone and telex communication links. It also needs liberal government regulations on banking and foreign exchange transactions, taxation, securities dealings, and work permits for expatriate staffs in the general environment of political and economic stability. It is also useful to have locally available internationally-oriented personnel and manpower in the legal, accounting, and clerical professions.

Within the framework of an international financial centre as described above, we will evaluate Hong Kong and Singapore as two key Asian financial centres. During the decade of 1970s, the East Asian region witnessed one of the fastest economic developments in the world. The region's economies have benefitted from the significant contribution made by Hong Kong and Singapore as Asian financial centres. Their continuing contribution will be needed in the coming decade for the Asian economy to maintain its dynamic progress. It is in this context that we shall evaluate and compare the respective roles played by Hong Kong and Singapore.

The Development of Singapore as the Asian Dollar Market

Singapore emerged as an international financial centre in 1968 when the Asian dollar market was started there. The Asian dollar market is part of the Eurodollar market in the sense that Eurodollars are US dollar-denominated deposits at banks located outside the United States. Since Asian dollars are the dollar deposits at banks located in Asia and more specifically in Singapore, Asian dollars are also Eurodollars.

The Asian dollar market was first launched by Singapore in 1968 when the Singapore Government allowed banks there to set up the Asian Currency Units (ACUs) to accept US dollar-denominated bank deposits without prior government approval. Foreign depositors were also exempted from paying the 40 per cent Singapore withholding tax on the interest earnings by non-residents from their Asian dollar deposits in Singapore.

Singapore had three important advantages which contributed to the successful initiation and continued expansion of the Asian dollar market. First, a strong banking sector had developed very early in Singapore with the necessary background and experience to start on this new venture. As early as 1860 the first British bank was established in Singapore. Most of the prominent domestically-incorporated banks were established in the 1930s. A moderate number of foreign bank branches were established before and after the Second World War.

Second, Singapore had a natural time-zone advantage. In the morning hours, Singapore could conduct business with Tokyo (1 hour ahead) and Sydney (2 hours ahead). In the afternoon, Singapore was in touch with London (8 hours behind) and the rest of the European centres. This meant that Singapore could trade with both sides of the world during a normal business day. Third, there was a reliable and responsive communications infrastructure: telephone, telex, air mail, and sea mail. In Singapore good communications were already in place and could be easily expanded to serve the needs of the new financial centre.

The growth of the Asian dollar market was helped by the active support of the Singapore Government especially the Monetary Authority of Singapore (MAS). The Government supported the market's development by gradually removing various restrictions, allowing more access to the domestic market, and expanding the areas of tax concessions. Restrictions on non-resident activities in ACUs are minimal and are being increasingly liberalized. As mentioned earlier, the Government eliminated in 1968 the 40 per cent withholding tax on interest paid to non-residents. In early 1972, stamp duty on negotiable certificates of deposit (CDs) was abolished. The tax rate on net income from offshore loans by ACUs was reduced from 40 per cent to 10 per cent in 1973. The Government also exempted the tax on Asia dollar bonds paid by non-residents, permitted the issuance of negotiable CDs denominated in US dollars to non-residents and among ACU banks, reduced the income tax to 10 per cent on fees, interest, or commissions received by ACUs, and exempted from Singapore estate duty non-resident deposits with ACUs and non-resident holdings of approved Asian dollar bonds.

Of all the concessionary moves made by the Singapore Government, another important one was the abolition of the 20 per cent liquidity requirement for foreign currency deposits. This move, effective from January 1972, allowed the Asian dollar market to compete on an equal footing with the Eurodollar market in Europe and other financial centres.

Because of active Government encouragement and support, the Asian dollar market has developed rapidly in the 1970s in parallel with the growing Asian economy. The market has also diversified into various sub-segments similar to those of the Euromarket. For example, there has developed an active Asian dollar inter-bank market in Singapore, and the Singapore inter-bank offer rate (SIBOR) has become almost as well known as the Eurodollar's London inter-bank offer rate (LIBOR). Asian dollar CDs, as well as the floating rate CDs, have been actively traded in Singapore since 1977. Similar to the Eurobonds, Asian dollar bonds were also developed in Singapore.

In December 1971, the first Asian dollar bond issue was floated by the Development Bank of Singapore for US$10 million. Issue activity was slow until 1976, with only three issues each in 1973 and 1975 and none in 1974. Asian dollar bonds are loosely defined as those which banks in Singapore are predominantly involved in underwriting and marketing. They are listed in the stock exchange of Singapore or Hong Kong, and not in Luxembourg or London on whose stock exchanges the majority of Eurobonds are listed. Some experts differentiate between Asian dollar bonds and 'Euroasian' bonds. A Euroasian issue includes European and Asian co-managers, underwriters, and selling group members. As a Euroasian issue, there is no restriction on whether the bonds are placed in Europe or Asia.

Some argue that the Asian dollar bond market is not a reality, since the placing power of Asian institutions is extremely limited and to a greater or lesser extent nearly all Asian bond issues have had to rely on support from Europe. Like Eurobonds, Asian dollar bonds are bearer instruments whose interest payments are free of withholding tax. The underwriting commissions are similar to those for Eurobond issues, ranging from 2 per cent to 2½ per cent. Asian dollar bonds are mainly sold to institutional investors in Asia, though a substantial portion of them is placed in Europe and the Middle East. Trading in the secondary market is fairly limited. Market makers, most of whom are also members of the Association of International Bond Dealers (AIBD), generally quote both a buy and sell price with a margin of ½ to 1 per cent depending on turnover and market conditions.

The gross size of the Asian dollar market in Singapore reached $86 billion in early 1982. While the Asian dollar market has diversified into various sub-markets similar to those of the Euromarket, it has failed to develop the equivalent of Asian Eurocredits. Eurocredits, which played the most important role in international banking in the 1970s, are medium- to long-term Eurodollar syndicated bank credits with floating interest rates tied to LIBOR. The Asian syndicated Eurocredit market was developed in Hong Kong instead of Singapore for reasons which will be discussed in the next section. Singapore has played only a supporting role for Hong Kong's Eurocredit activities which have become the dominant format in supplying international credits for Asian borrowers during the past decade.

The Challenge by Hong Kong

Since the early 1970s, Hong Kong has emerged as a major international financial centre for the Asia-Pacific region. There are many reasons for Hong Kong's rise as a financial centre. Among them are absence of foreign exchange control, low level of tax rates and simplicity of tax structure, and liberal Government policy towards the economy and the financial sector. There is complete freedom in the movement of funds into and out of the Colony. The standard tax rate is only 15 per cent and the corporate profit tax rate is 17 per cent, while there is no tax on dividends and capital gains. Hong Kong also enjoys a healthy and dynamic economy, and its growth rate is one of the highest in the world.

Geographically, Hong Kong is situated near the major capital importing countries in the Asia-Pacific region, which include Korea, Japan, Taiwan, the Philippines and Thailand. Hong Kong is China's second largest trading partner after Japan, and the most important source of foreign exchange, and there are active and growing two-way direct investments between China and Hong Kong. It has other advantages: its excellent communications, transport and service facilities, and its relative social and political stability.

However, Hong Kong's role as an Asian financial centre has been different from that of Singapore. The Government of Hong Kong first looked at the possibility of promoting a Singapore-type Asian dollar market in 1973. But the idea was rejected, partly because some leading banks in Hong Kong preferred to arrange deals from Hong Kong but to book the loans at bank branches outside Hong Kong so as to avoid Hong Kong profit tax on their earnings from international loans. However, this profit-tax argument became irrelevant in 1978 when the Government introduced measures to tax a portion of profits on any international loan, wherever booked, that a Hong Kong bank had played a significant role in 'arranging'.

Nevertheless, Hong Kong still maintained a 15 per cent withholding tax on foreign currency deposits by non-residents at banks located in Hong Kong. This withholding tax effectively barred development of an Asian dollar market in Hong Kong, because Hong Kong banks were unable to attract Asian dollar deposits in competition with Singapore, which does not levy the withholding tax.

Instead, Hong Kong has emerged as the dominant Asian centre for syndicating Eurocredits, far surpassing Singapore in this segment. Hong Kong is now the world's third most important Eurocredit syndication centre after London and New York. Singapore, which once rivalled Hong Kong in the Eurocredit business, slipped back to eighteenth place in 1981. There were two main reasons for this development. First, as mentioned earlier, Hong Kong is geographically close to the major Asian borrowers of Eurocredits, such as South Korea, Taiwan, Japan, Thailand, the Philippines, New Zealand, and Australia.

Second, Hong Kong has been much more willing than Singapore to grant work visas to expatriate bankers and other foreign businessmen. Eurocredits require close interaction among bankers in syndication, pricing, and marketing of the loans. Easy relocation of international bankers in Hong Kong has allowed banks there to develop the expertise required to become the Asian Eurocredit centre independent of other Eurocredit centres such as London and New York.

In contrast, Singapore has been relatively inflexible in granting work visas for non-Singapore expatriates there. This restriction has prevented international banks in Singapore from moving their staff around between Singapore and other financial centres, thereby crippling the development of Eurocredit expertise in Singapore.

The Development of Specialization in Hong Kong and Singapore

The difference in style between Hong Kong and Singapore has tended to encourage each to develop its own specialization, and these have complemented each other. Each place has both advantages and disadvantages in terms of its qualifications as a financial centre. There are many similarities between the two centres, such as a thriving economy, political stability, good sea and air transportation links, a hard-working English-speaking workforce, good communication facilities, a well-developed service infrastructure in legal, accounting and insurance sectors, an efficient British-influenced civil service, etc. In the 1970s, observers generally noted the complementary nature of the two Asian financial centres, rather than emphasizing the competition between the two for supremacy as 'the' Asian financial centre.

On closer observation, however, some important differences developed between Hong Kong and Singapore. In terms of geography, Singapore used to have the time-zone advantage, with overlapping business hours with the major Asia-Pacific financial centres such as Tokyo and Sydney and also the European centres such as London and Paris. This advantage has helped Singapore in the past to develop more active international money market trading activities than Hong Kong. Offshore currency dealings in Singapore have been extensive and sophisticated, able to connect the Asia-Pacific region with the Eurodollar market on a daily operational basis.

This was further helped by the fact that Singapore levies no withholding tax on non-resident deposits at the ACUs in Singapore, while in Hong Kong there was until 1982 a 15 per cent withholding tax which discouraged development of an offshore currency market in Hong Kong. Absence of any withholding tax in Singapore has attracted offshore funds not only from the Asian region but also from Europe, the Middle East and other non-Asian regions. This has made Singapore the funding centre for international loans to Asia-Pacific borrowers.

On the other hand, Hong Kong has the geographic advantage of being located near the major international borrowers such as Korea, Japan, the Philippines, Taiwan, and recently China. International banking, like a hotel business, is substantially affected by location. Proximity to these major borrowers has made Hong Kong important for the arrangement, syndication and management of Eurocredits to borrowers from the Asia-Pacific region. This is further helped by the liberal work permit rules for expatriates in Hong Kong, allowing easy transfer of financial professionals to Hong Kong.

Therefore, one can easily see why the two centres have developed their own specializations in international banking functions. This has resulted not only from the different geographical advantages of the two centres but also from the different government policies. Hong Kong's approach to financial development differs from that of Singapore in that it basically relies on private sector initiatives and not so much on government controls or government incentives. The government is content to provide only the general framework, but otherwise avoids any direct sponsoring role in stimulating the growth of Hong Kong as a financial centre. On the other hand, the Singapore Government has taken a more active role in promoting Singapore as an international financial centre.

Apart from funding and money market trading activities, Singapore has become the most important Asian market for long-term international bonds. It is true that some questions still remain as to whether Asian dollar bonds are genuinely 'Asian' or simply another name for Eurobonds. Nevertheless, Singapore has offered the only Asian alternative to the Eurobond market for international bond issuers. Many Asian as well as non-Asian borrowers have tapped the Singapore Asian dollar bond market as an alternative to Eurobonds. The fact that some of these Asian dollar bonds have been placed in Europe does not negate the role of Singapore as 'the' Asian international bond market. In contrast, Hong Kong's bond market is almost nonexistent as far as international borrowers are concerned.

Prospect

We have seen that both Hong Kong and Singapore have developed their own spheres of specialization as international financial centres. Nevertheless, specialization in the two centres may not be pushed too far. It is true that, up to now, Singapore has developed a broad base for a financial centre, including Asian dollar deposits, inter-bank markets, Asian dollar CDs, and Asian dollar bonds. Hong Kong, on the other hand, has served a somewhat narrower function in international finance, with its main role being that of a centre for marketing, arrangement, pricing and syndication for Eurocredits. Funding and booking for Eurocredits have been shared, but the greater part has been handled by Singapore.

However, a new development took place in early 1982 which may blur such specialization in the future. The Hong Kong Government finally removed the 15 per cent withholding tax on non-resident foreign currency deposits in Hong Kong. This will surely lead to development of a Singapore-type Asian dollar market in Hong Kong. Even though the future success of the Hong Kong Asian dollar market will not be known for some time, already one can sense heightened competition between the two centres.

Singapore still enjoys a profit tax advantage over Hong Kong for offshore banking, 10 per cent against 16.5 per cent, and further incentives may be considered by the Singapore Government now that Hong Kong has posed a direct challenge to the Singapore Asian dollar market. The Singapore Government has traditionally played a more active role than Hong Kong in nurturing its financial centre as 'the' Asian dollar market. However, Hong Kong has already established a solid international banking base for the Asia-Pacific basin, with its geographical proximity to the region as well as other advantages. With the development of an Asian dollar market now possible, Hong Kong is expected to pose a serious challenge to Singapore for a broad array of Asian dollar activities.

In the coming decade, therefore, it is likely that the two Asian financial centres will move away from specialization in different spheres, which have complemented each other in the past. Instead, both of them are expected to develop a wide array of financial services which will enable them to become truly independent international financial centres.

Over the short term, Hong Kong appears to possess the momentum and dynamism to outpace Singapore. It will be interesting to see how Singapore reacts to this renewed challenge from Hong Kong. At least one thing seems certain. Competition between Hong Kong and Singapore is bound to contribute to further development and strengthening of the two Asian financial centres to the benefit of their neighboring economies in Asia and the Pacific region.

References

Banker Research Unit (ed.), *Banking Structure and Sources of Finance in the Far East*, (3rd ed.), The Financial Times Business Publishing Ltd., London, 1980.

Bowring, Philip, 'Hong Kong: A Bid for the Asia Dollar', *Far Eastern Economic Review*, 5 March, 1982.

Goodstadt, Leo, 'How Hong Kong Came of Age as a Euromarket Centre', *Euromoney*, February 1982.

Herman, Colin C., 'Asian or Euroasian Bonds? A Significant Difference', *Asian Money Manager*, December 1976.

Koenig, Peter, 'HCA's Asian Dollar Adventure', *Institutional Investor* (International Edition), February 1982.

Lees, Francis A. and Eng, Maximo, *International Financial Markets*, Praeger Publishers, New York, 1975.

Martin, Ben, 'The Asian Dollar Bond Market Is a Charade, Not a Reality', *Euromoney*, November 1976.

Quirt, John, 'Hong Kong: The Foreign Banks Go Retail', *Institutional Investor* (International Edition), March 1982.

Skully, Michael T., *Merchant Banking in the Far East*, (2nd ed.), The Financial Times Business Publishing Ltd., London, 1980.

Yassukovich, Stanislas, 'Multinational Companies and Offshore Centres', *The Banker*, May 1974.

[24]

Excerpt from *Journal of Business Administration*, 17 (1 and 2), (Special Issue), 151–72.

7

STRATEGIC ADJUSTMENT OF INTERNATIONAL FINANCIAL CENTRES (IFCs) IN SMALL ECONOMIES: A COMPARATIVE STUDY OF HONG KONG AND SINGAPORE

Kam-Hon Lee and Ilan Vertinsky*

1.0 INTRODUCTION

"A financial centre is generally defined as a central location where the financial transactions of an area are coordinated and cleared" (Reed, 1981, p. 3). There are several reasons why financial transactions tend to be centralized geographically. Among the most important reasons are: (1) access to information stemming from proximity to rivals, complementary organizations, customers and markets; (2) the development of specialized technological and economic infra-structure including markets for production factors and services; (3) economies of density in inter-institutional transaction costs; (4) increased liquidity associated with the development of large and efficient financial markets; (5) specific inducements offered by governments which are not available elsewhere (e.g., in the form of subsidies, tax and regulatory concessions, etc.); and (6) economies of scope.

The process of centralization, however, is constrained by some diseconomies that work to limit the geographical scope of a financial centre at least for some types of transactions. Kindleberger (1974, pp. 10-11) points out that regional centres have the advantage of access to

---

*The Chinese University of Hong Kong and the University of British Columbia respectively. This study was funded in part by the Centre for International Business Studies at the University of B.C. We are grateful for insightful comments received from Dr. M. Goldberg, Dr. W.T. Stanbury, and Mr. T. Ursacki.

information concerning local players and business customers. But, more importantly, centralization limits face-to-face contacts with primary customers of financial intermediation services. Centralization of financial transactions may also be constrained by national regulatory regimes and other forms of formal and informal discrimination against foreigners and/or foreign institutions.

Several recent developments are changing the economic calculus of the centralization of financial transactions, thus creating both opportunities and threats to the economic health of some of the traditional financial centres of the world. These threats and opportunities are especially pronounced for those financial centres which assumed international pre-eminence without the advantage of a large and stable national economic base. Two important Pacific Rim international financial centres which face the challenge of strategic adjustment and repositioning in international financial markets in this decade are Hong Kong and Singapore. In this paper, we (1) analyze the alternative strategies which were chosen in each of these two economies to face the changing environment, and (2) present the results and implications of a survey of top bankers in Hong Kong and Singapore with respect to the attributes each must provide to enhance its position as an international financial centre.

2.0 THE CHANGING ENVIRONMENT

The world supply of money grew significantly in the last decade. This growth accelerated recently, reaching an annual rate of 20% during 1985 compared with a rate of 11% in 1981. The expansion of the world money supply was accompanied by a comparable growth in international financial markets. The international bond market, for example, grew from US $5 billion in 1970 to US $168 billion in 1985. Similarly, the Euro-Bond market grew to 19 times its original size during the same period. The trend towards globalization of financial markets is also well reflected in buying trends in equity markets. American investors held U.S. $90 billion of foreign company shares in 1985 as opposed to U.S. $21 billion in 1970, while foreigners held $90 billion of U.S. company shares in 1985 as opposed to $36 billion in 1970.

Technological change in information processing and communications has led to greater integration between financial markets in geographically distant locations. Governments have responded to the globalization of financial markets by moving toward deregulation of national financial markets and providing more access to foreigners, thus accelerating the process of globalization (e.g., the "big bang" in the U.K. in 1987). The integration of markets and the opportunities it created have brought about a trend toward around-the-clock operations. The extension of working hours has eroded some traditional time-zone advantages while creating others. A shift (temporary or permanent) toward debt "securitization" and a reduction in the role of traditional intermediaries, most notably banks, has created a stimulus for change in the strategies and management styles of the traditional financial institutions. Finally, the growing interdependence between financial markets and economies and the speed with which geographical financial flow patterns can alter are a source of variability and potential sharp discontinuities. (The size and speed of changing financial flow patterns make attempts to control them by single national actors infeasible, thus creating enormous uncertainties even for the largest economies.)

These changes in the environment mean that the strategic niches that Hong Kong and Singapore held in the past few decades may be exposed to competition resulting from further centralization (e.g., competition from Tokyo), or the entrance of new regional competitors (such as Sydney or Melbourne) in the arena as rival IFCs. Before assessing the strategic positions and future options of Hong Kong and Singapore, it is useful to outline briefly current theories concerning the formation of IFCs, to provide a framework for our analysis.

3.0 THEORIES OF IFC FORMATION

Scholars have speculated about the patterns of growth of financial centres generally, and IFCs specifically. They have focused on alternative causes leading to the concentration of international and domestic financial activities in a particular place. Some scholars have focused upon the "derived demand" for financial intermediation. Thus trade, production and investment patterns which create a surplus of funds and borrowing needs have been hypothesized to determine demand for financial intermediation (Vernon, 1960).

Other scholars emphasized the "supply" side, i.e., the ability to produce the services of international financial intermediation in a particular location at a competitive cost. Indeed, several authors have pointed out different important attributes of a financial centre that affect the quality and/or cost of producing financial services. For example, Ragazzi (1973) emphasized the importance of the existence of broad and efficient financial markets in the creation of an IFC. Kindleberger (1974) considered the externalities produced by the existence of a large banking sector in terms of specialization, joint facilities and services of other industries such as printing, accounting and legal services. He also emphasized the role of economies of scale that exist in financial markets due to higher liquidity and consequent lower transaction costs.

Other scholars have focused upon attributes of a location that attract depositors or lenders (e.g., derived demand for intermediation from "third" parties). Nadler et al. (1955) identify the following "necessary" conditions essential to the development of an IFC:

(1) a currency system that is stable and sound,
(2) constant substantial demand for and supply of the country's currency,
(3) a national balance of payments which is reasonably well adjusted,
(4) a sophisticated system of financial institutions,
(5) a system of branch or subsidiary foreign financial institutions free to operate without undue restrictions and discrimination,
(6) specialized institutions that supplement the role of commercial banking in foreign financial transactions, and
(7) location of the principal office of the nation's central bank in the centre.

Probably the most comprehensive study to date of factors influencing the development of international banking and finance centres is by Goldberg et al. (1987). In a multi-tier study consisting of a comprehensive, cross-national review of 42 countries as well as time-series studies of the U.S. and Great Britain and a pooled cross-sectional, time-series analysis of IFC development in 16 OECD nations, they obtained consistent relationships between attributes of IFCs and their national environment and measures of their size. The size of imports, the size of real GNP per capita, saving rates and offshore banking were significantly and positively associated with the size of an IFC. Interestingly, exports were found to be negatively related to the development of an IFC. This could be explained as the impact of neither exports nor imports alone, but the financial imbalances created by trade deficits which provide the impetus to the growth of a financial centre. These results confirm the historical importance of demand for financial intermediation in the development of an IFC, rather than supply advantages.

The historical approach provides one with ex-post identification of conditions that facilitate the growth of IFCs, but offers little insight into the possibility and the prescribed strategy of deliberately developing or inducing the growth of a particular IFC. Furthermore, while it is possible that demand variables dominated the past, supply variables could determine the competitive edge for future IFCs. Tan and Vertinsky (1987) investigated the circumstances and conditions under which alternative strategies for creating an IFC are feasible and effective. They concluded that: (1) marginal modification of supply advantages may shift the distribution of financial transaction concentrations within a national economy and affect, to some degree at least, the national pace of growth of international financial activities (mainly by enhancing agglomeration economies in the initial phase of growth); (2) an aggressive pro-active policy requires a flexible, highly centralized financial system; and (3) important conditions for the success of pro-active strategies are product innovation and sensitive adjustment to changing market environments. Specialization and product differentiation were identified as important strategic moves to ensure the resilience of IFC development in circumstances where existing demand-related advantages do not ensure the growth of an IFC.

In the following sections we attempt to assess the degrees to which the growth of IFCs in Hong Kong and Singapore were affected by demand pull, supply advantages, and deliberate public policies.

4.0 HONG KONG VERSUS SINGAPORE

4.1 An Historical Perspective on Two IFCs

Reed (1981), who studied the hierarchical structure of international banking centres and international financial centres from the beginning of this century, ranked Hong Kong as the fourth most important international banking centre in the year 1900, just behind London, New York and Paris. With the exception of a period during the Second World War, Hong Kong consistently ranked as one of the top international banking centres throughout this century. In the Asia Pacific region, Hong Kong ranked as the pre-eminent banking centre until the early 1930s when Yokohama outranked it. In 1935 Shanghai assumed the role of the pre-eminent regional centre. In 1940, Tokyo, Jakarta and Hong Kong achieved the same rank. In 1947, Shanghai, Hong Kong and Singapore emerged as the leading regional banking centres just behind London, New York and Paris in the global ranking. In the late 1950s Tokyo assumed the role of the pre-eminent regional banking centre while Hong Kong retained a position in the top 10 banking centres in the global ranking. Reed's (1981) cluster analysis to identify a hierarchy of international financial centres yielded similar results.

The ranking which Reed (1981) generated using multi-variate statistical methods corresponded well with information he obtained by interviewing a large sample of international finance executives who were asked to rank IFCs. The most significant difference between the rankings was the relatively higher ranks which Singapore and Hong Kong obtained in the interviews compared with a ranking based upon objective measures such as number of banks, financial assets, international linkages, etc. Reed (1981, p. 41) reports that "tradition, history, its importance to the People's Republic of China, and the large number of banks with offices there were cited as reasons for ranking Hong Kong highly."

Singapore, which was ranked among the top 10 global financial centres by the panel of international officials, was classified by Reed's statistical analysis in the top 10 only in 1947 and 1975. The interviewees, when asked why they ranked Singapore so highly, responded that their perception of Singapore's influence within the community of international financial centres may not be entirely accurate but that it was the centre of the "Asian dollar market." Singapore, an important deposit centre for the ASEAN countries, commanded the attention of the financial community through its innovation and aggressive pursuit of eminence as an international financial centre. These perceptions of each IFC form a basis for foreign direct investment decisions of financial service providers. The analysis of resilience of each of these financial centres must contrast the role of Hong Kong with that of Singapore. Hong Kong was a financial centre which traditionally handled transactions between China and the outside world as well as a large share of the financial transactions of the overseas Chinese. Singapore was an actively managed IFC creating and defending a new niche as an international financial centre by expanding on its traditional role as a regional deposit centre.

4.2 Hong Kong and Singapore: The Evolution of Present Financial Structures and Strategic Adjustments to Changing International Financial Markets

To assess the resilience of the financial systems in Hong Kong and Singapore, one must identify their natural and historical relative advantages, as well as the strengths and weaknesses of their respective institutions of management.

The most important attributes of Hong Kong and Singapore that led to their emergence as financial centres were their locations and roles as regional, central ports and their ties to London—the world's financial centre. These attributes continue to provide a basis for the maintenance and growth of a financial centre in each of the cities. Both cities now rank among the world's most important ports. In 1986, Hong Kong's Kwai Chung container terminal ranked as the third-largest container port in the world, topped only by New York and Rotterdam. In the same year, Singapore was the second-largest cargo-handling port in the world. Both cities continue to enjoy their historical and cultural ties with England, providing a Westernized outpost in the Asia Pacific Rim, while maintaining and cultivating traditional informal ties to regional networks of business information and financial flows. Their evolution as financial and trade centres has been accompanied by the development of an accommodating communications infrastructure. Both cities, for example, have busy and well-serviced airports, efficient telecommunications systems and significant computer service industries. Despite their relatively small populations and economies, both Hong Kong and Singapore are disproportionately significant in the realm of international trade. Exports in 1986 (including re-exports) totalled Cdn. $49.1 billion in Hong Kong and Cdn. $31.1 billion in Singapore, while imports reached Cdn. $49.2 billion and Cd. $35.3 billion respectively. Their position as regional trade centres in open economies creates derived demands for financial intermediation services. The presence of a critical mass of domestic and foreign banks has in turn created opportunities, rooted in economies of scale and centralization, for further development of the financial services sector in each city beyond the capacity indicated merely by derived demand for services from trade and domestic business transactions.

Indeed, in both cities the financial services sector is a significant direct contributor to national income and provides positive externalities to the development of other services (such as trade and communications) and investment ventures. The importance of the sector to the rapid development of each economy has meant that the respective governments pay close attention to the health of the sector. Their actions, however, have reflected differences in market opportunities, systems of government, and choice of strategies. The globalization of markets places both cities in direct competition with each other, with the increasingly dominant role of Tokyo as an emerging world centre, and with other secondary regional centres such as Melbourne and Sydney. In the next two sections we analyze the niches that Hong Kong and Singapore have occupied historically in international financial markets and their strategic adjustments as they have attempted to cope with a changing world. We start with an analysis of the evolution of their regulatory structures and the philosophies of strategic management which they reflect.

4.3 Hong Kong

The territory of Hong Kong was acquired by Britain in three stages during the 19th century. The Island of Hong Kong was ceded in perpetuity under the Treaty of Nanking in 1842. Parts of the Kowloon Peninsula and Stonecutter's Island were acquired in 1860, while the New Territories were acquired on a 99-year lease in 1898. For the past four decades the People's Republic of China (PRC) has reasserted its claims for sovereignty over the entire territory and engaged in lengthy negotiations with Great Britain. During that time it established a significant presence in the financial sector of the city as well as in other aspects of its economic life. It is the benefit that the PRC derived from using Hong Kong as its channel to the outside world that offered the Crown colony a certain measure of security and stability. Hong Kong's position as a world financial centre was also enhanced by the vigour of its own growing economy, as well as the benefits of serving as the door to China.

The "opening" of the economy of the PRC to trade and investment with the West in the mid-1970s provided an added stimulus to the growth of the city as a financial centre (Jao, 1983). The official signing in Beijing in late 1984 of the Sino-British agreement on Hong Kong meant the elimination of the immediate threats that failed negotiations could have brought about, although major uncertainties as to the fate of Hong Kong beyond 1997 remain, irrespective of the guaranties in the signed agreement. Thus Hong Kong, while benefitting from its links with the People's Republic of China, must contend with the fact that its long-term political risks put constraints on the type and stability of financial flows that the city is likely to attract.

The regulatory regime of the financial sector which has emerged over the past decade reflects, in part, the view of the authorities as to the attributes desired by those using Hong Kong's financial services.

The present three-tier system of regulation of banking services reflects a flexible "light touch" regulatory approach which evolved during the 1970s and 1980s. Though a formal ban was put on new banking licences from 1965 to 1972, the loose definition used to implement the ban permitted some overseas and local banks to open finance houses competing with licensed banks for deposits and banking services. In 1976 the government required the registration of these houses as deposit-taking companies (RDTC). These RDTCs remained unregulated as to the interest rates they paid, in contrast to the licensed banks which were regulated by a cartel that controlled interest rates. In 1981 non-licensed "banks" accounted for 36% of total deposits. To reverse the trend a new tier of deposit-taking companies was established—licensed deposit-taking companies (LDTC). These were subjected to minimum paid-up capital requirements and a minimal tenure in the industry of three years. The moratorium on the issuing of new bank licenses was lifted.

At the end of August 1981 there were 115 licensed banks in Hong Kong, with about 1200 branches. Eighty-one of the banks were foreign-owned. In March 1981, when the new legislation concerning deposit-taking companies was instituted, there were 342 such companies registered. Of these, about half were subsidiaries or joint ventures set up by foreign commercial banks, merchant banks and investment houses. Subsequent to the reforms, a number of deposit-takers took advantage of the opportunity to become banks, so that by June 1987 Hong Kong had 154 licensed banks, 35 licensed deposit-takers and 248 registered deposit-takers.

The regulation of banks was delegated to the Hong Kong Association of Bankers. This Association supervises banking standards and regulates charges and deposit interest rates. All licensed banks were required to be members.

The main thrust of government policy has been described as "positive non-intervention," a mix of light regulation designed to ensure stable growth for the industry, while maintaining a reputation for order sufficient to attract foreign banks and investors. Crises threatening the reputation or stability of the industry have been met by periodic reforms, the implementation of which ensured maximum flexibility and coordination with existing and potential providers of financial services.

Regular examinations of all banks and deposit-taking companies are carried out by the Office of the Commissioner of Banking and Deposit-Taking Companies. A number of bank collapses and problems in deposit-taking companies prompted the Hong Kong government to introduce new legislation in 1986. The new bill attempted to rationalize the regulation of banking services by providing a single regulatory framework for deposit-taking companies and banks, as well as reinforcing the supervisory powers of the banking commissioner.

Less than a year after the introduction of this legislation, plans were announced to introduce new guidelines to tighten supervision. The major objective was to "bring the territory's financial system into line with other financial centres" (EIU 2/87, p. 14). While tightening the regulatory regime on domestic companies the government decided to liberalize the requirement for foreign banks wanting to establish banks in Hong Kong. "Both moves highlight the government's desire to integrate Hong Kong fully into the international financial community, enhance its reputation as a financial centre and demonstrate that it is a serious competitor with the Tokyo market" (EIU 2/87, p. 14). Searching for an "optimal" regulatory regime, the government is attempting to reconcile the conflicting interests of different existing and potential service providers. While some of the reconciliation process will result in modified guidelines and regulations, much of it would be reflected in the process of "adaptive" implementation.

The attempt to balance demands for freedom and secrecy in the banking services sector and the need to defend a reputation for order and stability is characteristic of other sectors of the financial industry.

Periodic rationalization of natural growth processes, positive enhancement of the sector through removal of bottlenecks and slow, reactive rather than pro-active policies have also been essential characteristics of the role of the government in developing Hong Kong's stock and futures markets. The integration of the four separate exchanges into the unified Hong Kong Stock Exchange (opened in October 1986) took almost a decade to plan and implement. The supervisory structure was minimal and its style of implementation informal. The October 1987 global stock market crash ("Black Monday") led to a temporary closure of the market. The crash almost led to the collapse of the stock futures market which was averted only by a government arranged and financed bailout of losses.

The crisis triggered plans for reforms designed to maintain Hong

Kong's reputation and update the regulatory structure in ways that meet the emerging global demands for adequate regulation. Despite a self-promoted image of Hong Kong as a laissez-faire international market, it is clear that it is in fact a market carefully guided to respond to and meet competition from other international financial centres. The niche these policies imply is one of minimal regulation adapted periodically to satisfy international standards and expectations within the framework of a stable, predictable legal framework. The desired minimum is constantly assessed informally (through consultation with the community of financial service providers) and through periodic formal reviews.

4.4 Singapore

In contrast to Hong Kong, Singapore has sought to exploit the benefits of a strong, stable and pro-active government to stimulate growth in the financial services sector. The natural locational advantages of time zone and central position in international trade routes have been exploited to their fullest by deliberate government policy. A stable political and economic infrastructure coupled with liberal monetary and fiscal policies turned Singapore into a regional deposit centre for the ASEAN countries. Using this position as a base and taking advantage of its developed technological and institutional infrastructure, Singapore has deliberately sought to create for itself a niche as an international financial centre.

The 10-year development plan of 1975 envisaged Singapore as an international financial centre. The government guided the development of Singapore as an IFC through the following measures:

(1) liberalization of regulations pertaining to the operations of foreign financial institutions,
(2) liberalization of exchange control regulations,
(3) provision of tax incentives for offshore-oriented financial services,
(4) creation of new financial markets through legislation, tax incentives and direct participation using government spending power and its influence on private spending, and
(5) facilitation of the introduction of new financial instruments.

The attraction of foreign financial companies to Singapore fostered the development of a pool of expertise in financial services and helped generate the benefits of concentrating financial services (i.e., a higher level of liquidity, better access to information, and lower costs of inter-institutional transactions). The measures taken by the government led to an acceleration of growth rates of the banking and financial sector from 21% in 1975 to 34% in 1980. The share of the financial services sector in the gross domestic product grew from 7% in 1975 to 10% in 1984. In 1983 Singapore was served by 37 fully licensed commercial banks (of which 24 were foreign) and 13 restricted banks. In addition, there were 69 offshore banks, 69 representative offices of foreign banks, 49 merchant banks, 153 Asian Currency Units, four discount houses, 9 international money brokers, 79 insurance companies and 34 finance companies (Tan, 1985, p. 4). Favourable government policies were accompanied by public investment in the development of physical, technological, social and institutional infrastructures conducive to the development of an IFC. In particular, the government established a sophisticated international communications system and developed an unambiguous, stable legal and regulatory framework. These activities and the pattern of consistent, rapid economic growth and political stability have sustained the role of Singapore as a pre-eminent IFC.

In 1984 and 1985, for the first time in many years, Singapore experienced a reversal in this pattern of growth. The recession was accompanied by a reduction in the growth of the financial services sector from 10.5% in 1984 to 3.4% in 1985. This fact and the recognition of the new trends in the international financial markets led the government to adopt new strategies aimed at renewing the growth of financial services. The global trend toward deregulation, and especially the liberalization of Japan's financial markets, poses threats to the traditional market niche that Singapore occupies, but also creates opportunities. Seven potential, interlinked areas of growth identified by the Report of the Economic Committee in 1986 were as follows: (1) risk management, (2) funds management, (3) capital markets, (4) unlisted securities market, (5) financial and commodity futures, (6) financing of third-country trading, and (7) reinsurance and captive insurance companies. The targets have been modified, but the strategic posture of the recommendations of the influential Economic Committee was consistent with the past pattern of actions adopted by the Singapore government.

The government is expected to create a fiscal and regulatory environment conducive to the development of a vibrant capital market with a wide range of tradable instruments. Product innovation, fiscal incentives and a liberalized regulatory environment are to be accompanied by active efforts by the Monetary Authority of

Singapore (MAS) to improve liquidity in local financial markets. Similarly, the recommendations envisage the use of some of the large amount of compulsory individual savings controlled by the government to provide a domestic basis for a funds management industry. Finally, there is a clear recognition that the major asset of a financial centre lies in the expertise and ideas of its people. Thus the private sector (The Association of Banks) and the public sector (the University) were called upon to develop the appropriate manpower by setting up a banking school to cater to the training needs of the ASEAN region.

The government also adopted a clear policy that facilitates the recruitment of foreign experts while fostering the growth of domestic expertise. Implementation in Singapore is swift. To implement the objectives proposed by the Report, the Stock Exchange of Singapore Dealers Automated Quotation System opened on February 18, 1987. When this exchange did not obtain the critical mass to justify its existence, the government introduced a variety of measures to increase its liquidity and volume of transactions. Tax concessions were given to stimulate financial futures and gold trading in Simex. Similarly, tax concessions were introduced in the capital market for transactions involving non-residents. To encourage the orderly development of a bond market, liquidity requirements of banks were modified. To ensure an advantageous position in a 24-hour, global market the Stock Exchange of Singapore was encouraged to negotiate an agreement with the authorities in London and New York which would allow shares quoted in these centres to be listed electronically in Singapore. If successful, Singapore would be the first exchange in the Asian time zone to do so, generating a major advantage over its Pacific rivals.

5.0 THE QUEST FOR A FUTURE NICHE

Formal public policy pronouncements provide a vision and facilitate some preconditions for the evolution of a financial centre. Past actions of regulators and service providers shape the strategic style of a centre. The actual niche that the centre occupies in international markets, however, depends to a large extent on the actions of those who actually provide financial services and compete in these markets. The niche that service providers expect their IFC to occupy is reflected in the profile of attributes they consider important for its growth. For this reason, studying the perceptions of Hong

Kong and Singapore financial executives with regard to the importance of different attributes of the environment to the growth of the IFC may provide insights about the future niche of each centre's financial sector.

To provide the data for such a study a three-page questionnaire was designed, and interviews with key bankers were conducted. The main part of the questionnaire was concerned with importance judgment (on 5-point Likert-type scales) of attributes of a financial centre in terms of attribute contribution to centre growth. The attributes were those which may attract financial service providers by facilitating either (a) supply (e.g., low transaction costs, access to specialized labor markets, appropriate legal and political infrastructures, economies to scale through the existence of a large financial services sector); or (b) demand (e.g., finance of international trade and investment, proximity to a large base of borrowers and depositors) for financial intermediation. Attributes were identified on the basis of a literature search. Additional attributes were added on the basis of a pilot survey of both academic experts and practitioners. A total of 53 attributes were identified (see Appendix 1). Another part of the questionnaire requested the identification of the five most important of these attributes. A third section of the questionnaire was an unaided recall and ranking of the most important IFCs. The sample consisted of senior financial executives of banks with significant international activities. In each location the list of executives was developed through nomination of key local bankers. There were 28 useful responses in Hong Kong and 38 in Singapore (the respective response rates were above 60% in Hong Kong and 70% in Singapore).

The study showed a marked consensus between the two communities of bankers as to those attributes of a financial centre important for its success. Table 1 reports the attributes perceived to be the most important in contributing to success of IFCs. When we computed the mean scores and arranged the attributes in descending order, the first 12 attributes identified as most important by the Hong Kong sample were exactly the same as those indicated by the judgments of the Singapore sample. However, the orderings of the attributes in the two samples were somewhat different.

The key attributes selected by the two methods: (a) mean ranking (Table 1), and (b) frequency of mention as one of the five most important, were identical in 11 out of 12 cases in the combined sample.

Table 1

THE 12 MOST IMPORTANT ATTRIBUTES CONTRIBUTING TO SUCCESS OF IFC'S AS PERCEIVED BY BANKERS IN HONG KONG AND SINGAPORE (BASED ON MEAN SCORES)

IFC Attribute	Hong Kong[a]		Singapore[b]	
	Rank	Mean Score[c]	Rank	Mean Score[c]
Well developed communication links with the rest of the world	1	1.00	1	1.03
Organized and efficient domestic communication systems	2	1.46	3	1.47
A mature and sound legal system	3	1.54	8	1.55
A pool of expertise in legal services	3	1.54	11	1.63
A pool of expertise in financial services	5	1.57	4	1.50
Well developed transportation with the rest of the world	5	1.57	7	1.53
Favourable taxation policy for non-residents	5	1.57	12	1.68
A history of political stability in the country	8	1.67	4	1.50
Access to opportunities to trade between diversified financial instruments	9	1.68	8	1.55
An environment where opportunities to implement innovative financial instruments are encouraged	10	1.70	4	1.50
An unambiguous regulatory framework	11	1.75	2	1.39
Existence of a significant number of branches of the major international banks	12	1.86	10	1.61

Notes: (a) n = 28 (b) n = 38 (c) from 1 (very important) to 5 (not important)

Statistically significant differences ($p < 0.05$), however, were discovered between the importance ratings of Hong Kong and Singapore executives with regard to some important attributes. Executives in Singapore considered the following more important than Hong Kong executives: (1) access to government financial decision-makers, (2) convenient time zone, (3) proximity to a large base of savers, (4) ability of business community to communicate with policy makers in the country's central bank, (5) proximity to a large base of borrowers, (6) an unambiguous regulatory framework, and (7) an environment where opportunities to implement innovative financial instruments are encouraged.

The pattern and strong general consensus of ratings indicates that key attributes for obtaining a competitive edge in the new globalized international financial market in a relatively small economy are supply oriented. The technological infrastructure (e.g., a well developed external and internal communication system) is paramount. An accommodating regulatory system and the existence of a pool of expertise are next in line. Linkages with the international financial service providers are also included in the list of top-ranked attributes of an IFC.

The differences in importance ratings provide, however, a clue as to the different strategies each centre may assume. Service providers in Singapore indicated by their ratings the view that its future growth as a financial centre depends to a large extent on the continuation of the government's proactive management of its financial markets. Clarity of regulation and effective communications between service providers and regulators are important characteristics of a centre that attempts to position itself in a differentiated service niche through innovation. By contrast, Hong Kong executives, accustomed to an enhancing, but reactive management style of their IFC and aware of the limitations of public policy given Hong Kong's political position, seem to emphasize more cultural, environmental and infrastructure advantages. In particular, they emphasized ties with the British legal system, the possession of legal expertise, and a favourable tax regime. The differences also show the higher perceived dependence of Singapore upon regional demands for financial intermediation (e.g., proximity to borrowers and depositors of ASEAN). Many of Hong Kong's financial executives focused mainly upon new growth opportunities in world capital markets rather than those associated with China's trade and investment financing. These opportunities are being captured more and more by the PRC-owned Bank of China and its 12 sister banks (see Ko, 1986; and Jao, 1983).

To obtain additional insight into possible relationships of an IFC's perceived pre-eminence and environmental attributes judged to be important for its success, we have used correlation analysis. This methodology identifies the possible differentiating characteristics considered to contribute to the success of each city as an important IFC. The significant correlations for each community are presented in Table 2.

Table 2

CORRELATIONS OF IFC PRE-EMINENCE RATINGS AND IMPORTANCE OF IFC ATTRIBUTES BY LOCAL SERVICE PROVIDERS

I.	**Hong Kong** (n = 28)		
	1.	English is the working business language	0.52*
	2.	Access to political decision makers by local and foreign financial institutions	0.47*
	3.	A country that requires a minimum degree of financial disclosure	0.39*
	4.	Openness of the local business community to foreigners	0.39*
	5.	Availability of inexpensive support services	0.36*
	6.	Proximity to a large base of borrowers	0.34*
	7.	A city with a well-developed post-secondary education system	0.34*
II.	**Singapore** (n = 38)		
	1.	Proximity to other financial centres	0.35*
	2.	Proximity to a large base of savers	0.28**
	3.	Availability of inexpensive support services	0.27**

* significant at 0.05
** significant at 0.10

It appears that in Hong Kong those who value a more cosmopolitan business culture and language, minimal financial disclosure rules and proximity to borrowers, ranked the city higher than those who placed less importance upon these attributes. In Singapore, the local judgments of the pre-eminence of the city as an IFC are related to valuing proximity to other financial centres and a large base of savers and availability of inexpensive support services. Interviews with several bankers in each city confirmed our interpretation with regard to the nature of both financial centres and their likely attempts to position themselves in future markets.

Hong Kong was universally judged to be the more important financial centre. Its unique niche was identified by interviewees as stemming from: (1) its British legal traditions and legal and financial expertise, (2) its less constraining levels of regulation and disclosure, (3) its role in the investment in and trade flows to and from the People's Republic of China, as well as the internal demands for financial intermediation (see also Jao, 1983), (4) its role as a prime financial centre for overseas Chinese (see also Lee and Jao, 1982; Bualek, 1986; Chang, 1986; and Lim, 1986)—a role Singapore does not play because of its geographical position, and (5) opportunities for abnormal profits resulting from the structure of the domestic banking market (see also Hanley et al., 1987). Some of the interviewees pointed out the fact that these conditions favoured movement of relatively short-term risk money to Hong Kong.

Singapore was identified as a financial centre that developed from an historical base as a regional deposit centre into an IFC mainly through the force of the will of its government to create a niche in international markets. This was achieved through innovation and diversification of financial instruments, and aggressive maintenance of a competitive edge by: (a) enhancing the supply of support services, (b) the creation and maintenance of liquidity, (c) the importation of expertise, (d) the development of domestic expertise, and (e) the dynamic adaptive maintenance of internationally competitive tax and regulatory cost regimes.

Indeed, we have found our interviewees echoed Reed's contentions that it is the high international profile of innovation and attempts at niche creation that explain Singapore's pre-eminent position which exceeds its importance as judged by objective measures of stocks and flows.

6.0 CONCLUSION

Our comparison of Hong Kong and Singapore's strategies to defend and improve their traditional positions as pre-eminent IFCs in small economies results in two main conclusions. First, the globalization of markets can create opportunities for smaller IFCs if supply advantages (such as lower transaction costs, lower service costs, and lower taxes) can be maintained. In the past, growth of IFCs was motivated by demand advantages. Such demand advantages, and centralization and agglomeration economies accompanying them, explain the increasing role of London, New York and Tokyo in international financial markets. However, significant cost increases in these centres created opportunities for low-cost competitors in several service areas. And, second, IFCs in smaller economies may also create differentiated niches in international financial services markets by accommodating special market needs. Both Hong Kong with its reactive, non-interventionist, market-sensitive strategy of environmental management, and Singapore's proactive anticipation of a changing market environment, can respond effectively to changing needs which the more complex regulatory systems in other larger IFCs fail to identify or choose to ignore.

REFERENCES

Bualek, P., (1986) "The Growth and Development of Chinese Banks—Capitalists in Thailand (1932-1973)," a paper presented at the International Conference on Chinese Banking and Nation Building in Southeast Asia, Hong Kong, Oct. 10-11.

Chang, C.Y., (1986) "Localization and Chinese Banking in South East Asia," a paper presented at the International Conference on Chinese Banking and Nation Building in Southeast Asia, Hong Kong, Oct. 10-11.

Goldberg, M., R. Helsley, and M. Levi, (1987) "Factors Influencing the Development of International Banking and Finance Centres: A Cross National and Historical Evaluation," working paper, Faculty of Commerce and Business Administration, University of British Columbia, April.

Hanley, T.H., J.M. Rosenberg, C.A. D'Arista, and N.A. Mitchell, (1987) *The Hong Kong Banking System: An Intriguing Financial Services Center*, New York: Salomon Brothers Inc.

Jao, Y.C., (1983) "Hong Kong's Role in Financing China's Modernization," in A.J. Youngson (ed.), *Hong Kong and China: The Economic Nexus*, Hong Kong: Oxford University Press, pp. 77-103.

Kindleberger, C.P., (1974) *The Formation of Financial Centers: A Study in Comparative Economic History*, Princeton Studies in International Finance No. 36, Princeton: Princeton University Press.

Ko, C., (1986) "Bank of China Outperforms Local Rivals," *South China Morning Post*, January 13.

Lee, S.Y., and Y.C. Jao, (1982) *Financial Structures and Monetary Policies in Southeast Asia*, London: MacMillan, pp. 7-50.

Lim, H., (1986) "Chinese Banking and Indonesia's Economic Development," a paper presented at the International Conference on Chinese Banking and Nation Building in Southeast Asia, Hong Kong, Oct. 10-11.

Nadler, M. et al., (1955) *The Money Market and Its Institutions*, New York: Roland Press.

Ragazzi, G., (1973) "Theories of Determinants of Foreign Direct Investment," *International Monetary Fund Staff Papers*, Vol. 20, July, pp. 471-498.

Reed, H.C., (1981) *The Preeminence of International Financial Centers*, New York: Praeger Publishers.

Singapore, Ministry of Trade and Industry, (1986) *The Singapore Economy: New Directions*, Report of the Economic Committee, February.

Tan, C.H., (1985) *Financial Markets and Institutions in Singapore*, 4th Edition, Singapore University Press, National University of Singapore.

Tan, S., and I. Vertinsky, (1987) "Strategic Management of International Financial Centers: A Tale of Two Cities," in S.J. Khoury (ed.), *Recent Developments in International Banking and Finance*, Vol. II, Lexington: D.C. Heath.

Vernon, R., (1960) *Metropolis: 1985*, Cambridge, Mass.: Harvard University Press.

Additional Sources of Information

Economist Intelligence Unit (EIU), (1981-87) *Hong Kong and Macau* Country Reports, Annual and Quarterly (up to No. 3, 1987).

Economist Intelligence Unit (EIU), (1981-87) *Singapore* Country Reports, Annual and Quarterly (up to No. 3, 1987).

Hong Kong, (1980-1986) *Hong Kong Annual Reports*, The Government Printer.

Lloyds Bank Group, (1985/86) Economic Report: Hong Kong.

Lloyds Bank Group, (1985/86) Economic Report: Singapore.

Price Waterhouse, (1986) *Selected Financial Centres*, Summary of Banking and Tax Regulations, Canada.

APPENDIX 1: CHARACTERISTICS OF IFCS

1. Size of domestic economy
2. Proximity to other financial centres
3. Well-developed communication links with the rest of the world
4. Favourable taxation policy for non-residents
5. A pool of expertise in legal services
6. Favourable domestic taxation policy
7. Organized and efficient domestic communication systems
8. A pool of expertise in language translation services
9. Access to government financial decision-makers by local and foreign financial institutions
10. An unambiguous regulatory framework
11. Well-developed computer systems
12. Cost of renting office space
13. A pool of expertise in financial services
14. Stability of domestic currency
15. Access to political decision-makers by local and foreign financial institutions
16. Maturity and stability of the domestic financial system
17. A city with well-developed research institutes
18. English is the working business language
19. Availability of inexpensive support services (for example, office staff)
20. A history of political stability in the country
21. A convenient international time zone
22. Proximity to a large base of savers
23. A well-established reputation in financial affairs
24. Well-developed transportation links with the rest of the world
25. Access of residents to international currency markets
26. An environment where opportunities to implement innovative financial instruments are encouraged

27. A country that requires a minimum degree of financial disclosure
28. A history of financing and insuring international trade
29. A country that provides incentives for foreign investment
30. Existence of a recognized stock exchange
31. A city with well-developed post-secondary educational systems
32. Strong diplomatic ties with other nations
33. City with cosmopolitan cultural characteristics
34. Favourable reserve requirements
35. A basic framework of statutory protection with a wide measure of self-regulation
36. Openness of the local business community to foreigners
37. Access of foreigners to domestic currency markets
38. A country with a strong industrial and economic base
39. A mature and sound legal system
40. Access and opportunities to trade between diversified financial instruments (e.g., bonds, stocks, etc.)
41. Proximity of a city to industrial and commercial centres
42. Volume of exports of a country
43. Existence of a significant number of branches of the major international banks
44. Existence of a significant number of headquarters of some major banks
45. Ability of the business community to communicate with policy makers in the country's central bank
46. Convertibility of domestic currency
47. A city with an attractive physical environment
48. Proximity to a large base of borrowers
49. Volume of imports of a country
50. A high degree of diversification in deposit base and capital sources
51. Existence of significant number of the branch offices of trading companies
52. A high degree of sectoral diversification among potential borrowers
53. Existence of significant numbers of the head offices of manufacturing companies.

Name Index

Place Index